D0219069

Handbook of Probation

Handbook of Probation

Edited by

Loraine Gelsthorpe
and
Rod Morgan

WILLAN
PUBLISHING

Published by

Willan Publishing
Culmcott House
Mill Street, Uffculme
Cullompton, Devon
EX15 3AT, UK
Tel: +44(0)1884 840337
Fax: +44(0)1884 840251
e-mail: info@willanpublishing.co.uk
website: www.willanpublishing.co.uk

Published simultaneously in the USA and Canada by

Willan Publishing
c/o ISBS, 920 NE 58th Ave, Suite 300
Portland, Oregon 97213-3644, USA
Tel: +001(0)503 287 3093
Fax: +001(0)503 280 8832
e-mail: info@isbs.com
website: www.isbs.com

Hardback
ISBN-13: 978-1-84392-190-5

Paperback
ISBN-13: 978-1-84392-189-9

British Library Cataloguing-in-Publication Data

A catalogue record for this book is available from the British Library

Project management by Deer Park Productions, Tavistock, Devon
Typeset by GCS, Leighton Buzzard, Beds
Printed and bound by T.J. International, Padstow, Cornwall

Contents

List of abbreviations

ACE	Assessment, Case management and Evaluation system
ACOP	Association of Chief Officers of Probation
ACPOS	Association of Chief Probation Officers Scotland
ACPS	Advisory Council on the Penal System
ACR	automatic conditional release
ACTO	Advisory Committee on the Treatment of Offenders
ADSW	Association of Directors of Social Work
AGM	annual general meeting
ASB	anti-social behaviour
ASBO	Anti-Social Behaviour Order
ASBU	Anti-Social Behaviour Unit
ASPIRE	Assess – Sentence Plan – Implement – Review – Evaluate
ASSET	assessment tool used with young offenders
ATRs	alcohol treatment requirements
BASW	British Association of Social Workers
BCU	basic command unit
BCS	British Crime Survey
BME	black and minority ethnic group
CAB	Citizens' Advice Bureaux
CAF	Common Assessment Framework
CAFCASS	Children and Family Court Advisory and Support System
CARATS	Counselling, Assessment, Referral, Advice and Throughcare Services – in relation to drug treatment
CBI	Confederation of British Industries
CCETSW	Central Council for the Education and Training of Social Workers
CCTV	closed-circuit television

CDRPs	Crime and Disorder Reduction Partnerships
CETS	Church of England Temperance Society
CJA	Criminal Justice Act
CJAs	Community Justice Authorities
CJCSA	Criminal Justice and Court Services Act
CJIP	Criminal Justice Intervention Programme
CJNTO	Criminal Justice National Training Organisation
CJS	Criminal Justice Service
CLAN	Centrally Led Action Networks
CLS	Community Legal Service
C-NOMIS IT	Computerised National Offender Management Information System – Information Technology
COSLA	Convention of Scottish Location Authorities
CPA	Common Performance Assessment
CPO	Community Punishment Order
CPRO	Community Punishment and Rehabilitation Order
CPS	Crown Prosecution Service
CQSW	Certificate in Social Work
CRIMEPICS II	an industry standard interim outcome measure
CRO	Community Rehabilitation Order
CRO	Criminal Records Office
CRP	Crime Reduction Programme
CS	Community Service
CSO	Community Service Order
DATs	Drug Action Teams
DfES	Department for Education and Skills
DipPS	Diploma in Probation Studies
DipSW	Diploma in Social Work
DOMW	Director of Offender Management
DPAS	Discharged Prisoners' Aid Societies
DRRs	Drug Reduction Requirements
DTC	day training centre
DTO	Detention and Training Order
DTTOs	Drug Treatment and Testing Orders
DVPP	Domestic Violence Probation Project
ECHR	European Court of Human Rights
ECP	Enhanced Community Punishment
EFQM	European Foundation for Quality Management
eOASys	electronic version of the Offender Assessment System
EPI	Effective Practice Initiative
ETA	Euskadi Ta Askatasuna – 'Basque Homeland and Freedom'
ETE	education, training and employment
EWHC	England and Wales High Court
FOR	FOR – A change group work programme
GIAs	Gender Impact Assessments
HCR-20	20 Historical, Clinical and Risk Items

HDC	Home Detention Curfew
HMCIP	Her Majesty's Chief Inspector of Prisons
HMIP	Her Majesty's Inspectorate of Probation
HQ	headquarters
HRA	Human Rights Act
ICCP	Intensive Control and Change Programme
IDAP	Integrated Domestic Abuse Programme
ILPS	Inner London Probation Service
IMPACT	Intensive Matched Probation and After-Care Treatment
IP	Intensive Probation
IRA	Irish Republican Army
ISMs	Intensive Supervision and Monitoring Projects
ISSP	Intensive Supervision and Surveillance Programme
KPI	key performance indicator
LAAs	local area agreements
LASHs	local authority secure homes
LCJB	Local Criminal Justice Board
LSI-R	Level of Service Inventory – Revised
MAPPA	Multi-Agency Public Protection Arrangements
MATRIX	a quality standard for information, advice and guidance services
MORI	a market research company (Ipsos-MORI since 2005)
MPs	Members of Parliament
NACRO	National Association for the Care and Resettlement of Offenders
NADPAS	National Association of Discharged Prisoner's Aid Societies
NAO	National Audit Office
NAPO	National Association of Probation Officers
NAS	Needs Assessment Scale
NCJB	National Criminal Justice Board
NDPB	non-departmental public body
NHS	National Health Service
NI	Northern Ireland
NOMM	National Offender Management Model
NOMS	National Offender Management Service
NPD	National Probation Directorate
NPS	National Probation Service
NVQ	National Vocational Qualification
OASys	Offender Assessment System
OBTJ	offences brought to justice
OCJR	Office for Criminal Justice Reform
ODPM	Office of the Deputy Prime Minister
OFGEM	regulator for the UK's gas and electricity industries
OFSTED	official body for inspecting schools in the UK
OFTEL	UK regulator for the telecommunications industry

OLASS	Offenders' Learning and Skills Service
OLR	Order for Lifelong Restriction
ONS	Office for National Statistics
ORGS	Offender Group Reconviction Score
PBA	Probation Boards' Association
PC	Probation Circular (Home Office)
PDA	practice development assessor
PGA	Prisons and Probation Ombudsman
PHA	Public Health Approach
PIP	Performance Inspection Programme
PNC	Police National Computer
PO	Probation Officer
POPs	Prolific Offender Projects
POS	Persistent Offender Scheme
POS	Priority Offender Strategy
PPCU	Public Protection and Courts Unit
PPO	prolific persistent offender
PSO	Probation Service Officer
PSRs	pre-sentence reports
Q & E	quality and effectiveness
QPOS	Qualified Probation Officer Status
RAGF	Risk Assessment Guidance and Framework
RCP	Re-thinking Crime and Punishment
RCTs	randomised controlled trials
RDS	Research and Development Statistics
RJ	Restorative Justice
RLOs	Restriction of Liberty Orders
RMIS	Resource Management Information System
ROMs	Regional Offender Managers
SAOs	Supervised Attendance Orders
SERs	Social Enquiry Reports
SEU	Social Exclusion Unit
SFOs	serious further offences
SGC	Sentencing Guidelines Council
SIR	Social Inquiry Report
SLA	service level agreement
SMART	specific, measurable, achievable, realistic, targeted
SNOP	Statement of National Priorities and Objectives
SPOs	Senior Probation Officers
SRA	structured risk assessment
SRB	Single Regeneration Budget
SSPs	Safer Schools Partnerships
SSRs	specific sentence reports
STAC	Stop Think And Change
STCs	secure training centres
STO	Secure Training Order
STOP	Straight Thinking On Probation – a group work programme

SUGS	Supervision Grants Scheme
SWSG	Social Work Services Group
SWSI	Social Work Services Inspectorate
TPI	Targeted Policing Intitiative
TPOs	Trainee Probation Officers
TUC	Trades Union Council
VPS	victim personal statement
VSO	voluntary sector organisation
VSSs	Victim Support Schemes
WBPYSG	West Belfast Parents and Youth Support Groups
WEC	Work Education Centre
WHO	World Health Organization
WOATS	Women's Offending Action Teams
WORP	Women's Offending Reduction Programme
YIPs	Youth Inclusion Programmes
YISPs	Youth and Inclusion Support Panels
YJB	Youth Justice Board
YMCA	Young Men's Christian Association
YOI	Young Offender Institution
YOP	Youth Offender Panel
YOTs	Youth Offending Teams

Notes on contributors

Rob Allen is Director of the International Centre for Prison Studies at King's College, London, and was formerly a member of the Youth Justice Board for England and Wales.

Roy Bailey is an Honorary Senior Research Fellow in the Community and Criminal Justice Research Centre at De Montfort University, Leicester.

Kerry Baker is a Research Officer at the Centre for Criminology, University of Oxford and a Research Consultant to the Youth Justice Board.

Ros Burnett is Senior Research Fellow at the Centre for Criminology, University of Oxford.

Rob Canton is a former probation officer and now Professor of Community and Criminal Justice, De Montfort University, Leicester.

Tim Chapman spent 25 years working for the Probation Board for Northern Ireland. He is now an independent criminal justice consultant.

Stephen Farrall is a Senior Research Fellow at the Institute of Law, Politics and Justice, Keele University.

Loraine Gelsthorpe is Reader in Criminology and Criminal Justice, and Director of the MPhil Programme in Criminology at the Institute of Criminology, University of Cambridge; she is also a Fellow of Pembroke College.

Hannah Goodman is a Research Fellow in the Community and Criminal Justice Division of De Montfort University, Leicester.

Kevin Haines is Reader in Criminology and Youth Justice and Director of Research at the School of Human Sciences, University of Wales, Swansea.

Carol Hedderman is Professor of Criminology at the University of Leicester. She was previously an Assistant Director of the Home Office Research and Statistics Directorate with responsibility for prison and probation research and statistics.

Mike Hough is Director of the Institute for Criminal Policy Research at King's College, London.

Hazel Kemshall is Professor of Community and Criminal Justice at De Montfort University, Leicester.

Charlotte Knight is Principal Lecturer and Programme Leader of the MA in Community and Criminal Justice at De Montfort University, Leicester.

Gill McIvor is Professor of Criminology, Department of Applied Social Science, Lancaster University. She was formerly Director of the Social Work Research Centre at Stirling University.

Fergus McNeill is a Senior Lecturer in the Glasgow School of Social Work and a Network Leader in the Scottish Centre for Crime and Justice Research, University of Glasgow.

Mike Maguire is Professor of Criminology in the School of Humanities and Social Sciences at the University of Glamorgan, having taught at Cardiff University for many years.

George Mair is E. Rex Makin Professor of Criminal Justice at Liverpool John Moores University.

Rob C. Mawby is Reader in Criminal Justice at the Centre for Criminal Justice Policy and Research, UCE Birmingham.

Simon Merrington works as an independent research consultant in the area of probation and youth justice following a career in probation research and information.

Rod Morgan is Professor Emeritus at the University of Bristol and Visiting Professor at the London School of Economics. Until February 2007 he was Chairman of the Youth Justice Board for England and Wales and prior to that, HM Chief Inspector of Probation for England and Wales.

Mike Nellis is Professor of Criminal and Community Justice in the Glasgow School of Social Work, University of Strathclyde, having taught at the University of Birmingham for many years.

Tim Newburn is Professor of Criminology and Social Policy and Director of the Mannheim Centre for Criminology at the London School of Economics.

David O'Mahony is Reader at the Department of Law, Durham University, having previously taught in the Institute of Criminology and Criminal Justice at the School of Law, Queen's University, Belfast.

Peter Raynor is Professor of Criminology and Criminal Justice in the University of Wales, Swansea and a former probation officer.

Colin Roberts is University Lecturer at the Centre for Criminology and Fellow of Green College, University of Oxford.

Judith Rumgay is Reader in the Department of Social Policy, London School of Economics.

Stephen Stanley is an independent research consultant. He was formerly (until October 2006) the Head of Research for the London Probation Area.

Maurice Vanstone is Reader in Criminal Justice and Criminology at the Centre for Criminal Justice and Criminology, Swansea University.

Brian Williams was Professor of Community Justice and Victimology and Director of the Community and Criminal Justice Research Centre at De Montfort University, Leicester.

Jason Wood is a lecturer and researcher in the Faculty of Health and Life Sciences, De Montfort University, Leicester.

Anne Worrall is Professor of Criminology at Keele University and Head of the School of Criminology, Education, Sociology and Social Work.

Acknowledgements

We would like to thank the contributors for their continued faith in the Probation Service and its work with offenders. Thanks are also due to Joanne Garner at the Institute of Criminology, University of Cambridge, for her excellent administrative support towards the completion of this book. Finally, we are grateful to Brian Willan for his enduring enthusiasm and support for this project.

We would also we would like to make special mention of our colleague, Brian Williams, who has not only made a significant contribution to this book, but to the development of probation policy and training more generally. Brian's untimely death on 17 March 2007 means the loss of a committed and energetic supporter of the Probation Service.

Preface

Helen Edwards
(Chief Executive, National Offender Management Service)

I was very pleased to be invited to contribute to this book and I warmly welcome its publication. I am particularly glad to have the opportunity to reaffirm my appreciation for all that the Probation Service has achieved over the past hundred years and continues to deliver today. I see this centenary year as a milestone and not – as some have claimed – as a headstone.

The National Offender Management Service is making changes to the system for dealing with offenders. We were set up as a result of Lord Carter's 2003 report *Managing offenders, reducing crime*, and before that the 2002 Social Exclusion Unit report *Reducing re-offending by ex-prisoners*. At the heart of our package of reform is offender management. One person responsible for the offender throughout their sentence, ensuring the courts get the information they need, the right sentence plan is constructed and delivered and the most effective interventions are made both in custody and in the community. Already more than 200,000 offenders either are or have been subject to the new arrangements, which build on and extend the traditional role of the probation officer.

And probation will continue to be at the centre of the new system. We are aiming to establish a more diverse system involving the third and private sectors more, playing to the strengths of each. In practice however we envisage that public sector probation staff will be the offender managers – providing of course they can do this to the right standards, and I believe they can, particularly if we support them. We are also likely to look to probation trusts to be the main holders of contracts within local areas and to take forward their liaison and partnership roles with sentencers and local authorities. We very much recognise the professional skills and expertise of probation officers and want them to deliver what they do best. They are the local arm of our new system and an important part of the overall structure of delivery and accountability.

We recognise that we are asking a lot of offender managers. They have a tough job and need to be supported. Firstly through having the right tools to do the job and in particular through the improved assessment and case management systems in which we are investing. And secondly by our commissioners. Their job is to ensure that high quality services are available for offender managers to draw on, to ensure that sentence plans are delivered, the right interventions made and that offenders are resettled.

I recognise that we are making significant changes and that this can be difficult especially when people are already working very hard in what is always going to be a complex and sensitive environment. However, we are already beginning to see some encouraging results from new ways of working. I hope we can work together to ensure that probation in England and Wales enters its next hundred years with ever greater confidence and assurance.

Introduction

Loraine Gelsthorpe and Rod Morgan

Probation: change and challenge

This book captures and illustrates significant if not seismic changes to the Probation Service in recent years. At the turn of 2003–4 the Carter Report and the Home Office response to Carter was published (Carter Report 2003; Home Office 2004). The former proposed and the latter accepted that there should be fundamental changes in the way probation services are organised and delivered. Indeed, at that stage it seemed doubtful that there would continue to be something called a Probation Service. Since then there have been numerous discussions about the future direction of probation practice; those working within the Service have had to face a good deal of uncertainty, especially since the architects of the new organisational structure – the National Offender Management Service with concomitant Regional Offender Managers – left a good deal unsaid about future operations. But the publication of this book could not have been more timely since it coincides with the centenary anniversary of the founding of the Probation Service in the Probation of Offenders Act 1907. Moreover, the contributors to the book not only illustrate and take account of recent developments but get to the heart of the issues which make 'probation' such a controversial and captivating topic within the panoply of modern-day forms of social regulation and punishment.

In early 2005 an enabling Bill (the Management of Offenders and Sentencing Bill) granting the Home Secretary increased powers to direct Probation Boards (the local governing bodies) was introduced but lost because of a General Election in May 2005. Shortly thereafter it was announced that the Government had had second thoughts. Local Probation Boards (with a preponderance of community members) were now to be swept away and Probation Trusts formed. Probation Trusts (incorporating a wider range of community interests than hitherto and including a 'business mould') would have to compete with the voluntary and commercial sectors in putting bids to recently appointed Regional Offender Managers (ROMs) within a burgeoning National Offender Management Service (NOMS), already up and running within the Home Office: NOMS and the ROMs would commission custodial and community-based offender services. But it was not until 23 November 2006 that the probable future of probation was revealed with the introduction in Parliament of the Offender Management Bill. The Bill has been met with a good deal of concern and consternation on the part of the National Association of Probation Officers (NAPO) and the Probation Boards' Association (PBA), who see the Bill as the signal that the Probation Service is to be dismantled, and equally a good deal of political protectionism and persuasion on the part of the NOMS to both minimise and justify the changes. In essence, the Bill opens up the traditional probation functions to providers beyond the Probation Service. This is to be done on the basis of competition. But there are different perspectives on the significance and potential of this proposal. Drawing directly on various documents produced in response to the Bill (NOMS 2006; NAPO 2006; PBA 2006) the competing claims appear to be as follows: despite the move to abolish the 'Probation Service' as such and replace it with the 'probation function', the Government (in the form of the NOMS) envisages that local probation services (governed by Probation Trusts rather than Boards) will continue to play a central role, particularly in relation to offender management, but that other providers should have the opportunity to show what they can do, especially with regard to offender programme interventions. NAPO suggest that if the Bill becomes law, much probation work (including unpaid work and many accredited offender programmes) will immediately be subject to competition from voluntary and private sector providers. Moreover, whereas the NOMS claims that contracts will be awarded on the basis of performance, with providers demonstrating effectiveness and value for money being eligible for multi-year contracts, NAPO suggest that core probation work, and probation staff, will be liable to transfer to the private or voluntary sector 'by diktat', without effectiveness and relative value for money having been demonstrated. This fear has been fuelled by the stipulation, in 2006–7, that Probation Boards spend a minimum of 10 per cent of their budgets on services delivered by 'external' providers. Further, NAPO point out that duties in relation to victims, crime and disorder partnerships, and multi-agency protection arrangements will all be subject to contracts, so that the provider will not necessarily be the Probation Service. In response the NOMS argue that it is perfectly justifiable that other providers take on duties traditionally carried out by the Probation Service, if they can prove that they are better able to deliver.

NAPO have also expressed concern that if a Probation Board (Trust) is deemed to be 'underachieving' it is liable to be contracted out and excluded from putting in a bid for its own work, thereby further undermining the notion of open competition. One consequence of this would be that Boards might disappear, leaving no local state provider in future to bid when contracts come up for renewal. The NOMS, however, have indicated that they will use a range of measures to tackle Probation Board under-performance, and where a provider fails to improve, a new provider will be sought; any new provider would be required to develop strong local links in order to meet its obligations. This response arguably underestimates the degree to which local links and cooperative networks are formed over years and cannot be created as a matter of requirement. Moreover, as NAPO further argue, the introduction of competition will likely lead to reduced communication and cooperation between agencies, potentially undermining the aims of the NOMS to introduce better 'end-to-end management of offenders', reduce reoffending and increase public protection. The NOMS, on the other hand, allege that improvements have already been made in communications and that in any case the new C-NOMIS IT framework will ensure communications consistency with regard to core probation data. Further, the NOMS suggest that the commissioning process will itself actively reinforce cooperation (the Bill, it should be noted, contains measures to facilitate data-sharing between agencies).

NAPO also argue that the public service ethos of the Probation Service, its local accountability and links with sentencers will be lost as a result of the new governance framework (with Boards becoming Trusts and so on). Since there is no longer to be a requirement for magistrates, judges or local councillors to be Trust members, the Trusts are more likely to comprise persons drawn from the world of business and human resources rather than the local community. Trusts, as a consequence, will likely operate more commercially. By contrast, the Government argues that the membership of Trusts will be flexible to suit local needs in terms of numbers of members, skills and experience: the majority of Trust members are expected to be drawn from the local areas and new protocols will ensure proper liaison with sentencers. NAPO, however, fear that since probation services are to be commissioned regionally or nationally rather than locally this will limit the ability of providers to respond to local crime and offender needs: they question the practical feasibility of the NOMS' assertion that commissioners will statutorily be required to consult in order that services meet the specific needs of local communities.

Much of the above argument revolves around the issue of competition. NAPO argue that there is no evidence to support the Government's contention that competition drives up standards and no business case has ever been produced to demonstrate how it would. By contrast the NOMS claim that there *is* evidence from custodial and other sectors demonstrating that competition helps to drive up standards by introducing new service providers and incentivising existing providers to raise their game. Precisely what this evidence comprises remains open to question. Few commentators, for example, would dispute that prior to 1991 there were major problems in the occupational as well as the management culture of the Prison Service. Alison Liebling, one of the researchers who has looked closely at the contracting out of prisons management to commercial providers, has put it this way: 'These problems included indifferent or oppressive attitudes towards prisoners in many establishments, and a lack of responsiveness to management and Government requirements' (2006: 75). However, though contracting out has brought some benefits – new prison buildings, more positive and respectful staff–prisoner relationships, improved prisoner activity levels and so on (Liebling and Arnold 2004; National Audit Office 2003) – these outcomes appear to be related to the lower level of frustration experienced by prisoners in the less unionised, less traditionally 'anti-management' culture of the new prisons. But – and this is a 'but' writ large – it is impossible to say whether these findings are due to private sector management or high performance. In other words, the evidence on improvements cannot be attributed in straightforward fashion to the commercial contracting out of prisons; rather, the improvements are the result of a number of cumulative and complex moves towards 'high-performing' prisons. The two things are not synonymous, for there are also perceived weaknesses in private sector prisons in relation to security, safety, drug control and the use of authority in particular.

We might add that not only is it *not* clear that some of the problems which were thought to justify the introduction of contracted-out prisons have been overcome via privatisation, but it has not been demonstrated that privatisation was the *only* way to address the difficulties within the prison system. Moreover, since probation functions are really about 'people changing practice', it is unclear that the discipline of the marketplace is applicable in the field of probation. As Mike Hough indicates:

> The personal and social skills needed to persuade people to change their behaviour may not be readily engineered through conventional private sector management processes. We really need to know whether or not this is the case before we make any wholesale commitment to contestability in NOMS. (personal communication, cited in Liebling 2006: 75)

It is argued, for example, that contracting out to commercial providers those aspects of probation work in the management of property and hostel facilities such as cooking and cleaning has resulted in higher prices and a fall in standards (Fletcher 2006).

Of course NAPO seek to defend its members against the perceived implication that the dismantling of the National Probation Service will mean the end of probation as a profession and changed terms and conditions for officers. There are also doubts about the future of probation officer training and the role of collective bargaining. In response, the NOMS argue that probation will continue to be valued as a profession (with appropriate training and national standards) and maintain there is no plan to move away from collective bargaining.

The battle lines between the various parties to this contest are literally being drawn up as we write. NAPO and the PBA, among others, have garnered support from some MPs, peers and other supporters (the TUC and Howard League included). The Government, meanwhile, is claiming support for the Offender Management Bill provisions from Crime Concern and NACRO and it is clear that some national voluntary sector providers are forming alliances with commercial companies in order to enhance their prospects of bidding successfully for major probation contracts. Yet other voluntary sector organisations are arguing that probation services best belong with the Probation Service – as a body which has the appropriate expertise to work with offenders – and some have emphasised how important the voluntary element is to voluntary organisations' functioning. Thus the YMCA have pointed out that 'Charities need to go into potential Probation Service partnerships with their eyes wide open, otherwise they could come to represent a poisoned chalice rather than a golden opportunity' (YMCA 2006).

Notwithstanding these arguments and the late blueprint for the future of probation, the contributors to this volume have, by exploring both the history and current debate regarding the nature of the Probation Service, provided an account of how we have reached the present stage and, with an eye to the future, set out what might be lost and found in any new arrangements.

As indicated, publication of this book coincides with the one hundredth anniversary of what most probation historians take to be the foundation of the modern Probation Service in England and Wales – the passage and implementation of the Probation of Offenders Act 1907. It is indeed an irony that 2007 may well see the passage of a statute which effectively dismantles a national state service which, over the years, has established a positive international reputation and is celebrating its centenary. But so it is. This is part of the backcloth of change against which, in this brief introduction, we wish to highlight certain themes reflected in the chapters that follow.

Historical context

The police court missionaries whose work was institutionalised by the 1907 Act were committed to stopping the revolving-door syndrome which the repeated use of short-term imprisonment represented. During the House of Lords debate on the Act the Earl of Meath asserted optimistically: 'There can be no doubt whatever that [the Probation of Offenders Act] will prevent crime and, to a large extent, empty our jails' (5 August 1907). Though the early history of the service has in recent years undergone a good deal of revision, the hagiographic accounts of the early pioneers having given way to more sociologically informed histories of the prevailing cultural and political currents impacting on penal policy at the turn of the nineteenth century (see Garland 1985; McWilliams 1983, 1985), the optimism which the establishment of the service represented nevertheless remains a strong theme. In the 1960s Joan King's widely read handbook asserted that 'The great contribution of the probation service has been to the humanization of justice' (King 1969: 15). More than thirty years later, despite their acknowledgement of the importance of eugenics and mental hygiene for the foundation of probation, Peter Raynor and Maurice Vanstone (2002: 29) do not disavow this view: 'the humanitarian tradition of community supervision ... was a key driving force in the reform movement, and played an important role in the displacement of prison as a sentence of first resort'. This interpretation is now so embedded in the probation culture that contemporary commentators, as Mike Nellis notes in his chapter in this volume, look back wistfully on the past: 'The Probation Service's history and traditions are in stark contrast to the present political approach to offenders, with its emphasis on a punitive criminal justice system' (Buchanan and Millar 1997: 36).

What gave rise to this change of mood and the critical attacks on the Service from successive administrations, attacks the vehemence of which surprised as well as dismayed many probation officers who saw themselves as among the most dedicated of public servants? We can identify several contributory causes.

Social transformations

Social transformations since the 1950s have brought about what David Garland (2001) has depicted as a 'culture of control'. These include economic, technological and 'social' (family- and community-related) changes: the decline of manufacturing and the rise of the service industry, the emergence of a technologically driven society, increased mobility and changes in the structure of the family all feature here. In similar vein, sociological analyses of late modernity include consideration of changes in the sources of 'trust' and the growth of 'ontological insecurity' (Giddens 1990). At the risk of oversimplification, sociologists note that a 'risk society' has emerged in response to the erosion of localised trust which was previously embedded in kinship relations in settled communities. For Ulrich Beck:

> Risk may be defined as a systematic way of dealing with hazards and insecurities induced and introduced by modernization itself. Risks, as opposed to older dangers, are consequences which relate to the threatening force of modernization and its globalization of doubt. (1992: 21)

While the focus of key sociological authors in this area lies primarily on 'high consequences risks' of environmental degradation, nuclear proliferation and so on, the 'risk thesis' as such is that as societies have become more fragmented, there is a need to work harder to calculate risks in order to deal with life's contingencies. There is a notable pursuit of security (Zedner 2000, 2005). Mary Douglas, for example, has argued that in contemporary culture it is the language of risk that provides a 'common forensic vocabulary with which to hold persons accountable' (1992: 22). In this process the notion of risk is 'prised away' from its moorings within probability calculations and becomes a cultural keyword with much wider reference to debates about social life, accountability, crime, punishment and so on.

> This dialogue, the cultural process itself, is a contest to muster support for one kind of action rather than another ... The cultural dialogue is therefore best studied in its forensic moments. The concept of risk emerges as a key resource in modern times because of its uses as a forensic resource. (Douglas 1922: 24)

In other words, moments of intense controversy or recrimination (such as those engendered in debates about the neglect of professional duties in relation to offenders in the community, say) crystallise societal anxieties and expose lines of division about the competence, trustworthiness and legitimacy of the authorities. The culture of risk is thus transposed into a 'culture of blame'.

The emphasis on blame here is perhaps mirrored in the rise of individualism, with its associated hedonism, consumerism, and emphasis on 'individual rights'. While modernity[1] might be said to have opened up what Giddens (1991) calls the 'project of the self', this extends to the way in which market economies promote individualism and individual rights. Self-identity, Giddens (1991) suggests, has to be created and more or less continually reordered against a background of shifting day-to-day life experiences and the fragmentary tendencies of modern institutions. E-mail, video links and other technological changes, for example, serve to unify the experience of individuals. By contrast, our experience is dislocated by the diversifying contexts of human interaction (way beyond families and communities). Moreover, feelings of powerlessness are engendered by the increasing scale of our social universe, the deskilling effects of abstract systems (prompted by the process whereby local skills are expropriated into abstract systems and reorganised in light of technical and 'expert' knowledge) and concerns about the sources of authority. Tradition (reflected in religion and local community and kinship systems, for example) as a prime source of authority has been replaced by an indefinite pluralism of expertise. As Giddens puts it: 'Forms of traditional authority become "authorities" amongst others ...' and '... no longer an alternative to doubt' (1991: 195). This does not mean that people are perennially in doubt in their day-to-day lives; rather, most of us are buffered from extreme doubt by routine activities and investment in abstract systems of trust.

Finally, there is the issue of personalised versus commodified experience. Here the narrative of the self is constructed in circumstances in which personal appropriation is influenced by standardised influences on consumption (all shaped by capitalist market economies). Market-governed freedom of choice (in relation to the use of key services – hospitals and schools and so on – as well as commercial purchases) becomes an enveloping framework for individual self-expression and from this we see the emergence of a rights-based culture. Writing about the new stakeholding society in Britain, for instance, Will Hutton (1999) describes how the politicians have succeeded in creating a new language in which choice and individual rights have become the overwhelmingly dominant values rather than responsibility, mutuality or obligation and social duty. Even without this political framing of the issue, there is need to recognise that people have become vocal in asserting their rights. The arrival of the Human Rights Act 1998 was momentous in terms of the legal pursuit of human rights, its wider constitutional and juridical significance (Cheney *et al.* 1999) and, above all, in terms of its 'social' significance in bringing 'rights' to the fore of our thinking as a society. Beyond the assumed importance of choice such thinking is epitomised in 'me first' thinking and in the 'compensation' or 'personal injury' culture.

Even without sociological analyses, many of us can probably identify with something that Robert Putnam (2000) has described as the 'decline of social capital'. In *Bowling Alone* he describes how we have become increasingly disconnected from one another; informal connections of civil society (through churches, social clubs and local political activism) have largely disintegrated (though there are notable exceptions of course). Other social commentators have observed similar trends (see, for example, Richard Sennett's (1999) *Corrosion of Character* and Zygmund Bauman's (2003) *Liquid Love* – the very titles give a clue to the erosion of commitment, loyalty in the job market and our fastening onto short-term relationships instead).

Late modernity then is arguably 'a distinctive pattern of social, economic and cultural relations' which has 'brought with it a cluster of risks, insecurities and control problems that have played a crucial role in shaping our changing response to crime' (Garland 2001: viii). There are 'distinctive problems of social order that late modernity brings in its wake' (2001: ix).

These macro-level changes in society have arguably not only profoundly affected social and cultural life, but have shaped crime policies also. Garland (2001) identifies twelve features of change in crime policies since 1970, namely:

- the decline of the 'rehabilitative ideal';
- the re-emergence of punitive sanctions and expressive justice;
- changes in the emotional tone of crime policy (in response to a 'fearful, angry public', policy-makers have 'redramatised' crime);
- the return of the victim;
- a sense that 'above all, the public must be protected';
- the politicisation of crime control and the rise of a 'new populism';
- the renaissance of the prison;
- the transformation of criminological thought (from abnormal psychology, anomie/subcultures and labelling to control theories of various kinds, for example situational control and self-control);
- the growth of organised forms of crime prevention and community safety;
- civil society and the commercialisation of crime control;
- a 'new and all pervasive managerialism';
- a 'perpetual state of crisis'.

We rehearse one or two points from this list of features below. But valuable though this list is, it perhaps underemphasises the growing importance of technology (tagging and other forms of electronic surveillance and drug-testing for example) and arguably gives insufficient attention to the emergence of communitarianism in general and 'restorative justice' in particular. In Garland's analysis this is a neglected aspect of the 'return of the victim' in political criminal justice discourse. Hans Boutellier (2000), moves us on from the description of the emergence of the victim-based movement found in Garland's analysis to suggest that a focus on the victim in political and public arenas is becoming a key component of contemporary morality. That is, 'the victim' is presented as someone we can all identify with and thus serves as a touchstone for morality – a value base. Thus some critics have questioned the empirical realities of some of Garland's claims (see Matthews 2002 and the essays in Matravers 2005 – with Garland's responses) and certainly we know far too little about resistance to a 'culture of control' on the ground (see Chapter 17, this volume, on values and human rights).

These observations aside, all the themes above are in evidence within the book as authors outline the changes and prospects for the future of probation practice.

Managerialism

Managerialism is a second major theme which has contributed to the reshaping of probation. Garland, again, touches upon this development but for present purposes we think it deserves fuller attention in light of changes to the structure and delivery of probation.

The managerialist movement has been inextricably bound up in the reconstruction of public services in the UK from the 1980s onwards (Clarke *et al.* 2000). Its growth within the public sector, in the guise of what is today generally termed the 'modernising government' agenda, has been hugely important. The present framework, a development of ideas which constituted an aspect of Thatcherism, was fully articulated in the 1999 White Paper *Modernising Government* (Cabinet Office 1999). All government departments and agencies are subject now to Public Service Agreements (PSAs) setting out their lines of accountability, their aims and objectives, the resources to be made available to them following periodic spending reviews, their key performance indicators or targets and their plans for achieving greater productivity (for a general review see Faulkner 2006: chapters 2 and 20). The implication has been closer scrutiny and tighter managerial control by the centre of the minutiae of operational policy locally, and contracting out the provision of services in order to sharpen up the public sector whenever it is deemed sluggish. This is evident not just in the criminal justice system but throughout the public sector.

The Probation Service generally, and the work of individual officers in particular, has over time been subjected to tighter control from the centre and more closely monitored to ensure that published standards (see discussion below) are complied with. Prior to 2001 the more or less autonomous probation areas were already being subjected to the disciplines of a National Probation Service before that organisation came formally into being. Most commentators are agreed that this development was necessary to achieve greater consistency of practice and equitable application of court orders. But as several chapters in this volume (e.g. 3, 4, 8 and 17) explore, questions arise as to whether the developing managerialist framework for probation has been counterproductive in terms of the sensible exercise of professional discretion, loss of grassroots commitment and innovation and the driving out of practices not measured.

The politicisation of law and order

We can also identify a gradual party politicisation, from the 1970s onwards, of 'law and order'. Rising crime rates and a growing sense of insecurity (despite a decline in volume crime from the mid-1990s onwards) gave crime and anti-social behaviour (a more encompassing term favoured by New Labour since they came to power in 1997) a political salience it did not previously have. Politicians determined that policing, criminal justice and penal policy were no longer matters which could be left to expert committees, civil servants and professional practitioners: they became the increasingly high-profile stuff of election manifestos, hustings and speeches, policy statements and frequent legislative programmes. Today the major political parties jockey ever more intensively for the 'law and order' high ground, none of them secure in the knowledge that they enjoy voters' lasting confidence (for a historical review see Downes and Morgan 2007). The tendency has been for the political parties to seek to out-tough each other in order to demonstrate their governance credentials.

In the case of the Probation Service, there have been some specifically penal policy dynamics (see Bottoms *et al.* 2004: chapter 1) which combined with the pincer movement which gripped all criminal justices agencies as a result of the politicisation of law and order and managerialism. During the 1970s the predominantly rehabilitative view of probation-supervised community penalties was subject to a mood of profound penal scepticism as a consequence of what were widely typified as 'nothing works' reviews of the evidence as to effectiveness conducted on either side of the Atlantic (Martinson 1974; Brody 1976). In fact the reviews did not assert that *nothing* worked, it was more a question that nothing appeared to work much better than anything else. But scepticism about the effectiveness of all penalties marked the end of what some commentators have termed the period of 'penal welfarism'. Doubts about the rehabilitative ideal combined with other critiques, namely that the caring professions were representative of an overweening state, that treatment and preventive justifications led to interventions with little regard to the principle of proportionate justice, or simply that crime was insufficiently sanctioned in order generally to deter.

Periodising Probation Service development

The periodisation generally applied to the history of probation since the late 1960s comprises: the era of 'alternatives to custody' followed by the era of 'punishment in the community', which has been carried over, arguably more intensively, into the present period of *designer* penalties capable of being put together and varied for every offender and every occasion (a mixed economy or cafeteria approach, we might say).

If nothing-worked-much-better-than-anything-else then it initially seemed sensible to continue advocating community penalties supervised by the Probation Service on the grounds that they cost less and avoided some of the long-term deleterious effects of imprisonment. However, the introduction of community service and suspended imprisonment failed to halt the rise in the prison population and thus it was argued, adopting a 'just deserts' approach, that community penalties had to become penalties in their own right, sufficiently tough to be credible to sentencers and sufficiently distinctive for each to have its own place on the tariff ladder. To reinforce these messages we saw from 1989 onwards the development of National Standards, initially for particular penalties and then for probation supervision generally (see Hedderman and Hough 2004). Each edition of National Standards from 1992 onwards became tighter. Yet, paradoxically, the growing emphasis on enforcement, backed up by tighter monitoring by the Inspectorate of Probation as to how standards were being applied and community penalties enforced, fuelled the politicians' doubts. The evidence suggested that probation practices were changing too slowly in the direction the politicians required. From first the Conservatives and then New Labour there was more and more talk of introducing into the Service practitioners without traditional backgrounds or training and contracting out to the voluntary or commercial sectors some or all probation services.

The result has been a Service which for more than a decade now has been characterised by declining morale, internal feuding about desirable ways forward and, as a result of major structural changes, the introduction of new personnel and new intervention programmes, great uncertainty about the future and a corresponding lack of confidence.

In 2001 the 54 more-or-less autonomous local probation services were abolished to form the National Probation Service (NPS). Though the NPS was administratively divided into 42 areas coterminous with police, prosecution and court administrative areas, and though each area was (and at the time of writing still is) governed by local probation boards who continued to employ probation staff, the NPS was in reality steered by a National Probation Directorate (NPD) formed within the Home Office. The service became highly centralised with a service level agreement (SLA) woven tightly into the new Home Office managerial fabric which, in turn, was woven tightly into a tri-departmental (Home Office, the Department for Constitutional Affairs – formerly the Lord Chancellor's Department – and the Attorney General's Department) managerial framework for what began to be talked of as *the* criminal justice *service*. It had long been complained that the criminal justice *system* lacked systemic qualities. Now it began to have them.

Meanwhile the Service employed more and more staff without recognised probation qualifications so that, today, only approximately half of the Service's employees are qualified probation officers. Significant numbers of these new staff were taken on to deliver what became known as 'What Works' programmes, which very largely meant cognitive-behavioural and offending behaviour group-work programmes for which the NPD set participation targets for each probation area (see Mair 2004: chapter 2). In the late 1990s What Works programmes began to be presented as the evidence-based salvation for the Service. They were said to promise significant reductions in reoffending and it was on this basis that the NPD and the Home Office secured additional funding for the service from the Treasury. The *quid pro quo*, as required by the Modernising Government framework now in place, was target setting. As a result of this the Service arguably placed too many eggs in the cognitive-behavioural programmes basket, to the neglect of traditional casework relationships (as they used to be known), partnerships with other agencies to tackle offenders' typically multiple practical problems and use of volunteers.

The result, not surprisingly, was that the nationally rolled out What Works agenda failed to deliver the reductions in reoffending which pilot schemes, most of them originally delivered in custodial settings in North America, suggested would be the outcome. Meanwhile successive probation inspectorate reports indicated that the tightened Probation Standards were being inadequately complied with and medium- and high-risk offenders – a growing preoccupation – inadequately managed. These increasingly politicised concerns were focused on offenders on the cusp of custody or being supervised on licence. They were galvanised by scrutinies of a prison population which continued to rise and a series of high-profile dramatic crimes where the 'failures' of the Service were identified by inquiry reports requested by the Home Secretary following adverse media publicity arising out of these tragic events.

Scapegoating

During the 1990s and the first years of the new millennium the Probation Service has arguably been made the scapegoat for a penal system unsustainably overburdened by an increasing number of offenders subject to ever more intensive, punitive interventions. Imprisonment was used proportionately more with longer sentences being imposed (Hough *et al.* 2003; Ashworth 2007). The use of fines continued dramatically to decline and ever more demanding forms of supervision used in their place. If supervisees on licence were discounted the Probation Service found itself with larger caseloads comprising greater proportions of minor offenders with less serious offending histories (Morgan 2003). These trends were the cumulative consequence of the *penal populism* (Bottoms 1995) engineered by a growing body of piecemeal legislation and ratcheted up by regular doses of get-tough rhetoric from successive governments and their political opponents.

The many practical resettlement problems facing the record numbers of prisoners, particularly those serving short sentences whose release was unaccompanied by any form of supervision, went unaddressed and those medium- and long-term prisoners subject to licence were supervised by probation officers with little or no effective liaison arrangements with the Prison Service (Social Exclusion Unit 2002). Not surprisingly essential information often went unshared and the management of cases lacked continuity and progression (HMI Prisons/HMI Probation 2001).

These were the inadequacies – sentencing drift and the unjoined nature of the Prison and Probation Services – highlighted in Patrick Carter's 2003 report (Carter 2003). His two key propositions, that a NOMS be formed and probation services opened up to competition, a development first mooted but somewhat surprisingly not taken further following a Green Paper more than a decade earlier (Home Office 1990), reflects the prevailing neoliberal orthodoxy of our time. There was to be a purchaser-provider commissioning split to foster competition – *contestablity* as the government prefers to put it. This, it is assumed, and as we have described above, will drive up standards of delivery and enhance the effectiveness – reduced reoffending and better protection of the public – of services.

In 2005–6 the Government's apparent determination to pursue these fundamentally reformist policies wobbled, however. They were simultaneously pulled in several directions. The general confidence of the Government waned. The position of the Prime Minister, Tony Blair, became more and more precarious as a result of what were widely seen as highly controversial foreign policy misjudgements. Within the domestic sphere this general loss of confidence most affected the Home Office. There were two, forced changes of Home Secretary within 18 months and a mounting crisis over immigration policy and national security. In June 2006 this led an incoming Home Secretary, John Reid, to declare the department 'not fit for purpose'.

At about the same time there were published two probation Inspectorate inquiry reports on events leading up to the separate murders of John Monkton and Naomi Bryant, committed by offenders (Damien Hanson and Elliot White in the former case, and Anthony Rice in the latter) subject to probation supervision following release on licence. Both reports, particularly the former, identified serious Probation Service failings. In the case of Hanson and White the failings were such that the Chief Inspector described what had taken place as 'offender mismanagement' and 'collective failure' (HMIP 2006a: para. 14.1). In the case of Rice, the Chief Inspector concluded, more controversially and questionably, that in addition to Probation Service supervision failings there was, on the part of probation and other staff, an increasing focus on his [Rice's] 'human rights rather than on public protection' (HMIP 2006b: para. 11.26).

While ministers were digesting the Chief Inspector's conclusions and recommendations the public was assailed with horrifying reportage arising out of the trial, conviction and sentencing of four young men for the systematic torture, rape and murder of a 16-year-old schoolgirl, Mary-Ann Leneghan. Two of the young men were subject to probation supervision at the time of the murder and assessed as low-risk offenders. This apparently incomprehensible juxtaposition led to further vilification of the Probation Service. Despite the introduction some five years earlier of routine, systematic risk assessment of individual offenders (using a tool termed OASys) and increasingly elaborate monitoring arrangements for allegedly dangerous offenders (Multi-Agency Public Protection Arrangements, MAPPA) the service was lambasted for its failure to predict savagery, control depravity and protect the public from repeated harm. Yet the scapegoating pressure institutionally to reform the Service had to be set against a mounting penal crisis, the cumulative and wholly predictable consequence of more than a decade of short-termist, get-tough, political rhetoric and, arguably, a failure of other forms of governance stimulating general public insecurity. In August 2006 the prison population passed 79,000, an all-time record high, and the prison system virtually ran out of places. Little was done to divert the approaching crisis and, literally as we write, the prison population has risen above 80,000 with police cells brought back into use (last used extensively during the late 1980s) for Home Office prisoners.

Meanwhile, in the background, it became far from clear how the ROMs and NOMS were to commission probation services. Their database for assessing aggregate offender need was rudimentary, most of the ROMs had no experience of commissioning and no budget with which to work and, if these factors were not critical enough, they had no in-depth knowledge of local probation circumstances and the level of interest from and availability of potential not-for-profit and commercial providers. The evidence suggests that voluntary sector organisations (VSOs), for example, are either local or national, they are not regional. It is not clear that all the large VSOs are able to contribute the experience or legitimacy with users (offenders and their families) that the Probation Service lacks and, if that be true, that they are that different from the security companies who already hold contracts for managing custodial establishments and escorts (Morgan 2006).

Which brings us back to the point at which we began this Introduction. Despite the publication of the Offender Management Bill 2006, there remains, at the time of writing, great uncertainty about the future shape and operation of NOMS and the degree to which Probation Trusts, if they are actually formed, will continue to provide the services currently delivered by the

NPS, overseen locally by the Probation Boards. Meanwhile, mostly below the surface but increasingly breaking through it with a fury which demonstrates the passions aroused, there is much heartache within the Service about the manner in which probation has been rebadged and had its priorities reordered. The Probation Service has always involved coercion. From the very beginning in 1907 offenders who failed to lead a 'good and useful life' were brought back to court. To be put on probation, hence the use of the term, always involved a test, failure of which was punishment. But the test was undertaken by a Service whose role was to 'advise, assist and befriend' which is a far cry from the new NOMS offender management framework, hierarchically ordered according to the level of assessed risk of reoffending and harm, of 'Punish, Help, Change and Control' (Home Office 2006: para. 13.3). If the first obligation of the Probation Service is now to punish offenders, then, with supreme irony, Sir Alexander Paterson's famous dictum that offenders are sent to prison 'as a punishment, not for punishment' (Ruck 1951: 23) appears to have been forgotten by those who created a service to displace imprisonment. There is a world of difference between *enabling* offenders to comply with the orders of the court and becoming a punitive *enforcer*. It is a battle which rages within the minds of many practitioners and not a few managers. It is battle not just about appearances, important though appearances are. It is also about relationships, trust and evidence as to what *really works* in enabling humans to change their behaviour.

The shape of this volume

No text of this nature can hope to be comprehensive in its coverage. This one is no exception. The book includes comparison within the UK, but not beyond the UK (that would be a project in itself since it is some ten years since Hamai *et al.* (1995) attempted to look at probation round the world). There are *lacunae*. There is, for example, no chapter specifically covering the role of probation staff seconded to prisons, nor is their role in preparing parole reports covered. Likewise there is no specific attention to the historic and contemporary use of probation volunteers as opposed to general voluntary sector partnerships. But we believe we have covered all the principal aspects, institutional and conceptual, of probation theory, research and practice, that those thinking about joining the Probation Service, or working in or with it, will wish to consider. Further, the extensive bibliographies and guides to further reading provide our readers with pointers to where they may go to explore issues in greater depth. Finally, as we emphasised at the beginning of this Introduction, though there is never an ideal time to produce a text on a public service that is constantly undergoing change, this particular project was launched at a time presenting almost unique uncertainties about the future of the Service. The production of this book has been a long haul, but our sympathies are entirely with the long-suffering Probation Service which has continued to operate within this protracted and damaging political flux.

Part I: The Story of Probation in England and Wales, Scotland and Northern Ireland

Chapters 1 to 4 focus on the development, structure, staffing and operation of probation in England and Wales.

In Chapter 1 Mike Nellis outlines the emergence of the Probation Service in England and Wales in 1907 and records its detailed history to 1972. He documents its roots, principles of practice and the values inherent in its operation. It is a story of the Probation Service serving to humanise justice. Peter Raynor and Maurice Vanstone pick up the story of probation from the 1970s onwards in Chapter 2 and provide a critical commentary on the changes in probation practice towards a correctional service. In Chapter 3 Rod Morgan focuses on mainly contemporary issues relating to probation service governance and accountability. He does so in the broader context of general criminal justice governance and addresses the implications of the formation of the NOMS. In Chapter 4 Roy Bailey, Charlotte Knight and Brian Williams examine the effects of political and legislative changes upon probation management styles and staff, and consider the impact on recruitment and training as well as how staff in the front line have coped.

There then follows some scrutiny of provision elsewhere in Britain. In Chapter 5 Gill McIvor and Fergus McNeill outline the very different probation structures and practice in Scotland and in particular record how 'welfare' practices may not have been eclipsed, as expected, but reinscribed and relegitimated in and through new discourses of risk and protection. In Chapter 6 David O'Mahony and Tim Chapman focus on probation practice in Northern Ireland, which again rather departs from the story in England and Wales, not least because of the impact of the civil conflict between 1970 and 1995 and, thereafter, the impact of the peace process from 1995 onwards.

Part 2: Probation services: impact, prospects and potential in everyday practice

Chapters 7 to 14 revolve around probation practice. The focus here is on probation practice in light of research evidence, and how practice will likely be affected by the proposed structural changes related to the NOMS.

Chapter 7 by Kevin Haines and Rod Morgan concerns provision for offenders before and leading to court appearances. They consider the preparation of court reports as well as bail information and support work undertaken by the Service to support the making of appropriate sentencing decisions. In Chapter 8 Ros Burnett, Kerry Baker and Colin Roberts continue the focus on practice by describing and discussing assessment (including OASys and OGRS and other risk assessment tools), and supervision and intervention processes. Chapter 9 by George Mair and Rob Canton concerns the impact of probation work on sentencing. They discuss the role that probation plays in the panoply of community sentences and set out a number of challenges in making the purpose of probation clear in modern conceptions of community penalties. Chapter 10 by Rod Morgan and Tim Newburn both describes the role that the Probation Service has played in dealing with young offenders following the reform of youth justice in 1998 and sets out the case for closer cooperation between adult and juvenile systems so as to ensure continuity of care – a variation on the theme of 'end-to-end management'.

In Chapter 11 Loraine Gelsthorpe and Gill McIvor examine practice in terms of the diversity of offenders coming under the auspices of the Probation Service. They set out the various issues relating to women and minority ethnic groups in particular and give particular attention to the new 'duties' prompted by legislation relating to race, gender and disability. In Chapter 12 Stephen Farrall, Rob Mawby and Anne Worrall tackle some of the issues relating to prolific and persistent offenders and desistance from offending. The authors outline some of the tensions between the direction that the NOMS appears to be taking in relation to its rehabilitative role and what can be learned from the literature on desistance. Hazel Kemshall and Jason Wood continue this theme in Chapter 13 by looking at provision and the prospects for special groups of offenders, namely those presenting high risk of harm or reoffending and their implications for public protection. The chapter reviews the main legislative, policy and practice responses to these offenders and how the National Probation Service, in partnership with other agencies, is responding to the challenges. Finally, in this section, Mike Maguire outlines in Chapter 14 current research and challenges in relation to resettlement. In particular, he raises questions in relation to the need for continuity in offender management.

Part 3: What works in Probation?

Chapters 15 to 20 examine what is meant by effectiveness and what is known about it. This discussion necessarily involves paying attention to values, victims, the interests of the public at large and the different voices of probation staff and the offenders with whom they work.

In Chapter 15 Simon Merrington and Stephen Stanley critically examine what might be meant by 'effectiveness' and identify essential ingredients for what might count as 'good evidence'. Chapter 16 by Carol Hedderman examines the research evidence in relation to the effectiveness of community penalties supervised by the Probation Service. She points out that one of the biggest challenges for both researchers and practitioners who want to know what works in reducing reoffending might be to move away from examining the impact of discrete interventions to offender-focused interventions. In Chapter 17 Loraine Gelsthorpe, has regard to the 'different voices' represented in probation practice. She questions the juggernaut of control and managerialism implied by the structural changes to the Service. She identifies pockets of resistance and rehearses some of the changes in values noted earlier in the book, not least the part that a human rights culture might play alongside other values brought into play to counteract managerialism.

In Chapter 18 Brian Williams and Hannah Goodman address the implications of working for and with victims. They highlight the fact that NOMS has been created without much thought being given to its impact on victims of crime. They question the implicit assumption that mergers between services mean better services for victims. This theme is picked up in Chapter 19 by Judith Rumgay, who takes a critical look at partnerships and what might be lost and found through market competition in the provision of probation services. She questions whether the creation of new partnerships beyond those agencies which have been tried and tested in probation practice will prove beneficial or undo what already works. Finally, in Chapter 20, Rob Allen and Mike Hough take us to the voice of the public at large and attitudes towards community penalties. They examine factors which drive public opinion (including the role of the media), and give positive indications of ways in which public opinion can be changed – through better communication, the visibility of probation practice, and community participation. Positive steps in this direction, however, may be undone not only by the uncertainty which surrounds the future of the Probation Service, but by the prospect of a complex, multi-layered structure in which there are a number of different providers of services.

Notes

1 'Modernity' might be taken to mean the social transformation which emerged out of industrialisation. 'Late modernity', by contrast, might be taken to mean the period since the 1950s – as we move towards postmodernity (a state in which all certainties, concepts and practices become open to scrutiny and change). Postmodern architecture, for example, represents an inversion of the expected – with service pipes exposed on the outside of a building rather than inside and hidden (as in the Pompidou Centre in Paris). Postmodernity has connections with a position of relativism, however, and we are not there yet, as a culture. Hence the term 'late modernity' is used in the context of this introduction to denote a focus on some of the empirical (and observable) transformations presently taking place.

References

Ashworth, A. (2007) 'Sentencing', in M. Maguire, R. Morgan and R. Reiner (eds), *The Oxford Handbook of Criminology*, 4th edn. Oxford: Oxford University Press.

Bauman, Z. (2003) *Liquid Love*. Oxford: Polity.

Beck, U. (1992) *Risk Society: Towards a New Modernity* London: Sage.

Bottoms, A. E. (1995) 'The philosophy and politics of punishment and sentencing', in C.M.V. Clarkson and R. Morgan (eds), *The Politics of Sentencing Reform*. Oxford: Oxford University Press.

Bottoms, A.E., Rex, S. and Robinson, G. (eds) (2004) *Alternatives to Prison: Options for an Insecure Society*. Cullompton: Willan.

Boutellier, H. (2000) *Crime and Morality. The Significance of Criminal Justice in Post-modern Culture*. Dordrecht: Kluwer Academic.

Brody, S. (1976) *The Effectiveness of Sentencing*. London: HMSO.

Buchanan, J. and Millar, M. (1997) 'Probation: reclaiming a social work identity', *Probation Journal*, 44 (1): 32–46.

Cabinet Office (1999) *Modernising Government*, Cm 4310. London: Stationery Office.

Carter Report (2003) *Managing Offenders, Reducing Crime – A New Approach*. London: Prime Minister's Strategy Unit.

Cheney, D., Dickson, L., Fitzpatrick, J. and Uglow, S. (1999) *Criminal Justice and the Human Rights Act 1998*. Bristol: Jordan.

Clarke, J., Gewirtz, S. and McLaughlin, E. (2000) *New Managerialism. New Welfare?* London: Sage, in association with the Open University.

Douglas, M. (1992) *Risk and Blame: Essays in Cultural Theory*. London: Routledge.

Downes, D. and Morgan, R. (2007) 'No turning back: the politics of law and order into the millennium', in M. Maguire, R. Morgan and R. Reiner (eds), *The Oxford Handbook of Criminology*, 4th edn. Oxford: Oxford University Press.

Faulkner, D. (2006) *Crime, State and Citizen: A Field Full of Folk*. Winchester: Waterside Press.

Fletcher, H. (2006) *Offender Management Bill*, NAPO Briefing, 23 November. London: NAPO.

Garland, D. (1985) *Punishment and Welfare: A History of Penal Strategies*. Aldershot: Gower.

Garland, D. (2001) *The Culture of Control: Crime and Social Order in Contemporary Society*. Oxford: Oxford University Press.

Giddens, A. (1990) *The Consequences of Modernity*. Oxford: Polity Press.

Giddens, A. (1991) *Modernity and Self-Identity*. Cambridge: Polity Press.

Hamai, K., Villé, R., Harris, R., Hough, M. and Zvekic, U. (1995) *Probation Round the World*. London, Routledge.

Hedderman, C. and Hough, M. (2004) 'Getting tough or being effective: what matters?', in G. Mair (ed.), *What Matters in Probation*. Cullompton: Willan.

HMI Prisons/HMI Probation (2001) *Through the Prison Gate: A Joint Thematic Review by HM Inspectorates of Prison and Probation*. London: Home Office.

HMI Probation (2006a) *An Independent Review of a Serious Further Offence Case: Damien Hanson and Elliot White*. London: HMIP.

HMI Probation (2006b) *An Independent Review of a Serious Further Offence Case: Anthony Rice*. London: HMIP.

Home Office (1990) *Supervision and Punishment in the Community*, Cm 966. London: HMSO.

Home Office (2004) *Managing Offenders – Changing Lives*. London: Home Office.

Home Office (2006) *The NOMS Offender Management Model*. London: NOMS, Home Office.

Hough, M. (2006) Personal communication, cited in A. Liebling, 'Lessons from prison privatisation for probation', in M. Hough, R. Allen and U. Padel (eds), *Reshaping Probation and Prisons: The New Offender Management Framework*. Bristol: Policy Press.

Hough, M., Jacobson, J. and Millie, A. (2003) *The Decision to Imprison*. London: Prison Reform Trust.

Hutton, W. (1999) *The Stakeholding Society. Writings on Politics and Economics*. Cambridge: Polity Press.

King, J. (1969) *The Probation and After-Care Service*, 3rd edn. London: Butterworths.

Liebling, A. (2006) 'Lessons from prison privatisation for probation', in M. Hough, R. Allen and U. Padel (eds), *Reshaping Probation and Prisons: The New Offender Management Framework*. Bristol: Policy Press.

Liebling, A. and Arnold, H. (2004) *Prisons and Their Moral Performance. A Study of Values, Quality and Prison Life*. Oxford: Clarendon Press.

McWilliams, W. (1983) 'The Mission to the English police courts 1876–1936', *Howard Journal of Criminal Justice*, 22: 129–47.

McWilliams, W. (1985) 'The Mission transformed: professionalism of probation between the wars', *Howard Journal of Criminal Justice*, 24: 257–74.

Mair, G. (ed.) (2004) *What Matters in Probation*. Cullompton: Willan.

Martinson, R. (1974) 'What works? Questions and answers about prison reform', *The Public Interest*, 5: 22–54.

Matravers, M. (ed.) (2005) *Managing Modernity: Politics and the Culture of Control*. Abingdon: Routledge.

Matthews, R. (2002) 'Crime control in late modernity', *Theoretical Criminology*, 6 (2): 217–26.

Morgan, R. (2003) 'Thinking about the demand for probation services', *Probation Journal*, 50: 7–19.

Morgan, R. (2006) 'Working with volunteers and the voluntary sector: some lessons for probation from youth justice', in N. Tarry (ed.), *Returning to Its Roots? A New Role for the Third Sector in Probation*. London: Social Market Foundation/Rainer Foundation.

National Association of Probation Officers (NAPO) (2006) *Ten Reasons to Oppose the Bill*, leaflet. London: NAPO.

National Audit Office (2003) *The Operational Performance of PFI Prisons Report by the Comptroller and Auditor General HC Session 2002–2003: 18 June*, 2003. London: Stationery Office.

National Offender Management Service (NOMS) (2006) *The Offender Management Bill: The Facts*. See: www.noms.homeoffice.gov.uk.

Probation Boards' Association (2006) *Initial Reaction to the Offender Management Bill November 2006*. London: Probation Boards' Association.

Putnam, R. (2000) *Bowling Alone: The Collapse and Revival of American Community*. New York: Simon & Schuster.

Raynor, P. and Vanstone, M. (2002) *Understanding Community Penalties: Probation, Policy and Social Change*. Buckingham: Open University Press.

Ruck, S. (ed.) (1951) *Paterson on Prisons: Prisoners and Patients*. London: Hodder & Stoughton.

Sennett, R. (1999) *Corrosion of Character. The Personal Consequences of Work in the New Capitalism*. New York: W. W. Norton.

Social Exclusion Unit (2002) *Reducing Re-offending by Ex-prisoners*. London: Office of the Deputy Prime Minister (OPDM).

YMCA (2006) *Response to the Proposed Offender Management Bill*, Press Release, 15 November 2006. See: http://www.ymca.org.uk/pooled/articles?BF_NEWSART/view.asp?Q-BF_NEWSART_225143.

Zedner, L. (2000) 'The pursuit of security', in T. Hope and R. Sparks (eds), *Crime, Risk and Insecurity*. London: Routledge.

Zedner, L. (2005) 'Securing liberty in the face of terror: reflections from criminal justice', *Journal of Law and Society*, 32: 507–33.

The Story of Probation in England and Wales, Scotland and Northern Ireland

The chapters in this opening section trace the origins and development of probation in the United Kingdom and the manner in which, over time, it has taken different forms in Northern Ireland, Scotland, and England and Wales. Consideration is also given to the changing character of probation staff and the governance of the service in England and Wales with the onset of the National Offender Management Service (NOMS).

In Chapter 1 Mike Nellis chronicles the growth of the Probation Service to 1972, the year in which a major Criminal Justice Act brought to fruition a period which he characterises as one of probation 'modernisation and diversification'. Nellis emphasises that much of the history of early probation practice remains to be written, local sources and offender perspectives having been little drawn on. Further, he points out that the Probation of Offenders Act 1907, generally taken as the major administrative starting point, nevertheless drew on a common law tradition of 'preventive justice'. Moreover, although the reformist movement of the early twentieth century promoted welfare measures as a means of ensuring greater public safety, the Probation Service's role to 'advise, assist and befriend' also represented a toughening up of traditional court recognisances. By the 1930s probation had emerged as a branch of a broader social work profession, secularised (separated from its police court mission origins), with psychology and casework methods at its core. However, it was in the 1960s that the Service emerged from an organisational struggle between welfarism and criminal justice with a cultural tradition of what Nellis characterises as 'humanised justice'.

In Chapter 2 Peter Raynor and Maurice Vanstone take the probation story forward from the early 1970s to the present day. The paradox of the 1970s was that having established for itself what appeared to be a firm, distinctive professional foundation, the Probation Service was almost immediately faced with empirically based doubts about the validity of its 'treatment' approach. The offences which provided the rationale for officers' caseloads scarcely figured on what Raynor and Vanstone describe as the Service's radar screen. The authors describe in detail the evidence behind the infamous 'nothing works' debate and chart the lead-in to the 1984 Home Office Statement of National Priorities and Objectives (SNOP), the first major sign of growing government interest in the cost-effectiveness of the Service, the background to which was the increasing party politicisation of the 'law and order' debate. From then on every criminal justice agency, Probation included, operated in an increasingly politicised limelight. Raynor and Vanstone chart each stage of the Service's response to this challenge from the adoption of 'What Works' to the 'New Choreography' statement put out by the National Probation Directorate (NPD) following the creation of a national service in 2001. The optimistic high point of 'What Works' came and went rather soon in the new millennium. Raynor and Vanstone critically dissect exactly what went right and what went wrong operationally, assess how the probation caseload was changing, what led to the Carter Report and how the proposal that there be a NOMS was received and, during a period of devastating uncertainty, was reacted to. They conclude with a summary of the critical choices now facing the Service.

In Chapter 3 Rod Morgan provides an overview of this century-long probation history as far as the governance of the Service is concerned. He describes how, under the 1907 Act, probation officers were appointed locally by the courts and were officers of the court, and how their work came to be overseen by local probation committees comprising magistrates elected by their peers. He also describes how there came into existence within the Home Office a succession of offices to oversee the development of the Service and which gradually enhanced the powers of the Secretary of State. This included from 1936 an inspectorate which, during the 1990s, began operating as a sort of surrogate probation directorate before the NPD was created in 2001. In the post-War years the responsibilities of the Service were broadened and the control of the Secretary of State correspondingly strengthened. This included control over the purse strings. From the 1980s onwards the Home Office began to prescribe in ever greater detail what work probation officers would do and how local services were to be amalgamated. From the early 1990s onwards there was more and more talk of creating a market in the provision of probation services, an approach already being adopted in the management of prisons. The creation of the National Probation Service (NPS) in 2001 and the adoption of the Carter Report proposals for the creation of a NOMS-based purchaser–provider split was thus the culmination of a long process. Morgan analyses closely what the implications of the NOMS and the formation of probation trusts might be for the accountability of the Service. He concludes that the model currently proposed by the Government cannot, despite the emphasis on 'contestability', be interpreted as other than one of Home Office control centralisation with little or no local accountability for services that may be substantially fragmented.

Roy Bailey, Charlotte Knight and Brian Williams ask in Chapter 4 whether the Probation Service is currently 'fit for purpose', a question which the multiple changes and uncertainties of the last few years suggests others have answered in the negative. They focus on the aspects of management, the changing roles of practitioners, and staff performance and training in the light of the emphasis now being given to risk assessment and management and public protection. In light of the dwindling proportion of probation staff now comprising probation officers, the authors emphasise the importance of graduate-level professional training, the need for postgraduate programmes to foster senior management skills and the importance of developing a comprehensive in-service programme of training for Probation Service officers whose development and career prospects has so far been relatively neglected despite their growing number. Bailey, Knight and Williams also consider the implications of the gradual feminisation of the probation workforce given the increasing emphasis on the 'management' of offenders and tighter 'enforcement' of their court orders. They suggest that questions must be raised about suitable role models for the predominantly young, white, male caseload with which the Service works. More attention, they argue, needs to be given by senior probation managers to the relational aspects of probation work and rather less emphasis placed on targets.

The contrasting form taken by probation work in Scotland is the subject of Gill McIvor and Fergus McNeill's Chapter 5. Despite probation origins in Scotland not dissimilar to those in England and Wales, there is no separate probation service in Scotland. Probation work is undertaken by criminal justice social workers employed by the local authorities. McIvor and McNeill chronicle the fact that whereas moves in the 1960s to remove juveniles in trouble from the jurisdiction of the criminal courts largely failed in England and Wales, parallel moves in Scotland following the 1964 Kilbrandon Report largely succeeded and had an impact on provisions for adults in the Social Work Scotland Act 1968. Probation and after-care work was integrated in generic social work departments, representing the triumph of a penal-welfarist approach. However, as the authors go on to describe, probation work subsequently lost out within this framework such that the quality of supervision and the confidence of sentencers arguably declined. The result was growing control of probation services, through standard setting and the ring fencing of budgets, by the centre in a manner similar to that south of the border. Yet, McIvor and McNeill argue, the influence of correctionalism has been more attenuated in Scotland than in England and Wales. The number of community-based sentences has been broadened and 'What Works' has become a theme as elsewhere. But proposals to merge probation work with that of the Prison Service in Scotland have been abandoned in favour of a management of offenders organisational framework which has left probation work within social services subject to direction by regional community justice authorities. This framework, the authors suggest, has reinscribed Scotland's welfarist commitment within a new emphasis on public protection, that is the public is best protected by helping offenders solve their practical problems.

Probation has also followed a distinct course in Northern Ireland, though for reasons different to those in Scotland, as David O'Mahoney and Tim Chapman describe in Chapter 5. The early development of the service was similar to that in England and Wales, though few officers were appointed and probation orders were little used by the courts during the interwar period. Not until 1950 did the Secretary of State for Northern Ireland take responsibility for administering the Service which from then on was funded entirely by the centre. Yet, ironically, the 'Troubles' led to the Probation Service in Northern Ireland being granted greater autonomy from the civil service in the 1980s when the reverse course was being pursued on the mainland. A Probation Board representative of the whole community was established and granted considerable autonomy to engage community-based groups to assist in the supervision of offenders. The Service also adopted various means of disengaging itself from the political dimension of much offending behaviour in Northern Ireland. The corollary was that probation officers in Northern Ireland failed to challenge the sectarian attitudes rife within the province, though, ironically, the service engaged and developed partnerships with the divided Northern Ireland community to a greater extent than anywhere else in the United Kingdom. The peace process since 1995, as O'Mahoney and Chapman indicate, has seen the Northern Ireland probation service being drawn back into a mainstream debate similar to elsewhere – closer working with the prison service, 'What Works' programmes, a greater emphasis on public protection, etc. – but one legacy of the Troubles and the tradition of community engagement has advanced further in Northern Ireland than elsewhere – restorative justice.

Chapter 1

Humanising justice: the English Probation Service up to 1972

Mike Nellis

Introduction

> There can be no doubt whatever that [the Probation of Offenders Act] will prevent crime and, to a large extent, empty our jails. (Earl of Meath, House of Lords, 5 August 1907)

> The great contribution of the probation service has been to the humanisation of justice. (Joan King 1969: 15)

> The Probation Service's history and traditions are in stark contrast to the present political approach to offenders, with its emphasis on a punitive criminal justice system. (Buchanan and Millar 1997: 36)

As the Probation Service of England and Wales commemorates its centenary in 2007, one might reasonably ask who, nowadays, apart from historians, might be interested in the early history of probation in England – and why? A somewhat mythic 'origins and development of probation' story focused on 'police court missionaries' has long circulated within the service (Coddington 1950; Jarvis 1972; Osler 1995; North and Smith 2001), and probation veterans might well assume they have 'read it all before'. More recent employees and new trainees, on the other hand – unborn even in the year where this chapter ends – can have no *prima facie* reason for thinking that events prior to 1972 might have relevance to their present endeavours and ambitions. In their working world, the past few years have seen a concerted attempt by politicians and senior probation managers to distance the Service from what (in their terms) were unduly liberal and ineffective forms of practice. In the mission statement of the (then) newly formed National Probation Service (NPS), for example, its Director-General informed staff that she intended to 'lead the Service against the grain of its past history and traditions' (Wallis 2001: 5). To a large extent (and well before the advent of the NPS), incremental procedural and cultural 'detraditionalisation' had indeed been occurring, aided by generational change among service staff and wider social changes in British society. Thus, in spirit, style and terminology, the community supervision of offenders today differs substantially from what it was even 30 years ago, let alone a century ago (McWilliams 1987, 1994) – and it is still changing. Under the rubric of 'modernisation' – a New Labour watchword across the public services – 'past practices' in criminal justice, perhaps particularly in probation, have been variously represented by politicians as an anachronism, an embarrassment and a burden – never as a useful resource.

What is – or was – this 'probation tradition' that the new modernisers have set themselves against? Tradition in general is a mix of memory, myth, historical data, hallowed places, people and incidents, retold stories, practice wisdom and enduring institutional routines. It also tends to have a strong normative dimension – a sense of the way things *ought* to be, a distinctive 'moral imagination'. In a seminal work Hobsbawm and Ranger (1983) rightly argued that cultural, political and organisational traditions are invariably 'invented' to serve contemporary social and political purposes, while recognising that it is in the very nature of traditions to feel, not artificially constructed, but 'natural', 'objective' and 'given' to the people whose lives they govern. There is no doubt that, in the two decades preceding the creation of the NPS in 2000, many serving probation officers were conscious of 'their' tradition being eroded by the Government's increasing emphasis on coercion and punishment and much of their initial hostility to the proposed changes was articulated in terms of this (in their eyes) unwarranted loss. The faltering tradition was defined as 'social work', and was encapsulated in the motto 'advise, assist and befriend' – both terms denoting a broadly humanistic way of working with offenders. It acknowledged the largely socially disadvantaged position of probation's 'clients' (acquiring a 'socialist' tinge in the 1980s), emphasised their potential for rehabilitation, respected their individuality (and, in the 1990s, their cultural diversity), trusted them to cooperate with only a minimum of coercion and sought to shield them from the harsher elements of judicial and penal authority (including probation's own capacity to breach clients for non-compliance).

This chapter will be partly historiographical, but it will also seek to get the history itself right. It will inevitably draw on the work of existing probation historians while recognising how limited and partial our understanding of twentieth-century probation history actually remains. Independent professional historians have paid some attention to the nineteenth-century roots of probation (White 1978, 1979), but compared to both police history and prison history (which dominate histories of crime and punishment) probation has been hugely underexplored. Academic historians have been especially neglectful of twentieth-century *local* probation history, where what little we know comes from probation officers (or ex-probation officers or probation-officers-turned-academics) with a sideline interest in the history of their own profession. Journalistic, literary and cinematic sources which may illuminate probation history have been universally overlooked.

Dorothy Bochel (1976) provides a narrowly *administrative* history of probation, focusing on the legal and policy changes which constituted and transformed the Service up to 1972. With a broader remit than probation,

Bailey (1987) covers the 1914–48 period in more depth. Both contain only limited reference to the ideas which influenced probation, to actual probation practice and to the broader social and cultural context in which probation developed. Bill McWilliams's (1983, 1985, 1986, 1987) quartet on the *history of ideas* in probation rectified the first of these but neglected social and cultural factors and the detail of practice. The way he periodises ideational change in the service reflects the way issues were seen by professional leaders, penal reformers and textbook writers, rather than the perspectives of front-line staff who were few in number, initially part-time, badly paid, often worked in isolation and had little interest in abstract ideas. Eileen Younghusband (1978), social work trainer and juvenile court magistrate, provides more information than Bochel on what policy changes meant for probation practice, but she too concentrates on ideal rather than commonplace practice, and emphasises welfare rather than *penal* measures in probation's development. Probation officers Donald Bissell (1987), Martin Page (1992) and Charles Preece (1989) have deepened understanding of probation's development in Birmingham, London and Trecynon, Wales – the latter by writing about his formidable great-grandmother, a Welsh Salvationist who worked first as a police court missionary and later as a probation officer. Retired journalist Vincent Ryder (1995) has contributed a much needed study of the rural dimension of probation's development in Norfolk; Goodfellow (1987) does something more anecdotal for Bristol, as do North and Smith (2001) for Cornwall. Britain's island jurisdictions, Jersey for example, have clearly had rather idiosyncratic 'probation' histories (Miles 2004). Maurice Vanstone (2004), a probation officer turned academic, has recently written a rich, revisionist account of probation history, focused on actual practice but also utilising insights from the sociology of punishment. Whitehead and Statham (2006) have recently condensed the administrative history of probation into a single volume. Several theoretically and culturally informed histories of penal practice touch on probation in the Victorian and Edwardian period (Young 1976; Garland 1985; Weiner 1990), and while Kilcommins (2000) has provided a valuable genealogy of community service, developments between 1948 and 1972 still await an analysis of equivalent theoretical sophistication.

This chapter summarises and interprets key developments in probation (and its nineteenth-century precursors) over a hundred-year period, seeking simultaneously to illuminate the construction of a 'social work tradition' within the service. Historical observations will sometimes be highlighted because they echo contemporary concerns – notably the efforts of a modernising Labour government to 'abolish' probation in the late 1960s – and certain themes will be emphasised – the persistence of faith-based vocations, the invention and commemoration of probation tradition, and the image of probation in popular and literary culture – which are not particularly prominent in existing accounts. Nothing will be said about offender perspectives – probationers' own views of being 'on probation' – for there is paucity of data on this in the period in question, but any rounded understanding of what probation is or was, it must be admitted, is incomplete without this. The chapter will conclude by exploring the aptness (or otherwise) of Joan King's claim that probation in this period 'humanised justice', and by noting some features of the contemporary penal/welfare landscape which originated in the pre-1972 probation world. The service's own more recent history is continued in the next chapter by Peter Raynor and Maurice Vanstone.

The roots of probation

Contrary to the mythology which (over-privileges) the role of Victorian 'police court missionaries' in probation's inception – although, indubitably, they played a part – its antecedents lay equally in established judicial practice and in a *subsequent* penal reform initiative. A long common law tradition of 'preventive justice' (Blackstone 1769) – courts ensuring good behaviour without the application of punishment to people of 'whom there is probably ground to suspect of future misbehaviour' – was undoubtedly its seedbed. Bind-overs (applied to cheats, vagabonds, known thieves and prostitutes) and recognisances to keep the peace (applied to any case short of murder) were the main forms of preventive justice in the nineteenth century, and were sometimes used instead of prison. They acquired legal force in 1879, but the highly autonomous local magistrates retained discretion to deal with offenders in a variety of informal, extra-legal ways. Warwickshire magistrates, for instance, released certain young offenders back to their employees for supervision, but without using recognisances. As Recorder of Birmingham (after 1841) Matthew Davenport Hill (1792–1872) applied, publicised and had high hopes for this scheme, but it was never widely copied. The initiative by the Church of England Temperance Society (CETS), encouraged by a small donation from a Hertfordshire printer, Frederick Rainer (in 1876), to persuade magistrates at a South London Police Court to let two 'missionaries' supervise drunken offenders was an entirely separate development (Cassady 2001). It was emulated, unevenly, elsewhere in London and in other cities where the CETS already had branches, and by 1894 there were 70 missionaries – although by then the Howard Association was promoting an innovative North American system of 'probation' as a desirable means of reducing imprisonment for juvenile offenders in Britain.

From 1869 Massachusetts had had 'probation officers' who investigated and supported youngsters under 17 who were appearing in court. Motivated by Christian charity, a Boston shoemaker, John Augustus (1784–1859), had initiated this work in 1841, personally standing bail for an array of convicted adult drunkards, delinquent children and young prostitutes. Over a 30-day period he set individualised reform measures in place, pending the offender's return to court for sentence; those who had responded well to his reform measures were not sent to prison. After his death, the Massachusetts state authorities adopted and augmented his approach, with juveniles only, initially (up to 1891) under the auspices of the police (Panzarella 2002). 'Probation', as they renamed the work, was intended to 'watch over [the offender] and devise measures for his benefit, while still remaining at home', and was rapidly deemed successful. At the point at which the Howard Association drew probation's attention to the British government, juvenile prison was hardly used in Massachusetts, and the state was considering extending it to adults.

The Howard Association envisaged something a little different – specialised magistrates, each with a team of police officers or, preferably, volunteer helpers, assisting parents with the upbringing of their wayward children. An ambitious lawyer, Howard Vincent (1849–1908), and first Director of Criminal Investigation at Scotland Yard, also championed the Massachusetts scheme (which he had visited), seeing the use of police officers as a way of remedying the perceived leniency of recognisances. His Probation of First Offenders Bill 1886 – the first reference to 'probation' in English law – was enacted, but Parliament had seen fit to permit greater flexibility in the appointment of supervisers. Not all police forces wanted such a role, while the CETS understandably saw an opportunity to increase the numbers of missionaries. In the event, neither magistrates' courts nor Courts of Assize and Quarter Sessions made much use of the new law, having few resources to appoint supervisers, and preferring the flexibility of recognisances (which were not restricted to *first* offenders). Practice thus changed little, and in 1898 the Howard Association again pressed the government for Massachussetts-style improvements in dealing with juveniles. Prison Commissioner Evelyn Ruggles-Brise (a man wary of purely rehabilitative ideals) agreed to pursue this, but with a clear commitment to using police officers as supervisers rather than 'probation officers' (a term imported from America).

The Ruggles-Brise vision never, in fact, developed, and an incoming Liberal government placed greater emphasis on welfare measures as a means of ensuring public safety. The Probation of Offenders Act 1907 was part of a wave of initiatives of both government and civil society – specialist juvenile courts, specialist penal institutions (borstals) and the Boy Scouts – aimed at remoralising the nation's wayward youth, although probation was from the start also available for adults. The new Act, skilfully steered through Parliament by Home Office Under-Secretary Herbert Samuel (1870-1963), enabled both higher and lower courts to suspend punishment and discharge *offenders* – or even *defendants who were not convicted* – if they entered into a recognisance for between one and three years, one condition of which was supervision by a person named in the 'probation order'. Legislators believed that they were toughening up traditional recognisances, although at the same time the legally prescribed aim of probation – 'advise, assist and befriend' – emphasised its non-punitive character. The new measure was intended to have a wide application: there were no restrictions of age, criminal record or offence (except murder) on its use. The Act's many Parliamentary supporters had immense confidence in it, one claiming that 'there can be no doubt whatever that [it] will prevent crime and to a large extent empty our jails'. Critics were of two persuasions, some fearing that probation would weaken the deterrent function of the law, others that it would covertly extend 'the surveillance functions of the police' (Radzinowicz and Hood 1986: 643). Significantly, however, petty sessional areas (each one served by a bench of magistrates) were merely *permitted* – not *required* – to appoint probation officers.

The precise detail of probation practice evolved out of deliberation, dialogue and the dissemination of regulations – including the first set of Probation Rules – in the three years following the Act. Though not a sentence it was patently intended by government as a means of using prison less and to this end, according to a subsequent Departmental Committee, 'firmness is as necessary in a probation order as sympathy' (quoted in Radzinowicz and Hood 1986: 645). It was aimed at quite serious adult offenders as well as children, and was explicitly discouraged for trivial breaches of the peace. 'Probationers' (as those subject to probation were called, up to the 1960s) were required to report to their supervisors as required, to receive visits and notify any changes of address and employment. Youngsters were to be steered from crime by attendance and support at school, school-leavers by employment and the pursuit of suitable recreational activities; both groups were to be subject to moral exhortation and to lead 'an honest and industrious life'. They could be prohibited from mixing with undesirable people, visiting certain places or drinking alcohol. Requirements to reside in an 'approved home' were not initially available, although this was something magistrates were known to want (and later got), as was fine collection by probation officers, despite initial Home Office discouragement of the practice.

The Home Office saw probation as a means of stimulating developments in civil society rather than as a new specialist agency. They envisaged probation officers as employees of the local magistrates, acting as intermediaries between court and community, on whose resources they would draw to socialise offenders back into law abidingness. They strongly encouraged the formation of an association 'comprising and managed by the probation officers themselves' (quoted in Radzinowicz and Hood 1986: 645) to develop and disseminate probation expertise. In essence, the Home Office did not want the burden of costs entailed by central control of a new agency and any resultant bureaucracy. So who were the probation officers to be? The Home Office discouraged – but could not always prevent – the appointment of police officers as probation officers – and forbade the staff of Discharged Prisoner's Aid Societies from taking such posts, lest the taint of imprisonment infused probation. Neither they nor the Howard Association were keen on the police court missionaries: their Christian aspirations were respected, but they were often not well-educated and their temperance-orientation – securing attendance at church and encouraging pledges to avoid alcohol – overshadowed proper probation work. It was never a foregone conclusion that police court missionaries would dominate the first generation – or the later mythology – of probation officers: they came to do so because there were insufficient numbers of other 'people of good character' able and willing to do the job for such low pay. The missionaries – some of whom were adept publicists of their work (Holmes, T. 1902; Holmes, R. 1915, 1916, 1923) – at least had some relevant experience and tolerated the poor wages paid by the magistrates. Their stern moral outlook, characterised by the CETS historian as 'the seasoning of justice by mercy' (Ayscough 1923), was not itself at odds with what the Home Office wanted, so long as it was not expressed exclusively through demands for temperance.

Not all magistrates wanted to appoint missionaries or probation officers, particularly in rural areas, many of whose petty sessional areas were thought too small to warrant employing one. Some magistrates simply preferred the old, uncomplicated practice of making recognisances without probation requirements, others believed probation itself to be rather lenient. The expansion of specialist juvenile courts after 1908, committed to sparing juveniles the stigma of imprisonment, gradually increased the number of probation orders, and by 1913 a combination of 7,534 probation orders and 6,369 recognisances constituted 40 per cent of magistrates' courts' sentences (20 per cent of the convicted were fined, 30 per cent were imprisoned (90 per cent for under three months) and only one in twenty was whipped). Most probation orders were for juveniles and young men – 44 per cent under 16, 29 per cent between 16–21, and 27 per cent over 21 (Bochel 1976).

The consolidation of probation

The Home Office's hopes for an independent body which would drive probation forward were fulfilled by the formation of the National Association of Probation Officers (NAPO) in 1912, at the instigation of Sydney Edridge (d. 1934), Clerk of the Croydon Police Court, and the association's first chair. It aimed to advance probation work, to facilitate contacts between officers and to stimulate thinking about the reform of offenders. The Earl of Lytton accepted the presidency, initiating a tradition of formal and high-profile aristocratic support for probation which was to last into the 1960s. Edridge (though a religious man himself) envisaged probation as something distinct from the temperance work of the police court missionaries, and while acknowledging their occasional strengths, campaigned against their employment throughout his tenure. Unsurprisingly, missionaries tended not to join NAPO, resenting its formally secular ethos (and the designation 'probation officer'), and tension inevitably grew between them and the new organisation. Edridge encouraged the formation of local NAPO branches and established its journal (the prototype of today's *Probation Journal*). Although the Howard Association, and the newly formed Penal Reform League were to remain major independent champions of probation, NAPO eventually equalled them in influence, with the three organisations together pressing the Home Office to call recalcitrant magistrates to account, and to challenge the influence of the Church of England (and other denominational bodies) whose role as employers of the missionaries, alongside the magistracy, created a system of 'dual control' over probation that the 1907 Act had not anticipated.

Easing the tension created by dual control underpinned many of the reforms which probation underwent in the next 30 years. The Criminal Justice Act 1914 enabled the Home Office to subsidise the formation of a network of (non-denominational) philanthropic bodies concerned with offenders under 21, hoping thereby to increase the potential supply of probation officers, but the outbreak of the First World War meant the power was never implemented. It was not picked up after the peace, because rising juvenile delinquency during the war years led the Home Office to conclude that state initiatives, rather than those of philanthropic bodies, were necessary to deal with it. More significantly (for the long term, at least), the war years saw the emergence of Cecil Leeson (1883–1949), a Quaker and Birmingham probation officer who published 'the first book devoted entirely to probation'

(Bochel 1976: 64), based, significantly, on his observations of how probation had further developed in America (Leeson 1914). He argued for the better selection, training and payment of officers, insisting that such people were versed in psychology. He argued for more central control of probation in the Home Office, for the appointment of chief (or senior) probation officers and for a more open-minded attitude (than either the Home Office or existing probation officers showed) to the delegation of some work with offenders to trained and supervised volunteers. A young London magistrate, William Clarke Hall (1866–1932), much concerned with the welfare of young offenders, took up Leeson's ideas, while Leeson himself went on to become secretary of the Howard Association and later, in 1920, founded and ran the Magistrates' Association (conceived as a vanguard organisation for the liberal and progressive members of the magistracy), skilfully using both organisations to advance probation interests.

The post-War Probation Service was in poor shape. Twenty-five per cent of courts had still not appointed a probation officer. Many officers were part-time, overworked, badly paid and sometimes poor quality. A Home Office Departmental Committee (Home Office 1922) looked into this. The Howard League for Penal Reform (an amalgamation of the Howard Association and the Penal Reform League) ambitiously pressed them to create a Probation Commission, akin to the Prison Commission. While wanting improvements to probation, the Home Office resisted making probation officers 'a new class of civil servant' (quoted in Bochel 1976: 81) and hoped that the CETS and its equivalents could be persuaded to modernise. Thus pressured, the CETS notionally separated its police court work from its temperance work, allowed magistrates and social workers into its management structures and reorganised around county rather than diocesan boundaries. The Anglican Bishops nonetheless resisted appointing non-Anglicans as missionaries, even though this narrowed the pool of applicants. The London Police Court Mission was formed within the CETS to serve the capital (Bochel 1976: 92) and reinvigorated respect for the church's work, although in the provinces a reluctance to distance proper probation from missionary work caused the influence of denominational bodies to wane.

The need for improved probation officer training emerged as a point of contention in the Departmental Committee – and was to remain one throughout probation's history. Training for other types of social work had emerged in the Charity Organisation Society and the Settlement movement, increasingly linked to universities, and both NAPO, the Magistrates' Association and the Howard League wanted something similar for probation officers. Even the missionaries conceded its importance and the CETS was prepared to provide it. Partly with cost in mind, the Home Office was not initially convinced that probation officers needed to be university trained and was slow to act. It did create, within itself, an Advisory Committee on Probation (a lesser body than a Probation Commission) to put the probation ideal back on track, and, after legislation in 1923, began to pay half the cost of employing probation officers, whose appointment in petty sessional areas was finally made mandatory. Some area boundaries were combined or enlarged to make appointments viable, and police officers, even retired ones, were formally prohibited from taking up probation posts. Pay was improved, a career grade introduced and, in 1930, a proper training scheme introduced linked to universities in Manchester, Birmingham and London (although not of sufficient scope to train all probation officers).

The ascendancy of probation

Although never intended solely for juveniles, it was developments in juvenile justice – the desire to fulfil the immense promise of the juvenile court – which triggered the first phase of the process that was to lead to the ascendancy of probation officers over police court missionaries. The 1927 Molony Committee boldly sought new methods of reforming juvenile offenders. By arguing that neglected and delinquent children were one and the same, it increased the scope of social work and boosted the importance of probation reports in providing courts with a full understanding of the child before them (criticising magistrates who still did not utilise them). It discouraged probation involvement in supervising fine payment by 16–21-year-olds. It reaffirmed gender matching of women officers and probationers, highlighting the fact that only half of the 1,028 petty sessional areas had appointed a woman. It noted that London magistrates were by now making regular use of residence requirements, in homes rather than hostels, in order to avoid sending younger offenders to reformatory schools (which many magistrates and probation officers thought too punitive). Molony nonetheless discouraged this use of homes, fearing that an institutional dimension was creeping into probation, which had been conceived as 'treatment in the open' and should be kept pure. Hostels, however, were encouraged as a serious alternative to prison for 'working lads'. Molony gave broad encouragement to the now established (if still informal) involvement of probation officers in aftercare from both Borstal and reformatory schools, recommending that the Advisory Committee on Probation added 'Aftercare' to its name, which was duly done in 1928.

The legislation derived from the Molony Report – the Children and Young Persons Act 1933 – actually increased the scale and importance of local authorities' work with children rather than that of the Probation Service, although delinquents remained the preserve of the latter and in places it did become more involved in the supervision of truants (Rimmer 1995). To NAPO's chagrin, however, the Act seemingly attached more importance to school reports than to probation reports, and modernised reformatory schools, renaming them 'approved schools' in a bid to make them more popular with sentencers. These developments complicated the environment in which probation worked, but in many respects stimulated it to greater professionalism. Although NAPO still lacked a subscription-based membership (probation officer's pay was too low) the stature and talent of the people who ran it made this professionalism possible. The indefatigable Sydney Edridge retired after 16 years in 1928, but the trio who replaced him – Gertrude Tuckwell (recently appointed the first woman JP) as president, Charles William Slingsby Duncombe (the young Earl of Feversham) as vice-president and

William Clarke Hall as chair – were equally formidable. Feversham's wealth solved some immediate problems – the costs of an office, NAPOs first two salaried officers and a revamped journal – but he was to give valuable service to NAPO for 33 years, not least as a consistent champion of probation in the House of Lords. He brought in H.E. Norman, for whom he had worked in South Africa, to be NAPO's secretary, which proved to be a highly effective and popular appointment. Clarke Hall's reputation and influence grew – he was knighted in 1932 but died tragically the same year. One of his last acts was to initiate and finance the first *Handbook of Probation*, with entries on law, administration and practice by officers and members, edited by an established writer on criminal affairs, Mrs Le Measurier (1935). The Clarke Hall Fellowship which was subsequently set up in his name, promoted juvenile courts and subsidised NAPO for twelve years.

Stimulated partly by the growth of psychology (especially by the influence of Cyril Burt's (1925) *The Young Delinquent*) and partly by American developments in casework technique, Probation Service leaders (if not necessarily the grassroots) evolved a view during the 1930s that probation should best be seen as part of a wider social work 'profession'. They believed that incorporating psychological knowledge would increase the service's competence and give it a clearer identity with the public, distinct from the missionaries – and make it more credible with magistrates. Probation had still not achieved national cover, and some magistrates still showed 'ignorance and apathy' (Bochel 1976: 126) towards it, with some local committees appointing staff on the basis of personality rather than training. Caseloads remained impractically high. Officers were often isolated, too few were women, and their calibre poor – part-timers' other jobs included 'greengrocery or undertaking' (*ibid.*). Some were over 70 or 80 (*ibid.*).

Ironically, it was Home Office acknowledgement of the intense demands being made on courts and probation officers by 'matrimonial work' rather than criminal work which initiated decisive improvements in probation's standing. Conciliation with disputing parents, husbands and wives, acting as guardians *ad litem* in adoption cases, help with family budgeting, childrearing advice, hire purchase advice and assisting the wives of imprisoned men had developed informally since 1907, alongside – and entwined with – criminal work. NAPO wanted this recognised as a core probation task. A Departmental Committee on the Social Services in Courts of Summary Jurisdiction examined the matter – Feversham was a member of the Committee – and reported in 1936. The Committee's key conclusion was that the structural organisation of probation rather than its legislative framework needed improvement and that a clear break was needed with the CETS – in effect the ending of dual control. The need for casework skills was endorsed. In addition, inspecting the efficiency of the way in which the Home Office's grant aid was used, was seen *inter alia* as a way of pressuring magistrates to use probation more responsibly. The possibility of making probation officers into local government employees was examined but rejected, being seen at the time as tantamount to executive interference with independent sentencers (Bochel 1976: 128).

NAPO and the Home Office worked in unison to end dual control. They were not alone in seeing the dominance of the Anglican church in the management of probation as anachronistic and discriminatory. Christians of other denominations resented it (Rimmer 1995), though for Margery Fry (1874–1958), Chair of the Howard League (an agnostic, albeit one possessed of a Quaker conscience), 'free[ing] probation from its denominational ties' had become necessary because 'good candidates were being lost to the Probation Service because they could make no claim to a personal religion and could not imagine themselves working under a committee united by religious convictions' (Huws Jones 1966: 159). Although the CETS had increasingly been allowing some distance to develop between them and the Police Court Missions they had established, a temperance ethos still prevailed. Some missionaries nonetheless wanted to transfer to the employ of local probation committees, and the Missions reluctantly let them go. By such means dual control – but not Christian influence in probation – came to an end. Interestingly, William Temple (1881–1944), the Archbishop of Canterbury (formerly an Archbishop of York who had had oversight of the CETS), used the first Clarke Hall memorial lecture, to outline an 'ethics of penal action' for the Probation Service, with negligible reference to Christian principles and no evident nostalgia for police court missionaries (Temple 1934). The London Police Court Mission in fact went on to an illustrious future, among other things establishing Rainer House as a London base for trainee probation officers, a place which was eventually to become one of the probation services most revered and remembered institutions (Jacobs 2001).

The newly 'secularised', post-CETS service still fell far short of the professionalism that NAPO wanted. Many officers still worked in court corridors and yards or in nearby shops, and used their homes as offices. Despite NAPO, they had little sense of a corporate identity or a shared body of knowledge. Given their haphazard distribution across the country, many were isolated, and inspection visits (established in 1937) became the main 'source of information about the operation of the service as a whole' (Bochel 1976: 129). Most officers were still poorly paid and training had not flourished as well as expected, because recruits with only an elementary education could not make the most of what the university-linked courses offered (Bochel 1976: 144). A Probation Training Board was established in 1937 to improve training still further, strengthening links with universities and promoting a 'treatment ideal' based on casework (McWilliams 1985). Nonetheless, only an educated metropolitan elite, and *some* fieldworkers, took this seriously in the late 1930s. The practical outlook of many provincial probation officers was still shaped by their limited educational experience, varieties of Christian belief, varieties of eugenic thinking, and the views of the local magistrates for whom they worked. Faced with abjectly poor probationers and families during the Depression, many understandably saw casework as an unduly lofty aspiration and exerted influence in more down-to-earth ways.

The 1936 Committee noted the poor public image of probation, which was not helped by courts which themselves still confused binding over with probation, or by the still perfectly legal practice of sometimes ordering probation even if a conviction had not been made. The Committee insisted that probation mean release under supervision, *after conviction only*. They hoped that this 'would mean an end to the appearance in newspaper reports of the phrase "dismissed under the Probation of Offenders Act" which helped to encourage in the public mind the idea that probation was equivalent to being let off' (Bochel 1976: 147). The Committee recommended further stimulation of public interest in probation, along lines being pursued by NAPO and the Clarke Hall Fellowship – the public in this instance being no more than influential political elites and the educated middle classes.

The 1936 Committee's report 'became the blueprint for the probation service for the next quarter century' (Bochel 1976: 150) – envisaging a structure not dissimilar to that envisioned by Leeson in 1914. Some recommendations were implemented immediately – namely, recognition of matrimonial work (allowing the appointment of probation officers of the same religious persuasion as the conflicting parties), improved inspection and training and the creation of the Colonial Office Advisory Committee on penal affairs which the Howard League had pressed for to promote probation in Britain's colonies (Rose 1961 314–5). The remaining recommendations were incorporated in the Criminal Justice Bill 1938, whose aim (in respect of probation) was to simplify and consolidate a lot of accumulated legislation, to replace entering into a recognisance with 'consent' to probation, to introduce requirements for psychiatric treatment and to make women officers mandatory as supervisers of female probationers (thereby forcing magistrates to employ women). The many liberal penal measures in the Bill – including the proposal to remove magistrates' discretion to order probation without a conviction – proved controversial, and protracted parliamentary debate on the Bill as a whole prevented its enactment before the Second World War was declared.

The modernisation of probation

Ultimately, the Second World War boosted the fortunes of the Probation Service and paved the way for its becoming a distinct, if still subordinate, agency within the criminal justice system (although a sense of 'system' was barely apprehended at the time). Probation was designated a reserved occupation, and while some younger male officers opted for war service, Home Office commitment to new recruitment remained strong: there were 509 full-timers in 1939 and 750 in 1945 – 50 per cent of whom had been trained. More officers became principals and seniors, and more were women, who now routinely supervised under 14-year-old boys as well as girls and women in order to ensure that scarce male officers could concentrate on adults. Numbers of new probation orders rose from 29,000 in 1939 to 35,000 in 1943, the total number of people on probation reaching 50,000, reflecting in part wartime increases in crime (Smithies 1982). 'Some of the old inhibitions that had held back the development of the Probation Service were [now] beginning to fade' writes Ryder (1995: 27) and in a climate where Whitehall's general authority had massively increased, the Home Office became noticeably more directive with magistrates. Inspections of practice became more rigorous and critical and for the first time NAPO complained of central interference in local affairs (e.g. perfunctorily transferring officers to the 'reception areas' where evacuated youngsters had been sent). Evacuation undoubtedly undermined supervision;

foster families were not always informed if a youngster was on probation and delinquency increased in some reception areas. The separation of wives and families from serving soldiers brought new problems, or amplified old ones, and probation officers worked alongside Army Welfare Officers to ameliorate them. Some probationers joined the forces, some with their orders discharged, some not. Resources nationally became tight – a female officer whose male colleague had been assisted in purchasing his first car just before the war was told to 'stick to the buses' once war had been declared (Ryder 1995: 27). Sewell Stokes (1950), a journalist who worked as a probation officer at Bow Street magistrates court in wartime London, wrote a vivid, picaresque memoir of his experiences.

Even before the war had ended, increased official awareness of poverty and deprivation experienced by children and a nascent social democratic spirit were prompting reflection on the shape of postwar social services. NAPO was made anxious by rumours that probation would become centrally funded, and perhaps run on a regional basis. Magistrates – proprietorial about 'their' probation officers – had picked upon this by the end of the war, and the first task undertaken by the newly formed Advisory Committee on the Treatment of Offenders (ACTO) was to consider 'what more can be done to develop the Probation Service as a highly skilled profession requiring *not only a missionary spirit* but training and expert knowledge' (quoted in Bochel 1976: 164, emphasis added). Its unpublished report did not recommend major structural changes to the service. (The newly formed Principal Probation Officer's Conference – initiated by the Home Office in 1942 to bring more senior staff under its influence – was steadily to become another voice arguing for the distinctive contribution of probation, although in the period covered by this chapter, they were never as significant a body as NAPO, nor a rival to it.)

The Criminal Justice Act 1948 tackled a range of specifically post-War issues – including rising juvenile crime – but also carried forward some elements of the progressive spirit of the aborted 1938 Bill, which various Home Secretaries, MPs, penal reform and professional groups (the Howard League, the Institute for the Study and Treatment of Delinquency, NAPO) had kept alive (Coddington 1950). Reflecting the intentions of the 1936 Departmental Committee the Act established an administrative infrastructure for probation which was, in fact, to last into the 1970s, and indeed after that. It finally forbade the practice of using probation where there was no conviction, reaffirmed 'advise, assist and befriend' as the legal aim of probation supervision, and permitted the inclusion in an order of a requirement for mental treatment. While abolishing the birching of juveniles, it made concessions to punishment with the introduction of attendance centres for under 21-year-olds and military-style 'short, sharp shock' detention centres, neither of which had figured in the 1938 Bill. The spirit of these measures was somewhat contradicted by the simultaneous creation, in the 1948 Children's Act, of local authority Children's Departments to address problems of child neglect and, inevitably, the delinquency associated with it. Twenty years later, debates within and about these departments were to have a significant bearing on government thinking on the future of probation.

Unsurprisingly, this new, modernising, legislation did not effect immediate cultural change in the Probation Service. Older practices lingered on, with some officers (and magistrates) using the new 1949 probation rules to permit the inclusion of requirements in probation orders for youngsters to attend church and Sunday School, on the grounds that 'lack of religious training' lay behind the juvenile crime problem (quoted in *Justice of the Peace*, 9 July 1949: 433). Nonetheless, the service did begin to recruit younger people, some of whom were interested in new ways of working – notably adventure training and various sorts of groupwork, the latter owing something to the influence, on training courses, of placements in the Tavistock Clinic, the Henderson Hospital and some of the more progressive prisons and Borstals (Vanstone 2004: 97). Smaller probation services were merged into larger ones and, crucially, the early 1950s were the period in which probation changed from 'a predominantly part-time to a whole time service' (Younghusband 1978: 99). More senior and principal probation officers were appointed, and better clerical backup made available. The nine- to twelve-month training courses run at Rainer House grew more sophisticated, including lectures from staff at the Tavistock Clinic and the Institute for the Study and Treatment of Delinquency, as well as from academic criminologists like Max Grunhut and Hermann Mannheim. While celebrating the incorporation of 'new' insights from psychology and psychoanalysis in this period, an influential textbook, written by the joint secretary of the Home Office Probation Training Board, still emphasised the desirability of probation officers being people of 'truly Christian magnanimity and discernment', and assumed consonance between probation practice and 'Christian faith and teaching' (Glover 1949: 270–1).

NAPO became a more professional and more influential body during the 1950s, surviving on subscriptions without – except in respect of its journal – the patronage of the Clarke Hall Fellowship. Although Lord Feversham remained as president, it appointed its first probation officer as chair. Most fatefully, however, it appointed Frank Dawtry (1902–68) as its full-time secretary in 1948. Though not himself a probation officer – he had led the National Council for the Abolition of the Death Penalty and been secretary of a Discharged Prisoner's Aid Society – he was a man of exceptional talent, surefooted in the penal reform world and respected by the Home Office. He adroitly steered the service through the challenges of the next twenty years until his retirement in 1967, and died while still editor of *Probation*. Originally a Methodist, he subsequently joined the Society of Friends, and his intelligence, eloquence and temperament was emblematic of the sensibility which the service as a whole, at its best, sought to project. During Dawtry's tenure, NAPO representatives regularly attended international conferences and hosted foreign probation visitors, many of whom (quite reasonably) regarded the English service as the progenitor of their own and the model to which they should aspire.

Over and above the casebooks and memoirs produced by magistrates (Watson 1942/50; Page 1948; Henriques 1950) – which had been a perennial, and largely positive, source of public information about probation – the avenues through which the public might become better informed about the service were increasing. In the immediate postwar period, Ealing Studios made a number of popular movies which celebrated various public service organisations. One such, *I Believe in You* (1950 d. Basil Dearden), dealt with probation. Loosely based on Sewell Stokes, (1950) memoir but set after the war, it had the same production team as *The Blue Lamp* (1948), a film which famously helped shape a congenial image of British policing. Probation officer Henry Phipps, a middle-aged, newly retired colonial officer begins work (untrained) at a court in South London alongside a trained woman officer. Much of his work with the lowly denizens of the magistrate's court is rendered in rather comic terms, but in passing serious points are made about juvenile crime and contemporary probation practice. Phipps himself exhibits a wry, self-deprecating decency and spends a lot of time persuading a stern stipendary magistrate that certain youngsters have some good in them, are worth 'believing in' and can be helped. At the end, after a backstreet skirmish with a more incorrigible (and armed) delinquent, he takes over from the old-and-weary-but-still-dedicated senior probation officer, Mr Dove (Birkbeck 1982).

Melodrama apart, the film was true to the better aspects of the probation spirit, but glossed over its more desultory elements. Many officers in Wales worked from home – a practice which continued in some areas until 1976 (Minkes 2003). In a late 1950s study, researchers Rodgers and Dixon (1960) described probation in an unnamed 'northern town' as plagued by high staff turnover, scepticism about training and low morale, while John Barron Mays, a settlement warden in Liverpool, emphasised continuing flaws in probation practice:

> Confusion exists in the public mind regarding the seriousness of a probation order and it is often regarded as being nothing more than a let off. Parents do not always realise that their children can be brought back to court for the same offence if the probation officer is dissatisfied by the child's behaviour or the degree of parental cooperation. A suspicion that probation officers have a tendency to 'whitewash' offenders has arisen from time to time. Young officers quite wrongly feel it a personal failure if children under their care have to be brought back to court. There are factors beyond their control which may nullify their efforts for probation is essentially a matter of cooperation with the family and with other agencies and this cannot be compelled. Again some children are placed on probation for whom that particular treatment is quite unsuitable and much of the blame for failures in such cases must be charged against the magistrates. (Mays 1951: 4)

Public anxiety that probation entailed offenders 'being let off lightly' required constant rebuttal throughout the 1950s. Sheffield's principal probation officer, for example, explained tartly to a local newspaper that probation was 'not always understood' and that 'it checks the liberty' (*The Star* 19 March 1954). Nonetheless, by 1957, the year of its jubilee, the Probation Service demonstrably enjoyed an unprecedented level of official prestige, if not widespread public appreciation. There were at that point in time 104 probation areas, 1,250 probation officers, supervising 45,000 offenders, 4,000 children in need of care and protection and 7,000 ex-prisoners being resettled. Its first 50 years were commemorated by a long weekend of events starting with a private celebration organised by the Queen Mother at Lancaster House, a more public event at the Guildhall and NAPO's AGM at the London School of Economics. A by now frail and elderly Viscount Herbert Samuel (1957), the Under-Secretary of State who had piloted the 1907 Act through Parliament, spoke at the Guildhall, emphasising the extent to which probation was still a Christian vocation. An editorial in *Probation* (March 1957) referred to the police court missionaries as 'pathfinders' and clearly connected the work of modern probation officers to their cause. The Home Secretary's letter of congratulation to NAPO on the jubilee was printed on the front page of *Probation* (*idem*); his own speech (Butler 1957), emphasised the need to put probation on a more scientific, research-based footing, but he too portrayed the service primarily as a moralising force in the criminal justice system. An address by the Most Reverend Joost de Blank (1957) Archbishop of Cape Town, on 'working in faith', published later in the jubilee year, again reaffirmed the essentially Christian ethos of the Probation Service.

It is thus clear that by 1957 NAPO (and others) had successfully constructed the 'myth' of the police court missionaries as the *most significant* of probation's roots. The other roots – bindovers and the Howard Association's publicising of probation in Massachusetts, as well the tensions once entailed by dual control – were played down. This helpfully simplified a less than straightforward story, and NAPO was only able to celebrate its spiritual ancestry when it was actually free of the church's direct influence. Doubtless the narrative reflected the deep and genuine Christian faith of some contemporary probation leaders and champions, but it also served to give probation work a mystique and an authority, a 'transcendental justification' – in essence, a minimally secularised version of the original vision of John Augustus and Frederick Rainer – which a merely social or political authority could have bestowed. As significantly – although rather paradoxically given the earlier and much longed-for break with the CETS – it placed the Service once again within the orbit of the Anglican Church – a still prestigious institution to whose rituals and figureheads (including monarchs and princes) the state still deferred to signify and celebrate occasions of national moment. This in turn helped create an image of the Probation Service as distinctively and essentially 'British' – an image reinforced within NAPO by the sense that it was the hub connecting many Commonwealth probation services. This may also explain why no effort was made in the jubilee to acknowledge the long-forgotten *American* origins of the term 'probation officer'. Supressing the transatlantic connection further enabled NAPO to sustain an impression that the English service had been the first in the world, but even in European terms this was not strictly true.

The expansion and diversification of probation

The 1960s saw expansion and diversification in the Probation Service, in the context of decisive attempts to modernise criminal justice more generally. The White Paper *Penal Practice in a Changing Society* (Home Office 1959) had sought to orient the whole of penal policy towards scientifically based rehabilitation. The first major study of probation (undertaken by the University of Cambridge, Radzinowicz 1958) had shown a success rate (as measured by successful completion of an order and the avoidance of conviction over three years thereafter) for adults of 73.8 per cent and for juveniles of 62.4 per cent. This was a good enough result (despite acknowledged methodological limitations) to encourage continued investment in the service, and the personal encomium which Radzinowicz, the most esteemed criminologist in the land, gave probation probably increased its prestige still further. The report of the Streatfeild Committee (Home Office 1961) (which examined the work of the courts, not probation as such) echoed the spirit of the White Paper, emphasising that probation officers, armed with sounder understanding of the effects of sentencing on particular types of individual, could and should provide courts with more reliable information than hitherto. Doubtless influenced by Barbara Wootton, who was a member of the Committee, it significantly raised the prominence of social enquiry reports in the culture of the Probation Service, emphasising that offering guidance to sentencers was on par with all other aspects of modern probation work.

NAPO – conscious that probation's fortunes had, from 1909 on, always been improved by the recommendations of Departmental Committees – had pressed throughout the 1950s for an inquiry into the changing work of the service, and the White Paper created a pretext for the Home Office to agree to this. The Morison Committee sat between 1959 and 1962. It reaffirmed the idea of probation as something imposed instead of punishment (and not akin to a suspended *sentence* of imprisonment, which some magistrates, led by Sir Leo Page, were wanting it to become (see Nellis 2000)). It nonetheless emphasised that a disciplinary element was essential to probation's purpose and to its credibility with the public (para.s 9–11). It deflected arguments that the service might be improved if it were run by either local authorities or central government, and echoed Streatfeild's defence of retaining 'matrimonial work' in the service (and not given to another agency), because the Probation Service was publicly recognised for its expertise in this field. It did emphasise that probation committees needed to speak with one voice and learn from each other, and this prompted the establishment of the Central Council of Probation Committees in 1961, which was to remain a significant voice in the politics of probation until the turn of the twentieth century. Morison made a special effort to revitalise probation in Scotland where, it was now becoming clear, it was held in less esteem by the judiciary than it was in England and Wales. Much to NAPO's chagrin, despite the fact that in the 1958–61 situation 45 per cent of new probation staff were 'direct entrants', Morison did not accept the case for more university-based training of officers, conceding only that Rainer House was too London-focused, and that training should be decentralised around the country, with inspectorate staff and guest academics taking more part in it.

Morison (Home Office 1962a: para. 54) saw 'social casework' as the scientific basis of the Probation Service's claim to expertise and professional status, but with two caveats. Firstly, the Committee doubted whether the available scientific knowledge justified major changes in probation practice and disagreed with Streatfeild that probation officers should make recommendations to sentencers in their reports, simply because there was as yet no reliable evidential base for doing so. Secondly, casework was not seen as synonymous with 'treatment'; only some probationers required 'intensive therapy'; many others required mere 'help and advice' or just 'regular control' (para. 16). Morison's primary defence of probation was in any case grounded in its moral value to individual offenders and to society as a whole, not in terms of its scientifically established effectiveness (para. 59). In essence, the Committee straddled the positions taken by Eileen Younghusband and Barbara Wootton in contemporary debate on the nature of social work. Younghusband (a member of the Morison Committee) emphasised that in conditions of full employment and improved welfare provision probation officers could and should concentrate less on meeting material needs and more on using psychology to help emotionally needy individuals. Wootton tended to emphasise the continuing part that poverty, inequality and relative deprivation played in the genesis of delinquency, and as poverty was progressively 'rediscovered' in 1960s Britain her mockery of the pretensions of casework, her greater openness to *whatever* might work to reduce crime and not least her agnosticism – made her something of a hero to a rising generation of more street-wise probation officers who were uneasy with some aspects of the service's putative Christian heritage (Parkinson 1988).

When the 1960s began, probation's public profile had never been higher or more positive. Between 1959 and 1962 Associated Television showed a drama series, *Probation Officer*, made with the support and cooperation of the London service (Inner London Probation Service 2001). A journalist, John St John (1961), published an officially authorised, informative and well-received book about the reality of the modern Probation Service (whose cosmopolitan focus perhaps underplayed the service's backwardness in more provincial areas). One of several popular social work novels by Hertfordshire Childcare Officer John Stroud (1961) *Touch and Go* had a probation officer as the central character. Frank Fletcher was a rather morose family man who had entered probation after wartime experiences in a German POW camp – 'I wanted to do something constructive after the war ... to try to make up for all I could see around me' (p. 14). The novel opens with him moving from London to a new post in 'Kellingham', a fictionalised New Town (modelled on Stevenage) for no other reasons than that his wife wants to leave the city. The job proves more onerous than he had anticipated – the delinquents far more intractable – and having been at odds with the police superintendent throughout Fletcher is forced by the end to concede the merits of the latter's tough approach and moves despondently to a more congenial post in rural Ludlow. Stroud makes Kellingham symbolic of a soulless urban wasteland emerging in modern England, which exacerbates youthful propensities to crime. Stroud's veiled suggestion that casework-oriented probation officers might not be equal to the challenge posed by rebellious modern youth – was in fact prescient. Anthony Burgess (1962) worked a similar seam in *A Clockwork Orange*, but more darkly still; his rather sleazy probation-officer-of-the near-future is both allied quite closely to the police and utterly ineffectual, a man whose profession has outlived its usefulness, whose knowledge is obsolete.

Fred Jarvis, the Principal Probation Officer of Leicester and Rutland (who had in effect taken on Frank Dawtry's intellectual mantle, and begun producing an influential manual of probation practice (Jarvis 1969)), looked back on the early 1960s as a period of strangely unfulfilled promise. The service was held in greater official esteem than ever before, but yet lacked the substantive influence on criminal justice as a whole that its leaders and champions felt was its due:

> As well as being the year of the issue of the Morison Report, 1962 was the fiftieth anniversary of the National Association of Probation Officers. The occasion was marked by a reception at St James Palace attended by Princess Margaret, and a gathering at Croydon for an address by the Archbishop of Canterbury. Despite this recognition, the support of a *Times* leader, despite too a television series portraying week after week an unfailingly good and infinitely resourceful probation officer; despite all this the service seemed unable to command its proper status and effect its necessary development. (Jarvis 1972: 66)

Underlying Jarvis's sense of underachievement was an unspoken belief that if only it were given full rein the rehabilitative ideal would have an utterly transformative effect on criminal justice. Arguably, however, the dissonance which Jarvis felt existed between 'the real' and 'the ideal' arose because he judged actually existing probation not by feasible improvements but by wholly unrealisable aspirations premised on an unduly benign view of human nature, and inevitably found it wanting. Among probation elites, the belief that lawbreakers exhibited little more than tarnished goodness and were easily scrubbed up peaked in the early 1960s and it is probably fortunate that contingent developments elsewhere in penal policy (Morris 1989) tempered – rendered more realistic but never quite dashed – this naive ideal. In practice, the Streatfeild and Morison Reports did increase the scope and influence and raise the status of the Probation Service in significant ways, but as the decade progressed the tone of probation's claims within penal debate became more down to earth, still socially progressive, but less likely to appeal to abstract moral (or Christian) principles as the basis for whatever case was being made and more likely to appeal to 'evidence'. While faith remained privately important to some probation officers – Packer's (1963) account of a day in the life of a hard-pressed rural officer ended with him taking a Bible class in a Methodist chapel – its justifying narratives, as evidenced by contemporary textbooks (Herbert and Jarvis 1961; Monger 1964), became steadily more secular.

Policy developments in the 1960s drew probation more intimately into the experience and consequence of imprisonment. Such welfare work as had occurred in prisons before then was largely the responsibility of volunteers from local Discharged Prisoners Aid Societies. In 1961 their National Association agreed with the Home Office to pay prison welfare officers to work inside prisons. Michael Sorenson (1986) and Sallie Trotter (1969) were among the first appointed. Trotter had in fact been a probation officer, but many others were inadequately trained. Eventually all were replaced by probation officers. Many were women, despite their low numbers in the service generally. By

1965, 101 were in place, 294 by 1972. They served 2–3 years as members of the prison management team, helping prisoners cope with the regime, undertaking counselling, preparing them for release and – to a lesser extent – working with prisoner's families. Dual systems of accountability – to prison governors and to outside principal probation officers – caused tensions and some prison officers resented the usurping of the helping element of their role. The work brought home to probation officers the difficulties of doing social work in a prison setting and an inchoate sense emerged – echoing their earlier hostility to approved schools, but varying with the character of particular penal institutions – that prison-based probation officers were colluding with something harmful.

The Service's ambivalence towards penal institutions had been in evidence throughout the post-War period in its vacillating attitude towards probation hostels. Recurrent debates on which probationers were best served by them and on what their purpose was (work training or therapy) continued in the 1960s, questioning their amenability to casework (Leeves 1967; Monger 1969). Individual hostel wardens may have been clear about their task (see Cooks' 1958 memoir) but at different times in the 1960s NAPO recommended that hostels, most of which, but not all, were in the voluntary sector, be merged into the Approved School System or be taken over by the Prison Service. Neither Sinclair's (1971) otherwise well received empirical research on hostels nor the second Morison Report (Home Office 1962b) made practice more consistent, although more probation committees set up hostels of their own, mostly for homeless and alcoholic offenders (Palmer 1982).

Voluntary 'aftercare' for short-sentence ex-prisoners, both juvenile and adult, developed haphazardly after 1895 (see Forsythe 1991: 217–32). Probation officers (supplementing their part-time incomes) became informally involved in it in the late 1920s, alongside an array of volunteers and (with adult offenders) police officers whom they eventually displaced. The Discharged Prison's Aid Societies (local, but after 1936 nationally coordinated) and the Central After-Care Association (covering those released on licence from longer sentences) dominated aftercare from the 1930s onwards, but the ramshackle nature of the enterprise was subject to constant criticism (Pritt 1934; Dawtry 1948; Pakenham/Thompson Committee 1961), even after the Criminal Justice Act 1948 put probation officer involvement in aftercare on a more formal footing. Something much more streamlined was needed. ACTO (1963) recommended merging the voluntary and statutory forms of aftercare into a single service, run by probation; this was accepted and in 1965 the Probation Service was renamed the Probation and Aftercare Service to reflect its widened responsibilities. Incorporating this new work entailed both administrative and professional challenges, especially in large urban areas. Among other things it renewed probation interest in the recruitment of volunteers to assist in the supervision of less serious offenders, and in intensive aftercare for the more serious offenders, particularly those from Borstals (Barr 1971).

Even as aftercare arrangements were finally being consolidated – if not necessarily being made particularly more effective – the Home Office (1965) was considering new and more dramatic ways of managing the rising prison population. It took up a Labour Party Study Group (1964) recommendation for a parole system – the early release on licence of prisoners – adapted from the USA. Many probation officers opposed this – parole required more oversight than casework principles permitted, and focused on more serious offenders than the service routinely dealt with. NAPO supported *the idea* of parole, but resisted its introduction on the grounds of inadequate consultation, understaffing (the service was 200 below strength), failing recruitment and the only recent absorption of aftercare and prison welfare. Despite these complaints the Government introduced parole in the Criminal Justice Act 1967. The hastiness of its introduction had predictable results; within a year probation officers were struggling to meet deadlines for their reports (Thomas 1974). Wootton's (1978: 120) observation that while 'some probation officers regard[ed] these duties as damaging to their professional role, attitudes change as time passes, and more recent recruits to the service come to take these developments in their stride' proved true in relation to both aftercare and parole, and summed up the part that new recruits and rising generations have always played in the service's evolution.

The reprieve and renewal of probation

The mid-1960s were uncomfortable times for the Probation Service. Internal reconfigurations within the penal welfare complex generated by a modernising Labour government pulled in contradictory directions, some favouring the expansion and diversification of the service, others wanting it merged into an enlarged local authority Family Service. There was no significant enthusiasm for either option in the service itself, partly because it already felt overwhelmed by change. The profile of offenders coming probation's way was also changing – in metropolitan if not initially provincial areas – with drug use in particular posing new challenges (King 1969). Most fatefully of all, however, the Magistrates' Association – no longer as close to probation as it had been in the 1920s and more intimate with the Conservative than the Labour Party – was expressing dissatisfaction with the perceived leniency of probation, and the difficulty of regarding it as a serious alternative to prison.

Home Secretary Roy Jenkins responded to this latter concern in 1966 by asking the ACPS to explore the possibility of extending non-custodial penalties – for offenders over 17 – beyond probation orders and fines. Labour peer Barbara Wootton – a critic in equal measure of casework and of excessive imprisonment – was appointed to chair the resulting ACPS subcommittee on reducing the use of short custodial sentences for petty persistent offenders. The contribution of alcohol, drug use and mental disorder to offending in this group was left to other, pre-existing, advisory committees, but one reading of this split responsibility is that it represents the first signs of a divergence between the logic of 'social work' and the logic of 'penal reform'. The rehabilitative ideal had been seamlessly entwined with – indeed, defined by – 'social work' – since the 1930s, but it now became possible to envisage liberal penal measures which were not social work in the established 'casework' sense. Wootton herself was open to the possibility of developing an 'effective deterrent' in the community, and specifically asked for the broadening of her terms of reference to encompass the new concept of 'semi-custodial' penalties alongside non-custodial measures.

The subcommittee's report, in June 1970, was radical and wide ranging. The community service order was the measure to which they themselves attached most importance. It was envisaged as having reparative and deterrent as well as rehabilitative elements, was not necessarily to be restricted to imprisonable offences and could occasionally be combined with a probation order. Developing community service was considered preferable to the expansion of senior attendance centres, of which, at the time, they were only two (one run by the Prison Service, the other by local police). The intermittent element of attendance centre orders directed the subcommittee's attention to the broader concept of intermittent custody, but ultimately only weekend imprisonment, as used in New Zealand, was recommended. They addressed longstanding arguments about the desirability of combining probation with a fine or with a suspended sentence, envisaging the occasional creative use of both combinations (arguing, in the case of a suspended sentence, that an offender's consent should be dispensed with). A minority on the subcommittee, including Wootton herself, proposed the abandonment of imprisonment for fine default, better means of fine collection and more regard among sentencers for an offender's ability to pay.

In addition, deferment of sentence – in effect postponing a court's decision (a measure many magistrates had long wanted) – was thought helpful. So too were various forms of disqualification (prohibited employment and car use) and forfeiture considered, though not on a large scale. A need for more hostels was identified. Day centres for training offenders in semi-skilled work for a given number of weeks (another measure advocated by magistrates) were examined, but not recommended. Oddly perhaps, given the breadth of Wootton's knowledge, no reference was made to the prototype of what became known as 'electronic monitoring' – despite its inventor having promoted it in England as a new rehabilitative tool (Schwitzgebel 1963). This was an era in which even an 'answerphone' roused a sense of wonder among probation officers – apart from the pervasive general impact of buses, cars and telephones (not least on the siting of probation sub-offices) technology had had negligible bearing on the evolution of probation. It did though, in one probation officer's wildly imaginative projections of what probation might be like in the year 2000 (Goslin 1970).

The Wootton Report challenged key axioms of probation practice. It questioned the time-honoured separation of community-based and custodial penalties and was dubious about consent. It decentred rehabilitation (if not offender reintegration) as an 'end' and casework as a 'means'. It saw deterrence and reparation as legitimate aims of non-custodial strategies. Some in the service wondered how this ostensible shift from social work squared with the Labour government's larger plan to absorb probation into the mooted Family Service, and it would indeed have been interesting to see how this would have been resolved if Labour had won the 1970 General Election. In the event it was the Conservative Party which ensured that the

Probation Service remained a distinct organisation and which governed the implementation of the Wootton Report.

The Labour government's readiness to absorb probation into a larger social work entity was rooted in administrative anomalies which had emerged in the immediate postwar period. The formation of the Children's Departments in 1948 had created a new powerbase for workers with young offenders in both central and local government, the first time since 1907 that probation had had any (non-residential) competitors. To some, however, the Children's Act had not gone far enough – the juvenile court needed either to become more welfare-oriented or be replaced with non-judicial welfare panels (Fry *et al.* 1947). The Inglebly Committee's (Home Office 1960) rejection of this proved unacceptable to the ascendant social work interests (on the grounds that delinquents were largely emotionally maladjusted and should be spared the stigma of criminal proceedings). In alliance with these social workers, the Labour Party, first in opposition, then in government, picked up the issue; initially, it did propose the abolition of the juvenile court alongside the enlargement of the Children's Departments into Family Departments which would address the multiple needs of 'problem families' more comprehensively. Social workers concerned with the welfare of old, mentally ill and disabled people then pressed for their inclusion in any new Family Department. Reforms along these lines did occur in Scotland, where welfare panels for young offenders were created and where probation was absorbed into unified, generic local authority Social Work Departments (see McIvor and McNeil, this volume). In England and Wales the Seebohm Committee (Department of Health 1968) was tasked to examine the feasibility of such departments here, although probation was left outside its remit.

NAPO watched these developments with increasing misgivings. Unity with other social workers would mean increased professional strength and status. Nonetheless, although they had casework (and a tradition of home visiting) in common with other social workers, many officers did not fully accept the delinquency-as-maladjustment theory that increasingly dominated the Children's Departments. They baulked at the proposed abolition of the juvenile court because they believed, with Younghusband, that a psychoanalytic understanding of delinquency necessitated the kind of firm boundary-setting that only a court – not a welfare panel – could provide. They recognised too that there were issues about 'authority' and 'enforcement' in probation that other social workers did not face (Hunt 1964; Foren and Bailey 1968). NAPO was thus relieved when the government dropped the idea of abolishing juvenile courts, but alarmed when, in the post-Seebohm legislation, the government did propose absorbing probation (and education welfare and child guidance clinics) into the new local authority Social Service Departments. Only concerted resistance from NAPO, the Magistrates' Association (which wanted probation officers to remain as 'friends of the court' rather than as employees of the local authority) and the Conservative opposition averted this. In Parliament, the Conservatives made the issue so contentious that it was only by dropping it from the Bill that the government was able to get the legislation through before the 1970 election (Hall 1976).

Technically, the question of the Probation Service's future remained open, but in 1972 the Conservative government simply ratified its continuing separation from local authorities. For NAPO the end result (in England) was the best of all possible worlds. The Probation Service had emerged unscathed from a modernising government's attempt to 'abolish' it, and not all work with delinquents passed to the new 'untried' local authority departments, who took time to build up their expertise. NAPO had further rejected merger into the British Association of Social Workers (BASW), social work's new generic professional body, but had enthusiastically welcomed incorporation into generic social work training arrangements, under the auspices of the newly formed Central Council for the Education and Training of Social Workers (CCETSW). They anticipated – mistakenly, as it turned out – that what was distinctive about work with offenders would not be dissipated in the new generic curriculum.

Guided by the Magistrates' Association, the Conservative government implemented the Wootton Report selectively. Community service was regarded as too valuable to lose, and day centres, which the magistrates wanted even though Wootton had not, were established experimentally by the Criminal Justice Act 1972, to be run by probation. Weekend imprisonment was rejected. Many older, established probation officers still saw community service as alien to the social work ethos. Jarvis (1972: 69) conceded that it 'may alter [probation officers'] traditional pattern of working', and in the event a rising younger generation of officers embraced it, drawing Wootton's reforms into a narrative of probation tradition by recasting them as a renewal of the service's original mission to keep offenders out of custody, and conceding that a limited degree of modernisation was necessary. In retrospect, the Service should have engaged more fully with the philosophical and practical challenges which Wootton posed, for they were rooted in social and cultural changes which genuinely affected the amenability of young people to supervision, and they were to return in more insistent forms in the Younger Report (ACPS 1974) on young adult offenders.

Could the Service have discerned any clues about the changing times and its own prospects from the wider culture? It is interesting that the film of *A Clockwork Orange* (Kubrick 1971) – more influential and talked about than Burgess's novel had been a decade earlier – proved rather prescient about the future tone of British penal policy (Bennett 2001). The story was set in an unspecified near-future, and anticipated a government whose primary concern was with 'cutting down crime…and relieving the ghastly overcrowding in our prisons' by developing new behavioural control technologies which inhibit violence. To the government minister who had authorised use of 'the Ludovico technique' (crude aversion therapy), the 'higher ethics' were irrelevant; all that mattered was 'that it works'. The probation officer in the film (as in the book) is dreary, defeated and without personal authority. It falls to a Christian – a prison chaplain – to point out what is lost when an offender 'ceases to be a creature capable of moral choice' (Kubrick 1972), although he himself seems bereft of practical answers. While clearly hostile to the techno-pragmatism of the future government, the film also mocks liberals for tolerating the intolerance of predatory violence and for undervaluing the immediate and ongoing need for public protection. There were subtle warnings here for the Probation Service, which only a few were prepared to heed.

Probation and the humanisation of justice

By 1972 the Probation Service was a thoroughly respected and taken-for-granted presence within the English criminal justice system. Nonetheless, in what proved to be the last edition of *The Probation Handbook,* Joan King (1969) considered that its main achievement was more in the realm of sensibility than in the realm of structure: it may not have emptied the prisons as some supporters of the 1907 Act had anticipated, but it had nonetheless effected 'the humanisation of justice'. This entailed more than the mere individualisation of justice, for this could be done in cold, positivistic ways. 'Humanising' here meant two things. Firstly, an appreciation of depth psychology, in which a minority of Tavistock-influenced officers had developed real expertise. Secondly, attention to the social and personal characteristics of offenders (not just their assumed moral character), a willingness to show them kindness and respect, and to patiently educate them. This talent for 'tough love' was within the gift of a rather broader tranche of probation officers than the Tavistock's psychodynamic approach, and was what Wootton (1978: 120) had in mind when she said that 'a more dedicated company of men and women than those employed in the Probation Service would be hard to find in any profession'. Both forms of humanisation could – and were – expressed in secular terms, but sublimated traces of a Christian emphasis on the redeemability of fallen sinners remained. Faith, perhaps more privatised than before, continued to motivate some officers, and the service in this period still recruited a steady stream of would-be priests, or ex-priests, who found the Church itself to be an uncongenial employer. Archbishop William Temple (1942: 27) had been prescient in this respect. Observing the growing ascendancy of NAPO over the police court missions in the 1930s but without the misgivings one might have expected of a cleric once associated with the CETS, he wrote: 'nine tenths of the work of the Church in the world is done by Christian people fulfilling responsibilities and performing tasks which in themselves are not part of the official system of the Church at all'.

A humanistic sensibility – which approximated to what Bill McWilliams (1987) called 'personalism' – rather than a fully shared knowledge base was mostly what unified the outlook of probation officers from the 1960s onwards. A variety of theories, perspectives and 'practice wisdom' fed into it (via training arrangements) but officers retained considerable leeway in what they believed and much discretion in the way they acted towards offenders. Dick Mott's (1992) memoir of his years as a basic grade officer in the service (1960–84) perfectly illustrates McWilliams's (1987) point that expertise in this period was understood to be a matter of personal character and acquired skill – rather than the capacity to implement a prescribed programme or to give expression to a 'policy'. Significant influences on the sensibility included Mays's (1963) belief that social work with young offenders was largely about compensating for the effects of social disadvantage, journalistic accounts of 'insecure offenders'

(Fyvel 1961), ethnographies such as Willmott's (1966) 'adolescent boys of East London' and Tony Parker's early 'offender biographies' (see Soothill (1999) for an overview). All variants of the humanistic ethos – including the agnostic version promoted by Barbara Wootton – distanced themselves from punishment in some degree. Some actually prided themselves on being wholly non-punitive, and retribution, in particular (despite C.S. Lewis's (1949) humanistic defence of it), was deemed wholly incompatible with social work and inimical to effecting positive change in offenders.

Whatever its shortcomings, there can be no doubt that probation in twentieth-century Britain did humanise significant aspects of the administration of justice at root by ameliorating unnecessary harshness but in many respects going beyond this to something more proactive. At their best, probation officers showed kindness, understanding and respect to offenders at fateful and strained moments in their lives. While this was a genuine achievement, it is perhaps best understood as an aspect of a more general – liberal and proto-egalitarian if not wholly permissive – mood which had grown among the younger elements of the educated, metropolitan middle class in the post-War era. At the same time, its reach and depth should not be exaggerated. Ordinary probation officers were not necessarily ahead of liberal opinion in the 1960s, and the older ones may in some ways have been behind it. While white, heterosexual, working-class men were reasonably 'humanised' – their stories were listened to and penalties individualised in some degree – some probation officers believed that they offered 'by far the most rational and humane method of dealing with male homosexuals whose offence does not make imprisonment unavoidable' (St John 1961: 177), rather than being in the vanguard of the decriminalisation movement. And while lesbian relationships were not *per se* illegal, this did not prevent a well-meaning probation officer from referring a 'mannish young woman' (convicted of a 'non-sexual' offence) to a psychiatrist and asking the court for permission to buy her a set of 'more feminine clothes ... so that she could feel proud of being a woman' – which the woman rejected (*ibid.*: 77).

The limits of humanisation were apparent also in probation officer attitudes to 'battered wives': both John St John and Marjorie Todd (a journalist working temporarily as a probation officer) instance officers accepting that a wife's slovenly housekeeping would understandably provoke their husbands to violence and saw nothing too untoward about it themselves. Todd (1964: 95) notes that a Mrs Ali, an Anglo-Pakistani, was 'always surprised when Mr Ali threw her against a wall or down the stairs'. Attitudes to race itself were also skewed. St John expresses respect for a young West African probationer who refused to be treated as an inferior by a white tobacconist, although by hitting him he earned a month's imprisonment and a breach of his probation order. In passing, St John wonders if 'a coloured probation officer would have been more effective' at helping the probationer come to terms with discrimination (St John 1960: 152) but concludes resignedly that incoming 'coloured people' should probably follow the example of assimilated Jews and be less touchy about their race.

Such judgements suggest that the liberal humanistic sensibility of the early 1960s was still hedged by the unconscious constraints of white British – even imperial – identity. Nonetheless, this does not in itself invalidate King's true-at-the-time claim that aspects of administering justice had been humanised to a degree inconceivable in the moral imagination of the police court missionaries – to a point where, in the service itself, Ayscough's (1923) austere notion of 'seasoning justice by mercy' no longer seemed like the moral high ground. Punitive practices in community supervision were largely being subordinated not only to the considerations of decency that were the presumed due of (most) British citizens, but also to an approach which privileged the creation of a trust-based, non-moralising learning relationship in which a set of competencies, capacities and attitudes that were deemed to foster law-abidingingness were communicated to offenders, with minimum coercion, in the hope that they would choose to adopt them. In 1972, within the Service itself, this outlook – part treatment, part kindness (befriending) – was understood by a rising generation to be the acme of good practice, the apotheosis of probation tradition and a viable ideal for the future. Undeniably it had its strengths, but its somewhat benign view of an offender's tractability, its seeming indifference to its own effectiveness and its nonchalance towards crime victims guaranteed that its adequacy would be questioned in the years to come.

Lessons, legacies and heritage

Some of the events described in this chapter took place more than a century ago, and even 1972 lies beyond the 'living memory'of many of its readers. There are still nonetheless traces – indeed 'living legacies' – of these distant events in the contemporary penal landscape, some of which have had histories of their own entirely separate from the Probation Service itself, and it is with some of them that I will close. The London Police Court Mission changed its name to the Rainer Foundation (commemorating Frederick Rainer) in 1963, and went on to become a pioneer of 'intermediate treatment' for young offenders in the 1970s (a concept which drew in part on experimental work in post-War probation services and children's departments) and a hugely influential body in the provision of non-custodial alternatives in the 1980s (Nellis 1991). Rather ironically, the Rainer Foundation and the Greater Manchester NAPO Branch (1988) were later to clash over the politics of statutory and voluntary sector 'partnerships' which the Home Office was then encouraging as a means of providing alternatives to custody, although neither side seemed cognisant of the fact that, in slightly different incarnations, they had been rivals once before. The Clarke Hall Fellowship, which subsidised NAPO in its pre-membership era, is now located in the University of Cambridge's Institute of Criminology, and continues to fund probation-related events and conferences, while NAPO's very first chair and founder of its still extant journal has been commemorated by the Edridge Fund since 1934, a still active welfare fund for serving and retired officers.

The penal reform and offender services organisation, the National Association for the Care and Resettlement of Offenders (first shortened to NACRO, then to Nacro), owes its existence to the probation takeover of prison aftercare functions in 1965. It emerged out of the otherwise redundant National Association of Discharged Prisoner's Aid Societies and went on to become a larger and more influential organisation than NADPAS had ever been. Some smaller voluntary organisations also emerged from more idiosyncratic probation initiatives. The Simon Community, a leading homelessness charity, was founded in 1963 by London probation officer, Anton Wallich-Clifford (1974, 1976; see also Jones-Finer 2000), a Catholic who, inspired by Father Mario Borelli's work with street children in Naples, left the Service to set it up. Glebe House Therapeutic Community, now a national resource at the forefront of work with juvenile sex offenders, was initiated in 1965 by Geoffrey Brogden, a Quaker probation officer.

Napo, now badged as 'the probation union' (deliberately rendering its name in lower case letters), no longer enjoys – or seeks – the goodwill of the Home Office which had urged it into being in 1912. It no longer relies on the patronage of influential aristocrats, reflecting marked shifts in the class background and affiliation of probation officers and their champions which began in the 1960s. Questions of staff training and pay still preoccupy Napo, and it still represents staff involved in family court welfare work, even though they became a separate organisation, the Children and Family Court Advisory and Support Service (CAFCASS), in 2000. The Central Council of Probation and Aftercare Committees and the Principal Probation Officer's Conference (in its later incarnation as the Association of Chief Officers of Probation (ACOP)) remained closer to the Home Office for longer than Napo, but their joint successor, the Probation Boards Association, has also found itself marginalised as the prospect of local accountability for probation services ebbs away; indeed, the employer's association and the union, often at odds in the past, have found much common ground in the struggle to resist the National Offender Management Service (NOMS).

Lastly, although its crucial role was written out of the mid-century probation jubilee and eclipsed by a narrative focused on the police court missionaries, the most significant surviving reminder of probation's very origins in England and Wales is the Howard League for Penal Reform. As the Howard Association it drew attention to the Massachusetts 'probation' initiative which was eventually to be emulated here and which – later on – had in Margery Fry one of the Service's most ardent and effective champions. The League's house journal has remained a forum for both historical forward-looking debate about the Service, and several former chief probation officers have chaired the organisation or been otherwise associated with its working parties. When Frances Crook, the League's current secretary, took part in a 'Keep Probation – Keep It Public' rally on 11 May 2004 to challenge the subsuming of the Probation Service into NOMS and its exposure to private sector competition (Napo Bulletin, March 2004, issue 157: 12), she was upholding a concern for the moral vision and organisational form of probation whose foundations had been laid by her predecessors more than a century before.

Further reading

All the key histories of the Probation Service are mentioned in the text itself, so the key issue is perhaps less the detail of the period being covered, but how it could be interpreted. Insights could certainly be gained from reading probation history in the light of histories of Christian faith and the process of secularisation in twentieth-century Britain – religious motivation and spiritual ideals underpinned more of its face-to-face work with offenders and families throughout the period covered in this chapter, but that tends not to be acknowledged by secular historians. How much of the rehabilitative ideal, which probation defended so staunchly, was grounded in an essentially religious understanding of human nature, and how did religious faith 'persist' in social institutions in an ostensibly secular age? Most of the published probation histories tend to assume that the evolution of the service could not have been other than it was, especially in the social democratic framework within which it developed after the Second World War. But is this really so? Ken Pease's (1999) McWilliam's memorial lecture *The Probation Career of Altruism* pertinently wonders how the twentieth-century history of probation might have been different if a crime victim's movement had developed earlier than the 1980s – would probation's insistence upon the moral primacy of rehabilitation been as tenable if it had? Too little is known about the history of probation in local areas outside the big cities – even the whereabouts of relevant archives are not properly catalogued, and it is to be hoped that the centenary year will stimulate further interest in this. Some indication of the historical development of probation services in mainland Europe, and of the ways they were and were not entwined with the English service, is given in each of the chapters in Anton van Kalmthout and Jack Derks (2000) *Probation and Probation Services: A European Perspective*, but there is much more to be written here too.

References

Advisory Council on the Penal System (1970) *Non-Custodial and Semi-Custodial Penalties* (Wootton Report). London: HMSO.

Advisory Council on the Penal System (1974) *Young Adult Offenders* (Younger Report). London: HMSO.

Advisory Council on the Treatment of Offenders (1963) *The Organisation of After-Care*. London: HMSO.

Ayscough, H.H. (1923) *When Mercy Seasons Justice. A Short History of the Church of England in the Police Court*. London: Church of England Temperance Society.

Bailey, V. (1987) *Delinquency and Citizenship: Reclaiming the Young Offender*. Oxford: Clarendon Press.

Barr, H. (1971) *Volunteers in Prison Aftercare*. London: George Allen & Unwin.

Bennett, J. (2001) 'The clockwork continues: revisiting Stanley Kubricks "A Clockwork Orange"', *Prison Service Journal*, 134: 5–7.

Birkbeck, J. (1982) 'I believe in you', *Probation Journal*, 2 (3): 83–86.

Bissel, D. (1987) *Conscience, Courts and Community: A History of the Probation Service in the City of Birmingham*. Birmingham: West Midlands Probation Service.

Blackstone, W. (1769) *Commentaries on the Laws of England* Oxford: Clarendon Press.

Bochel, D. (1976) *Probation and After-care: Its Development in England and Wales*. Edinburgh: Scottish Academic Press.

Buchanan, J. and Millar, M. (1997) 'Probation: reclaiming a social work identity', *Probation Journal*, 44 (1): 32–6.

Burgess, A. (1962) *A Clockwork Orange*. Harmondsworth: Penguin.

Burt, C. (1925) *The Young Delinquent*. London: University of London.

Butler, R.A. (1957) 'My intention to promote progressive thought and action', *Probation*, 8 (6): 83–4.

Cassady, S. (2001) 'Frederick Rainer: the founder of probation?', *Probation Journal*, 48 (4): 287–9.

Coddington, F.J.O. (1950) 'The probation system under the Criminal Justice Act', in L. Radzinowicz and J.W.C. Turner (eds) *The Journal of Criminal Science Vol 2. – A Symposium on the Criminal Justice Act 1948*: 23–45. London: Macmillan.

Cooks, R.A.F. (1958) *Keep Them Out of Prison* London: Jarrolds.

Davies, M. (1969) *Probationers in Their Social Environment*. London: HMSO.

Dawtry, F. (1950) 'Aftercare and supervision under the Criminal Justice Act', in L. Radzinowicz and J.W.C. Turner (eds) *The Journal of Criminal Science Vol 2. – A Symposium on the Criminal Justice Act 1948*: 179–196. London: Macmillan.

Dawtry, F. (1968) (ed.) *Social Problems of Drug Abuse*. London: NAPO.

de Blank, J. (1957) 'Working in faith', *Probation*, 8 (8): 113–14.

Department of Health (1968) *Report of the Committee on Local Authority and Allied Personal Social Services* (Seebohm Report), Cmnd. 3703. London: HMSO.

Folkard, S., Lyon, K., Carver, M. M. and O'Leary, E. (1966) *Probation Research: A Preliminary Report*. London: HMSO.

Foren, R. and Bailey, R. (1968) *Authority in Social Casework*. Oxford: Pergamon Press.

Forsythe, W.J. (1991) *Penal Discipline, Reformatory Projects and the English Prison Commission 1891–1939*. Exeter: Exeter University Press.

Fry, M., Grunhut, M., Mannheim, H. and Rackham, C. D. (1947) *Lawless Youth: A Challenge to the New Europe. A Policy for the Juvenile Courts Prepared by the International Committee of the Howard League for Penal Reform*. London: George Allen & Unwin.

Fyvel, T. (1961) *The Insecure Offenders*. Harmondsworth: Penguin.

Garland, D. (1985) *Punishment and Welfare: A History of Penal Strategies*. Aldershot: Gower.

Garland, D. (2002) 'Of crimes and criminals', in M. Maguire, R. Morgan and R. Reiner R (eds), *The Oxford Handbook of Criminology*. Oxford: Oxford University Press.

Glover, E. (1949) *Probation and Re-education*. London: Routledge and Kegan Paul.

Goodfellow, J. (1987) *Missionaries to Managers: Memories of the Probation Service in the Bristol Area*. Bristol: Avon Probation Service.

Goslin, J. (1970) 'Social science fiction', *Probation*, 16 (3): 75–8.

Greater Manchester NAPO Branch (1988) 'Tackling offending: a reaction plan?', *Probation Journal*, 35 (4): 137–9.

Hall, P. (1976) *Reforming the Welfare*. London: Heinemann.

Halmos, P. (1965) *The Faith of the Counsellors*. London: Constable.

Henriques, B.L.Q. (1950) *The Indiscretions of a Magistrate*. London: The Non-Fiction Book Club.

Herbert, W.L. and Jarvis, F.V. (1961) *Dealing with Delinquents*. London: Methuen.

Hobsbawm, E. and Ranger, T. (eds) (1983) *The Invention of Tradition*. Cambridge: Cambridge University Press.

Holmes, R. (1915) *My Police Court Friends with the Colours*. London: William Blackwood & Sons.

Holmes, R. (1916) *Walter Greenway, Spy, and Others Sometime Criminal*. London: William Blackwood & Sons.

Holmes, R. (1923) *Them That Fall*. London: William Blackwood & Sons.

Holmes, T. (1902) *Pictures and Problems from the London Police Courts*. London: Edward Arnold.

Home Office (1910) *Report of the Departmental Committee on the Probation of Offenders Act*, Cmd 5001. London: Home Office.

Home Office (1922) *Report of the Departmental Committee on the Training, Appointment and Payment of Probation Officers*, Cmd 1601. London: Home Office.

Home Office (1927) *Report of the Departmental Committee on the Treatment of Young Offenders*, Cmnd 2831. London: Home Office.

Home Office (1934) *Report of the Departmental Committee on Imprisonment by Courts of Summary Jurisdiction in Default of Payment by Fines*. London: Home Office.

Home Office (1936) *Report of the Departmental Committee on the Social Services in Courts of Summary Jurisdiction*, Cmnd 5122. London: Home Office.

Home Office (1959) *Penal Practice in a Changing Society*, Cmd 645. London: Home Office.

Home Office (1960) *Report of the Committee on Children and Young Persons* (Ingelby Report), Cmnd 1191. London: Home Office.

Home Office (1961) *Report of the Departmental Committee on the Business of the Criminal Courts*, Cmnd 1289. London: Home Office.

Home Office (1962a) *Second Report of the Departmental Committee on the Probation Service*, Cmnd 1650. London: Home Office.

Home Office (1962b) *Report of the Departmental Committee on the Probation Service*, Cmnd 1800. London: Home Office.

Home Office (1965) *The Adult Offender*, Cmnd 2852. London: HMSO.

Hunt, A. (1964) 'Enforcement in probation casework', *British Journal of Delinquency*, 4: 239–52.

Huws Jones, E. (1966) *Margery Fry: The Essential Amateur*. Oxford: Oxford University Press.

Inner London Probation Service (2001) *Recollections of Probation in Inner London 1937–2001*. London: Inner London Probation Service.

Jacobs, B. (2001) 'Entering probation during the 1950s and 60s', *Probation Journal*, 48 (4): 280–6.

Jarvis, F. (1969) *The Probation Officer's Manual*. London: Butterworths.

Jarvis, F.V. (1972) *Advise, Assist and Befriend: A History of the Probation and Aftercare Service*. London: National Association of Probation Officers.

Jones, H. (1956/1965) *Crime and the Penal System*. London: University Tutorial Press.

Jones-Finer, C. (2000) 'Transnational fundraising in a good cause: a North–South European example' in C. Jones-Finer (ed.), *Transnational Social Policy*. Oxford: Blackwell.

Kilcommins, S. (2000) *The Introduction of Community Service Orders*. Chichester: Barry Rose Publications.

King, J. (1969) *The Probation and Aftercare Service* 3rd edn. London: Butterworths.

Kubrick, S. (1972) *A Clockwork Orange* (the screenplay). New York: Ballantyne Books (republished in 2000 by Southold, Suffolk: Screenpress Books).

Labour Party Study Group (1964) *Crime: A Challenge to Us All*. London: Labour Party.

Le Measurier, L. (1935) *A Handbook of Probation and Social Work of the Courts*. London: National Association of Probation Officers.

Leeson, C. (1914) *The Probation System*. London: P.S. King & Son.

Leeves, R. (1967) 'What criteria for selection for probation hostels?', *British Journal of Criminology*, 7: 207–14.

Lewis, C.S. (1949) 'The humanitarian theory of punishment'. *Twentieth Century*, March.

McWilliams, W. (1983) 'The mission to the English police courts – 1876–1936', *Howard Journal*, 22: 129–47.

McWilliams, W. (1985) 'The mission transformed: professionalisation of probation between the wars', *Howard Journal*, 24 (4): 257–74.

McWilliams, W. (1986) 'The English probation system and the diagnostic ideal', *Howard Journal*, 25: 41–60.

McWilliams, W. (1987) 'Probation, pragmatism and policy', *Howard Journal*, 26: 97–121.

McWilliams, W. (1994) 'Changing aims of the English probation service' in A. Duff, S. Marshall, R.E. Dobash and R.B. Dobash (eds), *Penal Theory and Practice: Tradition and Innovation in Criminal Justice*. Manchester: Manchester University Press.

Mays, J.B. (1951) *Juvenile Delinquency: Report of Discussions of a University Settlement Group*. Liverpool: Liverpool University Settlement.

Mays, J.B. (1963) *Crime and the Social Structure*. London: Faber.

Miles, H. (2004) 'The parish hall enquiry: a community-based alternative to formal court processing in the Channel Island of Jersey', *Probation Journal*, 51 (2): 133–42.

Minkes, J. (2003) *Probation in Powys*. (Available from the author at the University of Swansea.)

Monger, M. (1964) *Casework in Probation*. London: Butterworths.

Monger, M. (1969) *The English Probation Hostel*. Paper 6. London: National Association of Probation Officers.

Morris, T. (1989) *Crime and Criminal Justice Since 1945*. Oxford: Blackwell.

Mott, J.R. (1992) *Probation, Prison and Parole: A True Story of the Work of a Probation Officer*. Sussex: Temple House Books.

Nellis, M. (1991) 'The Development of Intermediate Treatment for Young Offenders in England and Wales 1960–1985'. Unpublished PhD thesis, University of Cambridge.

Nellis, M. (2000) 'Community penalties in historical perspective', in A.E. Bottoms, L. Gelsthorpe and S. Rex (eds), *Community Penalties: Change and Challenges*. Cullompton: Willan.

North, T. and Smith, C. (2001) *Two Into One Will Go. Recollections of the Cornwall Probation Service*. Exeter: Devon and Cornwall Probation Service.

Osler, A. (1995) *Introduction to the Probation Service* Winchester: Waterside Press.

Packer, E. (1963) 'A day in social work III – the probation officer', *New Society*, 8.

Page, L. (1948) *The Sentence of the Court*. London: Faber.

Page, M. (1992) *Crimefighters of London: A History of the Origins and Development of the London Probation Service 1876–1965*. London: Inner London Probation Service.

Pakenham/Thompson Committee (1961) *Problems of the Ex-Prisoner*. London: National Council of Social Service.

Palmer, S. (1982) 'Historical Developments and Changes in the Hostel Movement'. Paper presented to the National Conference of Probation Hostels; University of Lancaster July 1982. Unpublished.

Panzarella, R. (2002) 'Theory and practice of probation on bail in the report of John Augustus', *Federal Probation*, 66 (3): 38–42.

Parkinson, G. (1970) 'I give them money', *New Society*, February, 220–1.

Parkinson, G. (1988) '"Tailgunner Parkinson" column', *New Statesman and Society*, July, p. 32.

Pease, K. (1999) 'The probation career of altruism', *Howard Journal*, 38 (1): 2–16.

Preece, C. (1989) *Woman of the Valleys: The Story of Mother Shepherd*. London: Charles Preece (privately published).

Pritt, D.N. (1934) 'Reform of the criminal law', in C. Joad (ed.), *Manifesto of the Federation of Progressive Societies and Individuals* London: George Allen & Unwin.

Radzinowicz, L. (ed) (1958) *The Results of Probation: A Report of the Cambridge Department of Criminal Science* London: Macmillan.

Radzinowicz, L. and Hood, R. (1986) *The Emergence of Penal Policy in Victorian and Edwardian England*. Oxford: Oxford University Press.

Radzinowicz, L. and Turner, J.W.C. (eds) (1950) *The Journal of Criminal Science Vol 2. – A Symposium on the Criminal Justice Act 1948*. London: Macmillan.

Raynor, P. and Vanstone, M. (2002) *Understanding Community Penalties: Probation, Policy and Social Change*. Buckingham: Open University Press.

Rimmer, J. (1995) 'How social workers and probation officers in England conceived their roles and responsibilities in the 1930s and 1940s', in J. Schweiso and P. Pettit (eds), *Aspects of the History of British Social Work*. Reading: University of Reading, Bulmershe Papers.

Rodgers, B. and Dixon, J. (1959) *Portrait of Social Work: A Study of Social Services in Five Northern Towns*. Oxford: Oxford University Press.

Rose, G. (1961) *The Struggle for Penal Reform*. London: Stevens & Sons.

Ryder, V. (1995) *Daring to Care: History of Norfolk Probation Service*. Norwich: Norfolk Probation Area.

St. John, J. (1961) *Probation – The Second Chance*. London: Vista Books.

Samuel, H. (1957) 'Address', *Probation*, 8 (6): 80–2.

Schwitzgebel, R.R. (1963) 'Delinquents with tape recorders', *New Society*, January, pp. 11–12.

Sinclair, I. (1971) *Hostels for Probationers*, Home Office Research Unit 6. London: Home Office.

Smithies, E. (1982) *Crime in Wartime. A Social History of Crime in World War II*. London: George Allen & Unwin.

Soothill, K. (1999) *Criminal Conversations: An Anthology of the Work of Tony Parker*. London: Routledge.

Sorenson, M. (1986) *Working on Self-Respect: Writings on Offenders and Other Homeless People*. London: Peter Bedford Trust.

Stokes, S. (1950) *Court Circular: Experiences of a London Probation Officer*. London: Michael Joseph.

Stroud, J. (1961) *Touch and Go*. Harlow: Longmans.

Temple, W. (1934) *The Ethics of Penal Action*. The First Clarke Hall Lecture, delivered at Grays Inn, London, 19 March 1934. London: Clarke Hall Fellowship.

Temple, W. (1942) *Christianity and the Social Order: A Statement by the People's Archbishop that All Secular Policy Should Be Founded Upon Christian Truth*. Harmondsworth: Penguin.

Thomas, D.A. (1974) *Parole: Its Implications for the Criminal Justice and Penal Systems. Papers Presented to the Cropwood Round-table Conference December 1973*. Cambridge: University of Cambridge Institute of Criminology.

Todd, M. (1962) *Ever Such a Nice Lady*. London: Gollancz.

Trotter, S. (1969) *No Easy Road: A Study of the Theories and Problems Involved in the Rehabilitation of Offenders*. London: George Allen & Unwin.

van Kalmout, A.M. and Derks, J.T.M. (2000) *Probation and Probation Services: A European Perspective*. Nijmegen: Wolf Legal Publishers.

Vanstone, M. (2004) *Supervising Offenders in the Community: A History of Probation Theory and Practice*. Aldershot: Ashgate.

Wallich Clifford, A. (1974) *No Fixed Abode*. London: Macmillan.

Wallich Clifford, A. (1976) *Caring on Skid Row*. London: The Simon Community.

Wallis, E. (2001) *A New Choreography: An Integrated Strategy or the National Probation Service for England and Wales – Strategic Framework 2001–2004*. London: Home Office.

Watson, J. (1942/50) *The Child and the Magistrate*. London: Jonathan Cape.

Weiner, M.J. (1990) *Reconstructing the Criminal: Culture, Law and Policy in England 1830–1914*. Cambridge: Cambridge University Press.

Weston, B. (2001) 'The Probation Service in West Yorkshire: Arrangements for Organisation and Structure 1949–2001'. Unpublished. Available from Wakefield: West Yorkshire Probation Area.

White, S. (1978) 'The nineteenth-century origins of the pre-sentence report', *Australia and New Zealand Journal of Criminology*, 11: 157–78.

White, S. (1979) 'Howard Vincent and the development of probation in Australia, New Zealand and the United Kingdom', *Historical Studies*, 18, 598–617.

Whitehead, P. and Statham, R. (2006) *The History of Probation: Politics, Power and Cultural Change 1876–2005*. Crayford, Kent: Shaw & Sons.

Whitfield, D. (1998) *Introduction to the Probation Service*. Winchester: Waterside Press.

Willmott, P. (1966) *Adolescent Boys of East London*. Harmondsworth: Penguin.

Wootton, B. (1959) *Social Science and Social Pathology*. London: George Allen & Unwin.

Wootton, B. (1978) *Crime and Penal Policy: Reflections on Fifty Years' Experience*. London: George Allen & Unwin.

Young, P. (1976) 'A sociological analysis of the early history of probation', *British Journal of Law and Society*, 3: 44–58.

Younghusband, E. (1978) *Social Work in Britain 1950–1975: A Follow-up Study*. London: George Allen & Unwin.

Chapter 2

Towards a correctional service

Peter Raynor and Maurice Vanstone

As the last chapter has explained, at the beginning of the 1970s the Probation Service held a respected but unwittingly vulnerable position within the criminal justice system. During the next 30 years, century-old assumptions and practice orthodoxies that had underpinned the criminal justice system would be swept aside (Garland 2001) and the Probation Service would change from a closely knit federation of semi-autonomous local services to an accountable, centrally driven criminal justice agency. As Garland (at the end of that period) put it 'probation has had to struggle to maintain its credibility, as the ideals upon which it was based have been discredited and displaced' (2001: 177).

In this chapter we go beneath the surface of this broad theoretical analysis and explore the detail of that recent history in order to make sense of the Probation Service's position in this new order. In the process we look critically at the way the service has responded to the demise and rebirth of rehabilitation, the increased governance of policy and practice and the creation of the National Offender Management Service (NOMS). The chapter ends with an exploration of the critical choices facing both government and the agency itself.

Faith amid scepticism

Paradoxically, although the 1970s became the decade in which confidence in the efficacy of probation practice would be shaken, it followed a decade in which expansion inspired by the 1962 Morison Committee had been the norm (Home Office 1964), and it began with every sign that its immediate future was secured. In 1970 the Wootton Report was published. Given the task of enquiring into 'the adequacy of the existing powers of the courts to deal with offenders aged 17 and over without resort to custodial sentences' (Home Office 1970: 2), it appeared to be based on a consensual view that the effects of custody were detrimental to the chances of rehabilitation whereas community sentences might enhance them. The problem with community sentences was not their efficacy but rather their limitations. As the report authors put it: 'There is a widely held view amongst sentencers that many offenders are sentenced to imprisonment, not because this is in itself the sentence of choice, but, in effect, for lack of any appropriate alternative' (*ibid*.: 3).

In its pursuit of a solution to this problem, the committee looked to forms of community service (although compulsory, it was drawn from the long-established principle of voluntary service within the community and required consent); an increase in the use of attendance centres; what it described as semi-custodial penalties that combined community service and residential provision (intermittent custody); but no new form of non-custodial sentence 'designed exclusively' for the 'small' female custodial population. The community service experiment emerged from these broad ideas and what was clearly a confident endorsement of the continuation of the expanding role of the Probation Service which the committee welcomed 'heartily'. Subsequently, the day-training-centre experiment was placed alongside community service, influenced by Philip Priestley's idea of a community training centre to respond to the needs of a group of what might now be termed excluded ex-prisoners identified in a survey of 614 men discharged from Swansea, Cardiff, Gloucester and Bristol prisons (Vercoe 1970).

The histories of both the community service and day-training experiments have been thoroughly documented (Burney 1980; Fairhead and Wilkinson-Grey 1981; McIvor 1991; Pease *et al*. 1975; Vanstone 1985 and 1993; Vass and Weston 1990), so it is not the intention of this chapter to repeat them. Rather, they are highlighted in order to illustrate that at the beginning of the decade of scepticism, faith in the Probation Service as a provider of worthwhile work with offenders remained entrenched. The Wootton Report, as Nellis (2001) has argued, showed no particular commitment to rehabilitation, but community service which flowed from it was premised on the idea that people might change for the better or at least not reoffend. While reparation remained to the fore, during the experimental period many of the schemes tried to generate what might be loosely described as the therapeutic experience of doing good work, and the idea of contact with a range of experiences and influences had close links to notions of reform and change. For example, in the second reading of the Criminal Justice Bill 1972 Wootton said, 'in Cheshire offenders helped bathe totally disabled people and it was found that the sight of persons at a greater disadvantage than themselves had a beneficial effect' (*The Times*, 27 June 1972). However, one of the early innovators in this area of work warned that it should not be used 'as a treatment for those whose behaviour does not warrant such restriction of liberty' (West 1977: 116). Despite such concerns, community service is evidence of the credibility of the service which survived but nevertheless had its detractors – the Younger Report (Home Office 1974a) with its proposal for supervision and control orders justified by a desire to promote the acceptance by the public of non-custodial sentences is evidence of that detraction. The point is that although there is evidence of political interest in what the Probation Service could or not do, the age of accountability was still some way off and the broad acceptance of probation as a 'moral good' (Celnick and McWilliams 1991) still prevailed.

Treatment reinvented

It might be argued, therefore, that the Service was not in the kind of self-reflective shape properly to absorb the foundation-shaking research findings that loomed on the horizon. Nellis's point that 'the culture of the Service as a whole remained resolutely resistant to new thinking, and committed to a particular conception of "social work" that hardly seemed adequate to the challenges of real world criminal behaviour' (2001: 23–4) accurately portrays the general picture. However, an analysis of the detail of practice in the 1970s reveals examples of obstinate adherence to outmoded forms of 'social work' treatment alongside experimentation some of which was already influenced by the findings of research, and a significant measure of belief-driven activity that belies any notion of low confidence in the efficacy of probation supervision (see Raynor and Robinson 2005).

Some of this was evident in work with groups. Probation officers had been working with groups from the beginning of the Probation Service, and probation officers were being introduced to social psychology on training courses in the 1940s (Vanstone 2003). Moreover, some were engaging with the theoretical as well as the practical problems of working this way as early as the 1950s (Hawkins 1952). However, despite the fact that what Senior (1991) identifies as a significant increase in its use began in the early 1970s, it is safe to suggest that through the 1970s the generalised casework approach so confidently espoused in the previous decade (Holden 1960; Aylwin 1961; Sanders 1961; Haines 1967; Frayne 1968) was still pre-eminent. The following illustrations are not necessarily characteristic of all practice. Nevertheless, they are interesting because they claim an empirical base (and in this sense lay claim to being part of the history of 'What Works'), they have charismatic leading proponents, and their use spread largely because of individual commitment to and belief in the idea that they worked with people who offend.

Intermediate treatment is most associated perhaps with the investigation into the high care rates for young people (Thorpe et al. 1980), but it was facilitated by s. 19(2) of the Children and Young Persons Act 1969 and in probation largely took the form of outdoor activities with groups (Harding 1971; Carpenter and Gibbens 1973; Bunning 1975). Two schemes in the West Midlands and 'Wessex' were authorised by the Home Office as early as 1973 (Home Office 1973). It survived well into the 1980s and Lacey (1984) provided a theoretical construct for its application in prevention work. Heimler's (1975) Scale of Social Functioning was rooted in his experience in Buchenwald and Auschwitz, and initially developed through his work with the long-term unemployed. Application of the scale which measured the tension between an individual's levels of frustration and satisfaction with life was followed by the use of counselling techniques such as reflection and summarising and collaborative work on action plans. Officers attended support groups, and some who were given advanced training became trainers themselves (Morley 1986). Behaviour modification was introduced to the service on the back of an extensive body of evidence about its effectiveness in other helping fields (Jehu 1967; Hall 1974). Later, in the wake of Bottoms and McWilliams's (1979) 'Non-Treatment Paradigm', it was put forward as an alternative to the medical model (Remmington and Trusler 1981) and applied to, for example, alcohol problems, anti-social behaviour, parenting difficulties and shoplifting (Aust 1987). Transactional analysis was first introduced into this country in the late 1970s, and its more extensive use evolved in the 1980s, but it still serves as an example of the kind of influence on practice that was occurring during the period in which the pessimistic research findings commonly known as 'Nothing Works' were being published. Based on the work of Eric Berne (1964) and his three ego states – parent, adult and child – its use in probation began in the late 1970s. Midgley (1981) describes its application in terms of engaging with offenders' problems that originate from maladaptive behaviour in childhood which continues to impact on their decision-making and problem-solving. As an approach it survived into the 1990s in work with sex offenders (White 1992) and offenders involved in day centre-based group programmes (Hill *et al.* 1993). Two other significant innovations in practice, family therapy and task-centred casework, which were prominent in the IMPACT project (Folkard et al. 1976), gained significant currency with managers and officers and will be returned to later in the chapter.

Each of these approaches found their way into the curricula of the regional Staff Development Units which during this period of probation history played a significant role in promulgating different forms of practice. Indeed, the units' part in sustaining faith in rehabilitation has perhaps been understated in histories of the Service. Established at the end of the 1960s, they were superimposed on the previous *ad hoc* arrangement by which probation committees could organise in-service training for officers in consultation with the Home Office (Home Office 1965). Regional staff development officers were given responsibility to organise short residential courses in conjunction with the services in their particular region, and the outcome was a range of courses the content of which depended largely on their decisions. One aspect of their impact was the introduction of new, interesting methods which, among other things, offered a tangibility that contrasted with the mysticism of conventional casework. It must be remembered that from its beginnings in the 1930s, by the 1960s *casework* had gained a dominant position in the theoretical canon of probation practice (NAPO 1956; Dawtry 1958; Golding 1959; Holden 1960; Leeves 1963), and the Advanced Course in Social Casework at the Tavistock Clinic still retained its iconic status (Home Office 1965).

Pessimistic research findings versus innovation and optimistic practice

Doubts about the treatment model upon which probation practice had been built found early expression in C.S. Lewis's (1952) critical assault on what he termed 'the Humanitarian Theory of Punishment' which removed 'sentences from the hands of jurists' and placed 'them in the hands of technical experts whose special sciences do not even employ such categories as rights or justice' (p. 240). Wootton (1959) and later, Bean (1976) extended the critique, but it is the pessimistic research findings of the 1970s (Lipton *et al.* 1975; Brody 1976; Folkard *et al.* 1976) that are emphasised as the potential catalyst for the demoralisation of practitioners. Yet, as the above examples show, they came at a time when practitioners were being stimulated and enthused by refreshing and optimistic new methods, and policy-makers were being encouraged by significant investment (in the shape of community service and day-training centres) in the notion of an effective Probation Service. Their lack of impact on practice may well be attributed to the fact that they coincided with a change in the practice culture of the service characterised by a shedding of its casework credo. It is not as simple as this, of course, because casework of a sort probably survived (albeit in a wider model) in the daily routine of officers late into the century as the research of Boswell *et al.* (1993) demonstrates. However, interest in new methodology may partly explain why potentially demoralising research findings failed to dampen rehabilitative ardour. What rehabilitation meant to probation officers at this time is critical to unravelling a fuller explanation: the clues lie in practice itself.

The research that attracted the epithet 'Nothing Works', while it contained some evidence of effectiveness (in the case of IMPACT (Folkard *et al.* 1976) with non-recidivists with high self-perceived problems, and in the case of the North American research some successful young offender projects), provided evidence that seriously undermined probation-type supervision as 'a general-purpose "treatment" for crime' (Raynor and Vanstone 2002: 58). This was a potentially devastating blow to an agency like probation whose main objective is the reduction of crime, and its high-profile work emphasised this: for example, the London Day Training Centre was unambiguous about its purpose of helping offenders 'learn how to satisfy their needs in ways that will not bring them into continued conflict with the law, thus providing a greater protection for society through their rehabilitation' (Inner London Probation Service 1972). However, there is weight to the argument that during this period the Service was still wedded to its roots as a social work agency focused more on the needs of offenders than on offending itself. It was after all not until the mid-1980s that McGuire and Priestley (1985) set out to restore the offence as a focus for probation work, and even later when Boswell and her colleagues (1993) found prevention of offending as the most frequently stated purpose of supervision.

In contrast, each of the methods described above as illustrations of 1970s practice development was concerned with classic social work problems such as interpersonal skills, problem-solving, emotional stress, family disfunction, levels of frustration and satisfaction, employment, and alcohol abuse. Furthermore, two surveys of practice in the 1970s, although differing in their findings about the general approach to probation supervision, provide confirmation of the social work element. The first by Davies (1974) revealed evidence of the treatment model while the second by Willis (1980) suggested that officers were involved in more pragmatic, non-treatment work. The point, however, is that despite this difference both studies painted a picture of social work purpose and activity: it included information-seeking, advice-giving, assessment, therapeutic treatment and practical help focused on employment, health, leisure and material needs. Willis (1980), in particular, found little evidence of a concern with the offence.

Given, therefore, a practice culture so deeply entrenched in a social work tradition that the offence had disappeared off the radar screen, it is not surprising that research conclusions showing the ineffectiveness of offence reduction found little resonance with practitioners. Eventually, however, such conclusions did register with policy-makers, who then concentrated attention on diversion from custody as a prime objective of the service. The seeds of this change might have been planted not by the 'Nothing Works' research but rather by the most significant initiatives of the 1970s, namely community service and day training centres. Both were set up explicitly as alternatives to custody. The former was described as 'a form of treatment [...] designed primarily as a method of dealing with persons who might otherwise have been sentenced to short-terms of imprisonment', and the courts were urged to use it 'in lieu of custodial sentences' (Home Office 1974b: 8). The latter resulted directly from Priestley's (1970) idea of a community training centre to meet the needs of the short-term prisoner, and the Wootton Report's (Home Office 1970) recommendation of experimentation with the concept (Burney 1980; Mair 1988; Vanstone 1985, 1993; Vass and Weston 1990; Wright 1984). Both introduced managers and practitioners not just to the job of keeping individuals out of prison, which it can be argued has been a tradition going back to the police court missionaries, but to the practice of assessing risk of custody and monitoring success in reducing that risk. Therefore, by the time that negative research evidence encouraged a change in the direction of policy, the relevant experience and expertise was already in place. The combination of practitioner concern with the provision of social work help and manager concern with establishing probation as a viable community sentence alternative to custody unintentionally ensured the survival of the notion of helping offenders with their personal and social problems. It also ushered in a short period of stability in which the Service demonstrated a renewed assurance of its viability as a social welfare agency within the criminal justice system. In other words, the innovative trailblazing of the community service and day-training-centre experiment (and paradoxically the IMPACT experiment) combined with the social work ethos of the service partially obscured the 'Nothing Works' message.

Ironically, the decade after the publication of Martinson's (1974) infamous paper was, perhaps, the most innovative in the history of the Probation Service: a decade in which both practitioners and managers asserted their confidence in the ability of the Service to engage with the problems of offenders not simply through the application of new methods but also through new team-based strategies within which to apply those methods. It was a confident, creative era of virtual self-governance, and yet in retrospect it can be viewed as the twilight of the kind of managerial autonomy that each separate service had enjoyed for most of the century. So what is the evidence for describing probation activity of this period in this way? The illustrations that follow cannot be generalised to all services, but they do show the renewed vigour in which both practitioners and managers pursued their task: they are subdivided into the methodological and strategic.

As far as methods are concerned, the examples outlined earlier in this chapter give a flavour of the kind of innovation we mean, but two stand out in so far as they had the added respectability of being a part of government-sponsored experimentation. The first, Family Therapy, was propagated by regional staff development courses, but originally formed a significant part of the IMPACT experiment (Thornborough 1974; Ireland and Dawes 1975; Thompson and Clare 1978). It involved systemic intervention with families and drew probation officers into a mode of practice prescribed by an explicit theoretical and formulaic style of intervention (Walrond-Skinner 1979). The second, Task-Centred Casework, was also prominent in the IMPACT experiment, and perhaps has the strongest empirical credentials. It emanated from the initial findings of Reid and Shyne (1969) that structured short-term work on problems was associated with effectiveness. Subsequently, Reid and Epstein (1972) demonstrated that a focus on problems such as interpersonal conflict, role performance, social transition, insufficient resources and emotional stress underpinned by an emphasis on client choice and mutual agreement and framed by the pursuit of achievable, short-term objectives achieved positive results. The case for the use of short-term work in probation in the United Kingdom was made by Clulow (1974): then, following a Cropwood conference in 1978, and partly because of dissatisfaction with the outcome of the IMPACT experiment, it was decided that the Differential Treatment Unit team should set up its own project based on six-month periods of work within the framework of one-year probation orders (Dobson 1976). Subsequently, its influence was generalised to a significant proportion of the Probation Service (Vaisey 1976; Goldberg and Stanley 1979; Waters 1976; Harman 1978).

The period between the Criminal Justice Acts of 1972 and 1984 has been labelled the 'Age of Priestley and McGuire' (Senior 1991: 285). This may or not be entirely reflective of what was happening in the Probation Service, but as has been indicated earlier it was a time when groupwork became 'more widely recognised as a method of social work in Britain' (Brown *et al.* 1982) and had a significant influence on probation practice. For example, Adams and Howlett (1972) established three groups, one in which they used film-making as a kind of 'diversionary therapy', another in which they used discussion to increase empathy and another in which they attempted to help parents of probationers. Shaw and Crook (1977) went further and not only introduced an evaluative framework into their groupwork but also the idea that as one group ended it chose the participants of the next group by interview. Their evaluation focused on attendance, attitudinal change and reconviction rates – the latter involving the use of control groups. Fox and Weaver (1978; Weaver and Fox 1984) ran a voluntary group for non-violent sex offenders for ten years, involved the support of a consultant psychiatrist and monitored subsequent levels of self-control and social development. Nor was such work confined to probation supervision. Also with sex offenders, Shaw (1978a, 1978b) combined groupwork with the prescribing of a libido suppressant drug. Finally in this list of examples, Leach (1973) established a pre-release group for what he described as 'short-term recidivists' which involved seven weekly sessions before the end of sentence designed to change attitudes and formulate plans for post-release.

Practice initiatives of this kind were given a boost by the promulgation of the 'Social Skills and Problem Solving' model introduced by Priestley *et al.* (1978), through which officers were enthused to run groups on themes such as employment, money and rights. Equally significant, however, were attempts to change the structures within which officers worked with offenders, and in particular team approaches to the delivery of programmes. In arguing that officers need to learn how to work in teams before becoming group workers, Dobson (1975) describes how, following experience in the IMPACT experiment, his team changed the waiting room into an activity centre in which they offered a range of group activities that involved a number of methods later to become familiar in cognitive-behavioural work. Sutton (n.d.) went further by completely restructuring his team's approach to supervision, moving away from one-to-one supervision and filtering all probationers through an induction group in which their needs were assessed and contracts agreed. Probationers then moved on to 'treatment package situations' (p.3), including short-term one-to-one supervision, a social skills group, an alcohol group and family therapy; they could also attend a 'Thursday Club' and even do voluntary community service. Although not overtly based on systems theory, the influence is clear and showed itself in similar developments across the country.

The Shelton team project was described many years later by Millard (1989) as taking the idea of the probation office as a resource centre and the team as resource provider. In the same vein, the Preston West Team (1977: 93) developed a system whereby the weekly team meeting was the fulcrum of the team's response to probationers' needs: as they put it, '[we] decided to look in more detail at the needs of our clients, and the skills and facilities that we as a team could provide in order to best meet these needs'. Later, the teamwork principle was taken to further levels of sophistication in Gloucestershire using a model that involved: the allocation of tasks (work episodes) rather than cases; nominated officers with the role of overseeing the probationer through a process of review; intake groups for assessment and helping 'agency and client [decide] how and when to engage; a display board showing work in process and work allocated; team evaluation; and team reviews' (Stanley 1982: 501). Each of these approaches were underpinned by the concept of induction and induction group which, as Brown and Seymour (1984:1) explain, has the 'aim of assessment of individual need and induction into an agency system and what it offers' and 'replaces the traditional start on an individual casework basis'. Meanwhile, through the 'New Careers Project' (Davies 1974) and the setting up of the Barbican Centre in Gloucester (Foggart 1976), the practice of using ex-offenders (to help people in trouble) was established.

Each of these innovations was premised on the assumed deficiency of the traditional casework relationship and a belief in the potency of the group, and reading their stories leaves little sense of a concern with the ineffectiveness of probation exposed by research. In contrast, Bryant and his colleagues (1978: 110) redefined the probation order against a background of 'doubt about the competence of the Probation and After-Care Service and the efficacy of probation methods' and the broadening 'concept of differential treatment'. Through the use of a primary contract between the probationer and the court (focused on the sanction of the probation order) and a secondary contract between the probationer and the Service (focused on the needs of the probationers) they intended to separate 'social work provision from the routine oversight of offenders in the community' (p. 111). In essence, this was a modified version of an idea later put forward by Harris (1980) to resolve the care-versus-control dilemma, but it was also designed to ameliorate some of the core problems of the treatment model. The concerns of Bryant *et al.* and these other innovators were given a coherent philosophical and theoretical articulation later by Raynor (1985) and in Bottoms and McWilliams's (1979) seminal paper on the 'non-treatment paradigm'.

The creative energy of this period was not just spent on new methods and ways of implementing them: the social, cultural and political confines within which offenders lived their lives for the first time received attention. Some ten years before Walker and Beaumont's clarion call for socialist practice some officers were focusing their attention not on individuals but the broader context of their lives. Goff (1972) asked whether the Probation Service could become community-involved without there being a detrimental effect on statutory duties. In an affirmative answer to his own question he described how a local area team in Sheffield made contact with agencies, various services, politicians and clergy in an attempt to 'tap reservoirs of help' and coordinate intervention in a local estate. In the same year Mason drawing on the findings of Davies' (1969) study *Probationers in Their Environment*, asked whether the Service should be working with the environment rather than the individual. His position is unequivocal:

> Surely the answer lies in involvement with the community, in modifying the institutions which help to mould community behaviour, and by protesting through social action against injustice wherever it arises. (Mason 1972: 46)

In order to do this, he argued, probation officers should not hesitate to enter the political arena. Engaging with politics was the inevitable outcome of an interest in, and concern about, the needs of ethnic minority groups and women. Carrington and Denney's (1981) small study of Rastafarianism revealed for the first time probation officers' perceptions of Rastafarians, the methods of intervention being used and the views of Rastafarian offenders on probation. In the same year Worrall (1981) opened the eyes of the Service to the particular experiences of women in the courts.

Collectively, these innovations and developments suggest a vibrant service sure of its place (if not its function) within the criminal justice system and for whom governance was confined to its jurisdiction over probationers. They camouflage, however, a frailty that was to be exposed by the onset in 1984 of an unprecedented rise in governmental interest in what the Service was and should be doing. It began with the Statement of National Priorities and Objectives (SNOP) (Home Office 1984) which took the form of redefining and reordering the Services' objectives and putting public protection to the fore. But it continued with a full frontal attack on the language (and by implication philosophy) of the Service. To the disquiet of management and the direct opposition of the National Association of Probation Officers (NAPO) and some commentators (Rumgay 1989), a Green Paper (Home Office 1988) reformulated probation as punishment in the community.

Despite the level of opposition to such a fundamental change in philosophical direction, the Service was ill-placed to resist. This was due partly to doubts about its efficacy, but more to do with its disparate knowledge base. As this chapter has argued, the effect of the 'Nothing Works' research was not on practice but on policy. However, its most potent effect was in removing the wrapping from the theoretical foundations of the Service and revealing their disparity and flakiness. Information systems are important in this respect. They were introduced in the mid-1980s, and they served the purpose not of clarifying what the Service was doing and achieving, but rather allowing the government to dictate its terms of accountability. As Robinson (2001) has argued, the Service now became governed. At first, this manifested itself in a struggle over language, but new ways of prescribing the purpose and objectives of the Service were to result in a fundamental shift towards punishment in the community. However, an unlikely counter to this threat to the future of the Service emerged. Rehabilitation had been kept alive by the innovations outlined above, but it was about to be reinvigorated by the proponents of 'What Works'.

Investing in survival: the adoption of 'What Works'

In 1993 the Conservative government found itself seriously challenged by the emergence of New Labour as a more effective and potentially electable opposition. Part of the Government's resulting lurch to the right was the appointment of a new populist 'tough on crime' Home Secretary, Michael Howard. It is hard to overestimate the significance of this change for modern British penal policy: the pragmatic policy of relying on criminal justice professionals to keep prison numbers at reasonable levels was replaced by a populist strategy of both responding to and aggravating public concern about crime through a systematically punitive approach which could be presented as evidence of toughness – 'prison works'. Along with this went a sneering disregard for social workers and probation officers, represented in the popular right-wing press as a left-wing or liberal 'establishment', 'politically correct', soft on crime and on the side of offenders rather than victims. This stance did not win the next election for the Conservatives, but it did trigger a rise in prison numbers which has since proved unstoppable. For the Probation Service in England and Wales, Michael Howard's policies meant cutting resources and abolishing the long-standing practice of training probation officers on social work courses. For a short while they had no official training provision at all: the government talked instead of recruiting redundant military personnel, who would need no training because they were used to 'handling men'. Leaders of probation opinion, and particularly the Chief Probation Inspector Graham Smith, saw a clear threat to probation's survival, and came to the conclusion that the only way to ensure this was through demonstrable effectiveness in reducing reoffending by those under supervision. The time was ripe for the rediscovery of rehabilitation in the guise of the 'What Works' movement.

The origins of this movement, and the history of its adoption by the Probation Service in England and Wales, have been thoroughly reviewed elsewhere (for example, Raynor and Vanstone 2002; Raynor and Robinson 2005; from a more sceptical stance Mair 2004; and also Chapter 9, this volume). Readers interested in the full detail are referred to these sources. This chapter is mainly concerned with its impact on the shape and development of the Probation Service and its subsequent evolution. In brief, the existence of a body of research pointing to effective methods of work with offenders was already entering the British probation world in the late 1980s, not from the Home Office (where such research was still paralysed by the legacy of Martinson) but largely from other countries where reputable research on effective methods had continued. Work carried out in Canada and the USA was drawn to the attention of British audiences by the early 'What Works' conferences, in which James McGuire played a leading role (McGuire 1995); by a research review funded by the Scottish Office, which had never lost its commitment to rehabilitative penal methods (McIvor 1990); and by many other contributions. Particularly influential were two large meta-analyses of service and project evaluations which supported the argument that the right kind of intervention with offenders under supervision could make a significant difference to levels of reoffending (Andrews *et al.* 1990; Lipsey 1992). These meta-analyses tended to favour methods which were based on the now familiar principles of risk, need and responsivity (see Hedderman, this volume) and the use of cognitive-behavioural methods designed to help offenders to change anti-social beliefs and attitudes and acquire new skills for dealing with problems.

In addition, some local projects in Britain, which used structured forms of groupwork with persistent young adult offenders, had produced small but convincing positive results in the late 1980s (for example Raynor 1988; Roberts 1989) and a fully evaluated local pilot of a Canadian cognitive-behavioural programme was under way in a South Wales probation area by the summer of 1991 (see Raynor and Vanstone 1996, 1997). Although the full results of this project were not published until 1996, some early results were available in 1994 and were described by Christine Knott in McGuire's influential edited collection of 1995. This study showed that British probation officers could deliver this kind of programme, and there were indications of modest beneficial effects on programme completers, particularly in comparison with similar offenders who received custodial sentences. Programme members did not do significantly better, in terms of reconviction, than people who received 'ordinary' probation orders without a programme: the project was targeted on people who would otherwise have received a custodial sentence rather than a standard probation order, and custodial sentences were the key comparison group for the evaluation. In the 'Nothing Works' era these results would probably not have attracted much attention, and the widespread interest aroused by this project was itself an indicator of how the climate was beginning to change.

Implementation and first reorganisation: towards the 'New Choreography'

While this and other local experiments were proceeding, managers, practitioners and researchers who were interested in the possibilities of effective practice were actively disseminating the new ideas. In addition to the annual series of 'What Works' conferences, an influential conference at Green College, Oxford also helped to promote the new approaches, and in 1993 the Home Office organised a conference in Bath, followed by another conference in London in 1995 on 'Managing What Works'. This was followed by a circular (Home Office 1995) encouraging (or requiring) Probation Services to adopt effective methods and promising a follow-up inspection by Her Majesty's Inspectorate of Probation (HMIP). This was the first of a number of attempts to transform the service from the top down.

Other jurisdictions and agencies took rather different routes to the implementation of the new ideas. In Scotland, with different criminal justice legislation, there was a tradition of welfare-centred juvenile justice, and a criminal justice social work service was (and still is) provided by local authority social work departments rather than by a separate Probation Service. Consequently, the chosen development strategy emphasised education and incremental development in a context where implementation was necessarily devolved and localised. The Scottish Office (later, after political devolution, the Scottish Executive) funded an advanced university course for senior practitioners and a development unit, and aimed to influence service providers in the right direction by using its powers to set standards and fund services. In England and Wales (the policies come from England, since criminal justice powers are not yet devolved to the Welsh Assembly Government) rather different approaches emerged for young offenders, under the auspices of the Youth Justice Board (YJB), from those which were developed for adult offenders by the Probation Service and the Prison Service. The YJB, working through youth offending teams (YOTs) in each locality, encouraged experimentation and diversity by funding a wide variety of local schemes. This was probably a good way of engaging the energies and creativity of local agencies and practitioners, although it created problems for research and for consistency of practice.

The Probation Service adopted, by contrast, a highly centralised development strategy accompanied by a systematic programme of research. Instead of a simple inspection to follow up the 1995 circular, a research exercise was set up involving a detailed survey of probation areas by Andrew Underdown, a senior probation manager who was already closely involved in issues around effective practice. The results, eventually published in 1998 (Underdown 1998), after the election of a Labour government expected to be better disposed towards the Probation Service, were an eye-opener: of the 267 programmes which probation areas claimed they were running based on the principles of effective practice set out in the 1995 Circular, evidence of actual effectiveness based on reasonably convincing evaluation was available only for four (one of which was not actually included in the responses to the initial survey). One of the four was the Mid-Glamorgan STOP programme; the others were in London (Wilkinson 1997, 1998). Graham Smith's introduction to Underdown's report clearly shows the importance he attached to 'What Works' as a survival strategy for probation:

> This is the most important foreword I have ever written ... The report offers the Probation Service ... an opportunity to renew and revitalise community penalties ... the rewards will be immense in terms of increased confidence and public belief in and support for community sanctions. (Underdown 1998: iii)

The poor results of the Inspectorate's survey of current practice pointed to the need for a centrally managed initiative to introduce more effective forms of supervision. The Home Office's Probation Unit worked closely with the Inspectorate to develop the 'What Works' initiative; good publications were issued to promote awareness (Chapman and Hough 1998; McGuire 2000) and a number of promising programmes were identified for piloting and evaluation as 'Pathfinder' programmes, with support in due course from the government's Crime Reduction Programme (CRP). The Pathfinders included several cognitive-behavioural programmes but also included work on basic skills (improving literacy and numeracy to improve chances of employment), pro-social approaches to supervision in community service, and a number of joint projects run by Probation Services with prisons and in some cases voluntary organisations working on the resettlement of short-term prisoners after release.

In the meantime a new Probation Service was taking shape, to come formally into existence as the National Probation Service (NPS) for England and Wales in April 2001, replacing the old separate area Probation Services and explicitly committed to public protection and crime reduction. Instead of 54 separate Probation Services, each responsible to and employed by a local probation committee consisting largely of local magistrates, the NPS was a single organisation run by a director with a substantial central staff located in the Home Office (the National Probation Directorate (NPD)). Some local influence was still provided by the 42 area boards, each employing the staff in its own area (apart from the area's chief officer) but responsibility for policy moved to the centre and was implemented through a national management structure. The new areas were coterminous with police, court and crown prosecution service areas in order to facilitate multi-agency working in the criminal justice system (though they did not coincide with local authorities or with YOTs), and board members were chosen on the basis of relevant expertise, with much less representation of sentencers than on the old committees. The NPS started with an annual budget of about £500 million (roughly 4 per cent of overall spending on the criminal justice system). By the end of 2002 this figure was reported as £693 million, with 8,000 probation officers employed (including trainees) and 9,300 other staff (Home Office 2004a). Recent statements from the Probation Boards Association mention a staffing figure of 20,000 (PBA 2005).

The new structure had emerged from a substantial review of prison and Probation Services (Home Office 1998) which, among other possibilities, considered merging prisons and probation into a single correctional service, but (ironically, in view of later developments) concluded that this would be a step too far. The main aim of the changes was to create an organisation which could be more effectively managed and directed from the centre. Detailed national policies and targets were published in a document intriguingly entitled *A New Choreography* (NPS 2001) incorporating 'stretch objectives' designed to produce change, and performance was monitored. All this represented a considerable transformation over a very short period of time, and the new organisation was faced with the problem of how to maintain a sense of involvement among those groups which had less influence in the new structure than they had in the past. These groups included the magistrates who passed most of the community sentences and some of the Service's own staff. At the same time, the Service's new director chose to emphasise a decisive shift in direction by adopting the slogan 'Enforcement, Rehabilitation and Public Protection' (NPS 2001). The priority given to enforcement was not accidental, and some of the consequences are discussed below.

What went right and what went wrong?

The end of the twentieth century marked the high point of optimism for the 'What Works' movement in England and Wales – or at least its highest point to date. Promising programmes were identified and being piloted; the Joint Prisons and Probation Accreditation Panel (later Correctional Services Accreditation Panel) was set up in 1999 to apply some independent quality control to the programmes adopted by prisons and Probation Services, and substantial funding was attracted from the Treasury to finance programme implementation and research (though not without strings, such as hugely ambitious target numbers for programme completions and an unrealistically short period during which evaluations were to be completed: for fuller discussion of the problems of the Crime Reduction Programme see Hough 2004; Homel *et al.* 2005). A good example of the general optimism is provided by John Halliday in his influential review of sentencing (Halliday 2001), which provided the underpinning rationale for most of the 2003 Criminal Justice Act: '... if the programmes are developed and applied as intended ... reconviction rates might be reduced by 5–15 percentage points (i.e. from the present level of 56% within two years, to (perhaps) 40%)' (Halliday 2001: 7). It is not clear how Halliday arrived at this remarkable example of a 'best case' scenario, but clearly he had been talking with the Home Office and probation staff who were enthusiastically pressing ahead with 'What Works'.

More difficult times lay ahead. No correctional service anywhere in the world had tried to implement 'What Works' principles on such a scale, at such a speed and subject to such comprehensive scrutiny and evaluation. This inevitably led to a number of short cuts, sometimes running well ahead of or even contrary to the available evidence. For example, the targets for accredited programme completions set in 1999, which drove the pace of the roll-out of offending behaviour programmes, had been negotiated with Treasury officials without any systematic prior assessment of the characteristics of offenders under supervision and their suitability for programmes (Raynor 2007). The instrument which was designed to produce such assessments, the Offender Assessment System (OASys), originally promised for August 2000, is still not used for all offenders in the prison and Probation Services. The targets quickly proved too high for most probation areas to achieve and were eventually reduced, but not before consuming much time and effort and causing many problems for staff and managers. The creation of the NPS, although intended to promote effectiveness, diverted energy into new arrangements for governance and management and, in some cases, the complex and time-consuming amalgamation of areas. In some of the amalgamated areas this caused considerable disruption and delay in implementing the 'What Works' agenda.

Within the Pathfinders themselves, researchers noted a large number of implementation difficulties: projects were often not running in a fully developed form when the evidence which would be used to measure their effectiveness was collected. The results of the Pathfinder evaluations have been reviewed elsewhere (for example Raynor 2004, 2004a; Roberts 2004, 2004a; Harper and Chitty 2004; and Hedderman, this volume). For the purposes of this chapter, it is important to note what the evaluations teach us about the implementation of new service designs. Often, as in the resettlement study, local projects depended on small numbers of staff and were vulnerable to staff sickness or communication problems (Lewis *et al.* 2003). In all the Pathfinder studies, projects tended to make a slow start and not to achieve their target numbers; in the 'basic skills' and 'employment' Pathfinders (McMahon *et al.* 2004; Haslewood-Pocsik *et al.* 2004) numbers completing were so small that the evaluation could not be carried out as intended. In the 'offending behaviour' Pathfinders (for example Roberts 2004, 2004a; Hollin *et al.* 2004) the high levels of attrition, due in large part to enforcement action leading to the termination of orders for non-compliance, led to difficulties in interpreting evidence. Outcomes based on programme completers, when these are only a small proportion of those who start the programme, may show effects of the programme or may show simply the effects of whatever selection or self-selection processes led to those people, rather than others, completing it.

In addition, the top-down management style which was seen as necessary to drive implementation forward within the prescribed timescale (Blumsom 2004) alienated parts of the workforce, particularly probation officers who were used to a high degree of autonomy. Staff in some areas found their workloads spiralling out of control at the same time as demands to meet targets were increasing. At one stage (luckily after most of the Pathfinder data had been gathered) most probation areas were involved in industrial action over workloads, and the probation officers' union NAPO (2001) expressed its concern in conference resolutions which rejected aspects of the 'What Works' approach. In such circumstances researchers could hardly be surprised if some of the data quality was poor.

Reliance on central direction and a managerialist approach also contradicted some of the British evidence about how to engage staff in effective innovation (Raynor and Vanstone 2001): the STOP programme, like many other successful innovations, involved a substantial period of local discussion and a high level of input and ownership by local practitioners. Similar lessons are emerging from a new international interest in problems of effective implementation (Gendreau *et al.* 1999). Some warning notes might, however, have been sounded by an American study (Lipsey 1999) of differences between 'demonstration' and 'practical' interventions. The former are the special pilot projects which are often the source of the research covered in systematic reviews, and the latter are the routine implementations which follow organisational decisions to adopt new methods, as in the rapid roll-out of the Probation Service's new programmes. Better results are more commonly found among the 'demonstration' projects: in Lipsey's study the 196 'practical' programmes reviewed were on average half as effective as the 205 'demonstration' programmes. (Even this level of effectiveness depended heavily on a few programmes, as 57 per cent of the 'practical' programmes had no appreciable effect.) As he points out, 'rehabilitative programmes of a practical "real world" sort clearly can be effective; the challenge is to design and implement them so that they, in fact, are effective' (Lipsey 1999: 641).

Problems also arose from a tendency to be preoccupied with implementing programmes or 'interventions' rather than with providing an experience of supervision which would be effective as a whole. Although this had been pointed out by earlier British research (Raynor and Vanstone 1997), by Rod Morgan (2003) when, as Chief Inspector of Probation, he warned against 'programme fetishism', and by the Correctional Services Accreditation Panel (2003) which insisted on continuity as one of its accreditation criteria, little attention was paid to the need for effective case management until attrition rates started to cause concern. Recent Home Office research (Partridge 2004) has examined the merits of different case management models, and found strong support for 'generic' models which aim to keep offenders in contact with the same case manager/supervisor through the whole of their orders, as opposed to 'functional' models (favoured by managers but disliked by most staff and offenders) which break up supervision into separate tasks carried out by different people. Meanwhile research in other countries has pointed clearly to the benefits of continuity of contact with skilled practitioners (Trotter 1993; Dowden and Andrews 2004). The Pathfinder projects were not designed with this in mind, and the associated evaluations are therefore able to say little about its contribution to outcomes, which is likely to have been substantial.

A final criticism which can be made of the early 'What Works' years in England and Wales is their lack of a clear penal strategy. In other words, there does not seem to have been any clear shared vision of the pattern of sentencing which was intended to result from the initiative, or any clear policy regarding the functions and desirable levels of custodial and community sentencing. Although efforts were made, with only partial success, to ensure that programmes were not used for low-risk offenders, little else was done to eliminate the down-tariff drift of community sentences in general. This process had been going on throughout the 1990s (Raynor 1998; Morgan 2002): for example, only 12 per cent of new probationers in 1991 were first offenders, but by 2001 the figure was reported as 27 per cent (Home Office 2002). In a remarkable act of collective amnesia, probation's leaders made no connection between the 'What Works' agenda and their earlier strategy of reducing reliance on custodial sentences. For example, there was no attempt to promote programmes as an alternative to short custodial sentences. Indeed, following the lead of politicians, the idea of alternatives to custody was as completely forgotten as George Orwell's 'Oldspeak' (Orwell 1949). The potential impact of the 'What Works' initiative on the wider penal system was probably diminished as a result.

Overall, in spite of the hard work and undeniable achievements of many very able and dedicated staff, it is clear that the early results of the 'What Works' initiative were not impressive enough to bring about the radical change in the Probation Service's standing and prospects for which Graham Smith and others originally hoped. With hindsight, it is also clear that a three-year implementation timescale, with a major reorganisation in the middle, was never likely to be long enough to show clear benefit from such a complex process of change.

Two reorganisations and a funeral? The emergence of NOMS

If 1999–2000 was a high point of optimism about 'What Works' in England and Wales, 2003–4 may come to be seen as the low point. Although the 2003 Criminal Justice Act, influenced by Halliday's therapeutic optimism, clearly prioritised the reduction of reoffending at the expense of proportionality, it posed a number of new problems for probation services. For example, a new hybrid sentence of 'custody-plus', starting in prison and ending under supervision in the community, signalled a new approach to the widely criticised regime for short-sentence prisoners (Maguire *et al.* 2000) but would add considerably to the service's caseload. The new generic community sentence, with its 13 possible ingredients for sentencers to mix and match, posed new challenges in terms of case management and preventing tariff escalation. It risked overloading needy offenders with so many supposedly helpful requirements that the overall package would become too demanding and complex, and compliance would become almost impossible. In addition, new and rigorous requirements in relation to enforcement threatened other difficulties which are discussed further below. However, the main shock to hit the NPS in the winter of 2003–4 was the proposal to bring the prison and probation services together under the single organisational umbrella of a National Offender Management Service (NOMS). The threat which seemed to have been seen off in 1998 was suddenly revived.

Briefly, this proposal arose from a review of correctional services carried out by Patrick Carter, a businessman with experience of the private health care sector and highly regarded in Downing Street. His report (Carter 2003) offered a diagnosis of the system's problems with which few specialists would disagree, pointing to prison overcrowding, failure to help short-term prisoners, and the fact that for persistent offenders who pass repeatedly through the custodial and community systems, no one agency has the clear responsibility for managing the sentence as a whole in the way that offers the best prospect of reducing reoffending. The proposed alternative, known as 'end-to-end offender management', required, in Carter's view, a single agency to run it, namely NOMS. Under a Chief Executive and a National Offender Manager, ten Regional Offender Managers (ROMs) would 'commission' the services required, whether custodial or non-custodial, for the management of offenders in their region. (In Scotland, following a long consultation of the kind that was barely attempted in England and Wales, a proposal for a single correctional service was abandoned in favour of a strategy for better coordination of the existing services under the overall guidance of a new Community Justice Agency.) Even more controversial was Carter's proposal that the best way to improve the effectiveness of services in the community was to introduce contestability or market testing. This was already in limited use in the prison system but had not previously been a feature of probation except for an expectation, current during the 1990s but since lapsed, that they should spend a small proportion of area budgets (never more than 7 per cent) on 'partnerships'.

There is in fact a strong case for probation services to work more in partnership with other organisations, primarily because the range of services needed by offenders greatly exceeds what the Probation Service itself is equipped to supply. The current 'Reducing Re-offending Action Plan' (Home Office 2004b), based partly on work by the Social Exclusion Unit (SEU 2002) and others on the resettlement needs of prisoners, identifies seven 'pathways': accommodation; education, training and employment; mental and physical health; drugs and alcohol; finance, benefits and debt; children and families of offenders; and attitudes, thinking and behaviour. Intervention in relation to almost all of these requires collaboration with other organisations, and even the last (work on attitudes, thinking and behaviour) has a history of successful contracting out by some services (see, for example, Raynor 1988; Heath *et al.* 2002). It is much harder to see how the core of offender management, which coordinates these other elements and provides continuity and structure for the offender, can benefit from the fragmentation implied by contestability. For the purposes of this chapter, it is also important to note that the Carter proposals actually constituted a significant rupture in the 'What Works' project as it developed up to 2003. Instead of the careful and iterative process of piloting, evaluation and improvement, we are offered the market solution of contestability as if this guarantees better results. Perhaps this shows a loss of patience with the limited effectiveness of 'What Works' up to 2003; if so, it attaches far too much weight to research results produced at an early stage of implementation. In other ways, however, the NPS may have unwittingly paved the way for NOMS.

The nationalisation of a service which was formerly rooted in localities and at least to some degree in a sense of ownership by local sentencers may have made it more vulnerable to politically driven change: a single service based in London under the eye of the Home Office was arguably a more obvious focus of political awareness and target for political gestures than 54 locally based services involving hundreds of influential magistrates, particularly when the single service was seen as slow to meet its targets and overspent its budget.

At the time of writing it is still too soon to say how far, or in what ways, the Carter proposals are likely to be implemented. Both NAPO (2005) and the Probation Boards Association (PBA 2004, 2005) have produced powerful counter-arguments and there have been some contradictory messages from government: for example, government spokespeople regularly point out in reassuring tones that only a tiny proportion of the prisons estate is run by the private sector, but the 'NOMS Partial Regulatory Impact Assessment' (Home Office 2005a) assumes 50 per cent contracting out of Probation Service business within five years. And in 2004, following an energetic campaign by probation boards, Paul Goggins, then the relevant Minister, stated that 'better management of offenders and better services ... can best be achieved through the existing 42 probation boards' (Goggins 2004), but this apparent victory for the boards has been reversed by the latest developments discussed below.

Living with uncertainty: some critical choices

Two aspects of the Carter proposals and the NOMS 'reform' package which attracted wide-ranging support were the end-to-end offender management model and the underpinning aim of controlling the growth of imprisonment. This was to be achieved through the linked strategies of providing sentencers with guidance which no longer ignored the relative costs of different sentences, replacing short prison sentences with intermittent or hybrid custody/ community sentences, and encouraging a return to the widespread use of fines. Some commentators found these proposals sufficiently encouraging to offset doubts about the wisdom of yet another major criminal justice reorganisation. The proposals seemed to provide precisely that kind of strategic thinking about sentencing patterns and the intended shape of the penal system which had been lacking in the 'What Works' initiative. However, at the time of writing it is much less clear whether developments are still underpinned by these same principles, or whether other aspects of the package are now more salient. The final task of this chapter is to highlight some areas of major uncertainty where official guidance is currently confusing, contradictory or absent, and to consider their implications for the effectiveness of probation services.

Part of the reason for the continuing confusion seems, as so often in this story, to be political. We have already described how the Carter Report was seized on as the basis for policy announcements at the beginning of 2004, without a consultation period. Consultation was later offered on the details of implementation, but not the principles. It has been suggested that this haste arose from a perceived political need for another eye-catching 'big idea' in criminal justice to maintain the Government's stance of activism in relation to crime (Raynor 2004a). The 'correctional services review' which Patrick Carter led was owned by the government's Strategy Unit and had the flavour of Downing Street rather than the Home Office; perhaps the need for a 'big idea' was not unconnected with the expectation that 2005 would bring a General Election. The Labour Party manifesto (2005: 46) for that election included a section on 'crime and security' with a conspicuous emphasis on toughness and tabloid language (such as 'exclude yobs from town centres'). The NOMS reforms were mentioned briefly: we were told that 'voluntary organisations and the private sector will be offered greater opportunities to deliver offender services' (*ibid.*: 48) but nothing about any attempts to reduce prison overcrowding. Instead there was what looked like a boast that 'we have built over 16,000 more prison places than there were in 1997' (*ibid*.: 47). So contestability was important enough to go in the manifesto, but an end to the growth of imprisonment was not.

When Charles Clarke became Home Secretary later in the year, he set out some of his views on penal policy in a widely reported speech to the Prison Reform Trust, in which he emphasised the reduction of reoffending as a major goal of correctional services and gave very strong (and widely welcomed) support to the principle of community prisons (Clarke 2005). However, in the same week he or his officials briefed the *Guardian* newspaper (19 September 2005) to the effect that Patrick Carter's target of limiting prison numbers to 80,000 was being quietly abandoned, and sentencing guidelines would not after all include guidance on cost-effectiveness. Although the YJB has targets for the reduction of custodial sentencing on which it is making modest progress, it appears that this approach is deemed unsuitable for the adult sector. A few weeks later the Home Secretary published his proposals on *Restructuring Probation to Reduce Re-offending* (Home Office 2005b). These indicated that not just 'interventions' but also offender management services in the community would be subject to contestability, so that in principle all the functions of the Probation Service in a given geographical area could be transferred to a private or voluntary sector bidder and the area's probation board would disappear. Again contestability appeared as the priority. NAPO has consistently argued that the real driver of the NOMS proposals is the attempt to further New Labour's interest in (some would say obsession with) increasing the role of the private sector in public services: contestability, they say, simply means privatisation. This points to the first unresolved issue in the implementation of the NOMS reforms: are they driven, as the Carter report was at least partly driven, by evidence about what is effective in correctional services, or are they driven simply by a characteristically New Labour faith in the capacity of the private sector to transform public services? (For a review of the reasons why contestability is likely to create more problems for offender management than for 'interventions' see Raynor and Maguire 2006.)

Advocates of contestability will, of course, argue that it is intended as a strategy to improve effectiveness, including improvements in the performance of public sector staff and organisations subjected to the challenge of market testing. Home Office ministers and officials point to the example of the prisons and the role played by contestability in their improvement, but the evidence on this is not quite so clear and unambiguous as they claim (see, for example, Liebling 2006). In any case, part of the reason for contestability in prisons was to reduce the capacity of the Prison Officers' Association to block progress and defend outdated practices, and it is hardly credible to present NAPO as the same kind of obstacle. It is more accurate to see contestability as a political doctrine for which the evidence, however limited, is already regarded as conclusive. On 19 October 2005 a letter from the Public Services Directorate of the Confederation of British Industries (CBI) to a national newspaper confidently stated that: 'The current probation system is failing ... because of the high rates of re-offending. There is everything to gain from giving private and voluntary bodies the chance to cut crime' (Bentley 2005).

If the CBI has really discovered the magic bullet to cure offending, they have been keeping it pretty quiet until now. Or perhaps in the new contestability environment the rules of evidence are different. So the first of our critical choices is: will the development of NOMS be guided by the same evidence-based approach which underpinned the 'What Works' movement, or will it be driven simply by a formulaic belief in the capacity of the market to transform the public sector? The answer to this will probably depend on the amount and level of political interference in the implementation process.

A second critical choice will be between continued reliance on centralised managerialism and a degree of empowerment for local decision-makers to respond to local needs and characteristics. We have already described how the centralisation of management and development in the NPS reduced the real power and influence of the probation boards in comparison with the old probation committees, and the boards themselves were constituted in a way which reduced the number and influence of magistrates in the governance of the service. The proposed arrangements for commissioning in NOMS appear to envisage most commissioning of services being done at a regional level, and at the time of writing current proposals involve the replacement of probation boards by smaller more business-oriented trusts (Home Office 2005b), with less local representation and probably coterminous with new larger police authorities. The PBA (2005) is energetically resisting this, basing its arguments on the government's own commitment to involving local communities and local organisations in 'civil renewal': 'to empower citizens and their communities to work in partnership with public bodies to develop local solutions to local problems' (NOMS and YJB 2005). For example, the 'Community Payback' approach to community service aims to involve local people in the choice of 'visible unpaid work' to be undertaken by offenders under supervision. The probation boards, arguing the case for their own survival, stress the importance of the local agenda and local partnerships. However, in the larger probation areas the boards themselves are hardly local, and (if they survive) will need to develop a strategy to engage with the much smaller geographical units within which local responses to crime can actually be developed – at the level of petty sessional divisions, YOTs or local probation offices (for example, at the time of writing England and Wales have 42 probation boards and 156 YOTs). The proposals in *Restructuring Probation to Reduce Re-offending* seem to imply some recognition of past problems of over-centralised management: we are told that the NPD should become 'increasingly light touch' and that chief officers should be appointed and employed locally (as they were before 2001) rather than centrally. However, these measures are designed to facilitate contestability at regional level rather than to empower local communities.

Finally, and not before time, some clear thinking is needed about how far probation services are or should be involved in the explicit delivery of punishment. This is a complex argument to which it is impossible to do justice in this chapter and it is covered in more detail elsewhere in this volume. However, a few points are worth mentioning here. As outlined above, a significant obstacle to the success of the 'What Works' initiatives was the NPS's commitment to rigorous enforcement and the reduction of practitioners' discretion to show flexibility even in low-risk cases or with offenders whose lifestyles were so chaotic that the only realistic target would be improved compliance rather than full compliance. It is well known that the 2000 version of the National Standards on enforcement was made significantly more punitive by the personal intervention of a Home Office minister, and the latest version (NOMS 2005) shows no relaxation: indeed the new four-tier model of offender management assumes that all people under supervision require punishment, while only some require help, change or control.

This may mean no more than that the Service should be seeking to ensure that all offenders meet the requirements of their various sentences and licences, but in reality punishment is not a sensible priority for every sentence at every stage. For example, community sentences are still sometimes imposed on people who are seen as needing help rather than punishment, or are seen as less blameworthy because of the difficulties they face. Another example can be found in the new hybrid sentences such as 'custody-plus'. Is it sensible to understand the post-custodial resettlement phase as simply an extension of punishment, or is its main purpose the reintegration of people who have already served what they will undoubtedly see as the punitive part of their sentence? If we remember the important distinction between serving a sentence *as* punishment (i.e. offenders lose some freedom to use their time as they please) and serving it *for* punishment, with punitive content informed by punitive attitudes which are the direct opposites of 'What Works', then it is easier to get the enforcement issue into perspective. The main point of enforcement is surely to encourage compliance (for which it is one of several strategies, and not necessarily the most important or effective) and to allow review of orders which are not working and need to be revisited by sentencers. Currently nearly 9,000 people per year find themselves in prison as a result of enforcement of community sentences (Home Office RDS NOMS 2005) and implementation of the 2003 Criminal Justice Act is likely to make things worse, as courts cannot vary a requirement of a breached community sentence except by imposing a more rigorous requirement or a custodial sentence if the failure to comply is repeated. Research has also shown that probation areas with a highly rigorous approach to enforcement do not achieve lower levels of reconviction than those with a more flexible approach (Hearnden and Millie 2003). In short, the practice of enforcement in community sentences cries out for an evidence-based review, which it has not so far received because it has been seen as an inescapable political requirement.

Meanwhile, there is beginning to be more evidence that the improvements in consistency and performance that were part of the aim of the 'What Works' initiative are actually happening. The original three-year timescale was too short, but now, after roughly twice as long, targets for programme completions are being exceeded, rates of attrition (though still high) are reducing, and there is evidence of positive change during programmes in most of the areas assessed by routine psychometric testing (NPS 2005). Equally important, the case management and supervision process is now taken seriously as an essential support and reinforcement for other 'interventions' and sometimes as an intervention in itself, and national training programmes have been developed to equip a wide range of staff with useful approaches such as pro-social modelling and motivational interviewing. There is some foundation for the Director of Probation's claim that the service is delivering 'more ... than at any time in our history' (NPS 2005: 2). It is also clear that the Probation Service is capable of delivering work which benefits both offenders and the community, and which is in an intelligible line of descent from the traditions and aspirations which informed its past. It is less clear, at the time of writing, whether the latest reorganisation will consolidate or threaten these achievements, and the knee-jerk instability of current policy-making means that by the time this chapter appears in print the detailed proposals will almost certainly have changed. However, if the wrong choices are made about contestability, centralisation and enforcement, we could move quite quickly towards a situation where there is little left of the Probation Service of the past 100 years. An important vehicle for dialogue and reconciliation between society and its delinquent members will then be lost, and the necessary work of supervising offenders and helping them to stop offending will be done, if at all, by others. Such an outcome would be both extraordinary and perverse.

Further reading

Detailed histories of the Probation Service can be found in Vanstone's *Supervising Offenders in the Community: A History of Probation Theory and Practice* (2004) and Whitehead and Statham's *The History of Probation* (2006). These can be looked at alongside earlier histories like King's *The Probation and After-Care Service* (1969) and Bochel's *Probation and After-care: Its Development in England & Wales* (1976). Of course, for insight into the beginnings of Service accountability readers need go no further than McWilliams's 'Probation, pragmatism and policy' (1987). For general texts on contemporary probation issues readers should go to Worrall and Hoy's *Punishment in the Community* (2005), Nellis and Chui's *Moving Probation Forward* (2003), Burnett and Roberts's *What Works in Probation and Youth Justice* (2004) and Bottoms, Rex and Robinson's *Alternatives to Prison* (2004). *Reshaping Probation and Prisons* edited by Hough, Allen and Padel (2006) provides readers with critical accounts of NOMS and its implications.

It is important to place recent developments in probation within general social, cultural and political contexts, and the best elucidations of these can be found in Bottoms's 'The philosophy and politics of punishing and sentencing' (1995), Downes and Morgan's 'The skeletons in the cupboard: the politics of law and order at the turn of the millennium' (2002), Garland's *The Culture of Control* (2001), Tonry's *Punishment and Politics: Evidence and Emulation in the Making of English Crime Control Policy* (2004) and Young's *The Exclusive Society* (1999). Further exploration of the concept of risk can be found in Kemshall's *Risk in Probation Practice* (1998) and *Understanding Risk in Criminal Justice* (2005).

A greater understanding of probation service practice should follow from reading Trotter's *Working with Involuntary Clients* (1999), Bottoms and Stelman's excellent *Social Inquiry Reports* (1988) and Burnett and McNeill's 'The place of the officer–offender relationship in assisting offenders to desist from crime' (2005). In addition to 'What Works' related texts referred to in the chapter, readers can go to three excellent edited books, namely McGuire's *Offender Rehabilitation and Treatment* (2002), Harland's *Choosing Correctional Options that Work* (1996) and Bernfeld, Farrington and Leschied's *Offender Rehabilitation in Practice. Implementing and Evaluating Effective Programmes* (2001).

References

Adams, C. and Howlett, J. (1972) 'Working with clients in the group setting or diversionary therapy', *Probation Journal*, 18: 54–6.

Andrews, D.A., Zinger, I., Hoge, R.D., Bonta, J., Gendreau, P. and Cullen, F.T. (1990) 'Does correctional treatment work? A clinically relevant and psychologically informed meta-analysis', *Criminology*, 28: 369–404.

Aust, A. (1987) 'Gaining control of compulsive shop theft', *Probation Journal*, 34: 145–6.

Aylwin, G.D.L. (1961) 'Personality in probation work', *Probation*, 9: 178–9.

Bean, P. (1976) *Rehabilitation and Deviance*. London: Routledge & Kegan Paul.

Bentley, N. (2005) 'Letter', *Guardian*, 19 October.

Berne, E. (1964) *The Games People Play. The Basic Handbook of Transactional Analysis*. Santa Barbara, CA: Grove Press.

Bernfeld, G., Farrington, D.P. and Leschied, A. (2001) *Offender Rehabilitation in Practice. Implementing and Evaluating Effective Programmes*. Chichester: John Wiley & Sons.

Blumsom, M. (2004) 'First steps and beyond: the pathway to our knowledge of delivering programmes', *VISTA*, 8: 71–6.

Bochel, D. (1976) *Probation and After-care: Its Development in England & Wales*. Edinburgh: Scottish Academic Press.

Boswell, G., Davies, M. and Wright, A. (1993) *Contemporary Probation Practice*. Aldershot: Avebury.

Bottoms, A. (1995) 'The philosophy and politics of punishing and sentencing', in C. Clarkson and R. Morgan (eds), *The Politics of Sentencing Reform*. Oxford: Clarendon Press.

Bottoms, A. and McWilliams, W. (1979) 'A non-treatment paradigm for probation practice', *British Journal of Social Work*, 9: 159–202.

Bottoms, A. and Stelman, A. (1988) *Social Inquiry Reports*. Aldershot: Wildwood House.

Bottoms, A., Rex, S. and Robinson, G. (2004) *Alternatives to Prison*. Cullompton: Willan.

Brody, S.R. (1976) *The Effectiveness of Sentencing*. London: HMSO.

Brown, A. and Seymour, B. (eds) (1984) *Intake Groups for Clients: A Probation Innovation*. University of Bristol.

Brown, A., Caddick, B., Gardner, M. and Sleeman, S. (1982) 'Towards a British model of groupwork', *British Journal of Social Work*, 12: 587–603.

Bryant, M., Coker, J., Estlea, B., Himmel., S. and Knapp, T. (1978) 'Sentenced to social work', *Probation Journal*, 38: 123–6.

Bunning, M.R. (1975) 'The Summit Club', *Probation*, 22: 22–5.

Burnett, R. and McNeill, F. (2005) 'The place of the officer–offender relationship in assisting offenders to desist from crime', *Probation Journal*, 52: 221–42.

Burnett, R. and Roberts, C. (2004) *What Works in Probation and Youth Justice*. Cullompton: Willan.

Burney, E. (1980) *A Chance to Change*. London; NACRO.

Carpenter, M. and Gibbens, F. (1973) 'Combined operations (intermediate treatment)', *Probation*, 20: 84–7.

Carrington, B. and Denney, D. (1981) 'Young Rastafarians and the probation service', *Probation Journal*, 28: 111–17.

Carter, P. (2003) *Managing Offenders, Reducing Crime: A New Approach*. (Correctional Services Review). London: Home Office.

Celnick, A. and McWilliams, W. (1991) 'Helping, treating and doing good', *Probation Journal*, 38: 164–70.

Chapman, T. and Hough, M. (1998) *Evidence-Based Practice*. London: Home Office.

Clarke, C. (2005) *Where Next for Penal Policy*. Speech to Prison Reform Trust, 19 September.

Clulow, C. (1974) 'Time: a solution for the piecemeal operative?', *Probation Journal*, 21: 50–6.

Correctional Services Accreditation Panel (2003) *Report 2002–2003*. London: CSAP.

Davies, M. (1969) *Probationers in Their Social Environment*. London: HMSO.

Davies, M. (1974) *Social Work in the Environment. A Study of One Aspect of Probation Practice*. London: HMSO.

Davies, N. (1974) 'New careers for offenders', *Probation Journal*, 21: 80–3.

Dawtry, F. (1958) 'Whither probation', *British Journal of Delinquency*, VIII, 180–7.

Dobson, G. (1975) 'Team work before groupwork', *Probation Journal*, 22: 17–21.

Dobson, G. (1976) 'The Differential Treatment Unit: Part 1', *Probation Journal*, 23: 105–8.

Dowden, C. and Andrews, D. (2004) 'The importance of staff practice in delivering effective correctional treatment: a meta-analysis', *International Journal of Offender Therapy and Comparative Criminology*, 48: 203–14.

Downes, D. and Morgan, R. (2002) 'The skeletons in the cupboard: the politics of law and order at the turn of the millennium' in M. Maguire, R. Morgan and R. Reiner (eds), *The Oxford Handbook of Criminology*, 3rd edn. Oxford: Clarendon Press.

Fairhead, S. and Wilkinson-Grey, J. (1981) *Day Centres and Probation*, Home Office Research Unit Paper 4. London: Home Office.

Foggart, R.H. (1976) *The Barbican Centre: An Analysis of the Helping Relationship* Gloucestershire Probation Service.

Folkard, M.S., Smith, D.E. and Smith, D.D. (1976) *IMPACT. Intensive Matched Probation and After-Care Treatment. Volume 11. The Results of the Experiment*. Home Office Research Study 36. London: HMSO.

Fox, C. and Weaver, C. (1978) 'Groupwork with sexual offenders (an alternative approach)', *Probation Journal*, 25: 84–6.

Frayne, L. (1968) 'Supervision in social casework', *Probation*, 14: 84–8.

Garland, D. (2001) *The Culture of Control*. Oxford: Oxford University Press.

Gendreau, P., Goggin, C. and Smith, P. (1999) 'The forgotten issue in effective correctional treatment: program implementation', *International Journal of Offender Therapy and Comparative Criminology*, 43: 180–7.

Goff, D. (1972) 'An approach to community involvement', *Probation Journal*, 18: 68–72.

Goggins, P. (2004) *Statement by Minister for Prisons and Probation*, quoted in PBA (2005) *PBA Response to Restructuring Probation*. London: Probation Boards Association, p. 4.

Goldberg, E.M. and Stanley, S.J. (1979) 'A task centred approach to probation', in J. King (ed.), *Pressures and Change in the Probation Service*. Cambridge: Institute of Criminology.

Golding, R.R.W. (1959) 'A probation technique', *Probation*, 11: 9–11.

Guardian (2005) 'Clarke to scrap plan to peg prison numbers', 19 September, p. 4.

Haines, J. (1967) 'Satisfaction in probation work', *Probation*, 13: 75–80.

Hall, J. (1974) 'Penal institutions and behaviour modification', *Probation Journal*, 21: 46–50.

Halliday, J. (2001) *Making Punishments Work: Report of a Review of the Sentencing Framework for England and Wales*. London: Home Office.

Harding, J. (1971) 'Barge cruising: an experiment in group work', *Probation*, 17: 45–7.

Harland, A.T. (1996) *Choosing Correctional Options that Work*. Thousand Oaks, CA: Sage.

Harman, J. (1978) 'Crisis intervention (a form of diversion)', *Probation Journal*, 25: 115–21.

Harper, G. and Chitty, C. (2004) *The Impact of Corrections on Re-offending: A Review of 'What Works'*, Home Office Research Study No. 291. London: Home Office.

Harris, R.J. (1980) 'A changing service: the case for separating care and control in probation practice', *British Journal of Social Work*, 10: 163–84.

Haslewood-Pocsik, I., Merone, L. and Roberts, C. (2004) *The Evaluation of the Employment Pathfinder: Lessons from Phase 1 and a Survey for Phase 2.* Online Report 22/04. London: Home Office.

Hawkins, E. (1952) 'Some thoughts on the principles of group reporting', *Probation*, 6, 184–5.

Hearnden, I. and Millie, A. (2003) *Investigating Links between Probation Enforcement and Reconviction*, Online Report 41/03. London: Home Office.

Heath, B., Raynor, P. and Miles, H. (2002) 'What Works in Jersey: the first ten years', *VISTA*, 7: 202–8.

Heimler, E. (1975) *Survival in Society.* London: Weidenfield and Nicolson.

Hill, J., Thomas, S. and Vanstone, M. (1993) 'Opening doors with offenders: groupwork in a probation day centre', in A. Brown and B. Caddick, *Groupwork Practice in Probation.* London: Whiting and Birch.

Holden, G.E. (1960) 'The role of the caseworker', *Probation*. 9: 119–20.

Hollin, C., Palmer, E., McGuire, J., Hounsome, J., Hatcher, R., Bilby, C. and Clark, C. (2004) *Pathfinder Programmes in the Probation Service: A Retrospective Analysis*, Home Office Online Report 66/04. London: Home Office.

Home Office (1962) *Report of the Departmental Committee on the Work of the Probation Service*, Cmnd. 1650. London: HMSO.

Home Office (1964) *Recruitment and Training of Probation Officers*, Home Office Circular 43/1964. London: Home Office.

Home Office (1965) *Training of Serving Probation Officers*, Home Office Circular 274/1965. London: Home Office.

Home Office (1970) *Report of the Advisory Council on the Penal System: Non-Custodial and Semi-Custodial Penalties* (Wootton Report). London: HMSO.

Home Office (1973) *Intermediate Treatment Schemes*, Home Office Circular 207/1973 London: Home Office.

Home Office (1974) *Young Adult Offenders. Report of the Advisory Council on the Penal System.* London: HMSO.

Home Office (1974a) *Community Service by Offenders*, Home Office Circular 197/1974. London: Home Office.

Home Office (1984) *Probation Service in England and Wales: Statement of National Objectives and Priorities.* London: Home Office.

Home Office (1988) *Punishment, Custody and the Community*, Cm. 424. London: Home Office.

Home Office (1995) *Managing What Works: Conference Report and Guidance on Critical Success Factors for Probation Supervision Programmes*, Probation Circular 77/1995. London: Home Office.

Home Office (1998) *Joining Forces to Protect the Public: Prisons-Probation.* London: Home Office.

Home Office (2002) *Probation Statistics England and Wales 2001.* London: Home Office.

Home Office (2004) *Reducing Re-offending National Action Plan.* London: Home Office.

Home Office (2004a) *Probation Statistics in England and Wales 2002.* London: Home Office.

Home Office (2005a) *NOMS Partial Regulatory Impact Assessment.* London: Home Office.

Home Office (2005b) *Restructuring Probation to Reduce Re-offending.* London: Home Office.

Home Office RDS NOMS (2005) *Offender Management Statistics 2004*. London: Home Office.

Homel, P., Nutley, S., Webb, B. and Tilley, N. (2005) *Investing to Deliver: Reviewing the Implementation of the UK Crime Reduction Programme*, Home Office Research Study No. 281. London: Home Office.

Hough, M. (ed) (2004) *Criminal Justice*, 4 (3). Special Issue: *Evaluating the Crime Reduction Programme in England and Wales*.

Hough, M., Allen, R. and Padel, U. (eds) (2006) *Reshaping Probation and Prisons*. Bristol: Policy Press.

Howard, M. (1993) Speech to Conservative Party conference, October.

Inner London Probation Service (1972) *Proposal Paper for the Establishment of a Day Training Centre Within the Area*. Inner London Probation Service.

Ireland, M. and Dawes, J. (1975) 'Working with the client in his family', *Probation Journal*, 22: 113–16.

Jehu, D. (1967) *Learning Theory and Social Work*. London: Routledge & Kegan Paul.

Kemshall, H. (1998) *Risk in Probation Practice*. Aldershot: Ashgate.

Kemshall, H. (2005) *Understanding Risk in Criminal Justice*. Buckingham: Open University Press.

King, J. (1969) *The Probation and After-Care Service*, 3rd edn. London: Butterworth.

Knott, C. (1995) 'The STOP programme: reasoning and rehabilitation in a British setting' in McGuire, J. (ed.), *What Works*. Chichester: Wiley.

Labour Party (2005) *The Labour Party Manifesto*. London: The Labour Party.

Lacey, M. (1984) 'Intermediate treatment: a theory for practice', *Probation Journal*, 31: 104–7.

Leach, A. (1973) 'The pre-release group as a method of after-care', *Probation Journal*, 19: 25–7.

Leeves, R.E. (1963) 'The principles of probation', *Probation*, 10: 68–70.

Lewis, C.S. (1952) *Undeceptions. Essays on Theology and Ethics*, (ed.) W. Hooper. London: Geoffrey Bles.

Lewis, S., Vennard, J., Maguire, M., Raynor, P., Vanstone, M., Raybould, S. and Rix, A. (2003) *The Resettlement of Short-term Prisoners: An Evaluation of Seven Pathfinders*, RDS Occasional Paper No. 83. London: Home Office.

Liebling, A. (2006) 'Lessons from prison privatisation for probation', in M. Hough, R. Allen, and U. Padel (eds), *Reshaping Probation and Prisons*. Bristol: Policy Press.

Lipsey, M. (1992) 'Juvenile delinquency treatment: a meta-analytic enquiry into the variability of effects', in T. Cook, H. Cooper, D.S. Cordray, H. Hartmann, L.V. Hedges, R.L. Light, T.A. Louis and F. Mosteller (eds), *Meta-Analysis for Explanation: A Case-Book*. New York: Russell Sage.

Lipsey, M. (1999) 'Can rehabilitative programs reduce the recidivism of juvenile offenders? An inquiry into the effectiveness of practical programs', *Virginia Journal of Social Policy and the Law*, 6: 611–41.

Lipton, D., Martinson, R. and Wilks, J. (1975) *The Effectiveness of Correctional Treatment*. New York: Praeger.

McGuire, J. (ed.) (1995) *What Works: Reducing Reoffending*. Chichester: Wiley.

McGuire, J. (2000) *Cognitive-Behavioural Approaches*. London: Home Office.

McGuire, J. (2002) *Offender Rehabilitation and Treatment*. Chichester: Wiley.

McGuire, J. and Priestley, P. (1985) *Offending Behaviour: Skills and Stratagems for Going Straight*. London: Batsford.

McIvor, G. (1991) 'Community service work placements', *Howard Journal*, 30: 19–29.

McMahon, G., Hall, A., Hayward, G., Hudson, C. and Roberts, C. (2004) *Basic Skills Programmes in the Probation Service: An Evaluation of the Basic Skills Pathfinder*, Home Office Research Findings 203. London: Home Office.

McWilliams, W. (1987) 'Probation, pragmatism and policy', *Howard Journal*, 26: 97–121.

Maguire, M., Raynor, P., Vanstone, M. and Kynch, J. (2000) 'Voluntary after-care and the Probation Service: a case of diminishing responsibility', *Howard Journal of Criminal Justice*, 39: 234–48.

Mair, G. (1988) *Probation Day Centres*, Home Office Research and Planning Unit. London: HMSO.

Mair, G. (ed.) (2004) *What Matters in Probation*. Cullompton: Willan.

Martinson, R. (1974), 'What works? Questions and answers about prison reform', *Public Interest*, 5: 22–54.

Mason, J.H. (1972) 'Community involvement – case-work or politics', *Probation Journal*, 18: 44–7.

Midgley, D. (1981) 'Discovering TA', *Probation Journal*, 28: 9–11.

Millard, D. (1989), 'Looking backwards to the future', *Probation Journal*, 36: 18–21.

Morgan, R. (2002) 'Something has got to give', *HLM – the Howard League Magazine*, 20: 7–8.

Morgan, R. (2003) 'Foreword', *Her Majesty's Inspectorate of Probation Annual Report 2002/2003*. London: Home Office.

Morley, H. (1986) 'Heimler's human social functioning', *Probation Journal*, 33 (4): 140–2.

NAPO (1956) 'Casework supervision in the Probation Service', *Probation*, 8: 97–100.

NAPO (2001) 'AGM resolutions 2001', *NAPO News*, 134: 10–15.

NAPO (2005) *Restructuring Probation: What Works?* London: National Association of Probation Officers.

National Probation Service (2001) *A New Choreography*. London: Home Office.

National Probation Service (2005) *Performance Report 18 and Weighted Scorecard Q2 2005/06*. London: National Probation Service.

Nellis, M. (2001) 'Community penalties in historical perspective', in A. Bottoms, L. Gelsthorpe and S. Rex (eds), *Community Penalties. Change and Challenges*. Cullompton: Willan.

Nellis, M. and Chui, W.H. (2003) *Moving Probation Forward*. Harlow: Pearson Education.

NOMS (2005) *National Standards 2005*. London: National Offender Management Service.

NOMS and Youth Justice Board (2005) *NOMS and YJB Approach to Communities and Civil Renewal*. London: NOMS & YJB.

Orwell, G. (1949) *Nineteen Eighty-Four*. London: Secker & Warburg.

Partridge, S. (2004) *Examining Case Management Models for Community Sentences*, Home Office Online Report 17/04. London: Home Office.

Pease, K., Durkin, P., Earnshaw, Payne, D. and Thorpe, J. (1975) *Community Service Orders*, Home Office Research Study No. 29. London: Home Office.

Preston West Team (1977) 'Putting the sacred cows out to grass', *Probation Journal*, 24: 92–6.

Priestley, P. (1970) *The Problem of the Short Term Prisoner*. London: NACRO.

Priestley, P., McGuire, J., Flegg, D., Hemsley, V. and Welham, D. (1978) *Social Skills and Personal Problem Solving. A Handbook of Methods*. London: Tavistock.

Probation Boards Association (2004), *Response to 'Managing Offenders: Reducing Crime' and 'Reducing Crime: Changing Lives'*. London: Probation Boards Association.

Probation Boards Association (2005) *PBA Response to Restructuring Probation*. London: Probation Boards Association.

Raynor, P. (1985) *Social Work, Justice and Control*. Oxford: Blackwell.

Raynor, P. (1988) *Probation as an Alternative to Custody*. Aldershot: Avebury.

Raynor, P. (1998) 'Reading probation statistics: a critical comment', *VISTA*, 3: 181–5.

Raynor, P. (2004) 'Rehabilitative and reintegrative approaches' in A. Bottoms, Rex, S. and G. Robinson (eds), *Alternatives to Prison*. Cullompton: Willan.

Raynor, P. (2004a) 'The probation service "Pathfinders": finding the path and losing the way?', *Criminal Justice*, 4: 309–25.

Raynor, P. (2007) 'Risk and need in British probation: the contribution of LSI-R', *Psychology, Crime and Law* (forthcoming).

Raynor, P. and Maguire, M. (2006) 'End-to-end or end in tears? Prospects for the effectiveness of the National Offender Management Model', in M. Hough, R. Allen and U. Padel (eds) *Reshaping Probation and Prisons*. Bristol: Policy Press.

Raynor, P. and Robinson, G. (2005) *Rehabilitation, Crime and Justice*. Basingstoke: Palgrave Macmillan.

Raynor, P. and Vanstone, M. (1996) 'Reasoning and rehabilitation in Britain: the results of the Straight Thinking On Probation (STOP) programme', *International Journal of Offender Therapy and Comparative Criminology*, 40: 272–84.

Raynor, P. and Vanstone, M. (1997) *Straight Thinking On Probation (STOP): The Mid Glamorgan Experiment*, Probation Studies Unit Report No. 4. Oxford: University of Oxford Centre for Criminological Research.

Raynor, P. and Vanstone, M. (2001) 'Straight Thinking On Probation: evidence-based practice and the culture of curiosity', in G. Bernfeld, D. Farrington and A. Leschied (eds) *Offender Rehabilitation in Practice* Chichester: Wiley.

Raynor, P. and Vanstone, M. (2002) *Understanding Community Penalties: Probation, Policy and Social Context*. Buckingham: Open University Press.

Reid, W. J. and Epstein, L. (1972) *Task-Centred Casework*. New York: Columbia University Press.

Reid, W.J. and Shyne, A. (1969) *Brief and Extended Casework*. New York: Columbia University Press.

Remmington, B. and Trusler, P. (1981) 'Behavioural methods for the Probation Service', *Probation Journal*, 28: 52–5.

Roberts, C. (1989) *Hereford and Worcester Probation Service Young Offender Project: First Evaluation Report*. Oxford: Department of Social and Administrative Studies.

Roberts, C. (2004) 'An early evaluation of a cognitive offending behaviour programme ('Think First') in probation areas', *VISTA*, 8: 137–45.

Roberts, C. (2004a) 'Offending behaviour programmes: emerging evidence and implications for research' in R. Burnett and C. Roberts (eds) *What Works in Probation and Youth Justice*. Cullompton: Willan.

Robinson, G. (2001) 'Power, knowledge and What Works in probation', *Howard Journal*, 40: 235–54.

Rumgay, J. (1989) 'Talking tough: empty threats in probation practice', *Howard Journal*, 28: 177–86.

Sanders (1961) 'A time of re-birth', *Probation*, 9 (10): 141–4.

Senior, P. (1991) 'Groupwork in the Probation Service: care or control in the 1990s', *Groupwork*, 4: 284–95.

Shaw, R. (1978) 'The persistent sexual offender – control and rehabilitation', *Probation Journal*, 25: 9–13.

Shaw, R. (1978a) 'The persistent sexual offender – control and rehabilitation (a follow-up)', *Probation Journal*, 25: 61–3.

Shaw, R. and Crook, H. (1977) 'Group techniques', *Probation*, 24: 61–5.

Social Exclusion Unit (2002) *Reducing Re-offending by Ex-prisoners*. London: Office of the Deputy Prime Minister.

Stanley, A.R. (1982), 'A new structure for intake and allocation in a field probation unit', *British Journal of Social Work*, 12: 487–506.

Sutton, D. (n.d.) 'Central Bristol Area Team Probation Project'. Unpublished paper.

Thompson, L. and Clare, R. (1978) 'Family Therapy in probation', *Probation Journal*, 25: 79–83.

Thornborough, P. (1974) 'Impact in Inner London', *Probation Journal*, 21: 42–4.

Thorpe, D.H., Smith, D., Green, C.J. and Paley, J. (1980) *Out of Care*. London: Allen & Unwin.

Tonry, M. (2004) *Punishment and Politics: Evidence and Emulation in the Making of English Crime Control Policy*. Cullompton: Willan.

Trotter, C. (1993) *The Supervision of Offenders – What Works? A Study Undertaken in Community Based Corrections, Victoria*. Melbourne: Social Work Department, Monash University and Victoria Department of Justice.

Trotter, C. (1999) *Working with Involuntary Clients*. London: Sage.

Underdown, A. (1998) *Strategies for Effective Supervision: Report of the HMIP What Works Project*. London: Home Office.

Vaisey, R. (1976) 'The Differential Treatment Unit: part 2', *Probation Journal*, 23: 108–11.

Vanstone, M. (1985) 'Moving away from help? Policy and practice in probation day centres', *Howard Journal of Criminal Justice*, 24: 20–28.

Vanstone, M. (1993) 'A "missed opportunity" reassessed: the influence of the day training centre experiment on the criminal justice system and probation practice', *British Journal of Social Work*, 23: 213–29.

Vanstone, M. (2003) 'A history of the use of groups in probation work: Part one – from "clubbing the unclubbables" to therapeutic intervention', *Howard Journal*, 42: 69–86.

Vanstone, M. (2004) *Supervising Offenders in the Community: A History of Probation Theory and Practice*. Aldershot: Ashgate.

Vass, A.A. and Weston, A. (1990), 'Probation day centres as an alternative to custody: a "Trojan Horse" examined', *British Journal of Criminology*, 30: 189–206.

Vercoe, K. (1970) *Men Leaving Local Prisons*, South Wales and Severn Valley Region & Information Paper. NACRO.

Waldren-Skinner, S. (1979) *Family Therapy: The Treatment of Natural Systems*. London: Routledge & Kegan Paul.

Waters, R.W. (1976) 'The value of short-term work', *Probation Journal*, 23: 17–20.

Weaver, C. and Fox, C. (1984) 'Berkeley sex offenders group: a seven year evaluation', *Probation Journal*, 31: 143–6.

West, J. (1977) 'Community service orders – how different', *Probation Journal*, 24: 112–120.

White, C. (1992) 'A TA approach to child sex abusers', *Probation Journal*, 39: 36–40.

Whitehead, P. and Statham, R. (2006) *The History of Probation: Politics, Power and Cultural Change 1876–2005*. Crayford: Shaw & Sons.

Wilkinson, J. (1997) 'The impact of Ilderton motor project on motor vehicle crime and offending', *British Journal of Criminology*, 37: 568–81.

Wilkinson, J. (1998) 'Developing the Evidence Base for Probation Programmes'. PhD thesis, University of Surrey.

Willis, A. (1980) 'Young Men on Probation. A Survey of the Probation Experience of Young Adult Male Offenders and their Supervising Officers'. Unpublished Monograph.

Wootton, B. (1959) *Social Science and Social Pathology*. London: George Allen & Unwin.

Worrall, A. (1981) 'Out of place: female offenders in court', *Probation Journal*, 28 (3): 90–3.

Worrall, A. (1990) *Offending Women: Female Lawbreakers and the Criminal Justice System*. London: Routledge.

Worrall, A. and Hoy, C. (2005) *Punishment in the Community*. Cullompton: Willan.

Wright, A. (1984) *The Day Centre in Probation Practice*, Social Work Monograph 22. University of East Anglia.

Young, J. (1999) *The Exclusive Society*. London: Sage.

Chapter 3

Probation, governance and accountability

Rod Morgan

Introduction

At the time of writing, spring 2006, the future governance of the Probation Service in England and Wales remains uncertain. The Government has announced (Home Office 2005) its legislative intention fundamentally to change existing governance arrangements. But the enabling Bill has yet to be published and, given the doubts and opposition already signalled, it is by no means certain that the Government will get through all the changes it wishes. This chapter aims, therefore, to cover the following: first, to chart the evolution, until 2001, of local probation services; secondly, to describe the current National Probation Service (NPS) arrangements, accountability for which is shared between the Secretary of State at the centre and 42 area probation boards locally; thirdly, to describe the accompanying accountability mechanisms which surround probation work (inspection, complaints, serious incident investigations, etc.) and will likely continue to operate whatever structural changes are now made; fourthly, to describe the steps leading to the Government's announcement, in November 2005, that it proposes abandoning the existing model in favour of a centrally governed commissioning system in which local probation trusts will compete with voluntary and commercial providers of probation services; fifthly, to speculate on how the new governance and managerial arrangements, if legislated for after this text is put to bed, might work and what the advantages and drawbacks of such a system might be.

Governance pre-2001

From 1907, with the passage of the Probation of Offenders Act, until implementation in 2001 of the Criminal Justice and Courts Services Act 2000, probation services in England and Wales were both provided and administered locally. Their administration and governance became progressively more formalised, however, and over the years the financial and managerial control of the Home Office grew steadily, particularly from the 1980s onwards.

Probation officers have since 1907 been officers of the court. They were originally appointed by each court in which they served, the 1907 Act empowering courts to appoint paid officers. Though considerable use was made of the statute, a review undertaken 15 years later found that 215 courts had not appointed a single officer and the conditions of service of many were unsatisfactory (Home Office 1922). As a consequence in 1925 their appointment was made compulsory in all magistrates' courts. Their value remained unappreciated by many benches, however. The voluntary, police court, missionary origins of the service continued to influence recruitment and conditions of service. Many courts went on recruiting part-time officers on meagre salaries well into the 1930s (Home Office 1936) and the Police Court Mission, a Church of England organisation which continued to part finance some officers' salaries and expenses, did not finally cease employing officers until 1938. Prior to this date a system of 'dual control' by the Mission and the courts operated in many areas, a system which most officers wished to end (McWilliams 1983: 130).

In the inter-War period the work of probation officers became overseen by probation committees comprising magistrates elected by their peers. Meanwhile, as early as 1922 there was created a national Probation Advisory Committee (reconstituted as the Probation Advisory and Training Board in 1949 and the Advisory Council for Probation and After-Care in 1962) and, in 1936 within the Home Office, a section to oversee the development of the service (in the post-War period this became known as the Probation and After-Care Department) as well as a national probation inspectorate (Morgan 2004: 80) was created. This approach was put on a statutory footing by the Criminal Justice Act 1948. Each petty sessional area, or combinations of petty sessional areas if the Secretary of State determined, was designated a 'probation area', each of which was to have a probation committee and a case committee or committees. The former comprised magistrates and a recorder from the Court of Quarter Sessions and the latter magistrates and co-opted persons with such qualifications as were considered useful. Probation committees had the duty to appoint sufficient probation officers as the caseload of the area needed, to pay their officers' salaries and expenses and 'provide for the efficient carrying out' of their work (5th Schedule, s. 3). Rates of pay and expenses were laid down by the Secretary of State. Case committees had the duty to review the work of probation officers in individual cases (*ibid.*: s. 6).

The role of the probation services was steadily broadened in the post-War years. Officers became responsible for: discharged prisoners' aftercare and the statutory supervision of prisoners on licence; the throughcare of prisoners while in prison (later undertaken by officers seconded to prison service establishments); matrimonial conciliation to support the magistrates' courts' family jurisdiction and, after 1957, acting as welfare officers in divorce proceedings; fines enforcement by means of money payment supervision orders; the introduction of new sentences such as community service the management of which fell to the service; and so on. But the system of administration through local committees (albeit formally retitled probation and after-care committees after 1967) continued. By the late 1960s the cost of probation services, including probation training, was divided equally between the local authorities and central government, though parts of the services' role (the whole of the cost of prison-based welfare posts, for example) were met by the Exchequer. Administrative oversight of the services by the Home Office was tightened. The probation inspectorate was expanded to include after-care and prison welfare. Recruitment and training of officers was increasingly through a Home Office training course, which by 1965 accounted for two-thirds of all new recruits. A corporate, national, pay negotiating committee had already been established, with representatives of the local authorities, justices and the Home Office on one side and the National Association of Probation Officers (NAPO) on the other, implementation of the agreed salary scales falling to the Home Secretary.

That is, the structure and substance of governance was subtly changing. The steer from the centre became firmer. But this continued to rub along with the constitutional doctrine of devolved, local area services, now reduced through amalgamation to 59 in number. More robust challenges to these constitutional arrangements grew in the early 1980s out of the conjunction of the so-called 'nothing works' movement (or mood – see Martinson 1974; Brody 1976) which gained ascendancy in the late 1970s, the simultaneous 'penal crisis' (Bottoms and Preston 1980) resulting from the burgeoning prison population, and the election in 1979 of a Conservative administration under Margaret Thatcher dedicated to tough 'law and order' measures and committed to tighter control over public expenditure (Downes and Morgan 2007). The Probation Service, which in the view of one commentator had 'failed at rehabilitation ... failed at reducing the prison population ... and [was] committed to "soft" social work values which meant that offenders who deserved punishment received help instead' (Mair 1997: 1202), became a prime government managerial target and has remained so ever since.

In 1984 the Home Office published a *Statement of National Objectives and Priorities* (SNOP) which signalled the Home Secretary's intention to subject probation policy and practice to a degree of control never previously attempted (Raynor and Vanstone 2002: 77–8). Any pretence that probation services were locally autonomous, able to set their own priorities unfettered by government prescription, was now over. Henceforward the Home Office, which since 1974 had been paying 80 per cent of services' budgets, would prescribe in ever greater detail what work should be resourced and how tasks should be undertaken (see Home Office 1988, 1990a, 1990b). The Home Office did not accept that 'nothing worked' and laid down standards for probation work (Home Office 1992) the enforcement of which an expanded inspectorate, placed on a statutory footing in 1991, closely monitored in what were termed 'Efficiency and Effectiveness' inspections (HMIP 1993). These developments represented a challenge to the professional autonomy of individual probation officers, were associated with growing demands for management performance data and practice accountability, and were allied to increased pressure that practitioners adopt evidence-based working practices legitimated by Home Office and other research. The Home Office also directed ring-fenced funding for some probation-based initiatives which served the broader needs of the criminal justice system (for example, the 'hypothecated grant' for bail information and support schemes in 1992–4 – see Haines and Morgan, this volume).

There were already indications, however, that the Home Office doubted that its purposes could be achieved within the existing framework for governance. The 1990 Green Paper placed the writing clearly on the wall:

> The probation service has already responded to pressure for change. Over a short period of time there have been rapid improvements in consistency of standards, objectives and of management approach. These have been partly on the service's own initiative and partly in response to the Statement of National Objectives and Priorities published in 1984, the National Standards for Community Service Orders and further guidance from the Home Office. It cannot be taken for granted that the demands of the White Paper and the needs of the criminal justice system into the next century can be met by a collection of independent probation areas, loosely coordinated, with varying management structures and a professional base established in a working environment bearing little relationship to today's. It must also be asked what enhanced role can be played by the voluntary and private sector. (Home Office 1990b: para. 1.5)

The Green Paper set out three options, with arguments for and against each, for establishing a national probation service, either as a division within the Home Office or as an executive agency (as the Prison Service became in 1992) or as a non-departmental public body (NDPB) (*ibid.*: para.s 8.11–14). These options, when set alongside ideas for creating a market of providers of different probation services sketched out in a preceding Green Paper (Home Office 1988), presaged the reforms which, in the new millennium, New Labour have determined to pursue:

> One possibility would be for the probation service to contract with other services, and private and voluntary organisations, to obtain some of the components of punishment in the community. The probation service would supervise the order, but would not in itself be responsible for providing all the elements.
>
> Another possibility would be to set up a new organisation to organise punishment in the community. It would not itself supervise offenders or provide facilities directly, but would contract with other services and organisations to do so. (Home Office 1988: para.s 4.3–4)

Some of the managerial problems to be faced were set out in an Audit Commission analysis. The then 56 area services differed hugely in size, the largest, the Inner London Probation Service (ILPS), with over 1,000 staff, being on its own as large as the smallest 13 area services combined, with the smallest, the City of London Service, having only five officers (Audit Commission 1989: para. 22). Divisions of labour within probation services, partly as a consequence of size, differed greatly, some being dominated by individual casework generalists, highly resistant to the developing Home

Office-driven managerialist controls. In each area the chief probation officer was accountable to his or her probation committee one-third of whose members might by now be co-opted members, though their composition differed anomalously, depending on the type of local authority. In outer London and in the former metropolitan counties there was a requirement to co-opt elected local authority members. This was not the case in the shire counties (though this was changed by the Criminal Justice Act 1988).

Probation services were, as a result, delicately balanced between three interest groups – sentencers and the courts, the local authorities and the Home Office. The Home Office provided most of the money and had the greatest interest in how effectively it was spent (not least in terms of consequences for other parts of the criminal justice system), but as yet had 'limited direction in how the service is used or how big probation budgets should be. The local authorities ... have limited financial interest in probation ... but have considerable influence over its size. The courts have no financial interest in the probation service at all, but they determine how it should be used' (*ibid.*: para. 172).

In the event the then Conservative government, on the basis of these Green Paper-inspired discussions, took limited statutory measures (Criminal Justice Act 1991) to increase Home Office leverage over probation services. The probation inspectorate was made a statutory body with the Secretary of State empowered to direct aspects of its activities. The Secretary of State took default powers with respect to 'failing' probation committees. The 80 per cent of the budget contributed by the Home Office was henceforth cash-limited, meaning that any overspend had to be met by the local authority. And existing powers to amalgamate services were extended to Inner London. The government stepped back from taking a further measure, floated in the 1990 Green Paper (para. 5.26), that the Secretary of State be empowered to determine the employment of particular candidates as chief officers as opposed to approving candidate short lists. The government's decision document noted that performance-related pay had been introduced for chief and deputy chief officers, the implication being that the Home Office was by other means increasingly able to influence both the selection, performance and tenure of senior officers (see Wasik and Taylor 1994: 159–60).

The Home Office piper was now better able to call the probation tune, and did so. The number of area services was reduced to 54 and national standards for the supervision of offenders were laid down (Home Office 1992). In 1995 a further Green Paper (Home Office 1995) was published. This proposed that the various community sentences (probation, community service, combination orders, etc.) be amalgamated to form a single, portfolio community order with the courts deciding precisely what requirements to attach in individual cases. This suggested that the role of many probation staff might shift further from being professional assessors of individual offender's needs and likely responses to being administrators of differentiated punishments in the community. In such a case the requirement that officers have higher education, social work-type, professional qualifications, a requirement already doubted as necessary by Home Secretary Michael Howard, was called fundamentally into question. Yet, somewhat surprisingly, given that their proposals were based on the premise that community sentences were 'poorly understood … failed to command the confidence of the public despite the greater prominence and extra resources given to probation services in recent years … [and were] still widely regarded as a soft option' (*ibid.*: para. 4.4), the outgoing Conservative government failed to pursue the contracting out developments they had mooted.

The results of the managerial initiatives taken by the Conservative administration failed, after 1997, to convince the incoming New Labour government that structural change was not required, however. As David Faulkner, a former senior Home Office director, has described the period:

> The service suffered a series of public attacks and humiliations, from both Conservative and Labour governments … Opinions will vary on the extent to which they were deserved or justified … Statistics of re-offending did not show the hoped-for improvement, and those for failure to comply with court orders suggested that breaches were too often complacently ignored. Both were represented as evidence that too many officers were 'on the side of the offender' and neglecting their duty to protect the public, and that the service's management was too often ineffective and incompetent. (Faulkner 2001: 313)

The Probation Service was widely referred to as a 'failing service'. Moreover, the landscape of contiguous services, notably the prison and youth justice services, in whose operations many probation officers were now embedded, underwent fundamental, structural changes suggesting that the probation services were unlikely to be allowed to remain in their present form. The new executive prisons agency had from 1992 contracted out the management of some new prisons to commercial companies and many independent commentators, some of whom had not favoured the initiative, concluded that, despite teething problems, the development had been positive both in terms of improved regimes delivered in the contracted-out establishments and the knock-on consequences for the state service (see Morgan 2002: 1147–9). In 1998, following the Crime and Disorder Act, the youth justice system was reformed. Multi-agency, local authority youth offending teams (YOTs), to which probation officers were initially seconded (many remain seconded), were created, overseen by an NDPB, the Youth Justice Board (YJB), with considerable commissioning and purchasing responsibilities and powers.

Meanwhile, New Labour settled into government and announced a review of both the prison and probation services. The expanded probation inspectorate, in the absence of any substantial managerial capacity within the Home Office, collected performance data from local services in the course of their inspections and published a series of thematic reviews (HMIP 1998a, 1998b, 1999a, 1999b) suggesting how practice might be made more effective. The Government determined, however, that these initiatives did not suffice. Following its review of services (Home Office 1998), it introduced and, in the face of considerable opposition in the House of Lords, got through the Criminal Justice and Court Services Act 2000 (CJCSA), which in spring 2001 created the National Probation Service (NPS). The new framework constituted a compromise. The Home Office review inclined toward forging a combined 'correctional service' out of the probation and prison services, but noted from experience overseas (Canada, Australia, New Zealand and Scandinavia) that 'no country has moved with one giant step from completely separate organisations to complete integration. There has always been a gradualist approach, with central HQ merger first and then moves towards other (local) mergers' (*ibid.*: Appendix C, 3). The review accordingly favoured, as a first step, either the formation of regional probation agency services or a national probation agency on the lines of the then Prison Service. In the event, the risks acknowledged by the review of 'some disruption to established local links between probation services and local authorities, voluntary groups, the courts and local criminal justice agencies' (*ibid.*: 13), combined with a powerful lobby in Parliament in favour of the retention of strong local connections and accountability, led to the creation of the NPS, but with local probation boards.

At the same time a fresh, thoroughgoing review of the sentencing framework under John Halliday (Home Office 2001) picked up on the 1995 Green Paper proposals that there be a portfolio community sentence. The Halliday recommendations formed the basis of the provisions in the Criminal Justice Act 2003. All of this is to say that New Labour reinvigorated and implemented most of the Conservative Party's core ideas (many of which originated from the Home Office), and with respect to the marketisation of probation services now underway, now proposes implementing the most radical of them on a scale not contemplated by the Conservatives.

A national service: trials and tribulations

The functions of the NPS established in 2001 are:

- To assist the courts in deciding appropriate sentences and to supervise and rehabilitate offenders by giving effect to community sentences, supervising prisoners released on licence and providing accommodation in approved premises (CJCSA, s. 1 – those family-related duties previously undertaken by local probation services were hived off to a new, separate, national service, the Children and Family Court Advisory and Support Service (CAFCASS)).

Further:

- All persons with duties relating to the NPS are to have regard to five aims when exercising their functions: the protection of the public, the reduction of offending, the proper punishment of offenders, ensuring offenders' awareness of the effects of crime on victims and the public, and the rehabilitation of offenders (CJCSA, s. 2).

The constitution of the NPS is as follows:

- The Service is subject to the direction of a National Director, supported by a National Probation Directorate (NPD), who is accountable to the Secretary of State: neither this office or the Directorate, which is part of the Home Office, has a statutory basis. They exist to support the Secretary of State whose function is to ensure that provision is made throughout England and Wales for the purposes set out in s. 1 (CJCSA, s. 3).

- For administrative purposes England and Wales has been divided into 42 probation areas (the number may be altered by the Secretary of State), coterminous with court, CPS and police boundaries, for each of which there is a probation board comprising the chief officer and representatives of the local community appointed by the Secretary of State plus a judge appointed by the Lord Chancellor (CJCSA, ss. 4–5 and Schedule 1).

- Probation boards are, with the exception of chief officers (who are separate post-holder Crown Servants appointed by the Secretary of State), the employers of the probation staff in their area and are responsible for ensuring that there is sufficient provision in their areas for the purposes of s. 1 (CJCSA, s. 5(1)–(2)).

- It is for the Secretary of State to determine whether provisions made by boards are sufficient. He has default powers over boards in the event of his deciding that they are failing to perform their functions or not providing good value for money. He may make a 'management order' replacing any or all members of a board including the chief officer (CJCSA, ss. 5 and 10).

The 54 former probation services were reduced, by amalgamation, to 42 probation areas, each with their own probation board. The 42 areas are coterminous with the administrative structure of the police, CPS and the courts, though not the Prison Service, and are grouped in nine English regions, each with their own regional government office, plus Wales, for each of which the NPD appointed a regional probation manager. This involved the creation of some very large areas, notably London, where five former probation services were reduced to one, with an offender caseload comprising 23 per cent of the work of England and Wales.

Jack Straw, when Home Secretary, appointed Eithne Wallis, a former chief probation officer, to manage the transition to the national service, and his successor, David Blunkett, subsequently appointed her as the first National Director of the Service. Over the next three years the National Probation Directorate (NPD), the central administrative arm of the Service, grew in size with a staff, at its height, of approximately 350. At the time of writing (spring 2006), however, the NPD is rapidly shrinking, a large proportion of its staff having moved across to the National Offender Management Service (NOMS), as the commissioning functions of that body develop preparatory to passage of the enabling legislation for the proposed new structure, which the Government has announced it intends shortly to introduce (enabling legislation was introduced in early 2005 but aborted – see below – and has since been repeatedly put back). During this transitional period the division of labour and precise functions of the burgeoning NOMS – which, ironically, already has a staff in excess of 1,000 – and the withering NPD are in flux and difficult to delineate. Ever since 2001 a junior minister (or ministers) within the Home Office ministerial team has been given responsibility for probation and prisons and, subsequently, NOMS. It is to this minister, and the relevant permanent secretary, that both the National Director of the NPS, the Director of NOMS and HM Chief Inspector of Probation, reports. With the appointment in 2004 of Martin Narey, previously Director General of the Prison Service and then Commissioner of Correctional Services, as the first National Offender Management Director, he rather than the National Director of the NPS became the prominent, publicly visible manager of the Service. Though Martin Narey resigned at the end of 2005 and was replaced, though without permanent secretary status, by Helen Edwards, formerly Director of the National Association for the Care and Resettlement of Offenders (NACRO), the new locus of influence was preserved. Policy-making power now resides with NOMS not the NPD. Indeed a question mark now hangs over the future existence of the NPD.

Founder members of the 42 probation boards, each of which has between seven and 15 members, chairs being part-time paid appointees and their colleagues receiving *per diem* fees and expenses, were appointed in 2001. Members, who are eligible for reappointment, serve for three years. Depending on the number on the board, the other members generally comprise four magistrates and two elected members of local authorities from within the area. One member is a Lord Chancellor-appointed judge from the locality. The remaining members are drawn from the public living or working in the area. The chief officer, who is responsible for the day-to-day running of the local area, is the only executive (staff) member of the board.

Prior to 2001 the Association of Chief Officers of Probation (ACOP) was an influential body that spoke for local services and exercised some influence over the direction of policy. ACOP ceased to exist in March 2001 and, perhaps surprisingly given the turbulent and uncertain time that the NPS has since suffered, no successor organisation (like the Association of Chief Police Officers (ACPO) or the weaker Prison Governors' Association (PGA) or the fledgling Association of YOT Managers) has emerged exclusively to represent the views of chief officers. Some of ACOP's functions were transferred to the Probation Boards Association (PBA), membership of which is open to all boards and their members, including chief officers, on a board subscription basis. The relationship between the PBA and the NPD has at times been an abrasive one, not least because the PBA, which has a full-time chief executive, Martin Wargent, a former chief probation officer, and secretariat, sought to represent boards' interests by resisting what the PBA saw during the period 2001–4 as the centralising diktats of the NPD (see, for example, Wargent 2002). In this struggle the position of chief officers was difficult and compromised, not having a representative body of their own and, though members of the PBA, being Crown servants appointed by the NPD, acting on behalf of the Secretary of State.

The PBA's *Handbook* (2001) describes boards as responsible for:

- establishing the strategy for the work of the area, within the policy framework and resources set out by the Home Secretary;
- preparing an annual area plan and budget, which contains both national and local priorities and takes account of national performance measures set by the NPD; the plan is submitted to the Director General of the NPS for agreement;
- contracts with other organisations to provide services, e.g. employment, education and training for offenders;
- ensuring that it is a good employer;
- meeting together at least four times, and as far as practical ten times, a year, those meetings being held in public;
- monitoring and assessing the area's performance against the annual plan with the aim of continually improving performance;
- reviewing the financial management and probity of the board.

It was probably inevitable that the relationship between the PBA and the NPD would prove difficult given that establishing the NPS involved ensuring a common administrative and managerial framework as well as greater consistency across the country in how offenders were worked with. Though, for example, the previous, 54, more-or-less-autonomous, probation services subscribed to a common National Negotiating Committee-agreed staff salary and working conditions scheme, they interpreted it differently and the working conditions and salaries of non-probation staff differed. Their estates arrangements (ownership and maintenance of buildings, office services, etc.) varied. And they had different IT tie-ups with their local authorities. The NPD took over the management of most of these aspects of policy. The consequence was some employee disaffection locally and many boards, whose members included commercially-minded persons familiar with local labour and property services market conditions, resented their lack of control as NPS employers. Many thought the financial consequences of NPD decisions for their budgets disadvantageous (these issues are hinted at in HMIP 2003b: para. 3.8). With the emergence of NOMS, the centre of the PBA's attention has shifted from the NPD to it.

Contextual accountability arrangements

One cannot, by definition, be accountable *to* someone unless it is clear what one is accountable *for*. Which is why defining the outcomes of a service, and agreeing some priorities and procedures for delivering those outcomes, are essential components for achieving accountability. *External* accountability rests crucially on the chain of *internal* managerial control and the collection of performance data. One may argue about whether managerial controls are appropriate – whether they are excessive in number or inappropriately targeted, stifle innovation, allow sufficient scope for professional judgement and discretion, etc. – but without paper or electronic performance traces, and means for monitoring those traces, any true accountability is rendered nugatory. In this section we consider what further accountability mechanisms support the existing governance arrangements.

Published statistics and performance data

There is no legislative requirement, as there is for the Prison Service (see Morgan 2002: 1140–2), for the Secretary of State to produce and publish an NPS annual report or for certain operational statistics to be laid before Parliament. The Probation Service has for many years nonetheless done so. Until 2003 *Probation Statistics* were published annually by the Home Office, aggregating and analysing data returned by the local probation services until 2001 and thereafter the area administrations of the NPS. The *Probation Statistics* were never as extensive or sophisticated as the *Prison Statistics*, but they were a valuable source of accessible data on such issues as the changing characteristics of the probation caseload, the number and nature of reports written by probation staff, the characterstics of probation staff, etc. In 2004, however, they were replaced (as were the *Prison Statistics*) by an annual volume of *Offender Management Caseload Statistics* prepared by the branch of the Home Office Research Development and Statistics Directorate attached to NOMS (Home Office 2004b). Parallel changes were made to the annually published *Criminal Statistics*. It will no doubt take time for the precise format of the new statistics, along with the reports of NOMS and the Home Office more generally, to settle down. In the short term, however, the situation is most unsatisfactory with consequential difficulties for those wishing to understand and call the Service to account. Many data that were formerly published routinely or intermittently (for example, the characterstics of probation staff, the nature of recommendations made in pre-sentence reports or the proportion of offenders remanded in custody and subsequently receiving non-custodial sentences) are no longer published or made easily accessible. Information about NOMS, the work of the Probation Service and its offender caseload is currently fragmented and relatively incoherent. It will not be easy, for example, for readers to find out what staff are employed where, how the NOMS and NPS budget is dispensed and how the nature of offender assessment and supervision is changing. The operation of the Probation Service is today arguably less transparent than for many a year.

Her Majesty's Inspectorate of the National Probation Service for England and Wales

There has existed, as we have noted, a probation inspectorate since 1936, though not put on a statutory footing until 1993. The current statutory authority is the Criminal Justice and Courts Services Act 2000, ss. 6 and 7. The Secretary of State appoints HM Chief Inspector and determines his staff and resources. The inspectorate is required to inspect the provisions made by each local probation board under s. 5 of the Act and the Secretary of State may direct the inspectorate to make those assessments according to criteria specified in directions. The Secretary of State may direct that particular reports be submitted, but whatever reports are submitted or requested, copies must be laid before Parliament.

How statutory inspection arrangements work in practice is often opaque, though in the case of the probation inspectorate the nature of operational changes made in recent years have been described rather fully:

> Inspectorates have a variety of functions – public interest accountability, giving independent advice to Ministers, identifying good and bad practice, driving up performance, safeguarding the interests of the customers, users and other beneficiaries of services, and so on. But the manner in which they fulfil these functions depends ... on the nature and the organisation of whatever service they inspect ... there is, and should be, a symbiotic relationship between what an inspectorate does and the character of the inspected service. (Morgan 2004: 81)

The Chief Inspector argued that, following the creation of the NPS and the NPD in 2001, it was necessary and sensible for HMIP to change its approach and methodology. Prior to 2001, he suggests, HMIP had to some extent operated as a surrogate NPD in relation to the 'more-or-less autonomous probation services'. There were no national performance data other than those collected by HMIP. The inspection programme was essentially a form of performance management, focused on compliance by probation staff with the National Standards for Supervision introduced in 1992 and updated since. With the creation of the NPD, it was appropriate for it, and not HMIP, to manage the system, routinely collect performance data and check on their reliability and validity. Henceforth HMIP would certainly use those performance data, but it would concentrate its inspectoral effort less on *processes* and more on *objectives* and *outcomes*, giving greater attention to *users* (offenders) and looking not just at what the NPS itself does, but also at what is achieved in *partnership* with other agencies and bodies. Further, inspections were now to be less *routine* and more *targeted*, depending on what the management data and other indicators suggested were the risks and needs. The corollary was that more inspectoral effort was to be devoted to *thematic* reports, looking at data *across* probation areas (*ibid.*: 82–4).

To sum up, the Chief Inspector's account was that now that there existed a framework for managerial control *by* the Home Office, HMIP could and should operate more like an independent inspectorate and less like the management arm *of* the Home Office.

The annual reports of HMIP show unequivocally that, in accordance with this manifesto, the inspectorate has since 2001 devoted less of its time to routine area inspections and more to thematically focused reports on aspects of probation performance, attempting to look at the relationship between what the Chief Inspector has described as the potentially virtuous triangle of offender *assessments*, *interventions* and *outcomes* (*ibid.*: 84; HMIP 2003a: chapter 5; HMIP 2004).

The data from these routine and thematic reports should assist not just the public at large, ministers and Home Office advisors to assess the merits and shortcomings of policy and practice across the country, but also members of probation boards to see how local provision compares with practice elsewhere.

In 2003, *inter alia*, HMIP published, as we have seen, its initial assessment of the governance of probation areas by probation boards, a key aspect of the new structure (HMIP 2003b). The review was superficially encouraging. Boards had been appointed and settled into their new roles pretty smoothly. They were responsive to national priorities and were adopting a systematic approach to area planning, strategic development and policy review. But there was a sting in the tail of the report which, given that the Government had at that stage not given an indication that they intended abolishing boards as currently constituted, was potentially devastating. Did boards, the inspectorate asked, add value? If boards did not exist could other structures and processes very easily take over their responsibilities? HMIP did not answer either of their own questions with negative assessments. But neither did they 'find evidence to contradict' them. The statement arguably provided another nail for the coffin of the 2001 arrangements.

In 2003, in a public lecture commenting, *inter alia*, on a Cabinet Office review of regulation and inspection arrangements across Whitehall, the Chief Inspector floated the proposition that HMIP, together with the four other inspectorates of criminal justice services, be abolished and a single criminal justice system inspectorate be created (Morgan 2004). This proposition was subsequently adopted by the Government (CJS 2005) and enabling legislation introduced. But the amalgamation proposal has since been abandoned in favour of greater administrative integration of inspectorate budgets and collaborative working.

The Prisons and Probation Ombudsman

Unlike HMIP, the Prisons and Probation Ombudsman (PPO) has not yet been placed on a statutory basis and until 2001 the Ombudsman dealt only with prisons-related complaints. In 2001 the Ombudsman had added to his remit 'the provision of an independent complaints service for offenders under the supervision of the National Probation Service' (PPO 2002: 14).

Persons eligible to make complaints to the PPO are offenders who either are, or have been, under the supervision of the NPS, or have had pre-sentence reports (PSRs) prepared on them, or who live, or have lived, in NPS hostel accommodation, and have failed to get satisfaction from complaints made through the NPS internal system. The PPO does not normally consider complaints made on behalf of offenders by organisations or other individuals and decisions made by ministers or persons acting on behalf of ministers are excluded. However, the actions of agencies acting on behalf of the NPS – for example, contracted out supervision or surveillance such as community service or electronic surveillance – is included. Complainants must normally contact the PPO within one month of receiving a substantive decision from the probation board to their internal complaint and he will not normally accept a complaint after a delay of one year unless the delay is somehow the fault of the NPS or is very serious. When complaints are judged eligible the PPO has unfettered access to all documents relevant to his investigation. He communicates his findings in writing to complainants, copies his reports to the relevant persons in the NPS, and may make recommendations to the Home Secretary, the National Director or the probation board, as appropriate.

The PPO has to date received very few complaints from probation-related offenders – 97 in the first six months, and 192, 282 and 309 respectively in the three years March 2002–5. Only a tiny proportion, 10 and 13 per cent respectively in the last two years, were found to be eligible, invariably because the internal complaints system had not been exhausted. This is a much lower absolute number and proportion than that for the Prison Service (typically between 40 and 50 per cent). Moreover, nearly all the complaints so far received have been from prisoners, usually complaining about issues relating to their recall or release – mostly the fairness or accuracy of parole reports – or alleged failures of probation officers to maintain contact with, or provide information to, them while in prison. Remarkably few complaints have so far been upheld, two fully and ten partially in 2003–4 and only one fully and six partially in 2004–5 (PPO 2002, 2003, 2004, 2005). The PPO reports that the complaints he receives from prisoners regarding the NPS are typically more complex than those he receives about the Prison Service because they normally relate to the alleged actions of individual officers (HMIP 2004: 52). It is reassuring, therefore, that he has so far seldom found the Service wanting. Complaints regarding alleged racism, inaccuracy or unfairness in probation reports have rarely been even partially upheld. A high proportion of complaints, including some not strictly eligible, are resolved by the PPO with the NPS informally. It is usually a matter of re-establishing effective communications between the Service and the prisoner concerned.

The emergence of NOMS

Proposals that probation services be subject to a puchaser–provider split with a view to stimulating market competition between providers have, as we have seen, been in the air since the early 1990s. However, most commentators will take the 2003 Carter Report as the starting point for the creation of NOMS. This is for the very good reason that Patrick Carter, a successful businessman who has undertaken several policy reviews on behalf of Prime Minister Blair, recommended that the agency, combining the objectives and functions of both the probation and prison services, be formed and his recommendation was immediately adopted (Home Office 2004a). Next came some brief Home Office consultation papers in 2004, and in early 2005 publication of the Management of Offenders and Sentencing Bill. The Bill was lost because of the June 2005 general election. The Bill provided, crucially (clause 2), that the Secretary of State be empowered to direct probation boards to contract for the provision of specified probation services with specified persons, or that the board not provide certain services as directed. This was in keeping with the then plan that probation boards be retained but that Regional Offender Managers (ROMs), already appointed by spring 2005, commission probation and prison services which might be tendered for by voluntary and private agencies as well as probation boards.

Between the 2005 general election and early autumn 2005 this plan was amended. In October 2005 the Home Office published a more radical plan for NOMS (Home Office 2005). It announced that it intended introducing an amended Bill in December 2005, a plan then put back to early summer 2006 (the expectation at the time of writing, May 2006). This is where matters now stand. The current proposals include the following:

- Abolishing probation boards as currently constituted and creating in their place, in however many areas the Secretary of State shall determine, probation trusts, the members of which would continue to be appointed by the Secretary of State, but which will likely be smaller than the existing boards. 'It is not proposed to replicate the detailed legislative prescriptions on the appointment process for, or membership and constitution ... so as to create flexibility ... as contractual arrangements change' (para. 15). However, since trusts 'will no longer be the sole providers of probation services' there is no longer a case for a Crown Court judge necessarily to be a member (para. 18). Further, if trusts 'are to operate with greater freedom' it makes sense for them to be able to choose, employ and line manage their own chief officer (para. 20).

- Giving the Secretary of State the statutory duty to make arrangements with others to provide probation services. This will mean that either the National Offender Manager or the ten ROMs, acting on behalf of the Secretary of State, 'will enter into arrangements, through contracts or service level agreements (SLAs), with other organisations in the public, private or voluntary and community sectors to provide them for him' (para. 10). These 'other organisations' are to include the local probation trusts.

- This is not intended to mean, however, that certain probation services are to be reserved for probation trusts or that trusts will be given contracts or SLAs: they may fail to win any contracts, something NOMS envisages (para.s 25–6). Either the National Offender Manager nationally, or the ROMs regionally, 'will commission services from whichever organisation is best placed to deliver them. They will be free to commission across probation area boundaries and across the custody/community divide' (para. 11).

- Separating the commissioning of 'offender management' and probation 'interventions' (para. 11), though it is envisaged that both could be provided by the same agency (NOMS 2005: para. 35).

- Giving the Secretary of State 'powers of last resort'. If trusts lose all of their business, they will cease to exist. However, the Secretary of State will be empowered 'to recreate a trust to take over an alternative provider in case of failure and/or to create a "shadow trust" to bid for work on behalf of the public sector in a future market test, with a full trust being set up if the bid is successful' (para. 26).

- Creating, at the outset, 42 probation trusts for the existing 42 probation areas. However, the Secretary of State is to be empowered to amend their number and boundaries 'to keep pace with changes elsewhere' in the criminal justice system. 'It is proposed that this be done administratively rather than, as at present, by means of a parliamentary procedure' (para. 27).

Before dissecting these proposals, we should go back to the Carter Report in order to chart the direction and distance so far travelled.

In his letter to the Prime Minister which serves as the preface to his report, Carter wrote as follows:

> Despite recent improvements, a new approach is needed to break down the silos of prisons and probation and ensure a better focus on managing offenders ... The Report calls for a new National Offender Management Service (NOMS) responsible for reducing re-offending. It separates the case management of offenders from the provision of prison places, treatment services or community programmes (whether they are in the public, private or voluntary sectors).

In fact, most of the Carter Report was not devoted to structural change, but rather to sentencing policy and practice and the enforcement of sentences, aspects of which were judged, either explicitly or by implication, to be seriously flawed. Too many minor or first-time offenders, for example, were receiving more punitive sentences whereas 'the system needs to improve its grip on persistent offenders' (Carter 2003: 18). There was unwarranted sentencing disparity and 'poor self-governance in respect of sentencing practice' (*ibid.:* 20). Carter also observed, however, that the prison and probation services remained largely detached from each other. 'A more strategic approach to the end-to-end management of offenders across their sentence is needed' and 'no front line organisation ultimately owns the target for reduced offending'. This was in 'sharp contrast to the Youth Justice Board, which has a clear aim to "prevent offending by children and young people". They have a strong focus on managing young offenders (through the Youth Offending Teams). This structure ... appears to have made a significant impact on rates of re-offending' (*ibid.:* 23).

This reference to the YJB is instructive, for the YJB does not *manage* YOTs (see Morgan and Newburn, this volume). YOTs constitute devolved, multi-agency and largely locally financed, local government teams. The YJB *monitors* YOTs' performance and partly finances them, providing each with a core grant and ring-fenced funds for innovative offender interventions. YOTs themselves determine whether to deliver interventions in-house or contract out. However, the YJB does commission custodial places for juvenile offenders, and does so from a variety of providers. This arrangement has been judged generally to work well (Audit Commission 2004), though reoffending has so far reduced only marginally and the factors contributing to that reduction are debatable. This is is an issue to which we shall return.

Carter concluded that introducing private sector prisons had worked well and that the benefits of competition, which had hitherto scarcely been tested with regard to front-line probation services, should be given greater scope in the prison and probation services generally. In a brief, six-page chapter, he sketched out 'A New Approach to Managing Offenders'. The essence of Carter's proposals was that a NOMS:

> should be established, led by a single Chief Executive, with a clear objective to punish offenders and help reduce reoffending. Within

the service there should be a single person responsible for offenders. This would be separate from day-to-day responsibility for prisons and probation. (Carter 2003: 33).

Thereafter Carter provided only the lightest of sketches as to what this should mean in organisational practice, though two concepts were emphasised both in his script and diagrammatically. 'Offender management' should be fundamentally separated from 'operations', by which Carter meant the running of prisons and specific offender interventions within them, and 'community interventions and punishment' (*ibid.*: 36–7).

The Home Office response to these proposals was published within a fortnight: as the Home Secretary emphasised, the Carter Report had 'been developed closely with the Home Office'. He also asserted that many of the day-to-day tasks of probation and prison staff 'would not greatly change'. But they would be more integrated by offender managers, who would be 'largely Probation Officers' (Home Office 2004a: Foreword). Despite the progress that had been made by both the probation and prison services the Home Office asserted that it was 'still all too easy for offenders to fall between the gap between the services' (*ibid.*: para. 25), a scarcely veiled reference to the shortcomings of sentence planning and prisoner resettlement arrangements (see HMIP 2001; Social Exclusion Unit 2002). Great emphasis was placed on the benefits already achieved by contracting out the construction and management of prisons to the private sector, benefits that needed to be replicated across the probation and prisons field.

The appointment of Martin Narey as Chief Executive of NOMS was announced immediately and a National Offender Manager, Christine Knott (formerly Chief Officer, Greater Manchester Probation Area), later in the year. NOMS came formally into existence on 1 June 2005, most of its staff transferring from the NPD and Prison Service HQ. It became widely known that the Home Office estimated that approximately 70 per cent of the staff currently employed by probation boards would be needed for offender management-related work, and that the NOMS view was they would ideally be line managed by NOMS regional managers (ROMs), whose appointment would follow as soon as possible. It was also widely assumed that the Home Office would wish to be rid of probation boards, considered to be too large and unwieldy and to add no real value (see discussion of HMIP 2003b above).

The PBA published its initial response to Carter and the Home Office paper in February 2004. The Association was 'dismayed' that such 'far-reaching decisions' for a 'costly reorganisation' should have been taken without any business case being presented or consultation offered. Carter's analysis of sentencing trends was welcomed and the proposition that offenders be subject to improved end-to-end sentence management accepted. But the Government was reminded that 90 per cent of offenders were subject to non-custodial sentences and there should be no weakening of the vital links with local services such as policing, health, housing and education. Moreover for local accountability to be convincing, local governors had to have the 'power to put things right'. The Association welcomed the proposition that the not-for-profit sector be more involved in delivering probation services and had no objection in principle to contracting out some services to the commercial sector. But it had concerns about the cost-effectiveness of the implied processes involved in commissioning, contract specification, monitoring and management (PBA 2004a).

In May 2004 NOMS issued an 'organogram' for the structure it had in mind, accompanied by the briefest of scripts (NOMS 2004). The diagram placed purchasers and providers on either side of a central, vertical line, at the top of which was the NOMS Chief Executive, Martin Narey, to whom both puchasers and providers were to be accountable. The 42 probation areas and boards were swept away as was the title 'probation'. On the provider side the latter was replaced by a 'Director of Public Sector Interventions' working with a National Management Board, and on the puchaser side were the ten ROMs each with a Commissioning Advisory Board and a Regional Management Board to oversee commissioning and offender management respectively. This was the framework envisaged for transferring the estimated 70 per cent of probation staff to be line managed by the ROMs.

This model was met with scarcely disguised incredulity in many quarters. The PBA's published response was almost a model of ironic restraint. What of the developing benefits of the 42 coterminous criminal justice areas each with their Local Criminal Justice Boad (LCJB)? Why this elaborate, bureaucratic structure at regional level when practically all of probation's statutory and non-statutory duties, obligations and partnership structures were at the 42 areas level? What of Chancellor Gordon Brown's recent statement that the Government was intent on pursuing policies which will move 'us forward from the era of an Old Britain weakened by the man in Whithall knows best towards a 'New Britain strengthened by local centres awash with initiative, energy and dynamism'? The organogram had allegedly emerged, once again, without consultation: the PBA considered that the Service could be 'on the brink of a chaotic period which would result in real harm'. It was all a 'recipe for disaster' (PBA 2004b).

As a result of this and other expressions of doubt a compromise was reached. In July 2004 the Home Secretary announced that it had been decided not to pursue the national/regional approach, and in January 2005 the Management of Offenders and Sentencing Bill was published providing for the retention of area probation boards, but empowering the Secretary of State to direct what services they should and should not provide. In response the PBA announced that boards looked forward to developing their commissioning role with NOMS (PBA 2005b).

By 2005 the ten ROMs had been appointed and a pathfinder project announced in the north-west to begin testing the new framework for offender management. The Home Office plans to begin transferring probation area staff to be line managed by the ROMs had been abandoned: it could not legally be done. A new approach was forged. Probation boards would be abolished but be replaced by trusts, and instead of moving across to be line-managed by the ROMs, probation staff, whether involved in offender management or the delivery of interventions, would likely move about between whichever providers, public, private or voluntary sector, successfully tendered to the ROMs or the National Offender Manager for contracts or SLAs. The implicit vertical dividing line between offender management and the delivery of specific interventions of the 2004 organogram had also been abandoned: it would now be possible, apparently, for the same providers to both manage offenders *and* deliver particular services – as probation areas do currently. This was the plan announced in October 2005, with an enabling Bill promised by the end of the year.

Having suffered almost two decades of scarcely concealed criticism and hostility from successive ministers, Conservative and Labour; having endured the fundamental change in structure and working practices inherent in the creation of a national service in 2001; and now, for the 18 months since the beginning of 2004, having faced great uncertainty about their future employment – probation staff, particularly senior managers, unsurprisingly reported low morale and little confidence in the proposed arrangements (PBA 2005b). Their views were reportedly widely shared by probation board members.

NOMS: likely prospects

Let us assume that the Government introduces, and successfully secures passage of, the enabling Bill outlined in October 2005 (Home Office 2005). What might the proposed arrangements for NOMS and the NPS mean in practice?

The first point to be made is that there are inumerable, important details to the proposed framework that have yet to be made clear. For example:

- There has not yet been set out any statement of the principles which should govern the proposed market in probation services. (This was accomplished for prisons through the provisions in the Criminal Justice Act 1991 for the appointment of a Crown 'controller' in each privately managed prison, etc.) Are any aspects of probation work – the preparation of court reports, for example – to be exempted from the services for which non-public bodies might contract? And, if not, would non-public agencies preparing court reports be eligible also to deliver interventions possibly proposed in those court reports? Would such overlaps not embody conflicts of interest?

- It is not yet clear what characteristics probation trust members are to have and whether there is to be any semblance of local accountability to constituent local authorities and the courts either through the trusts or, should trusts fail to secure contracts or SLAs, through other providers or the ROMs.

- Reference is made in the October 2005 statement to: 'local partnership arrangements' and the 'significant advantages [which] have accrued from coterminosity of geographical boundaries between local [criminal justice] agencies'; and to boards' statutory and non-statutory duties other than the provision of probation sevices (Home Office 2005: para. 27). However, it is far from clear how these duties will satisfactorily be met given the uncertainty and possible flux in the number and range of possible future providers of probation services. Probation areas, for example, are statutory partners of YOTs, and are obliged to contribute resources to them: how are these obligations in future to be met? Probation areas are currently represented, through their chief officers, on the LCJBs: how are probation services, critical to joint criminal justice system effectiveness, to be represented in future?

- Further, as noted earlier, external accountability rests crucially on the chain of internal managerial accountability and there is a symbiotic relationship between internal performance management and external inspection. How are these relationships in future to be structured, not least that the Government proposes that the criminal justice inspectorates should work more collaboratively?

In addition, there are fundamental, operational issues, the discussion of which is beyond the scope of this chapter, which have implications for governance and about which serious doubts are entertained as to the likely effectiveness of the proposed structure. For example, the connection between changing the direction of the sentencing trend and structural reorganisation of the probation and prison services was singularly opaque in the Carter Report, and remains opaque in the operational plans for NOMS (see, for example, Hedderman 2006). Many commentators have from the outset considered that the prospects for launching NOMS successfully would be poor were the prison and probation services to be overwhelmed by a rising prison population. At the time of writing, May 2006, the prison population stands at over 77,000, a record high. Further, there are substantial doubts regarding the model of offender management being implemented: what will work administratively will not necessarily be effective from offenders' standpoint (see Partridge 2004; PA Consulting Group and MORI 2005; Robinson 2005; Raynor and Maguire 2006). These doubts will be exacerbated if the relationships between offenders and their supervisors is fragmented by the division between offender management and delivery of particular offender programmes by a multiplicity of agencies.

This brings us to the question of accountability, local and national. The structure and conceptual basis of the 2004 organogram has been largely abandoned, but the position of one person within it, the NOMS Chief Executive in the Home Office, remains intact. Both the commissioning and delivery of offender management and all custody and community-based sanctions are henceforth to be accountable to the Chief Executive of NOMS and, through her, the Secretary of State, who is to be empowered to both appoint the members of probation trusts and determine the content and recipients of all service provider contracts and SLAs. There remains the possibility that the Secretary of State may decide, administratively, that there should be links between the membership of trusts and the judiciary, the local authorities and other bodies: this is one question about which the Home Office sought the views of stakeholders (Home Office 2005: para.s 16–18). But it is difficult to interpret the Government's proposals as not representing a significant shift towards centralised command, as is and has been the case with the Prison

Service. This is the exact opposite of that for which the Government itself and several commentators (see Faulkner 2006), as well as the PBA, have argued. Even if the Secretary of State decides that there should be such membership links, the trusts will no longer determine what services they provide locally: those decisions will rest with the ROMs or the National Offender Manager. In such a case, if local communities wish to question the manner in which offenders are or are not supervised, their recourse would appear to be to ROM offices at regional government level. There will be no democratic local connection, as there is not with prisons.

This restructuring plan rests on the twin propositions that the elected government will discern the wishes of the judiciary and the community at large, that the National Offender Manager and the ROMs will interpret how those wishes are to be shaped to local circumstances and needs, and a more open, competitive market will secure enhanced effectiveness and value for money. If the corollary of these arrangements leads on the one hand to lack of continuity in supervisory relationships with offenders and on the other fragmentation of probation services as far as local partnerships are concerned, then the consequences for both reduced reoffending and effectively joined up criminal justice policy will be jeopardised.

As if these structural uncertainties and process outcomes were not enough, the criminal justice and local government landscape within which probation services are delivered is itself changing fundamentally. In autumn 2005 the Home Secretary announced that he proposed amalgamating police forces. Though his successor, in summer 2006, put these plans on hold, few commentators doubt that they will eventually be resuscitated, with knock-on consequences for the organisation of other criminal justice services. Meanwhile, within local government the development of childen's trusts and local area agreements will potentially transform the delivery of services with consequences for the operation of YOTs and, thus, their partnerhips with probation services. For all these reasons it is difficult to foresee the reality of probation governance and accountability in the short to medium term.

Further reading

For a general history of the Probation Service, including aspects of its governance, Peter Raynor and Maurice Vanstone's *Understanding Community Penalties: Probation, Policy and Social Change* (2002) is an excellent introduction. The website of the Probation Boards Association (http://www.probationboards.co.uk) provides authoritative guidance to the governance provisions of the existing framework. To get to grips with the turmoil surrounding recent changes in the governance of the service, both made and proposed, there is no substitute for reading the key official documents, principally the Carter Report, *Managing Offenders, Reducing Crime – A New Approach* (2003), and the Home Office responses *Managing Offenders – Changing Lives* (2004a) and *Restructuring Probation to Reduce Re-offending* (2005). Chapters 20 and 23 of David Faulkner's *Crime, State and Citizen: A Field Full of Folk* (2006) and a collection of essays edited by Mike Hough, Rob Allen and Una Padel, *Reshaping Probation and Prisons: The New Offender Management Framework* (2006), sketch aspects of the argument about future policy directions.

References

Audit Commission (1989) *The Probation Service: Promoting Value for Money*. London: Audit Commission.

Audit Commission (2004) *Youth Justice 2004: A Review of the Reformed Youth Justice System*. London: Audit Commission.

Bottoms, A. E. and Preston, R. H. (eds) (1980) *The Coming Penal Crisis: A Criminological and Theological Exploration*. Edinburgh: Scottish Academic Press.

Brody, S. (1976) *The Effectiveness of Sentencing: A Review of the Literature*, Home Office Research Study No. 35. London: HMSO.

Carter Report (2003) *Managing Offenders, Reducing Crime – A New Approach*. London: Prime Minister's Strategy Unit.

Criminal Justice Service (2005) *Inspection Reform: Establishing an Inspectorate for Justice, Community Safety and Custody – Policy Statement*. London: CJS.

Downes, D. and Morgan, R. (2007) 'No turning back: the politics of law and order into the new millennnium', in M. Maguire, R. Morgan and R. Reiner (eds), *Oxford Handbook of Criminology*, 4th edn. Oxford: Oxford University Press.

Faulkner, D. (2001) *Crime, State and Citizen: A Field Full of Folk*, 2nd edn. Winchester: Waterside Press.

Faulkner, D. (2006) 'A modern service, fit for pupose?', in M. Hough, R. Allen and U. Padel (eds), *Reshaping Prisons and Probation: The New Offender Management Framework*. Bristol: Policy Press.

Hedderman, C. (2006) 'Keeping a lid on the prison population – will NOMS help?', in M. Hough, R. Allen and U. Padel (eds), *Reshaping Prisons and Probation: The New Offender Management Framework*. Bristol: Policy Press.

Her Majesty's Inspectorate of Probation (1993) *Annual Report 1992–3*. London: Home Office.

Her Majesty's Inspectorate of Probation (1998a) *Strategies for Effective Offender Supervision*. London: HMIP.

Her Majesty's Inspectorate of Probation (1998b) *Delivering an Enhanced Level of Community Supervision*. London: HMIP.

Her Majesty's Inspectorate of Probation (1999a) *Offender Assessment Supervision Planning*. London: HMIP.

Her Majesty's Inspectorate of Probation (1999b) *The Victim Perspective*. London: HMIP.

Her Majesty's Inspectorate of Probation (2001) *Through the Prison Gate*. London: HMIP.

Her Majesty's Inspectorate of Probation (2003a) *2002/2003 Annual Report*. London: HMIP.

Her Majesty's Inspectorate of Probation (2003b) *From Aspirations to Reality: An Inspection of the Governance of Probation Areas by Probation Boards*. London: HMIP.

Her Majesty's Inspectorate of Probation (2004) *2003/2004 Annual Report*. London: HMIP.

Home Office (1922) *Report of the Committee on Training, Appointment and Payment of Probation Officers*, Cmd 1601. London: Home Office.

Home Office (1936) *Report of the Committee on Social Services in Courts of Summary Jurisdiction*, Cmd 5122. London: Home Office.

Home Office (1988) *Punishment, Custody and the Community*, Cm 424. London: HMSO.

Home Office (1990a) *Crime, Justice and Protecting the Public*, Cm 965. London: HMSO.

Home Office (1990b) *Supervision and Punishment in the Community*, Cm 966. London: HMSO.

Home Office (1992) *National Standards for the Supervision of Offenders in the Community*. London: Home Office.

Home Office (1995) *Strengthening Punishment in the Community*. London: Home Office.

Home Office (2001) *Making Punishments Work: Report of a Review of the Sentencing Framework for England and Wales*. London: Home Office.

Home Office (2004a) *Managing Offenders – Changing Lives*. London: Home Office.

Home Office (2004b) *Offender Management Caseload Statistics 2003*, Statistical Bulletin 15/04. London: Home Office.

Home Office (2005) *Restructuring Probation to Reduce Re-offending*. London: Home Office.

Hough, M., Allen, R. and Padel, U. (eds) (2006) *Reshaping Probation and Prisons: The New Offender Management Framework*. Bristol: Policy Press.

Mair, G. (1997) 'Community penalties and probation', in M. Maguire, R. Morgan and R. Reiner (eds), *Oxford Handbook of Criminology*, 2nd edn. Oxford: Oxford University Press.

Martinson, R. (1974) 'What works? Questions and answers about prison reform', *Public Interest*, 35: 22–54

McWilliams, W. (1983) 'The mission to the English police courts 1876–1936', *Howard Journal*, 22: 129–47.

McWilliams, W. (1985) 'The mission transformed: professionalism of probation between the wars', *Howard Journal*, 24: 257–74.

McWilliams, W. (1990) 'Probation practice and the management ideal', *Probation Journal*, 37: 60–7.

McWilliams, W. and Pease, K. (1990) 'Probation practice and an end to punishment', *Howard Journal*, 29: 14–24.

Morgan, R. (2002) 'Imprisonment: a brief history, the contemporary scene, and likely prospects', in M. Maguire, R. Morgan and R. Reiner (eds), *The Oxford Handbook of Criminology*, 3rd edn. Oxford: Oxford University Press.

Morgan, R. (2004) 'Thinking about the future of probation inspection', *Howard Journal*, 43: 79–92.

Morison Report (1962) *Report of the Departmental Committee on the Probation Service*, Cmnd 1650. London: HMSO.

National Offender Management Service (2004) *National Offender Management Service (NOMS) Organisational Design – Consultation Paper*. London: NOMS.

National Offender Management Service (2005) *Partial Regulatory Impact Assessment: Restructuring Probation to Reduce Offending*, November. London: NOMS.

National Probation Service (2001) *A New Choreography: An Integrated Strategy for the National Probation Service for England and Wales – Strategic Framework 2001–2004*. London: Home Office.

PA Consulting and MORI (2005) *Action Research Study of the Implementation of the National Offender Management Model in the North West Pathfinder*. London: Home Office.

Partridge, S. (2004) *Examining Case Management Models for Community Sentences*, Home Office Online Report 17/04. London: Home Office.

Prison and Probation Ombudsman (2002) *Annual Report 2001–2: The Pursuit of Decency*. London: PPO.

Prison and Probation Ombudsman (2003) *Annual Report 2002–3: Towards Resettlement*. London: PPO.

Prison and Probation Ombudsman (2004) *Annual Report 2003–4*, Cm 6256. London: PPO.

Prison and Probation Ombudsman (2005) *Annual Report 2004–5*, Cm 6612. London: PPO.

Probation Boards Association (2001) *Handbook*, 3rd edn. London: PBA.

Probation Boards Association (2004a) *'Managing Offenders, Reducing Crime and Managing Offenders, Changing Lives' – The Government's Plans for Transforming the Management of Offenders – Outline Response from the PBA*, February. London: PBA.

Probation Boards Association (2004b) *Home Office Consultation on NOMS Organisational Design – Response from the Probation Boards Association*. London: PBA.

Probation Boards Association (2005a) *'Managing Offenders, Reducing Crime* and *Managing Offenders, Changing Lives' – The Government's Plans for Transforming the Management of Offenders – Full Response from the PBA*. London: PBA.

Probation Boards Association (2005b) *The View of Chief Officers on the Development of a National Offender Management Service*. London: PBA.

Raynor, P. and Maguire, M. (2006) 'End-to-end or end in tears? Prospects for the effectiveness of the national offender management model', in M. Hough, R. Allen and U. Padel (eds), *Reshaping Prisons and Probation: The New Offender Management Framework*. Bristol: Policy Press.

Raynor, P. and Vanstone, M. (2002) *Understanding Community Penalties: Probation, Policy and Social Change*. Buckingham: Open University Press.

Robinson, G. (2005) 'What works in offender management?', *Howard Journal*, 44 (3): 307–18.

Social Exclusion Unit (2002) *Reducing Re-offending by Ex-prisoners*. London: Social Exclusion Unit.

Wargent, M. (2002) 'The new governance of probation', *Howard Journal*, 41 (2): 182–200.

Wasik, M. and Taylor, R. D. (1994) *Criminal Justice Act 1991*, 2nd edn. London: Blackstone.

Chapter 4

The Probation Service as part of **NOMS** in England and Wales: fit for purpose?

Roy Bailey, Charlotte Knight and Brian Williams[1]

Introduction

In recent decades, the Probation Service has been subject to almost continuous change. The uncertainty and upheaval surrounding the creation of the National Offender Management Service (NOMS) in the period since 2003 has, however, been of a different order. In this chapter, we examine some of the effects these political and legislative changes have had upon management styles and upon the staff concerned. Three principle sources of material are used: the available literature, research undertaken specifically for this chapter[2] and the authors' own experience spanning the period under discussion.

Context

The Probation Service was subject to little overt political direction from central government prior to the 1980s, but it has long been riven by internal ideological debate. Whether the Service can be described as 'fit for purpose' depends upon whether there is a consensus as to what that purpose is and should be (Robinson and McNeill 2004; Wing Hong Chui and Nellis 2003).

In its early days probation was guided by a sense of Christian mission, an approach which remained influential to some degree until the 1970s. The organisation of its work was also greatly influenced by the introduction of American-inspired case work methods in the 1930s, which led to a greater sense of professionalism and independence from the courts.

From the 1960s, the religious motivation of probation staff was largely replaced by a humanistic approach, influenced by social scientists involved in social work training. In the 1950s and 1960s probation was torn by conflict between those advocating 'traditional' methods of offender supervision and the newcomers, often graduates trained at the Tavistock Clinic or other centres of psychotherapeutic education, with a different view of case work. The staff who were part of this 'psychiatric deluge' achieved a degree of dominance until their understanding of the purpose of probation was in turn challenged by the advocates of a sociological view of the world, exemplified by labelling theory and 'radical non-intervention' which contributed to the pessimism of the 'nothing works' view of work with offenders.

Such views were supplanted by managerialism, which later maintained its hegemony by incorporating or coopting a very different set of psychological theories in the shape of cognitive behavioural approaches to offender management and the development of a 'What Works' agenda of effective practice.

In addition to the move towards targeting effective methods of reducing offending, the Home Office instruction to chief probation officers to set up and maintain registers of Potentially Dangerous Offenders (Home Office 1988) began the process of placing the assessment and management of offender risk at the centre of the Probation Service's work (Knight 2003). This increasing focus on concerns of public protection and away from the welfare of offenders has marked a significant shift along the continuum of 'care and control' that has defined probation practice over the years. Meanwhile, central government had begun to intervene much more confidently in the management and policies of the Probation Service than in the past (Mair 2004a). Naturally, staff training has been a site of ideological conflict for much of the last 50 years, and training issues are considered more fully later in this chapter.

This very brief review of the changing paradigms of probation work does not do justice to history, but others have addressed this in greater detail and it is not the main purpose of this chapter to retell this story (see Cavadino and Dignan 2002; McWilliams 1981, 1987; Raynor and Vanstone 2002; Wargent 2002; Williams 1995). Suffice it to say that these internal debates have influenced the roles of practitioners and managers as much as external pressures, and that the internal and external pressures interacted with one another.

Until the Probation Service began to grow more rapidly and the growing cost of running it came under increasing scrutiny, it was subject to little interest from central government in comparison with the other, larger criminal justice agencies. With the incorporation of work within prisons after the Probation Service took over the role of voluntary through-care agencies in the mid-1960s, and the introduction of new court orders, probation was subject to a period of sustained growth in the period until the early 1990s. Also during this period, scepticism about the effectiveness of the treatment model in particular and probation in general was fuelled by Martinson's influential research (and hardly challenged by his subsequent, less well-publicised recantation) (Martinson 1974, 1979). As part of a wider quest for value for money and greater accountability, the Home Office imposed increased central control from 1984, both through more prescriptive policies and by using the Audit Commission, the National Audit Office and HM Inspectorate of Probation as tools for enforcing the implementation of its policies (Home Office 1984; Cavadino and Dignan 2002). National Standards, which imposed standardised practice at the level of the supervision of individual offenders, were introduced in 1992 and tightened up periodically in subsequent years. Financial cuts were imposed and privatisation was first threatened and then gradually introduced in the 1990s.[3]

A series of reorganisations and repackaging attempts created an unsettling sense of continual change within the Probation Service in the period from 1990, with a cascade of green and white papers, criminal justice acts and structural reviews. The Probation Service in England and Wales began to take a distinctive path in the early 1990s, largely jettisoning its commitment to the social inclusion of offenders and the promotion of their welfare, in favour of an agenda dominated by public protection concerns. This was in distinct contrast to the development of policy in Scotland and Northern Ireland (Robinson and McNeill 2004; Criminal Justice Review Group 2000). The Victim's Charter (Home Office 1990, 1996a) was introduced without widespread consultation or additional funding, and required the Probation Service to change its culture and its priorities in order to accommodate the needs of victims of crime, in a small way initially, but necessitating the provision of a contact service to thousands of victims every year from 1996 (Williams 1999). The Criminal Justice and Court Services Act 2000 created a National Probation Service from 2001, which was then brought under a joint management structure with the Prison Service in the period from 2004, in the form of the National Offender Management Service (NOMS). Resources were initially increased after the election of a new government in 1997, but further financial restrictions were imposed after a brief 'honeymoon' period. Whether NOMS, which brings together the Prison and Probation Services under one organisational umbrella, can indeed offer the 'seamless' offender case management service proposed remains open to speculation. The performance management culture of the National Probation Service seems set to continue into NOMS. It has been suggested that this culture has 'sapped the pioneering spirit of probation and de-skilled and de-professionalised its core staff. We see staff who are shell-shocked, overworked and suffering from stress, low morale and subject to crippling performance management processes which deaden the profession' (Senior 2004: 1). Quite a substantial number of respondents in the research for this chapter reflect this perspective.

Changes in management

Criminal justice agencies have all been affected by managerialism, which combines 'a bureaucratic quest for greater cost-efficiency and more effective planning with a more overtly political quest for more effective forms of social regulation' (Cavadino and Dignan 2002: 139). This has used techniques and philosophies borrowed from the private sector, in an attempt to raise standards of service, promote greater accountability and increase the value obtained for the money expended. Not all senior managers in probation feel that the Home Office version of managerialism is effective: as one put it, 'Just as health and other agencies are seeing the error of an over-emphasis on targets, probation has acquired more and is being told that its existence now depends on achieving some clumsily set numeric targets' (Wargent 2002: 40).

It appears that many managers and practitioners find it difficult to understand the purpose of some of these targets and what relation they are intended to bear to addressing the priorities and purposes of probation work.

However, the private scepticism of senior managements is often masked by public discretion. Although many chief officers doubted the wisdom of the rapid and wholesale implementation of cognitive behavioural group work in the late 1990s, for example, most saw it as a political imperative which had possible benefits for the Probation Service as well as obvious drawbacks (Mair 2004b). Nevertheless, managers are necessarily more concerned about the public credibility and legitimacy of the Service than practitioners, and many embraced the change of emphasis towards reducing reoffending and ensuring public protection, symbolised for example by tighter breach policies, greater engagement with victims and the growth of multi-agency public protection work, as affording welcome evidence that the Service could be trusted to improve public safety (Robinson and McNeill 2004). (It should be added that many practitioners also frame their accounts of how they work in terms of public protection and legitimacy, although in so doing they may often 'reinscribe existing purposes and practices within evolving ideologies' (Robinson and McNeill 2004: 292).)

In practice, senior managers' public embrace of cognitive behavioural group work as the driving force for more effective work with offenders has been stymied, according to some commentators, by the very management techniques and targets used to impose it (Mair 2004b). Offender groups have been swamped by referrals, not always appropriate, in order to keep up the numbers and try to meet Home Office targets for successful completions. Because of large numbers of inappropriate referrals, completion rates have been low – but staff have continued to feel pressured to make more and more referrals (Fletcher 2004). A vicious spiral appears to be in operation.

A large majority of our respondents identified changes in the way the probation services are managed during their time employed within it, and 71 per cent considered that their role had changed in the time they had occupied it. Nevertheless, 87 per cent said that they were clear about the expectations and responsibilities of their roles. Despite the changes, then, and regardless of staff views of these changes, expectations and responsibilities have been clearly identified to staff in the great majority of cases.

Asked to expand on these changes, our respondents identified a range of issues. The most common response related to a greater focus on targets, sometimes at the expense of the quality of practice, greater accountability and an associated increase in the burden of bureaucratic demands; and a reduction in discretion, not only for practitioners but also for middle managers.

Changing roles for practitioners

The boundary between the role of the qualified probation officer (PO) and that of probation service officers (PSOs) has been the subject of debate and dispute from an early stage, and this debate, which began in the 1970s, continues.[4] PSOs (initially called 'ancillaries' when first appointed in the early 1970s) were recruited for a range of specialist and generic duties; they supported teams of probation officers in their work with individuals and groups, they supervised offenders undertaking community service work,[5] they undertook court duty or they worked as assistant wardens in hostels. In many cases they went on to train as probation officers, treating the ancillary role as a preparatory one in career terms. Some, however, saw the PSO role as one which should be defended in its own right rather than as 'ancillary' to that of the probation officer. There was a need for specialist staff to undertake a variety of roles for which the traditional salary and hierarchical structures did not provide, including the supervision of offenders undertaking unpaid work under community supervision orders. The Home Office controlled the number of probation officers who could be appointed, but expressed no view in the early days about numbers of ancillary staff. This enabled chief officers from the 1970s to appoint specialist senior staff who were not probation officers, such as IT specialists and human resource managers, and to develop new services such as community service using unqualified staff.

The National Association of Probation Officers has campaigned for many years to defend 'role boundaries'. However, with the temporary abolition of the professional qualification for probation officers in 1996, many posts for qualified staff remained vacant until the first graduates of the new training arrangements began to arrive in 2000. The need for services to maintain core activities accelerated the already evolving tendency for PSO roles to overlap with those of probation officers. Other changes added to this erosion of the traditional boundaries to the probation officer role. For example courts could, from 1999, request specific sentence reports (SSRs) to be prepared at court without the need for an adjournment. In cases where the issue in question was an individual offender's suitability for a community punishment order, PSOs in some areas were asked to undertake the preparation of SSRs and it was well within their capabilities and experience to do so. When SSRs were replaced by fast-delivery and oral pre-sentence reports, PSOs continued to prepare them. Similarly, group work (especially when it had to be delivered using a prescriptive manual) lent itself to the skills and experience of staff without formal social work qualifications, some of whom were qualified as teachers or had degrees in subjects such as psychology or criminology. The decision to identify Level 3 of an NVQ as an appropriate standard of qualifications for the running of core, offending behaviour group work programmes, with the higher-risk offender groups such as those for sex offenders being run by probation officers (Level 4 NVQ), set the standard from which further role boundary erosion has emerged.

Not all PSOs have welcomed these developments, seeing themselves as underpaid and inadequately trained for the responsibilities which were increasingly being entrusted to them. Further specialist PSO posts were being created to develop and deliver new areas of work, an obvious example being liaison with victims of crime. In many cases these staff received no training beyond a period of 'sitting next to Nellie' which did not equip them to undertake the role with any degree of confidence,[6] and this was remarked upon repeatedly by the Inspectorate (HMIP 2000, 2003). Our respondents reflected these concerns, with PSO respondents commenting upon the increased levels of responsibility involved in their roles and the requirement to 'deal with higher-risk offenders' and manage their own caseloads. However, some PSOs responding to our questionnaire welcomed these changes: 'Five years ago my role was as a kind of assistant to a PO with no real responsibility for case management. Now I manage my own cases, office duty, breaches; I also do jobs that are specific to PSOs, i.e. court duty, HDCs.'[7]

There was a degree of frustration about the continuation of existing structures: 'Management keep blurring distinctions between the PSO and PO role saying it is good for development. But the only way to develop is to stop being a PSO and become a PO.'

Work with victims is at times emotionally demanding, and it requires extensive knowledge of the structure and operation of the criminal justice system, since an essential part of the task is to explain to victims what will happen to 'their' offender. Without adequate preparatory training, this is an unnecessarily stressful task, although a few PSOs felt that it could be managed: respondents to the questionnaire said, for example: 'Because of an excellent line manager I am able to clarify this if it seems a bit blurred.' 'I have helped to develop team meetings to address such issues as victim work.'

During a somewhat longer period, probation officers also saw their traditional roles changing. Whereas a probation officer in the 1980s might be described as a semi-autonomous professional, the rise of National Standards and a changing approach to professional supervision eroded this discretion and introduced a different relationship with the offenders under a main grade practitioner's supervision. Indeed, many would argue that the notion of working with offenders to encourage changed behaviour by means of a professional 'relationship' gradually became all but obsolete. Probation officers became case managers, spending less time face to face with Service users and more of that time administering standardised assessment tools or delivering specified programmes. Increasingly, work was outsourced to partner agencies specialising in housing, employment, drug and alcohol treatment, literacy and skills training and so on. New specialisms were introduced for main grade probation staff, and a new grade of senior practitioner came into being in some areas. Thus probation teams in some areas began to take on new names such as Public Protection Teams, Programmes Teams, Think First Teams, Drug Treatment and Testing Order Teams, Intensive Supervision Teams, Case Management Units and so on (these examples were drawn at random from the *NAPO Probation Directory*). Again, our respondents reflected these changes. One wrote on the questionnaire: 'I used to have a mix of risky and less risky cases – now whole caseload is domestic abuse, sex offenders and violence, so very stressful.'

In interview, another respondent said: 'My role now feels like one of a highly paid administrator – I receive no job satisfaction whatsoever; the job I trained for no longer exists.'

Another reflected the changes described above: 'There is an expectation that I will not undertake "social work" with offenders; in reality, you need a relationship with offenders before any work can be done. The resources are not out there to case manage properly, so I often end up doing most of the work but getting little credit for it.'

The complexity of the new training arrangements also necessitated the establishment of specialist units in a number of probation areas in order to accommodate increased numbers of trainees. These new titles reflect a response on the Service's part to changing national policies – but the extent to which they differ from place to place suggests a degree of fragmentation. It was clear from some questionnaires that the role of Practice Development Assessor[8] offered job satisfaction to those undertaking this role, but also additional work, for example in supervising PSOs as well as trainees.

However, the values of complex organisations cannot necessarily be changed effectively either by central diktat or by administrative reorganisation. There is evidence that some practitioners (and some managers) cling resolutely, if often covertly, to the values which initially attracted them to probation work, and in so doing ensure the preservation and continuation of currently marginalised strands of 'diversity of purpose and approach' (Robinson and McNeil 2004: 297: the argument is developed throughout the chapter quoted, and this brief extract does not do justice to it).

Training issues

The Home Office introduced the first training course for probation officers in 1930, and in 1946 a training centre was established at Rainer House in Chelsea. By the 1950s the Home Office monopoly on probation officer training was being challenged by universities as they began to offer diploma courses in probation work. Following the report of the Morison Committee in 1962, which expressed the view that the Home Office training was not providing probation officers with the broad knowledge base needed, and the Seebohm Report, leading to the establishment of the Central Council for Education and Training in Social Work (CCETSW) in 1971, there was a rapid growth in the Certificate in Social Work (CQSW) courses offering probation options (Pillay 2000; Knight 2002). These were replaced by the Diploma in Social Work (DipSW) in 1989 and continued to be the pre-qualifying training route for all probation officers until the abolition of the probation pathway in 1996. The embedding of probation training within social work education was staunchly defended by many throughout this 25-year period (Wing Hong Chui and Nellis 2003) on the premise that work with offenders required very similar skills and values. This was in recognition of the fact that some of the knowledge base was inevitably more specialised, including criminological perspectives and legislation. While there had been an ongoing debate about the quality and amount of this specialised knowledge as taught within the probation pathways, the advocates of this approach to training were able to argue that the detailed 'nuts and bolts' of the job could be learnt within the practice placements and confirmation year in post. There is evidence from some of the practitioners interviewed for this chapter who were trained during this period of their continued valuing of the multidisciplinary approach to their training and the values underpinning this. For example, questionnaires referred to:

No casework advice. What we actually do with people simply does not matter: emphasis is all on how we do it.

Work oriented to comply with National Standards and inspectors rather than client centred as in the past.

Senior management structure too unyielding and supports disengagement from knowing what is really happening in practice.

Some respondents expanded on such comments in interview. For example, one said: 'We have moved from a "corner shop" personal service to a "supermarket" stack 'em high and sell 'em cheap service. We are all about systems.'

The Dews Report, commissioned in 1994 by the Home Office (Dews and Watts 1994) as a result of a Departmental scrutiny of policy, while recognising that probation work required some of the same skills and underpinning knowledge as social work, nevertheless made the case for a distinct and separate subject. It recommended the abolition of the social work qualification for probation officer training and the removal of training from higher education, to be replaced by on-the-job training and the achievement of Qualified Probation Officer Status (QPOS). The following two years saw active campaigning by a number of interest groups to challenge this and to maintain the place of probation officer training within higher education (Pillay 2000), including mounting a strong challenge to the Dews Report's main proposal for an entirely work-based route. The removal of professional training from higher education and the creation of Qualified Probation Officer Status were seen as a very inadequate basis for probation officer qualifying training (Pillay 2000: 23).

In 1995 the Probation Rules (secondary legislation) had been amended to remove the requirement for probation officers to hold the Diploma in Social Work (or equivalent). NAPO sought to overturn this through a judicial review, which was ultimately lost in February 1996, leaving the field open for the new Home Secretary to announce the new qualification of a Diploma in Probation Studies in 1997.

The new award was identified as being located in higher education and combined with a National Vocational Qualification (NVQ) (Knight and Ward 2001). It was structured as an employment-based programme, to be delivered in partnership with Probation Services via regional consortia, and practice learning was to comprise 50 per cent of the degree. This latter was to be achieved via a foundation practice period in phase one of the degree and the successful completion of an NVQ 4 in Community Justice in phase two.

The new arrangements provided for the juxtaposition of degree-level academic input and ongoing probation practice, a particular strength in relation to the opportunities for the integration of theory and practice. The apparent failure of previous training arrangements to address this issue adequately was one factor in their demise. The role of the Practice Development Assessor (PDA) has been a crucial one in this development, in managing, and representing to the trainee, the relationship between academic and practice teaching and assessment (Knight and White 2001). While many PDAs, particularly those who were previously qualified as practice teachers under DipSW arrangements, have risen to the challenges of the new arrangements with creativity and energy, others have felt inadequately supported by their managers, some of whom have yet to grasp the full significance of the new training arrangements and identify trainees as members of staff rather than students.

The failure to identify and develop an appropriate learning programme and qualification for PDAs has resulted in many seeing the role as primarily a stepping stone into management rather than a career pathway in its own right. While attempts were initially made to address their training needs, this still risks being identified primarily as a competence-led process using the concept of 'cluster (NVQ) units', rather than a learning and development programme linked to academic credits at post-qualifying level.

Although trainee probation officers carry smaller caseloads than their predecessors under the previous training arrangements, they are under considerably more pressure during their training for a number of reasons. First they are undertaking an undergraduate degree – which in normal circumstances is spread over three years with long vacations each summer – within two years with only a few short breaks. Secondly, there are additional pressures arising from the combination of this degree with an NVQ for which evidence has to be collected throughout the training. Thirdly, they combine student status with employment by an individual probation area, and this can generate considerable tensions for individuals caught between the sometimes differing priorities of universities and probation areas.

The new training scheme has been running only a few years, and opinions vary on its merits and drawbacks. Some trainees report finding it an intellectually stimulating experience, offering them opportunities to explore critically the ways recent developments are taking criminal justice and to integrate theoretical knowledge with probation practice (Jarvis 2002), while others have expressed frustration that there is no time to think or reflect because of the many different forms of assessment which are central to the curriculum and the shortened time period of the programme (Knight 2002). More than one critic has argued that the curriculum is excessively skills-focused and lacks intellectual rigour (McGowan 2002; Nellis 2003). All of these authors write from the perspective of their experience of a single training programme and the application of the curriculum clearly varies from region to region. The 2002/03 round of re-tendering for the probation training contract saw the original nine university providers reduced to five nationally and an increased focus on distance and e-enabled learning as the prime method of delivery. Those who have inspected the programmes nationally have assessed them positively, although they had only a limited opportunity to obtain a consumer perspective (CJNTO 2001; HMIP 2001, 2003).

While the universities which run the degree programmes and the PDAs who supervise and assess the practice would arguably maintain that the primary focus and outcomes of a university degree are the development of skills in reflective practice and critical analysis, this goal may not be universally shared within the National Offender Management Service. Critical thinkers can find themselves in uncomfortable positions within a service that increasingly requires compliance and conformity to national standards and procedures. The 'What Works' industry is, at its best, formulated on rigorous and constantly updated empirical research, undertaken jointly by academic and practice-based researchers and embedded within the culture of the organisation. Sadly, the current target-driven culture values the achievement of targets set to a given, prescriptive model of intervention (cognitive behavioural programmes and enforcement) over and above any other models of change that continue to hold currency within the broader remit of 'What Works', such as solution-focused brief therapy, narratives or family work.

Whether the complex and costly training arrangements embodied within the DipPS will continue beyond the current Home Office contracts with universities to deliver them is a matter of some speculation. What is without doubt is the importance of retaining a qualification structure within higher education. To allow an erosion of the significance of graduate routes into practice would place the Probation Service as the poor relation to other comparable public sector organisations, including social work, teaching and nursing. The damage to the credibility of the Service in terms of its work with high-risk offenders would be immense. Proper consideration should be given to developing a comprehensive qualifications structure that enables staff at all levels to undertake a combination of in-service learning and development, and practice-based competence recognised via the NVQ structure and awarded credit within HE programmes, and to enabling staff to enter and leave such HE programmes at various times and stages to suit their career development needs. Graduates of the DipPS, while appropriately well versed in current psychological models of change, hold a curiosity and research-minded approach to new and alternative methods of intervention that the Probation Service and the National Offender Management Service would do well to heed rather than stifle.

Throughout this period, the rapid growth in numbers of Probation Service officers has not been matched by a concomitant growth in training for this group of staff. The Certificate in Community Justice, set at NVQ Level 3 and with underpinning knowledge identified at level one of an undergraduate degree, was launched in the late 1990s with an expectation that this would become the appropriate qualification for this staff group. While taken up by three universities, and notably supported financially by one large probation area, the Certificate has not developed in the manner originally envisaged. The reasons for this are not straightforward, and in part relate to the failure to conceptualise a full qualifications framework at the time of the planning for the DipPS. However, the most significant reason for its failure to become embedded within a qualifications framework has been the lack of financial backing from the centre. The DipPS has been successful because it has attracted very substantial funding from the centre which provides for the salaries of the trainees and of their PDAs, for their university fees and for the area and consortia infrastructure, and which identifies trainees as supernumerary to the work of the probation area in which they are located. In most instances no such arrangements were made to support the Certificate and it is unsurprising that its take up has been small and that universities have been reluctant to invest heavily in its development. This is unfortunate as, properly developed and structured on a national basis, it could have provided both a qualification in its own right for staff content to work at this level of operation and a stepping stone to qualification as a probation officer for those staff who wished to progress.

The introduction of the PSO Induction programme has been an important step towards instituting a coherent, national framework for this particular group of staff, albeit based on in-service training rather than external (FE or HE) accreditation. The attempts to link the PSO learning units to the Certificate and enable staff to work for credit accumulation within a recognised HE framework of qualifications such as that provided by the Certificate, have happened only in fragmented and localised ways. While, as noted above, this grade of staff is increasingly expected to take on higher-risk work with offenders in terms of both assessment and intervention, the failure adequately to address their training needs is regrettable. If this grade of staff is to undertake OASys assessments of low- to middle-risk offenders without the knowledge and theory base provided by the current DipPS qualifications, the bureaucratic demands of the OASys form are likely to take precedence and limit the ability to understand and adequately predict subtle and complex risk factors.

In addition to the pre-qualifying training arrangements for probation officers, there has been a well-embedded tradition of in-service training arrangements for all probation staff over many years. The 'confirmation year' for newly qualified probation officers, prior to the introduction of the DipPS, included, in many areas, regular and supported training programmes for new staff as an induction into the role coupled with a protected caseload. Staff could then expect to be offered a range of training opportunities both in-service and externally provided, in both generic and specialist areas of practice. Perhaps the most well-structured and formalised of these were for staff moving into senior roles and staff seconded to work in prisons. Increasingly, with the plethora of new criminal justice legislation from the 1990s onwards, the in-service provision has been geared to instructive training on the implications of new legislation and policy development. This training has had as its focus the instruction of staff in new methods and formulae, rather than primarily their educational or career development needs, suggesting an instrumental and technocratic rather than educational approach to training. However, there continued to be exceptions to this, including specialist training on complex areas of practice such as work with sex offenders, mentally disordered offenders and domestic violence, which enabled the continuing development of experienced staff in the honing of their practice skills and practice wisdom as bedrocks of probation practice.

A qualifications framework needs to be conceptualised to take into account the continuing professional development needs of qualified probation officers and managers, for example as constructed under the post-qualifying framework for social workers. While some universities have maintained and developed postgraduate certificates, diplomas and master's routes that offer a range of educational qualifications for probation staff, there has been no drive to construct this within a coherent national framework. Some of the obvious opportunities within this would be the development of a PDA national award, systematic learning opportunities for senior probation officers and other management roles, and for specialist areas of probation practice such as working with high-risk offenders.

Recruitment and staff composition

Staff are increasingly recruited to practitioner roles within the Service via assessment centres that require candidates to be processed through a series of problem-solving and psychometric testing arrangements to assess their suitability to work with offenders. This has been driven by the demands of the Accreditation Framework for group work with offenders, such that in order to be a group worker, tutor or treatment manager on these programmes, staff have first to have been assessed as suitable.

One of the most startling trends in recent years has been the large increase in women at main grade levels within the Service. The Dews Report (Dews 1994) identified the alleged over representation of young women and black people in the former qualifying training arrangements and urged the government to encourage the application by older (including ex-services) men.

> Although many older people do train there is evidence of a trend to a younger, unmarried predominately female recruitment base. There could be various reasons for this but it is clear that the present training system is difficult or impossible for people with commitments. The Probation Service may thus be being denied a source of recruits with much to offer. (Dews 1994: 28)

Dews placed the blame for the failure to attract a more mature and more male workforce on the training arrangements. Interestingly, the DipPS has continued to attract a preponderance of young, white females at each stage of the assessment and selection process and through to recruitment, which suggests there are other factors at play here. Black applicants have been reasonably well represented although there continue to be retention issues. Figures for the first intake of trainee probation officers in 1998 showed that 15.1 per cent of the applicants and 11.3 per cent of the trainees appointed were from minority ethnic groups (HMIP 2000a: 108). The original HMIP Inspection of Race Equality in the Service[9] identified that although 80 per cent of services had agreed a strategy with their local consortium for the recruitment of trainee probation officers (TPOs), a lower proportion had specific strategies for minority ethnic recruitment and few were proactive. The follow-up Inspection Report (HMIP 2004) identified that in June 2001 the joint progress report noted that further work was to be undertaken for a model national framework for TPO recruitment and selection as well as developing a standard national recruitment process. The second inspection of DipPS programmes, undertaken jointly by HMIP and the Community Justice National Training Organisation between January and March 2003, found that all 'Consortia had worked hard to establish a proactive approach to recruiting a diverse group of TPOs'.

Responses to the Inspectorate's questionnaire sent to minority ethnic staff showed that 45 per cent had been encouraged to apply for promotion and had been offered help by the service in progressing their careers. Although this proportion was considered acceptable by HMIP, given the range of ambition, ability and aptitude reflected in any staff group, it had clearly not proved sufficient to secure the promotion of minority ethnic staff in any numbers, as demonstrated in the past ten years (HMIP 2000: 132). Minority ethnic staff consistently remarked on their perception of being excluded from the informal networks to which they believed white staff had access. Five of the ten services had no managers from minority ethnic groups. Of those that did, minority ethnic managers described varying levels of support in their managerial role, although 85 per cent described their relationship with their line manager as good or excellent, as did 89 per cent with white colleagues (HMIP 2000: 136).

The feminisation of the workforce, with increasing numbers of women now occupying senior manager roles (of 42 chief officers nationally 17 are women and 25 are men), is an interesting phenomenon, given the changing focus on the role as 'correctional' 'managerial' and 'authoritarian' – more traditionally recognised to be 'masculine' traits. Until the 1970s, the Service had a preponderance of men at all levels, with the image of the probation officer carrying an air of 'authority' which was attractive to men leaving the armed forces and changing career. While it is possible to argue that current pay scales are unlikely to be as attractive to men as to women, this economic fact alone seems insufficient to explain the current trend of female recruitment. One sustainable argument may be the ongoing attractiveness of 'enabling change in others' for women. Another may lie in the heavy reliance on skills of 'problem-solving' at the assessment centre stage. While problem-solving *per se* is clearly not the prerogative of women, it is possible that women are more willing to admit to having problems of their own and finding solutions to these than are men in the highly charged and competitive arena of a recruitment process. Whatever the reasons, it is increasingly the case that many probation offices are staffed primarily if not solely by women. While women are as able as men to work with high-risk and dangerous behaviour (and sometimes their skills in defusing tension and conflict management may make them better able than men), there nevertheless have to be questions raised about the absence of role models for the predominantly male and young offender population with which the Probation Service works.

Coping with change

A staff satisfaction survey undertaken in the Thames Valley Probation Area in 2003 found high levels of general satisfaction among staff at all levels, but serious dissatisfaction with specific issues. Notable among these were increasing workloads, low pay and a feeling that 'more could be done to help them prepare for and cope with change' (PWR 2003: 1).

Our research with staff across two probation areas identifies some broad themes including generally high levels of satisfaction by PSO level staff, but decidedly poor morale among POs and SPOs. This related, as noted above, to feeling devalued, having less discretion than in the past and consequently feeling deskilled, and increased workloads. It was aggravated by insecurity, stress and a sense of being powerless in the face of rapid and sometimes poorly understood change (see the sections above entitled 'Changing roles for practitioners' and 'Training issues').

126

Cannings (2002: 47) noted that demoralisation affected staff at the most senior levels also: 'It is said that a number of Chief Officers in the new regime feel disheartened because they feel that they have lost both authority and status'.

It seems that remaining the same is not a realistic option for probation work at all levels – but staff find it increasingly difficult to relate the changes which are being made to the changing purposes of the service for which they work. For some, this is a matter of regret at the pace of change and inadequate consultation; for a few, it raises questions about whether they wish to continue working in a profession which has changed completely from the one they originally chose to join.

Conclusion

It is difficult to gain an accurate picture of an organisation in the midst of rapid change, and some of the comments quoted here may relate simply to the cynicism of respondents or their anxiety about change *per se*. As we noted earlier, the fitness for purpose of any public service depends to a large extent on whether there is widespread agreement about what that purpose should be. To some extent, the unity of purpose of probation staff has been dissipated by the way in which the current programme of change has been handled at a national level: staff have not been kept well informed and the reasons for some changes are not apparent. On top of this, the timetable for the changes has altered unpredictably, with unsurprising consequences for morale. Nevertheless, there do appear to be some lessons that the new National Offender Management Service can learn and some worrying tendencies which might still be reversed.

For example, there is perhaps an undue emphasis at present upon targets at the expense of 'relational work' (see Robinson 2005). Linked to this, it is clear that many staff feel that the present targets place undue emphasis upon the technocratic and bureaucratic at the expense of the use of professional discretion, and for many this is linked with issues of trust. Secondly, change needs to be managed, not merely by diktat, but by involving staff in and consulting them about the process. Thirdly, we have identified a range of issues relating to staff training. The new offender management model lends itself to the development of a continuum of training directly relating to the 'tiers of risk' for which staff are responsible (NOMS 2005). Externally validated qualifications could thus be developed to meet the needs of staff for different levels of responsibility, including continuing professional development for those with qualifications. Staff currently feel undervalued: if the National Offender Management Service is to continue to develop and enhance the notion of evidence-based practice, there will be a continuing need for critically minded staff capable of developing research-based practice. Training will also increasingly need to be multidisciplinary in its approach, enabling prison and community-based staff to work together more effectively. Finally, given the recurrent nature of the theme of change and its consequences for staff throughout this chapter, it may be that an articulated model of management of change needs to be developed, shared and discussed, and then included in qualifying and continuing staff development.

Notes

1   The authors wish to thank Avril Aust and Jackie Stevenson for their help with the field research and for their comments on earlier versions of this chapter. Thanks are also due to PERT (the Probation Education and Research Trust) for a grant which assisted with the cost of the field research.

2   The research was conducted in two probation areas, and 157 staff of various grades grades (senior probation officer (SPO), probation officer (PO) and probation service officer (PSO)) responded to the postal questionnaire. Of these, a small number were then interviewed face to face.

3   It was not only practitioners who found privatisation threatening: see, for example, Martin Wargent's reference (2002: 41) to 'a slavish approach to contracting out services'.

4   For example, the 2005 AGM of the National Association of Probation Officers debated several motions on 'role boundaries'.

5   The community service order was formally renamed the community punishment order in 2001, and under the Criminal Justice Act 2003 it became 'unpaid work' as a possible requirement of a community order – but most people (including sentencers) continue to refer to it by the traditional name.

6   The Home Office provided a programme of 'cascade' training in 1996 (Home Office 1996a) but this was never updated or repeated despite rapid turnover of staff and increasing legal requirements in respect of services to victims introduced in 1996 and 2001.

7   This refers to home detention curfews.

8   Practice Development Assessors replaced practice teachers on the introduction of the Diploma in Probation Studies and have a somewhat different role.

9   *Towards Race Equality* (HMIP 2000b).

Further reading

It is difficult to recommend topical reading in such a rapidly changing field. However, the following texts are particularly useful (see Reference section for full details), given that qualification. George Mair's (2004) edited collection, *What Matters in Probation*, is a useful introduction to the 'What Works?' debate and a pointer towards a less sterile set of questions about work with offenders in the future. Gwen Robinson's (2005) article entitled 'What works in offender management' applies these issues to everyday practice in an engaging way, as do the chapters in Wing Hong Chui and Mike Nellis's (2003) book *Moving Probation Forward*. Charlotte Knight's chapter entitled 'Training for a modern service' in Ward *et al.*'s (2002) book goes into greater detail on the need for a training continuum than we have been able to in this chapter. So, too, does Mike Nellis's (2003) article 'Probation training and the community justice curriculum'.

References

Beaumont, W. and Mistry, T. (1996) 'Doing a good job under duress', *Probation Journal*, 43 (4): 200–4.

Cannings, J. (2002) 'A walk around the lake', *VISTA*, 7 (1): 46–51.

Cavadino, M. and Dignan, J. (2002) *The Penal System: An Introduction*, 3rd edn. London: Sage.

Community Justice National Training Organisation (2001) *Review of Academic Structures to Support Level 4 S/NVQ 5 in the Community Justice Sector*. London: CJNTO.

Criminal Justice Review Group (2000) *Review of the Criminal Justice System in Northern Ireland*. Belfast: Stationery Office.

Dews, V. and Watts, J. (1994) *Review of Probation Officer Recruitment and Qualifying Training*. London: Home Office.

Fletcher, H. (2004) 'Programmes, targets and offenders', *NAPO News*, February, p. 5.

HM Inspectorate of Probation (2000) *The Victim Perspective: Ensuring the Victim Matters*. London: Home Office.

HM Inspectorate of Probation (2000b) *Towards Race Equality*, Thematic Inspection Report. London: HM Inspectorate of Probation.

HM Inspectorate of Probation (2001) *The Diploma in Probation Studies*. London: Home Office.

HM Inspectorate of Probation (2003) *Valuing the Victim*. London: Home Office.

Home Office (1984) *Statement of National Objectives and Priorities for the Probation Service*. London: Home Office.

Home Office (1988) *The Registration and Review of Serious Offenders*, Home Office Letter to Chief Probation Officers, July. London: Home Office.

Home Office (1990) *Victim's Charter: A Statement of the Rights of Victims of Crime*. London: Home Office Public Relations Branch.

Home Office (1996) *The Victim's Charter: A Statement of Service Standards for Victims of Crime*. London: Home Office Communications Directorate.

Home Office (1996b) *Training Materials for Contact with Victims*, Probation Circular 21/96. London: Home Office.

Jarvis, S. (2002) 'A critical review: "Integrating knowledge and practice"', *British Journal of Community Justice*, 1 (1): 65–78.

Knight, C. (2002) 'Training for a modern service', in D. Ward, J. Scott and M. Lacey (eds), *Probation: Working for Justice*. Oxford: Oxford University Press.

Knight, C. (2003) 'The assessment process in work with offenders', in J. Horwath and S. Shardlow (eds), *Making Links Across Specialisms: Understanding Modern Social Work Practice*. Lyme Regis: Russell House.

Knight, C. and Ward, D. (2001) 'Qualifying probation training: implications for social work education', *Social Work Education*, 20 (2): pp. 175–86.

Knight, C. and White, K. (2001) 'The integration of theory and practice within the Diploma in Probation Studies: how is it achieved?', *Probation Journal*, 48 (3): 203–10.

McGowan, V. (2002) 'The NVQ: a means to an end?', *Probation Journal*, 49 (1): 35–9.

McWilliams, W. (1981) 'The probation officer at court: from friend to acquaintance', *Howard Journal of Criminal Justice*, 20: 97–116.

McWilliams, W. (1987) 'Probation, pragmatism and policy', *Howard Journal of Criminal Justice*, 26: 97–21.

Mair, G. (2004a) 'The origins of What Works in England and Wales: a house built on sand?', in G. Mair (ed.) *What Matters in Probation*. Cullompton: Willan.

Mair, G. (2004b) 'What Works: a view from the chiefs', in G. Mair (ed.) *What Matters in Probation*. Cullompton: Willan.

Martinson, R. (1974) 'What Works? – questions and answers about prison reform', *Public Interest*, 35: 22–54.

Martinson, R. (1979) 'New findings, new views: a note of caution regarding sentencing reform', *Hofstra Law Review*, 7: 243–58.

Morgan, R. and Smith, A. (2003) 'The Future Role and Workload of the National Probation Service', unpublished paper. London: HM Inspectorate of Probation.

National Offender Management Service (2005) *The NOMS Offender Management Model Version 1*, January. London: NOMS.

National Probation Service for England and Wales, and the Home Office Communications Directorate (2001) *A New Choreography. An Integrated Strategy for the National Probation Service for England and Wales*. London: Home Office.

Nellis, M. (2003) 'Probation training and the community justice curriculum', *British Journal of Social Work*, 33 (7): 943–55.

Pay and Workforce Research (2003) *National Probation Service Thames Valley Area Staff Survey 2003: Summary*. Aylesbury: NPS Thames Valley.

Pillay, C. (ed.) (2000) *Building the Future: The Creation of the Diploma in Probation Studies*. London: NAPO.

Pitts, S. (1998) 'What works in probation service practice and management? The contribution of quality standards', *VISTA*, 4 (1): 57–72.

Raynor, P. and Vanstone, M. (2002) *Understanding Community Penalties: Probation, Policy and Social Change*. Buckingham: Open University Press.

Robinson, G. (2005) 'What works in offender management', *Howard Journal of Criminal Justice*, 44 (3): 307–18.

Robinson, G. and McNeill, F. (2004) 'Purposes matter: examining the "ends" of probation', in G. Mair (ed.), *What Matters in Probation*. Cullompton: Willan.

Senior, P. (2004) 'NOMS – the National Community Justice Service?', *British Journal of Community Justice*, 2 (3): 1–5.

Ward, D. (1996) 'Probation training: celebration or wake?', in S. Jackson and M. Preston-Shoot (eds) *Educating Social Workers in a Changing Policy Context*. London: Whiting & Birch.

Wargent, M. (2002) 'Leading backwards from the front?', *VISTA*, 7 (1): 38–45.

Williams, B. (1995) 'Social work with prisoners in England and Wales: from missionary zeal to street-level bureaucracy', in J. Schwieso and P. Pettit (eds.), *Aspects of the History of British Social Work*. Reading: Faculty of Education and Community Studies, University of Reading.

Williams, B. (1999) *Working with Victims of Crime: Policies, Politics and Practice*. London: Jessica Kingsley.

Wing Hong Chui and Nellis, M. (2003) *Moving Probation Forward. Evidence, Arguments and Practice*. Harlow: Pearson Longman.

Chapter 5

Probation in Scotland: past, present and future

Gill McIvor and Fergus McNeill

Introduction

This chapter offers an account of the distinctive features of criminal justice social work in Scotland. It employs a historical perspective to describe how probation practice and its organisation and ethos have evolved and in so doing aims to capture criminal justice social work in transition.

The first section of the chapter examines the organisation and practice of probation prior to and following the Kilbrandon Report and the Social Work Scotland Act 1968, including the impact of generic arrangements for service delivery on social work with offenders. This is followed by a discussion of the centralisation of funding of criminal justice social work services and the introduction of national objectives and standards in the 1990s in the context of a broader policy commitment to penal reductionism. More recent developments in policy, practice and training are then discussed. These developments include the emergence of protecting the public by reducing reoffending as the key aim and task for criminal justice social work agencies and evolving approaches to developing effective practice to this end.

The impact of changing forms of governance is a key theme throughout the chapter. This includes analysis of the impact of local government reorganisation in the mid-1990s resulting in the 'Tough Options' consultation paper, the creation of 'groupings' of local authorities to deliver criminal justice social work services and, most recently, the establishment of Community Justice Authorities. The concept of 'risk' in transition is explored and linked to developments such as the establishment of the Risk Management Authority. The chapter concludes with some observations about the possible future direction of criminal justice social work in the light of the unprecedented policy and legislative change since devolution in 1999.

From punishment to supervision to treatment[1]

The starting point for this chapter is recognition of the distinctive arrangements that pertain in Scotland for the supervision of offenders in the community. Scotland, unlike the rest of the UK, does not have a separate probation service: the functions undertaken by probation officers are, instead, the responsibility of criminal justice social workers employed by local authorities. However, these different organisational arrangements – and differences in underlying ethos – belie somewhat similar origins and familiar changes in the purpose and focus of probation practice throughout much of the last century as the following brief historical analysis will illustrate.

Glasgow was among the first parts of Scotland (and of the UK) to establish a recognisable probation service delivered by the state as opposed to a charitable agency (Scottish Office 1947: 5). The Glasgow service was established as early as 1905 and a very brief history of its first 50 years was published by the City of Glasgow Probation Area Committee in 1955 (City of Glasgow 1955). This document suggests that the origins of probation in Glasgow were linked to public concern about the excessive use of custody for fine defaulters. The authors note that a report on judicial statistics for Scotland revealed that 43,000 people were received into prison on these grounds in 1904 (16,000 from Glasgow alone) at the rate of 800 per week and that in Scotland at that time one person in 75 of the population was sent to prison compared to one person in 145 in England and Wales (City of Glasgow 1955: 9).

Probation emerged in Glasgow as a response to this penal crisis largely because of the efforts of Bailie John Bruce Murray, a local councillor who had taken a 'great interest in the treatment of offenders and who had studied the workings of the Probation Service in various parts of the United States of America' (City of Glasgow 1955: 9). Murray persuaded the Glasgow Corporation (or Council) to appoint a special committee (in June 1905) to investigate establishing a trial for a system of probation. On 14 December 1905, the committee submitted a report which was approved by the Corporation, recommending that the Chief Constable be invited to select police officers for each District Police Court to act, in plain clothes, as probation officers of the court. Their duties were to include daily attendance at the courts to receive instruction from magistrates in cases that they deemed suitable for probation; to make enquiries as to the offenders' circumstances and their offence, for the guidance of the courts; to observe and supervise the probationer in line with the method suggested by the magistrate during the period fixed for continuation, caution or otherwise;[2] and to make reports to the magistrate. Six police officers of the rank of detective sergeant were subsequently appointed. Shortly afterwards, three women were appointed by the Chief Constable as probation officers to work with child offenders. By 1919, there were eleven (male) police officers working as probation officers and five women probation officers.

Although an apparently humanitarian desire to reduce the use of imprisonment motivated the Glasgow initiative, the initial emphasis seems to have been primarily on delivering supervision rather than care or treatment. The Glasgow history notes that it was the Probation of Offenders (Scotland) Act 1931 that 'completely revolutionised the Probation Service in Glasgow and the idea of treatment, training and reformation of Probationers superseded that of supervision' (City of Glasgow 1955: 11). As well as effectively creating a comprehensive set of local services by establishing probation committees in each local authority, the 1931 Act created a Central Probation Council to advise the Secretary of State. In terms of the governance of practice, however, one of the most intriguing provisions of the 1931 Act was that it expressly prohibited the appointment of serving or former police officers as probation staff, indicating both that this may have been a common practice in Scotland beyond Glasgow and that it had fallen out of favour. The change in staffing arrangements seems to have been closely associated with the transition from supervision to treatment. The significance of the new 'science' for the authors of the Glasgow history is evidenced, for example, in the assertion that 'treatment' must be an individual process following on from some kind of selection (if not diagnosis). Their discussion of selection reflects the assumption that only some offenders are 'reclaimable'; probation 'should be applied only to those in whom wrong-doing is not habitual and whose age, record, or home circumstances, give reasonable hope of reformation' (City of Glasgow 1955: 7).

In the development of a treatment approach to probation practice, it seems likely that women officers played a pivotal role. Though their role was initially limited to juvenile offenders, it seems significant that, in Glasgow, the five women officers recruited in the police-probation era were the only survivors of the 1931 Act's proscription of police-probation officers. The Glasgow history acknowledges that 'the knowledge and experience of these women were of great help in setting the stumbling feet of the newcomers [one woman and six men] on the right road' (City of Glasgow 1955: 13). In the light of other sources, this role as experienced staff in a reconfigured service after 1931 may have given women probation officers in Glasgow (and others like them throughout Scotland), the opportunity to advance the treatment ideal, an ideal that had been developing in and through their work with juveniles even before the 1931 Act.

Mahood (1995) locates probation primarily among a range of evolving institutions associated with the child-saving movement, drawing on the accounts of early probation officers and their contemporaries to describe the role that probation played in extending the reach of the state into families' lives and 'rescuing' children from 'vicious homes' (Mahood 1995: 59–60). However, probation (even as treatment) was not simply an alternative to institutional or punitive measures; it could be used both as a prelude to or an adjunct of both institutionalisation and corporal punishment.[3] That said, by the 1930s, perhaps as a result of the influence of women staff, it seems to have been more common for probation to be cast as an alternative to such measures:

> A boy gets into trouble because he has not learnt to adapt himself to the life of the community. What is needed is that he should be re-educated, and the probation system was devised for this purpose. A brief experience of pain cannot alter a boy's point of view or teach him how to direct his energy or control his impulses. All it can do, and unfortunately often does, is to make the boy a 'swank' and prove to his friends that he is

'tough'. Vanity makes him repeat his offence. (Winifred Elkin, Howard League for Penal Reform, *Glasgow Herald*, 28 October 1937, quoted in Mahood 2002: 453)

Probation's slow but steady development as a measure for both adults and juveniles suffered as a result of the Second World War, following which the transition to peace and the lifting of wartime restrictions and disciplines gave rise to concerns about increases in criminal activity. The Criminal Justice (Scotland) Act 1949 created new duties for the Service and its officers, including the provision of 'social reports' on those aged 17–21 and pre-trial reports on children (previously provided by education authorities). Reports were to focus upon treatment and causation, reflecting the 'scientific' discourse of offender-oriented treatment and presaging the Streatfeild Report's (1961) high tide of optimism about the potential of social science to produce a more effective and rational approach to sentencing.

Though the statistics provided in the Glasgow history reveal significant increases in the business of the Service between 1932 and 1954 (with the number of orders rising from 1,313 to 2,019), this was accounted for by an increase in the number of juveniles under supervision. By contrast, the use of probation with adult offenders declined. As a Scottish Office booklet, *The Probation Service in Scotland: Its Objects and Its Organisation* (1947) indicated, this decline was not confined to Glasgow. It was attributed by the Glasgow history directly to the numbers of the adult male population engaged in military service during the war years when probation for adult offenders 'had fallen into disuse' (City of Glasgow 1955: 20). Though the Criminal Justice (Scotland) Act 1949 gave the courts new powers to make wider use of probation with adult offenders and the number of orders began to increase slowly thereafter, the reluctance to use probation as a disposal for adult offenders was an enduring problem in Scotland. This was seen by the Morison Report (1962) to reflect a stubborn misconception that 'a person placed on probation has been "let off"' (Morison Report 1962: 3). The Morison Committee simultaneously acknowledged the punitive element inherent in supervision (that is, the requirement to 'submit to supervision' (Morison Report 1962: 3)) and stressed an essentially benevolent and offender-centred view of rehabilitation as restoration to full citizenship.

The later versions of *The Probation Service in Scotland* revised and reissued in 1955 and in 1961 (Scottish Office 1955, 1961) clearly represented efforts to continue to promote the use of probation, especially with adult offenders. They offered greater guidance to sentencers on the kinds of cases for which probation might be appropriate, clearly seeking to promote the use of probation in the middle ground between 'minor offences committed by those with clean records and good home backgrounds, and grave offences where there would be an undue risk in allowing the offender to remain at liberty' (Scottish Office 1955: 6; 1961: 6). They also focused on the character, previous record and attitudes of offenders and what these factors suggested in terms of prospects for success. In this regard they suggested that adults may fare *better* than children because they may be more cooperative, can look ahead and stand a better chance of surviving the 'difficult first three months' (Scottish

Office 1955: 6; 1961: 6). Although the absolute numbers of probation orders rose unevenly from 3,666 in 1951 to 4,558 in 1959, probation's share of the increasing number of disposals in the same period declined from 3.76 per cent to 2.87 per cent and probation continued to be a much more popular disposal option for juveniles than adults.

Welfare and responsibility

Ultimately, the problem in advancing the use of probation among adult offenders may have been the undoing of the probation service in Scotland. The publication of the Kilbrandon Report (1964) revolutionised juvenile justice in Scotland through its determination to remove children in trouble (whether for offending behaviour or on grounds of care and protection) from the criminal courts. Though Kilbrandon's most significant and enduring legacy is the Scottish Children's Hearings System, the 'Kilbrandon philosophy', which established the pre-eminence of a welfare-based approach predicated on social education principles, also affected the ideology and organisation of adult criminal justice in Scotland (Moore and Whyte 1998). Most significantly in this context, the report led to the integration of probation and aftercare services in generic social work departments. Offenders were thus placed alongside others deemed to be in need of social work services, the common duty of which was to 'promote social welfare' (Social Work (Scotland) Act 1968: section 12). The disbanding of the Scottish Probation Service and the establishment of generic social work departments under the Social Work (Scotland) Act 1968 have therefore been seen as representing the triumph of a penal-welfarist philosophy (McIvor and Williams 1999). However, there were also two important pragmatic reasons for the ultimate demise of the Service. First, the limited use of probation with adults meant that in some areas caseloads (once juveniles had been moved on to the social work departments) would have been insufficient to sustain an independent service. Secondly, and equally importantly, in the 1960s probation staff were better trained than most other social workers and therefore their knowledge and skills were seen as vital resources for the new social work departments.

By the late 1970s, however, commentators in academic and professional journals were expressing concerns about the viability of probation and aftercare services when subsumed within the social welfare functions of the social work departments (Marsland 1977; Moore 1978; Nelson 1977). Despite the assumption by local authorities of wider responsibilities with respect to the community-based supervision of offenders (community service was made widely available in Scotland in 1979 following a short pilot), the priority accorded to social work with offenders had become eroded in the generic social work departments by the pressing requirements of child protection work and other statutory duties, with the result that cases remained unallocated or the quality of supervision was often poor (McIvor 1996). There ensued a progressive loss of confidence in probation supervision by the courts, causing one sheriff to describe probation as the 'sick man of the criminal justice system' (Lothian 1991).

135

The use of probation declined in Scotland in the 1980s while the rate of imprisonment increased and prisons were overcrowded and characterised by prisoner unrest. In response, a policy of penal reductionism was articulated as 'The Way Ahead' by the then Scottish Secretary (Rifkind 1989) in an address to the Howard League Scotland that was to provide a blueprint for policy over and beyond the next decade. The key elements of the address focused on improving prison conditions and decreasing the use of imprisonment through the strengthening of existing disposals (increasing the *number* of options available to the courts was not thought likely in itself to achieve this policy objective). The strengthening of probation and community service was to be pursued through the introduction in 1991[4] of full central government funding for these disposals and by the introduction of National Objectives and Standards for these and most other criminal justice social work services (Social Work Services Group (SWSG) 1991). This introduction of ring-fenced funding tied to new standards was interpreted by some as 'official' recognition that such services had indeed fallen into a state of comparative neglect in the generic era (Huntingford 1992; Moore and Whyte 1998) – a state which had to be corrected if the prison population was to be reduced.

At this point, criminal justice social work looked set to follow the 'alternatives to custody' model which had already taken root in England and Wales. Indeed, the first objective delineated in the new National Objectives and Standards (SWSG 1991) was 'to enable a reduction in the incidence of custody ... where it is used for lack of a suitable, available community based social work disposal' (s. 12.1). Though probation in Scotland was never required to negotiate the ideological traverse towards punishment in the community, a focus on reducing reoffending, informed from the outset by emerging research evidence (McIvor 1990; SWSG 1991), was nonetheless seen as being critical to the enhanced credibility of community penalties on which reduction in the use of custody was thought to depend (e.g. Paterson and Tombs 1998).

A concern to stress the responsibilisation of the offender but to balance it explicitly (though usually more quietly and discreetly) with notions of tolerance and inclusion has been evident in Scottish penal policy since the introduction of the standards (SWSG 1991). Paterson and Tombs (1998), for example, describe the 'responsibility model' of practice initiated by the standards as recognising 'both that offenders make active choices in their behaviour and that choice is always situated within a person's particular social and personal context' (p.xii). By the late 1990s, although there was evidence of a hardening of the rhetoric around community penalties, the link between crime and social exclusion continued to be recognised:

> Criminal justice social work services are often dealing with the consequences of exclusion and it follows that ... offenders ... should be able to access services and resources which can assist in their reintegration. (Scottish Office 1998: s. 2.2.1)

Similar sentiments were expressed by the First Minister in 2003 when he outlined his vision for the future of criminal justice in Scotland (McConnell 2003: 11):

There is a balance to be struck. A balance between protection and punishment – and the chance for those who have done wrong to change their behaviour and re-engage with the community as full and productive members.

The same theme underpinned the third of the *Criminal Justice Social Work Services: National Priorities for 2001–2002 and Onwards*, which was to 'Promote the social inclusion of offenders through rehabilitation, so reducing the level of offending' (Justice Department 2001: 3). In this context, rehabilitation was cast as the means of progressing towards two compatible and interdependent ends: not only the reduction of reoffending but also the social inclusion of offenders. This reading of rehabilitation remained entirely consistent with the social welfare philosophy underlying the Social Work (Scotland) Act 1968. South of the border, by contrast, there was little evidence in similar strategic documents to indicate that the promotion of offenders' welfare or social inclusion were regarded as laudable ends in their own right. Indeed, where 'rehabilitation' was articulated as an aim in official documentation, it was 'rehabilitation-as-treatment' or 'correctionalism' which was inferred: that is, the reduction of reoffending risk via the application of accredited, 'rehabilitative' programmes of intervention (see NPS 2001: 7; Robinson and McNeill 2004).

Although it appears that being governed by New Labour in London and Edinburgh had produced some predictable convergences of penal ideologies and related policy and organisational changes north and south of the border, the influence of correctionalism in Scotland has been somewhat more attenuated than in England and Wales (Robinson and McNeill 2004). Although, as we will discuss later in this chapter, the recent National Strategy for the Management of Offenders (Scottish Executive 2006a) makes no explicit reference to reducing the use of custody, as late as 2005 in Scotland (unlike in England and Wales) there was evidence of a continuing, if somewhat more qualified, commitment to penal reductionism or 'anti-custodialism' (Nellis 1995). This was reflected in the second of the National Priorities which is to 'Reduce the use of unnecessary custody by providing effective community disposals' (Justice Department 2001: 3) and in recent enquiries by the Scottish Parliament's cross-party Justice 1 Committee into the use of alternatives to custody in Scotland and internationally (Eley *et al.* 2005). As we will see in the next section, it has also been consistently evidenced in the expansion of disposals and initiatives aimed, among other things, at encouraging the courts to make greater use of non-custodial sanctions.

The expansion of non-custodial options

Following the introduction of 100 per cent funding and National Standards the use of both probation and community service in Scotland rose markedly, though the prison population and proportionate use of imprisonment also continued to rise (McIvor 1996) and has generally continued on a steady upward trajectory to this day (Scottish Executive 2006b). This increasing use of imprisonment must be set against the fact that since 1993/4 there has been a steady annual decrease in Scotland in the number of recorded crimes, with crimes of dishonesty in particular (including housebreaking (burglary) and theft of or from vehicles) having fallen markedly from a high of around 425,000 recorded incidents in 1991 to 210,365 cases in 2004/5 (Scottish Executive 2005a).

Although Rifkind had explicitly rejected the expansion of sentencing options, it appears that during the 1990s confidence in the ability of probation and community service alone to halt or even reverse rising prisoner numbers had begun to erode. It was also recognised that action was required to reduce the numbers of people remanded in custody prior to conviction or sentence and to reduce the numbers received into custody for defaulting on payment of fines.

With respect to the latter group, although the proportion of those fined who were imprisoned for default was small, fine defaulters represented a high proportion of prison receptions. Supervised attendance orders (SAOs) – which substituted the unpaid portion of a fine for a period of 10–60 hours of constructive activity designated and supervised by the social work department – were first introduced in Scotland under section 62 of the Law Reform (Miscellaneous Provisions) (Scotland) Act 1990.[5] Following an evaluation of pilot schemes introduced in 1992 (Brown 1994) they were gradually introduced throughout Scotland during the 1990s, though further pilots enabling the courts to impose SAOs at first sentence for 16- and 17-year-olds without the means to pay a fine were suspended when it was found that the high breach rate had resulted in a significant number of 16- and 17-years-olds serving custodial sentences (Levy and McIvor 2001). Custodial receptions for fine default have declined following the national roll-out of SAOs and – in part to address the relatively high incidence of imprisonment for default among women – the mandatory use of SAOs for default in respect of fines up to £500 is currently being piloted in two sites.

Other initiatives that have been introduced during this period have been aimed at enabling the courts to deal more effectively with particular 'problems' or groups of offenders. Regarded as particularly appropriate for those facing a custodial sentence or to contain the behaviour of persistent offenders who posed a nuisance to their communities, electronically monitored restriction of liberty orders (RLOs) have been rolled out across Scotland since May 2002 after being piloted in three sites (Lobley and Smith 2000). Introduced under s. 245A of the Criminal Procedure (Scotland) Act 1995, RLOs require offenders to be restricted to a particular location for up to 12 hours a day for a period of up to 12 months or to avoid a particular location for up to 12 months. The use of electronically monitored bail is currently being piloted and proposals in the Criminal Justice Plan (Scottish Executive 2004c) for the introduction of Home Detention Curfews for prisoners serving sentences of more than three months gained legislative expression in the Management of Offenders (Scotland) Act 2005.

The introduction of two pilot Youth Courts in 2003 and 2004 was also aimed at addressing the behaviour of 'persistent' 16- and 17-year-old offenders (persistent being defined as three or more 'episodes' of offending within a period of six months) or those of the same age whose circumstances or offending suggested that such intervention might be necessary. The Youth Courts are characterised by fast-track processing of cases, the availability of a wider range of age-appropriate services and resources and ongoing judicial overview. Evaluation of the first pilot site suggested that target timescales were generally being met; however, it was still too soon to assess the impact of participation in the Youth Court on young people's offending behaviour (Popham *et al.* 2005). A parallel scheme to fast-track younger offenders to and through children's hearings was abandoned following the initial pilot phase when it became apparent that outcomes were no better for young people who took part in fast-track in comparison with similar young people dealt with under existing procedures in comparison areas (Hill *et al.* 2005).

Dealing with drug-related offending has been a priority issue in recent years and Scotland, in common with other western jurisdictions, has sought to develop more effective ways of responding to drug-related crime. Drug treatment and testing orders (DTTOs) were introduced in two pilot sites in Scotland (under the UK-wide Crime and Disorder Act 1998) and have subsequently been subject to national roll-out. DTTOs differed from existing community penalties in a number of important respects. First, they allowed for the regular drug testing of offenders as a requirement of the court. Secondly, they emphasised the case management role of the supervising officer, who would be responsible for coordinating service provision rather than directly providing services. Thirdly, and perhaps most significantly, they included provision for sentencers to take an active role in reviewing the progress of offenders on orders by bringing them back to court on a regular basis (or, alternatively, scrutinising progress through paper-based reviews). The pilot DTTO schemes that had previously been introduced in England had met with varying degrees of success (Turnbull *et al.* 2000). However, results from the Scottish pilots were more encouraging, with evidence of reductions in self-reported drug use (Eley *et al.* 2000) and reconviction (McIvor 2004a). DTTOs drew upon the drug court model that had evolved during the 1990s in the United States but have been criticised for representing a 'watered down' version of that model insofar as they do not allow for the development of the coordinated multi-professional team approach which characterises drug courts in other jurisdictions (Bean 2002). Alert to the shortcomings of DTTOs in this respect, and following a review of international developments in drug courts (Walker 2001), the Scottish Executive decided to build upon the experience of the DTTO pilot sites by introducing pilot drug courts in Glasgow and Fife. The Glasgow drug court became operational in November 2001 and the Fife drug court made its first orders in September 2002. A further three-year period of pilot funding was granted in March 2006 following an evaluation of their first two years of operation (McIvor *et al.* 2006). The Scottish Executive's interest in problem-solving courts was extended in 2004 with the introduction of a pilot domestic abuse court in Glasgow.

The pilot drug courts had succeeded in engaging effectively with offenders with lengthy histories of drug misuse and drug-related crime and linking them into treatment and other services. However, professionals had expressed concern that they were less effective in engaging with women. Encouraging the use of community-based alternatives to imprisonment for women had been a priority policy area since the late 1990s following the suicide of seven women in Scotland's only dedicated female prison. Despite this, as in other jurisdictions, the rate of female imprisonment has continued to rise at an unprecedented rate to an all-time high (Scottish Consortium on Crime and Criminal Justice 2006). The drug testing of prisoners had revealed that most women received into Scottish prisons were drug users (Scottish Prison Service 2000) yet imprisonment did not appear to break the cycle of drug use and drug-related crime. In 2003 the 218 Time Out Centre was established in Glasgow with a view to providing the courts with a residential and non-residential alternative to custody for women and offering a resource for women whose offending might place them at risk of imprisonment in the future. Initial evaluation of the Time Out Centre suggested that it is a resource that has been broadly welcomed by professionals and service users alike (Loucks *et al.* 2006), though more time will be required for its impact upon recidivism to be assessed. It is unlikely that the resource-intensive, holistic approach that has been developed at 218 could be replicated across Scotland. However, it is probable that elements of practice developed by the Time Out Centre – and, indeed by criminal justice social workers in other locations – could be adapted for use in other parts of the country.

The development of 'evidence-based' probation practice

At the same time as the range of community-based disposals has increased, there has been a commitment in Scotland, as in the rest of the UK, to the development of 'evidence-based' probation practice. The National Objectives and Standards introduced in 1991 provided a framework aimed at raising minimum standards of practice but they did not, in themselves, provide detailed guidance on the methods and approaches that might be adopted to increase the likelihood that supervision might impact positively upon offenders' behaviour. Subsequent initiatives have been more directly concerned with increasing the effectiveness of work undertaken with offenders in the community or on release from prison (McIvor 2004a). These include: the introduction in 1993 of a Masters degree and associated advanced practice award in criminal justice social work and the establishment in 1999 of the Criminal Justice Social Work Development Centre for Scotland at the Universities of Edinburgh and Stirling (both with funding provided by the Scottish Executive); the convening in 1998 of the Getting Best Results (GBR) Steering Group which brought together representatives from central government, local authorities, the independent sector and academics to provide leadership, direction and coordination in the development of effective practice in the community supervision of offenders;[6] and, most recently, the establishment of an Effective Practice Unit in the Community Justice Division of the Justice Department.

A key task for the GBR Steering Group was the development of a framework for the accreditation of community-based programmes and providers. Accreditation was originally introduced in Scotland by the Scottish

Prison Service in 1996. A separate Community Justice Accreditation Panel was established in 2003,[7] based on the work undertaken by the GBR accreditation sub-group, with the first programme (a sex offender programme) receiving accreditation in 2005. The Prison and Community Justice Panels were formally merged in 2006 (as the Scottish Accreditation Panel for Offender Programmes) and the new panel has been tasked with devising a common framework for accreditation across the prison and community settings. The principal reasons for merging the panels appear to have been twofold: first, the anticipated volume of work and the pool of expertise available to draw upon made it unlikely that two separate panels could be indefinitely sustained; second, the creation of a joint accreditation panel would facilitate a closer working relationship between Scottish prisons and local authorities, as was encouraged by the 'Tripartite Group' – a group of representatives from the Scottish Executive, Scottish Prison Service and local authorities that was established in 2001 to explore ways of promoting closer partnership working, especially in relation to the transitional arrangements for prisoners returning to the community (Scottish Executive 2002) – and by the creation in 2006 of Community Justice Authorities.

The governance of criminal justice social work: rehabilitation and correctionalism in Scotland

The unprecedented rate of legislative change and associated development of new penal initiatives must also be set against a background of organisational change and increasingly centralised regulation of practice. The introduction of ring-fenced central government funding of statutory social work services to the criminal justice system brought with it increased requirements of accountability on the part of local authority social work departments with respect to both the quantity and quality of the services they provided. Local authorities were required to institute mechanisms for quality assurance and in 1992 the Social Work Services Inspectorate (SWSI) replaced the existing Scottish Office social work advisory service. The new Inspectorate embarked upon a programme of desktop and field inspections of criminal justice social work services, beginning with a national inspection that focused upon the arrangements that were being made by local authorities to implement National Standards (Social Work Services Inspectorate 1993). A programme of thematic and area-based inspections has continued, more recently under the auspices of the Social Work Inspection Agency which replaced SWSI in 2005 and which has a further reduced advisory function.

When 100-per-cent funding and National Standards were introduced in 1991, social work services were the responsibility of 12 regional and three island authorities under a two-tier local government structure. An immediate impact of the new funding arrangements was to encourage the reorganisation of criminal justice social work services at the local level along specialist lines, through the creation of designated teams or individual workers who were devoted entirely or primarily to this area of work and through the appointment of managers with specific responsibility for criminal justice social work services (McIvor 1996). While these arrangements were deemed necessary to facilitate strategic planning and resource allocation (enabling local authorities more easily to account for how ring-fenced money was being spent), they also enabled the more efficient delivery of specialist training and encouraged the development of relevant expertise. Significant challenges were subsequently posed by local government reorganisation in 1996 which resulted in the creation of 32 single-tier authorities. Not only did this bring about the organisational disruption that is almost inevitably associated with structural reform but also resulted in the creation of social work departments, some of which were unlikely to be able to deliver efficiently and effectively the increasing range of services for which they had been ascribed responsibility.

The practical constraints upon service delivery and development that arose from local government reorganisation were also recognised by the Scottish Office whose 1998 consultation paper *Community Sentencing: The Tough Option* set out three options for the future provision of criminal justice social work services: the *status quo*, a single centralised service or the creation of 'groupings' of local authorities with shared responsibility for service delivery (Scottish Office 1998). Following the consultation, the then Justice Minister in October 1999 invited local authorities to come forward with proposals for the restructuring of criminal justice social work to enable a smaller number of inter-authority groupings to be established (Scottish Executive 1999). Such arrangements were regarded by central government as having both strategic and operational advantages – giving a strong local authority voice and identity to criminal justice social work services while enabling local authorities to benefit from economies of scale and to redirect increased resources to front-line services – though little centralised guidance was issued with respect to how they were to be managed. The resultant 'Tough Options Groupings', consisting of eight partnership groupings, three unitary authorities and three island authorities, came into effect in April 2002.

These very different, if somewhat unstable, systemic contexts for probation in Scotland might have been seen as a protective factor against the adoption of the crude reductionism of correctional approaches and of increasingly punitive penal politics that characterised developments elsewhere in the UK in the 1990s. However, the 2003 election campaign signalled further significant changes to the organisational context of probation in Scotland. The Scottish Labour Party's Manifesto for the Scottish Parliamentary election campaign in May 2003 (eight months ahead of the publication of the Carter Report (2004) in England and Wales) promised the creation of a single agency or 'Correctional Service for Scotland' – staffed by professionals and covering prison and community-based sentences – to 'maximise the impact of punishment, rehabilitation and protection offered by our justice system' (Scottish Labour 2003). The Partnership Agreement between Scottish Labour and the Scottish Liberal Democrats, published following the elections, moderated this position slightly by undertaking to 'publish *proposals for consultation* for a single agency to deliver custodial and non-custodial sentences in Scotland with the aim of reducing reoffending rates' (Scottish Executive 2003, emphasis added).

COSLA (the Convention of Scottish Local Authorities) and ADSW (the Association of Directors of Social Work) responded to the Labour manifesto commitment by pledging to fight 'tooth and nail' against the proposed measures, arguing that there was no justification for such changes and no evidence that they would work to cut reoffending (*The Scotsman*, 9 May 2003). Following the election they commissioned a report from the International Centre for Prison Studies to explore whether the available international evidence supported the proposed organisational changes. The resulting report was submitted as a response to the Consultation on Reducing Reoffending (Scottish Executive 2004a) which reiterated the First Minister's previously stated position that 'the *status quo* is not an option' (McConnell 2003: 21). However, in a conference speech towards the end of 2003, the report's author concluded that 'there is no evidence that particular organisational arrangements for the delivery of criminal justice provision in any one country lead to higher or lower use of imprisonment or affect re-offending rates' (Coyle 2003: 12).

In the introduction to the Reducing Reoffending consultation the Justice Minister acknowledged that 'the answer to reducing reoffending does not simply lie in more imprisonment … The prison population continues to expand, in many cases with offenders who might actually be suitable for non-custodial penalties' (Scottish Executive 2004a: 4–5). Neither, however, was the answer seen to lie in increasing the availability and use of community-based disposals, since the growth in the prison population had paralleled an increased use of alternatives such as community service and probation. In certain respects there are echoes of similar policy concerns, articulated by Rifkind (1989), that preceded the introduction of 100 per cent funding of criminal justice social work: an apparent commitment to anti-custodialism (albeit attenuated in the later consultation document) and a recognition that simply making more alternatives available was unlikely in itself to have an impact on the prison population. In both cases, moreover, organisational change is proposed as a potential solution, though this would be achieved only indirectly through arrangements necessary at the local level to facilitate the allocation of ring-fenced funds. Importantly, however, the policy emphasis has shifted from a primary concern to reduce the rate of imprisonment and a subsidiary concern to bring about reductions in crime to a primary interest in reducing recidivism linked, as we will argue later in this chapter, to an increasing preoccupation with the effective management of offender risk.

The analysis of responses to the Reducing Reoffending consultation highlighted widespread lack of support among consultees for the bringing together of the Scottish Prison Service and criminal justice social work services under a single correctional agency structure (Scottish Executive 2004b). Concerns were voiced that a single agency would not necessarily be any more effective in tackling reoffending, would fail to address the complex needs of offenders and would reduce the ability of relevant agencies to manage risk. At an organisational level, the proposed arrangements were thought unlikely to reconcile differences between organisations while excluding some agencies and resulting in a loss of accountability, responsiveness and independence at the local level. Some consultees believed that the proposals could impact adversely on the status, skills and professional recognition of social work staff and that the associated bureaucracy and disruption could divert resources from front-line service provision (Scottish Executive 2004b).

In the face of strong opposition to the establishment of a single agency, the Criminal Justice Plan, published in December 2004, set out proposals for the creation, instead, of Community Justice Authorities (CJAs) (Scottish Executive 2004c). Following a consultation which sought views on their functions, structure and constitution and the role of partner organisations (Scottish Executive 2005b), the Justice Minister announced that eight CJAs would be established to facilitate strategic planning across areas and between partner agencies, with some agencies (including the police, courts, prosecution, prisons, Victim Support Scotland, health boards and relevant voluntary agencies) becoming statutory partners within the CJAs. It is intended that the CJAs will redesign services around the following offender groups: less serious/ first-time offenders; offenders with mental health problems; offenders with substance misuse problems; persistent offenders, including young offenders coming through from the youth system; prisoners needing resettlement and rehabilitation services; violent, serious and sex offenders; and women offenders (Scottish Executive 2006a). The Management of Offenders (Scotland) Act 2005 provided for the creation of the CJAs, which came into effect on 3 April 2006. In the first year their primary responsibility will be to produce a strategic plan for their area in consultation with statutory and non-statutory partner bodies. Thereafter their responsibilities will include the allocation of resources across and monitoring of criminal justice social work services.

A National Advisory Body on Offender Management, chaired by the Justice Minister, was established in March 2006. Described as a 'new body to tackle Scotland's high re-offending rates' (Scottish Executive 2006c) and with a membership consisting of representatives from the Convention of Scottish Local Authorities, the Association of Directors of Social Work, the voluntary sector, Victim Support Scotland, ACPOS, the Parole Board, the Risk Management Authority and a range of experts, its roles are to develop and review the national strategy for managing offenders, provide advice to enhance offender management practice and support the work of the new Community Justice Authorities. The first National Strategy on Offender Management (Scottish Executive 2006a) was published in May 2006, aimed at encouraging 'a set of common aims and expected outcomes centred on increased public protection and delivering a consistent approach to managing offenders in prison and in the community' (Scottish Executive 2006d).

Therefore while recent policy developments signal a closer role for central government and other agencies in determining the strategic direction of offender management in Scotland, Scottish policy has, in the face of strongly voiced opposition, stopped short of the organisational changes brought about through the creation of the National Offender Management Service in England and Wales.

Risk and public protection

In Scotland the focus and purpose of probation has changed over the last 100 years from punishment to supervision to treatment to welfare to responsibility and, more recently, to public protection (McNeill 2005). As in England and Wales, this has had an important influence on the content and purpose of social enquiry reports (SERs). For example, although the most recent National Standards for social enquiry reports describe the purpose of reports as being to 'provide the court with information and advice they need in deciding on the most appropriate way to deal with offenders' (Scottish Executive 2000: para. 1.5) this includes 'assessing the risk of re-offending, and in more serious cases the risk of possible harm to others … [and] requires an investigation of offending behaviour and of the offender's circumstances, attitudes and motivation to change' (Social Work Services Group 2000: para. 1.6). Here, then, as in the rest of the UK, assessment practice is increasingly driven by concerns about risk and, as in England and Wales, this has had important implications for the focus of assessments and the manner in which they are undertaken. The increasing use of structured approaches to assessment – and, in particular, the use of actuarial methods for the assessment of risk – reflected the growing influence of managerialism and 'actuarial justice' (Feeley and Simon 1992) upon probation practice in Scotland and in the rest of the UK.

The initial focus of actuarial tools – reflecting the anti-custodial objectives of criminal justice social work practice at the time – was on predicting the likelihood of a custodial sentence being imposed by the courts, the intention being to assist practitioners to identify those offenders for whom alternatives to imprisonment should be considered. In Scotland the National Objectives and Standards for Social Work Services to the Criminal Justice System (SWSG 1991) provided detailed guidance on the appropriate content of reports and encouraged social workers to target community-based social work disposals upon offenders who would otherwise be at risk of receiving a sentence of imprisonment. A standardised instrument for measuring risk of custody – the Dunscore – developed in the early 1990s for use in the Scottish context (Creamer *et al.* 1993) was widely used by social workers to assist in identifying those offenders for whom probation or community service might be recommended as an alternative to custody.

During the 1990s, however, with an increasing emphasis upon effective practice and increasing policy preoccupation with public protection, the emphasis shifted from assessing risk of custody to assessing the risk of reconviction and the risk of harm. Early tools – such as the Offender Group Reconviction Score (OGRS) (Copas 1995) that predicted the percentage likelihood of being reconvicted in England and Wales – were based purely upon static historical data (such as sex, age, number of previous convictions, etc.). Subsequent tools have become more sophisticated and include a structured assessment of the offender's circumstances and needs. The first tool of this kind to be widely used in Scotland (as in England and Wales) was the Level of Service Inventory – Revised (LSI-R) (Andrews and Bonta 1995). The Social Work Services Inspectorate subsequently developed the Risk Assessment Guidance and Framework (RAGF), which was a structured tool combining actuarial indicators with clinical or professional judgements. It incorporated assessments of risk of re-offending, criminogenic need and risk of harm. The RAGF used the same predictive factors as OGRS but there was no algorithm to determine precise levels of risk and judgements were made using 'high', 'medium' or 'low' descriptions (SWSI 2000). Practitioners who had used the RAGF regarded its ability to identify risk of harm, its ease of use, its compatibility with other risk assessment procedures and its ability to predict violent offending as strengths. It was also viewed by social workers as assisting professional judgements of risk and encouraging a more structured approach to assessment and case planning (McIvor and Kemshall 2002).

By the mid-to-late 1990s the growing emphasis on public protection across the UK coincided with the introduction of significantly higher risk populations of offenders to probation caseloads. In Scotland, legislative changes in the early 1990s required all prisoners serving sentences in excess of four years to undertake community supervision on release either on parole or on (compulsory) non-parole licences (Prisoners and Criminal Proceedings (Scotland) Act 1993). Subsequently, advances in both the rhetoric and the practice of public protection were rapid. Although it did not appear as an objective in the original standards (SWSG 1991), by the time of the publication of *The Tough Option* (Scottish Office 1998) the then Minister responsible was declaring both that 'Our paramount aim is public safety' (s. 1.2) and that the pursuit of reductions in the use of custody 'must be consistent with the wider objective of promoting public and community safety' (s. 1.2.3). Revisions to the Scottish Standards on throughcare services (SWSG 1996) and court reports (SWSG 2000), as well as other central reports and guidance (SWSI 1997, 1998), both presaged and reflected this shift in emphasis. (For a more detailed discussion of the emergence and pre-eminence of public protection in official discourses and in practitioners' accounts on both sides of the border, see Robinson and McNeill (2004).)

This concern with enhancing public protection has focused in particular upon serious violent and sexual offenders who are regarded as posing a significant risk of harm. Policy interest in the risks posed by sexual and violent offenders can be traced to *A Commitment to Protect* (SWSI 1997) followed by the MacLean Report in 2000 and the Cosgrove Report in 2001. In terms of shaping further legislation and policy, the MacLean Report was particularly influential insofar as two of its main recommendations – the introduction of an order for lifelong restriction (OLR) and the establishment of a new body for ensuring the effective assessment and management of risk (the Risk Management Authority) – gained expression in the Criminal Justice (Scotland) Act 2003. The Risk Management Authority was established as a non-departmental public body in the autumn of 2004. Its roles include policy advice, identifying best practice, commissioning and undertaking research, standard setting for risk assessment and management, accreditation of risk assessors and risk assessment methods, and approving offender risk management plans.

The Risk Management Authority is concerned essentially with those offenders who are deemed to pose the greatest risk. However, other recent legislative and policy changes in Scotland have had a broader focus upon managing the transition of prisoners between prison and the community. Since the revision of early release arrangements in 1993, the majority of short sentence prisoners have not been subject to statutory supervision on leaving prison,[8] though most have been entitled to voluntary assistance from the social work department in the 12-month post-custody period. Throughcare has long been acknowledged to be one of the most poorly developed of the criminal justice social work services, not least because of the practical difficulties involved in providing a consistent service to prisoners located across the prison estate (McIvor and Barry 1998). The Tripartite Group that was established in 2001 identified three priority groups for voluntary post-release support – sexual offenders and those who committed offences against children, young offenders and offenders with drug problems[9] – and recommended the establishment of specialist local authority throughcare services to better engage with prisoners during their sentences and after release.

More far-reaching proposals were, however, heralded by a review of early release arrangements by the Sentencing Commission for Scotland (2006). The proposals, which at the time of writing are subject to consultation (Scottish Executive 2006e), are that prisoners sentenced to more than 14 days will serve at least one half of the sentence in prison and will be subject to supervision on licence in the community for the remainder of the sentence. The proposals, if implemented, will have significant implications for criminal justice social work where the workload is likely to shift towards resettlement work and away from community disposals. Indeed, a growing emphasis upon prisoner resettlement/reintegration can also be discerned from the creation, structure and objectives of the new Community Justice Authorities and in the National Strategy for the Management of Offenders (Scottish Executive 2006a) where ex-prisoners are identified as one of the priority groups around whom services should be developed.

The future of criminal justice social work

The recurring themes in the century of probation in Scotland are not difficult to discern. On one level, the story is simple: for the last 100 years the Scottish courts have consistently sent disproportionate and unacceptable numbers of the population to jail. Though penal politics, public sensibilities and sentencing practices have all changed in various ways over the last 100 years, the problem of securing reductions in the financial and human costs associated with imprisonment endures. In this context, the story is also about the pursuit of quality and effectiveness within probation work and with it the credibility on which the success of probation as a force for penal reductionism was thought to depend. As McNeill (2005) has argued, probation's various changes of identity – from supervision to treatment to welfare to responsibility to public protection – might be best understood primarily as a series of distinctive discursive constructs seeking to appeal to changing penal cultures and sentiments. This is not to say that these changing identities were or are mere artefacts; far from it, they represent shifting attempts to realise new and better penal practices in the interests of offenders, in the interests of communities and, ultimately, in the interests of justice. The changing means and methods of assessment and supervision and the changing organisational arrangements for criminal justice social work represent reinventions of the same core purposes around sponsoring constructive changes both in individual offenders and in the system of justice itself.

With respect to the future of criminal justice social work, the evidence points towards both continuity and change. Since Rifkind's (1989) decision to embark on a penal reductionist path, Scottish policy has been characterised by its focus on reducing the use of custody, enhancing the social inclusion of offenders and, latterly, protecting the public by reducing reoffending. Though the policy emphasis has shifted at times in the degree of emphasis given to each of these aims, ministers and civil servants have tended to recognise their interdependence. Against this backdrop, perhaps the most significant and worrying contemporary change is the absence of any explicit commitment to reducing the use of custody in the new national strategy (Scottish Executive 2006a). When set alongside the introduction of the dehumanising discourse of 'offender management'[10] and the currently proposed changes to prisoner release arrangements, the apparent abandonment of penal reductionism could signal the emergence of a Service focused much more narrowly than hitherto on protecting the public by working with prison service colleagues to develop better resettlement policies and practices. While this attention to working with those *exiting* Scottish prisons is both necessary and overdue, with the use of imprisonment and the duration of sentences rising in Scotland it hardly seems to be the time to be distracted from the question of inappropriate *entry* to prison.

In terms of continuity, the new national strategy confirms the ongoing direction of Scottish policy since the *Tough Option* paper (Scottish Office 1998) in that the overarching 'shared aim' of offender management services is 'to reduce both the amount of offending and the amount of serious harm caused by those already known to the criminal justice system' (Scottish Executive 2006a: 3). Moreover, the specific target for such services is defined as a 2 per cent reduction in reconviction rates in all types of sentence by March 2008. Interestingly, the strategy sets out to explain its focus on reoffending in some detail and it is worth quoting the relevant section in full here:

> All offending matters. But the community has a specific right to expect public agencies to use their contact with known offenders to reduce the risk that they will offend again, particularly in those cases which raise the most serious concerns about public protection. At the moment, most offending is reoffending. Of those convicted of a crime or offence in 2002, two-thirds had at least one previous conviction.
>
> This has an impact not only on individual victims and hard-pressed communities but also on offenders and their families. This is why a central theme of the overall strategy and a key component of our drive to reduce reoffending is Closing the Opportunity Gap and tackling social exclusion and poverty. The strategy will therefore depend for much of its success on helping offenders and their families access the services they need, such as advice on financial services, benefits and sustainable support, and also for these services to recognise offenders and their families as groups who should have equal access to their services. (Scottish Executive 2006: 3–4)

While the first paragraph in this excerpt emphasises the importance, in the public interest, of reducing reoffending, the second paragraph helpfully and unequivocally reasserts the importance of enhancing the social inclusion of (ex-)offenders. Admittedly, this is primarily cast as an instrumental necessity in the pursuit of the overarching goal of reducing reoffending, but in places the tone of the strategy comes close to advancing the notion of rights-based rehabilitation (see Lewis 2005). Though this commitment to social inclusion is somewhat ironic, given the exclusionary impact of imprisonment (Social Exclusion Unit 2002) and the plan's silence on reducing the use of imprisonment, it leaves open (and perhaps even requires) the continuation of probation's long-standing association with social work in Scotland.

There is no doubt that the character of probation work in Scotland has been and continues to be profoundly influenced by this association. Robinson and McNeill (2004), for example, note that Scottish criminal justice social workers, while accepting public protection as their overarching aim, typically insist that protecting communities *requires* helping offenders, that the social work relationship is their primary vehicle for change, and that both offending behaviour and their efforts to bring about change have to be located in their wider social contexts. That similar messages have emerged recently from desistance research may account in part for its developing influence on Scottish policy and practice (McNeill 2004; McNeill *et al.* 2005).

In this sense then, there is perhaps some evidence in Scotland that traditional 'welfare' practices, rather than being eclipsed, have been reinscribed and relegitimated in and through the new discourses of risk and protection associated with the 'Culture of Control' (Feeley and Simon 1992; Garland 2001; O'Malley 2004). Of course, this kind of hybridisation of welfare and risk is far from benign and unproblematic (Hannah-Moffat 2005). Necessarily, it will be some time before we can say whether the process of reinscription and relegitimation, set within the context of the new socio-political settlement that has followed devolution, will lead to a fundamental adulteration of the humanitarianism that has shaped probation's history in Scotland, as elsewhere. It does seem clear, however, that criminal justice social work is at a critical stage in its evolution during which, as well as changes in its political and organisational contexts, fundamental questions arise about its purposes, values and practices.

Notes

1 This section of the chapter draws heavily on a paper previously published by one of the authors in *Probation Journal* (McNeill 2005). We are grateful to the editor of that journal for permission to use the material here.

2 Under Scots Law, continuations can be used both for administrative reasons and as purposeful deferrals of sentence to a specific future date. In the latter case, the offender can be required to be of good behaviour in the intervening period. A caution (pronounced 'kay-shun') requires the accused to lodge a sum of money with the court for a fixed period. The sum is forfeit in the event of further offending.

3 For example, the Chief Constable of Edinburgh suggested in evidence to the Young Offenders (Scotland) Committee in 1925 that birching should be an extension of the probation officer's role as surrogate parent (Mahood 2002).

4 One hundred per cent funding had previously been introduced for community service in 1989 to better enable local authorities to meet the demands for orders by the courts.

5 Proposals for the introduction of unit fines in Scotland had failed to survive the passage of the Law Reform (Miscellaneous Provisions) Scotland Bill 1989.

6 Specific areas addressed by this initiative included the revision of National Standards, staff development and training, quality assurance, and the development of a national framework for monitoring and evaluation. Additionally, a Pathfinder Provider Initiative was launched in 2000, adopting a different focus to the programme-based approach that had been introduced in England and Wales. Instead the Scottish Pathfinders were tasked with developing mechanisms to support the pursuit of effective practice at all levels of the organisation.

7 There was an overlap of membership with the Scottish Prison Service panel to encourage the development of a consistent approach to accreditation and to ease the proposed transition to a joint panel. It was also anticipated that the Community Justice Accreditation Panel would in due course also assume responsibility for the accreditation of youth justice programmes though this would require a slightly differing approach that recognised the more systemic and holistic approach to supervision in this context.

8 Only prisoners serving sentences of four years or more were eligible to apply for parole and only those with shorter sentences who were made subject to specific requirements by the courts were supervised for a period following their return to the community.

9 A Transitional Care Initiative had been introduced by the Scottish Prison Service and Cranstoun Drug Services to provide short-term prisoners with drug problems with support during the first 12 weeks following release. The Transitional Care initiative formally ended in July 2005 with the introduction of a new national Throughcare Addiction Service (TAS) for prisoners with drug problems in Scotland (MacRae *et al.* 2006).

10 It is interesting to note that the impact of the discourse of 'offender management' in Scotland (to describe the national policy focus) has been offset by the contemporaneous introduction of the term 'community justice' (to describe the bodies responsible at the local level for strategy and service delivery).

Further reading

For those interested in the historical development of probation in Scotland, McNeill (2005), 'Remembering probation in Scotland', provides an analysis of developments in philosophy and practice prior to the introduction of the Social Work (Scotland) Act 1968. An analysis and overview of more recent developments in policy and practice is provided in McIvor (2004b), 'Getting personal: developments in policy, practice and research in Scotland', in Mair's edited collection *What Matters in Probation*. The edited collection by Duff and Hutton (1999) *Criminal Justice in Scotland* offers a broader analysis of the Scottish criminal justice system, including chapters on criminal justice social work, gender and youth justice. The forthcoming book (2007) by McNeill and Whyte, *Reducing Re-offending: Social Work and Community Justice in Scotland*, provides analyses not only of contemporary challenges in historical and comparative context, but also of the legal contexts of criminal justice social work practice. McNeill and Whyte also develop arguments about the best ways forward for social work and community justice practice in Scotland. The contemporary policy context for criminal justice social work is provided by the National Strategy published by the Scottish Executive (2006), *Reducing Reoffending: National Strategy for the Management of Offenders*.

References

Andrews, D.A. and Bonta, J. (1995) *The Level of Service Inventory – Revised Manual*. Toronto: Multi-Health Systems.

Bean, P. (2002) *Drugs and Crime*. Cullompton: Willan.

Brown, L. (1994) *A Fine on Time: The Monitoring and Evaluation of the Pilot Supervised Attendance Order Scheme*. Edinburgh: Scottish Office Central Research Unit.

Carter, P. (2004) *Managing Offenders, Reducing Crime. A New Approach*. London: Strategy Unit, Home Office.

City of Glasgow (1955) *Probation. A Brief Survey of Fifty Years of the Probation Service of the City of Glasgow 1905–1955*. Glasgow: City of Glasgow Probation Area Committee.

Copas, J. (1995) 'On using crime statistics for prediction', in M. Walker (ed.), *Interpreting Crime Statistics*. Oxford: Clarendon Press.

Cosgrove, Lady (2001) *Reducing the Risk: Improving the Response to Sex Offending. Report of the Expert Panel on Sex Offending*. Edinburgh: Scottish Executive.

Coyle, A. (2003) *Joining up Criminal Justice Services: Scotland in an International Context*. Speech to the ADSW Conference, Dunblane.

Creamer, A., Ennis, E. and Williams, B. (1993) *The Dunscore: A Method for Predicting Risk of Custody within the Scottish Context and Its Use in Social Enquiry Practice*. Dundee: University of Dundee Department of Social Work.

Duff, P. and Hutton, N. (eds) (1999) *Criminal Justice in Scotland*. Aldershot: Ashgate

Eley, S., McIvor, G., Malloch, M. and Munro, B. (2005) *A Comparative Review of Alternatives to Custody: Lessons from Finland, Sweden and Western Australia*. Scottish Parliament Justice 1 Committee. Available at: http://www.scottish.parliament.uk/business/committees/justice1/reports-05/j1r05-custody-01.htm

Eley, S., Gallop, K., McIvor, G., Morgan, K. and Yates, R. (2002) *Drug Treatment and Testing Orders: Evaluation of The Scottish Pilots*. Edinburgh: Scottish Executive Social Research.

Feeley, M. and Simon, J. (1992) 'The new penology: notes on the emerging strategy of corrections and its implications', *Criminology*, 30 (4): 449–74.

Garland, D. (2001) *The Culture of Control: Crime and Social Order in Contemporary Society*. Oxford: Oxford University Press.

Hannah-Moffat, K. (2005) 'Criminogenic needs and the transformative risk subject: hybridizations of risk/need in penality', *Punishment and Society*, 7 (1): 29–51.

Hill, M., Walker, M., Moodie, K., Wallace, B., Bannister, J., Khan, F., McIvor, G. and Kendrick, A. (2005) *Fast Track Children's Hearings Pilot*. Edinburgh: Scottish Executive Social Research.

Huntingford, T. (1992) 'The introduction of 100% central government funding for social work with offenders', *Local Government Policy Making*, 19: 36–43.

Justice Department (2001) *Criminal Justice Social Work Services: National Priorities for 2001–2002 and Onwards*. Edinburgh: Scottish Executive.

Kilbrandon Report (1964) *Children and Young Persons (Scotland)*, Cmnd 2306. Edinburgh: HMSO.

Levy, L. and McIvor, G. (2001) *National Evaluation of the Operation and Impact of Supervised Attendance Orders*. Edinburgh: Scottish Executive Central Research Unit.

Lewis, S. (2005) 'Rehabilitation: headline or footnote in the new penal policy?', *Probation Journal*, 52 (2): 119–35.

Lobley, D. and Smith, D. (2000) *Evaluation of Electronically Monitored Restriction of Liberty Orders*. Edinburgh: Scottish Executive Central Research Unit.

Lothian, A. (1991) 'A prescription for the sick man of the system', *The Glasgow Herald*, 9 January.

Loucks, N., Malloch, M., McIvor, G. and Gelsthorpe, L. (2006) *Evaluation of the 218 Centre*. Edinburgh: Scottish Executive Social Research.

McConnell, J. (2003) *Respect, Responsibility and Rehabilitation in Modern Scotland,* Apex Lecture 1, September. Edinburgh: Scottish Executive.

McIvor, G. (1990) *Sanctions for Serious or Persistent Offenders: A Review of the Literature.* Social Work Research Centre, University of Stirling.

McIvor, G. (1996) 'Recent developments in Scotland', in G. McIvor (ed.), *Working with Offenders: Research Highlights in Social Work 26.* London: Jessica Kingsley.

McIvor, G. (2004a) *Reconviction Following Drug Treatment and Testing Orders.* Edinburgh: Scottish Executive Social Research.

McIvor, G. (2004b) 'Getting personal: developments in policy, practice and research in Scotland', in G. Mair (ed.), *What Matters in Probation.* Cullompton: Willan.

McIvor, G. and Barry, M. (1998) *Social Work and Criminal Justice Volume 7: Community-based Throughcare.* Edinburgh: Stationery Office.

McIvor, G. and Kemshall, H. (2002) *Serious Violent and Sexual Offenders: The Use of Risk Assessment Tools in Scotland.* Edinburgh: Scottish Executive Social Research.

McIvor, G. and Williams, B. (1999) 'Community based penalties', in P. Duff and N. Hutton (eds), *Criminal Justice in Scotland.* Aldershot: Ashgate.

McIvor, G., Barnsdale, L., Malloch, M., Eley, S. and Yates, R. (2006) *The Operation and Effectiveness of the Scottish Drug Court Pilots.* Edinburgh: Scottish Executive Social Research.

MacLean Report (2000) *A Report of the Committee on Serious Violent and Sexual Offenders* Edinburgh: Scottish Executive.

McNeill, F. (2004) 'Desistance, rehabilitation and correctionalism: prospects and developments in Scotland', *Howard Journal of Criminal Justice,* 43 (4): 420–36.

McNeill, F. (2005) 'Remembering probation in Scotland', *Probation Journal,* 52 (1): 23–38.

McNeill, F. and Whyte B. (2007) *Reducing Re-offending: Social Work and Community Justice in Scotland.* Cullompton: Willan.

McNeill, F., Batchelor, S., Burnett, R. and Knox, J. (2005) *21st Century Social Work Reducing Reoffending: Key Skills.* Edinburgh: Scottish Executive.

MacRae, R., McIvor, G., Malloch, M., Barry, M. and Murray, L. (2006) *Evaluation of the Scottish Prison Service Transitional Care Initiative.* Edinburgh: Scottish Executive Social Research.

Mahood, L. (1995) *Policing Gender, Class and Family. Britain, 1850–1940.* London: UCL Press.

Mahood, L. (2002) '"Give him a doing": the birching of young offenders in Scotland', *Canadian Journal of History,* 37 (3): 439–58.

Marsland, M. (1977) 'The decline of probation in Scotland', *Social Work Today,* 8 (23): 17–18.

Moore, G. (1978) 'Crisis in Scotland', *Howard Journal,* 17 (1): 32–40.

Moore, G. and Whyte, B. (1998) *Moore and Wood's Social Work and Criminal Law in Scotland,* 3rd edn. Edinburgh: Mercat Press.

Morison Report (1962) *Report of the Departmental Committee on the Probation Service,* Cmnd 1650. London: HMSO.

National Probation Service (2001) *A New Choreography.* London: Home Office.

Nellis, M. (1995) 'Probation values for the 1990s', *Howard Journal,* 34 (1): 19–44.

Nelson, S. (1977) 'Why Scotland's after-care is lagging', *Community Care,* 14 (12): 87.

O'Malley, P. (2004) 'The uncertain promise of risk', *Australian and New Zealand Journal of Criminology,* 37 (3): 323–43.

Paterson. F. and Tombs, J. (1998) *Social Work and Criminal Justice Volume 1: The Policy Context.* Edinburgh: Stationery Office.

Popham, F., McIvor, G., Brown, A., Eley, S., Malloch, M., Piacentini, L. and Walters, R. (2005) *Evaluation of the Hamilton Sheriff Youth Court.* Edinburgh: Scottish Executive Social Research.

Rifkind, M. (1989) 'Penal policy: the way ahead', *Howard Journal*, 28: 81–90.

Robinson, G. and McNeill F. (2004) 'Purposes matter: the ends of probation', in G. Mair (ed.), *What Matters in Probation*. Cullompton: Willan.

Scottish Consortium on Crime and Criminal Justice (2006) *Women in Prison in Scotland: An Unmet Commitment*. Edinburgh: Scottish Consortium on Crime and Criminal Justice.

Scottish Executive (1999) *Minister Outlines Way Forward For Criminal Justice Social Work*. Scottish Executive News Release: SE1070/1999.

Scottish Executive (2002) *Tripartite Group Report – Throughcare: Developing the Service*. Edinburgh: Scottish Executive.

Scottish Executive (2003) *A Partnership for a Better Scotland*. Available at: http://www.scotland.gov.uk/library5/government/pfbs.pdf

Scottish Executive (2004a) *Reduce, Rehabilitate, Reform: A Consultation on Reducing Reoffending in Scotland*. Edinburgh: Scottish Executive.

Scottish Executive (2004b) *Consultation on Reducing Reoffending in Scotland: Analysis of Responses*. Edinburgh: Scottish Executive.

Scottish Executive (2004c) *Scotland's Criminal Justice Plan*. Edinburgh: Scottish Executive.

Scottish Executive (2005a) *Recorded Crime in Scotland, 2004–5*. Edinburgh: Scottish Executive.

Scottish Executive (2005b) *Supporting Safer, Stronger Communities: Consultation on Community Justice Authorities*. Edinburgh: Scottish Executive.

Scottish Executive (2006a) *Reducing Reoffending: National Strategy for the Management of Offenders*. Edinburgh: Scottish Executive.

Scottish Executive (2006b) *Statistical Bulletin Criminal Justice Series: CrJ/2006/3: Criminal Proceedings in Scottish Courts, 2004/05*. Edinburgh: Scottish Executive.

Scottish Executive (2006c) *National Advisory Body on Offender Management*. Available at: http://www.scotland.gov.uk/News/Releases/2006/03/20150733.

Scottish Executive (2006d) *National Strategy of Offender Management*. Available at: http://www.scotland.gov.uk/News/Releases/2006/05/22104805.

Scottish Executive (2006e) *Release and Post Custody Management of Offenders*. Edinburgh: Scottish Executive.

Scottish Labour (2003) *Scottish Labour Manifesto 2003: On Your Side*. Available at: http://www.scottishlabour.org.uk/manifesto/

Scottish Office (1947) *The Probation Service in Scotland. Its Objects and Its Organisation*. Edinburgh: HMSO.

Scottish Office (1955) *The Probation Service in Scotland*. Edinburgh: HMSO.

Scottish Office (1961) *The Probation Service in Scotland*. Edinburgh: HMSO.

Scottish Office (1998) *Community Sentencing: The Tough Option: Review of Criminal Justice Social Work Services*. Edinburgh: Scottish Office Home Department.

Scottish Prison Service (2000) *Partnership and Co-ordination: SPS Action on Drugs*. Edinburgh: Scottish Prison Service.

Sentencing Commission for Scotland (2006) *Early Release from Prison and Supervision of Prisoners on Their Release*. Edinburgh: Sentencing Commission for Scotland.

Social Exclusion Unit (2002) *Reducing Re-offending by Ex-prisoners*. London: Social Exclusion Unit.

Social Work Services Group (1991) *National Objectives and Standards for Social Work Services in the Criminal Justice System*. Edinburgh: Social Work Services Group.

Social Work Services Group (1996) *Part 2 – Service Standards: Throughcare*. Edinburgh: Social Work Services Group.

Social Work Services Group (2000) *National Standards for Social Enquiry and Related Reports and Court Based Social Work Services*. Edinburgh: Social Work Services Group.

Social Work Services Inspectorate (1993) *Social Work Services in the Criminal Justice System: Achieving National Standards*. Edinburgh: Scottish Office.

Social Work Services Inspectorate (1997) *A Commitment to Protect. Supervising Sex Offenders: Proposals for More Effective Practice*. Edinburgh: Scottish Office.

Social Work Services Inspectorate (1998) *Management and Assessment of Risk in Social Work Services*. Edinburgh: Scottish Office.

Social Work Services Inspectorate (2000) *Risk Assessment Guidance and Framework*. Edinburgh: Scottish Executive.

Streatfeild Report (1961) *Report of the Interdepartmental Committee on the Business of the Higher Criminal Courts*, Cmnd 1289. London: HMSO.

Tombs, J. (2004) *A Unique Punishment: Sentencing and the Prison Population in Scotland*. Edinburgh: Scottish Consortium on Crime and Criminal Justice.

Turnbull, P. J., McSweeney, T., Webster, R., Edmunds, M. and Hough, M. (2000) *Drug Treatment and Testing Orders: Final Evaluation Report*, Home Office Research Study No. 212. London: Home Office.

Walker, J. (2001) *International Experience of Drug Courts*. Edinburgh: Scottish Executive Central Research Unit.

Chapter 6

Probation, the state and community – delivering probation services in Northern Ireland

David O'Mahony and Tim Chapman

Introduction

In this chapter we look at how probation services have evolved and developed in Northern Ireland. This is a history of a service structurally independent from, yet influenced by, policy and practice developments in probation services in England and Wales. It is also about probation officers and managers struggling to perform a professional role in a society in which criminal justice has provoked highly contentious political issues often resulting in violence. Thus, while probation practice in Northern Ireland has many similarities to England and Wales, it also has significant and interesting differences. Its unique historical development, the civil conflict and the peace process in Northern Ireland have all forced probation to examine its relationship to the state, to offenders and to communities. The practice that emerged from this critical examination may have lessons for other probation services.

We have chosen to describe the development of the Probation Service in Northern Ireland in three phases:

- The origins of probation in Northern Ireland up to the emergence of a modern service 1907–70;
- Probation and the civil conflict in Northern Ireland 1970–95;
- Probation and the peace process in Northern Ireland 1995–2004.

The origins of probation in Northern Ireland up to the emergence of a modern service 1907–70

The origins and early development of probation in Northern Ireland can best be understood if it is looked at over three distinct periods The first is its initial formation and early development from the Probation of Offenders Act 1907 to 1938 just prior to the Second World War. During the next period from 1938 to 1948 attempts were made to develop and 'professionalise' the Service.

But it was only in the third period between 1948 and 1970 that a modern Probation Service along the British lines emerge.

The roots and early development of probation in Northern Ireland 1907–38

The very early roots of probation work in Northern Ireland appear to have been similar to those that had evolved in England at the turn of the century. Missionaries and Christian groups had established informal ways of providing help to individuals brought before the courts (Gadd 1996). The courts could bind over offenders to the supervision of these missionaries, giving them a chance to 'mend their ways' in the community rather than being fined or sent to prison. However, there was no formal or legal system of probation supervision available until the enactment of the Probation of Offenders Act in 1907. The Act allowed for the establishment of probation services for courts across the whole of Britain and Ireland. Despite sharing this same basic legislation, the actual development of probation in Northern Ireland was quite different to that in England and Wales. Indeed, as will be explained below, the early development of probation in Northern Ireland was largely hampered by a series of ineffective mechanisms that were put in place to establish the service, persistent problems over funding and a general lack of 'professional status' for the service or probation officers at the time.

Following the enactment of the Probation of Offenders Act 1907 and the Probation Rules (Northern Ireland) 1928, the basic duties and expectations of probation officers were established and in many respects these were similar to those in the rest of the United Kingdom. Probation officers were expected to carry out their duties and follow directions given by the court. They were required to visit the homes of probationers and make enquiries as to their behaviour, employment and way of life and prepare reports for the court. Officers were required to keep in close contact with the probationer and meet with them at least weekly for the first month (unless directed otherwise) and, where the probationer was a juvenile, to make enquiries as to their school attendance and progress.

Overall, the role of the probation officer was to 'advise, assist and befriend' the probationer. Their role was very much a helping hand and service-based role, where probation officers were expected to help their clients, with such things as finding employment and, as far as possible, securing the help of others, such as social and religious groups, in the rehabilitation of offenders.

In relation to work with juveniles, the role of the probation officer was also to enable the young person to start a new life without shutting him off from the rest of the community. Probation officers were expected to gain the confidence of the young person's parents in this process, or where the young person had been removed from the home and committed to the care of a 'fit person' the probation officer would assist the 'fit person', by helping the juvenile find employment with assistance from religious groups and social agencies.

The appointment of probation officers was solely decided upon by the judiciary and under the Probation of Offenders Act 1907, as it applied to

Ireland, probation officers were supposed to be appointed to districts under the recommendation of the local justices. This was changed under the Summary Jurisdiction and Criminal Justice Act (Northern Ireland) in 1935, whereby the Ministry of Home Affairs became the appointing authority, though all appointments were still made on the recommendation of resident magistrates.

There were no formal skill requirements for probation officers in the early development of the service. Rather, this was a matter for the resident magistrates to decide. They simply had to draw up a list of persons they considered fit for the job, and this would be passed to the Ministry of Home Affairs for the appointment to take place. As set out in the Probation Rules (Northern Ireland) 1936:

> For the purpose of appointing a Probation Officer for any Petty Sessions district ... the Resident Magistrates for such Petty Sessions district shall submit to the Ministry of Home Affairs the name of the person considered fit for appointment. (Article 1, Probation Rules (Northern Ireland) 1936)

The selection of the 'right type' of candidate was therefore completely left to the discretion of the resident magistrates. Furthermore, at this stage there was no system of professional development or training for probation officers.

It is perhaps not surprising that the probation service in Northern Ireland did not flourish in the early years. There were a number of reasons for this, but the most obvious following the passage of the Probation of Offenders Act 1907 was the fact that there was nothing in the legislation to compel local authorities to appoint probation officers in their local areas. Since local authorities had to absorb all of the costs of paying for probation officers, it appears that this was a major disincentive for local courts to appoint them. A similar situation existed in England and Wales up to 1925 (prior to the passing of the Criminal Justice Act 1925). As the English Report of the Departmental Committee on the Social Services (1936) notes, by 1922 'no less than 215 Courts had failed to take steps to appoint a probation officer'. But this situation was rectified in England and Wales by the Criminal Justice Act 1925 which made the appointment of probation officers compulsory and the Secretary of State was empowered to regulate their salaries and conditions and a proportion of their salaries was to be paid from the National Exchequer towards these costs (which had previously been paid by the local authorities).

In Northern Ireland similar legislation to the Criminal Justice Act 1925 was not enacted. The Summary Jurisdiction and Criminal Justice Act (Northern Ireland) of 1935 did go some way towards addressing the problem by making the Ministry of Home Affairs responsible for their appointment. However, it did not make their appointment compulsory. So, while there was a considerable growth in the use of probation in England and Wales up to the mid-1930s, whereby the percentage of adults found guilty of indictable offences (in courts of summary jurisdiction) and placed on probation rose from 11 per cent in 1910 to 19 per cent in 1933 – and in the juvenile courts this rose from 26 per cent in 1910 to 54 per cent in 1933 – the available statistics for Northern Ireland showed that only 4 per cent of adults and 14 per cent of juveniles were placed on probation in 1936.

Few reliable statistics on probation were collected in Northern Ireland until the mid-1920s, which is a reflection of the fact that there appeared to be a low priority placed on probation or the development of the service. All of the available statistics from Northern Ireland show that the courts made little use of probation supervision, particularly prior to the mid-1930s. Indeed, of the probation orders made, these were largely restricted to a small number of juvenile cases. The use of probation orders was also only confined to the larger towns such as Belfast, Coleraine, Ballymena and Derry. Outside these towns there was practically no probation orders made by the courts whatsoever. Looking at the figures for 1935, for example, a total of only 126 individuals were placed under probation supervision in Northern Ireland and of these 119 were made in Belfast, 2 in Ballymena and 5 in Coleraine (*Report on the Administration of Home Office Services* (NI) 1936). There were no probation orders made in any of the other courts across Northern Ireland. Looking more closely at the statistics for that year, it was also evident that probation was almost exclusively used for juveniles or young offenders – 75 per cent of those given probation supervision were under 16 years of age, a further 24 per cent were between 16 and 21, and only less than 1 per cent were over 21.

As mentioned earlier, the infrequent use of probation supervision in Northern Ireland was largely attributable to the lack of probation officers. An order of probation supervision could not be made if there wasn't an available probation officer to recommend probation or supervise the case, and at this time there simply were no probation officers available to the courts outside a few of the major towns. The available statistics from 1937 give a good insight into the extent of the problem. In that year there were only ten probation officers in the whole of Northern Ireland (in the few towns mentioned above). It is also noteworthy that none of these probation officers were employed on a full-time basis: the few urban courts with probation officers effectively had to rely on the goodwill of these civic-minded individuals.

Attempts to promote the development of probation services 1938–48

The first serious attempt to address the inadequate development of the Probation Service in Northern Ireland was undertaken by a Home Affairs Committee assigned to examine 'The Protection and Welfare of the Young and the Treatment of Young Offenders' which was chaired by Sir Robert Lynn and reported in 1938. The 'Lynn Committee', as it became known, was set up to consider what aspects of the English Children and Young Persons Act of 1933 might be incorporated into Northern Irish legislation. But the committee also examined the probation system and made specific recommendations for its development.

The Lynn Committee in its deliberations was strongly influenced by developments in the probation system in England and in particular the impact of the English Criminal Justice Act of 1925. They were also heavily influenced by what they described as 'the very valuable report' of the English Departmental Committee on the Social Services in Courts of Summary Jurisdiction.[1] The committee felt that the English Committee's findings would be 'of the greatest assistance to the authorities in Northern Ireland in building up what, we hope, come to be regarded as one of the essential public services' (Lynn Committee 1938: 65).

The Lynn Committee recognised that the Probation Service in Northern Ireland was considerably underdeveloped, especially by comparison to services in England. They noted that 'little use is made of probation in Northern Ireland [and] ... the remarkably small number of adults placed on probation' (p. 69). The Committee pointed out that the underdevelopment of the Service was primarily due to the failure to appoint sufficient numbers of probation officers, but also recognised that this was a result of inadequate mechanisms put in place to fund the service and the poor pay and conditions that existed for probation officers themselves.

When the Committee reviewed the pay and conditions for probation officers, they noted that probation officers were only paid according to the number of cases they supervised and their rate of pay was wholly inadequate. The Committee commented, 'under the existing system it would be quite impossible for a probation officer to live on his fees' (p. 79), and that '...under the present system it is absolutely necessary for the probation officers to have some other occupation or means of subsistence besides the supervision of offenders'. Furthermore, they stated '... it is self-evident that the existing scales of remuneration would be wholly inadequate for qualified full-time officers' and while the existing probation officers appeared to have taken up the probation work though a sense of vocation '... this should not be a reason for underpaying them' (p. 90). They described the situation in 1937 where in Belfast, three of the five officers were women, two of which were police officers who could only supervise a few cases and, of the two men, one worked as a court missionary and the other worked for the Catholic Discharged Prisoners' Aid Society. The other five officers outside Belfast were all men working on a part-time basis (Lynn Committee 1938).

In relation to the desire to have an effective probation service, the Committee were wholly supportive of probation as an effective intervention and when reviewing the available statistics on individuals who had been given probation orders, the Committee noted that, when it was used, it had been 'highly successful'. They observed that the vast majority of those given probation supervision had completed their supervision successfully. Though no information was available at the time on the conduct of probationers after their period of supervision, the Committee concluded '... there is little doubt that where it is properly applied probation is in the majority of cases a most valuable and successful form of treatment' (p. 71). The Committee also drew evidence from the English Report of the Departmental Committee on the Social Services (1936) which suggested:

> ... there is no reason to doubt that the majority of probationers not only respond at the outset to the opportunity given to them to mend their ways, but definitely turn their backs on a life of crime ... [and] ... 'if

the Probation Service is adequately organised and the courts operate proper discrimination after enquiry into the selection of cases, the results obtained will fully justify the confidence placed in the system. (pp. 44–5)

The Lynn Committee recommended major changes to the whole system of probation for Northern Ireland. Specifically they recommended that one or more probation officers should be present at every juvenile court and all the important courts of summary jurisdiction. They suggested that for juveniles probation should be extended so as to be made available as a form of treatment for both 'delinquent' and 'neglected' children alike and that juvenile courts should be required to consider probation supervision as a suitable form of treatment for all offenders. They felt that there should also be a similar requirement to consider probation for all young offenders between 17 and 21 years of age. The Committee recommended that probation officers should be given proper training and paid appropriately to attract the necessary full-time professional staff. They recommended that probation officers should be appointed directly by the Ministry of Home Affairs and that half of the funding for the Service should come from central government, with the other half from local authorities.

The Lynn Committee effectively put in place a series of recommendations that could have directly addressed the very problems that had hampered the successful development of the Probation Service in Northern Ireland up to this time. Their considerable insight and recognition of the problems facing the service coupled with a strong belief that probation was worthwhile and effective, if given the chance, meant there was the potential for the Service to emerge from years of neglect. However, this opportunity was to be lost at this time, as world events overtook local matters with the outbreak of hostilities that marked the start of the Second World War.

Post-War developments and the emergence of modern probation 1948–70

The question of probation reform was not addressed again until after the war, when the Northern Ireland government published the report *The Protection and Welfare of the Young and the Treatment of the Young Offender* in 1948. This report looked at the whole area of youth justice and revisited the recommendations of the Lynn Committee, particularly relating to the development of probation services. The report noted that there continued to be a severe shortage of probation officers and that outside Belfast, many of the courts did not have probation representation and thus were unable to make use of probation supervision. The report went on to make a series of recommendations for new legislation to develop the Service. They recommended that new measures dealing with how the probation system should be expanded so as to allow for the appointment of either full-time or part-time probation officers for each of the courts across Northern Ireland. It was also recommended that a probation officer should be required to attend all juvenile court sittings. However, the report was by no means as fundamental in its call for reform, nor as comprehensive in its recommendations, as the Lynn Committee had been. In many respects the report was a product of the difficult economic and social conditions that existed following the Second World War. So, rather than calling for a whole new probation system that should be properly funded and professional as envisaged by Lynn, the report suggested that existing probation services should be improved and practices should be consolidated and coordinated with work being done by church and voluntary organisations in the community.

The resulting legislation the Probation Act (Northern Ireland) 1950 put into place many of the recommendations from the report on *The Protection and Welfare of the Young and the Treatment of the Young Offender*. It was the first major revision of the law relating to probation services in Northern Ireland since the Probation of Offenders Act 1907 and in many respects helped to establish the basis for the modern-day Probation Service. The new Probation Act made a number of significant changes for the Service. Importantly the Act dealt with the problem of leaving the recruitment of probation officers up to the discretion of the judiciary, which had not even been given guidance as to the skills that probation officers should possess. It also dealt with the inadequate financial arrangement of making local authorities responsible for paying for the Service, which had dogged its earlier development. The Act made central government wholly responsible for the funding of the Service. The Secretary of State for Northern Ireland was also made responsible for the appointment of probation officers, establishing their pay, conditions and professional training. Probation, therefore, following the 1950 Act was in a position to develop as a properly funded, professional service that was administered directly by the central government department responsible for law and order.

Though the Probation Act 1950 was the first major revision of the Probation Service, elements of the early 1907 legislation were kept intact. For instance, the Act reinforced the basic duties of the probation officers to 'advise, assist and befriend' their clients. But the 1950 Act had some significant shortcomings. In particular, it did not require the appointment of probation officers for all courts, as Lynn had recommended previously. Rather, it only required the Ministry to appoint probation officers for districts 'as it thinks necessary' (s. 12.1), leaving the growth of the service on a now familiar, less than sure footing.

There was a steady development of the Probation Service in the years following the Probation Act 1950 with the appointment of probation officers and the establishment of a system of professional training. But the Service was still not expanding in the same way as other probation departments across the UK, and by comparison remained considerably underdeveloped. By 1977 this was formally recognised in a consultation document issued by the Children and Young Persons Review Group which noted 'the failure of the Northern Ireland [probation] Service to achieve the same development as services in England and Wales' (p. 45). Essentially, by the mid-1970s, probation was still only involved with juvenile courts by about half as much as comparable services in England and Wales, and as commented by the review group, it was involved 'hardly at all in the adult court' (p. 45).

In the early 1970s there had also been a major review of social services provision in Northern Ireland. Part of this review led to a debate as to

161

whether probation should continue to be administered separately by the ministry responsible for law and order, or whether it should be absorbed into social services departments of the Health and Social Services Boards which had been established in 1973. Thinking at the time had been influenced by developments in the rest of the UK, where for example in England and Wales probation was managed by probation and aftercare committees with strong social services links, and in Scotland it had been completely integrated into local authority generic social work departments and thus had ceased to exist as a separate service. The Review Group's consultation document asked whether the service in Northern Ireland needed to be administered differently, for example by being merged with social services, and whether its problems and difficulties might 'have been attributable to the present form of administration' (p. 47). It very much seemed that the Review Group were looking to change the whole way the Service was administered and sought to correct its underdevelopment by tackling how it was managed.

Probation and civil conflict in Northern Ireland 1970–95

During this period there was relatively little legislation on probation. The government was preoccupied with the violence of the civil conflict. This situation not only posed many threats to the Probation Service but also provided many opportunities to develop an effective and relevant practice without too much interference from policy-makers. In fact the most important piece of legislation, The Probation Board (Northern Ireland) Order 1982, provided the Service with considerable autonomy from the civil service.

In this section we will describe the emergence of the Probation Board, the impact of the 'Troubles' on probation practice, the Board's unique relationship with the community during this period and the development of effective practice in Northern Ireland.

The emergence of the modern Probation Board

In 1979, following their period of consultation, the Children and Young Persons Review Group chaired by Sir Harold Black published their recommendations. The 'Black Report', as it became known, was a fundamental review of the whole system of youth justice and made a number of significant recommendations regarding the operation of the Probation Service. The report took a very different approach to the whole issue of delivering justice to young people and much of what it proposed was dramatically different to developments and trends that had been occurring in the rest of the UK.

The report recognised that a completely different approach would be necessary in Northern Ireland, as the problems facing the jurisdiction and particularly the criminal justice system were immense. This was a time when there had been over ten years of violent civil unrest marking the 'Troubles' and Northern Ireland was also facing severe social and economic problems. There were deep concerns regarding the impact of the violent conflict on a whole generation of young people and a recognition that the conflict had driven communities into isolation, eroded the very authority of the state and undermined the legitimacy of the criminal justice system.

It was against this backdrop that Black's recommendations were formulated. One of the central themes of the report was the recognition that an integrated approach to dealing with young offenders was necessary and it stressed the importance of developing a whole range of preventative and diversionary work in the community. This, as Black stated, would have to involve the family, schools and community, all working together. He emphasised the need to divert offenders away from the justice system, and that only cases which posed a real or serious threat to society should be brought before the courts.

Unlike developments in England and Wales and Scotland, where issues of welfare and justice for children were increasingly merging, the report recommended that young people who offend and children facing care or protection proceedings should be managed and treated completely separately. It was recommended that juvenile offenders should be dealt with within the criminal justice system and child welfare issues should be completely divorced from offence proceedings.

Black looked at how the probation system might best be placed to develop its potential and effectively discharge its functions given the situation facing Northern Ireland and the criminal justice system at that time. Since, under the model he proposed, criminal justice and welfare issues were to be separated, it made no sense to have the Service administered through social service departments, as had been proposed (in their consultation document in 1977). Nor did he think the existing arrangement of running the Service directly through the Northern Ireland Office had worked effectively in the past. But more importantly, he recognised there were major legitimacy problems facing the criminal justice system, particularly the police, who were not seen as representative of the whole community, nor indeed independent. Essentially, the criminal justice system at this time did not have the support of significant sections of the community.

Black felt that for probation to work and to be able to deliver non-custodial disposals, it was vital for it to be able to work in the community and to be accepted by the whole community. He recommended, therefore, that the Service be managed in a completely novel manner. A single service was to be managed by a 'board' that was to be drawn from and representative of the community, and to be seen as outside direct government and Northern Ireland Office control. As he proposed:

> if the Service is to enjoy fully the confidence of the community, which will be essential if it is to carry out its work successfully, we consider that this can be better achieved if the community participates directly in the management of the Service. (p. 53)

It was recommended 'that the Probation Service be administered by a Board drawn from a wide spectrum of the community in Northern Ireland'.

Not only did Black recommend a radically different way of managing probation services by actively engaging the community in its activities, he also saw it as a way of engaging the community in a much broader agenda of community safety and crime prevention. As the report states:

> The main thrust of the Service's activities, as we see it, will be the provision of a specialist service to the courts and involvement *with the community* in the management of the offender. (italics added, p. 53)

The resulting legislation, the Probation Board (Northern Ireland) Order 1982, took on Black's recommendations and brought into existence the modern Probation Board. For the first time the legislation required that probation officers be appointed by the Board for all the petty session courts across Northern Ireland, directly addressing the uneven patchwork of services detectable up until then. More fundamentally, however, the establishment of the Board was a major departure from what existed before in Northern Ireland and elsewhere in the UK, in that it drew cross-community representation into the overall strategic management of the Service. Significantly, it gave the Board the power to fund directly local community groups and organisations if they could help in the supervision of offenders, or if they were seen as helpful in crime prevention generally. The Board was also given the power to determine probation policy and to monitor its effectiveness. The net effect was the establishment of an independent board that was rooted in the communities it had to serve and given the mandate to support and fund local community initiatives delivering schemes for offenders or crime prevention.

The impact of the 'Troubles'

The story of probation in Northern Ireland during over 25 years of the 'Troubles' is similar to many of the stories of individuals, communities and organisations – a struggle to find space to create some sense of normality within a highly volatile and often dangerous political conflict. In the case of the Probation Service normality represented the ability to provide a useful and relevant service to offenders and to the communities in which they lived and committed their offences. Like other probation services they worked through courts, prisons and local communities, except that in Northern Ireland between the late 1960s and the mid-1990s courts, prisons and communities were very different to those in probation areas throughout Britain.

The history of Northern Ireland has been formed by political and often violent conflict over its legitimacy as a state (see generally Whyte 1991, and McGarry and O'Leary 1995). This state needed to deploy the police, courts and prisons to control paramilitary violence. The criminal justice system, designed to process and control criminal offenders, has been adapted to manage people who are organised to break the law for political purposes. Although the criminal justice system also pursued loyalist paramilitaries, it was perceived by republicans as part of the state apparatus directed against them (Ruane and Todd 1996). This is compounded by the fact that police officers and prison officers are predominantly from the Protestant community.

Many of the most bitter and violent struggles have focused on the institutions of criminal justice. These include policing practices such as the use of emergency legislation to arrest and interrogate suspects, as well as releasing confidential information to loyalists, the use of internment, Diplock courts and the 'supergrass' trials, special category status, segregation and hunger strikes in the prisons (McEvoy 2001). Many judges, magistrates, police officers and prison officers have been killed by paramilitary organisations.

The probation service is an integral part of the criminal justice system. How has it managed to operate with integrity throughout every community in Northern Ireland and to survive without any of its staff coming to serious harm? Early in the 'Troubles' the government introduced through emergency legislation mandatory custodial sentences for any young person convicted of rioting. The provision of individualised assessment in the form of reports to the juvenile court became an absurd exercise. This led to probation officers perceiving a contradiction between rehabilitation and the realities of political conflict. In 1975 the National Association of Probation Officers (NAPO) developed a policy on politically motivated offenders which enabled officers to resist preparing court reports on people who had committed offences for political purposes and supervising them on statutory orders. This was designed to preserve the professional integrity, the personal safety and the political neutrality of probation officers.

This policy, which from time to time has been under pressure from government, courts and management, has enabled the Probation Service to avoid political manipulation and to establish its non-sectarian credentials. This resulted in the Service's capacity to operate within the most militant communities while protecting staff from the threat of violence. While every other agency in the criminal justice system has struggled to recruit Catholics, the Probation Service has always had a mixed-religion workforce.

In addition to the policy on politically motivated offenders the Probation Board, while it cooperated with the police, courts and prisons, was careful during the 'Troubles' to maintain a distance and to preserve its independence from these bodies. This was necessary to preserve its neutrality. This was especially critical in its relations with the Prison Service.[2]

Crawford (2003) describes how paramilitary prisoners struggled to live as normally as possible in the compound of Long Kesh and later in the H Blocks of the Maze prison. These prisoners had the political power and organisational capacity to gain a position of relative autonomy from the prison authorities. Their 'special category' status helped them maintain a level of self-respect and dignity through physical and psychological independence from the prison. Crawford believes that this set of arrangements avoided many of the negative effects of normal incarceration and that this was borne out by the finding that reconviction rates for politically motivated prisoners were much lower than for ordinary prisoners.

These prisoners resisted the state's attempts to criminalise them. Although they were convicted of criminal offences, the court procedures were determined by emergency provisions which many individuals refused to recognise. Once imprisoned they did not see themselves as in need of rehabilitation. They did, however, acknowledge that they had basic welfare needs mostly in relation to communicating with families and legal representatives (McEvoy et al. 1999).

The Prison Welfare Departments staffed by the Probation Service provided a link with the outside world. This involved acting on a list of requests from prisoners' representatives rather than interviewing individual prisoners. Probation officers had to be careful to avoid identification with either the prison authorities or the prisoners. In spite of continuous tension and periods of intense conflict, often violent, over the years probation officers achieved respect for their role from both sides. Their sensitivity to all parties during the hunger strike was especially appreciated (McEvoy 2001).

As time went on the Welfare Departments tried to develop their role. They recognised that offending or other therapeutic programmes were inappropriate. Yet it was clear that prisoners needed support both to cope with long sentences and in preparation for release. The Probation Board began to deliver 'seminars' on such things as child development so that prisoners could understand their children and support their partners in parenting. The Board also funded external organisations to provide courses in a range of activities such as yoga and drama. These programmes allowed prisoners to address their needs without seeing themselves as clients of a service addressing their offending. This model of practice provides a glimpse of how a probation service might work with individuals who had the power to command real respect.

Most of the time during the 'Troubles' the Northern Ireland Office was preoccupied with more pressing problems than the operations of probation and left it much to its own devices. Thus the Probation Service in Northern Ireland found for itself a depoliticised space within a highly political environment. It used this space both to engage with politically motivated prisoners and to work with ordinary offenders with a mixed workforce in all communities.

To some extent this strategy was common to many other statutory agencies in Northern Ireland as Pinkerton (1998: 18) observes:

> During the early period of the present round of the Troubles, the longest and most vicious in Northern Ireland's history, the British government attempted to manage the crisis by depoliticising it. The crisis of legitimacy was reset as a series of technical security, economic and social problems to be solved by apolitical, professional experts.

However, this strategy was not without its costs to the Probation Board. While in England and Wales probation services were addressing the oppressive nature of racism, in Northern Ireland the Service's commitment to being non-sectarian inhibited it from challenging sectarianism in the community and in the criminal justice system in spite of clear evidence of inequality and oppressive behaviour. The lack of local politics, while avoiding the excesses of populist criminal justice policies, resulted in a lower level of transparency and accountability than the general public has a right to expect. The Board like other public services has tried to address this problem through publishing annual reports and business plans.

Probation's relationship with the community

This lack of local democracy could have resulted, as Pinkerton (1998) suggests, in a disengagement from civil society. Was this the case in relation to the Probation Board?

While Northern Ireland has had and continues to have a low 'ordinary' crime rate (non-terrorist related crime) relative to other western societies,[3] the most deprived communities have suffered from very high rates of crime and disorder. These communities, in which most offenders in Northern Ireland live, experience high levels of unemployment and are dependent for income and services on a state to which many feel deeply antagonistic. It is in these environments that paramilitary organisations operate. The most deprived communities tend to be Catholic.

Political neutrality allowed probation officers to operate normally in these communities. Taking advantage of this, officers did not simply retreat into the protected world of professional social work. The choice was made to engage with the most marginalised communities through the use of a community development budget to develop partnerships. In doing so, probation's so-called 'technocratic', apolitical response to offending encountered these communities' subjective experience of crime and their political response to the state.

While many probation services in England and Wales were struggling to spend up to 5 per cent of their budget on partnerships, the Probation Board for Northern Ireland's community development funds were almost 20 per cent of its total budget. Much of this was used to purchase services such as hostels for homeless and high-risk offenders, vocational training workshops and Prison Link, a service for prisoners' families in partnerships with the Northern Ireland Association for the Care and Resettlement of Offenders (NIACRO). A significant proportion of funds was invested in partnerships with local community groups committed to crime prevention.

Political marginalisation and deprivation had resulted in the growth of a vibrant network of community organisations delivering services to the unemployed, to women, to the elderly and to youth. Many groups sought to divert young people from offending. They were motivated by the perception that the criminal justice system had failed to protect them and to contain youth crime. They were also concerned about the vicious punishments being inflicted on young people by paramilitary organisations for anti-social behaviour (Feenan 2002). These included warnings to young people and parents, exclusion from the community, beatings, bullet wounds through various limbs ('knee-cappings') and killings in the case of drug dealers. While these draconian measures were supported by many beleaguered members of the public, they proved no more effective in reducing offending than the state's system of punishments.

Chapman and Pinkerton (1987) described how the conditions causing a virtual epidemic of car crime or 'joyriding' in west Belfast created a fundamental change in probation practice. Probation officers were faced with clear evidence of the ineffectiveness of the traditional casework method and had to adopt a community-based approach which entailed case management and referral to community-run projects.

Why did 'joyriding' rather than any other form of crime cause such a radical change? Primarily this was because it was the one crime which penetrated the blanket media coverage of violent politically motivated offences to enter the public consciousness. The mobile nature of the crime connected the middle class who owned the cars with the 'joyriders' who disproportionately came from the deprived estates of west Belfast. Driving stolen cars recklessly is both a highly dangerous and public crime. As Chapman (1995: 130) commented:

Joyriders in west Belfast are prime targets for this process of 'demonisation'. Their offending is prolific and persistent and very destructive and dangerous. It is also highly visible and as such appears defiant of, rather than deviant from, social norms. Most crime tends to be secretive and hidden. As a group these young people tend to justify and celebrate their offending and show little or no remorse or sense of responsibility.

Once in west Belfast young people showed off to their friends by driving recklessly. This resulted in several deaths of pedestrians and legal drivers. The local community were outraged and put pressure on the IRA to control this activity. As far as the security forces were concerned joyriders' reactions to security measures, such as driving through road blocks set up by the Army or police, made them indistinguishable from terrorists or at least just as dangerous. In one incident three young people who had driven through an Army checkpoint were shot dead. Others were killed or killed others through road accidents. Many were shot by paramilitaries.

In the early 1980s the west Belfast Auto Project, modelled on a similar project in London, engaged young people involved in car crime. While it was managed by Extern, a voluntary organisation, it had been set up and staffed by local people concerned with the problem. It was funded by the Probation Board and the Department of Health and Social Services. Although it was evaluated as effective in reducing reoffending, it was closed due to its high costs and its failure to win sufficient support in the community. Several attempts to replace it foundered primarily through lack of organisational and financial expertise.

In the late 1980s and early 1990s joyriding once again became a major public issue. Several deaths were caused by the crime. It was clear that the offenders were marginalised in an already marginalised community. This is confirmed by research into joyriders elsewhere (Light *et al.* 1993). They were excluded from both statutory and community resources. The only people who remained to offer support were parents, mainly mothers. It was with the West Belfast Parents and Youth Support Groups (WBPYSG) that the Probation Board chose to form an alliance. Out of this the Turas project was born.

This partnership involved a team of probation officers and community workers employed by two very different organisations working together. This not only created management difficulties for both organisations, but also generated some very innovative practice (Chapman 1995). It was basically an outreach project appealing to the concerns of mothers and the community for someone to take young people engaged in dangerous activities off the streets at times when they were at most risk – late at night, particularly at weekends. Activities and drop-in facilities were offered at these times. This enabled the project to engage with the highest-risk offenders in a way that other approaches had been unable to do. This had an immediate effect on the number of cars stolen at those times. Eventually the team succeeded in involving serious offenders in offending programmes, the Duke of Edinburgh Award, drama, art and football. Parents were also involved in a parent support group.

After three years the contract was completed to the satisfaction of all parties. Consultations with the community revealed that local people were more concerned about drug use among young people than car crime. Consequently the Probation Board funded a drug outreach project.

These innovations in practice challenged the social work base of the Probation Service. This was reflected in staffing. The Probation Board has recruited staff with youth and community work qualifications and ex-offenders through a New Careers project. These initiatives have transformed the way probation works with offenders in Northern Ireland. Activities and programmes usually delivered in the evenings and weekends when offenders are most at risk became the norm.

The development of effective practice

In some respects the Probation Service was in the vanguard of the effectiveness approach to practice. *The Report of the Children and Young Person's Review Group* (the Black Report) published in 1979 outlined a policy aimed at 'a realistic balance between welfare and justice' (para. 5.58) which maintained the Probation Service as the lead agency for juvenile offenders and placed it clearly within the justice framework, thus weakening its social work value base. This corresponded to the Chief Probation Officer's vision of punishment in the community (Griffiths 1982). The challenge of the Black Report to the Probation Service was assessed by Chapman (1983: 108):

> The Service needs to develop more sophisticated methods of assessment and a variety of effective programmes which help the young person and the scapegoating group to change their way of interacting. The potential for doing this exists within present practice but to be fully realised it demands changes in the internal management structure, the development of specialisms within community oriented teams, greater liaison with other statutory agencies and voluntary organisations, and a commitment to research into *what works* in helping young people.

One of the Government's first responses to the recommendations of the Black Report was to establish the Probation Board as an agency managed by a board separate from the Northern Ireland Office. This occurred in 1982 as a consequence of the Probation Board (NI) Order. Each successive Board has been chaired by a local business leader. This provided the Chief Probation Officer with the opportunity to initiate 'managerialism' in the Probation Service. The Chief Probation Officer had engaged management consultants to introduce 'management by objectives'. This introduced an orientation towards results rather than process which paved the way to effective practice. Many other probation services in England and Wales followed this lead by contracting consultants to develop a similar management practice in their areas.

Alongside the community-based initiatives described above this commitment to effectiveness nurtured the development of a range of programmes based upon the 'What Works' research. As the politics of violence decreased and Northern Ireland crept towards a peace process, the Probation Board like other probation services became increasingly influenced by research into effective practice. This was facilitated by the Northern Ireland Treatment of Offenders Order 1989 which introduced statutory provision for day centres and specified activities. The Corporate Plan for 1992 to 1997 committed the Board to a strategy to deliver an increased intensity and improved quality of intervention in response to levels of risk of offending.

A range of cognitive behavioural programmes was designed to suit local culture and styles of delivery. These addressed anger management, alcohol and drug use, and car crime (joyriding) and disqualified drivers. The most intensive programme was targeted at the most high-risk offender. This programme was called Stop Think And Change (STAC). It was delivered throughout Northern Ireland but primarily at the Belfast Probation Centre. It required the offender to attend three full days a week. A version for the employed was delivered in the evenings and weekends. It combined modules developing responsibility for offending and victim awareness with a range of cognitive skills. What made it distinctive was its emphasis on the context of gender for offending. This programme was evaluated as having a measurable positive impact on criminogenic needs such as motivation to change, victim awareness, personal responsibility, moral attitude, impulsivity and empathy. A limited reconviction study also reported promising results in reducing reoffending (Chapman and Doran 1998).

STAC was reviewed generally favourably in an HM Inspectorate of Probation publication, *Strategies for Effective Offender Supervision* (Underdown 1998). Shortly after this a member of the Probation Board's senior management was asked to write with Michael Hough an effective practice guide for HM Inspectorate of Probation (Chapman and Hough 1998).

Other innovative approaches included a residential cognitive behavioural programme, the Ramoan programme, which enabled intensive group and individual work on offending. This was particularly useful for high-risk offenders from rural communities. The ineffectiveness of the criminal justice system to protect women from domestic violence led to a close working relationship with Women's Aid and the delivery of a programme for perpetrators. Similarly the Probation Board pioneered a day centre dedicated to the provision of structured programmes for and intensive supervision of sex offenders. In 1993 a report (Social Services Inspectorate 1993) was published by the Social Services Inspectorate into the circumstances of the offences of a sex offender who had been supervised by the Probation Board. While the report confirmed that the individual had not committed the offences while subject to probation supervision, it had the effect of concentrating the minds of the Probation Board on the critical importance of risk management.

In relation to youth offending the Board developed a range of interventions ranging from diversionary adventure learning activities through the Duke of Edinburgh Award to intensive supervision of persistent offenders through the Watershed programme which provided an intensive programme of assessment, restorative justice, residential work, learning activities and personal coaching over a nine-month period.

Probation and the peace process in Northern Ireland 1995–2004

The Probation Service has not only survived around 25 years of violent conflict in Northern Ireland but has also developed a distinctive practice which has been described as inclusive (Chapman 1998). This is an approach which:

- is responsive to community concerns over crime;
- bypasses, when necessary, the institutional systems of accessing services, e.g. through court orders;
- is based upon partnership with those closest to the problem;
- reaches out to the most marginalised by delivering services at the most appropriate times and places;
- is delivered by a flexible and multi-skilled staff group.

This distinctive approach to probation, combining 'managerialism' and partnership with the community with the principles of 'What Works', has clearly been influential beyond Northern Ireland. Underlying this approach was a fundamental belief in the possibility of positive individual change in spite of significant social obstacles.

Given the radical changes that probation practice has undergone due to the Northern Irish conflict, how will the Probation Board adapt to a post-conflict situation?

The Good Friday Agreement provided the political will and the stability to conduct a fundamental review of the criminal justice system in Northern Ireland (Criminal Justice Review Group 2000). This Review has set the agenda for the role and reform of the Probation Board. It also signalled the intention of government to take a stronger lead in criminal justice policy than previously. Freed of the security priorities of the civil conflict the Northern Ireland Office directed its attention to the management of ordinary offenders. This included inspecting the practice of the Probation Board. This had not occurred throughout the 'Troubles'. The Board was not fully prepared for such scrutiny. The impact of inspection was to direct attention towards the importance of conforming to and monitoring standards of practice agreed with government and the courts.[4] This marked a fundamental change in the internal culture of the Probation Board.

Post-conflict legislation relating to probation has emphasised public protection rather than rehabilitation. For instance, the Criminal Justice (Northern Ireland) Order 1996 provided for custody probation orders and licences for sex offenders.[5] The Criminal Justice (Northern Ireland) Order 1998 arranged for the monitoring and multi-agency risk management of sex offenders.

There are no indications that Northern Ireland will develop a similar structure to the National Offender Management Service (NOMS) currently being put in place in England and Wales. It is unlikely that such an elaborate restructuring would be appropriate for a relatively small area such as Northern Ireland. The Criminal Justice Review Implementation Plan (2003) will drive the development of a closer relationship between the Probation Board and the Prison Service. This is intended to provide structured release packages for prisoners and to ensure continuity and consistency in the delivery of accredited and evaluated programmes in prisons and in the community. This should involve joint arrangements for training and the accreditation, monitoring and evaluation of programmes. The two organisations have already agreed a common assessment system and adopted some offending behaviour programmes from England and Wales. A Programme Approval Group has been set up to assure the quality of programmes delivered, to make arrangements for accreditation and to ensure that programmes are evaluated.

The government intends to devolve the responsibilities for criminal justice to a Department of Justice and a locally elected minister (Review of the Criminal Justice System in Northern Ireland 2002).[6] Once this occurs the Probation Board is likely to become a Next Steps agency subject to more direct accountability to the local Assembly. This will facilitate more complementary structural arrangements with the Prison Service and may result in a similar structure to the National Offender Management Service in England and Wales. Though this may mean probation is less able to decide on its policies and will have to concentrate more on delivering services, ministerial accountability should mean greater openness and transparency and could open up new possibilities for change and innovation responsive to local needs.

Peace also brought the so-called 'Peace Dividend'. Significant funds were invested by the European Union in supporting the peace process. This meant that many community groups which previously depended upon Probation Board funding were receiving much higher sums from a variety of sources.

The government has produced a community safety strategy which requires local authorities to form community safety partnerships that will develop and implement local plans to prevent crime and the fear of crime (Community Safety Unit 2003). The Probation Board will take its place in these partnerships. However, with 26 partnerships covering the whole of Northern Ireland it is difficult to envisage how the Board will have the resources to participate actively in all of these. Furthermore it appears the Community Safety Unit and newly created Youth Justice Agency will take over the funding of some of the crime prevention projects previously funded through probation. It is likely, however, that it will be able to advise these partnerships on arrangements to manage the risk of specific high-risk offenders. The Board has also had a budget of nearly £2 million for community-based projects. Much of this has been committed to essential services such as hostel accommodation; however, this has recently been reallocated directly to the housing authority (the Housing Executive). Therefore it appears there will be a reduction in probation's community involvement through crime prevention initiatives, as these are increasingly being absorbed by other agencies.

The Criminal Justice Review was strongly in favour of the development of restorative justice in Northern Ireland. The police had already implemented a successful pilot scheme (O'Mahony et al. 2002). However, there was also a growing community-based network of restorative justice projects set up as alternatives to paramilitary punishments. These initiatives were viewed with suspicion by the government, the police and the courts. The community projects had connections with paramilitary organisations and particularly on the republican side were not prepared to collaborate with the police.

The Criminal Justice Review agreed with the government's position – that community restorative justice posed a threat to human rights.

In the meantime the youth justice system in Northern Ireland is undergoing a truly radical process of change (O'Mahony and Deazley 2002). The use of custody for young offenders has been dramatically reduced, primarily through the Criminal Justice (Northern Ireland) Order 1996, which restricted the use of custody to only the most serious offenders and the Justice (Children) (Northern Ireland) Order 1997, which allows for short determinate juvenile justice centre orders to be served partly in juvenile justice centres and partly through supervision in the community by the Probation Board (Chapman 1997).

The Justice (Northern Ireland) Act 2002 provided for the introduction of the Youth Conference Service. This Service currently provides restorative youth conferences for young people who commit offences other than low-risk offenders who will be cautioned in a restorative manner by the police and the most serious offenders. The Service takes referrals from the Prosecution Service directly or from the Youth Court. Diversionary conferences result in voluntary agreements made by young people to make reparation and to prevent reoffending. Court-referred conferences result in similar agreements enforced through a Youth Conference Order. This is being piloted in greater Belfast and the west of the province (Tyrone and Fermanagh). Once it covers the whole of Northern Ireland and is fully accepted by the Youth Courts, it will severely restrict the Probation Board's role within the youth justice system.

However, the Criminal Justice Review has recommended that restorative justice should be found a place within the current sentencing framework for adults. This offers the Probation Board an opportunity to develop its work in this area. Furthermore, the custody probation order has proved popular with the courts and nearly half of adult offenders in custody currently are under such orders. It appears that probation will be well placed to move further into the management of released prisoners. It may also increasingly provide specific programmes for high-risk offenders addressing their needs such as in education, employment, anger management and drug and alcohol addiction.

Conclusions

Where does this leave the Probation Board? It seems likely that it will follow the English model for probation rather than continue to develop a specifically Northern Irish approach. There are indications that relationships with local communities will become less important than relationships with a Department of Justice and more specifically the Prison Service. The Board's long history of innovative and effective work with young people may be very much reduced in favour of the management of the risk that adult offenders pose in the community. New practice may include electronic monitoring. Increasingly probation officers will work collaboratively with the police and prison services through accredited programmes. Risk management will continue to develop through multi-agency panels and a common computerised information system to supervise registers of sexual, violent and other high-risk offenders. It is also likely that the Board will become more involved with victims of crime through restorative justice and through providing information to victims on the release of offenders from prison.

Probation in Northern Ireland has had to adapt itself greatly over time to meet the needs of both the community it serves and its clients, and the state which provides its funds. At times this has been a difficult balancing act, but it has also provided the service with the opportunity to shape its own direction. Once the local assembly takes on responsibility for criminal justice, the depoliticised space to develop probation practice that the Board experienced during the civil conflict may well be considered a 'golden age'.

Appendix: A chronology of the development of probation in Northern Ireland

1907	Probation of Offenders Act	Act to establish a probation service across Britain and Ireland
1914	Criminal Justice Administration Act	Extending the availability of probation as an option for 16–21-year-old fine defaulters.
1928	Probation Rules (Northern Ireland)	Set out the principal duties for probation officers
1935	Summary Jurisdiction and Criminal Justice Act (Northern Ireland)	Ministry of Home Affairs made appointing authority for probation officers
1936	Probation Rules (NI)	Appointment of probation officers by Ministry made under recommendation of resident magistrates
1938	Lynn Committee Report	Review of criminal justice arrangements (including probation) for young people in Northern Ireland
1948	Northern Ireland government report on *The Protection and Welfare of the Young and the Treatment of the Young Offender*	Brought forward recommendations made by Lynn Committee
1950	Probation Act (NI)	Secretary of State for Northern Ireland to pay and appoint probation officers
1977	Children and Young Persons Review Group, Consultation	Consultation exercise to review legislation and services for young offenders, with a review of probation services
1979	Black Report	Report of the Children and Young Persons Review Group
1982	Probation Board (NI) Order	Establishment of the modern Probation Board for Northern Ireland
1996	Criminal Justice (NI) Order	Redefined the role of probation officers
1997	Criminal Justice (Children) (Northern Ireland) Order	Reformed the custody of young offenders
2002	Justice (Northern Ireland) Act	Established the Youth Conference Service

Notes

1 *Report of the Departmental Committee on the Social Services in Courts of Summary Jurisdiction* (1936), Cmd. 5122.

2 Prisons in Northern Ireland have gone through considerable change during and following the conflict. The most dramatic changes occurred with the onset of the 'Troubles' and use of internment without trial in the early 1970s. The prison population rose from around 600 in the late 1960s to a high of nearly 3,000 in 1978. The population then stabilised at around 2,500 in the mid-1980s and fell to below 2,000 in the mid-1990s. The most significant decline in the population occurred in the late 1990s, particularly after the Good Friday Agreement and following the enactment of the Sentences Act 1998 which saw the early release of political prisoners. The population fell to below 1,000 in 2001 and was just over 1,000 in 2002 (Northern Ireland Office 2004a). Placing these figures in context, Northern Ireland went from an extremely high rate of imprisonment in the 1970s and 1980s to currently having one of the lowest rates of imprisonment in Europe. The 'World Prison Population List' (Walmsley 2003) shows that in 2001 Northern Ireland had 50 prisoners per 100,000 population, compared to 125 in England and Wales, 120 in Scotland and 80 in the Republic of Ireland. For an excellent review of the issues faced by prisons over this period see McEvoy (2001).

3 Northern Ireland, despite the conflict, has had and continues to have a relatively low 'ordinary' crime rate. Looking at the levels of police recorded crime (non-terrorist related), it has typically had a crime rate of about half that found in England and Wales. In the decade 1992–2002, for example, the recorded crime rate in Northern Ireland averaged about 4,000 per 100,000 population compared with about 8,000 per 100,000 in England and Wales. The notable exception to this is the higher rates of some serious offences in Northern Ireland, such as murder and rape. While recently there has been a narrowing of the gap between the two jurisdictions, it appears that much of this has been caused by new Home Office counting rules, which have had much more of an impact in Northern Ireland than in England and Wales (Northern Ireland Research and Statistics Agency 2003).

   Victimisation surveys also confirm this generally low crime rate and in the International Crime Victimisation Survey (Kury 2003), Northern Ireland had the lowest victimisation rate of any of the participating countries. Only 15 per cent of those questioned in Northern Ireland had been a victim of crime in the previous year, compared with an average of 21 per cent and 27 per cent found in England and Wales.

4 The result was the development and publication of a clear management statement in April 1999 (Probation Board for Northern Ireland 1999).

5 Recent available statistics for probation supervision in Northern Ireland show that between 1987 and 1997 the numbers of those who have commenced criminal supervision (probation and community service) have remained relatively stable, fluctuating between 1,500 and 2,000 individuals (Commentary on Northern Ireland Crime Statistics 2003). Voluntary supervision on release from prison is also provided by the Probation Service. Until relatively recently there was no parole system or statutory after-care – unlike in England and Wales. In 1996 licences for sex offenders and custody probation orders were introduced. Custody probation orders combine a period in custody followed by a period under probation supervision in the community. Recently, there has been a slight decline in new probation orders being made by the courts and the total caseload in 2002 was 3,033 individuals (Commentary on Northern Ireland Crime Statistics 2003).

In 2002, 70 per cent of the probation caseload was made up of probation orders, community service orders and combination orders, 19 per cent were custody probation orders and 1 per cent were juvenile justice orders. The remaining 10 per cent were made up of sex offender, life sentence or Great Britain transfer licences.

Between 1998 and 2002 there has been a slight but steady decline in the number of probation orders made by the courts. However, there has been an increase in the number of custody probation orders over the same period (NIO 2003).

In terms of the workload of those on probation supervision, the most marked difference in the past 20 years has been the changing profile of offenders. Whereas most of those placed on probation 20 years ago were petty or first-time offenders, this has moved to a much greater concentration on higher-risk offenders where probation has been given as an alternative to custody, or on post-custody supervision. At present about half of those in custody are under probation supervision, serving custody probation orders.

6 Devolved government, or the elected Assembly, was suspended in October 2002 and at present Northern Ireland is governed by ministers appointed by the government at Westminster.

Further reading

For a good general review of probation arrangements in Northern Ireland, see Blair (2000) *Prisons and Probation: Research Report 6, Review of the Criminal Justice System in Northern Ireland*. Chapman also gives a review of key probation issues, particularly from a social work perspective, in *The Same but Different: Probation Practice in Northern Ireland in Social Work and Social Change in Northern Ireland* (1998). Otherwise for general information about the probation Board for Northern Ireland and its current operation see their website: http://www.pbni.org.uk/

For information about the juvenile justice system in Northern Ireland see O'Mahony and Deazley (2002) *Juvenile Crime and Justice: Research Report 17, Review of the Criminal Justice System in Northern Ireland*, and for more recent information, especially regarding the introduction of youth conferencing arrangements see O'Mahony and Campbell (2006) 'Mainstreaming restorative justice for young offenders through youth conferencing'. Issues of restorative justice and community justice are dealt with in O'Mahony and Doak (2006) 'The enigma of "community" and the exigency of engagement: restorative youth conferencing in Northern Ireland'.

The Northern Ireland Office publishes most of the statistical information on the operation of the criminal justice system, which can be viewed from their website at: http://www.nio.gov.uk/. There are also useful publications which review this statistical information such as the Northern Ireland Office's *Digest of Information on the Northern Ireland Criminal Justice System 4* (2004b) or the *Commentary on Northern Ireland Crime Statistics* (NIO 2003).

For more general information about Northern Ireland and its political context see Whyte (1991) *Interpreting Northern Ireland* or Ruane and Todd (1996) *The Dynamics of Conflict in Northern Ireland: Power, Conflict and Emancipation*.

For an excellent review of the issues relating to imprisonment in Northern Ireland over the period of the conflict see McEvoy (2001) *Paramilitary Imprisonment in Northern Ireland: Resistance, Management and Release*.

References

Blair, C. (2000) *Prisons and Probation: Research Report 6, Review of the Criminal Justice System in Northern Ireland*. Belfast: Stationery Office.

Chapman, T. (1983) 'The Black Report and probation practice', in B. Caul, J. Pinkerton and F. Powell (eds), *The Juvenile Justice System in Northern Ireland*. Belfast: Ulster Polytechnic.

Chapman, T. (1995) 'Creating a culture of change: a case study of a car crime project in Belfast', in J. Maguire (ed.), *What Works: Reducing Re-Offending*. Chichester: Wiley.

Chapman, T. (1997) 'The Criminal Justice (Children) (Northern Ireland) Order: a long time coming – was it worth the wait?', *Child Care in Practice*, 4 (2): 130–7.

Chapman, T. (1998) *The Same but Different: Probation Practice in Northern Ireland in Social Work and Social Change in Northern Ireland*. London: CCETSW (NI).

Chapman, T. and Doran, P. (1998) *Working with High Risk Offenders in Challenge and Change: Celebrating Good Practice in Social Work in Northern Ireland*. London: CCETSW (NI).

Chapman, T. and Hough, M. (1998) *Evidence Based Practice: A Guide to Effective Practice*. London: HM Inspectorate of Probation.

Chapman, T. and Pinkerton, J. (1987) 'Contradictions in community', *Probation Journal*, 34 (1): 13–16.

Children and Young Persons Review Group (1977) *Legislation and Services for Children and Young Persons in Northern Ireland: A Consultative Document for the Children and Young Persons Review Group*. Belfast: HMSO.

Community Safety Unit (2003) *Creating a Safer Northern Ireland Through Partnership: A Strategy Document*. Belfast: Community Safety Unit.

Crawford, C. (2003) *Inside the UDA: Volunteers and Violence*. London: Pluto Press.

Criminal Justice Review (2003) *Criminal Justice Review Implementation Plan*. Belfast: Stationery Office.

Criminal Justice Review Group (2000) *Review of the Criminal Justice System in Northern Ireland*. Belfast: HMSO.

Feenan, D. (2002) 'Researching paramilitary violence in Northern Ireland', *International Journal of Social Research Methodology*, 5 (2): 147–63.

Gadd, B. (1996) 'Probation in Northern Ireland', in G. McIvor (ed.), *Working with Offenders*. London: Jessica Kingsley.

Griffiths, W. A. (1982) 'Supervision in the community', *Justice of the Peace*, 21 August, pp. 514–15.

Kury, H. (ed.) (2003) 'International comparison of crime and victimization: the ICVS', *International Journal of Comparative Criminology*, 2 (1).

Light, R., Nee, C. and Ingham, H. (1993) *Car Theft: The Offender's Perspective*, Home Office Research Study. London: HMSO.

Lynn Committee (1938) *The Protection and Welfare of the Young and the Treatment of Young Offenders*. Belfast: HMSO.

McEvoy, K. (2001) *Paramilitary Imprisonment in Northern Ireland: Resistance, Management and Release*. Oxford: Oxford University Press.

McEvoy, K., O'Mahony, D., Horner, C. and Lyner, O. (1999) 'The home front: the families of politically motivated prisoners in Northern Ireland', *British Journal of Criminology*, 39: 175–97.

McGarry, J. and O'Leary, B. (eds) (1995) *Explaining Northern Ireland, Broken Images*. Oxford: Blackwell.

Northern Ireland Office (2003) *Commentary on Northern Ireland Crime Statistics*. Belfast: Northern Ireland Office, Statistics and Research Branch.

Northern Ireland Office (2004a) *The Northern Ireland Prison Population in 2003*, Research and Statistical Bulletin 2/2004. Belfast: Northern Ireland Office

Northern Ireland Office (2004b) *Digest of Information on the Northern Ireland Criminal Justice System 4*. Belfast: Northern Ireland Office, Statistics and Research Branch.

O'Mahony, D. and Campbell, C. (2006) 'Mainstreaming restorative justice for young offenders through youth conferencing', in J. Junger-tas and S. Decker (eds), *International Handbook of Youth Justice*. Amsterdam: Springer Academic Press.

O'Mahony, D. and Deazley, R. (2002) *Juvenile Crime and Justice: Research Report 17, Review of the Criminal Justice System in Northern Ireland*. Belfast: Stationery Office.

O'Mahony, D. and Doak, J. (2006) 'The enigma of "community" and the exigency of engagement: restorative youth conferencing in Northern Ireland', *British Journal of Community Justice*, 4: 9–25.

O'Mahony, D., Chapman, T. and Doak, J. (2002) *Restorative Cautioning: A Study of Police Based Restorative Cautioning Pilots in Northern Ireland*, Research and Statistical Series No. 4. Belfast: Northern Ireland Office.

Pinkerton, J. (1998) *Social Work and the Troubles: New Opportunities for Engagement in Social Work and Social Change in Northern Ireland*. London: CCETSW (NI).

Probation Board for Northern Ireland (1999) *Probation Board for Northern Ireland Management Statement*. Belfast: Northern Ireland Office.

Protection and Welfare of the Young and the Treatment of the Young Offender, The (1948) Belfast: HMSO.

Report of the Children and Young Persons Review Group (The Black Report) (1979) Belfast: HMSO.

Review of the Criminal Justice System in Northern Ireland (2002) London: Stationery Office.

Report of the Departmental Committee on the Social Services in Courts of Summary Jurisdiction, Cmnd. 5122 (1936) London: Home Office.

Report on the Administration of Home Office Services (NI) (1936) Belfast: HMSO.

Ruane, J. and Todd, J. (1996) *The Dynamics of Conflict in Northern Ireland: Power, Conflict and Emancipation*. Cambridge: Cambridge University Press.

Social Services Inspectorate (1993) *An Abuse of Trust*. Belfast: DHSS.

Underdown, A. (1998) *Strategies for Effective Offender Supervision*. London: HM Inspectorate of Probation.

Walmsley, R. (2003) *World Prison Population List*, Home Office Findings 188. London: Home Office.

Whyte, J. (1991) *Interpreting Northern Ireland*. Oxford: Oxford University Press.

Part 2

Probation services: impact, prospects and potential in everyday practice

In this part of the book the contributors focus on probation practice in everyday life and particularly the challenges that probation staff face in addressing the new demands created by the politicisation of criminal justice. The chapters describe past practice, but more particularly the changes over the past few years and the prospects for an effective role in relation to offenders, their needs, and the creation of 'justice' in terms of sentencing.

In Chapter 7 Kevin Haines and Rod Morgan carefully discuss two areas of the court-related (as opposed to supervisory) work of the Service: court reports and then bail information and support. Probation court reports have their origins in the 1930s as 'home circumstances reports' and have undergone several transformations since. Their current use revolves around the task of helping the sentencer decide whether a custodial sentence or a community sentence is warranted, but there are controversies about the great number of reports which are prepared, about the expense, about the absence of reports in relation to black and minority ethnic group offenders, possible gender biases, and about the ways in which value judgements are subtly presented as 'professional assessments', all of which the authors touch on.

The Probation Service's pre-trial agenda (bail information for example) has perhaps been dominated by an overall lack of commitment from Government and concomitant geographical variation in the delivery of such services. This is surprising given that the Prison Service is overburdened and that pre-trial information might usefully be deployed to establish offenders' community ties so as to avoid imprisonment. By contrast, the idea of quicker and slimmer 'reports for the court' has increasingly received attention, but as the authors suggest, whether the two issues can be married so as to control better the remand population remains to be seen.

What do probation staff actually do? In Chapter 8 Ros Burnett, Kerry Baker and Colin Roberts provide an effective outline of the supervision, assessment and intervention tasks as of old and as they appear at the dawn of the NOMS. Under the auspices of NOMS, the authors suggest that many of the traditional probation functions will change and that those pursuits will become narrower in concept and delivery. But at the same time, they identify a number of new tasks and challenges for those working with offenders. In particular, the authors suggest that an offence-based approach should not exclude a person-orientation in assessment and planning. In other words, there is scope still for probation tasks to be 'humanising' within the world of criminal justice.

Who gets probation? George Mair and Rob Canton address this question in Chapter 9 by describing sentencing patterns as well as changes to the law which signify a changing clientele and purpose. They also discuss the different ways in which community penalties (especially those concerning probation) are used as sentences, the trends in use and the topical issues of compliance and enforcement. The history of the development of community penalties is paved with unintended consequences. Mair and Canton thus speculate on the implications of the new community order created by the 2003 Criminal Justice Act. Probation is no longer to be the monopoly provider of community penalties and this brave (or foolish) new world may bring a fresh crisis of confidence.

Over the years probation officers have become less involved with young offenders than they once were, particularly since the inception of youth justice reforms heralded by the 1998 Crime and Disorder Act. Yet probation officers do continue to make a contribution (both financially and with personnel) to the newly created multi-agency youth offending teams (YOTs). Rod Morgan and Tim Newburn turn to both the nature and adequacy of the contribution, not least because of the increasing recognition that some young offenders will persist in their offending and go on to be assessed and supervised by probation staff, among others, working within the newly created NOMS. The authors pose some challenging questions as to ways in which probation staff can contribute to the threefold task of ensuring care, consistency and continuity in the transition of young people to adulthood.

Young offenders are traditionally seen as a special group of offenders with distinctive needs. But over the years there has been increasing attention to the distinctive needs of women (and men to some extent) too. In Chapter 11 Loraine Gelsthorpe and Gill McIvor explore the extent to which diversity and difference has been recognised in rhetoric and reality. There have been many observations of differential treatment of course, but some of this has been based on myths, muddles and misconceptions as to what might be appropriate. Thus the authors also examine the extent to which differentiation on grounds of race/ethnicity or gender, for example, can really be justified. Their critical theme is one of 'legitimate differentiation' and ways in which probation might aim to do justice to difference without blurring equality of treatment with the 'same' treatment.

In Chapter 12 Stephen Farrall, Rob Mawby and Anne Worrall turn our attention to another distinctive group of offenders: those who persist in offending and who are perhaps the most challenging to a sentencing system designed to deter and rehabilitate or protect the public. Their chapter places policy and practice within the probation field firmly within the theoretical framework of recent literature on desistance. This is important because there is no point in looking at intensive surveillance or supervision or other mechanisms of crime reduction without drawing on what is known about desistance from research in this area. Explorations in this direction thus lead the authors to suggest that the relationship between 'primary desistance' (any lull or gap in the pattern of offending) and 'secondary desistance' (the assumption of a role or identity as a non-offender') is of the essence. It is arguable that secondary desistance will only happen when personal, social and economic factors are favourable – all of which raises questions about the precise role that probation interventions (or related agency interventions) can play in encouraging or facilitating enduring desistance.

Chapter 13 also revolves around a special group of offenders. Here, Hazel Kemshall and Jason Wood explore the public protection aim of the National Probation Service in relation to the management of high-risk offenders. The authors examine key legislative, policy and practice responses to these offenders, and critically discuss how the NPS is responding to the challenges. Importantly, the authors compare and contrast two models of risk management. While the Government has opted for a 'community protection' model, there are lessons to be learned from the alternative 'public health' model. Potentially, there may be real gains in broadening risk management beyond the coercive strategies relating to community protection, to include 'integrative' approaches so that high-risk offenders are less isolated and excluded and more people know how to identify 'warning signals' for risky behaviour.

In Chapter 14 Mike Maguire describes the long tradition of probation work with offenders released from prison. He charts the changes in this work over the years, the changes in focus and language, and then the demise of voluntary after-care for offenders released from prison in the early 1990s. But he also records and discusses the revival of the resettlement agenda and associated theories, aims and models underpinning the different approaches to resettlement practice. Building on the common 'zig-zag' movement that offenders make towards change identified in the previous chapter, Maguire outlines some of the central tenets of desistance and critically discusses not only recent research findings on the effectiveness of policies and practices, but the prospects for effectiveness as the concept of resettlement is remoulded within the 2003 Criminal Justice Act and within the NOMs. While the picture for resettlement was very bleak a decade or so ago when the problems of those leaving prison were virtually ignored, serious thought is now being given to sustainable solutions.

Chapter 7

Services before trial and sentence: achievement, decline and potential

Kevin Haines and Rod Morgan

Introduction

The Probation Service in England and Wales grew out of the oral representation, initially by volunteers, of defendants at court. Court-related services, as opposed to the supervision of penal sanctions, continues to be a core ingredient of probation work. In this chapter we aim to describe and critically assess two areas of the work of the Service before trial and sentence. Following historical and context-setting sections we consider, first, the preparation of reports on defendants for sentencers better to enable them to sentence appropriately. Secondly, we consider the bail information and support work undertaken by the Service to assist the court make appropriate bail or remand decisions pre-trial or sentence. In the concluding section we review future prospects and the place that both these areas of work are likely to have, or might have, in the future.

Probation: origins and philosophical setting

The Probation Service has formally existed in England and Wales for almost a century and, depending on the historical account, individuals have engaged in aspects of the work eventually incorporated into the state service for a good deal longer (see Raynor and Vanstone 2002: chapter 2; Nellis, this volume). The early history of these efforts has been subject to close attention by penal theorists seeking to analyse the social origins of the work, the motivations of the pioneers and the factors informing their cooption by the criminal justice system (see, for example, Rothman 1980; Garland 1985). The philanthropic efforts of the early police court missionaries were driven by the desire to 'rescue' or 'save' individual offenders from what were held to be their morally depraved circumstances. The representation by volunteers of 'deserving' offenders in court aimed to avoid, initially through substitution by recognisances or fines or, in the case of juveniles, charity-run industrial or reform schools, sentences of imprisonment. This voluntary, conscience-inspired work was eventually moulded by Home Office civil servants into the developing, administrative, penal complex of what Garland has termed 'individualisation', whereby offenders became subjects of assessment, classification and reformative processes. In the twentieth century a hierarchy of sentences was gradually developed and it became the role of probation officers to apply diagnostic and curative expertise to enable the court to settle on what was deemed the appropriate sentence, *just* according to the culpability of the offender and the seriousness of the offence, and *effective* in terms of realising the reformative potential of the offender.

Given that court reports and bail-related interventions are strategically so important for remand and sentencing policy, they have been subject to remarkably little research or managerial attention. There have been bursts of research, on court reports in the 1980s and on bail interventions a few years later, but little or no work has been conducted more recently. Why, relatively speaking, so little attention? The reason, arguably, involves sensitive issues or even taboos. Who is qualified to do what probation work and can defendants, prior to an admission of guilt, be engaged with?

The Probation Service has had a long-standing reluctance, almost an injunction against, being involved with defendants prior to a finding of guilt. This has impeded the development of bail-related work. It is today normal practice for pre-sentence reports (PSRs) to be prepared following conviction and for adjournments to be given for the purpose (this was less the case in the past because the higher courts then sat only intermittently and adjournments prior to sentence were often not practicable). But the Service's general resistance to pre-trial work goes beyond these operational considerations and prompts questions regarding what the Probation Service is for and who determines that issue.

There is today less dispute about the answers to these questions. There was a time when it was cogently argued that probation officers largely determined the role of probation, individually and collectively through their practices (McWilliams 1983, 1985, 1986). Such a claim is no longer tenable. The management of probation has long been a controversial and contested matter. Some have argued that throughout its history the senior management of the Service failed to provide strong professional or organisational leadership in shaping the role or purpose of the Probation Service: that they were either indifferent to, or distracted from, managing core activities (Beaumont 1995; Hankinson and Stephens 1986; McWilliams 1992; Vanstone 1995). At no time in its history was such a strong lead needed than in the 1980s when there was some attempt by Home Office civil servants to coordinate the direction of the Service and get it to move centre stage in community-based networks for working with offenders (Faulkner 1989; McWilliams 1987). The Service's response was weak and during the remainder of the 1980s and 1990s local probation services were subjected to increasing Home Office scrutiny and control (Humphrey 1991). With the formation of the National Probation Service (NPS) in 2001, and to an even greater extent the development of NOMS in 2004–5, the Service has been drawn into the ambit of Home Office and general government managerialism (Peters 1986) and control.

Scope for professional taboos – like not undertaking pre-trial work – is, as a consequence, radically reducing. How these developments are to be regarded depends on one's view of government policy, which arguably transmits mixed messages as far probation work is concerned. These mixed messages relate to where the Probation Service should lie on what we may term the penal–social welfare continuum. If placed at the penal end, probation is unequivocally part of the punitive apparatus of the state. It exists to assess risk of reoffending and harm, to punish and control offenders through tough and demanding community sentences which impose strict restrictions, resolutely enforced, on offenders' movement and behaviour and emphasises engagement in offending behaviour programmes. The role of the Service is to enforce the conditions of community sentences as structured by Government and imposed by the courts. Toughening the language of probation reflects this approach (Morgan 2003a). In this model probation is seen as an extension of physical imprisonment, transferring restrictions on liberty from institution to the community, most recently exemplified in the construct 'end-to-end offender management' which lies at the heart of the NOMS project, unifying prison and probation practically and symbolically.

In the social welfare model of probation the Service remains a criminal justice agency, but is an organisation which works through relationships with individuals (as opposed to managing sentences) largely in the community. In order to carry out this function the Service has important work to do in the criminal justice system (for example, maintaining a presence in court and undertaking targeted report writing) but the majority of its work is achieved through a wide range of community networks designed to meet offenders' welfare needs. There is a long history to this strand of probation work (Smith *et al.* 1993) but in more recent times it is exemplified by exhortations for probation to form an active part of local inter-agency strategies (Brittan 1984) and the partnership approach (Audit Commission 1989; Home Office 1990, 1992a). For probation to realise a welfare, community-based approach and attract resources, it must become an active partner within community networks. A current example is the 'Supporting People' programme which in 2003 drew together nine different funding streams, including Transitional Housing Benefit. The government allocated to the programme £1.801 bn in 2004/5 to fund housing-related support services for over one million vulnerable people, including victims of domestic violence, older people and those with mental health problems. The programme now funds an estimated 250,000 units of housing-related support, compared to fewer than 100,000 in 2000 (ODPM 2003). It follows that any probation area seeking housing provision for those with whom it works must be actively engaged with those persons in the local authority responsible for administering the 'Supporting People' strategy in their area.

The penal and welfare-oriented models of probation are of course not stark alternatives. Probation work necessarily involves elements of both. Our starting point, however, is that the penal model has in recent years been in the ascendant and is currently dominant, politically, symbolically and culturally within the service itself. Yet our assumption is also that if the Probation Service is to function efficiently and effectively to reduce offending and protect the public it must successfully operate as one community-based organisation among a network of community-based service providing organisations. Probation has hitherto struggled in this regard (Fullwood 1989) and a recent appraisal from the Probation Inspectorate has highlighted the fact that the community welfare approach has been given lower priority than the penal (HMIP 2002).

The tensions concerning the place of probation work on the penal–social welfare continuum are clearly evidenced in Probation Circular 65/2005 *National Standards (2005) and National Offender Management Model: Application of Tiering Framework* (NPS 2005c) which sets out a managerialist framework for probation work ranging from punish – help – change – control. The framework is complex as will be its implementation. There is a need to assess the impact of government priorities for the Service, not least in relation to those which attract core funding. As we will show, government 'messages' about the role of the Probation Service, Home Office managerialism and the allocation of resources have acute implications for the work of the service in writing reports for courts and pre-trial services.

The origins of reports for courts

The individualisation of sentencing involves information about defendants being provided to the court and the provision of this information is a defining characteristic of past and present probation practice. In England and Wales in the early 1900s, probation officers became the servants of the court and the advice that they gave to the courts was gradually routinised in the form of written reports. These formal written reports were first used systematically from the 1930s onwards in the juvenile court (where they were called 'home circumstances reports') and subsequently in the adult courts, particularly the higher courts where the seriousness of the cases dealt with made the more severe sanctions of supervision in the community and imprisonment likely. These pre-trial reports, initially termed social enquiry reports (SERs) and now pre-sentence reports (PSRs), were subjected to a major review in 1960–1 when the Streatfeild Committee on the *Business of the Criminal Courts* was charged to consider existing arrangements.

The climate of opinion within which Streatfeild worked was one of confidence that decision-making could increasingly be informed by scientific knowledge as to 'what works', though that phrase, now current, was not then employed. Great emphasis was placed on the promise of research and prediction. Streatfeild anticipated that 'research studies will advance to the point ... [that we shall] discover to what extent the chances of an offender not being re-convicted depend on the form of the sentence imposed, and then to indicate, in respect of individual offenders, whether one form of sentence which the court has in mind is likely to have a different effect from another' (Streatfeild 1961: para. 278). Streatfeild declared that 'our cardinal principle throughout is that sentences should be based on reliable, comprehensive information relevant to what the court is seeking to do' (*ibid.*: para. 336). The purpose of court reports was defined as follows:

to provide information about the offender and his background which will help the court in determining the most suitable method of dealing with him. Originally, the information was used primarily where the court was considering putting the offender on probation, but it has also been found helpful where the court is considering whether any other form of sentence might divert the offender from crime. In addition, the information has been found relevant to the court's assessment of culpability ... the courts now give increasing weight to the social and domestic background of the offender. (*ibid*.: para. 333)

Streatfeild also endorsed a practice already encouraged in some courts, that probation officers conclude their SERs with an opinion about the likely response of offenders to probation or another sentence. This practice the Committee said 'should be regarded as an integral part of the probation officer's function' (*ibid*.: para. 339), stressing that such opinions should be grounded on substantial experience and have regard to the results of research. This experience and knowledge should be the object of both probation officers' training and supervision (*ibid*.: para. 342).

Though Streatfeild made recommendations regarding the circumstances in which SERs *should* be prepared, there were few circumstances in which the law *required* that an SER be prepared. It was not unknown in the early 1970s for an offender who had never spoken to a probation officer to find himself on probation (Ford 1972: 8). Practice made that circumstance increasingly rare, however. A succession of Home Office circulars endorsed Streatfeild's recommendations and added to the categories of cases in which an SER was expected. By the 1970s reports were being prepared 'in almost all juvenile court cases, in the vast majority of higher court cases, and in a significant and growing minority of magistrates' court cases' (*ibid*.: 9). Further, though Streatfeild recommended that reports conclude with an 'opinion' regarding only one issue in the court's mind, namely how the offender might respond to a particular sentence in terms of the likelihood of reoffending – a recommendation which a Department Committee on the Probation Service pronounced unfeasible on the grounds that probation officers were not equipped by either experience or research to make such judgements (Morison Report 1962: para. 41) – this nicety was largely lost on practitioners. It became general practice for officers to conclude their SERs with general sentence recommendations or, to use the term now preferred, 'proposals'.

The number of court reports hugely increased and by the early 1980s some 200,000 were being prepared annually. The number of PSRs prepared for the courts has continued to rise, to such an extent that several probation areas found difficulty in meeting the targets set down by the NPD of 15 days for their preparation (NPD 2001: 32). Procedures were streamlined. Home visits, which in the early days was regarded as an important aspect of data gathering, were now seldom undertaken, reliance being placed on the risk assessment tool, OASys, introduced at the turn of the millennium. Templates for report writers were introduced, and later eOASys. But the evidence suggests that the principal device introduced to improve performance – specific sentence reports (SSRs), designed to address, briefly, the suitability of a particular sentence announced by the court and prepared quickly, generally on the same day – served to add to, rather than displace, the number of PSRs written (Home Office 2004a: table 1.2; NPS 2005a: para. 2.4).

This issue is vital. The confidence of sentencers in the Probation Service rests crucially on the good quality and timely provision of court reports. As far as the courts are concerned, this is the most regular, visible service that probation officers provide. Moreover, it was the London area, the largest and most visible part of the NPS, accounting for 23 per cent of the national caseload, that reportedly performed worst. The problem was summed up by the Chief Inspector. He reported that in correspondence the Lord Chief Justice had quoted a fellow judge as saying: 'If the Probation Service cannot deliver the court reports requested of it, how can the judiciary have confidence that it can adequately supervise offenders?' (HMIP 2003: para. 8). The following year the Inspectorate reported that the problem persisted. The Chief Inspector considered that more radical thinking was needed. Were all the reports being requested necessary? Did every case assessment have, in the first instance, to be grounded on full use of the service's new risk assessment tool, OASys (HMIP 2004a: para. 12)? This was the background against which, following the Carter Report (2003), the embryonic NOMS grasped the nettle of court report overload and developed the current approach to court reports which we describe below.

In the early 1960s the Streatfeild Report put at the heart of court report work the qualified probation officer well versed in criminological research and the experienced probation officer familiar with patterns of offender behaviour. Qualified probation officers today comprise only 47 per cent of probation staff and preparing court reports generally remains their preserve. Is this a shibboleth which should be questioned? Does the development of algorithmic risk assessment tools mean that court report work could reasonably be undertaken by many experienced probation staff with a modicum of training? As Bailey *et al.* (this volume) show, in practice and for what seem to be largely workload-related issues, many Probation Service officers are now engaged in the preparation of court reports (as well, increasingly, as other aspects of probation practice), although what may be termed 'principled objections' remain.

Court reports: current thinking

Current thinking about court report work within the Probation Service is heavily influenced by the following data and trends:

- The number of court reports requested and delivered has risen significantly faster than has the number of cases dealt with by the courts. In 2003, 244,492 reports were prepared, slightly fewer than in 2002, but 18 per cent higher than in 1993 (Home Office 2004a: para. 2.1 and table 1.2). By contrast the number of cases, indictable and summary, heard in the courts was 2,014,200 in 2003, an increase of only 3 per cent on the number in 1993 (Home Office 2004b: table 3A).

- Some probation areas have in recent years been unable to meet National Standards in delivering this increased workload with the consequence that cases have been delayed, the courts have expressed dissatisfaction and confidence in the service has to some extent diminished. Further, efforts hitherto to stem this rising demand for reports, or to simplify and thus make less burdensome the form that some court reports take, have not been notably successful (see discussion of SSRs above).

- The upward trend in the proportion of cases for which reports have been prepared has accompanied a downward trend in the proportion of cases fined and upward trends in the proportions of cases dealt with by means of community sentences, more intensive community sentences and custodial sentences (Hough *et al.* 2004). These concomitant trends have been in line with the sentencing proposals made in court reports, which rarely propose fines or discharges. The consequence is that probation caseloads have progressively silted up with offenders whose offences and offending careers are of relatively low seriousness (Carter 2003; Morgan 2003b).

The latter trends are clear, but simply stating them leaves many questions unanswered regarding the *directions* of influence. There is, however, further evidence on the connection. In 1989 the Audit Commission compared sentencing across local probation services in which the proportionate demand for court reports differed significantly. The findings were that the proportionate take up of court reports made no difference to the proportionate use of custody but the greater the take-up of reports the greater the proportionate use of community sentences and the lower the proportionate use of fines and discharges. That is, probation officers tend to propose greater use of their own services, and their proposals tend to be acceded to (Audit Commission 1989: para.s 70–80; see also Thorpe 1979 and Roberts and Roberts 1982).

Two questions arise from these concurrent trends. To what extend is there concordance between probation report proposals and subsequent sentencing decisions? And, to the extent that there is concordance, what does it signify?

Assessing concordance between report proposals and sentencing decisions is by no means straightforward because of the complexity of current sentences and because reports do not always contain sentencing proposals (the most recent official estimate is that 21 per cent of reports do not – Home Office 2002). Community sentences, for example, vary greatly in duration and the number of conditions which may be incorporated. Moreover, though only a small proportion of reports explicitly propose custodial sentences, a fair proportion of reports containing no proposal implicitly assume, indeed accept, that a custodial sentence will inevitably be the outcome (see Stanley and Murphy 1984). Nevertheless, most studies that have explored the phenomenon have concluded that there is broad concordance in about three- to four-fifths of cases in which court reports have been presented.

As to what concordance signifies, and whether high or low rates are desirable, there are several possibilities. As Carter and Wilkins (1967) early pointed out there may be at least four explanations at work. First, sentencers may agree with probation officers because of their high regard for their experience or expertise. Secondly, there will be some cases in which the appropriate sentence is regarded by everyone as 'obvious'. Thirdly, probation officers may anticipate, or second-guess, the sentence they believe the court will in any case impose. And, fourthly, both probation officers and sentencers may entirely agree about the factors which *should* determine sentence.

Two studies have attempted to assess the degree to which these four possibilities apply. In one (Mott 1977) magistrates were given basic facts about the offence and offender and asked to arrive at a provisional sentencing decision before being presented with a court report. In 10 per cent of the cases there was no agreement at either stage, in two-thirds of the cases the magistrates agreed with the probation officers without a report being seen and in a quarter of cases the magistrates changed their views in line with the reports' recommendations after they had been seen. This suggested that probation reports *can* be influential in changing sentencers' views, but that this is so in probably only a quarter of cases. Hine *et al.* (1978) also considered the relationship, albeit by means of a sentencing exercise rather than actual cases. The method here was to provide sentencers with information about a number of cases in three experimental situations, first on the basis of basic information including police antecedents, secondly with the addition of the social information contained in a court report and, thirdly, with the addition of a court report recommendation. The finding here was that in a small proportion of cases the addition of the report recommendation did make a difference and that it could be in the direction both towards and away from custody.

What neither of these studies reveals, however, is the degree to which, through a process akin to apprenticeship, both probation officers and sentencers (particularly magistrates) socialise each other through doing the job, that is adjust their practice to each other over time. The degree to which this happens with probation officers may be dependent on local organisation for producing court reports. In predominantly rural areas the production of court reports is generally not a specialised probation task but is part of all officers' supervision caseloads. In urban and major metropolitan centres by contrast there tend to be specialised court teams whose sole task is the production of PSRs and other court-related tasks. What is clear is that if effective sentencing is the criterion, by which we mean sentencing that results in justice and reduced offending, neither high or low concordance rates are self-evidently desirable. Sentencers' occasional complaints that court report proposals are 'unrealistic' (Burney 1979; Shapland 1981) need to be put in the context of considerable variation in sentencing patterns between courts, the so-called 'court culture' and 'justice by geography' phenomenon (Flood-Page and Mackie 1998: 127–9; Carter 2003; Home Office 2005b: chapter 5). What is also clear, however, is that, over time sentencing has for a variety of reasons drifted towards increased punitiveness and intervention, a process which the provision of more court reports has apparently done little effectively to challenge and may have encouraged (see Stanley and Murphy 1984; Morgan 2003b).

Despite the fact that there is currently the lowest rate of unemployment for many years, sentencers' use of fines in indictable cases has dramatically declined. The Government has accepted the central message of the Carter Report regarding 'sentencing drift' and is committed to resuscitating the use of fines in those cases where community sentences are not warranted. It is entirely consistent with this objective (given that PSR writers seldom recommend fines) that the Sentencing Guidelines Council (SGC) has issued guidance, in relation to the Criminal Justice Act 2003 (CJA), which has heavily underlined the circumstances in which PSRs are unnecessary, or may be unnecessary, and that where the court considers a PSR necessary it should ideally make a *detailed written request* for one, something generally not done hitherto.

A PSR is 'pivotal', the SGC has stated, 'in helping a sentencer decide whether to impose a custodial sentence or ... a community sentence'. Further, if the court has:

> reached the provisional view that a community sentence is the most appropriate disposal, the sentencer should request a pre-sentence report, indicating which of the three sentencing ranges [low, medium or high] is relevant and the purpose(s) of sentencing which the package of requirements is required to fulfill ... the most helpful way to do this would be to produce a written note for the report writer. (SGC 2004: para. 1.1.16)

However, 'there will be occasions when any type of report may be unnecessary despite the intention to pass a community sentence though this is likely to be infrequent. A court could consider dispensing' with a PSR for adults:

- where the offence is within the 'low' range of seriousness;
- where the court is minded to impose a community sentence with a single requirement, such as an exclusion requirement;
- where the sentence will not require the involvement of the Probation Service (e.g. an electronically-monitored curfew (SGC 2004: para. 1.1.17)).

The report writing procedure which, in line with this SGC guidance, became operational in April 2005 (NPS 2005a) is as follows:

- PSRs should only be written when the court makes a *written* request indicating which level of seriousness the offence lies in and which of the purposes set out in the CJA (s. 142(1)) – punishment, deterrence, rehabilitation, public protection and reparation – the court has in mind.

- PSRs *need not be written* (CJA, s. 158(1)(a) removes that requirement) in cases, usually in the 'low' seriousness band, when the court requires limited, or only a specific piece of, information. In these circumstances an *oral report* will suffice.

- Written PSRs take one of two forms, 'fast delivery' or 'standard delivery'. The former replace the 'same-day' or SSR reports introduced in 1999 (Home Office 1999) and should normally be produced on the same day, but should always be completed in less than five days. Standard-delivery PSRs are subject to the established production target of 'within 15 days'.

- Fast-delivery PSRs will usually be undertaken without a full OASys assessment (the really time-consuming element in court report production) but *must*, along with oral reports, be based on an OGRS 'likelihood of reconviction' score, and application of the OASys Risk of Harm screening tool (see Chapters 8 and 13, this volume, for details) and whatever Basic Skills screening tools are approved by the NPD.

- If a fast-delivery PSR is initially judged appropriate, but: the OGRS score is 41 or more; or if the OASys Risk of Harm screening tool suggests that a full risk of harm analysis is required; or if any other factor (for example, a mental health concern) comes to light which suggests that a full OASys assessment would be desirable; then the report writer should either consider requesting, or should request, an adjournment to prepare a standard-delivery PSR.

- Standard-delivery PSRs are based on full OASys assessments, employ an e-OASys template (so that OASys information can be 'pulled through' into a PSR Word document and edited as necessary) and have the sub-headings – 'Sources of information', 'Offence analysis', 'Offender assessment', 'Assessment of risk of harm to the public and likelihood of reoffending' and 'Conclusion' (including a sentence proposal) which have previously been set out in the Probation National Standards and which are now built into the PSR template.

The current advice is notable for stressing that probation officers 'will need to use their professional judgement to gauge which type of report is suitable for each individual case' (NPS 2005a: para. 5.4). For example, there are many 'custodial cases' that are 'straightforward', where sentencers do not require the level of analysis afforded by a standard-delivery PSR and where a fast-delivery report will suffice. In other cases the issue for the court will be simply a question of the sentence of imprisonment length, for which no NPS assistance is necessary. If no report is requested in such cases none should be prepared: an OASys assessment can always be prepared post-sentence.

As for sentencing proposals, the guidance for probation officers is in line with that given to sentencers by the SGC. 'Sentencers should consider all of the disposals available (within or below the threshold passed) ... so that even where the threshold for a community sentence has been passed, a financial penalty or discharge may still be an appropriate penalty' (SGC 2004: para. 1.36). Probation reports must make a sentencing proposal 'consistent with the Court's direction of seriousness range and sentencing purpose'. But this will not necessarily mean that the report writer 'will concur with the Court's provisional view ... there will be cases where it is appropriate to recommend to the Court that a fine or discharge is considered rather than a Community Order, or a Community Order imposed rather than a custodial sentence' (NPS 2005a: para.s 7.2–3). Cases where this would be appropriate are set out – for example, where the assessment uncovers mitigating factors such as mental illness or a low level of maturity, which, when presented to the court, could lead it to conclude that the offender's culpability is less than might have been thought. In particular it is stressed that 'in cases of low likelihood of conviction and low risk of harm, proposals in reports should generally be for fines and conditional discharges' except in those cases where the level of seriousness suggests otherwise (PC 53/2004: 3).

As for the preparation of reports, the guidance is set out in detail in the NPS National Standards. Reports shall be based on 'at least one face-to-face interview [which can be via video link] with the offender' – the assumption that reports will be prepared post-conviction or admission is clear – and the content shall be 'objective, impartial, free from discriminatory language and stereotype, balanced and factually accurate'. Finally, PSRs should 'make clear, in an outline sentence plan, what requirements are envisaged, including outline timescales, and how the [proposed] sentence is likely to be implemented, including any plans for sequencing interventions' (NOMS/NPS 2005: 8).

It remains to be seen what effect the latest guidance and new arrangements will have. It already seems clear, for example, that judges will resist the proposition that they should complete a form requesting a PSR, setting out their assessment of the case and the sentencing purpose/s to be fulfilled. They dislike the suggestion that fellow sentencers might feel bound by such assessments (personal communications). In the absence of written requests the Probation Service will almost inevitably continue to prepare PSRs in cases where, arguably, they are not wanted or needed. It is difficult to predict, therefore, how the arrangements will affect the number of PSRs prepared, the types of cases in which they are and are not prepared, the manner in which requests for reports are met (the proportion of oral, fast-delivery and standard-delivery PSRs), the pattern of proposals made in reports and, above all, sentencing trends.

There will almost certainly be rubbing points. Probation officers will produce oral or fast-delivery PSRs which will not be to the liking of sentencers and will no doubt be chided by some judges and magistrates for the manner in which they have exercised their discretion. There will continue to be complaints about 'unrealistic' proposals. Further, despite the fact that all officers will in future be using e-OASys templates, there will continue to be variation in the quality and content of PSRs, not least because a completed OASys, like any other risk assessment tool, is only as good as the information fed into it and the skill of the person processing the available information. Managers and the Inspectorate of Probation should scrutinise closely the new arrangements which will ideally be the subject of fresh, commissioned research. There are a few lessons from the history of court report research which need to be remembered in this regard.

First, PSRs, or the lack of them, are likely to continue to play some part in the substantial over-representation of minority ethnic groups at the 'deeper' end of the criminal justice and penal system. A number of studies have considered the degree to which, *inter alia*, minority ethnic offenders are: sentenced without benefit of reports; are the subject of reports *not* containing sentencing proposals; are the subject of reports resulting in more punitive sentencing proposals; or whose reports contain prejudicial material (for a general review see Morgan 2006). The research has mostly generated inconsistent conclusions, but two pieces of recent, sophisticated evidence are of concern.

Relating his findings to the over-representation of black offenders within the prison population, Hood's 1992 study *Race and Sentencing* concluded that most of the over-representation was attributable to their greater number appearing for sentence, but 10 per cent was due to legal case factors (the greater seriousness of offences or the number of previous convictions, for example) and 20 per cent to other non-legitimate factors. Court reports figured in the account. Significantly higher proportions of Afro-Caribbeans and Asians than whites had not had a court report prepared and of these, whether or not they pleaded guilty, a significantly higher proportion received a custodial sentence. Court reports for white as opposed to black or Asian defendants were much more likely to propose probation. Some commentators (see Bowling and Phillips 2002: 184) have argued that Hood's analysis provided a conservative estimate of the impact of 'race effects' within the criminal justice system on the grounds that not all the factors he controlled for are race neutral and Hood was unable to assess the impact of cumulative, criminal career considerations. What is clear, however, is that Hood's research provided the Probation Service with unequivocal statistical evidence that the absence, and to some extent the content, of court reports contributed to a process the outcome of which was racially discriminating. This evidence the Inspectorate of Probation subsequently acted on in two thematic reports (HMIP 2000, 2004a).

In 2000 the Inspectorate found, on the basis of reading samples of PSRs, that reports on black, Asian and white defendants differed in a number of respects, some of which may legitimately have been related to differences in the case profiles, not controlled for. Notable, however, was the fact that the inspectors judged PSRs prepared for black defendants to be significantly less likely to be satisfactory in quality than reports on 'other', white and Asian defendants. These 'worrying' findings (HMIP 2000: para. 4.47) went unexplained, neither the reports' authors or their subjects having been interviewed. What the findings suggested, however, is that, for whatever reason, probation officers tend not to engage as well with black as other offenders and this is reflected in the depth and quality of the reports they write about them. Further, the differential persists, albeit to a lesser degree and in the context of a significant overall improvement in the quality of reports prepared (HMIP 2004b).

Secondly, some of the differences relating to race found in reports may apply also to gender. A relatively recent study (Gelsthorpe and Raynor 1995: 194) found that while 'there was no clear evidence of sexist language or assumptions' in the PSRs studied, women were more likely than men to be recommended for probation and less likely to be recommended for community service. Further, women were also more likely to be the subject of reports of a slightly lower quality 'largely because their offending was less adequately covered'. It is unclear why this should be so, but it is a finding which monitoring exercises should bear in mind.

This leads, thirdly, into a long-standing concern about the tendency for reports to present material embedded with *value judgements* as if they *were professional assessments* (Curran and Chambers 1982; Bottoms and McWilliams 1986). To the extent that this remains the case – and the introduction of quality control mechanisms may have changed matters (Raynor *et al.* 1995) – the tendency may be explained by the fact that though National Standards stress the need to be 'objective and impartial', in fact officers may regard PSRs as 'strategic documents involved in "persuasive communication" with the courts' (Curran and Chambers 1982).

Fourthly, even if, as the latest SGC and NPD/NOMS guidance seeks, the number of reports written is reduced and the resuscitation of penalties less intrusive and costly than community penalties achieved, there is nevertheless a danger that the current emphasis on risk assessment and evaluating offenders' motivation to change and the 'actions required to improve motivation' (National Standards 2002) will lead report writers ambitiously to overstate the potency of interventions and propose community sentences incorporating more requirements than the NPS can sustainably deliver or the evidence suggests will be effective. This, historically, has been the tendency of PSR report writers. It is a danger which the Criminal Justice Act 2003, with its 12 possible requirements attaching to a community order (s. 177(1)), plus electronic monitoring, places centre stage.

Pre-trial services: background and origins

The Probation Service has a history of practitioner 'bottom-up' initiatives, often leading to developments which have influenced the Service nationally or become enshrined in Home Office policy. So it was with pre-trial services.

Most cases which come before the courts, particularly when they follow arrest and are of moderate or high seriousness, cannot be dealt with on the first occasion. Time is needed to gather prosecution evidence and for the defence to give legal advice before pleas are taken. In the minority of cases in which trials take place evidence has to be assembled and witnesses called. Thus, whether or not the defendant has been held in police custody or granted police bail prior to first court appearance, adjournments are frequently requested and granted, in which circumstance the court must determine what is to happen to the defendant. In English law the court has four main options: to release on unconditional bail, to release on conditional bail, to release on bail subject to a surety or security or to remand in custody.

To remand in custody is by definition a serious and costly decision. Defendants are subject to the presumption of innocence and denial of their liberty at this stage can have consequences as severe as a short custodial sentence. Some defendants remanded in custody subsequently have their cases dropped while others are found not guilty. A significant proportion of those remanded in custody and convicted receive a sentence other than custody – the proportion was 46 per cent of males and 73 per cent of females in 1972 (King and Morgan 1976: 2) and it remains just less than two-fifths today (Home Office 2003: table 5.8). The evidence suggests that in like-for-like cases defendants remanded in custody have a greater likelihood of being sentenced to custody than those granted bail. Precisely why this should be the case is a matter for conjecture. It may be a consequence of both appearances (presentation in court) or the fact that after a spell in custody defendants are less likely to have other things going for them (functioning supportive relationships, accommodation, employment, etc.) which might mitigate the sentence of the court. A clutch of official and unofficial studies in the early 1970s (Bottomley 1970; Davies 1971; King 1971; Simon and Weatheritt 1974) focused on this relationship. This was partly because, at the time, the inherently disadvantageous consequences of a remand in custody were exacerbated by the fact that remand prisoners, despite the presumption of innocence, were subject to prison conditions significantly more oppressive that those for sentenced prisoners (King and Morgan 1976; for a general review see Morgan 1994). Their conditions worsened as prison overcrowding increased with growth of the prison population from the 1950s to the 1980s (see Morgan 1997: 1137).

Courts routinely make bail/remand decisions – often in a relative vacuum of verified information about the defendant. Pre-trial services directly address this decision-making process. Bail information, as its name implies, involves the Service checking the social circumstances of a defendant (usually focusing on address and home circumstances, employment and community ties) and reporting this verified information to the court to promote better and more effective bail/remand decision-making. Bail support comprises an enhanced service that aims to provide a range of services which directly address objections to bail and give the court greater confidence in a non-custodial remand. Bail support services may include the provision of suitable accommodation (sometimes in probation or voluntary-run bail hostels) and a mixture of support and management/surveillance of defendants. Such services may be provided in direct response to a request from the court (in practice this has been mainly limited to a request for a bail hostel place). Or they may be provided proactively as part of a strategy to reduce custodial remands in cases where a modicum of community-based services can directly address objections to bail, support defendants through to trial/sentencing and manage public protection.

Tentative practitioner provision of bail information in the early 1970s led to a larger demonstration project (in 16 areas) supported by the Home Office (Probation Circular 155/75) and facilitated by the Vera Institute of Justice (for a detailed account of the history and chronology of pre-trial services work, see Drakeford et al. 2001; Haines and Octigan 1999). But the idea never really took off in the 1970s. This was partly because, in the short term, the Bail Act 1976 greatly reduced the number of untried and unsentenced receptions into custody. It was also because the Home Office provided no additional funds and the idea of 'pre-trial' services transgressed some professional culture considerations. Defence solicitors considered schemes to intrude on their territory and probation officers were ambivalent about getting involved with defendants prior to conviction: it was not considered appropriate that SERs be prepared at that stage because of the presumption of innocence (Drakeford et al. 2001: 13). As a consequence there was only one bail hostel at the end of the 1970s and little more was heard of the 16 bail information schemes.

The positive effects of the Bail Act 1976 were relatively short-lived, however. The remand population more than doubled between 1978 and 1988 (Cavadino and Gibson 1993) such that the proportion of the prison population comprising remand prisoners rose from 8 to 22 per cent between 1975 and the late 1980s (Ashworth 1994). Home Office interest in developing pre-trial services was reawakened. What became known as the 'hypothecated grant' for pre-trial services was promulgated through the 1991 'cash limits formula' (CPO 23/1991). This initiative provided ring-fenced funds (on application, for years 1992/3/4) for probation services to provide pre-trial services. Further, from 1995 to 1998 the Home Office established national and local coordinators for bail information schemes and launched the Public Interest Case Assessment (Crisp *et al.* 1995) and the Bail Process Projects (Morgan and Henderson 1998).

Most local probation services successfully applied for the hypothecated grant (Haines and Octigan 1999) and pre-trial service provision peaked between 1992 and 1995. Thirty-five of the 54 probation services were providing court-based bail information and 15 were providing bail support services of some kind. Closer examination revealed a less optimistic picture, however. Not all probation services applied for the hypothecated grant and not all those that did reapplied consistently throughout the period of the grant. Pre-trial service provision was never brought into mainstream practice, or even the mainstream practice of dedicated court teams. Stand-alone units, often comprising unqualified probation staff – a relative novelty at that time – were the main providers of pre-trial services. Moreover, at the same time that some probation services were developing pre-trial services others were closing theirs. The overall response of the Probation Service to the hypothecated grant, and the opportunity it presented for the Service to move centre stage in the provision of pre-trial services, was opportunistic and piecemeal. Research evidenced some commitment to pre-trial services by probation staff at all levels of the Service, but there was also a degree of opportunism in seeking funding from the hypothecated grant without any particular evidence of short- or long-term commitment. However, the one factor that appears to have dominated the response of probation to the pre-trial services agenda has been the overall general lack of commitment from Government and the failure to place pre-trial service provision on either a statutory footing or to make it a high priority for the Service (Haines and Octigan 1999).

The effectiveness and decline of pre-trial services

Research on bail information schemes consistently demonstrated positive effects. Warner and McIvor (1994) concluded that the provision of bail information reports diverted between 19 and 29 per cent of defendants from a custodial remand. For homeless defendants the impact was more dramatic, 15 per cent receiving bail where no bail information was provided compared to 72 per cent when it was (Home Office 1992b). The provision of bail information reports was also shown to increase, by 22 per cent, CPS requests for bail (Godson and Mitchell 1991). Prison-based schemes were likewise judged successful. Nottingham and Mitchell (1994), surveying 14 prisons, showed that between 25 and 49 per cent of prisoners received bail where bail information was provided. In a further five prisons these figures rose to between 50 and 74 per cent (see also Williams 1992). Women prisoners also benefited (Beamer 1991; Wilkinson 1990).

The hypothecated grant was nevertheless withdrawn in 1995 and though the funds were drawn into mainstream probation budgets, the provision of pre-trial services fell into decline. This decline has persisted to the present. Bail support services have all but disappeared from practice and bail hostels have closed. Dedicated bail beds in what are now termed 'approved premises' have been largely lost as a result of the NPS priority that serious offenders, often on parole, be accommodated (Burnett and Eaton 2004). Few, if any, probation areas now promote bail beds and many make such places available only on direct request from the court. Further, the provision of bail information reports has fallen from a high of 24,779 in 1997 to just 5,677 in 2003 (NAO 2004). In a relatively short space, bail information services have reduced from being a widespread specialist practice (with dedicated staff working daily in the courts) to a responsive service of court teams whose priority is the production of PSRs.

Why, given the continued upward rise in the prison population at the turn of the millennium, were bail-related services allowed to collapse? Several interacting factors were influential. Pre-trial services were not mainstreamed into probation practice, then, as now, dominated by writing court reports and supervising offenders. Throughout the 1990s probation managers were uncertain about the future of the Service and reluctant to commit themselves to work not considered mainstream. Pre-trial services conflicted with the traditional probation injunction against working with defendants before an admission or finding of guilt. Moreover, following withdrawal of the hypothecated grant probation managers were squeezed financially and directed their limited resources at other, higher priorities. Consideration of the nature and size of the remand population was, from the probation perspective, relegated to the background.

According to *A New Choreography*, the strategy document which launched the NPS in 2001, one of the Service's 'stretch' objectives was 'providing courts with good information and pre-trial services' (NPD 2001: 31–2). However, though the Home Secretary was reportedly giving 'new emphasis' to bail such that it was 'up to the NPS to re-evaluate the totality of its bail provision and produce new strategies with others for greater provision', the NPD *stretched* itself not at all. Bail information and support services further declined.

Pre-trial services: prison or probation?

'A vision for the future of the Probation Service is one in which a fully articulated set of court-focused remand services, firmly located within the public protection and effectiveness agendas, can be mobilised to reduce, wherever possible, unnecessary and inappropriate remands in custody' (Haines and Octigan 1999). This vision has never been fully or even adequately realised and neither the Home Office, its executive departments or the Probation

Service have consistently taken pre-trial services seriously. Although, as we have seen, the Home Office and the Probation Service have over the past 30 years engaged with the pre-trial services agenda, the engagement has been fitful, marginal and unsustained (Drakeford *et al.* 2001). Moreover, despite the growing emphasis on managing the criminal justice system, the remand population and pre-trial services have been surprisingly neglected.

Fluctuations in the remand population in the 1970s and 1980s have been referred to above. During the 1990s to the present the remand population has grown steadily. In October 2005 the prison population reached yet another peak of 78,000, with remand prisoners growing the fastest.

The response of the Prison Service to the increased number of remand and trial committals and, arguably, the lack of court-based bail information schemes has been, *inter alia*, to give priority to prison-based bail information schemes. Prison Service Order No. 6101 'Bail Information Schemes' (September 1999), notes that 'it has, until recently, been Prison Service policy to *encourage* rather than *require* all local prisons and remand centres to have comprehensive bail information schemes in place. Following the provision of funding in the Comprehensive Spending Review, it is now a *mandatory* requirement' (Prison Service 1999, original emphasis).

Noting that staffing is a matter for local resolution and may involve prison or probation staff, the mandatory requirements of these prison-based, second or subsequent appearance, bail information schemes are that:

- they match the National Standards set by the ACOP Bail Practice Committee;
- data are provided on a quarterly basis for monitoring purposes;
- bail information officers receive approved training by attending nationally approved courses at the Prison Service College;
- bail information, in the form of a report, is supplied to the court duty officer;
- information presented to the CPS should always have been verified by at least one other source – which should be noted in the report;
- only defendants who are 17 and over should be interviewed, with their consent;
- interviews focus on issues which maximise the defendant's right to apply for bail;
- managers draw up a clear interview targeting policy and issue it to all relevant staff. The policy should be in line with National Standards for bail practice, having regard to equal opportunities and anti-discriminatory practice.

In answer to the question: 'Why do schemes exist?', PSO 6101 states that:

> The aim is to enable the courts to make better informed bail decisions, with the possibility that the number of defendants held in custody awaiting trial is reduced. It is in the interest of the Prison Service to promote development of bail information schemes as a means of reducing prison population.

Routine monitoring data suggest that schemes are in place in all remand prisons. In a letter to prison governors (August 2005) the Prison Service Director of Operations noted the 'significant population pressure' the prison system is currently experiencing, with a convicted population growth of 2 per cent over the last year and an increase in the remand population of 4 per cent. Among the options open to the Service he stressed the contribution of bail information schemes to 'help prisoners who can be bailed to be so'. He emphasised the need to target:

- those defendants most likely bailable – those, not charged with particularly serious offences, who pose no threat to victims or witnesses, who do not have a poor bail history and have, or can be found, accommodation or can show other evidence of stability and reliability;
- black or minority ethnic defendants – because of the evidence that they are disproportionately remanded in custody;
- prisoners considered particularly vulnerable in custody;
- female defendants, also disproportionately remanded in custody.

The first complete set of annual monitoring data for 2004 (compiled but unpublished, provided by the Prison Service) reveals the data given in Table 7.1.

No further breakdown of the data in Table 7.1 is currently available and there is as yet no evaluation of whether prison-based bail information services are fully realising their potential. The above data provide only the barest indication of the possible success of prison-based bail information schemes. Thus their cost-effectiveness remains untested. We do not know what proportion of these prisoners would likely have been released without the bail information intervention. Nevertheless the data indicate that over 3,000 defendants per year are being released from remand in custody following bail information who might otherwise have spent longer on remand. Further, the fact that these schemes are funded, are comprehensive, have the support of senior management and are guided by targeting criteria means that their effectiveness *could* be measured.

In contrast to these prison-based pre-trial services, community-based services remain in their pre-millennium state of collapse. The current state

Table 7.1 Prison service bail information monitoring data 2004

Total number of remand prisoners eligible for bail	41,090
Total number interviewed	19,680
Number of bail information reports sent to the CPS	9,509
Number of bail information reports sent to the CPS as % of eligible remands	23%
Number of bail information reports sent to the CPS as % of those interviewed	48%
Number released by court following bail information report	3,387
Percentage of bail information reports followed by release	36%
Percentage of eligible remands released	8%

of pre-trial service provision across the Probation Service is desultory. What remains of those bail information services developed under the hypothecated grant of the early 1990s is a responsive service provided by court teams. Proactive bail support services have virtually disappeared. Practically all that remains is a responsive bail hostel placement function.

This lacklustre picture exists despite an avowed Home Office commitment to court-based bail information (though notably not bail support) services, unaccompanied by any support strategy. A 2000 probation circular on 'Bail Information' stated:

> This circular ... explains why it is necessary for services to provide comprehensive court-based bail information in all areas and sets out the minimum requirements they are expected to meet. It also covers compliance with National Standards, the bail information KPI which was introduced in 1999–2000, and advice on establishing closer links with the prison service to ensure that court-based and prison-based schemes operate in a complementary and efficient way. (NPS 2000)

Key features of the circular include:

- a clear requirement that chief officers ensure that comprehensive court-based bail information services are provided, though recognising that this is not a statutory requirement;

- that bail information provision should be part of the role of court teams (and not a separate, specialist or stand-alone service) and that such services should be first appearance schemes (with prison-based schemes providing subsequent appearance bail information);

- a recognition that, in the future, bail information services may form part of a wider remand management system, but that now and in the immediate future bail information services should be provided in accordance with the provisions of PC 29/2000;

- that a bail information service should provide factual and verified information to the CPS to assist in the determination of grounds for requesting courts to grant bail rather than remand in custody;

- a concern to maintain the highest standards of fairness and justice, while reducing delays and dealing with defendants quickly and efficiently and with proper concern to make the best use of limited remand facilities;

- that in order to provide an effective bail information service the probation service requires information from other criminal justice agencies and should ensure arrangements are in place to secure access to this information;

- that bail information services can also provide *insights* into a defendant's character, social/personal circumstances and community ties and that enquiry into these areas is a proper function of bail information – thus reflecting concerns that form part of a community-based vision of the role and function of the Probation Service.

Although it is noted that Probation Services play no part in collecting the required information, emphasis is placed on their meeting the KPI and targets for bail information (KPI 9, promulgated through PC 22/1999), which is defined as:

The proportion of prosecutors who:

(a) consider that bail information actually makes a difference to their recommendation to the court;
(b) consider that bail information reports cover everything needed;
(c) are satisfied that bail information reports are objective, including information on risk where relevant.

The associated targets for the KPI are: (a) 80 per cent, (b) 90 per cent and (c) 90 per cent.

Finally, PC 29/2000 states that the provision of comprehensive court-based bail information is Government policy and enjoys ministerial support.

Despite the clear messages emphasised by PC 29/2000 a subsequent circular, PC 19/2005 'Bail Information Schemes', (NPS 2005b) confirmed the continued national decline in bail information provision. This decline is attributed to two factors: first, the withdrawal of probation resources from non-statutory work and, secondly, the 2002 Probation Priority Framework Guidance, which gave bail information work 'medium priority'. High priority was attached to statutory functions only – reports completed by court teams and the Service's enforcement activities.

Pre-trial services now and in the future

PC 19/2005 nevertheless indicates the importance attached to bail information and places it firmly on the agenda for now and in the future. Indeed, the circular's primary purpose is to inform probation areas of a forthcoming cost-benefit review of bail information schemes to be undertaken by the NPD 'in the coming months' as a result of a recommendation from the National Audit Office (NAO 2004: 12). Chief officers are instructed to prepare for this review by reassessing their local priorities and identifying temporary targeting criteria for bail information work in advance of the review. PC 19/2005 also indicates that a review is taking place of bail places in approved premises and alternative provision.

Work carried out for the Comprehensive Spending Review reports that in cases where bail information is provided, 41 per cent of defendants received a custodial remand compared to 56 per cent where no bail information was available. On this limited basis, estimated net savings of about £9 million per year were posited with a potential to achieve an additional £18 million per year if comprehensive bail information services, with supporting bail hostel places, were made available nationally (see PC 29/2000). Other estimates, based on the introduction nationally of a comprehensive remand management strategy (embracing bail information and bail support), suggest that these savings could be in the order of over £100 million per year (Drakeford *et al.* 2001). Addressing the NAO findings Edward Leigh MP, in a session of the Parliamentary Committee of Public Accounts, stated that:

> The whole bail process needs to be managed much more effectively. It is currently unclear, for each stage of the process, which criminal justice agency is in charge. This 'pass the parcel' attitude is a recipe for confusion. (Press Notice No. 22 of Session 2004–05, dated 16 June 2005)

What confidence or expectations can we have for the future of pre-trial services based on the conditions that pertain now compared to those that existed in the early 1990s? Salient features of the current terrain include:

- clearer Government policy and ministerial support for pre-trial services, both bail information and support and a wider remand strategy;

- relegation of bail information and support services to the non-statutory 'medium priority' level and the absence of any financial commitment to their operation;

- some focused interest in the bail process by Government institutions (such as the NAO as referred to above) but as yet a lack of clear messages about both the policy and financial benefits to be gained from comprehensive bail information;

- as yet no clear, consistent policy message from NOMS, the NPD and the Prison Service about provision of a 'joined up' bail information service with supporting performance targets;

- the provision of comprehensive prison-based bail information services but as yet no firm commitment to undertake evaluations of both prison- and community-based bail information services in order to see whether the positive research outcomes recorded in the early 1990s remain applicable today.

Some of the key elements, necessary for the development of effective pre-trial services are in evidence now that were lacking in the 1970s, 1980s and 1990s – notably an integrated, inter-departmental criminal justice policy planning process and an 'institutional' interest in the bail process. Key characteristics of the contemporary English system include: policy setting, priority frameworks (tied to financial issues), standards and performance indicators, management frameworks and training, etc. However, the structures and processes that these general characteristics embody have yet to be applied systematically to bail/remand decision-making. This is largely true for the one aspect of pre-trial services which has received the most direct attention, namely bail information, and is wholly true for remand management generally. Thus the management (tied inevitably to the priorities set for the Service) of and professional engagement with pre-trial services remain on the fringes of practice.

Conclusion

Why should the Probation Service engage in the provision of services before trial and sentence? Pre-trial services and the provision of PSRs warrant different answers to this question.

The Probation Service currently derives little benefit and bears additional costs from delivering pre-trial services. Such services are non-statutory. They are provided either for the benefit of defendants who would otherwise be remanded in custody, or for the benefit of other criminal justice agencies (the courts, CPS or prisons – and their reduced workloads, delays and/or costs) and the improved operation of the criminal justice system generally, or for all of these. The performance of the Probation Service is neither measured nor rewarded for delivering pre-trial services with the consequence that probation managers cannot afford to give them priority, and do not.

By contrast the preparation of court reports is the Service's statutory duty. It is the primary vehicle through which the Service represents itself to, and gains credibility with, the courts. It is subject to performance targets and measurement. And it is the principal means by which the Service draws offenders into its professional sphere of competence – the supervision of community-based sanctions, whether in their own right or following release from custody. It follows that the delivery of PSRs is very much the high priority focus of probation managers' attentions and, unless pushed, they will not likely challenge the current view that this work should largely remain the function of their most qualified staff.

From the Service's current standpoint, therefore, there are very good reasons for *not* providing pre-trial services and *for* delivering high quality court reports. Without a major initiative from the inter-departmental National Criminal Justice Board (NCJB), the Home Office and NOMS, this state of affairs will not change.

There are good reasons, however, why the Probation Service should be incentivised to undertake pre-trial services on behalf of, and for the better management of, the criminal justice system. Remands of accused persons in custody who could safely be managed in the community involves profligate use of expensive, overburdened, prison resources and does not accord with the twin principles of the presumption of innocence and the minimum use of restrictions on liberty to secure the ends of justice. Further, with the formation of the NCJB and NOMS there are now in place the inter-departmental planning mechanisms to set reducing targets for the proportionate use and duration of remands in custody to the achievement of which the NPS could significantly contribute. To the extent that it is argued that the CPS is better equipped than was the case a decade ago to establish defendants' community ties and, thus, that probation bail information and support services will no longer be cost effective, that is a matter for fresh empirical investigation. All the research evidence currently available supports the proposition that such services were cost-effective in the early to mid 1990s and would likely prove to be so were they resuscitated today.

By contrast, the evidence suggests that the NPS continues, almost certainly counter-productively as far as the more punitive sentencing trend is concerned, to provide PSRs many of which are over-elaborate and unnecessary, and this despite successive attempts in recent years at managing down provision. The introduction of OGRS as opposed to OASys-backed fast-delivery PSRs, and the attempt to encourage greater use of oral reports, represents a significant step forward, not least because the initiative is congruent with advice to sentencers from the newly operational SGC. However, there are already signs that the guidance so far offered by the SGC and the NPD will prove insufficient significantly to turn back the increasing production tide of full PSRs recommending more intrusive community penalties. The present guidance needs the backing of targets and monitoring exercises which can be overseen by middle probation managers. These exercises should have as their focus the production of oral and fast-delivery PSRs at the *expense* of standard-delivery PSRs, an increased proportion of proposals for discharges and fines and close attention to the quality of reports on women and minority ethnic defendants set against clearly articulated and well developed national and local strategic priorities for probation services. Moreover, given the fact that only a minority of NPS staff are now qualified probation officers, it is increasingly difficult to sustain objections as to why many of the non-probation officer but nonetheless well qualified NPS staff (see Bailey *et al.*, this volume) could not undertake much of the work currently done by the dedicated court teams. Given the formal acceptance that PSRs can now take a variety of forms, and need not necessarily be written, resistance to such a move looks more and more like a restrictive practice.

All of this should be done better to align the distribution of scarce probation resources to the supervision of those offenders whose risk of reoffending and of causing significant harm is moderate or high. If the NPS is to remove from its books many of those minor offenders who, frankly, do not warrant its professional services (Morgan 2003b; Carter 2003), then that objective must begin with well-targeted pre-trial information and support services and more parsimonious PSRs both in terms of their production, form and proposals.

Finally, it remains to be seen whether the intended NOMS framework, as announced in *Restructuring Probation to Reduce Re-offending* in October 2005 (Home Office 2005a), is introduced and interpreted. Among the probation services which will be contracted out to probation trusts or voluntary or commercial providers, either nationally or regionally, are both pre-trial services and the preparation of court reports. There would be fundamental objections of principle to contracting out the preparation of court reports to any commercial or even voluntary provider, particularly if they were also the providers of any form of supervision or management of custody, there being fundamental conflicts of interest. Moreover, if the initial assessment of offenders, including the preparation of PSRs, is to be an integral aspect of offender management, and judicial confidence is to be maintained, there may be less scope for contracting out to not-for-profit and commercial providers than some of the early discussion suggests. Nevertheless many commercial and voluntary sector organisations believe they have the capacity to be effective, ethical and professional providers of a variety of criminal justice services. The extent to which this is a valid claim, backed up by increasing experience, will provide a major challenge to state probation services, many of whose staff, whose morale has in recent years been notoriously low, may welcome the opportunity to transfer to smaller, focused and potentially better managed organisations. What is clear is that the proposed NOMS arrangements represent a shift towards total managerial control by Whitehall of all probation services. It would be surprising were that not to be accompanied by resuscitation of pre-trial services in order better to control the remand prison population and further rationalise the preparation of court reports, both their form and number.

Further reading

Probation Circular 18/2005, *Criminal Justice Act 2003 – New Sentences and the New Report Framework*, (NPS 2005a) sets out the latest official thinking about reports for courts. It describes the new PSR framework and how it fits with new sentences introduced by the Criminal Justice Act 2003.

The absence of recent empirical research on the preparation of court reports is reflected in the fact that Gelsthorpe and Raynor (1995), 'Quality and effectiveness in probation officers' reports to sentencers', is one of the most recent studies examining issues of quality and effectiveness in court report writing.

Drakeford *et al.* (2001) in *Pre-Trial Services and the Future of Probation* provide the most recent comprehensive account of pre-trial services, exploring the development of this area of work to its peak in the 1980s and subsequent decline.

References

Ashworth, A. (1994) *The Criminal Process: An Evaluative Study*. Oxford: Clarendon Press.

Audit Commission (1989) *Promoting Value for Money in the Probation Service*. London: HMSO.

Beamer, S. (1991) 'A Study of HMP Holloway's Bail Unit – Users and Staff's Perspectives'. Unpublished MSc thesis, London: LSE.

Beaumont, B. (1995) 'Managerialism and the probation service', in B. Williams (ed.), *Probation Values*. Birmingham: Venture Press.

Bottomley, A. K. (1970) *Prison Before Trial*, Occasional Papers in Social Administration No. 39. London: Bell.

Bottoms, A.E. and McWilliams, W. (1986) 'Social enquiry reports twenty-five years after the Streatfeild Report', in P. Bean and D. Whynes (eds), *Barbara Wootton: Social Science and Public Policy*. London: Tavistock.

Bowling, B. and Phillips, C. (2002) *Racism, Crime and Justice*. London: Longman.

Brittan, L. (1984) 'A strategy for criminal justice', *Howard Journal*, 23 (1): 3–10.

Burnett, R. and Eaton, G. (2004) *Factors Associated with Effective Practice in Approved Premises: A Literature Review*, Online Report 65/04. London: Home Office.

Burney, E. (1979) *JP: Magistrate, Court and Community*. London: Hutchinson.

Carter, P. (2003) *Managing Offenders, Reducing Crime: A New Approach*. London: Home Office and Strategy Unit.

Carter, R.M. and Wilkins, L.T. (1967) 'Some factors in sentencing policy', *Journal of Criminal Law, Criminology and Police Science*, 58 (4): 503–14.

Cavadino, P. and Gibson, B. (1993) *Bail, the Law, Best Practice, and the Debate*. Winchester: Waterside Press.

Crisp, D., Whittaker, C. and Harris, J. (1995) *Public Interest Case Assessment Schemes*. London: Home Office.

Curran, J.H. and Chambers, G.A. (1982) *Social Enquiry Reports in Scotland*. Edinburgh: HMSO.

Davies, C. (1971) 'Pre-trial imprisonment: a Liverpool study', *British Journal of Criminology*, 2: 32–48.

Drakeford, M., Haines, K., Cotton, B. and Octigan, M. (2001) *Pre-Trial Services and the Future of Probation*. Cardiff: University of Wales Press.

Faulkner, D. (1989) 'The future of the probation service: a view from government', in R. Shaw and K. Haines (eds), *The Criminal Justice System: A Central Role for the Probation Service*. Cambridge: Institute of Criminology.

Flood-Page, C. and Mackie, A. (1998) *Sentencing Practice: An Examination of Decisions in Magistrates' Courts and the Crown Court in the mid-1990s*, Research Study 180. London: Home Office.

Ford, P. (1972) *Advising Sentencers: A Study of Recommendations Made by Probation Officers to the Courts*, Occasional Paper No. 5. Oxford: Oxford University Penal Research Unit.

Fullwood, C. (1989) 'Probation, community and inter-agency dimensions: a future look', in R. Shaw and K. Haines (eds), *The Criminal Justice System: A Central Role for the Probation Service*. Cambridge: Institute of Criminology.

Garland, D. (1985) *Punishment and Welfare: A History of Penal Strategies*. Aldershot: Gower.

Gelsthorpe, L. and Raynor, P. (1995) 'Quality and effectiveness in probation officers' reports to sentencers', *British Journal of Criminology*, 35 (2): 188–200.

Godson, D. and Mitchell, C. (1991) *Bail Information Schemes in English Magistrates Courts*. London: Inner London Probation Service.

Haines, K. (1996) *Understanding Modern Juvenile Justice*. Aldershot: Avebury.

Haines, K. and Octigan, M. (1999) *Reducing Remands in Custody: The Probation Service and Remand Services*. London: ACOP.

Hankinson, I. and Stephens, D. (1986) 'Ever decreasing circles: practitioners and probation bureaucracy', *Probation Journal*, 33 (1): 17–19.

Hine, J., McWilliams, W. and Pease, K. (1978) 'Recommendations, social information and sentencing', *Howard Journal*, 17: 91–100.

HM Inspectorate of Probation (2000) *Towards Race Equality: A Thematic Report*. London: HMIP.

HM Inspectorate of Probation (2002) *Probation Service Workload Prioritisation – Report of an HMIP National Survey*. London: HMIP.

HM Inspectorate of Probation (2003) *2002/3 Annual Report*. London: HMIP.

HM Inspectorate of Probation (2004a) *2003/4 Annual Report*. London: HMIP.

HM Inspectorate of Probation (2004b) *Towards Race Equality: Follow-Up Inspection Report*. London: HMIP.

Home Office (1978) *The Sentence of the Court – A Handbook for Courts on the Treatment of Offenders*. London: HMSO.

Home Office (1990) *Partnership in Dealing with Offenders in the Community*. London: Home Office.

Home Office (1992a) *Partnership in Dealing with Offenders in the Community: A Decision Document*. London: Home Office.

Home Office (1992b) *Bail Information Schemes: Practice and Effect*, Research Paper No. 69. London: Home Office.

Home Office (1999) *Pre-Sentence Reports and Specific Sentence Reports*, Probation Circular 85/99. Home Office: Probation Unit.

Home Office (2002) *Probation Statistics England and Wales 2001*. London: National Statistics.

Home Office (2003) *Criminal Statistics England and Wales 2002*. London: National Statistics.

Home Office (2004a) *Offender Management Caseload Statistics England and Wales*, Statistical Report No. 15/04. London: National Statistics.

Home Office (2004b) *Criminal Statistics England and Wales 2003*, Cm 6361. London: National Statistics.

Home Office (2005a) *Restructuring Probation to Reduce Re-offending*. London: Home Office.

Home Office (2005b) *Sentencing Statistics 2004*, Statistical Bulletin No. 15/05. London: National Statistics.

Hood, R. (1992) *Race and Sentencing*. Oxford: Clarendon Press.

Hough, M., Jacobson, J. and Millie, A. (2003) *The Decision to Imprison: Sentencing and the Prison Population*. London: Prison Reform Trust.

Humphrey, C. (1991) 'Calling on the experts: the Financial Management Initiative (FMI), private sector consultants and the probation service', *Howard Journal*, 30 (1): 1–18.

King, M. (1971) *Bail or Custody*. London: Cobden Trust.

King, R.D. and Morgan, R. (1976) *A Taste of Prison: Custodial Conditions for Trial and Remand Prisoners*. London: Routledge & Kegan Paul.

Lloyd, C. (1986) *Response to SNOP*. Cambridge: Institute of Criminology.

McWilliams, W. (1983) 'The Mission to the English police courts 1876–1936', *Howard Journal*, 22: 129–47.

McWilliams, W. (1985) 'The Mission transformed: professionalism of probation between the wars', *Howard Journal*, 24: 257–74.

McWilliams, W. (1986) 'The English probation system and the diagnostic ideal', *Howard Journal*, 25: 241–60.

McWilliams, W. (1987) 'Probation, pragmatism and policy', *Howard Journal*, 26: 97–121.

McWilliams, W. (1992) 'The rise and development of management thought', in R. Statham and P. Whitehead (eds), *Managing the Probation Service*. Harlow: Longman.

Morgan, R. (1994) 'An awkward anomaly: remand prisoners', in E. Player and M. Jenkins (eds), *Prisons After Woolf: Reform Through Riot*. London: Routledge.

Morgan, R. (1997) 'Imprisonment: current concerns and a brief history since 1945', in M. Maguire, R. Morgan and R. Reiner (eds), *Oxford Handbook of Criminology*, 3rd edn. Oxford: Oxford University Press.

Morgan, R. (2003a) *Carcentricity: Fatal Attractions*. Annual McClintock Lecture, Edinburgh.

Morgan, R. (2003b) 'Thinking about the demand for probation services', *Probation Journal*, 50: 7–19.

Morgan, R. (2006) 'Race, probation and inspections', in S. Lewis, P. Raynor, D. Smith and A. Wardak (eds), *Race and Probation*. Cullompton: Willan.

Morgan, P. and Henderson, P. (1998) *Remand Decisions and Offending on Bail: Evaluation of the Bail Process Project*, Home Office Research Study 184. London: Home Office.

Morison Report (1962) *Report of the Departmental Committee on the Probation Service*, Cmnd 1650. London: HMSO.

Mott, J. (1977) 'Decision making and social inquiry reports in one juvenile court: an examination', *British Journal of Social Work*, 14 (4): 361–78.

National Audit Office (2004) *Facing Justice: Tackling Defendants' Non-attendance at Court*. London: NAO.

National Probation Directorate (2001) *A New Choreography: An Integrated Strategy for the National Probation Service for England and Wales – Strategic Framework 2001–2004*. London: NPD.

National Probation Service (2000) *Bail Information*, Probation Circular 29/2000. Home Office: National Probation Service.

National Probation Service (2005a) *Criminal Justice Act 2003 – New Sentences and the New Report Framework*, Probation Circular 18/2005. Home Office: National Probation Service.

National Probation Service (2005b) *Bail Information Schemes*, Probation Circular 19/2005. Home Office: National Probation Service.

National Probation Service (2005c) *National Standards (2005) and National Offender Management Model: Application of Tiering Framework*, Probation Circular 65/2005. London: Home Office.

NOMS/NPS (2005) *National Standards 2005*. London: NOMS/NPS.

Nottingham, S. and Mitchell, C. (1993) *Bail Information Schemes in Prisons*, Review of Prison Service Agency Action Plan. London: Home Office.

Office of the Deputy Prime Minister (2003) *Supporting People (England) Directions 2003*. London: ODPM.

Peters, A. (1986) 'Main currents in criminal law theory', in J. Van Dijk, C. Haffmans, F. Rüter, J. Schutte and S. Stolwijk (eds), *Criminal Law in Action: An Overview of Current Issues in Western Societies*. Arnhem: Gouda Quint BV.

Prison Service (1999) *Bail Information Schemes*, Prison Service Order No. 6101. London: Home Office.

Raynor, P. and Vanstone, M. (2002) *Understanding Community Penalties: Probation, Policy and Social Change*. Buckingham: Open University Press.

Raynor, P., Gelsthorpe, L. and Tisi, A. (1995) 'Quality assurance, pre-sentence reports and the probation service', *British Journal of Social Work*, 25 (4): 477–88.

Roberts, J. and Roberts, C. (1982) 'Social enquiry reports and sentencing', *Howard Journal*, 21: 76–93.

Rothman, D. (1980) *Conscience and Convenience: The Asylum and Its Alternatives in Progressive America*. Boston: Little, Brown.

Sentencing Guidelines Council (2004) *New Sentences: Criminal Justice Act 2003 – Guideline*. London: SGC.

Shapland, J. (1981) *Between Conviction and Sentence: The Process of Mitigation*. London: Routledge & Kegan Paul.

Shaw, R. (1992) 'Corporate management in probation', in R. Statham and P. Whitehead (eds), *Managing the Probation Service*. Harlow: Longman.

Simon, F. and Weatheritt, M. (1974) *The Use of Bail and Custody by London Magistrates' Courts Before and After the Criminal Justice Act 1967*, Research Study No. 20. London: Home Office.

Smith, D., Paylor, I. and Mitchell, P. (1993) 'Partnership between the independent sector and the probation service', *Howard Journal*, 32: 25–39.

Stanley, S.J. and Murphy, B. (1984) *Inner London Probation Service: Survey of Social Enquiry Reports*. London: ILPS.

Streatfeild Report (1961) *Report of the Interdepartmental Report on the Business of the Criminal Courts*, Cmnd 1289. London: HMSO.

Thorpe, J. (1979) *Social Inquiry Reports: A Survey*, Home Office Research Studies 48. London: Home Office.

Vanstone, M. (1995) 'Managerialism and the ethics of management', in R. Hugman and D. Smith (eds), *Ethical Issues in Social Work*. London: Routledge.

Warner, S. and McIvor, G. (1994) *Pre-Trial Services in Scotland: An Evaluation of Two Experimental Bail Information & Accommodation Schemes*. Scottish Office: Central Research Unit.

Wilkinson, J. (1990) 'The Holloway Bail Unit: Review of the First Year', unpublished report. London: ILPS.

Williams, B. (1992) *Bail Information – An Evaluation of the Scheme at HMP Moorland*. Bradford: Haughton Publishing.

Chapter 8

Assessment, supervision and intervention: fundamental practice in probation

Ros Burnett, Kerry Baker and Colin Roberts

If asked 'What do you do?', a likely answer from practitioners at any point in the hundred-year history of the Probation Service would include descriptions of 'assessment', 'supervision' and 'intervention', although not necessarily using precisely those terms. These three concepts are loaded with various connotations but, in essence, they still stand as overarching headings for most core practice with offenders. They involve skills and activities that are complementary and interlinked, although 'intervention' in the broadest sense[1] has always included referrals to other services, while 'assessment' and 'supervision' have been more exclusively provided 'in-house'. With the advent of commissioning and contestability, following the Correctional Service Review (Carter 2004; Home Office 2004a), interventions are decreasingly likely to be provided from within the Probation Service. The aim of this chapter is to gain insight into contemporary probation practice: first, by providing snapshots of supervision, assessment and intervention[2] at different points in probation's history; secondly, by looking at how they are to be played out at the dawn of the National Offender Management Service (NOMS); and thirdly, by examining key themes in recent critiques of trends affecting practice.

The long road of traditional practice

A retrospective look at probation practice throughout most of the twentieth century shows diverse influences, from the temperance movement to public sector managerialism (see Chapters 1 and 2 for an account of the historical context). This grounding in numerous, sometimes conflicting, ideologies combined with a culture of autonomous practice resulted in a 'marked theoretical eclecticism [being] a feature of the Probation Service throughout its history' (Raynor 2002: 1173). Despite this variability, the underlying model of practice for working with offenders remained much the same for several decades. Writing in the mid-1990s, Mair (1997: 1203) commented that, while group work and specialist activities had increased, 'the practical tasks associated with probation work remain very much as they were in 1907' when the Probation Service first came into being. A similar observation, though restricted to a shorter period, was made by Raynor and Vanstone (2002: 40) in noting that the practice and ideologies in place by the early 1930s included 'most of the ingredients of an approach to community supervision of offenders that were to prevail for at least the next 40 years'.

Placed under the supervision of the Probation Service

Throughout the distinct eras of probation history, the central idea underlying supervision remained that officers should 'advise, assist and befriend' offenders, with the main objective being to change individual behaviour. Practitioners worked through a personal (one-to-one) working relationship with their probationers, and this relationship was regarded as a *sine qua non* for influencing the change process (Burnett 2004; Burnett and McNeill, 2005). Early practice progressed from a mission to redeem by Christian moralisation and friendly encouragement to a treatment model applying psychology and casework techniques (Raynor and Vanstone 2002). Imported from psychoanalytical psychiatry, casework was initially heavily influenced by Freudian concepts, but later came to be used more loosely to refer to all one-to-one work; for example, the influential report of the Morison Committee (Home Office 1962: 24) defined casework simply as 'the creation and utilisation for the benefit of an individual who needs help with personal problems, of a relationship between himself and a trained social worker'.

'Supervision' was (and remains[3]) a generic term for oversight by the Probation Service. It is one of those fuzzy concepts that has diverse meanings, some of which are seemingly oppositional (dictionary definitions include 'management' and 'control' as well as 'oversight' and 'watching over'). As such, it embraces the dichotomy of care and control (or mentoring and monitoring) that was an enduring characteristic of probation practice. The tensions between these elements of supervision were an accepted characteristic of the job: to become a probation officer was to sign up for the dual role of being an 'officer of the court' while, at the same time, being expected to 'help' the offender. As conveyed by the Morison Committee report: 'the probation officer's prime concern is with the well-being of an individual, but he is also the agent of a system concerned with the protection of society' (Home Office 1962: 23).

Another enduring feature of traditional practice was the autonomy of the supervisor. The probation officer to whom an individual offender was known was deemed the best judge of what that individual needed and was given free rein, within principled limits, to determine the content of supervision (Raynor *et al.* 1994). Therefore, *how* supervision was delivered varied widely with the practitioner's supervisory style and perception of what was required, as well as the probationer's responsiveness to what was presented.

Traditional assessment methods and purposes

Assessment, like supervision, has been a constant component of probation work, though its focus and goals have changed, reflecting shifts in legislation and penal trends. For example, in the era characterised by McWilliams (1986) as 'saving souls', assessment (although this term may not have been used) attempted to determine which offenders were reformable. In the 'diagnostic' era, attention switched to identifying offenders who were 'treatable'.

Within the casework model, assessment was closely woven with supervision, and – seen in terms of a diagnosis of psychosocial needs – could itself be considered part of the supervision process, often leading into one-to-one work similar in style to counselling approaches and reflecting psychodynamic and other theoretical perspectives on the causes of offending behaviour. At the beginning of the 1960s (Home Office 1962: 24), assessment, or the 'exposition' of a probationer's problems, was described as a 'lengthy and exacting process' that depended on developing trust and interpersonal skills:

> [The caseworker's] first task is to win the confidence of the person needing help, and often that of his family, since only with their co-operation can the full picture emerge: they cannot be treated as passive conveyors of information. The caseworker must build gradually upon the individual's own account of himself, however incomplete and inarticulate. Rare sensitivity may be needed in establishing and developing the casework relationship at this stage, and sympathetic interest must be matched by objective and critical analysis of the data obtained. (Home Office 1962: 24)

Two critical features of assessment in the casework era can be helpfully identified here, the first of which was the close link with social work practice. Although there were, for example, differences of opinion about the most appropriate practice framework for the preparation of social enquiry reports (the forerunners of pre-sentence reports), there still appeared to be general agreement that these reports should be 'written by a person trained in social work' (Bottoms and Stelman 1988: 39) thus reflecting social work knowledge and values. The second key feature was the persistence of 'clinical' approaches to assessment, wherein information was collected through interviews, observation and interpretation of secondary sources (such as previous records) to produce an individualised assessment of the personal and situational factors contributing to an offender's behaviour. The assessor considered the significance of this information in the light of theory and their own experience before reaching a conclusion. As in supervision more generally, the quality of the relationship between the worker and offender was seen as being critical to the assessment process and much emphasis was placed on a probation officer's professional expertise in interpreting the meaning and significance of the information thus provided.

Early interventions

The concept of 'intervention', insofar as it was explicitly used in early practice, was likely to be preceded by the adjective 'therapeutic' and, as such, linked with 'medical' or 'treatment' models of practice. If we apply the concept more broadly, however, then it covers court sentences and mandatory conditions within sentences (see Chapter 9); interventions to address social and environmental problems; group work and skills training; and other services and specialist resources to which offenders may be referred as part of their sentence. Within the confines of this chapter, we are necessarily selective.

According to one school of thought, probation practice has never been sufficiently focused on the social and economic problems faced by the majority of probationers (e.g. Walker and Beaumont 1981). By the 1960s, described by some as the 'heyday' of probation (Chui and Nellis 2003), the official view was that 'crime is not primarily the product of economic hardships' (Home Office 1962: 25), although concession was made at the beginning of supervision 'for altering external influences by helping the individual to change his home or economic circumstances' (Home Office 1962: 25). However, the main targets for change were the individual's attitudes, beliefs and corresponding behaviour. Raynor and Vanstone (2002: 38) suggest that supervision facilitated this 'process of individualization' and was intended to awaken conscience and influence individual thinking and behaviour. Yet, when Davies (1974) carried out research for the Home Office to investigate the social and environmental circumstances of probationers, he found that such difficulties were more extensive than had been recognised and that practice was not geared to addressing such needs. He pointed out, though, that 'caseworkers in practice have never entirely turned their backs on the client's environment' (1969: 6). Indeed, during the 1970s and beyond, although the 'textbook' version of traditional practice retained a psychological bias, contributions to discussion by practitioners reflect a more practical orientation in everyday work:

> Probation officers spend a significant amount of time in negotiating on behalf of clients with other agencies – phoning and writing to the DHSS, housing departments and fuel boards or arranging nursery places. (Kirwin 1985: 41)

Group-work interventions were developed in the 1960s and 1970s and applied by practitioners themselves, though at first limited mainly to psychodynamic methods (Raynor et al. 1994) and support groups for prisoners' wives. A step change came when the 1972 Criminal Justice Act made provision for piloting 'day training centres' in which the dominant approach was group-work; while these were not extended they were the prototype for 'day centres', later named 'probation centres', which provided courts with an alternative to custodial sentences for relatively serious offenders. The programmes applied in these centres were significant in orientating practitioners to group work approaches as part of their mainstream practice (Vanstone 1993).

Interventions, in the sense of methods, became more innovative during the 'nothing works' era. Raynor observes that 'practitioners had to find their own sources of optimism and belief in what they were doing, and the "nothing works" era actually became a period of creativity and enthusiasm in the development of new methods and approaches' (2002: 1182). Most notably, James Maguire and Philip Priestley introduced courses for offenders on life skills and problem-solving to the Service, thereby importing the principles of social learning theory into mainstream probation. These were well-received by probation staff many of whom signed up for training in what was an early example of cognitive and behavioural work (McGuire and Priestley 1985). This approach was backed up by the publication of manuals to aid both one-to-one and group-work applications.

Group work methods had been slow to take off in the Probation Service. Long regarded as an optional extra, their application in services depended on individual initiative and a willingness to work extra hours (Senior 1985). However, a survey (Caddick 1991) of group-work practice in probation services in the late 1980s identified no fewer than 1,500 group-work programmes being delivered, and concluded that no longer could such types of interventions be considered 'marginal' in probation practice. The subject range of typical groups included: general offending behaviour, motor offending, sex offending, social skills, alcohol education, drug addiction, anger control, leisure activities and hostel residence.

One of the reasons why group work found favour among practitioners, especially following the promotion of the 'non-treatment paradigm' (Bottoms and McWilliams 1979), was that groups were seen as empowering for participants because they were removed from the authority of the caseworker in standard one-to-one practice (Vanstone 2004). It was not until the mid-1990s that group work was promoted on a national level, not least because of its perceived cost-effectiveness compared to more expensive individual counselling. Before then, opportunities for offenders to attend such groups remained largely a matter for the initiative of the supervising officer.

Practice at the crossroads

It was partly because practice was so individualised (in more ways than one: the officer knows best what is right for this person) that it was enabled to continue in the same form for so long, free from managerial and Government interference, and despite external events and influences that might reasonably have been expected to impact on it. To summarise the preceding, in the traditional model of practice, probation officers typically assessed and prepared court reports on defendants, and subsequently supervised those who became the responsibility of the Probation Service and, where possible, provided or acquired supplementary interventions to support the supervision plan. This *modus operandi* was largely impervious to the negative messages from research on the ineffectiveness of practice to reduce reoffending: practitioners continued to believe in the potential of their clients to change for the better, and in the value of their practice in supporting such change (Nellis and Chui 2003). Nevertheless, although the rehabilitative ideal continued to motivate practitioners, the Probation Service increasingly came under pressure from central government to reform its operations and adopt new methods.

There is no single turning point or dividing line to mark a separation between traditional and contemporary practice. Rather, as chronicled in Chapter 2, there were several turning points and junctures leading to modifications in policy and practice. However, the 1990s, as noted by Raynor (2002: 1192) 'were a period of fundamental transformation in our understanding of how offenders could be supervised successfully in the community'. Cognitive-behavioural group-work programmes became the favoured method of intervention: they were seen as expedient because of their cost-effectiveness and because their comparative effectiveness in reducing reoffending was indicated by an accumulation of meta-analytical research reviews and the promulgation of principles for effective practice:

> Key components of an effective approach, which at the beginning of the decade were the focus of interest for only a few researchers and practitioners, were by its end part of an officially recognized and endorsed strategy, underpinned by some serious research (not yet enough) and prompting a considerable reorganization of the process of supervising offenders. (Raynor 2002: 1192)

By 2001, when the 54 independent probation services in England and Wales were reorganised to form one service, a definite paradigm shift and change of ethos had taken place, on a policy level at least. The resulting National Probation Service (NPS) was firmly identified as a 'law enforcement agency delivering community punishments' (Wallis 2001). Approaches to 'assessment', 'supervision' and 'intervention' were heavily implicated in these transformations.

More than the alternating bad and good news from research into probation effectiveness, it was the managerial approach of Thatcherism, with its focus on audit, performance indicators and cost-effectiveness, that first pushed the Probation Service to redefine its work within a new framework of accountability and evaluation (Faulkner 2006; Raynor and Vanstone 2002). Probation services, like other public services, were called upon to demonstrate efficiency and cost-effectiveness (Audit Commission 1989). It became increasingly apparent that provision varied widely from one service to another, and from one officer to another, reflecting the 'virtually unlimited discretion' that practitioners were allowed in working with offenders (Mair 2004a: 30), as well differences in local resources and management practices (Burnett 1996). Studies, such as Roberts *et al.* (1996) and Underdown (1998), pointed to the need for a systematic case-management approach to be applied to facilitate the accountability and standardisation of individual practice, to act as a framework for the supervision of offenders during their attendance on programmes and to review the effectiveness of methods applied.

The advancement of assessment tools

A crucial component of case-management approaches was the development and use of assessment tools. While attempts to systematise the process of assessment may not be particularly new, the widespread use of such tools in practice is a more recent development. For example, tools to assist and guide decisions regarding who should be eligible for parole have been available since the 1920s although they were not widely used until the 1970s (Glaser 1985).

The subsequent proliferation of risk assessment tools in probation and youth justice services illustrates how systematic and structured approaches came to be used in relation to all types of offenders (rather than just those engaged in violent or sexual offending for example) and by many practitioners (rather than being the preserve of specialists).

Among the tools designed for use with adult offenders, the Offender Group Reconviction Scale (OGRS) was developed in the 1990s as a reconviction predictor using demographic data from a large sample of offenders (Home Office 1996). Probation areas began to develop their own assessment scales, for example the Berkshire Probation Service Assessment Framework (BPS), and a Home Office-commissioned study produced the Needs Assessment Scale (NAS) (Aubrey and Hough 1997). Other tools had a more specific focus, for example predicting risk of custody (Bale 1989).

The Level of Service Inventory Revised (LSI-R) was originally developed in Canada and arose from discussions 'about how to select offenders who required more intensive supervision at a time when caseloads were rising and decisions had to be made about priorities' (Raynor *et al.* 2000: 9). Following testing of its predictive validity, the tool began to be used within the UK and was subsequently adopted by approximately 20 probation areas. One perceived advantage of using LSI-R to improve assessment practice was that it 'shared a common theoretical base with the emerging "what works" literature' (Raynor *et al.* 2000: 12).

The Assessment, Case Management and Evaluation System (ACE), designed jointly by Warwickshire Probation Service and the University of Oxford, was another tool used widely by probation services. It was not designed primarily as a research instrument nor, importantly, as a risk predictor. Rather, it grew out of a recognition by Warwickshire that the data available to assess the effectiveness of probation supervision practice were limited and that, before effective practice could be analysed, information about the actual work being done with offenders needed to be systematically recorded in some way. The initial aim of the ACE project therefore was to design a 'methodical and consistent means of collecting information with a view to ongoing evaluation of practice' (Roberts *et al.* 1996: 2). In order to reflect the complexity of offending behaviour, the designers wanted to create a 'system which would reflect the diversity of factors appertaining to offenders and their behaviour and the diversity of aims and methods used in their supervision by probation staff and partnership agencies' (Roberts *et al.* 1996: 2). Other key features of ACE were an integral supervision plan designed for practitioners to set out a relevant programme of work that would follow on from assessment, and a self-assessment form to promote offender involvement in the process.

It is worth noting that, as with interventions, some of the initial development in the use of assessment tools in the probation context was driven by local services who saw it as a means to demonstrate the effectiveness of their work with offenders; moreover, practitioners were closely involved in the design and implementation of such tools. The origins of ACE in particular exemplify this, and a number of other local services chose to use either ACE or the LSI-R (Raynor *et al.* 2000) before the Home Office began to develop the Offender Assessment System (OASys).[4] This is not to say that practitioners welcomed them with open arms. A number of user studies in relation to both ACE and LSI-R highlighted that practitioners were concerned about assessment tools being time-consuming, to complete and potentially detracting from their professional skills, but also that they appreciated the comprehensive and systematic approach that such tools could promote (Robinson 2003; Aye-Maung and Hammond 2000).

Towards evidence-based interventions

The re-emergence of optimism in the effectiveness of interventions and Home Office initiatives to promote evidence-based practice, as detailed more fully in Chapters 15 and 16, led to key developments for the delivery of interventions. Bolstered by encouraging research findings from Canada and the USA and some promising studies (Roberts 1992; Raynor and Vanstone 1997) of effective community-based programmes in England and Wales, the Home Office in 1998 launched its own 'what works' agenda, otherwise known as the Effective Practice Initiative. This followed a series of service-led 'what works' conferences, and the publication of a report prepared by Andrew Underdown (1998) for HM Inspectorate of Probation. He surveyed 267 programmes delivered by local probation services, of which only four had been systematically evaluated. The new Labour government was committed to evidence-based public policy and this initiative in offender supervision fitted well into the overall criminal justice policy objectives (Faulkner 2006). Later in the same year the Home Office published a guide to evidence-based practice for practitioners (Chapman and Hough 1998). In July 1999 the then Home Office Probation Unit was successful in obtaining Treasury funding from the Crime Reduction Programme to develop a range of 'Pathfinder' programmes.

These Pathfinders included programmes for general offending behaviour, domestic violence, sex offenders and drug abusers. Later there were also Pathfinders for short-term prisoners, offenders with basic skills needs, unemployed offenders, women offenders and offenders subject to 'enhanced' community punishment orders. Probation areas were invited or selected to deliver pilot versions of group-work programmes, under the oversight of the newly created Joint Accreditation Panel (subsequently renamed the Correctional Services Accreditation Panel).

Other fundamental changes affecting the delivery and implementation of interventions were: the requirement introduced by the 1998 Crime and Disorder Act for local managers to participate in partnership arrangements (Rumgay 2004); revised National Standards in April 2000 with further specification of contact and attendance requirements, enforcement procedures, and prison and parole release conditions (Hedderman and Hough 2004); and the introduction of electronic monitoring, curfews, drug treatment and testing orders (DTTOs) and drug abstinence orders. These new responsibilities and the centralisation of probation governance enabled the detail of practice and choice of interventions to be removed from the domain of local practitioners and management, and to be designed and directed centrally.

The new National Probation Directorate (NPD) required probation areas to provide only *accredited* cognitive and behavioural programmes, with a limited degree of choice from four general offending behaviour programmes (e.g. Think First; Reasoning and Rehabilitation; Enhanced Thinking Skills; the One-to-One programme). Challenging targets were set for their delivery in all areas, including testing of staff (Kemshall *et al*. 2004), accreditation criteria (Rex *et al*. 2003) and performance indicators for attendance and completion rates.

Numerous critics have pointed out that the NPD was over-ambitious and over-zealous in its adoption of the accredited cognitive-behavioural programmes and its pursuit of high targets and strict enforcement standards (Rex 2001; Merrington and Stanley 2000; Mair 2004a, 2004b). The then Chief Inspector of Probation, Professor Rod Morgan (2003), went as far as to describe some aspects of the process as indicating 'programme fetishism', or a policy of putting too many 'eggs in one basket'. The early evaluations of the community-based programmes had less than encouraging findings (Hollin *et al*. 2002; Stewart-Ong *et al*. 2004; Roberts 2004). While outcomes for offenders who completed programmes were more positive, this could largely be ascribed to a selection effect. All the early evaluations showed high levels of attrition, with many offenders not even commencing programmes and up to half of those who did start programmes then failing to complete (Hollin *et al*. 2002; Kemshall *et al*. 2002; Stewart-Ong *et al*. 2004). There were major problems with implementation and delivery, partly because of insufficient provision for motivating offenders to attend programmes, partly because of design failures, and partly because of organisational problems, including lack of support for supervisory staff (Haslewood-Pócsik and McMahon 2004; Roberts 2004).

From casework to case management

As cognitive-behavioural group-work programmes became the focal point of practice, so conventional one-to-one counselling as an intervention in its own right became increasingly marginalised – though in England and Wales more so than in Scotland (see Chapter 5). There are a number of factors that help to explain why relationship-based one-to-one practice became discredited on a policy level (Burnett 2004; Burnett and McNeill 2005). In particular, counselling and one-to-one work had been identified as ineffective in most (not all) meta-analytical reviews of 'what works'. It was associated with unstructured and non-directive approaches that provided insufficient structure and purpose, and with autonomous and idiosyncratic practice that failed to address offending behaviour.

A growing body of research has found, however, that it is this relational element in supervision and offender management that practitioners frequently flag up as the indispensable foundation of effective practice with offenders (Burnett 1996; McNeill 2003) and that offenders themselves often identify as the factor that makes a key difference (Barry 2000; Rex 1999). Indeed, even though one-to-one work has been unfashionable for more than two decades (Kirwin 1985; Burnett 2004), it persisted as an element of case management. Some of the skills involved became redefined as specific approaches, such as 'motivational interviewing', 'mentoring', 'relapse prevention' and 'pro-social modelling'. Arguably, however, these approaches and others, such as 'crisis intervention' and 'solution-focused counselling', though not always labelled as such, have long been included in the probation officer's 'professional tool box' (Fleet and Annison 2003: 130).

Route 'NOMS'

In January 2005, the first version of the National Offender Management Model was issued (NOMS 2005a).[5] Aimed at staff and organisations that make up NOMS, this model is intended to provide a shared framework for the staff and organisations within NOMS involved in applying the 'components and processes of effective work with offenders' (para. 1.1). It was further developed in Probation Circular 65/2005 (NPS 2005a) which sets out tiering arrangements to be used in offender management. The scope of interventions and plans for procuring and providing them are described in *Reducing Re-offending – A National Action Plan* (Home Office 2004a) and the report on *Restructuring Probation to Reduce Reoffending* (NOMS 2005b). The above-named documents together provide some insight into the 'state of the art' for assessment, supervision and interventions in twenty-first century probation.

The core features of the National Offender Management Model (henceforth referred to as the OM model) are as follows:

- The NOMS model is built around an *Offender-Focussed Human Service Approach* to work with individual offenders.
- Within it is a *Single Concept of Sentence Implementation*, which incorporates a *Single Language* and a *Single, Core End-to-End Process*.
- It is a *Differentiated Approach*, enabling different resources and styles to be matched to different cases.
- But a *'One Sentence: One Manager'* structure is considered to be the baseline against which all delivery arrangements are judged.
- It is a *Brokerage Approach* in which an Offender Manager brokers resources, but does not commission or purchase them.
- And in order to deliver the required coherence to an offender, the model incorporates a *New Concept of Teamwork*.
- Finally, it is a *Whole System Approach*, which requires that organisational support functions support the core business process of Offender Management.

(NOMS 2005a: para. 2, emphasis in the original)

For purposes of locating the place and functions of assessment, supervision and interventions within this new framework, the first thing to note is that they remain interrelated operations. The model binds together assessment (including continuous risk assessment and review), supervision planning and brokerage of interventions, as may be discerned in Figure 8.1, adapted from the report on the OM model (NOMS 2005a).

Our triad of fundamental tasks is therefore alive and well within this model, but, far from being business as usual, there are some distinctive new aspects that require further description.

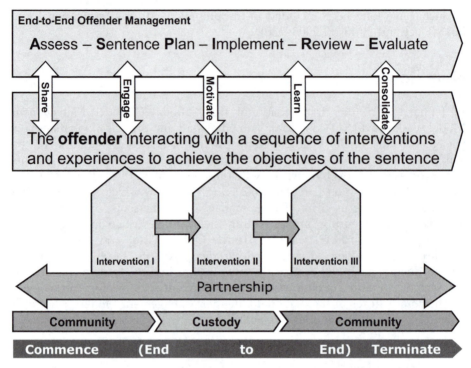

Note: This is a simplified version of the core model, adapted from Appendix C of NOMS (2005a). The original also includes two-way arrows to show the interrelationship between the activities of offender management and the interventions. Further arrows denote teamwork relationships and relationships with the offender.

Figure 8.1 The NOMS offender management model

Supervision as an element of offender management

In the new offender management model, the concept of 'supervision' is subordinate to the more embracing role of 'offender management' and is one of three 'threads' (the other two being 'management' and 'administration') within the end-to-end management process. Offender management is described as a process that is focused on the individual offender rather than on specific stages or activities, and the sentence is to be viewed as a whole, including both custodial and community elements. This approach conceives of the sentence as a journey for the offender, which is – applying the principle of 'one sentence, one manager' – overseen by the offender manager (2005a: para. 3.4). While technically the supervisor may be a different person from the offender manager, both roles are expected to be performed by the same person (para. 3.52) unless the offender is in distant custody, is attending an intensive programme, or there are acute staff shortages (para. 3.24).

Regarding what is meant by a 'human services approach' the report explains that specific staff behaviours, labelled 'core correctional practice' were identified by Dowden and Andrews (2004) as effective in influencing change. Following Dowden and Andrews these are:

- the firm, fair and clear use of authority
- modelling pro-social and anti-criminal attitudes, cognition and behaviours
- teaching concrete problem solving skills
- using community resources (brokerage)
- forming and working through warm, open and enthusiastic relationships.

(NOMS 2005a: para. 3.45)

The model also incorporates the 'four Cs' introduced by Holt (2002): consistency, continuity, commitment and consolidation.

The management thread in the process includes: assessment; planning; allocation of resources; ensuring the plan is implemented; monitoring progress; enforcement if necessary; reviewing, reassessment and replanning; and evaluation. The model uses the acronym ASPIRE (Assess – Sentence Plan – Implement – Review – Evaluate) as a mnemonic for these elements in the management process (see Figure 8.1). Initial assessment leads to formulation of a sentence plan, implementation of which involves 'brokering' (securing and deploying) the required interventions and identifying who will be responsible for delivering the plan. The management role requires some direct contact with the offender.

The concept of 'supervision' in this model is reserved for day-to-day contact intended to encourage the supervisee's compliance and motivation. In specifying this, it is assumed that: 'Most offenders will not cooperate actively with their Sentence Plan simply because one exists' (2005a: 8), and it is noted that intensity of supervision will vary depending on the supervisee's level of risk, motivation and responsiveness. The administrative element is there to deal with the 'complex web of standards and procedures' (2005a: 9) including record-keeping, scheduling, arranging appointments and filing.

Assessment as an element of offender management

These new specifications for probation practice show a continued emphasis on the importance of assessment (NPS 2005a; NOMS 2005a), while probation officers themselves continue to identify assessment as a key practice skill (Bracken 2003), not least because they are aware that the impact of their assessments can be momentous for offenders, and for the community, if mistakes are made.[6] A number of assessment tools are currently used in probation services across the UK. In Northern Ireland, for example, ACE continues to be used while in Scotland a variety of tools are used, in particular LSI-R and the RAGF (Risk Assessment Guidance Framework) for more serious violent and sexual offenders (McIvor et al. 2002). However, it could be argued that the introduction of OASys in England and Wales has moved the use of assessment tools in criminal justice into a new era – this is evident in the much greater level of centralised control over the development of the tool and in the way that it has become the basis for the offender management model and the tiering framework (NPS 2005a).

OASys was designed jointly by the Prison and Probation Services as a standard assessment tool that could be used across both community and custodial settings. Although its origins predate the advent of NOMS, the concept of a shared assessment tool clearly fits neatly into these more recent organisational developments. More specifically, OASys (NPS 2005b: 2) was designed to:

- assess how likely an offender is to be reconvicted
- identify and classify offending-related needs, including basic personality characteristics, cognitive behavioural problems and social variables
- assess risk of harm (to self, general public, known adults, children, staff and other prisoners)
- assist with management of risk of harm
- link assessments and sentence plans
- indicate any need for further specialist assessments
- measure how an offender changes during the period of sentence.

Although OASys is clearly identified as the central assessment tool for NOMS, other tools are of course also used. For example, the 'Sex Offender Strategy' states that case managers should also use Risk Matrix 2000,[7] the Structured Risk Assessment (SRA) for dynamic risk factors and Acute Risk Checklists (NPS 2004b). Another example of a specialist assessment tool would be the Spousal Assault Risk Assessment Tool used with perpetrators of domestic violence. In the case of very high-risk offenders who require referral to Multi-Agency Public Protection Arrangements (MAPPA), guidance states that 'other systems of risk assessment may be used in addition to OASys' as long as they meet certain specified criteria regarding validity and reliability (NPS 2004c: 29). The importance attached to the use of such additional tools is seen by the fact that the Inspectorate has criticised areas which were seen as failing to use additional specialised assessment tools when required (HMI Probation 2004).

The pivotal role of assessment is also evident in the introduction of a 'tiering framework' to determine which level of resources is required in any particular case. This sets out four levels or types of case management approach: Tier 1 – Punish; Tier 2 – Help; Tier 3 – Change; and Tier 4 – Control. The assessed likelihood of reoffending (measured by OASys or OGRS scores), the assessed risk of causing serious harm and assessments of suitability for particular intervention programmes (presumably based on both OASys and the results of any other specialist assessment tools used) are the key criteria for allocating cases to the different tiers. These tiers are not mutually exclusive, but are layered one on the other, so that each involves the interventions of all lower levels as well as those specified at its own level (see Figure 8.2). Other facets of the assessment should then provide the basis for a 'single Sentence Plan, which specifies who will do what and when to achieve the objectives of the sentence, and intermediate targets' (NPS 2005a: 8). The tiering framework was introduced in order to rationalise the use of scarce resources and in acknowledgement of research findings indicating counterproductive results when low-risk offenders receive high levels of intervention.

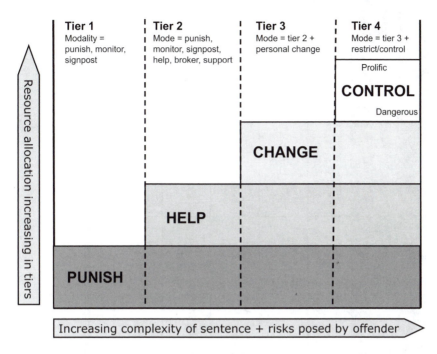

Note: Reproduced with permission from NOMS (2005a).

Figure 8.2 The NOMS tiering framework for resource allocation

Interventions in NOMS

The National Offender Management Model includes a typology of interventions, set out in diagrammatic form as shown in Figure 8.3.

Although planned intervention continues to stress cognitive-behavioural and social learning, these are now set into the broader context of the entire period during which the individual is under supervision, and are seen as processes that need to be nurtured.

The changing face of interventions has been determined also by new legislation, with the concept of intervention now being used in its broadest sense to refer to requirements that are made as part of a court sentence, whether for punishment, rehabilitation or public protection. The Criminal Justice Act 2003, which became operational in April 2005, enables courts to combine options from a menu of provisions and requirements which can be individually tailored for each offender into a generic community sentence.

In the first three months following its implementation, 7,600 community sentences were passed (16 per cent of all sentences passed during that period). Of these, 3,733 offenders were ordered to perform unpaid work (previously known as community service and later community punishment), of which 2,527 were stand-alone requirements (i.e. not combined with supervision requirements); 4,198 supervision requirements were imposed, of which 1,179 were stand-alone. The largest number of requirements for a

Punitive Interventions	Constructive Interventions					Restrictive Interventions
	Rehabilitative Interventions				Restorative Interventions	
	Supporting Protective Factors	Reducing Barrier Factors	Change Programmes	Re-Integration		
To implement the punitive element of the sentence	To protect or promote the positive desistance factors in an offenders life/situation	To reduce or eliminate factors which stand in the way of change	To learn new, pro-social attitudes and ways of behaving	To consolidate the new learning and promote citizenship	To make good the damage done by the offending	To control behaviour for public protection
Imprisonment	Maintaining family ties	Tackle homelessness	Accredited Offending Behaviour Programmes	Employment market skills training	Visible Unpaid Work	Prohibited Activity
Unpaid Work	Retaining work	Tackle acute drug or alcohol addiction	Medical treatment for drug or alcohol addiction	Benefits, debt and money management	Indirect Mediation	Curfew
Attendance Centre	Retaining accommodation	Tackle chronic lack of motivation	Some life and social skills training	Independent living support	Victim Offender Mediation	Mobility Restriction
Curfew	Maintaining good health	Address engulfing mental health issues		Relapse prevention	Direct Reparation	Surveillance

Shaded interventions cross-reference to inter-agency Pathways in National Reducing Re-offending Action Plan

Note: Reproduced with permission from NOMS (2005a).

Figure 8.3 The NOMS typology of interventions

single order was five (in only eight individual cases), while 13 per cent had three requirements and 30 per cent had two requirements (NPS 2005e). It is obviously still too early to draw any firm conclusions from this short period since implementation of CJA 2003. While the early signs are that courts have a preference for combining the wide range of interventions that are available to them, this may turn out to be an untypical picture in the long run once courts have adjusted to the new sentencing framework.

The most frequently imposed requirement, to date, has been attendance on accredited programmes: in the three months following implementation of CJA 2003 there were 2,040 such requirements, mostly combined with supervision (NPS 2005e). Currently there are 17 programmes accredited for use by probation areas, the majority of which are group-work programmes, dealing with: aggression and anger management (two programmes); substance abuse (three); general offending (four); sex offending (three); domestic violence and abuse (two); and a women's programme on acquisitive crime. There are two one-to-one (individual) programmes, one on general offending behaviour and one on substance misuse, and the two domestic abuse programmes have a mixture of group and individual sessions.

A key part of the *National Action Plan for Reducing Re-offending* (Home Office 2004b) is the introduction of seven individual 'Pathways' for the planning and delivery of intervention. A controversial aspect is the proposal for commissioning and contestability in their delivery (Carter 2004), whereby the Pathway interventions will be offered for tender, on a regional basis, to existing statutory services, voluntary agencies and the private sector. A positive aspect is that the thorough investigation by the Social Exclusion Unit (2002) in the resettlement needs of ex-prisoners had a powerful influence on the identification of the seven pathways, which are as follows:

1 *Accommodation.* This includes approved premises (hostels), supported housing, special short tenancies and locally negotiated access to local authority accommodation, housing associations and private tenancies. Areas will be expected to set up Accommodation Coordination and Referral Units to develop and manage this provision.

2 *Education, training and employment.* In August 2005 the new Offenders' Learning and Skills Service (OLASS) went live in three regions and is expected to be rolled out in the other six regions by August 2006. The intention is to provide a better, more integrated service to improve the quality and quantity of learning and skills provision. In relation to employment and employability, JobCentre Plus has been the main government provider, and a whole series of different programmes are being developed for specific offender groups. A new integrated employment Pathfinder was established in seven probation areas in 2004.

3 *Mental and physical health.* There is a joint plan with the NHS to improve access to primary care for offenders, but the detail in relation to offenders in the community remains vague.

4 *Drugs and alcohol.* Much of the resource and provision will come from the Criminal Justice Interventions Programme (CJIP), which is a national

strategy for tackling substance misuse by offenders. Five hundred million pounds is being spent on developing integrated treatment facilities for drug misusing offenders. The intention is a 'seamless' system, including residential drug treatment centres. The local Drug Action Teams (DATs) already have local links with probation areas to fund and coordinate a range of interventions. Drug treatment and testing orders (DTTOs), now replaced by drug reduction requirements (DRRs), will continue to be the responsibility of probation areas, but the treatment component will be provided by the DAT. Alcohol treatment requirements (ATRs) have been introduced for offenders with serious alcohol abuse problems, and there is an accredited programme for drink drivers (Drink Impaired Driver Scheme).

5 *Finance, benefits and debt.* Offenders currently access relevant services through voluntary agencies, for example the Citizens' Advice Bureaux (CAB) and other local services which advise on debt. The Community Legal Service (CLS) became responsible in 2005 for contracting debt advice services.

6 *Children and families of offenders.* The increasing Government policy emphasis on children's needs, as exemplified in the Green Paper, *Every Child Matters* (DfES 2003), is not mirrored by substantive content in this Pathway. The only provision currently operating for offenders' children and families is via the locally managed Sure Start Partnerships, which serve areas with high levels of deprivation and provide for children aged under five years – some of whom are likely to be the children of known offenders – and their families.

7 *Attitudes, thinking and behaviour.* Existing provision of accredited cognitive-behavioural programmes will continue to be the main means of delivering interventions under this Pathway. However, it is now recognised that the emphasis solely on accredited programmes drains resources away from other potentially valuable pre-accredited activities and programmes, resulting in unhelpful postponements or cancellations of other needed programmes. In the future, non-accredited interventions under this pathway will be permitted, subject to a new system of vetting which will replace the Correctional Services Accreditation Panel system. There are also plans to review the eligibility and suitability criteria for attending accredited programmes, to ensure that offenders unable to learn from them are supervised in a more individualised way.

The newly established Interventions Department of the NPS is expected to provide guidance about how interventions should be matched to offender characteristics and on the sequencing of selected interventions. The Tiering Framework, discussed above, and the 2005 National Standards (NPS 2005a) contain requirements that each sentenced adult offender should be allocated to one of the four offender case management tiers. There are also plans to encourage greater use of multi-modal interventions under the 2003 Criminal Justice Act powers for the imposition of generic community sentences. The various forms of interventions from the seven pathways will be combined in different ways and sequenced more carefully, based on experience gained through the Intensive Control and Change Programme (ICCP) project for young adult offenders.

Navigating through hazards

The new framework for offender management described above, in contrast to the traditional model of assessment, supervision and intervention that survived so many decades, amounts to a major reconstruction of practice in work with offenders. Critics of the route that probation has taken in becoming part of NOMS see several danger points on the road ahead that have crucial implications for interventions to promote rehabilitation and desistance from crime. Among criticisms made of recent probation reforms, those most directly relevant to practice are: that the purpose of working with offenders has shifted from rehabilitation to public protection and punishment; that the changes are resulting in fragmentation and depersonalisation of practice; that practitioners are being progressively deskilled, undermined and deprofessionalised; and that the Probation Service has been coopted into the moral engineering and responsibilisation agenda of late modern liberal states. These issues are not mutually exclusive but, in order to identify distinct aspects, will be considered under the separate headings of punitive controlism, depersonalisation, deprofessionalisation and responsibilisation. We will evaluate the applicability of these concerns to contemporary practice in the light of the latest strategy and policy documents on the NOMS approach to offender management, and with reference to recent reviews of practice skills in reducing reoffending.

Punitive controlism

At the turn of the century, after years of upheaval, the Probation Service was able to find a new sense of direction by redefining its purpose as risk management and reducing reoffending, and this remodelling was seen as compatible with the people-centred approach and rehabilitative ideals that had previously defined the Service (Roberts 1997; Walters 1997). There has always been an element of control in probation supervision, as noted earlier. The perennial debates in probation literature about achieving the correct balance between care and control are testimony to this. Likewise, risk assessment, with a view to public protection, has consistently featured among the core skills of practice (Hopkinson and Rex 2003).

However, probation practice over the last two decades has become enmeshed in the public protection agenda, with the result that the care–control counterbalance is now angled more sharply towards control. For practitioners this has meant a much greater emphasis on surveillance (electronic tagging) and enforcement (breach proceedings). This repositioning is set to remain; the breach provisions attached to the new sentences introduced by the Criminal Justice Act 2003 place ever greater emphasis on the offender manager's role as 'enforcer' (Nacro 2004). 'Public protection' is clearly being placed ahead of 'reducing reoffending' in the Government's strategy for managing offenders

(Home Office 2006). Recent adverse publicity against the competence of the Service, following serious reoffending by individuals subject to probation supervision, will reinforce procedures which favour greater restrictions against the liberty of ex-offenders (HMI Probation 2006).[8]

But it is the penal agenda of retribution, fuelled by punitive-populism, that has most threatened radically to shift the purpose of probation, from one of caring control to one of punitive control. Again, this is not a new development – it dates back to the toughening up of community penalties in the early 1990s – but when the NPS website lists '[t]he proper punishment of offenders in the community' as its third aim, when practice models incorporate 'punish' as a task at every risk assessment level of offending behaviour (see Figure 8.2), and when the Chief Inspector of Probation echoes this in describing the Probation Service as 'heading towards a new purpose to "Punish, Help, Change and Control" offenders' (Foreword to HMI Probation 2006), then there are understandable concerns that the quintessential nature of probation is being turned on its head. Added to these, the 2003 Criminal Justice Act and the five-year strategy promote much greater use of unpaid work as a punitive requirement of community orders, made visible to the community and overseen by the Probation Service.

Looking back at practitioner perspectives over the decades, and as chronicled by Raynor (1985: 42), few issues have aroused more hostility and discomfort than measures that increase 'controlism': in other words, 'an explicit identification with punishment and control, in which the Service's role will be to develop a wider range of punishments in the community'. Punitive controlism is also deplored by academic experts, among whom the consensus view is that punishment and rehabilitation are incompatible (Nellis and Gelsthorpe 2003; Hedderman 2005). Critics are concerned that actuarial approaches into assessment inadvertently support such controlism by focusing on the worst possible outcomes in terms of risk to others (Tuddenham 2000) and by decontextualising offending behaviour from the difficult circumstances which led to it (Hannah-Moffat and Shaw 2001). Particularly repellent is the specified direction to 'Punish', incorporated within the tiering framework, as part of probation work with all individuals subject to offender management, thereby overtly involving practitioners in the role of punishment.

That probation officers should be implicated so closely in dishing out punishment to make sure that offenders pay for their crimes is a development that many would regard as at odds with the humanistic tradition of probation practice, wherein 'offenders should be individualised and treated as people, with respect and care, and helped rather than coerced to change' (Nellis and Gelsthorpe 2003: 228). It was axiomatic in traditional practice that probation officers helped offenders. Helping and assistance were also self-evident in the concepts of 'through-care' and 'after-care' in relation to those in custody. Few at the time would have questioned Kirwin's (1985: 40) observation that:

> One concept which consistently appears in descriptions of our job is that we are 'helpers'. Magistrates put people on probation so that we can 'help' them; we say in our reports that someone might benefit from the 'assistance' of a probation officer.

Yet when we 'fast forward' to the last few years, examination of policy documents reveals that the concepts of 'caring' and 'helping' have been erased from official parlance about probation (Burnett and McNeill 2005). Chief executives have stressed that probation practice is not social work (e.g. Wallis, quoted in Brindle 2002) and recruitment literature has indicated that it is inappropriate for practitioners to be friendly towards the people they supervise (e.g. London Probation Service 2004).

However, while it is clear that the balance between care and control has shifted on a policy level, it remains questionable whether apprehensions of a dominantly punitive role for probation will be realised. First, it is doubtful whether the rehabilitative purpose for the Service's existence has ever been entirely vanquished within practice (Robinson 1999) or removed from official plans, even though it has increasingly been overshadowed by other legislative purposes and objectives. Secondly, alongside the rhetoric about punishment and the prioritising of public protection, policy documents and leader speeches have a strong thematic bias towards reducing reoffending as the central objective, with references to punishment being somewhat muted or made subservient to the goal of reducing recidivism (Clarke 2005; Hill 2005; Home Office 2006). Thirdly, there are alternative categories and conceptualisations of 'punishment' which do not exclude respect and care towards the individuals being punished. One position is that appropriate punishment can contribute to rehabilitation by communicating to offenders what is morally unacceptable behaviour (Duff 2000). While some Government rhetoric may have deliberately played up to a retribution-based notion of punishment to appease a revenge-hungry section of the public, the broader penal policy together with national action plans for interventions to reduce reoffending seems to be aligned with the goals of widening access to education, heath and housing (Clarke 2005). Unpaid work, under the heading of 'Community Payback' in place of the previous label 'Community Punishment', gives more focus to reparation, and any calculation of how much this is a retributionist form of punishment that is incompatible with rehabilitation should take account of other requirements in an individual's sentence intended to meet needs and provide positive incentives.

Depersonalisation

Some commentators have portrayed the emergence of 'offender management' and risk-based offender categorisation as leading to a fragmentation in the delivery of practice that is unhelpful to both offenders and staff. Robinson (2005) likened the process of management and referral from one specialist intervention to another as a 'pass the parcel' approach in which there would be little opportunity for the supervising probation officer to carry out face-to-face work and build a relationship with the offender. This echoes with misgivings that practitioners themselves have long articulated in response to the advance of what was formerly called case management (Burnett 1996). Specialist models of practice that emerged in the 1990s, whereby some teams were divided into those who carried out and prepared reports, those who supervised and managed cases, and those who delivered programmes (Boswell *et al.* 1993), further distanced staff from opportunities to relate to offenders as individuals. Research by Robinson found that: '[p]ractitioners were no longer encouraged to think of individual probationers as "their" offenders, but instead to concentrate on the full and accurate completion of increasingly complex assessment paperwork with a view to enhancing offenders' referrability within the new systematic framework' (2005: 310).

It may be difficult to envisage how the NOMS approach to practice, with its battalion of interventions, partner agencies and differentiated staff roles applied to sentences with compound requirements, can do anything other than exacerbate such trends of depersonalisation. As is acknowledged, the OM model 'involves different people from different agencies, doing different things with the same offender, at different stages of the sentence' (NOMS 2005a: 13). Much depends though on how well the planned strategies within the OM model are realised in practice. If the principles laid down in the strategy documents are adhered to in reality, then practice may become *less* fragmented and depersonalised than has been the case in recent years. As outlined earlier, it is intended that the offender manager will in most cases also be the supervisor, who will be there throughout the sentence and at the hub of the team delivering interventions, providing a 'thread of continuity, binding issue-specific interventions into a coherent whole' (NOMS 2005a: 13). The guidelines advocate this because 'management tasks, such as planning, provide an ideal vehicle for some of the supervisory processes, like relationship forming' (NOMS 2005a: 9). The desirability of combining these roles is also linked to cost considerations and avoiding risks following from breakdowns in communication that can occur when roles are split.

A key test will be whether the circumstances which are allowed to circumvent this more ideal arrangement (specified in para. 3.34) will mean that changes of supervisor and a remote, impersonal offender manager become the rule rather than the exception. Achieving continuity and consistency will be complicated by the removal of probationers to far flung prisons in cases of breach and further offending leading to custodial sentences. It will also be challenged by the tiering of provision according to risk level. The assigned level of risk is unlikely to remain static, and, as acknowledged by the evaluation of the North-West Pathfinder, it is not clear how case continuity will be maintained when a case is transferred to a higher or lower level of risk. It is, in any case, a matter of continuing debate whether continuity of supervisor is so important. The team model for offender management, in which staff on different professional levels each have some involvement, allows for some continuity even though the supervision responsibility may be passed up or down the hierarchy of staff roles (see Figure 8.4).

Notwithstanding the flexibility of role allowed by this team-based responsibility for working with offenders, the development of personalised practitioner–offender relationships remains a critical factor in shaping the success of practice in NOMS. It is heartening therefore that the OM model, as specified in Version 1, shows the influence of studies which reaffirm the critical role of relationship.[9] Most notably, the model explicitly incorporates Dowden and Andrews' (2004) specified 'pre-requisites' of what they call 'core correctional services' (listed above). One of these specifies that practitioners should form and work through 'warm, open and enthusiastic relationships'.

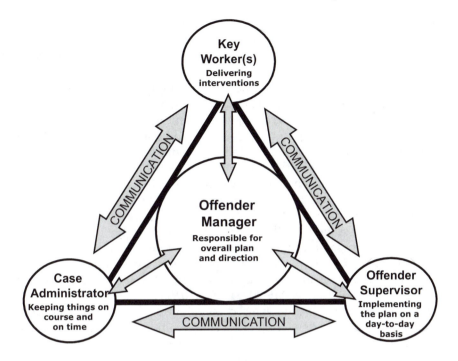

Note: Reproduced with permission from NOMS (2005a).

Figure 8.4   The offender management team

A stress on the need to 'engage with the offender as an individual' is also prominent in the foreword of the recent annual report of HMI Probation (Bridges 2005), and Charles Clarke's (2005) speech to the Prison Reform Trust referred to the need for an individualised response to offenders, with 'one person being responsible for each offender throughout their time in prison and on probation' (2005: 3).

A key yardstick of viability will be how the OM model is experienced by those being 'managed'. As expressed by the incumbent National Offender Manager, the offender's experience is the 'litmus test of offender management' (Knott, cited in PA Consultancy Group and MORI 2005: 8). The North-West Pathfinder evaluation of the OM model (PA Consultancy Group and MORI 2005) found that probationers value 'continuity of relationship' with the same practitioners, and that a significant factor in their participation with their sentence plan was the quality of relationships with staff (feeling supported, being heard, clarity of explanations given, being treated as an individual).

The offender's experience of group-work programmes is also pivotal. Cognitive-behavioural and social learning processes continue to be emphasised within the OM approach, within the broader context of a sentence plan. Group-work programmes are now required to include motivational elements in order to gain accreditation. Nevertheless, if not complemented by appropriate one-to-one attention, being referred to groups may exacerbate a sense of being treated like an object rather than a person. Detractors criticise what they see as one-size-fits-all programmes, designed for white adult males and unresponsive to the learning needs of women and minority ethnic groups (Shaw and Hannah-Moffat 2004).

Yet, in a powerful defence of the much maligned cognitive-behavioural programmes, McGuire (2005) points out that such criticism is largely invalid on the following grounds. Programmes are meant to be integrated as part of a supervision plan in which group sessions should be followed up in individual sessions. While programmes are not tailored to different categories of possible participants, it is implicit in the principle of responsivity that sessions should be adapted to the needs of those participating; also the research basis for the formulation of programmes has tended to include multi-ethnic samples and, while more work is needed in specifying how programmes can meet the needs of different sections of the community, 'considerable efforts have been made to adapt programmes for a variety of client needs' (McGuire 2005: 273). It is encouraging to see that plans for implementing the OM model stress that 'how' interventions are delivered is just as important as the content or the 'what' of the experience (NOMS 2005a: para. 3.9).

The appropriateness of this renewed attention to the processes and quality of interpersonal skills in delivering interventions, and in offender management, is supported by meta-analytical reviews in the mental health sector that show the significant role of process variables, such as accurate empathy, respect and warmth, in achieving positive outcomes in interventions (Lambert and Ogles 2004; McNeill *et al.* 2005). Indeed, some studies show that 'extra-therapeutic' factors ('client variables' and chance factors) contribute more to beneficial outcomes than do either 'therapist variables' or the interventions themselves. This of course does not contradict findings that some interventions are more effective than others in impacting on outcomes, but it does highlight the importance of additional factors over and above interventions.

In particular, the cooperation and engagement of the participant are recognised as paramount, with considerable research being undertaken to apply motivational interviewing and other approaches such as pro-social modelling to work with offenders (e.g. McMurran 2002; Trotter 1999). Such is the importance of motivation and, related to this, compliance (Bottoms 2001; Hopkinson and Rex 2003) it has been suggested by some that the key question should be, not simply 'What works?' but rather, 'What works to gain compliance?' (Hedderman and Hough 2004; Robinson and Dignan 2004). In the context of offending behaviour rather than, more broadly, in the mental health field where much contact is on voluntary basis, gaining cooperation and engagement is inevitably more difficult, creating greater challenges for practitioners. For those interventions that are outsourced from the voluntary and private sector it remains to be seen whether personnel delivering the interventions will have the requisite skills to engage and retain the interest of participants.

The relational element is also important for assessment. It is within the context of such a collaboration that the best assessment can take place. Making an assessment relies on an underlying assumption that people, and the society in which they live, are to some extent 'knowable'. But what is it that probation officers are trying to 'know' and how do they come to acquire this understanding? Given the current emphasis on risk, it is important to remember that assessment should be about *understanding* behaviour as well as predicting it, and is a 'matter of trying to *make sense of* a particular person's problems or behaviour in relation to his unique social environment' (Davies 1993: 156). It is only by developing trust, goodwill and empathy that the practitioner can gain access to that environment, and that the offender can be encouraged to disclose salient information. In this regard, it is worth noting that the person being assessed also brings subjective expertise to the process, and that their contribution can be vital (Smale and Tuson 1993). Again, drawing out this information calls for a more personalised approach, as well as professional integrity and knowledge.

Deprofessionalisation

Probation practice has traditionally been regarded as requiring considerable professionalism and discretion in order to carry out the role effectively, to deal with difficult issues without prejudice and to merit the trust of the public (Lacey 1995: 18). Practitioners have a 'difficult path ... to tread between engaging and working effectively with serious offenders and carrying out their responsibilities towards victims and the wider public', and the work 'demands a very high degree of skill in addition to commitment' (Jones *et al.* 1995: 142, 158). The managerial approach to practice, with its reliance on desk-bound, formulaic monitoring, has been seen as reducing skilled practitioners to 'minions who merely follow procedures from this or that manual' (Nellis and Chui 2003: 274).

The advent of NOMS compounds these concerns. Commissioning and contestability and the radical restructuring involved are viewed as significant threats to the professionalism of probation, endangering standards, principles and values, and jeopardising probation officer training and qualification (McKnight 2005). It is feared that the reformed working practices will demean and drive away existing trained staff and discourage others from taking up training to join the service (Nellis and Chui 2003). In place of professionally trained officers, the majority of staff will be untrained entrants, who will take up the work for short periods in between other jobs without any in-depth understanding of the social and psychological bases for the behaviour in which they are intervening. Staff shortages and difficulties in recruiting trained staff in some areas have already resulted in the deployment of 'Probation Service officers' instead of trained 'probation officers' as group-work tutors and offender managers.

Predating NOMS, however, the compulsory use of formalised assessment tools and monitoring procedures has long been implicated in such perceptions of deprofessionalisation. Since their introduction, practitioners have tended to be wary of assessment tools, seeing them as mindless, tick-box procedures taking up time that would normally be used to better effect in interviewing and making nuanced judgements (Roberts *et al.* 1996; Robinson 2003). Similarly, case management approaches (now termed offender management) have been regarded as a threat to practitioners' direct work with offenders because of the additional time needed for bureaucratic tasks and because of the increased emphasis on referring probationers to other services. The pivotal use of OASys and the OM model in NOMS exacerbates these trends.

Another way in which NOMS is seen as imperilling professional standards and roles lies in the division between the offender management and service provision arms of the organisation. Some view this division as likely to result in the transference of more professionally challenging and interesting aspects of their role to services that are less qualified to do them, leaving probation staff with more mundane and bureaucratic tasks. But the most vehement objections to the 'purchaser–provider split' centre around the prospect of services being commissioned from the private sector to the extent that probation will cease to exist as a public sector service. Most worrying is the prospect of 'private companies tender[ing] for services perceived as simple and deliverable by low-paid, poorly trained workers who can be dumped off when the inevitable disaster occurs' (Barkley 2005).[10]

Can better prospects for professional skills, job security and morale within the Probation Service be realistically envisioned? There is no doubt that many more interventions are to be provided by outside services, but it is less certain how many of the existing interventions provided in-house will be retained. The Director of the NPS recently offered the reassurance that: 'With 200,000 offenders on supervision in the community currently, an additional 40,000 who will come through custody plus and 250,000 reports a year *there is clearly no shortage of work*' (Hill 2005, our emphasis). According to official rhetoric, commissioning and contestability will improve both the quality and range of interventions. If there is truth in these predictions they are to be welcomed.[11]

With regard to apprehensions of a trade-off between professionalism and managerialism, the allusions to a split between offender management and interventions are somewhat misleading. First, the supervisory aspect of offender management is arguably an intervention in its own right, functioning to promote desistance (Burnett 2004). Secondly, supervision supports interventions not in an adjunctive way but integrally. To carry out this role with, often, resistant people who have complex problems, requires great skill, specialist training and the highest level of commitment. Likewise, the skilled application of OASys and other assessment tools demands rigorous training and professionalism (Baker 2004).

An insightful appraisal of how aspects of managerialism, such as actuarial risk assessment, impinge on probation's claim to professionalism has been provided by Robinson (2003). Borrowing from Jamous and Peloille (1970, cited in Robinson 2003), she notes that the rise in 'technicality' in probation practice (those aspects of work that can be prescribed and subject to routine practices) has been accompanied by a corresponding fall in 'indeterminacy' (aspects of work based on professional knowledge, interpretation and judgement). Investigation of practice revealed, however, that practitioners regard offenders' problems as too complex and ambiguous safely to be left to technical prescription, while the need for defensible decisions means that there will always be a place for trained professional judgement in the service. Robinson (2003) concludes that a 'professional future' for the Service lies in achieving a positive, working balance between technicality and indeterminacy.

There is no doubt that the complexity of the new framework for offender management and arrangements for the delivery and provision of interventions leave much scope for professional judgement – as well as other interpersonal skills and qualities that are called for in helping people to change.

The task of assessment is challenging, requiring utmost care.[12] The OM model emphasises that 'resources follow risk' (NOMS 2005a: 16). While this may sound simple, the reality is more complex because a number of different risks have to be weighed up in any individual case, including the likelihood of reoffending, the risk of harm and risks which some cases pose to the organisation. In this context, an assessment needs to demonstrate clarity in identifying and analysing the significance of these different types of risks. Training and experience is needed, as well as intuition and empathy. In the wrong hands, the use of systematic assessment procedures carry dangers, such as over-reliance on statistical predictions generated by assessment tools giving an 'illusion of clarity' (Bhui 1999), or leading to practitioners either inferring too much or being too cautious (Kemshall 1996), and giving rise to defensive rather than defensible decisions (Tuddenham 2000) which may result in disproportionate sentences and unnecessary restrictions on liberty. On the other hand, a failure to carry out 'risk of harm' assessments or to act on them can have disastrous consequences (as the murder of John Monckton made only too clear).

Similarly, effective deployment of interventions in offender management will not be straightforward. Simultaneous application of the tiering framework and appropriate use of the seven Pathways is likely to create a level of complexity that some practitioners will find difficult to operate and to describe clearly to external stakeholders. It will be impractical to individualise sentence plans in the way that is intended if the tiering framework is applied too rigidly or if pathway interventions are viewed too narrowly. Offenders with complex needs will require more than one of the pathways to be initiated, and in such cases prioritisation will be an important issue. Other needs may be easily identified but not readily met, for example, a lack of satisfactory accommodation. Finally, and also calling for high levels of professional knowledge and judgement, the implementation of multi-faceted sentences that combine punitive, rehabilitative and public protection interventions is likely to prove more complex than envisaged.[13]

Responsibilisation

Another critical view of NOMS sees it as the latest manifestation of consecutive governments' attempts to turn probation into an agency which ignores the social causes of crime and perpetuates the social exclusion of individuals who are already disadvantaged and marginalised (Drakeford and Vanstone 2000), resulting in an increased prison population (Rumgay 2005). In an extension of this perspective, Kemshall (2002) utilises the concept of 'responsibilisation' to argue that large-scale cognitive-behavioural intervention in probation replaces welfare provision with required self-reliance and self-control. In this scenario, the state's role becomes that of facilitator and educator: people are required to self-regulate and make sensible choices and those who do not are seen as responsible for their own misfortunes. 'Disadvantage and exclusion are re-framed as matters of choice and not of structural processes' (Kemshall 2002: 43) because those who break the law are provided with opportunities to correct their way and to be morally and cognitively re-educated.

The notion of 'responsibilisation', in a probation context, echoes with what some have decried as mistaken 'individuation' in probation work: a tendency to see the individual as at fault rather than the widespread social problems that lead to crime (Walker and Beaumont 1981). Citing Radzinowicz's (1958: xii) formulation of probation as 'a form of social service preventing crime by a readjustment of the culprit', Raynor and Vanstone (2002: 50) contend that community supervision has always 'been driven largely by attempts to change individual behaviour rather than the social environment in which that has been played out'. Such a perspective has led some authors to question the logic of training individuals to tackle their cognitive-behavioural deficits when it seems more likely that deficits in social capital are holding them back (Farrall 2002), as well as 'special problems of poverty, long-term unemployment and addictions, and sometimes long histories of abuse and abusive behaviour, which are not amenable, in any straightforward way, to the inculcation of social or cognitive skills' (Jones *et al.* 1995: 13). For these reasons, group programmes are seen as too narrowly focused on intra-individual processes and actions while neglecting environmental difficulties.

Similarly, some authors also see the utilisation of risk-needs assessment tools as serving to pathologise individual behaviour (Horsefield 2003) and to 'restrict interventions and responses to the personal domain of individual change and away from broader concerns with structural issues' (Kemshall 2002: 49; Shaw and Hannah-Moffat 2004). There are also criticisms of OASys which reflect the wider debate about the current focus on 'risk' and public protection as the goal of probation practice (see earlier discussion), including the question of whether need should be redefined as part of the risk paradigm (Hannah-Moffat and Shaw 2001), or whether a 'strengths-based approach' that places more emphasis on protective factors would be preferable to the current search for offending-related problems.

In response to arguments that programmes addressing cognitive and social skills are irrelevant, McGuire (2005: 258) reminds us of the accumulation of meta-analyses and integrative reviews which consolidate previous findings of effectiveness:

> Perhaps now [the debate about what works] is less of a debate than an 'agenda', as surely very few remain who doubt that there is convincing evidence of the possibility of reducing recidivism among persistent offenders.

Yet, as he further points out:

> [There are] some authors who have continued to regard the empirical base with disbelief and derision ... and dismissal of it has been enshrined in resolutions at annual conferences of the National Association of Probation Officers. (McGuire 2005: 261)

Such arguments against cognitive-behavioural programmes seem to misrepresent the supervisory context within which it was always intended they would take place. As McGuire contends, it is invalid to argue that a focus on cognitive-behavioural elements is tantamount to ignoring other factors that contribute to offending behaviour and 'it is a false dichotomy to suggest that researching how better to work with individuals or engaging in practice informed by research *ipso facto* constitutes a rejection of the importance of social change' (2005: 274). Amid such widespread denouncement of cognitive-behavioural group programmes this defence brings a salutary sense of perspective.

Clearly, social factors should also be addressed from within the Service and in partnership with other services, and the intervention pathways may bring welcome improvements in such provision. A concern, though, is that the tiering framework (PC 65/2005) will exclude provision to some people in dire need who are assessed as low risk. A first-tier offender will be eligible only for punishment and not be eligible for referral to sources of help with social needs (for example accommodation, debt). It is not clear how magistrates will deal with numerous offenders who present little risk but have multiple social and personal problems. Women offenders, for example, generally commit less serious offences and have fewer previous convictions (Gelsthorpe and Morris 2002): it follows that they will more typically be assessed as of low risk and so will fall into tier 1, resulting in a sentence of punishment alone, whereby the only requirement on probation officers will be that of monitoring or enforcement. Sentencers, and practitioners, may find it hard to accept that such offenders are no longer to receive active help from the Probation Service.

Essentials for the road ahead

In contrasting traditional and contemporary assessment, supervision and intervention, the most overt changes in each of these three areas of practice respectively are: the transition from unstructured and arbitrary assessment decisions to the use of systematic and validated assessment tools; the movement from one-to-one casework as the principal *modus operandi* to a team-based offender management approach; and the progression from exceptional and arbitrary use of interventions to the systematic utilisation of a package of interventions, sequenced and delivered in accordance with an end-to-end sentence plan. Perhaps the greatest change of general applicability to practice – now formalised in the principle of 'resources following risk' – is that those subject to 'offender management' are higher-end offenders and therefore the stakes have been raised.

The standard of probation practice has advanced greatly since supervision practice was described as pretentious (Wootton 1959), since assessment followed the 'kitchen sink school' of report-writing (Raynor 1980) and since 'intervention' for the majority of probationers was confined to one-to-one chats and occasional home visits. Anyone with a longer memory of probation practice will surely acknowledge that, whatever its former strengths, the Service was long in need of systems to ensure standardisation and accountability and to provide evidence of it effectiveness, and that therefore the advancement of these within recent probation history is generally to be welcomed.

The critical themes considered in the foregoing section, however, are based on the view that reforms have moved too far in the opposite direction or have been accompanied by other counterproductive shifts. In describing developments at different stages along the road to NOMS, we have argued here that practice has at times veered in undesirable directions, particularly in its diversion to one-track pursuit of cognitive-behavioural group-work programmes. But in reviewing recent moves on a practice level, we also find encouraging indications of improved 'in-house' provision for working with offenders and, if the soundbites are to be believed, for a broader range of high-quality interventions to be drawn on in a holistic approach to rehabilitation. The main caveats here though are that sufficient funding should be available to carry through these strategies, and that the following prior conditions and ongoing principles are met.

1 Working effectively with people at risk of reoffending is at least as challenging a role as several other professional occupations and therefore equally requires substantial and high-level training to equip practitioners with appropriate professional skills. A recent analysis of the practice skills required to reduce reoffending (McNeill et al. 2005), constructed from a literature review of effective practice in rehabilitation of offenders and in psychotherapy and counselling, identified the following skill sets as necessary in work to reduce reoffending:

   – Skill Set 1: Building relationships that support change
   – Skill Set 2: Assessing risks, needs and strengths
   – Skill Set 3: Research-based planning and delivery of interventions
   – Skill Set 4: Managing change.

2 In particular, and in accordance with Skills Set 1 above, the power of the offender-practitioner relationship in gaining the trust and cooperation of individuals who might otherwise be resistant, and in influencing them to engage in the steps towards change, should not be underestimated. The development of a 'collaboration' or 'working alliance' may be preferred terms. McNeill et al. (2005) identify the ability to build and utilise relationships as a discrete skill set in its own right (including communication, counselling and interpersonal skills) but point out that it underpins each of the other skill sets and each aspect of the supervision process.

3 It is essential for there to be sufficient numbers of practitioners to allow time for this important face-to-face work to take place, including visits where necessary to custodial institutions. Current staff shortages and the transference of prisoners to distant prisons militate against this. In this respect, expert commentators have welcomed the move away from a national prison estate towards community prisons (Nacro 2004).

4 A linked requirement is for staff to be demonstrably valued in the form of higher salaries, supervisory support and training opportunities. It is on record that sick rates for the Probation Service are very high (Hill 2005) and

that morale is low (Knott 2004). Once appropriate staff have been attained, it is vital that there are procedures and resources for looking after their morale. Moreover, the Service needs to ensure that it attracts suitable staff. The 'resources follow risk' principle serves to underline that practitioners now spend most of their time with medium- to high-risk offenders, and the complexity and challenge of that work should not be underestimated, whether in terms of the rewards and support that are offered or in recruitment of in-house staff and the outsourcing of interventions.

5 The present focus on the *sentence* as the offender manager's 'project' – perhaps a new variant on the offence-focused approach of recent years – should not exclude the adoption of a *person-centred approach* to assessment and sentence planning. Accurate assessment requires empathy and is partly dependent on the trust, cooperation and subsequent disclosure of information by individuals who are enabled to share their own perspective (Smale and Tuson 1993), and research into effective practice in changing behaviour has shown the importance of utilising the individual's own frame of reference (Burnett *et al.* 2005). More generally, in fulfilling the 'human services approach' (Dowden and Andrews 2004), the Service needs people-centred staff who care about the interests and potential of individuals with whom they work as well as achieving the targets of the Service.

6 Sentence plans should give sufficient weight to the environmental and economic context of individuals' behaviour, so that the focus on personal and behavioural issues (influencing human capital) in supporting individuals to desist from crime is complemented by interventions to improve their economic and social capital. In recent years, as discussed above, the Probation Service has been widely criticised for concentrating its resources on interventions to change individuals 'inside' while neglecting the 'outside' factors that are linked to repeat offending. NOMS provides an ideal opportunity for an extension of services and interventions to redress that imbalance.

7 It will be necessary for the concept of end-to-end management to include joined-up assessment, supervision and intervention as well as integrated custodial and community sentence planning. A danger is that the separation of management from services in the restructuring of the Probation Service could drive a wedge between interventions that are outsourced and those with the key role of supervising, engaging and motivating people referred to interventions. It will be good for practice if market-testing does indeed raise standards, but bad for practice if it results in a major divide between processes that have always been, and should remain, qualitatively related.

8 Finally, some thought might be given to finding alternatives for the following labels: 'punish' in the tiering framework, and 'offender'. It is the task of courts to punish, whereas probation staff monitor the enforcement of the penalty imposed: 'monitor' might therefore be a suitable substitute for 'punish'. With regard to those on the receiving end of probation intervention, the objective is that they will not be 'offenders' during and following the sentence. Labelling them as such *throughout* their sentence

can only serve to reinforce this aspect of their identity and thus seems counterproductive in efforts to encourage change. In this regard, there is some comfort to be found in the current use by the Home Office[14] of the concept of 'probation' to refer to all forms of supervision by offender managers, regardless of sentence. Given that this seems to be a use of the term 'probation' according to its literal meaning, perhaps it could be taken as a signal for the Service to now refer to all their charges as 'probationers'. This at least contains the idea of a being in a temporary state and travelling forward hopefully.

Notes

1 The concept of interventions is sometimes used to refer to court sentences. Specific sentences are discussed in Chapter 9 of this volume, and in this chapter we confine ourselves to interventions that are delivered or brokered by practitioners following sentences.

2 Each of these areas of practice is multifaceted in its own right, and it is not possible to do more than identify some of the main features in the space available. Likewise, we are limited to descriptions of practice applicable to offenders in general without detailing diversity provision and arrangements for working with specific categories such as dangerous and prolific offenders.

3 The latest probation statistics for England and Wales lists 'nine main types of supervision', including seven court orders as well as pre-release and post-release supervision (Home Office 2005: 8).

4 OASys is discussed later in this chapter. For young offenders (10–17) the Youth Justice Board developed the Asset assessment tool (Baker 2005).

5 It should be emphasised that our discussion in this chapter refers to Version 1 of the model, and that a second version is currently being drafted.

6 For example, risk assessments provided in court reports for those convicted of specified offences under the Criminal Justice Act 2003 will inform courts' decisions about 'dangerousness' and the subsequent imposition of indeterminate custodial sentences.

7 This tool is also used by police and prison services. Risk Matrix 2000 has different scales for predicting sexual and non-sexual violent recidivism.

8 Subsequent enquiries suggest that, in the case of John Monkton's murder, there had been Probation Service lapses in carrying out appropriate assessments and following procedures, but that in the case of those who murdered Mary Ann Leneghan, it seems that the assessments were reasonable and staff acted appropriately. The latter may prove to be an example of the fact that, however rigorous the procedures, there will always be an element of unpredictability and offender management services cannot completely control for risk.

9 Several such studies are summarised in appendices of the report (NOMS 2005a).

10 Regarding the quality of in-house provision, it is pertinent that the evaluation of the resettlement Pathfinder found probation-led projects produced consistently better results than the voluntary-organisation-led projects (Lewis *et al.* 2003).

11 The NW Pathfinder evaluation (PA Consultancy and MORI 2005) indicates that areas continue to differ in their provision of interventions and that many gaps remain.

12 As is increasingly apparent. See note 8.

13 The Intensive Control and Change Programme (ICCP), developed for 18 to 20-year-olds, has demonstrated the difficulties faced in delivering a multimodal community sentence which provides a balanced combination of punitive and rehabilitative elements (Partridge *et al.* 2005).

14 http://www.homeoffice.gov.uk/justice/probation/ (accessed 20 October 2005).

Further reading

For a review of developments, progress and limitations in introducing evidence-based interventions into the Probation Service, covering assessment, supervision and intervention programmes, see Burnett and Roberts (2004), *What Works in Probation and Youth Justice: Developing Evidence-Based Practice.* The collection edited by Mair (2004), *What Matters in Probation*, includes numerous chapters which critically appraise these developments. The latest guidance for practitioners bringing assessment, supervision and interventions together under the ambit of offender management is *The NOMS Offender Management Model* published by the National Offender Management Service (2006). McNeill *et al.* (2005) in *21ˢᵗ Century Social Work – Reducing Re-offending: Key Practice Skills* provide an analysis of key practice skills in reducing reoffending based on emerging evidence about desistance and a review of effective practice in psychotherapy and counselling.

References

Aubrey, R. and Hough, M. (1997) *Assessing Offenders' Needs: Assessment Scales for the Probation Service*, Home Office Research Study No. 166. London: Home Office.

Audit Commission (1989) *The Probation Service: Promoting Value for Money.* London: HMSO.

Aye-Maung, N. and Hammond, N. (2000) *Risk of Re-Offending and Needs Assessments: The User's Perspective.* London: Home Office.

Baker, K. (2005) 'Assessment in youth justice: professional discretion and the use of Asset', *Youth Justice*, 5 (2): 106–22.

Bale, D. J. (1989) 'The Cambridgeshire Risk of Custody Scale', in G. Mair (ed.), *Risk Prediction and Probation: Papers from a Research and Planning Unit Workshop*, Paper 56. London: Home Office.

Barkley, A. (2005) 'A wake, or a wake-up for probation', Letter to *Guardian*, 19 October.

Barry, M. (2000) 'The mentor/monitor debate in criminal justice: "what works" for offenders', *British Journal of Social Work*, 30: 575–95.

Bhui, H. S. (1999) 'Race, racism and risk assessment: linking theory to practice with black mentally disordered offenders', *Probation Journal*, 46 (3): 171–81.

Boswell, G., Davies, M. and Wright, A. (1993) *Contemporary Probation Practice.* Aldershot: Avebury.

Bottoms, A. E. (2001) 'Compliance and community penalties', in A. Bottoms, L. Gelsthorpe and S. Rex (eds), *Community Penalties: Change and Challenges.* Cullompton: Willan.

Bottoms, A. E. and McWilliams, W. (1979) 'A non-treatment paradigm for probation practice', *British Journal of Social Work*, 9 (2): 159–202.

Bottoms, A. and Stelman, A. (1988) *Social Enquiry Reports.* Aldershot: Wildwood House.

Bracken, D. (2003) 'Skills and knowledge for contemporary probation practice', *Probation Journal*, 50 (2): 101–14.

Bridges, A. (2005) 'The long haul: improving effectiveness in the criminal justice system', Foreword in *HMI Probation 2004/2005 Annual Report*. London: HMIP.

Brindle, D. (2002) 'Tough makeover for probation service', *Guardian*, 20 March.

Burnett, R. (1996) *Fitting Supervision to Offenders: Assessment and Allocation Decisions in the Probation Service*, Home Office Research Study No. 153. London: Home Office Research and Statistics Directorate.

Burnett, R. (2004) 'One-to-one ways of promoting desistance: in search of an evidence base', in R. Burnett and C. Roberts (eds), *What Works in Probation and Youth Justice: Developing Evidence-Based Practice*. Cullompton: Willan.

Burnett, R. and McNeill, F. (2005) 'The place of the officer–offender relationship in assisting offenders to desist from crime', *Probation Journal*, 52 (3): 221–42.

Burnett, R. and Roberts, C. (eds) (2004) *What Works in Probation and Youth Justice: Developing Evidence-Based Practice*. Cullompton: Willan.

Burnett, R., Bachelor, S. and McNeill, F. (2005) 'Practice skills in reducing reoffending: lessons from psychotherapy and counselling', *Criminal Justice Matters*, 61 (Autumn): 32–41.

Caddick, B. (1991) 'A survey of groupwork in the Probation Services in England and Wales', *Groupwork*, 4 (3): 197–214.

Carter, P. (2004) *Managing Offenders, Reducing Crime: A New Approach*. London: Home Office Strategy Unit.

Chapman, T. and Hough, M. (1998) *Evidence Based Practice: A Guide to Effective Practice*. London: HMIP.

Chui, W. H. and Nellis, M. (2003) 'Creating the national probation service – new wine, old bottles?', in W.H. Chui and M. Nellis (eds), *Moving Probation Forward: Evidence, Arguments and Practice*. Harlow: Pearson Education.

Clarke, C. (2005) *Where Next for Penal Policy?* Speech to the Prison Reform Trust, 19 September.

Davies, M. (1969) *Probationers in Their Social Environment: A Study of Male Probationers Aged 17–20*, Home Office Research Study No. 2. London: Home Office.

DfES (2003) *Every Child Matters*, Green Paper. London: Department for Education and Skills.

Dowden, C. and Andrews, D. (2004) 'The importance of staff practice in delivering effective correctional treatment: a meta-analysis', *International Journal of Offender Therapy and Comparative Criminology*, 48 (2): 203–14.

Drakeford, M. and Vanstone, M. (2000) 'Social exclusion and the politics of criminal justice: a tale of two administrations', *Howard Journal*, 39: 369–81.

Duff, R. A. (2000) *Punishment, Communication and Community*. Oxford: Oxford University Press.

Farrall, S. (2002) *Rethinking What Works with Offenders: Probation, Social Context and Desistance from Crime*. Cullompton: Willan.

Faulkner, D. (2006) *Crime, State and Citizen: A Field Full of Folk*, 2nd edn. Winchester: Waterside Press.

Fleet, F. and Annison, J. (2003) 'In support of effectiveness: facilitating participation and sustaining change', in W. H. Chui and M. Nellis (eds), *Moving Probation Forward: Evidence, Arguments and Practice*. Harlow: Pearson Education.

Gelsthorpe, L. and Morris, A. (2002) 'Women's imprisonment in England and Wales: a penal paradox', *Criminal Justice*, 2 (3): 277–301.

Glaser, D. (1985) 'Who gets probation and parole: case study versus actuarial decision making', *Crime and Delinquency*, 31 (3): 367–78.

Hannah-Moffat, K. and Shaw, M. (2001) *Taking Risks: Incorporating Gender and Culture into the Classification and Assessment of Federally Sentenced Women in Canada*. Ontario: Status of Women Canada.

Haslewood-Pócsik, I. and McMahon, G. (2004) 'Probation interventions to address basic skills and employment needs', in R. Burnett and C. Roberts (eds), *What Works in Probation and Youth Justice: Developing Evidence-Based Practice*. Cullompton: Willan.

Hedderman, C. (2005) *Eighty Thousand Not Out: The Rising Prison Population in England and Wales*. Inaugural lecture, 25 October, University of Leicester.

Hedderman, C. and Hough, M. (2004) 'Getting tough or being effective: what matters?', in G. Mair (ed.), *What Matters in Probation*. Cullompton: Willan.

Hill, R. (2005) Speech by the Director of the National Probation Service for England and Wales to the NAPO Annual Conference, Llandudno, 14 October.

HMI Probation (2004) *Effective Supervision Inspection of the National Probation Service for England and Wales: Report on Hampshire Probation Area*. London: Home Office.

HMI Probation (2006) *An Independent Review of a Serious Further Offence Case: Damien Hanson and Elliot White*. London: HMI Probation.

Hollin, C., McGuire, J., Palmer, E., Bilby, C., Hatcher, R. and Holmes, A. (2002) *Introducing Pathfinder Programmes into the Probation Service: A Interim Report*, Home Office Research Study No. 247. London: Home Office.

Holt, P. (2002) 'Case management evaluation: pathways to progress', *VISTA*, 7 (1): 16–25.

Home Office (1962) *Report of the Departmental Committee on the Work of the Probation Service* (The Morison Report), Cmnd 1650. London: HMSO.

Home Office (1996) *Guidance for the Probation Service on the Offender Group Reconviction Scale*. London: Home Office.

Home Office (2004a) *Reducing Crime, Changing Lives: The Government's Plans for Transforming the Management of Offenders*. London: Home Office.

Home Office (2004b) *Reducing Re-Offending: National Action Plan, Reference Document*. London: Home Office.

Home Office (2005) *Probation Statistics England and Wales. Quarterly Brief, October to December 2004*. London: NOMS.

Home Office (2006) *A Five-Year Strategy for Protecting the Public and Reducing Re-offending*, Cm 6717. London: Stationery Office.

Hopkinson, J. and Rex, S. (2003) 'Essential skills in working with offenders', in W.H. Chui and M. Nellis (eds), *Moving Probation Forward: Evidence, Arguments and Practice*. Harlow: Pearson Education.

Horsefield, A. (2003) 'Risk assessment: who needs it?', *Probation Journal*, 50 (4): 374–9.

Jones, A., Kroll, B., Pitts, J. and Taylor, A. (1995) *Probation Practice*. London: Pitman Publishing.

Jones, L. (2002) 'An individual case formulation approach to the assessment of motivation', in M. McMurran (ed.), *Motivating Offenders to Change: A Guide to Enhancing Engagement in Therapy*. Chichester: Wiley.

Kemshall, H. (1996) *Reviewing Risk: A Review of Research on the Assessment and Management of Risk and Dangerousness, Implications for Policy and Practice in the Probation Service*. Croydon: Home Office.

Kemshall, H. (2002) 'Effective practice in probation: an example of "advanced liberal" responsibilisation?', *Howard Journal*, 41 (1): 41–58.

Kemshall, H., Holt, P., Bailey, R. and Boswell, G. (2004) 'Beyond programmes: organisational and cultural issues in the implementation of What Works', in G. Mair (ed.), *What Matters in Probation*. Cullompton: Willan.

Kemshall, H., Canton, R. and Dominey, J. with Bailey, R., Simpkin, B. and Yates, S. (2002) *The Effective Management of Programme Attrition. Report for the NPS*. Leicester: De Montfort University.

Kirwin, K. (1985) 'Probation and supervision', in H. Walker and B. Beaumont (eds), *Working With Offenders*. London: Macmillan.

Knott, C. (2004) 'Evidence-based practice in the National Probation Service', in R. Burnett and C. Roberts (eds), *What Works in Probation and Youth Justice: Developing Evidence-Based Practice*. Cullompton: Willan.

Lacey, M. (1995) 'Working for justice: fairness', in D. Ward and M. Lacey (eds), *Probation: Working for Justice*. London: Whiting & Birch.

Lambert, M. J. and Ogles, B. M. (2004) 'The efficacy and effectiveness of psychotherapy', in M. J. Lambert (ed.), *Bergin & Garfield's Handbook of Psychotherapy and Behavior Change*, 5th edn. New York: Wiley.

Lewis, S., Maguire, M., Raynor, P., Vanstone, M. and Vennard, J. (2003) *The Resettlement of Short-term Prisoners: An Evaluation of Seven Pathfinders*, Research Findings 200. London: Home Office.

London Probation Service (2004) *Profile of a Probation Officer*. http://www.london-probation.org.uk/index.cfm?articleid=411 (accessed 4 February 2004).

McGuire, J. (2005) 'Is research working? Revisiting the research and effective practice agenda', in J. Winstone and F. Pakes (eds), *Community Justice: Issues for Probation and Criminal Justice*. Cullompton: Willan.

McGuire, J. and Priestley, P. (1985) *Offending Behaviour: Skills and Stratagems for Going Straight*. London: Batsford Academic & Educational.

McIvor, G., Kemshall, H. and Levy, G. (2002) *Serious Violent and Sexual Offenders: The Use of Risk Assessment Tools in Scotland*. Edinburgh: Scottish Executive.

McMurran, M. (2002) 'Motivation to change: selection criterion or treatment need?', in M. McMurran (ed.), *Motivating Offenders to Change: A Guide to Enhancing Engagement in Therapy*. Chichester: Wiley.

McNeill, F. (2003) 'Desistance-focused probation practice', in W. H. Chui and M. Nellis (eds), *Moving Probation Forward: Evidence, Arguments and Practice*. Harlow: Pearson Longman.

McNeill, F., Bachelor, S., Burnett, R. and Knox, J. (2005) *21st Century Social Work – Reducing Re-offending: Key Practice Skills*. Edinburgh: Scottish Executive.

McWilliams, W. (1986) 'The English probation system and the diagnostic ideal', *Howard Journal*, 25 (4): 241–60.

Mair, G. (1997) 'Community penalties and the Probation Service', in M. Maguire, R. Morgan and R. Reiner (eds), *The Oxford Handbook of Criminology*, 2nd edn. Oxford: Clarendon Press.

Mair, G. (2000) 'Credible accreditation?', *Probation Journal*, 47: 268–71.

Mair, G. (2004a) 'The origins of What Works in England and Wales: a house built on sand?', in G. Mair (ed.), *What Matters in Probation*. Cullompton: Willan.

Mair, G. (2004b) 'What works: a view from the chiefs', in G. Mair (ed.), *What Matters in Probation*. Cullompton: Willan.

Merrington, S. and Stanley, S. (2000) 'Doubts about the What Works initiative', *Probation Journal*, 47: 272–5.

Morgan, R. (2003) 'Foreword', in *HMIP Annual Report 2002/2003*. London: Home Office.

Nacro (2004) *NOMS: Will it Work?* London: Nacro.

Nellis, M. and Chui, W. H. (2003) 'The end of probation', in W. H. Chui and M. Nellis (eds), *Moving Probation Forward: Evidence, Arguments and Practice*. Harlow: Pearson Education.

Nellis, M. and Gelsthorpe, L. (2003) 'Human rights and the probation values debate', in W. H. Chui and M. Nellis (eds), *Moving Probation Forward: Evidence, Arguments and Practice*. Harlow: Pearson Education.

NOMS (2005a) *The NOMS Offender Management Model. Version 1*. London: Home Office.

NOMS (2005b) *Restructuring Probation to Reduce Re-Offending*. London: Home Office.

NOMS (2006) *The NOMS Offender Management Model*. London: Home Office.

NPS (2004a) 'Accredited Programmes Performance Report 2002–2003', *What Works Bulletin*, January. London: NPS.

NPS (2004b) *Sex Offender Strategy for the National Probation Service*. London: Home Office.

NPS (2004c) *The MAPPA Guidance*, Probation Circular 54/2004. London: Home Office.

NPS (2005a) *National Standards (2005) and National Offender Management Model: Application of Tiering Framework*, Probation Circular, 65/2005. London: Home Office.

NPS (2005b) *National Probation Service Briefing: OASys Information*, Issue 26. London: Home Office.

NPS (2005c) *National Standards 2005*. London: Home Office.

NPS (2005d) *Offender Assessment System (OASys) Quality Management Plan*, Probation Circular 48/2005. London: Home Office.

NPS (2005e) *Intervention News*, Issue 21. London: NPS.

PA Consultancy Group and MORI (2005) *Action Research Study of the Implementation of the National Offender Management Model in the North West Pathfinder*, Home Office Online Report 32/05. See: http://www.noms.homeoffice.gov.uk/downloads/Action_research_study_NOMS_Model_NW_Pathfinder.pdf

Partridge, S., Harris, J., Abram, M. and Scholes, J. (2005) *The Intensive Control and Change Programme Pilots: A Study of Implementation in the First Year*, Online Report 48/05. London: Home Office.

Radzinowicz, L. (ed.) (1958) *The Results of Probation: A Report of the Cambridge Department of Criminal Science*. London: Macmillan.

Raynor, P. (1980) 'Is there any sense in social inquiry reports?', *Probation Journal*, 27: 78–84.

Raynor, P. (2002) 'Community penalties: probation, punishment and "what works"', in M. Maguire, R. Morgan and R. Reiner (eds), *The Oxford Handbook of Criminology*, 3rd edn. Oxford: Oxford University Press.

Raynor, P. and Vanstone, M. (2002) *Understanding Community Penalties*. Buckingham: Open University Press.

Raynor, P., Smith, D. and Vanstone, M. (1994) *Effective Probation Practice. British Association of Social Workers*. London: Macmillan.

Raynor, P., Kynch, J., Roberts, C. and Merrington, S. (2000) *Risk and Need Assessment in Probation Services: An Evaluation*, Home Office Research Study No. 211. London: Home Office.

Rex, S. (1999) 'Desistance from offending: experiences of probation', *Howard Journal*, 38 (4): 366–83.

Rex, S. (2001) 'Beyond cognitive-behaviouralism? Reflections on the effectiveness literature', in A. Bottoms, L. Gelsthorpe and S. Rex (eds), *Community Penalties: Change and Challenges*. Cullompton: Willan.

Rex, S., Lieb, R., Bottoms, A. and Wilson, L. (2003) *Accrediting Offender Programmes: A Process-based Evaluation of the Joint Prison/Probation Services Accreditation Panel*, Home Office Research Study No. 273. London: Home Office Research, Development and Statistics Directorate.

Roberts, C. (1992) *The Hereford and Worcester Probation Service Young Offender Project: First Evaluation Report*. Oxford: Department of Social and Administrative Studies, University of Oxford.

Roberts, C. (2004) 'Offending behaviour programmes: emerging evidence and the implications for practice', in R. Burnett and C. Roberts (eds), *What Works in Probation and Youth Justice: Developing Evidence-Based Practice*. Cullompton: Willan.

Roberts, C., Burnett, R., Kirby, A. and Hamill, H. (1996) *A System for Evaluating Probation Practice: Report of a Method Devised and Piloted by the Oxford Probation Studies Unit and Warwickshire Probation Service*, Probation Studies Unit Report No. 1. Oxford: Centre for Criminological Research.

Roberts, J. (1997) 'Roles and identity', in R. Burnett (ed.), *The Probation Service: Responding to Change*, Probation Studies Unit Report No. 3. Oxford: Centre for Criminological Research.

Robinson, G. (1999) 'Risk management and rehabilitation in the probation service: collision and collusion', *Howard Journal*, 38 (4): 421–33.

Robinson, G. (2003) 'Technicality and indeterminacy in probation practice: a case study', *British Journal of Social Work*, 33 (5): 593–610.

Robinson, G. (2005) 'What works in offender management?', *Howard Journal*, 44 (3): 307–18.

Robinson, G. and Dignan, J. (2004) 'Sentence management', in A. Bottoms, S. Rex and G. Robinson (eds), *Alternatives to Prison: Options for an Insecure Society*. Cullompton: Willan.

Rumgay, J. (2004) 'The barking dog? Partnership and effective practice', in G. Mair (ed.), *What Matters in Probation*. Cullompton: Willan.

Rumgay, J. (2005) 'Counterblast: NOMS bombs?', *Howard Journal*, 44 (2): 206–8.

Senior, P. (1985) 'Groupwork with offenders', in H. Walker and B. Beaumont (eds), *Working With Offenders*. London: Macmillan.

Shaw, M. and Hannah-Moffat, K. (2004) 'How cognitive skills forgot about gender and diversity', in G. Mair (ed.), *What Matters in Probation*. Cullompton: Willan.

Smale, G. and Tuson, G. (1993) *Empowerment, Assessment, Care Management and the Skilled Worker*. London: HMSO.

Social Exclusion Unit (2002) *Reducing Re-Offending by Ex-prisoners*. London: Social Exclusion Unit.

Stewart-Ong, G., Harsent, L., Roberts, C., Al-Attar, Z. and Burnett, R. (2004) *Think First Prospective Research Study: Effectiveness and Reducing Attrition*, NPD Evaluation Findings. London: NPD.

Trotter, C. (1999) *Working with Involuntary Clients: A Guide to Practice*. London: Sage.

Tuddenham, R. (2000) 'Beyond defensible decision-making: towards reflexive assessment of risk and dangerousness', *Probation Journal*, 47 (3): 173–83.

Underdown, A. (1998) *Strategies for Effective Offender Supervision: Report of the HMIP What Works Project*. London: HMIP.

Vanstone, M. (1993) 'A "missed opportunity" reassessed: the influence of the Day Training Centre experiment on the criminal justice system and probation practice', *British Journal of Social Work*, 23 (3): 213–29.

Vanstone, M. (2000) 'Cognitive-behavioural work with offenders in the UK: a history of influential endeavour', *Howard Journal*, 3 (2): 171–83.

Vanstone, M. (2004) 'A history of the use of groups in probation work: Part Two – from negotiated treatment to evidence-based practice in an accountable service', *Howard Journal*, 43 (2): 180–202.

Walker, H. and Beaumont, B. (1981) *Probation Work: Critical Theory and Socialist Practice*. Oxford: Blackwell.

Wallis, E. (2001) *A New Choreography: An Integrated Strategy for the National Probation Service for England and Wales*. London: Home Office.

Walters, J. (1997) 'Response to David Garland "Probation and the reconfiguration of crime control"', in R. Burnett (ed.), *The Probation Service: Responding to Change*, Probation Studies Unit Report No. 3. Oxford: Centre for Criminological Research.

Wootton, B. (1959) *Social Science and Social Pathology*. London: Allen & Unwin.

Chapter 9

Sentencing, community penalties and the role of the Probation Service

George Mair and Rob Canton

Introduction

As recently as 1990 it would have been perceived as academic pedantry to discuss community penalties and the role of the Probation Service. For all intents and purposes (and with the exception of senior attendance centres) community penalties *were* the Probation Service as far as offenders aged 18 and over were concerned. But even as the 1991 Criminal Justice Act passed into law, there were straws in the wind that – with the benefit of 15 years' hindsight – should have been recognised as presaging a sea change for community penalties and the Probation Service. The 1991 Act had changed the way in which probation was seen by introducing a just deserts framework for sentencing that meant community penalties (a new generic term) were now officially sentences in their own right rather than alternatives to custody. The first trials of electronic monitoring had taken place (see Mair and Nee 1990) and, although by no means demonstrating unequivocal success, the use of 'tagging' was not about to disappear for good. A new sentence – the combination order – the first since the community service order in 1972, had been introduced. And the idea of partnership working was being actively encouraged by the Home Office (Home Office 1990a, 1991), partly for positive reasons such as the provision of wider opportunities to work with offenders, but also partly as a threat to Probation Services by reminding them that other agencies and organisations could take over their work.

Each of these developments has increased its significance in the intervening 15 years. Other developments too – of equal if not greater significance – need to be acknowledged: the centralisation of the Probation Service under direct Home Office control; the introduction of the What Works agenda; the ubiquity of risk assessment and the implementation of OASys; increasingly close working relations with the police. All of the developments noted provide the context in which the details of this chapter are grounded and we will return to their significance in our concluding section. At present, we only wish to emphasise the number of recent developments and their significance; it would be easy to make a case for probation having undergone more radical change in a shorter period of time than any other traditional criminal justice agency. Just how far this has had an impact upon the use of community penalties will be one of the major themes of the chapter.

In this chapter we are concerned with community penalties as sentences and how they are used and enforced in the sentencing process. The first section will focus on the various community penalties that have been – and currently are – available to the courts. The growth of such penalties, changing conceptions about them and the implications of the present situation with the generic community order will all be discussed, as will the changing role of the Probation Service. The next section will examine sentencing trends for community penalties using official data from the annual Criminal Statistics and Probation Statistics. The kinds of offenders who receive community penalties, the offences for which community penalties are made and consistency of use will be studied. The third part of the chapter discusses issues around compliance and enforcement. The former has only recently become an area of interest thanks to the work of Tony Bottoms (2001), while the latter (intimately related as it is to compliance) was for some considerable time left on the margins of probation and only with government efforts in the 1990s to 'toughen up' the Probation Service did it begin to receive empirical attention. The fourth section examines several probation programmes in detail in order to demonstrate how they operate in practice during the course of the order. Finally, we draw some conclusions from our analysis and speculate what the future might hold for community penalties and the Probation Service.

We are, of course, only too aware that since 4 April 2005 the situation has changed dramatically. For offences committed since 4 April the new community order has replaced the various community sentences, although the latter are still available for offences committed prior to 4 April. For the purposes of the chapter the basis of our discussion will be pre-4 April. This is partly because the 'old' set of community penalties is still in use, partly because statistical material on the use of the new order is sparse; and partly because it is still very early days for the community order. Despite our focus on community penalties rather than the community order, we will speculate wherever possible on the implications of the new order.

Sentences

The introduction of the probation order (with a maximum period of supervision of three years and no minimum) with the passing of the Probation of Offenders Act 1907 fixed an image of the order that has dogged it ever since. By providing that a probation order could be made by the court without proceeding to a conviction (similar to entering into a recognisance), and by classing probation in the same section of the Act as discharge, the order was irredeemably tainted with the idea of being a soft option; 'it was equivalent to letting the offender off' (King 1969: 8). Despite the 1948 Criminal Justice Act changing such provisions, this image of probation not being a proper punishment has persisted and can be seen to lie behind public perceptions of community penalties, sentencer confidence in them and much of the legislation relating to them since their beginnings.

The original idea of probation as help for an offender who was willing to embrace the offer of assistance in overcoming his or her problems, as offering a second chance for those who had slipped, does not seem to have unduly obstructed its growth. Although there were concerns about the abilities of the police court missionaries, a lack of any consistent training for those who worked as probation officers, no overall control of probation work and considerable disruption caused by the First World War, in 1923 there were almost 20,000 individuals placed on probation (with roughly one quarter of them for non-indictable offences). To provide some context, in the same year 31,000 individuals received a custodial sentence. For the first 40 years of its existence, the probation order was in a monopoly position as a sentence offering some form of supervision and its popularity can be seen by data for 1938 when 31,500 offenders were placed on probation and 22,000 received a custodial sentence. In that year, the probation order was the most commonly used sentence for indictable offences (see Rutherford 1986: 129).

The 1948 Criminal Justice Act kept the maximum period of a probation order at three years but added a minimum of one year. It differentiated the order from a discharge, and it made provision for a wider range of requirements to be added to the order. The Act also introduced attendance centres for offenders aged 12–20, and these could be used for imprisonable offences or for breach of a probation order. While it took ten years for the first senior attendance centre for 17–20-year-olds to be set up (in Manchester in December 1958), and it was only during the 1980s that a number of senior attendance centres were opened, the centres are significant in that they broke the monopoly of the Probation Service in providing a community-based sentence for those aged 17+ (the centres are run by prison officers and police officers – for a full account of the development of senior attendance centres see Mair 1991). In 1950, a total of 31,000 individuals were placed on probation, nine-tenths of whom had been convicted of indictable offences (Haxby 1978: 301–14).

By the 1950s the Probation Service had changed, as McWilliams has demonstrated so well (1983, 1985, 1986). But while the growth of the Service had necessitated a hierarchical structure, a bureaucracy, formal training and a much more professional approach to working with offenders, the practice of dealing with offenders had not changed very much at all. While the religious impulse that had driven the early probation officers had receded, and a scientific approach to casework with offenders had taken its place, the idea of helping individuals with problems remained at the core of the probation order. The 1950s and 1960s may well have been the high-point of the rehabilitative ideal, but only in so far as there was little in the way of questioning the basis of probation work and a naive assumption that good works were effective (although precisely what that might mean remained opaque). In 1961, 45,000 individuals were placed on probation, an increase of 45 per cent from 1950, although this was due to the rise in the overall numbers going through the courts rather than any increased demand for the probation order.

The significance of crime in the early 1960s can be seen in the title of a White Paper published in 1964 *The War against Crime in England and Wales*

1959–1964 (Home Office 1964). The White Paper suggested that a fundamental reassessment of the penal system was required to provide answers to questions about the effectiveness of existing sentences, whether new sentences were advisable, how these might be developed and the like. The first step was the appointment of a Royal Commission on the Penal System but this never reported (indeed it remains the only Royal Commission never to report; for the reasons, see Mair 1991: 72). The 1967 Criminal Justice Act was focused upon diversion from custody as a result of a sudden rise in the prison population and introduced parole and the suspended sentence. A House of Commons Estimates Committee Report (1967) also addressed the issue of prison overcrowding, and in 1966 the Advisory Council on the Penal System (ACPS) had been asked to look into the question of the range of non-custodial penalties. The question of new court sentences and the need for alternatives to custody came together in the ACPS study (1970), generally known as the Wootton Report after its chair Baroness Wootton, that recommended the introduction of the community service order.

The proposed new order was aimed to appeal to

> … adherents of different varieties of penal philosophy. To some, it would be simply a more constructive and cheaper alternative to short sentences of imprisonment; by others it would be seen as introducing into the penal system a new dimension with an emphasis on reparation to the community; others again would regard it as a means of giving effect to the old adage that the punishment should fit the crime; while still others would stress the value of bringing offenders into close touch with those members of the community who are most in need of help and support. (ACPS 1970: 13)

While the ACPS report claimed that the 'different approaches are by no means incompatible' (ACPS 1970: 13), Baroness Wootton herself admitted some years later that she was 'slightly ashamed' of the way in which the ACPS had tried to make the proposed new order appeal to all shades of penal opinion (Wootton 1978: 128). There is little doubt that the confusion about the aim of community service sown by ACPS (with good intentions) has persisted ever since.

The Government was persuaded by the ACPS recommendation and the 1972 Criminal Justice Act introduced the community service order (CSO) where an offender of 17 or over convicted of an offence *punishable by imprisonment* could be required to undertake unpaid work for between 40 and 240 hours. The tensions around community service, set out as virtues by the ACPS, were not resolved by legislation so that it remained unclear whether the CSO was a sentence in its own right or an alternative to custody (not, it should be emphasised, the same thing as only to be used for offences punishable by imprisonment). Many probation staff were not happy with the new sentence as it contained no possibility of help with problems that led to offending. But the CSO ushered in a new conception of community penalties as alternatives to custody and as an unintended consequence began the process of uptariffing that has haunted the introduction of new community penalties ever since.

The initial research on CSOs (Pease *et al.* 1977) suggested that only around half of those sentenced to a CSO were diverted from custody, implying that the other half had been sentenced more punitively as in the absence of the CSO they would have received a probation order or even a fine. In addition, breach of a CSO – with its semi-official aim of being an alternative to custody – would be more likely to lead to a custodial sentence.

The 1972 Act also introduced a requirement that could be added to a probation order to attend a day training centre (DTC) for up to 60 days. While only four day training centres were ever formally set up, the DTC experiment remains significant for several reasons: first, as Vanstone and Raynor (1981: 89) argue, the centres (unlike community service) 'always had a clear purpose as an alternative to custody, and the available evidence is that they have stuck to it, refusing to be diverted into just another non-custodial option at the lower end of the tariff'; second, DTCs institutionalised group work as an approach to dealing with offenders – an approach that, as Vanstone has shown, has 'moved from a marginalized activity of a few enthusiasts to the centre of the effective practice project' (2004: 191); and third, they seem to have been responsible for the growth of probation day centres which required fewer resources than DTCs (see Smith 1982). The number of day centres proliferated rapidly during the 1980s and the DTCs were allowed to mutate into day centres.

The idea of probation (with an added requirement) and community service both offering alternatives to custody was enhanced by the publication in 1974 of Robert Martinson's now infamous article 'What Works?: questions and answers about prison reform' (Martinson 1974). While the arguments over precisely what Martinson did and did not claim in the article have provided a mini-academic industry since its publication, the implications for probation were profound. Martinson's attack on the efficacy of rehabilitation, alongside arguments from the left about the unfettered discretion of probation officers and from the right about rehabilitation being soft on crime, all fed into the remaking of probation and community service as alternatives to custody. As the prison population was rising throughout the 1970s and 1980s, this conception of the two disposals fitted neatly with the times. There is no evidence that probation officers lost morale in the wake of Martinson or changed their practice in any way (and it is notable that in David Haxby's important book *Probation: A Changing Service* (1978) there is no mention of Martinson, although his UK equivalent Stephen Brody (1976) is mentioned briefly, and Haxby does argue in favour of a community correctional service). The terminology of alternatives to and diversion from custody, however, had entered the language and would define probation for almost 20 years.

One clear step in encouraging the idea of probation as an alternative to custody was the growth from the 1980s onwards of additional requirements that could be added to the straight probation order in order to 'toughen it up' (and with the same potentially serious unintended consequences with regard to uptariffing as the introduction of the CSO had caused). Some requirements had been available from the beginnings of the probation order (e.g. abstention from alcohol under the 1907 Act, conditions of residence under the Criminal Justice (Administration) Act 1914), but with the 1982 Criminal Justice Act two significant requirements were added: to participate in specified activities and to attend a day centre, either of which could be for up to 60 days. Day centres in particular were acknowledged as an important resource and by the mid-1980s there were estimated to be more than 80 such centres in existence in England and Wales, although they were by no means equally distributed across all probation areas (some areas simply decided not to have any day centres as they did not agree with the idea of statutory attendance as part of a court order). A Home Office study of the centres (Mair 1988) argued that greater consistency and standardisation were needed for the centres, and noted that the centres did seem to be used around half of the time as an alternative to custody, which was their main aim (cf. the community service order, above). As the research was being completed (1987), day centre conditions accounted for 2,400 persons (6 per cent) commencing probation supervision. At the same time, a condition to participate in specified activities accounted for a further 5 per cent (the two requirements accounted for just over half of the 8,500 additional requirements made).

During the 1990s more additional requirements (mostly to do with drug or alcohol treatment) were introduced. In 1981, nine out of ten probation orders had been made with no additional requirements; by 1997 this figure had dropped to two out of three; and by 2003 – as a result of the What Works strategy – only half of the probation orders made by the courts had no requirements (see Table 9.3 below). One logical response to this development was to make the probation order completely dependent upon requirements, a development that came to fruition with the community order in 2003.

Despite the articulation of the 'Nothing Works' ideology and its implicit counsel of despair about rehabilitation, and the redefinition of probation as an alternative to custody, probation officers almost certainly continued to work in the same ways, using the same methods they had always used. The problem with this was that their methods of work were difficult to pin down, based as they were on a variety of social work/psychological methods that were very much left to individual officers to dispense within the confines of one-to-one casework. In addition, as the prison population continued to rise throughout the 1980s, the efficacy of the Probation Service in serving to divert offenders from custody was increasingly called into question. At the same time, the Conservative administration was introducing ideas about economy, efficiency and effectiveness across the public sector, asking questions about the accountability of such services, and making moves to open up these services to competition with private sector or voluntary organisations. Adding to this toxic mix, law and order was very much at the forefront of policy, and the Probation Service continued to be seen as soft on law and order (for example, probation staff insisted upon using the term clients until a Home Office instruction that offenders had to be used instead). In addition, the Home Office had an open-ended commitment to fund 80 per cent of Probation Services' budgets yet had no input to planning that budget. It is, with hindsight, not at all surprising that Government began to take an interest in asserting control over the Probation Service from 1984 onwards with the publication of the Statement of National Objectives and Priorities (Home Office 1984).

The seminal Green Paper *Punishment, Custody and the Community* (Home Office 1988) yoked together in its title the concepts of punishment and custody with that of community in a trinity that at the time appeared rather unholy but that quickly became acceptable language. Punishment had never been seen as an aspect of probation work or as part of the remit of the Probation Service, and linking custody with community can now be seen as prefiguring the idea of the seamless sentence that came to fruition with the 2003 Criminal Justice Act. The idea of community punishment was born in the Green Paper, but so too were official suggestions about greater surveillance of offenders (perhaps by using the new technology offered by electronic monitoring), and the 'possibility of setting up a new organisation to take responsibility for the arrangements for punishment in the community, and providing services through contracts with other organisations' (Home Office 1988: 18). A new sentence was also proposed (the supervision and restriction order – although, in the event, a different title was used, that proposed was significant), and while three options were mentioned for introducing it, with two of these seen as impracticable, it is interesting – especially in the light of the introduction of the community order in 2003 – to note the reasons given for not scrapping the probation and community service orders and replacing them with an entirely new sentence:

> A new order, which replaced existing orders, would also be flexible and the courts would still be able to give some offenders a disposal which amounted to a probation order without any punitive elements. On the other hand, it might encourage the courts to impose too severe a penalty and make them more reluctant to use supervision a second time for an offender who had failed to complete an earlier order satisfactorily. (Home Office 1988: 14–15)

By 2003, worries about imposing 'too severe a penalty' or sentencers being over-keen to impose a custodial sentence in cases of breach of a community penalty had obviously diminished.

Other developments too pointed towards a more rigorous, demanding and controlling Probation Service. In 1989 the Government introduced National Standards for community service orders in order to ensure greater consistency in the way CSOs were designed and thus encourage greater use by the courts. And in the same year, the Home Office began discussing an experimental intensive probation (IP) project that began in April 1990 in nine Probation Services. This IP scheme differed from the earlier IMPACT project (see Folkard *et al.* 1974; Folkard, Smith and Smith 1976) in that in the latter intensive essentially meant more social work help, while in the IP schemes intensive meant more demanding, more controlling (Mair *et al.* 1994).

The 1991 Criminal Justice Act changed the context of probation for ever. Although more symbolic than substantive, the status of probation as not being a sentence of the court was changed; the probation order now became a sentence and, as such, could be combined with another penalty in respect of a single offence. The Act stated clearly where it was desirable to use a probation order: either to rehabilitate the offender or to protect the public from harm by the offender (CJA 1991: s. 8). The new sentence promised in the Green Paper was introduced: the simplistic appeal of a sentence that offered help (probation) as well as a dose of punishment (community service) was embodied in the aptly named combination order, where the supervision element could be between 12 and 36 months, while the community service part could be between 40 and 100 hours. Another new sentence appeared too: despite the equivocal results from the trials of electronic monitoring as a condition of bail (Mair and Nee 1990) the curfew order became a court sentence for offenders aged 16 and over. The order could be made for a period of up to six months and for between two and 12 hours in any one day. Perhaps most significantly, the curfew order could be subject to electronic monitoring (indeed, curfew orders became synonymous with electronic monitoring or tagging).

The 1991 Act also introduced a new legislative framework for sentencing – just deserts (or 'desserts' as the White Paper *Crime, Justice and Protecting the Public* (Home Office 1990b) put it). With this, community sentences, or community orders (defined as probation, community service, the combination order, curfew orders, supervision orders and attendance centre orders) became sentences in their own right, to be used when the offence 'was serious enough to warrant such a sentence' (CJA 1991: s. 6). Custody was to be used where the offence 'was so serious that only such a sentence can be justified for the offence' (CJA 1991: s. 1)

The 1991 Act was welcomed cautiously by probation officers (Mair and May 1995), but the new terminology (community punishment), the blurring at the edges between community sentences and custody, the introduction of the curfew order with its emphasis on surveillance should each have been enough to send out warning signals to the Probation Service. The Association of Chief Officers of Probation (ACOP) and the National Association of Probation Officers (NAPO) had both been so opposed to the idea of electronic monitoring that probation officers had lost the opportunity of being named as responsible officers for the curfew order. While the virtual non-development of senior attendance centres posed no threat to the Probation Service monopoly in providing community penalties for those aged 17 and upwards, the introduction of the curfew order was a more substantial threat to that monopoly. The companies responsible for providing electronic monitoring services were not traditional criminal justice agencies – they were in business to make profits for their shareholders and were likely to market their products aggressively.

As a result of the Act, there were now more community sentences, more additional requirements that could be added to probation or combination orders, and a greater emphasis on surveillance and control of offenders (and thus an increased likelihood of breach and the possibility of imprisonment). And the environment in which the Probation Service was operating was shortly to become even more threatening. When the retreat from the principles of the 1991 Act began with the 1993 Criminal Justice Act, there was little immediate direct impact upon the Probation Service, but soon after with the arrival of Michael Howard as Home Secretary and the promulgation of his new policy of 'prison works', the Service came under pressure. Howard began to question the effectiveness of community penalties, he criticised the social work foundation of probation and set up a review of its training (Dews and Watts 1994), he criticised recruitment practice, and he slashed budgets. Ironically, as this onslaught on probation was underway, the so-called What Works agenda was coming to the notice of the Home Office, partly via a series of conferences arranged by Greater Manchester and Hereford and Worcester Probation Services, and partly as a result of evangelising by the then Chief Inspector of Probation (Graham Smith) and the head of the Home Office Research and Statistics Directorate (Chris Nuttall). Smith and Nuttall pushed the What Works (or Effective Practice) agenda for all it was worth and while one might speculate how much might have been achieved if the Conservatives had remained in power, they were suitably rewarded by the good fortune of a newly elected Labour government that was very keen on effectiveness and delighted by their claims of evidence based practice (see Mair 2004). While the pressure on probation seemed to have been lifted, in fact it only shifted to another tack – modernisation.

Four official documents published in 1998 may have led the Probation Service to believe that the environment for community penalties was becoming less dangerous (Chapman and Hough 1998; Goldblatt and Lewis 1998; Home Office 1998a; Underdown 1998), but the Crime and Disorder Act of that year introduced a number of new court orders – most of them aimed at young offenders and thus not relevant for the Probation Service – that served notice that there was considerable continuity between the increased punitiveness of the previous Conservative administration and that of the new Labour government. The Act introduced the drug treatment and testing order (DTTO) and one indication of how far the Probation Service had moved from its roots in social work was that there was no sign of discontent over the new order; ten years earlier it is likely that NAPO would have pressed hard for industrial action over such an order and its members would have refused to cooperate with its demands.

The most important manifestation of the modernisation agenda also appeared in 1998 with the publication of the Consultation Document *Joining Forces to Protect the Public* (Home Office 1998b). This document proposed a unified national Probation Service, suggested changing the names and terminology associated with community penalties, discussed a major reorganisation of the service and advocated much closer joint working with the Prison Service. This was the price the Probation Service was expected to pay for its continued existence and the relevant legislation appeared in the Criminal Justice and Court Services Act 2000.

The Act made provision for the creation of a National Probation Service (NPS) fully funded by the Home Office, with 42 areas (down from 54) that were coterminous with police force areas. The names of the three main orders were changed: the probation order became the community rehabilitation order (CRO); the community service order became the community punishment order (CPO); and the combination order became (with a singular lack of imagination) the community punishment and rehabilitation order (CPRO). The terminology of punishment and rehabilitation emphasised the Government's determination to end the perception of probation as not being sufficiently tough. This was reinforced by ending probation's responsibility for family court welfare services by creating the Children and Family Court Advisory and Support Service (CAFCASS) as a separate organisation. The National Probation Service therefore became a fully fledged criminal justice agency for the first time. In addition, the Act required the establishment of Multi-Agency Public Protection Panels whereby the police and probation are expected to work closely together to manage the risks posed by sexual and other dangerous offenders. The Act also introduced two new community penalties: the exclusion order where an offender could be ordered not to enter a certain area for up to 12 months and the drug abstinence order.

By 2001 when the major provisions of the Act were implemented, there were three main community penalties (the CRO, CPO and CPRO) with more than 15 separate requirements that could be added to the CRO or the CPRO; the NPS also ran DTTOs (which were proving popular with the courts although their attrition rate was quite high – see Turnbull *et al.* 2000) and still supervised money payment supervision orders (though the number of these made annually was decreasing steadily). Senior attendance centres continued to exist in some parts of the country, although their use had also been decreasing. Curfew orders, despite some years of rather slow and erratic development, were beginning to be used more often. The last two sentences, of course, were not NPS owned and in the case of many of the requirements that could be added to the CRO and CPRO non-probation staff were involved. The monopoly position of the Probation Service had been eradicated and while it is easy to see advantages in this development (a wider range of expertise to work with offenders, for example), the disadvantage is clear – if other agencies or organisations could carry out probation-type work with offenders, then why should the NPS 'own' the CRO, CPO and CPRO?

The major organisational changes introduced in 2001 were given little time to bed down. Within two years the Carter Report made the case for a single corrections service (prefigured by the renaming of the Joint Accreditation Panel in summer 2002 as the Correctional Services Accreditation Panel), a National Offender Management Service (NOMS) that would 'ensure the end-to-end management of offenders, regardless of whether they were given a custodial or community sentence' (Carter 2003: 33). The Government's response was positive and its rhetoric was robust:

> Believing that offenders in the community will reduce their re-offending through occasional interviews with probation officers is also naïve. Therefore, in the community we have introduced rigorous supervision with much more use of electronic monitoring and demanding sentences such as the drug testing and treatment order and as a result we are reducing rates of re-offending. (Home Office 2004: 9)

At the same time as the Carter Report was published the Criminal Justice Act 2003 received royal assent. Here, the 1988 Green Paper dismissed option of a brand new order that would replace existing orders (see above) was embraced and the CRO, CPO, CPRO, DTTO (and senior attendance centres) were all scrapped and replaced by a new community order with 12 possible requirements to take effect from 4 April 2005 (offences committed prior to that date continued to receive the old-style sentences so that a twin-track system would be running in the courts for some months).

- supervision (for a maximum of 36 months);
- unpaid work (40–300 hours);
- accredited programme (for the number of sessions in the programme);
- drug rehabilitation (6–36 months and consent required);
- alcohol treatment (6–36 months and consent required);
- mental health treatment (up to 36 months and consent required);
- residence (up to 36 months);
- specified activity (up to 60 days);
- prohibited activity (36 months);
- exclusion (up to 24 months);
- curfew (up to 6 months for 2–12 hours per day);
- attendance centre (12–36 hours).

The money payment supervision order remained although its use by probation staff was not encouraged (see Home Office 2005a: 76). Suitable combinations of requirements were suggested for probation staff (one of which included five requirements), although it was also made clear that as long as the court took account of the compatibility of requirements with each other 'and their suitability for the offender and the resulting overall restriction of liberty being commensurate with the seriousness of the offending' (Home Office 2005a: 53) then any combination of requirements could be made. This immediately raises the possibility of offenders being weighted down with requirements ('condition creep') that could simply prove too demanding, leading to failure and – almost inevitably – a custodial sentence. The new order has been available only since 4 April 2005 and it is too early to make any definitive judgements about how it is being used, but a Home Office sentencing exercise in 1995 carried out to test how sentencers might use such powers (as had been proposed in the Green Paper *Strengthening Punishment in the Community* (Home Office 1995)), suggested that when confronted with freedom to choose a range of options, sentencers tended to opt for more rather than less (Mortimer and Mair 1995). Early data from the Home Office covering April–September 2005 suggest that half of community orders had only a single requirement, while one-third had two requirements (15 per cent had three requirements). A supervision requirement made up 36 per cent of requirements, while unpaid work made up 32 per cent (Home Office 2006a).[1]

The boundaries between custody and community were virtually eradicated in the 2003 Act with the suspended sentence order (custody minus), intermittent custody and custody plus (implementation of the latter, due in autumn 2006, has been deferred), all including a licence period with more or less the same range of requirements available for the community order and therefore involving the intervention of an offender manager who was likely to be a probation officer (unless the requirement was a curfew, exclusion or attendance centre). While the details of NOMS remain vague, the pushing together of Prison and Probation is underway, and with contestability the dominance of the Probation Service in the area of community penalties may be seriously undermined.

Community penalties and the Probation Service have come a long way in the last 100 years – although it is notable that most of the changes have taken place since 1991. Local control of Probation Services has ended and thus the scope for discretion (and inconsistencies associated with it) has been reined in; the fragmented growth in the number of separate community penalties has been halted; probation has lost its foundations in social work and become a fully fledged criminal justice agency; whatever public opinion may think, there can be little doubt that community penalties have been made more rigorous and demanding (the results of this will be interesting); probation's power-base as the supplier of community penalties has been weakened; and the impact of contestability could have profound consequences. In addition, as other chapters demonstrate, qualified probation officers no longer dominate work with offenders as Probation Service officers increasingly are involved in this; risk/needs assessment (OASys) has become a crucial task, emphasising the significance of allocating individuals to the most appropriate programmes (or mix of requirements); the introduction of contestability could lead to much greater instability among probation staff; and pressure to meet government targets (with financial penalties for failure) could lead to corner-cutting and difficult decision-making.

Overall, the current environment for the Probation Service is fraught with danger. A ship that, 20 years ago, seemed reasonably secure and able to negotiate any kind of sea is now leaking, has been patched up in various ways, has a new (and relatively inexperienced) crew and is heading into uncharted – and probably stormy – waters. In the next part of this chapter we will examine recent trends in the use of community penalties and discuss how these relate to this situation.

Sentencing

As noted above, in 1950 a total of 31,000 probation orders were made by the courts; by 1961 this number had increased to 45,000 and by 1970 it was 53,400. This represents a 72 per cent increase which, on the surface, seems substantial. However, as Barr and O'Leary (1966) and Haxby (1978) point out, the trend was downwards.

> ... Barr and O'Leary showed that in the period up to 1961, although the number of persons placed on probation each year continued to grow, the proportion of offenders being placed on probation was declining ... Since 1961 the general decline in the use of probation for indictable offences has continued. (Haxby 1978: 123)

It is important to note that this trend (and it will be examined further below) began during the 1950s and is thus not a new phenomenon but a deeply entrenched one.

Of the 53,400 probation orders made in 1970, 41 per cent were for offenders under the age of 17 – a proportion that had been dropping since 1950 when the figure had been 61 per cent. Clearly, juvenile offenders had made up a substantial part of probation's core market but, with the Children and Young Person's Act 1969, probation for those under 17 was replaced by the supervision order. This provision came into effect on 1 January 1971 and courts increasingly began to nominate the local authority to supervise younger offenders (in effect, this meant social workers), which meant that the number of probation orders made by the courts began to decrease considerably in the early 1970s: in 1971 only 32,690 probation orders were made; in 1972 the figure was 33,139; and in 1973 30,518 (dropping to approximately the same number as had been made in 1950).

In 1972 (the year before the introduction of the community service order) 25 per cent of probation orders were made on female offenders; 21 per cent of orders were made in the higher courts; 14 per cent of probation orders were made for non-indictable offences; and the most common offences for which a probation order was made were theft and burglary which between them accounted for more than 50 per cent of orders. Probation orders made up 7.5 per cent of sentences for indictable offences, although there was a considerable difference between its use for males and females: 6 per cent of males sentenced for indictable offences received a probation order, while for females the figure was 14 per cent.

Having outlined the use of probation in 1972, we now turn to examine more recent trends. Between 1984 and 2004 (Table 9.1), the number of probation orders made by the courts had increased by 48 per cent, and by 20 per cent in the past decade. On the face of it, the community rehabilitation order would

Table 9.1 Use of the CRO, CPO and CPRO by the courts 1983–2004 (thousands)

Year	CRO	CPO	CPRO	Total no. of sentences
1983	38.7	35.2	–	2,096.5
1984	40.9	37.9	–	1,963.5
1985	42.4	38.3	–	1,911.3
1986	40.1	35.1	–	1,895.0
1987	42.2	35.9	–	1,554.8
1988	43.6	35.3	–	1,555.4
1989	43.9	33.7	–	1,532.1
1990	47.7	38.6	–	1,513.9
1991	47.5	42.5	–	1,503.9
1992	43.9	44.1	1.3	1,519.9
1993	43.8	48.0	8.9	1,425.0
1994	50.5	49.5	12.4	1,407.1
1995	49.4	48.3	14.6	1,354.3
1996	50.9	45.9	17.3	1,437.8
1997	54.1	47.1	19.5	1,384.7
1998	58.2	48.6	21.2	1,468.9
1999	58.4	49.6	20.7	1,408.0
2000	56.5	50.0	19.2	1,424.3
2001	58.9	49.8	14.7	1,348.5
2002	63.8	50.8	15.5	1,419.6
2003	63.2	50.4	15.1	1,479.8
2004	60.7	53.9	15.9	1,536.8

seem to be in reasonable health, yet further examination of the available statistics places question marks against such an optimistic assessment. The growth in the number of CROs has been almost exclusively as a result of use for summary offences (see Table 9.2). In 1984, 12 per cent of probation orders were made for summary offences, while by 2004 this figure had increased to 45.7 per cent. These data demonstrate very clearly a major change in the way in which the CRO has been used by the courts in the past 20 years: to put it bluntly, the CRO has slipped quite dramatically down-tariff and has been increasingly used for summary offences.

Are similar trends discernible in the case of the other two main community penalties – the CPO and the CPRO? Between 1984 and 2004, there was a 42 per cent increase in the number of CPOs (a 9 per cent increase in the past decade) suggesting that the CPO, too, would appear to be in a healthy state. With regard to the CPRO, the initial picture is a little different. There was considerable growth in the use of the CPRO in its first few years of existence so that by 1998 21,200 orders were made. However, numbers began to fall after this so that by 2004 only 15,900 CPROs were made. The decrease in use of the CPRO is almost certainly a result of the Effective Practice Initiative which began in 1998 and which encouraged the use of probation with an additional requirement – mostly based on a cognitive-behavioural programme. But as Table 9.2 shows, both the CPO and the CPRO are characterised by the same

Table 9.2 Use of CRO, CPO and CPRO for summary offences 1983–2004 (%)

Year	CRO	CPO	CPRO
1983	12.4	10.8	–
1984	12.0	11.6	–
1985	12.3	11.7	–
1986	13.2	13.1	–
1987	14.7	13.4	–
1988	16.5	13.9	–
1989	27.1	30.3	–
1990	27.5	30.6	–
1991	28.0	30.6	–
1992	26.9	29.3	30.8
1993	29.8	31.5	31.9
1994	31.6	33.5	34.6
1995	33.4	37.0	38.9
1996	34.9	38.3	40.8
1997	34.4	38.6	40.3
1998	34.0	37.7	39.6
1999	33.3	38.5	40.2
2000	34.0	40.1	41.0
2001	34.9	43.3	45.3
2002	37.3	45.0	45.0
2003	41.3	46.7	45.9
2004	45.7	49.6	46.9

trend that is evident for the CRO; the growth of both sentences has been for summary offences, suggesting a move down-tariff. This trend was exacerbated by changes in the Criminal Justice Act 1988 whereby some triable-either-way offences were reclassified as summary offences, but the general shift is evident prior to 1988 and continued after that date (and, of course, the CPRO did not exist at the time of the 1988 Act). Thus, in almost half of all cases, the three main community penalties are currently used for what are, by definition, less serious offenders. (Morgan (2003) has also noted this trend.)

The curfew order is in a similar position with 45.4 per cent of these being used for summary offences in 2004; 15,142 were sentenced to a curfew order in 2004, a considerable increase over the 1,577 curfew orders made in 1991. The drug treatment and testing order, however, bucks this trend as in 2004 only 9 per cent of these were made for summary offences; a total of 8,596 DTTOs were made in 2004. Given the relative novelty of these two sentences, clear trends are not discernible.

The most common sentence in the Crown Court is imprisonment, while in the magistrates' courts it remains the fine, although use of the fine has decreased considerably over the past 25 years. More than three-quarters of CROs, CPOs and CPROs are made in the magistrates' courts. CPOs and CPROs are more likely than CROs to be made in the Crown Court and this is probably a reflection of their original objective in targeting the risk-of-custody market. What may be significant, however, is a slow but steady increase in the use of CROs and CPOs in the magistrates' courts during the past decade. Up to the early 1990s, more of both orders were being made in the Crown Court, but this trend shifted direction so that in 2004 just over one in ten CROs was made in the Crown Court and fewer than one in seven CPOs. The down-tariff move of community penalties noted earlier would seem to be confirmed by their distribution in the courts.

The emasculation of community penalties is highlighted further by examining the offences for which they are used; burglary and theft are the key offences here. In 1991, one-third of CROs were made for offences of theft, while by 2004 this figure had decreased to 23 per cent; the figures for CPOs are 26 per cent and 15 per cent, while for the CPRO they are 22 per cent in 1993 and 13 per cent in 2004. The use of the three sentences for burglaries has almost been eradicated completely; in 2004 only 4 per cent of CROs were for burglaries, 3 per cent of CPOs and 7 per cent of CPROs. The seriousness with which burglary as an offence is now viewed by the courts has led to a perception that community penalties are no longer effective for such offences. The result is that those convicted of burglary (and, to a lesser extent, theft) are now routinely imprisoned for offences which are no different in terms of their seriousness than they were when community sentences were seen as effective and commensurate penalties for these offences. By comparison with use for burglary, theft and summary offences, the use of the three sentences for other types of offences has hardly shifted at all.

This very clear trend in the use of community sentences for less serious offences has been accompanied by another development. The availability of additional requirements that could be added to a probation order was partly to permit specialist interventions (such as mental treatment by a qualified medical person) but also to make the order more rigorous and demanding with a view to encouraging sentencers to see such an order as offering a credible alternative to custody. The introduction of requirements such as attendance at a probation day centre or participation in specified activities in the 1982 Criminal Justice Act were very much aimed at 'toughening up' the claims of the probation order to offer an alternative to a custodial sentence. Table 9.3 shows the use of additional requirements since 1985 when only 15 per cent of probation orders were made by the courts with an additional requirement. As can be seen from the table, this figure has increased consistently since that time so that in 2004 only half of CROs were made without an additional requirement. As Hough *et al.* (2003) have argued, while there is little evidence to prove that offending within offence categories has become more serious

Table 9.3 Persons starting CROs with added requirements 1985–2004 (%)

Requirement	1985	1989	1995	1997	1999	2000	2002	2003	2004
Non-residential mental treatment	2.3	2.0	1.0	1.0	0.9	1.0	0.5	0.4	0.3
Residential mental treatment	0.5	0.3	0.1	0.1	0.1	0.1	–	–	–
Residence in app. prob. hostel	3.2	2.5	1.6	1.5	1.3	1.2	0.8	0.5	0.4
Res. in other inst.	0.5	0.6	0.2	0.1	–	–	–	–	–
Other res. req.	0.6	0.9	0.6	0.7	0.6	0.5	0.6	0.7	0.3
Prob. centre/ acc. prog.	4.3	6.5	5.3	4.1	4.7	4.3	10.8	35.0	36.8
Report to spec. person spec. place	0.1	1.2	1.4	1.5	1.5	1.4	0.8	0.2	–
Participate in specified activities	2.0	7.6	14.7	19.6	19.5	19.9	22.2	11.1	8.0
Mental treat. by qual. med. person	–	–	0.7	0.6	0.5	0.5	0.3	0.2	0.2
Res. drug or alcohol treatment	–	–	0.7	0.6	0.5	0.5	0.1	0.1	0.1
Non-res. drug/ alcohol treatment	–	–	1.6	2.0	2.8	3.3	1.3	1.0	0.9
Drug/alc. treat. by qual. med. person	–	–	1.1	1.2	2.0	2.0	1.1	0.9	0.7
Drug abs. req.							0.5	1.0	1.2
Other reqs.	2.3	2.9	2.3	2.7	1.9	2.2	1.7	2.2	4.5
No add. reqs.	85.2	77.2	71.6	67.0	67.3	66.9	62.1	50.3	50.6
Total number	41,750	43,280	48,271	51,509	55,903	53,930	58,478	60,200	59,485

or that offenders have become more prolific, it does seem that sentencers' perceptions are of an increasing seriousness of crime (no doubt partly fuelled by Government rhetoric and the media). The result is that, as Table 9.3 shows, offenders who – 15 years ago – would have received a probation order with no added requirements are now much more likely to have a requirement added to their order. The same trend is evident in the case of the CPRO: in 1993, 83 per cent of combination orders had no additional requirements while by 2004 this figure had dropped to 52 per cent. Tougher sentences are being handed out with no evidence that the offences concerned are any more serious. Indeed, given that more community sentences are being made for summary offences, it is interesting to pose the question of how many such sentences are being made with additional requirements?

It is certainly the case that the increased use of additional requirements is to some extent a result of the Effective Practice Initiative which encouraged the use of CROs with an additional requirement. But the trend was underway prior to the full impact of the EPI being felt (from 2000 onwards), and it also raises questions about the targeting of the EPI and the loading-up of additional requirements on offenders simply because of the demands of policy. The shift towards using added requirements can be seen as paving the way to the new community order, for if the CRO and the CPRO were increasingly being defined in practice as including conditions, and the CPRO involved supervision and unpaid work, then reformatting the community order as a set of requirements became a logical next step.

The length of orders made by the courts has declined. Short CROs (12 months or less) and short CPOs (40–99 hours) are roughly twice as likely now as they were 20 years ago. It may be significant, however, that the average length of a CRO has recently been increasing from 15.9 months in 2001 to 16.8 months in 2004. It will be particularly interesting to monitor this development as the supervision requirement of the new community order becomes more common (see below). There is considerable potential in the supervision requirement for the use of short periods of supervision, but just how far probation officers will take advantage of such potential and how far courts will use it is much too early to say. The trend towards shorter community sentences fits well with the trends already noted: increased use in the lower courts, less use for burglary and theft, increased use for summary offences. All of these developments suggest that community sentences are not dealing with serious, high-risk offenders – despite considerable claims to the contrary.

What are the characteristics of those given community sentences by the courts? Traditionally, probation supervision has been seen as being more appropriate for women and community service as more suited to men. We noted earlier the considerable growth in the number of CROs since 1993 but the small increase in the number of CPOs; for males there was a 34 per cent increase in CROs compared to a 62 per cent increase for females, while the respective figures for CPOs are 8 per cent for men and 120 per cent for women. However, the proportion of women being made subject to supervision has declined by 10 per cent since 1983 (from 29 per cent to 19 per cent), while the percentage of women sentenced to community punishment has doubled in the last decade (from 6 per cent in 1993 to 12 per cent in 2004). This may be a result of the courts slowly taking into account feminist critiques of the use of the CRO and the CPO as well as probation officers making changes in pre-sentence reports. With regard to the CPRO, in 2004 91 per cent were made on males, while for the DTTO the percentage was 79 per cent. In 2004, 82 per cent of those sentenced by the courts were male and 18 per cent female, so that the use of the CRO and the DTTO now almost reflect this split while males are still over-represented in the CPO and the CPRO.

Differential use of community sentences according to gender may be due to a variety of factors: different patterns of offending, bias in PSRs, discriminatory use of sentences by the courts. Tables 9.4 and 9.5 compare males and females starting CROs according to their offences. While for most

Table 9.4 Males starting CROs by offence 1996–2004 (%)

Offence	1996	1997	1998	1999	2000	2001	2002	2003	2004
Violence	8.7	9.2	10.0	9.8	9.7	9.5	9.9	10.2	10.3
Sexual	2.1	2.0	1.9	1.9	1.7	1.6	1.6	1.6	1.6
Robbery	0.5	0.4	0.5	0.4	0.3	0.3	0.3	0.3	0.2
Burglary	11.6	10.4	9.1	8.1	6.9	6.4	6.2	6.1	5.4
Theft	24.2	23.6	22.2	22.3	24.3	24.8	23.2	20.2	18.0
Fraud	3.6	3.1	3.3	3.1	3.2	3.0	2.9	2.3	2.1
Crim. damage	2.3	2.1	2.4	2.5	2.8	2.7	2.6	2.7	4.1
Motoring	1.2	1.0	1.0	1.0	0.9	1.0	1.0	1.2	1.1
Other	10.7	11.8	12.5	12.2	11.4	10.9	10.4	10.4	9.7
Summary	35.0	36.2	36.9	38.3	38.4	39.6	41.7	44.8	47.3
Total no.	39,735	41,258	44,016	43,793	42,101	43,094	46,193	48,865	48,009

Source: Home Office Probation Statistics annual.

Table 9.5 Females starting CROs by offence 1996–2004 (%)

Offence	1996	1997	1998	1999	2000	2001	2002	2003	2004
Violence	7.9	8.2	8.6	8.8	8.0	7.4	8.1	8.8	9.8
Sexual	0.1	0.2	0.2	0.2	0.1	0.1	0.2	0.2	0.2
Robbery	0.6	0.6	0.5	0.4	0.4	0.4	0.4	0.4	0.3
Burglary	3.1	2.9	2.8	2.7	2.5	2.0	2.2	2.7	2.3
Theft	41.6	40.2	37.6	37.0	39.0	40.6	40.2	38.2	33.8
Fraud	11.2	10.1	10.3	10.5	10.7	9.0	8.9	8.3	7.1
Crim. damage	1.4	1.6	1.5	1.5	1.5	1.5	1.5	1.8	2.6
Motoring	0.5	0.4	0.4	0.5	0.4	0.4	0.4	0.5	0.4
Other	10.0	10.6	11.9	11.6	10.0	9.3	8.8	9.0	8.2
Summary	23.1	25.0	25.9	26.6	27.2	29.1	29.1	29.8	35.0
Total no.	9,370	10,251	11,498	12,061	11,829	11,376	12,285	11,749	11,476

Source: Home Office Probation Statistics annual.

offence types there is little difference in the use of the CRO, women are less likely than men to receive a CRO for burglary and more likely to receive one for fraud than men. These differences may have something to do with the differential involvement of women in these types of offences: in 2004 29 per cent of those sentenced for fraud were female compared to 71 per cent who were male, while for offences of burglary the respective figures were 5 per cent and 95 per cent. With regard to offences of theft women are almost twice as likely to be given a CRO than men (in 2004 22 per cent of those sentenced for indictable offences of theft were female compared to 78 per cent male). Unless female thieves are committing different types of theft than males (which is a possibility) this is an interesting disparity that requires further investigation. Women are also more likely to receive a CRO for an indictable offence than men (65 per cent *v* 53 per cent).

The differences found in the use of CROs for men and women are, to a large degree, replicated in the case of CPOs and CPROs, although the use of the CPO for indictable and summary offences is almost similar for men and women. Such disparities in the use of community sentences in respect of gender suggest the need for further research into this matter.

In the early days of probation the vast majority of probation orders were made on juvenile offenders. Due to legislation, juveniles no longer figure in probation caseloads and, as Table 9.6 shows, very few 16–17-year-olds are now sentenced to a CRO. The age profile of those made subject to a CRO has become older: the proportion of those aged 20 and under has decreased by 11 per cent since 1993, while the proportion of those aged 30 and over has increased by almost 20 per cent. Age distribution is similar for men and women.

In the case of CPOs, there has been little change in the proportion of orders made on those aged 20 and under, but since 1993 there has been an 11 per cent increase in those starting CPOs aged 30 and over. Again, those being sentenced to CPOs are older. The age distribution, however, is different for CPOs when gender is taken into account, as females sentenced to CPOs tend to be older than males. With regard to CPROs the age distribution in 2004 was similar to that for the CPO, and those sentenced to a CPRO have also got older in the past decade: in 1993 24 per cent were 30 or older, while in 2004 the figure was 34 per cent. Again, women sentenced to CPROs tend to be older than men. Overall, those who are sentenced to CROs are older than those sentenced to CPOs, who in turn are older than those receiving CPROs.

As discussed earlier, the length of both CROs and CPOs has decreased over the past 20 years. Women are more likely to receive shorter CROs and CPOs than men: in 2004 the average length of a CRO was 17 months for a man and 16.2 months for a woman, while the average length of a CPO was 117.3 hours and 105.8 hours respectively.

Somewhat ironically, given their oft-stated commitment to race equality, the Probation Service has lagged seriously behind the Prison Service in collecting data on ethnicity. The Prison Service has been collecting and analysing such data since 1986. Probation – after a great deal of debate about how to collect such data – began ethnic monitoring in 1992. However, as

Table 9.6 Persons starting CROs by age 1993–2004 (%)

Age	1993	1994	1995	1996	1997	1998	1999	2000	2001	2002	2003	2004
16–17	4.0	3.7	4.0	4.5	4.8	4.9	4.4	2.6	1.0	0.6	0.5	0.4
18–20	22.2	19.6	18.7	17.7	17.0	17.0	17.6	18.0	18.0	16.7	15.6	14.5
21–29	43.8	43.2	42.3	41.5	40.1	38.5	38.3	38.4	38.6	38.5	37.3	36.3
30–39	19.5	21.9	22.8	23.9	25.1	25.9	26.2	27.2	27.9	28.6	29.5	30.0
40–49	7.6	8.3	8.5	8.7	9.0	9.5	9.3	9.8	10.1	11.2	12.2	13.5
50+	2.9	3.3	3.6	3.6	3.9	4.2	4.1	4.0	4.3	4.4	4.7	5.2
Total no.	42,861	49,504	48,271	49,105	51,509	55,514	55,854	53,930	54,470	58,478	60,614	59,485

the Home Office itself admits '... after an initial good start, the proportion of ethnic data missing rose substantially from the mid-1990s. Figures were consequently omitted from the 1999 and subsequent statistical publications on race and the criminal justice system' (Home Office 2005b: 4). The problems have, it is claimed, been resolved and some very sketchy data appear in the 2004 Offender Management Caseload Statistics (Home Office 2005c: 23–4). This, however, does not take us very far (especially as data from London are missing) except to note that the data show 'an over-representation of black offenders for those starting court order supervision by the Probation Service' (Home Office 2005d: 13). We have already noted that there appear to be some unexplained disparities between women and men with regard to community penalties, and this is also the case with regard to black and ethnic minorities. Given the NPS commitment to diversity – which now covers even wider topics than gender and ethnicity – one might be apprehensive about how far equal treatment applies in practice, although the question of monitoring diversity is a complicated one. (These issues are discussed in much greater detail in Chapter 11).

The 2001 Probation Statistics (Home Office 2002a) included data showing the previous criminal record of those sentenced to community penalties, going back to 1991. Tables 9.7 and 9.8 set out this information, and it confirms quite dramatically the 'tariff slippage' of community penalties that was noted above. Just over one-third of those commencing CROs in 2001 had served a previous custodial sentence, fewer than one in five of those starting CPOs (a consistent decrease since 1991), and one-third of those commencing CPROs (again a consistent decrease since their introduction in 1992). Increasingly, all three sentences were dealing with first offenders (and it should be borne in mind that half of CROs and CPROs had additional requirements) – indeed for those starting CPOs (a sentence that had started life unofficially aimed as an alternative to custody) half were first offenders. Interestingly, such data were missing from the 2002 Probation Statistics due to the introduction of a new system for collecting data. When information about previous criminal history reappeared in the Offender Management Caseload Statistics 2003 the

Table 9.7 Percentage of those commencing community penalties with a previous custodial sentence 1991–2001

Community penalty	1991	1992	1993	1994	1995	1996	1997	1998	1999	2000	2001
Community rehabilitation order	37	39	43	42	41	38	37	35	34	35	36
Community punishment order	33	32	32	29	27	24	22	20	20	19	18
Community punishment and rehab. order	–	45	49	48	42	39	37	34	34	34	33

Table 9.8 Percentage of those commencing community penalties with no previous convictions 1991–2001

Community penalty	1991	1992	1993	1994	1995	1996	1997	1998	1999	2000	2001
Community rehabilitation order	11	–	12	15	16	18	19	21	24	26	27
Community punishment order	14	–	19	25	28	32	34	37	42	47	51
Community punishment and rehab. order	–	–	10	13	15	17	19	20	23	27	28

picture had changed. There were no data on offenders' previous custodial experience, and the data on previous convictions suggested that, while the percentage of those commencing community penalties with no previous conviction had indeed been increasing (at least in the case of the CPO and CPRO), the situation was not quite as bad as the earlier data had shown. The data for 2002 suggest that only 12 per cent of those starting a CPO had no previous convictions; for CPOs the figure was 32 per cent, and for CPROs it was 19 per cent (Home Office 2005c: 39). Unfortunately, there is no discussion in the published statistics about the disparity between the earlier figures and the revised data, except a brief note to acknowledge the technical changes to data collection.

In 2004, almost 139,000 persons were sentenced to a community penalty (not counting another 15,000 who received a curfew order) compared to 106,300 who were sentenced to immediate custody. From this point of view the crucial importance of community penalties is very clear. But the increasing use of community penalties for less serious offences and offenders and the increased use of additional requirements suggest increased levels of punitiveness – even though the length of orders has decreased slightly. And the increasingly aging population of those sentenced to a community order is a noteworthy development (and one that is also evident in the custodial population).

The use of community penalties will be – to some extent – driven by the way in which they are perceived by sentencers. One of the key issues behind such perceptions is how well community penalties are enforced and in the next section of this chapter we examine compliance and enforcement issues.

Enforcement and compliance

The overwhelming importance of enforcement to the NPS is signalled by the fact that it is the first of the three official aims of the Service: enforcement, rehabilitation and public protection. This contrasts sharply with the situation ten years ago, when enforcement of community penalties tended to be seen as one of the more distasteful tasks of a probation officer and to be avoided if at all possible. Lax and inconsistent practice with regard to enforcement is indefensible, and the introduction of National Standards began the process of tightening up the enforcement of community penalties.

No matter how onerous the requirements of a community sentence it comes to little unless it is enforced – unless non-compliance meets a clear and firm response. It is to be noted that this particular challenge of enforcement is peculiar to community penalties: community penalties require people to do things – to keep appointments as instructed, to participate in activities, to work, to refrain from things – which, left to themselves, they might choose not to do. This creates the possibility of default. It is true that the best prisons try to engage the active participation of their inmates (Pryor 2001). Nevertheless, a passive or recalcitrant prisoner is still being punished; an unenforced community penalty, by contrast, is indistinguishable from impunity.

The recent history of enforcement has been reliably documented elsewhere (Windlesham 2001; Hedderman and Hough 2004; Canton and Eadie 2005). The matter came to particular prominence in 1999 when the Association of Chief Officers of Probation (ACOP) tried to pre-empt anticipated criticism of shortcomings in enforcement by commissioning an audit of practice. To no one's surprise, the first audit (Hedderman 1999) exposed a significant gap between probation practice and the stipulations of National Standards. Follow-up audits demonstrated improvement (Hedderman and Hearnden 2000, 2001).

Welcoming the findings of the second audit in April 2000, ACOP's chair said: 'Enforcement is for probation what waiting lists are for hospitals, detection rates are for the police and exam results are for schools.' (*Guardian*, 12 April 2000: 6). The comparison is almost too apt: all such headline statistics invite scepticism about whether the right things are being measured in the right ways and suspicions of sleight of hand in counting rules, the introduction of perverse incentives and distorting effects on practice. Such figures seem all too vulnerable to manipulation for political ends. And in the particular matter of enforcement is the public to expect high or low rates of breach? Would a high rate demonstrate the Probation Service's robust response to non-compliance – or failure to engage offenders effectively in the process of supervision? Would a low rate show the Service's success in gaining compliance and giving effect to the orders of the court – or that officers were negligent in their response to breach?

Strict enforcement, as prescribed by National Standards, appeared as an innocently uncontroversial objective; it was to be achieved by circumscribing ever more tightly officers' discretion. In particular, since failure to attend as instructed has always been the most common reason for breach (Ellis *et al.* 1996), successive editions of National Standards have limited the number of unacceptable absences permitted before breach action has to be taken. Discretion became even more tightly constrained.

Doubts, however, were beginning to be expressed. Lord Windlesham astutely pointed out that the demands of a community sentence typically weigh most heavily on those least able to comply (Windlesham 2001: 259) – a point that raises questions of justice as well as effectiveness. The established trend to impose additional requirements in the quest for punitive credibility, on which we have already commented, not only leads sometimes to a weight of imposition that some offenders will struggle to bear. Generally, the more that is asked of someone, the greater the *potential* for default. If, at the same time, enforcement is to be practised more stringently, the greater the likelihood of actual breach.

This could lead to the 'backlash' phenomenon (Bottoms 1987) by which custodial 'alternatives' can accelerate some offenders into prison, offsetting at least part of their diversionary effect. This upshot has been made even more likely by another aspect of the quest for credibility: if offenders fail to comply, they must expect additional punishment. It is the clear intention of successive legislative measures to increase penalties for non-compliance and to increase the likelihood of an immediate custodial sentence for default.[2]

At the same time, however, the proportion of those actually sent to immediate custody for breach of a community sentence has been (slightly) decreasing (NOMS 2005a; Canton and Eadie 2005). This is in contrast to the response to non-compliance during post-custodial supervision, where tougher enforcement practice (as much as, or more than, levels of reoffending) is leading to appreciably higher levels of recall to prison (Solomon 2005). Maruna (2004), noting the substantial inflationary effect of recalls on prison populations in parts of the USA, argues that England and Wales may be following a similar trajectory. While the evidence in relation to community sentence enforcement practice is inconclusive, then, the potential is clear; the Government has put in place a framework to facilitate the immediate incarceration of those in breach of the requirements of their community orders. In particular, the Criminal Justice Act 2003 allows imprisonment for breach of a community order even when the original offence was not punishable by imprisonment (Sch. 8).

Enforcement is an important topic in its own right, but the assumption that it supports the other two aims of the NPS (rehabilitation and public protection) is open to question. Hearnden and Millie (2004) were unable to find any positive association between 'tough' enforcement and reduced levels of reconviction. On the contrary, any premature ending of an effective programme, including curtailment through precipitate breach, is likely to make the intervention less effective in reducing reoffending (Raynor 2004). Tough talking to offenders about enforcement by emphasising the punitive consequences of non-compliance, as Hearnden and Millie (2004) point out, amounts to threatening people who have already shown themselves to be unimpressed by the prospects of punishment – and who, for that matter, are not particularly skilled 'means–ends' thinkers. 'Tough' enforcement can also, by estranging the offender, subvert a risk management strategy (Canton 2005).

The political preoccupation with enforcement is rather akin to closing the stable door after the horse has bolted. Greater attention to compliance – examining in detail what makes offenders comply with what is expected of them – might be a much more productive approach than sanctioning them for failure to comply.

Bottoms (2001) offers a rich analysis here. He identifies several dimensions to the question of compliance: most people in most circumstances, to be sure, take account of the anticipated costs and benefits of their actions, but other considerations are influential too. Bottoms distinguishes 'constraint-based' compliance (for example, the extent to which conduct is guided or circumscribed by physical restrictions) and 'compliance based on habit and routine' (typically unreflective patterns of conduct which, characteristically, cognitive-behavioural programmes are attempting to inculcate).

Most important for present purposes is what Bottoms terms 'normative compliance', a concept which itself has a number of dimensions. Among these is the idea of *attachment* – for example, 'attachment' to a member of staff who demonstrates concern for and interest in the offender may support compliance (Rex 1999). The concept of *legitimacy* is also relevant – people are more likely to comply with expectations on them and to accept decisions when these are seen to be fair and reasonable. It is legitimate to insist that people desist from offending, but it is also legitimate for offenders to expect that they are given reasonable opportunities and support to achieve this. What this entails for practice in the administration of community penalties has been explored by a number of commentators (for example, Rex 1999, 2005; Trotter 1999; Cherry 2005). Among the things that constitute legitimacy is a sense of being respected as an individual – attention to the many ways in which people differ, being listened to and understood.

The key point is that these different aspects of compliance are all significant and must be made to work together. Enforcement policy has limited itself by concentrating on a single dimension – the instrumental/prudential consideration of punishment for non-compliance – and may in the process have undermined the chances of enhancing compliance through its neglect of normative aspects like legitimacy.

At the same time, whatever the character of national policy, at local and at practice level there are several imaginative and successful initiatives to engage with offenders. Kemshall and Canton (2002) found a number of creative attempts to identify and overcome practical obstacles to compliance and to enhance motivation. These include the provision of transport in appropriate cases, appointment cards, phoning and texting as reminders, Breakfast Clubs, and access to gym and leisure facilities. Successful completion of a programme may be acknowledged through the presentation of a reward or a certificate – which might be highly prized by those who are unused to achievement and praise. Probation officers have long offered the incentive of early discharge from an order on the grounds of good progress. All such initiatives represent an attempt to make the several dimensions of compliance work together.

Robinson and McNeill (2004) warn that the relationship between 'official' and 'front-line' accounts of practice is never straightforward, as practitioners struggle to reconcile the requirements of policy and their own conceptions of good practice – or even just getting the job done. In the matter of enforcement, probation staff continue to have to make judgements – for example, about whether an absence should be deemed to be 'acceptable' or not. There has been little research undertaken about how such judgements are made, but it may well be that staff make sensible and realistic decisions about this which sometimes depart from the formal stipulations of policy. For instance, an offender who arrives late for an appointment – or even makes contact on the following day – but is plainly making efforts to meet the requirements of the order may get the benefit of a sympathetic interpretation of what is formally a failure to comply. It is to be noted that Ellis and colleagues (1996) found that officers welcomed the structure of National Standards, but nevertheless deployed them flexibly. While the position has no doubt changed as Standards have become the established framework of practice, there remains a degree of latitude.

Part of the difficulty is that auditable standards of enforcement have a very narrow conception of what counts as compliance: essentially compliance is keeping appointments. But is mere attendance sufficient? How are we to weigh the relative levels of compliance between, say, an offender who invariably attends the probation office but determinedly avoids any attempt to 'address offending behaviour' and, on the other hand, an erratic attender who shows a significant – if variable – commitment to avoid reoffending? It is at least arguable that the preoccupation with (auditable) attendance has had a negative effect on the character of probation practice. In some settings, the need to register contacts has deteriorated into a sterile exercise of signing in – a practice deeply resented by service users (Kemshall *et al.* 2001) which detracts significantly from the legitimacy of the experience, as well as undermining motivation – and no doubt with a similarly demotivating effect on staff as well.

To follow the kind of approach implied by Bottoms (2001) would be not only more fruitful, but much more ambitious because it would inquire about how supervisors might engage the *active* consent and participation of offenders. This rounded model of compliance offers ideas not just about how the formal requirements of the order may be fulfilled, but how the various dimensions of compliance can be deployed in a way that might lead to enduring change.

A compliance strategy, in particular, would have a much fuller and more subtle understanding of motivation. Practitioners have developed a sophisticated appreciation of the complexity and lability of motivation, involving, for example, ideas like the 'cycle of change' and methods like motivational interviewing and pro-social modelling (see, for example, Trotter 1999; Fleet and Annison 2003; Cherry 2005). It is both striking and ironic, therefore, that enforcement policy resolutely ignores these insights and concentrates on a coercive approach which is known to be of limited effect. The realities of practice, of course, require probation officers to work with the complexities of motivation, but it remains the case that audits and inspections are more likely to focus on formal conformity with Standards.

A tacit assumption of enforcement policy (as opposed to practice) is that offenders are typically recalcitrant and keen to backslide. An alternative motif, often invoked by those who are less enthusiastic about the Standards, is that many offenders live 'chaotic lifestyles' and are incapable of keeping appointments. But recalcitrance and chaos are just two among many reasons why people may not comply with the requirements of an order. 'Can't and 'won't' are better seen as ends of a spectrum than as mutually exclusive alternatives, since default more typically involves a complex dynamic between ability, opportunity and motivation. Unless the reasons for non-compliance are appreciated in the individual case, the response may make future compliance still less likely. For example, few things are more demotivating than hopelessness – a sense that change is impossible – and if the supervising officer's response fails to recognise this (perhaps through threats of breach action) then this sense of hopelessness is only likely to be confirmed.

In the next part of the chapter we examine three different community interventions. The challenges for compliance and enforcement, as well as the different aims and objectives of these interventions, are discussed. While much government rhetoric would argue that traditional problems and difficulties with community penalties have been resolved as a result of policy initiatives, we would – to the contrary – suggest that tensions, both old and new, continue to characterise community interventions.

Community interventions – some practical considerations

The three penalties we consider in this section have, for most of their history, been discrete sentences of the court. As we have noted earlier, however, they have now (since 4 April 2005) been subsumed under a single generic community order as a result of the Criminal Justice Act 2003, and they can be imposed as specific requirements of such an order. In what follows we discuss the interventions individually, but we should emphasise that the three interventions could easily be part of a single community order and thus the need to manage the three parts together is paramount. If the introduction of the combination order (the CPRO) led to tensions between those who managed community service and those who supervised offenders under probation orders, the potential for even greater tensions between various groups of staff – some not members of the NPS – would seem to be considerable.

Think First – an offending behaviour programme

In order to establish 'what works', an intervention has to be specified precisely. Since probation officers have deployed such a diverse and eclectic range of supervision styles and methods, it has proved difficult to evaluate the effectiveness of their work. The idea of a *programme* seems to offer a solution to this problem. A programme has been defined as 'a planned series of interventions over a specified and bounded time period which ... [will usually] be characterised by a sequence of activities, designed to achieve clearly defined objectives based on an identifiable theoretical model or empirical evidence. It can be replicated with different offenders to achieve the same results'[3] (Chapman and Hough 1998: 6). The core What Works principle of *programme integrity* – which insists that a programme must be delivered exactly as intended – makes evaluation a simpler matter, as well as guarding against the chances that a significant departure from the programme might prejudice its effectiveness.

Some programmes are targeted at particular types of offence, but there are also generic offending behaviour programmes (for general discussion, see

Chui 2003; Crow 2001; Roberts 2004). Among the most widely used is Think First. This programme consists of 22 two-hour sessions delivered to groups of offenders. Eligible participants are those assessed as at medium to high risk of reoffending, although in some cases higher- (and lower-) risk offenders may be accepted. Offenders attend preparatory sessions, which are likely to include taking psychometric tests to appraise their attitudes and cognitive skills (failure may preclude acceptance on the programme), and are required to participate in a number of post-programme sessions besides. Offenders are taught skills of problem-solving, social skills and skills of self-control (National Probation Service 2003a). There are possibilities of some 'catch-up' sessions for those who miss parts of the programme, but these are necessarily limited since the coherence of the programme depends on attendance at sessions in due sequence.

Quite apart from the intellectual and emotional demands of the programme, Think First therefore calls for a considerable period of sustained commitment and sufficient personal organisation to attend regularly over several months (some areas run a group every week, while others run two groups a week). Other programmes are typically no less demanding.

It is not, therefore, surprising that rates of attrition or drop-out have always been a substantial challenge for accredited programmes (see, for example, the attrition rates reported in the latest *Annual Report for Accredited Programmes* (NOMS 2005b)). Less obviously, it was quickly discovered that a large proportion of offenders never even began programmes.[4] Indeed, five years ago *A New Choreography* noted that '... the biggest issue is the drop-out rate between order commencement and the start of the programme' (National Probation Service 2001: 26).

Ways of addressing the problem of failure to start programmes or early drop-out have been suggested by Kemshall and Canton (2002). They noted that among the factors that might be influential were:

- pre-group preparation and joining information (including the quality and use made of promotional material and information leaflets);
- the experience of 'waiting time' and perceptions of case management;
- offender expectations of programme content and delivery.

Motivation, not surprisingly, was identified as critical, as were attempts by staff to identify practices that might sustain or conversely undermine this motivation. Our earlier consideration of compliance suggests that an important consideration here is the extent to which participants might see the relevance of the programme to themselves – an aspect of its legitimacy. Roberts (2004) found that levels of satisfaction with the content of Think First increased progressively over time among participants in the programme. One possible interpretation of this is that the rationale of the programme takes time to become clear to its participants. A further possibility in that case is that those who drop out – especially at an early stage – are manifesting the very cognitive shortcomings that made them suitable for the programme in the first place. Areas, of course, have been under significant pressure to meet targets and are therefore at risk of referring to programmes those who were unlikely to attend or who were otherwise unsuitable (Hollin *et al.* 2004; Kemshall and Canton 2002). This too risks detracting from the legitimacy of the intervention.

Chapman and Hough (1998) emphasised that a 'programme' is better seen as the whole process of supervision – not just participation in the group. The manner in which the offender manager helps the offender to make connections between the generalised teaching about problem-solving in the group sessions and the particular application of these lessons to his/her own circumstances and offending propensities is crucial. The What Works principle of *responsivity* is relevant here. This insists that the way in which offenders learn is a key variable and accordingly methods must be adapted to their learning styles and preferences. It is not easy to see how this might be accommodated in a group programme, especially one that respects programme integrity. The involvement of the offender manager, by contrast, gives opportunities for the personal attention which responsivity requires. It is significant that Roberts (2004) found frequency of contact with the case manager to be positively correlated with attendance levels at Think First – although characteristically the causal relationships are far from clear.

Under pressure to manage large workloads, supervisors and their managers may think that adequate levels of contact are already being achieved and themselves see offenders less frequently while they are participating in the accredited programme. Nevertheless, it is plain that the case manager role is critical throughout and that there must be a sufficient level of personal contact. Stewart-Ong and colleagues (2004) found that programme completion and subsequent lower reconviction rates were associated with sound case management and intensive individual supervision, especially at the start of the programme. Noting variable liaison between the programme tutors and the offender manager, Kemshall and Canton (2002) warned that there should be no sense of the group programme being a separate exercise from supervision by the offender manager. Referral to a specialised unit is always at risk of this kind of organisational separation and the corresponding challenge of integrating the different components of supervision coherently has more recently been emphasised in the NOMS Offender Management Model, which proposes that each case should be treated as a 'project' (NOMS 2005c: 3.56).

Although evaluation is complex and findings can be interpreted in different ways, there are signs of a promising correlation between programme completion and lower reconvictions (Roberts 2004). Non-completers of Think First, however, do much less well. Yet the single most common reason for early departure from the programme is breach for non-compliance (Kemshall and Canton 2002) – a specific instance of the way in which the priorities of enforcement and of reducing reconviction may not always comfortably fit together.

Unpaid work

Unpaid work is the most recent term for what was previously known as the community punishment order, although it is probably best known in its original incarnation of the community service order. The history of community service (CS) could be written around changes of conception in its purpose and the dynamics of trying to reconcile tensions among competing purposes. As noted earlier, these tensions were inherent from the beginning and CS has struggled to reconcile themes of punishment, reparation and rehabilitation (indeed, as we write, unpaid work has been reconceptualised as 'Community Payback' – see Home Office 2006b).

Even on its introduction in six 'pilot' areas, CS had local differences of emphasis. In most of these areas, though, the attempt was made to stress the *punitive* character of the new measure: it had to be seen as a credible alternative to prison and the restriction involved in giving time and labour was accordingly emphasised. It is to be noted that this loss of time and labour is what constituted the punishment: at that stage, there was no suggestion at a policy level that the tasks undertaken should in themselves be unpleasant or punitive. This did not, of course, mean that tasks should be undemanding, but they had to have worth and meaning. Supporters of that view were encouraged by the later research findings of McIvor (1992), who showed that offenders' perception of the worth of their work, in addition to its intrinsic value, influenced their commitment and their participation: where the work was found to be meaningful, there were fewer enforcement problems. Such experiences, moreover, were associated with lower rates of reconviction.

At the same time, however, if CS was to be a credible alternative to prison, it had to be shown to be sufficiently punitive in its character and administration – and it is surely no coincidence that the first ever National Standards were introduced for CS. These Standards, as well as tightening enforcement procedures, insisted that at least a proportion of every order should involve tough and physically laborious toil as a way of demonstrating the order's punitive content.

From the beginning, the viability of the scheme depended on its gaining referrals – work had to be undertaken reliably and well and the *reparative* potential of CS would only be achieved if the work undertaken was of genuine benefit to the community. The Probation Service was sometimes reticent about the *rehabilitative* aspects of the scheme. It had always been hoped, of course, that the effect of useful work – notably work on behalf of 'those members of the community who are most in need of help and support' (ACPS 1970: 13) – would change offenders' attitudes for the better, but CS was not meant to be a rival to the probation order which was intended to remain as the principal rehabilitative community sanction.

So the claims of rehabilitation and reparation were, at this stage, in sufficient harmony – both calling for meaningful and useful work whose value was transparent to the workers and the beneficiaries. The requirements of punishment, on the other hand, called at least for rigorous implementation, less choice of work by offenders, hard tasks and firm enforcement – and perhaps for laborious and tedious work that would be seen as punitive.

Despite some initial unease, probation staff managed to accommodate to the idea that CS had a punitive element; on the other hand, characterising the probation order in such a way would have been quite unacceptable. This difference has to some extent been reflected in the approach to the enforcement of the two penalties. Ellis *et al.* (1996) found that CS was enforced much more robustly than probation. More recently, Rex (2005) found that the staff in CS and in 'field' probation units have significantly different ideas about what the respective measures are for and what messages they do and should convey – as indeed do offenders, victims and magistrates.

When probation shifted emphasis away from punishment towards effectiveness and 'what works', it was initially unclear where CS might fit. It was anticipated that CS would make a substantial contribution to the numbers of offenders going through accredited programmes, but this could only be accomplished if CS explicitly structured the scheme around a rehabilitative purpose and was able to demonstrate its potential to the satisfaction of the Accreditation Panel. As a result, Pathfinders were established and enhanced community punishment (ECP) was to emerge (Rex and Gelsthorpe 2002; Rex et al. 2003; Gelsthorpe and Rex 2004). Presenting itself in the language of effective practice (National Probation Service 2003b), ECP represented an assimilation of CS into the mainstream of evidence-led, crime-reductive probation practice. As with other interventions, the attempt to attend to dynamic risk factors would shape the individual's experience of his/her order (National Probation Directorate 2003). A proportion of the order could be fulfilled through participation in appropriate educational and training schemes. Official views are positive:

> Community Punishment is particularly valuable in providing opportunities for learning in real situations and in a very concrete and practical way, in contrast to the more conceptual learning methods of other forms of supervision. Enhanced CP enables this contact to be used to target a range of dynamic risk factors. (National Probation Directorate 2003: 5)

Yet might this preoccupation with demonstrable effectiveness push out the reparative aspect of CS? It would indeed be an irony if the reparative aspirations of CS – the only well established adult sentence with a plausibly restorative function – were to be attenuated at just the time when 'making reparation' was instated for the first time as one of the statutory purposes of sentencing (CJA 2003, s. 142). On the other hand, the recent emphasis on Community Payback has reaffirmed the importance of demonstrating the genuine value to the community of the work undertaken (Home Office 2006b).

How does this play out in practice? In one area, there are three broad types of working group:

- working directly with needy people, for example the elderly;
- practical work – painting and decorating, gardening;
- workshop on the premises.

Typically the whole of the order is spent in one of these activities, although it is possible to change for a particular reason. Any and all of these can be a portal to employment-related training and so constitute 'guided skills learning'.

While breach action may be taken for misbehaviour or for poor work, this is relatively rare and much the most usual occasion for breach is non-attendance. Once breach action has been initiated, some areas suspend the order while waiting for the court appearance, while in other areas offenders are encouraged to continue which often leads to a completion. These differences of approach, again, originate in differences of view about the weight to be given to the various purposes of the order.

While the causal connections are unclear, obtaining (and retaining) employment is strongly associated with reduced levels of reconviction (Department for Education and Skills 2005). Responding to this, enhanced CP is intended to improve offenders' employment prospects. What, then, of those who are already employed? Increased proportions of offenders who receive this penalty are in work – one aspect, perhaps, of the trend noted previously towards using CPO for less serious offenders. Enabling offenders to complete their CPOs without prejudice to their gainful employment calls for ever more flexible working arrangements, including, for instance, the possibility of working at evenings and weekends. As well as having implications for the management of these activities, this also raises questions of equity – the same number of hours is a much heavier burden on an offender with extensive employment or domestic commitments. If the overall demand is excessive, the likelihood of non-compliance is correspondingly increased. At the same time, the demands of the penalty could strain or destabilise personal circumstances that support desistance. Once again there may be a tension between the punitive and the rehabilitative aspirations of unpaid work.

In summary, then, we would argue that CS has always had to try to reconcile a number of disparate and potentially competing purposes. The point can be most readily grasped by imagining a CS scheme that gives emphasis to punishment, and another that gives priority to reducing reoffending – or to reparation, or to social inclusion. These differences of conception would be reflected in the 'target group' (the offenders thought suitable for the measure), the tasks undertaken, the manner of enforcement, and the way in which the scheme is represented to courts, victims, offenders and the public. At times, CS has emphasised different aspects of all these purposes, but most schemes in practice have had to find ways of doing justice to them all.

Perhaps the greatest threat facing unpaid work is that it is all too easy to see it as a prime candidate for contestability – not just by the nature of its practice, but also because of its structural position within probation. Indeed Roger Hill (2005) has recently noted that he sees unpaid work as being 'particularly vulnerable to contestability' and expressed his desire to 'strengthen it' and make the NPS the provider of choice. It is quite possible that success in these terms could lead to unpaid work becoming even more tempting to other organisations to bid for it – another unintended consequence.

Drug treatment and testing orders

If the purposes of CS are contested, the purpose of the next measure to be considered at first seems unambiguous: to reduce the incidence of drug use and consequently the offending to which it is related. The drug treatment and testing order (now the drug rehabilitation requirement) was introduced as part of the Crime and Disorder Act 1998. Presented in response to the recognition that substance misuse was often associated with high levels of offending to support a habit, the measure was initially piloted in three areas and made nationally available from October 2000.

Probation, typically in partnership with other agencies, oversees the DTTO. Testing (by urine sample or oral fluid) is undertaken regularly. Turnbull and colleagues found that staff in the first pilots felt that:

- tests worked well in reinforcing good progress in stopping drug use;
- frequent testing was expensive and pointless for those who continued to use drugs;
- tests could be destructive to the motivation of those who were reducing their drug use but not managing to stop it completely. (Turnbull et al. 2000: 80)

Treatment can take a variety of forms, including therapy (conventional and complementary), education and general social support. Health care can include detoxification and the prescribing of substitutes. Since substance misusers typically experience other health problems as well as those directly associated with their substance use, more general health advice and support are offered too. DTTOs involved an extremely high level of contact – on five days a week for a total of 20 hours in the first 13 weeks of the order (Home Office 2002b: E6) – although this has been modified for the drug rehabilitation requirement by the 2005 National Standards and depends on the relevant community sentence 'band' (National Probation Service 2005: SS8.11)

Despite high rates of reconviction (in itself not surprising since heavily convicted offenders were deliberately targeted) and evidence of continuing problems with inter-agency working, there were some encouraging findings from the early research on DTTO. Turnbull et al. (2000), evaluating the pilots, found in a number of cases reductions in substance usage, expenditure on drugs and acquisitive crime which were sustained after follow-up. Turner (2004) noted marked improvements in very many respects for some participants, although one-third of those still in treatment at six months had not made a lot of progress. At the same time, Turner also found that half of those offenders on DTTOs had stopped attending by the fourteenth week of the order and that just 2 per cent were still attending at six months. While this does not mean that those who dropped out gained no benefit, Hough and colleagues (2003) found that the reconviction rates of completers were much lower than for non-completers and most overviews of DTTO (for example, Turnbull et al. 2000; Hough and Mitchell 2003; National Audit Office 2004) have concluded that retention is therefore a principal challenge.

How then are substance users to be engaged and retained in the programme? Hough (1996) in a review of the literature had concluded that coercion was just as effective in treating drug users as was voluntary treatment. Hough and Mitchell too showed that 'coerced treatment is no less effective than treatment on a voluntary basis' (2003: 42), recognising that many substance users are ambivalent about their usage. Motivation, after all, changes: one person may at first attend under compulsion, but quickly become convinced of the value of the programme; another, attending voluntarily, may be put off by their first impressions of the programme or lose hope in their ability to change. Rumgay (2004) suggests that, while external constraints may contribute to entry to a programme, continuing involvement calls for internal commitment. Once more we encounter the difficulty of ensuring that the coercive factors *support* the attempts to engage and motivate participants.

Turnbull *et al.* (2000) found differences in enforcement practice between the three pilot sites. Most breach was for non-attendance rather than on the grounds of continuing substance use disclosed by the tests: there was a (locally variable) recognition that not all tests would be 'clean'. Recognition of the complexity of testing and treatment for a relapsing condition led the National Standards to specify that:

> Refusal to provide a sample shall always be interpreted as an unacceptable failure to comply with the requirements of the order. Positive tests need to be seen in the context of the offender's overall response to the order. Persistent test failures when indicative of a failure to engage with the order or of unsatisfactory progress shall lead to the initiation of breach proceedings. (Home Office 2002b)

The insistence that refusal must count as an unacceptable failure to comply is retained in the new Standards covering DRR (National Probation Service 2005: SS8.11), but there is less guidance about how to respond to persistent positive tests. Indeed, rather than devise a separate set of Standards for the enforcement of drug rehabilitation requirements, the 2005 Standards assimilate this group of offenders into others. Rumgay notes, however, that relapse is characteristic of substance misusers and discusses how 'lack of access to alternative social worlds' (2004: 252) undermines their attempts to desist. Motivation here, then, is even more than usually labile and the challenges of inducing compliance all the more demanding.

In an instructive study of the views of DTTO participants, Powell and colleagues (2006) found that many participants did not resent the external constraints imposed by the court and the Probation Service. The court not only imposed DTTO, it should be noted, but also regularly reviewed the progress of an order. While this no doubt has a deterrent effect, many offenders in Powell's study confirmed Rumgay's view that it was the encouragement of the review – the interest shown in the progress of the individual – that is at least as influential as any deterrent.

The practice of review may become a feature of other community order requirements (under CJA 2003, s. 178) and the experience of DTTO here could be instructive. Sentencers are not well placed to see the consequences of their decisions and one potential advantage of review is that it might expose them to some of the real difficulties involved in responding to the changes in motivation and in circumstances as orders progress. On the other hand, as McKittrick and Rex (2003) point out, if sentencers are to be actively involved in the management of supervision, is their impartiality in jeopardy if they are called upon to exercise their judicial authority in relation to breach proceedings or other formal applications? However that may be, the review process affords another example of the importance of finding ways to make sure that modes of promoting compliance work together, that normative and instrumental considerations are mutually supportive.

The DTTO was always seen as an interdisciplinary project, with probation managing an order that depended on the involvement of a number of other agencies. While such an approach is surely sensible, Turnbull *et al.* (2000) and the National Audit Office (2004) found that the aspirations of partnership working were not so easily achieved. Rumgay (2004: 256) summarised the difficulties as follows: 'the absence of clear role boundaries, poor coordination of professional effort, perceived threats to professional autonomy and conflicting views about treatment and punishment'.

There is of course no inevitable correlation between the level of involvement required on therapeutic grounds and the appropriate punitive level of intervention. Nor, as Rumgay points out, will optimum levels of motivation necessarily coincide with the timing of criminal justice interventions (2004: 261). Immanent tensions between the therapeutic and punitive character of the measure may also be exposed and aggravated by the increased numbers that the drug rehabilitation requirement is likely to attract (an issue that may be exacerbated by the presence of a number of other requirements). We have seen earlier that the DTTO, against the trend of other community punishments, has held a high tariff position, with the measure aiming – successfully – at the mostly heavily convicted offenders. The new requirement, by contrast, will be available at all community order levels or 'bands'. Tariff level and treatment need, again, may often not coincide and the priorities of probation may not be shared by all of its partners.

Conclusions

The role of the Probation Service as *de facto* monopoly provider of community sentences is drawing to an end. Since its beginnings in 1907, the Probation Service has always worked with other organisations, but the practical issues of being in competition with such organisations poses real problems for the NPS. In the past, probation has led (if that is not a contradiction) partnership working; now (if the concept of contestability is implemented) it is going to have to bid against other organisations. While the culture of the Service has changed considerably over the past decade, it is not (yet?) that of a hard-nosed quasi-commercial organisation tendering for programmes that will be held to close account with regard to economy, efficiency and effectiveness. Indeed, if probation were to become such an organisation, it is difficult to see how it could retain the confidence of sentencers – and despite persistent government claims to the contrary, the NPS does seem to have the confidence of magistrates (MORI 2003). While – as we have shown – there are serious questions about trends in the use of community penalties, we should not lose sight of the fact that more offenders are sentenced to community penalties annually than are sent to custody. It is by no means empty rhetoric to claim that if we did not have community penalties we would have to invent them.

One of the themes that has appeared consistently in this chapter has been that of unintended consequences (good intentions – disastrous consequences is one of the models used by Stan Cohen (1985) to explain correctional change). By their nature, these are difficult to predict and deal with but they do seem to have bedevilled many of the community policy initiatives of the past 30 years. Given the regularity with which they appear, it is surely possible for policy-makers to try to take greater account of them and to plan how to deal with them if they emerge and begin to undermine a new initiative. Much faster feedback in relation to the implementation of new policies and greater reliance on pilot testing (with less urgency for national roll-out) would help here.

But the problem of the 'silting up' of community sentences with less serious offenders remains and has implications for many of the issues we discuss in the remainder of this conclusion. Morgan (2003) has made various proposals that, if implemented, might halt or reverse the trend. The Coulsfield Inquiry (2004) has examined ways in which community sentences could become more effective alternatives to custody (see also the essays contained in Bottoms *et al.* 2004). The Sentencing Guidelines Council might be successful in constraining sentencing, but it is unlikely that the Council will have any real impact in the immediate future; Wasik (2004: 308) notes that it has 'an enormous task ahead of it'. Such suggestions could only be effective if backed up with considerable political will – which seems unlikely to be forthcoming at present. Without such a change (and, of course, the possibility of further unintended consequences), addressing the rest of the issues we pick out here will be akin to moving the deckchairs on the *Titanic*.

While the introduction of a National Probation Service, the Effective Practice Initiative, the Correctional Services Accreditation Panel and OASys have all gone some way to reducing some of the inconsistencies that plagued the Probation Service in the past, there remain tensions that challenge the NPS and require resolution. How such tensions are dealt with will have consequences for the use of community penalties and therefore the role of the NPS:

- the increasingly blurred (if not almost eradicated) boundaries between custody and community;
- the centralisation of the NPS and the potential fragmentation of regional provision of services;
- partnership working versus competitive tendering for programmes;
- increased use of community penalties for less serious offenders versus the potential of the community order to overload requirements;
- the aging of the community penalties population versus the public and political obsession with young offenders;
- a rhetorical commitment to diversity and justice but a serious dearth of statistical data to monitor diversity;
- the need to take (and be seen to take) enforcement seriously without breaching too many offenders;
- the need to shift the balance from enforcement to compliance without compromising credibility.

In addition, the structure of the community order with its various possible requirements also throws into stark relief issues that have always lain behind community penalties in one way or another. Indeed, these issues are likely to become even more significant if NOMS and contestability are implemented along the lines of the Government's proposals (Home Office 2005e, 2005f). Successful targeting of appropriate offenders for programmes is one of the keystone principles of effective practice, but with pressure from the centre to hit challenging targets in terms of numbers, this could all too easily lead to inappropriate offenders being targeted – with consequences for effectiveness. Further, 'success' – no matter how it is measured – leads to pressure to expand programmes and take more offenders thus relaxing strict targeting, again with potentially negative consequences. Fitting a series of requirements to the needs/risks of offenders is going to be a difficult puzzle to resolve. Morgan (2003: 16) has shown that 'The proportion of offenders with low likelihood of reoffending on community punishment is … higher than that for assessed offenders subsequently fined or given conditional discharges'. And while this suggests that there is considerable scope for using risk assessment for targeting offenders with higher levels of risk, recent events (e.g. the murders of John Monckton and Mary-Ann Leneghan) are likely to militate against this.

The attrition rate for accredited programmes requires urgent attention. Admittedly, rates have improved slightly recently (NOMS 2005b), but this is an issue that has serious consequences as those who drop out (or never start) have significantly higher reconviction rates than those who complete programmes. With a variety of requirements to meet, offenders are more likely not to attend all. If some of those requirements are run by agencies/organisations other than the NPS, the task of keeping account of offenders' attendance and behaviour becomes more difficult. The role of offender manager will be crucial.

Indeed, the whole issue of staffing and offender management generally could be another problem. There were tensions between CS staff and those who supervised probation orders, and these tensions were raised again with the introduction of the combination order. Similar tensions have been noted between drugs agency staff and probation staff with regard to the DTTO. With a slew of possible requirements with various objectives and with different types and levels of staff, the potential for staff to disagree and find it difficult to work together is considerable. If contestability opens up the provision of some programmes to agencies new to the NPS, working together could become even more problematic. Ultimately, trying to ensure that the community order works in an integrated way will be the key challenge for the NPS and NOMS in the future.

It is perhaps ironic that commentators are beginning to acknowledge again the importance of the supervisor/offender relationship, at a time when that relationship has become more attenuated than ever. Robinson (2005) has drawn attention to research findings that suggest that the quality of the relationship with the supervisor is a critical factor in changing people and warns that this might be jeopardised by any model of case management that fragments the experience of supervision. She notes the irony that while the significance of 'relational' factors has become unfashionable in accounts of probation supervision, its value is being reaffirmed in the context of community punishment schemes. Dowden and Andrews (2004) too have reaffirmed the importance of the personal characteristics of criminal justice staff in enabling offenders to change. Like Robinson, there is no particular approach that we would seek to defend, but a model that involves referral to a range of interventions, defining people mainly in terms of their criminogenic needs, may find it hard to retain these influential personal influences.

Helping offenders to make sense of a disparate bundle of requirements and to understand that there is a coherent and organised sense to the package as a whole is a topic that has been ignored. Sue Rex's (2005) recent work on community punishment as communication has argued cogently for the importance of clarifying the messages articulated by punishment, and it would not be conducive to effectiveness if messages were to be confusing or contradictory.

It is all too easy to be negative about the future of community penalties and the NPS. Government proposals as set out in *Restructuring Probation to Reduce Re-offending* (Home Office 2005e) are badly thought out and seem to be looking for change for its own sake. Probation has been under some form of threat for at least a decade and has survived; it is still widely used by the courts, would appear to have the confidence of sentencers (a very important pressure group) and is at least as effective as prison. As it approaches its 100th anniversary, it is to be hoped that the service will not simply survive, but thrive for at least another 100 years.

Notes

1 See Mair, Cross and Taylor (2007) for an assessment of the use and impact of the community order and the suspended sentence order.
2 The Powers of Criminal Courts (Sentencing) Act 2000; the Criminal Justice and Court Services Act 2000, s. 53 sets a clear presumption of custody on breach; the Criminal Justice Act 2003, Schedule 8 envisages heavier penalties and the possibility of imprisonment.
3 We have omitted that part of the definition that says that a programme must be able to demonstrate positive change. No doubt this is a desirable feature of programmes, but it is unhelpful to make this part of the *definition*. This would make 'an unsuccessful programme' a contradiction in terms and, conversely, 'an effective programme' a tautology.
4 The logistics of running groups, incidentally, introduces another element to the problem of enforcement: absence not only has its implications for the individual, but for others in the group – and even, if too many people drop out, for the viability of the group itself. (A similar problem confronts community punishment/ unpaid work projects that require groups of participants.)

Further reading

The character of community punishment and the associated legal framework – indeed the very terms for community penalties – have been changing apace in recent years. Ian Brownlee's (1998) *Community Punishment: A Critical Introduction* remains an excellent introduction. Successive editions of *The Oxford Handbook of Criminology*, edited by Mike Maguire, Rod Morgan and Robert Reiner, have provided authoritative and reliable chapters on this topic. *Punishment in the Community: Managing Offenders, Making Choices* by Anne Worrall and Clare Hoy is a sound review of the subject, as is *Understanding Community Penalties* by Peter Raynor and Maurice Vanstone (2002). Three edited collections – *Community Penalties: Change and Challenges* (2001) edited by Anthony Bottoms, Loraine Gelsthorpe and Sue Rex, *What Matters in Probation* (2004) edited by George Mair and *Alternatives to Prison: Options for an Insecure Society* (2004) edited by Anthony Bottoms, Sue Rex and Gwen Robinson – contain many instructive and influential chapters. An important recent contribution is *Reforming Community Penalties* (2005) by Sue Rex, which goes beyond instrumental 'what works' accounts of community penalties to explore their communicative achievement and potential. The websites of the National Probation Service (http://www.probation.homeoffice.gov. uk/) and the National Offender Management Service (http://www.noms.homeoffice. gov.uk/) are also accessible sources of information at a time of rapid change.

References

Advisory Council on the Penal System (1970) *Non-Custodial and Semi-Custodial Penalties.* London: HMSO.

Barr, H. and O'Leary, E. (1966) *Trends and Regional Comparisons in Probation (England and Wales)*, Home Office Studies in the Causes of Delinquency and the Treatment of Offenders No. 8. London: HMSO.

Bottoms, A. (1987) 'Limiting prison use: experience in England and Wales', *Howard Journal*, 26: 177–202.

Bottoms, A. (2001) 'Compliance and community penalties', in A. Bottoms, L. Gelsthorpe and S. Rex (eds), *Community Penalties: Change and Challenges*. Cullompton: Willan.

Bottoms, A., Gelsthorpe, L. and Rex, S. (eds), (2001) *Community Penalties: Change and Challenges*. Cullompton: Willan.

Bottoms, A., Rex, S. and Robinson, G. (eds), (2004) *Alternatives to Prison: Options for an Insecure Society*. Cullompton: Willan.

Brody, S. (1976) *The Effectiveness of Sentencing: A Review of the Literature*, Home Office Research Study No. 35. London: HMSO.

Brownlee, I. (1998) *Community Punishment: A Critical Introduction*. Harlow: Longman.

Canton, R. (2005) 'Risk assessment and compliance in probation and mental health practice', in B. Littlechild and D. Fearns (eds), *Mental Disorder and Criminal Justice: Policy, Provision and Practice*. Lyme Regis: Russell House.

Canton, R. and Eadie, T. (2005) 'From enforcement to compliance: implications for supervising officers', *VISTA*, 9: 152–8.

Carter, P. (2003) *Managing Offenders, Reducing Crime*. London: Strategy Unit.

Chapman, T. and Hough, M. (1998) *Evidence Based Practice: A Guide to Effective Practice*. London: HMIP.

Cherry, S. (2005) *Transforming Behaviour: Pro-social Modelling in Practice*. Cullompton: Willan.

Chui, W.H. (2003) 'What works in reducing reoffending: principles and programmes', in W.H. Chui and M. Nellis (eds), *Moving Probation Forward: Evidence, Arguments and Practice*. Harlow: Pearson.

Cohen, S. (1985) *Visions of Social Control: Crime, Punishment and Classification*. Cambridge: Polity Press.

Coulsfield, Lord (2004) *Crime, Courts and Confidence: Report of an Independent Inquiry into Alternatives to Prison*. Prepared for the Esmée Fairbairn Foundation. Available online at: http://www.rethinking.org.uk/coulsfield/index.shtml (accessed December 2006).

Crow, I. (2001) *The Treatment and Rehabilitation of Offenders*. London: Sage.

Department for Education and Skills (2005) *Reducing Reoffending through Skills and Employment*, Cm 6702. Available online at: http://www.official-documents.co.uk/document/cm67/6702/6702.pdf (accessed March 2006).

Dews, V. and Watts, J. (1994) *Review of Probation Officer Recruitment and Training*. London: Home Office.

Dowden, C. and Andrews, D. (2004) 'The importance of staff practice in delivering effective correctional treatment: a meta-analytic review of core correctional practice', *International Journal of Offender Therapy and Comparative Criminology*, 48: 203–14.

Ellis, T., Hedderman, C. and Mortimer, E. (1996) *Enforcing Community Penalties*, Home Office Research Study No. 158. London: Home Office.

Fleet, F. and Annison, J. (2003) 'In support of effectiveness: facilitating participation and sustaining change', in W.H. Chui and M. Nellis (eds), *Moving Probation Forward: Evidence, Arguments and Practice*. Harlow: Pearson.

Folkard, M.S., Fowles, A.J., McWilliams, B.C., Williams, W., Smith, D.D., Smith, D.E. and Walmsley, G.R. (1974) *IMPACT Intensive Matched Probation and After-Care Treatment: Volume 1 The Design of the Probation Experiment and an Interim Evaluation*, Home Office Research Study No. 24. London: HMSO.

Folkard, M.S., Smith, D.E. and Smith, D.D. (1976) *IMPACT: Volume 2 The Results of the Experiment*, Home Office Research Study No. 36. London: HMSO.

Gelsthorpe, L. and Rex, S. (2004) 'Community service as reintegration: exploring the potential', in G. Mair (ed.), *What Matters in Probation*. Cullompton: Willan.

Goldblatt, P. and Lewis, C. (1998) *Reducing Offending: An Assessment of Research Evidence on Ways of Dealing with Offending Behaviour*, Home Office Research Study No. 187. London: Home Office.

Haxby, D. (1978) *Probation: A Changing Service*. London: Constable.

Hearnden, I. and Millie, A. (2004) 'Does tougher enforcement lead to lower conviction?', *Probation Journal*, 51: 48–59.

Hedderman, C. (1999) *ACOP Enforcement Survey: Stage 1*. London: ACOP. Available at: http://www.kcl.ac.uk/icpr/ (accessed May 2005).

Hedderman, C. and Hearnden, I. (2000) *Improving Enforcement: The Second ACOP Enforcement Audit*. London: ACOP. Available at: http://www.sbu.ac.uk/cpru (accessed May 2005).

Hedderman, C. and Hearnden, I. (2001) *Setting New Standards for Enforcement: The Third ACOP Audit*. London: ACOP. Available at: http://www.kcl.ac.uk/depsta/law/research/icpr/publications/acop3.shtml (accessed November 2005).

Hedderman, C. and Hough, M. (2004) 'Getting tough or being effective: what matters?', in G. Mair (ed.), *What Matters in Probation*. Cullompton: Willan.

Hill, R. (2005) Speech to the Napo Conference, Llandudno, 14 October. Available online at: http://www.probation.homeoffice.gov.uk/output/Page307.asp

Hollin, C., Palmer, E., McGuire, J., Hounsome, J., Hatcher, R., Bilby, C. and Clark, C. (2004) *Pathfinder Programmes in the Probation Service: A Retrospective Analysis*, Home Office Online Report No 66/04. Available online at: http://www.homeoffice.gov.uk/rds/pdfs04/rdsolr6604.pdf (accessed April 2006).

Home Office (1964) *The War against Crime in England and Wales 1959–1964*. London: HMSO.

Home Office (1984) *Probation Service in England and Wales: Statement of National Objectives and Priorities*. London: Home Office.

Home Office (1988) *Punishment, Custody and the Community*, Cm 424. London: HMSO.

Home Office (1990a) *Partnership in Dealing with Offenders in the Community: A Discussion Paper*. London: Home Office.

Home Office (1990b) *Crime, Justice and Protecting the Public*, Cm 965. London: HMSO.

Home Office (1991) *Partnership in Dealing with Offenders in the Community: A Decision Document*. London: Home Office.

Home Office (1995) *Strengthening Punishment in the Community: A Consultation Document*, Cm 2780. London: HMSO.

Home Office (1998a) *Effective Practice Initiative: National Implementation Plan for the Supervision of Offenders*, Probation Circular 35/1998. London: Home Office.

Home Office (1998b) *Joining Forces to Protect the Public: Prisons-Probation A Consultation Document*. London: Home Office.

Home Office (2002a) *Probation Statistics England and Wales 2001*. London: Home Office.

Home Office (2002b) *National Standards for the Supervision of Offenders in the Community*. London: Home Office.

Home Office (2004) *Reducing Crime – Changing Lives: The Government's Plans for Transforming the Management of Offenders*. London: Home Office.

Home Office (2005a) *Criminal Justice Act 2003: Implementation on 4 April*, Probation Circular 25/2005. London: Home Office.

Home Office (2005b) *Statistics on Race and the Criminal Justice System – 2004*. London: Home Office.

Home Office (2005c) *Offender Management Caseload Statistics 2004*, Home Office Statistical Bulletin 17/05. London: Home Office.

Home Office (2005d) *Race and the Criminal Justice System: An Overview to the Complete Statistics 2003–2004*. London: Home Office.

Home Office (2005e) *Restructuring Probation to Reduce Re-offending*. London: Home Office.

Home Office (2005f) *NOMS Change Programme: Strategic Business Case*. London: Home Office.

Home Office (2006a) *Offender Management Caseload Statistics Quarterly Brief: July to September 2005 England and Wales*. Available at: http://www.homeoffice.gov.uk/rds/pdfs06/omcsq305.pdf (accessed 3 April 2006).

Home Office (2006b) *A Five Year Strategy for Protecting the Public and Reducing Re-offending*. London: Stationery Office.

Hough, M. (1996) *Drugs Misuse and the Criminal Justice System: A Review of the Literature*, DPI Paper 15. London: Home Office.

Hough, M. and Mitchell, D. (2003) 'Drug-dependent offenders and *Justice for All*', in M. Tonry (ed.), *Confronting Crime: Crime Control Policy under New Labour*. Cullompton: Willan.

Hough, M., Clancy, A., McSweeney, T. and Turnbull, P. (2003) *The Impact of Drug Treatment and Testing Orders on Offending: Two-year Reconviction Results*, Home Office Research Findings No. 184. London: Home Office.

Hough, M., Jacobson, J. and Millie, A. (2003) *The Decision to Imprison: Sentencing and the Prison Population*. London: Prison Reform Trust.

House of Commons (1967) *Eleventh Report from the Estimates Committee: Session 1966–67, Prisons, Borstals and Detention Centres*. London: HMSO.

Kemshall, H. and Canton, R. (2002) *The Effective Management of Programme Attrition*. Available at: http//www.dmu.ac.uk/faculties/hls/research/commcrimjustice/commcrimjus.jsp (accessed February 2006).

Kemshall, H., Holt, P., Bailey, R. and Boswell, G. (2001) *The Implementation of Effective Practice in the Northwest Region*. Leicester: De Montfort University.

King, J.F.S. (1969) *The Probation and After-Care Service* 3rd edn. London: Butterworths.

McIvor, G. (1992) *Sentenced to Serve*. Aldershot: Avebury.

McKittrick, N. and Rex, S. (2003) 'Sentence management: a new role for the judiciary?', in M. Tonry (ed.), *Confronting Crime: Crime Control Policy under New Labour*. Cullompton: Willan.

McWilliams, W. (1983) 'The mission to the English police courts 1876–1936', *Howard Journal*, 22: 129–47.

McWilliams, W. (1985) 'The mission transformed: professionalisation of probation between the wars', *Howard Journal*, 24: 257–74.

McWilliams, W. (1986) 'The English probation system and the diagnostic ideal', *Howard Journal*, 25: 241–60.

Maguire, M., Morgan, R. and Reiner, R. (eds) (2007) *The Oxford Handbook of Criminology*, 4th edn. Oxford: Oxford University Press.

Mair, G. (1988) *Probation Day Centres*, Home Office Research Study No. 100. London: HMSO.

Mair, G. (1991) *Part Time Punishment? The Origins and Development of Senior Attendance Centres*. London: HMSO.

Mair, G. (2004) 'The origins of what works in England and Wales: a house built on sand?', in G. Mair (ed.), *What Matters in Probation*. Cullompton: Willan.

Mair, G., Lloyd, C., Nee, C. and Sibbitt, R. (1994) *Intensive Probation in England and Wales: An Evaluation*, Home Office Research Study No. 133. London: HMSO.

Mair, G., Cross, N. and Taylor, S. (2007) *The Use and Impact of the Community Order and the Suspended Sentence Order*. London: Centre for Crime and Justice Studies.

Mair, G. and May, C. (1995) *Practitioners' Views of the Criminal Justice Act: A Survey of Criminal Justice Agencies*, Research and Planning Unit Paper 91. London: Home Office.

Mair, G. and Nee, C. (1990) *Electronic Monitoring: The Trials and their Results*, Home Office Research Study No. 120. London: HMSO.

Martinson, R. (1974) 'What Works? Questions and answers about prison reform', *Public Interest*, 35: 22–54.

Maruna, S. (2004) '"California Dreamin": are we heading toward a national offender "waste management" service?', *Criminal Justice Matters*, 56: 6–7.

Morgan, R. (2003) 'Thinking about the demand for probation services', *Probation Journal*, 50: 7–19.

MORI (2003) *Magistrates' Perceptions of the Probation Service*. London: National Probation Service.

Mortimer, E. and Mair, G. (1995) 'Integrating Community Sentences: Results from the Green Paper Sentencing Exercises'. Unpublished report to the Home Office.

National Audit Office (2004) *The Drug Treatment and Testing Order: Early Lessons*. London: National Audit Office.

National Offender Management Service (2005a) *Probation Statistics October–December 2004*. London: NOMS.

National Offender Management Service (2005b) *Annual Report for Accredited Programmes 2004–2005*. London: NOMS.

National Offender Management Service (2005c) *The NOMS Offender Management Model*. Available online at: http://www.probation.homeoffice.gov.uk/files/pdf/NOMS%20 Offender%20Management%20Model.pdf (accessed January 2006).

National Probation Directorate (2003) *A Brief Introduction to Enhanced Community Punishment*. Available online at: http://www.probation.homeoffice.gov.uk/files/ pdf/ECP%20Scheme%20-%20Edition%202%20-%20A%20Brief%20Introduction%20to %20Enhanced%20CP.pdf (accessed January 2006).

National Probation Service (2001) *A New Choreography: An Integrated Strategy for the National Probation Service for England and Wales*. London: NPS.

National Probation Service (2003a) *Think First: Information for Sentencers*. Available online at: http://www.probation.homeoffice.gov.uk/files/pdf/think_first_information_for_sentencers.pdf (accessed January 2006).

National Probation Service (2003b) *Enhanced Community Punishment: Important Information for Sentencers*. Available online at: http://www.probation.homeoffice.gov.uk/files/pdf/Info%20for%20sentencers%204.pdf (accessed January 2006).

National Probation Service (2005) *National Standards for the Supervision of Offenders in the Community*. Available online at: http://www.probation.homeoffice.gov.uk/files/pdf/PC15%202005.pdf (accessed January 2006).

Pease, K., Billingham, S. and Earnshaw, I. (1977) *Community Service Assessed in 1976*, Home Office Research Study No. 139. London: HMSO.

Powell, C. L., Bamber, D. and Christie, M. M. (2006) 'Drug Treatment and Testing Orders: offender views and implications for drug treatment in the criminal justice system', *Drugs: Education, Prevention and Policy*, in press.

Pryor, S. (2001) *The Responsible Prisoner*. Available online at: http://inspectorates. homeoffice.gov.uk/hmiprisons/thematic-reports1/the-responsible-prisoner. pdf?view=Binary (accessed April 2006).

Raynor, P. (2004) 'Rehabilitative and reintegrative approaches', in A. Bottoms, S. Rex and G. Robinson (eds), *Alternatives to Prison: Options for an Insecure Society*. Cullompton: Willan.

Raynor, P. and Vanstone, M. (2002) *Understanding Community Penalties*. Buckingham: Open University Press.

Rex, S. (1999) 'Desistance from offending: experiences of probation', *Howard Journal*, 38: 366–83.

Rex, S. (2005) *Reforming Community Penalties*. Cullompton: Willan.

Rex, S. and Gelsthorpe, L. (2002) 'The role of Community Service in reducing offending: evaluating Pathfinder projects in the UK', *Howard Journal*, 41: 311–25.

Rex, S., Gelsthorpe, L., Roberts, C. and Jordan, P. (2003) *Crime Reduction Programme. An Evaluation of Community Service Pathfinder Projects: Final Report 2002*, RDS Occasional Paper No. 87. London: Home Office.

Roberts, C. (2004) 'Offending behaviour programmes: emerging evidence and implications for practice', in R. Burnett and C. Roberts (eds), *What Works in Probation and Youth Justice: Developing Evidence-based Practice*. Cullompton: Willan.

Robinson, G. (2005) 'What Works in offender management?', *Howard Journal*, 44: 307–18.

Robinson, G. and McNeill, F. (2004) 'Purposes matter: explaining the ends of probation', in G. Mair (ed.), *What Matters in Probation*. Cullompton: Willan.

Rumgay, J. (2004) 'Dealing with substance-misusing offenders in the community', in A. Bottoms, S. Rex and G. Robinson (eds), *Alternatives to Prison: Options for an Insecure Society*. Cullompton: Willan.

Rutherford, A. (1986) *Prisons and the Process of Justice*. Oxford: Oxford University Press.

Smith, L.J.F. (1982) *Day Training Centres*, Home Office Research Bulletin 14: 34–7.

Solomon, E. (2005) 'Returning to punishment: prison recalls', *Criminal Justice Matters*, 60: 24–5.

Stewart-Ong, G., Harsent, L., Roberts, C., Burnett, R. and Al-Attar, Z. (2004) *Think First Prospective Research Study: Effectiveness and Reducing Attrition*. Available online at: http://www.probation.homeoffice.gov.uk/files/pdf/Think%20First%20Research%20Study%202004.pdf (accessed April 2006).

Trotter, C. (1999) *Working with Involuntary Clients: A Guide to Practice*. London: Sage.

Turnbull, P.J., McSweeney, T., Webster, R., Edmunds, M. and Hough, M. (2000) *Drug Treatment and Testing Orders: Final Evaluation Report*, Home Office Research Study No. 212. London: Home Office.

Turner, R. (2004) 'The impact of drug treatment and testing orders in West Yorkshire: six-month outcomes', *Probation Journal*, 51: 116–32.

Underdown, A. (1998) *Strategies for Effective Supervision: Report of the HMIP What Works Project.* London: HMIP.

Vanstone, M. (2004) 'A history of the use of groups in probation work: Part Two – from negotiated treatment to evidence-based practice in an accountable service', *Howard Journal*, 43: 180–202.

Vanstone, M. and Raynor, P. (1981) 'Diversion from prison – a partial success and a missed opportunity', *Probation Journal*, 28: 85–9.

Wasik, M. (2004) 'What guides sentencing decision?', in A. Bottoms, S. Rex and G. Robinson (eds), *Alternatives to Prison: Options for an Insecure Society.* Cullompton: Willan.

Windlesham, D. (2001) *Dispensing Justice: Responses to Crime Volume 4.* Oxford: Oxford University Press.

Wootton, B. (1978) *Crime and Penal Policy: Reflections on Fifty Years Experience.* London: Allen & Unwin.

Worrall, A. and Hoy, C. (2005) *Punishment in the Community: Managing Offenders, Making Choices*, 2nd edn. Cullompton: Willan.

Chapter 10

Youth justice

Rod Morgan and Tim Newburn

The Probation Service has from its inception taken some responsibility for juvenile offenders. But over the years the manner and degree to which offending by children and young people has been dealt with in the criminal justice system has changed and with it the engagement of probation officers. In 1998 the system for dealing with the criminal offences of children and young persons in England and Wales was fundamentally reformed by the Crime and Disorder Act. Multi-agency youth offending teams (YOTs) were established, of which seconded probation officers became a part. Because the Probation Service contributes financially and with personnel to YOTs, this chapter will focus on the current arrangements, the nature of the contribution which probation makes and the connection issues which will arise with the inception of the National Offender Management Service (NOMS). These connections are vital because, regrettably, a high proportion of adult offenders supervised by probation officers were first convicted while they were children, that is when they were aged 10–17. If children and young people are to be criminalised – a contentious issue – it is desirable for the adult and youth justice systems to work closely together, to the greatest possible extent ensuring care, consistency and continuity in the transition of young people to adulthood.

We begin with a brief historical sketch of the background to the 1998 reforms and the prior involvement of the Probation Service with juveniles.

The emergence of juvenile justice and the background to the 1998 reforms

A separate system of juvenile justice began to emerge in the second half of the nineteenth century. Social reformers campaigned to protect children from danger and exploitation and as part of this sought to remove them from the 'adult' prison system. Reformatories and industrial schools were introduced for the 'dangerous' and 'perishing' classes respectively. Although initially part of the educational rather than the penal system, they housed children aged between 7 and 14 who had been convicted of vagrancy. Juvenile courts emerged at the beginning of the twentieth century. The 1908 Children Act created the juvenile court — special sittings of the magistrates' courts in the early years - empowered to act in criminal, begging and vagrancy cases. The probation officers appointed following the Probation of Offenders Act 1907 worked in both the adult and the juvenile courts. Meanwhile the separation of young offenders from adults was taken further with the creation of 'borstals' (for 16-21-year-olds, the 'juvenile-adult category') and the 'welfare principle' was later reinforced by the Children and Young Persons Act 1933 which prohibited capital punishment for under-18s and reorganised the reformatory and industrial schools as 'approved schools' to provide juvenile offenders with education and training.

In the post-War period the twin-track welfare and penal justice approaches became more apparent. In addition to remand centres, attendance centres, support for probation hostels and abolition of corporal punishment, the Criminal Justice Act 1948 also introduced detention centres designed to accommodate short, unpleasant sentences for young offenders not unlike the 'short, sharp shock' experiment of the early 1980s. Meanwhile the Children Act 1948 sought to end the placement of neglected children in approved schools alongside offenders, and local authority children's departments with their own resources for residential care were established.

A strong welfarist imperative continued to influence juvenile justice policy throughout the 1950s and most of the 1960s. Though the recommendation of the Ingleby Committee that the age of criminal responsibility be raised from 8 to 14 was not adopted, the Children and Young Persons Act 1963 did raise it to 10. Further, the Act abolished the system of approved schools and the remand homes or remand centres for juveniles which existed alongside them: they were replaced by community homes with residential and educational facilities. Care was preferred over criminal proceedings and the circumstances in which court proceedings were possible were narrowed. The intention was that the juvenile court become a welfare-providing agency of last resort, referral happening only in those cases in which informal and voluntary agreement had not been reached between the local authority, the juvenile and parents. It was also intended that detention centres and borstals for juveniles be phased out to be replaced by a new form of intervention – intermediate treatment. This, according to Rutherford (1986: 57), 'was less a policy of decarceration than a reiteration of the traditional welfare abhorrence of the prison system'.

The 1969 Act was arguably the high point of 'welfarism'. The victory of the Conservative Party in the 1970 general election put paid to any possibility of full implementation. The consequence was that juvenile courts continued to function largely as before: criminal proceedings for 10–14-year-olds continued, powers in relation to 14–16-year-olds were not restricted and the minimum age for a borstal sentence was not increased. Perhaps most significantly, although care proceedings on the commission of an offence were made possible, such powers were used exceedingly sparingly.

Partial implementation of the 1969 Act resulted in consequences which many commentators viewed as tragic. People were led to believe that the system was becoming softer and softer when in reality the reverse was largely the case (Thorpe *et al.* 1980). Though only partly implemented, the Act became the major scapegoat for the perceived ills of juvenile crime and justice in the 1970s. The 'welfare' model which the Act represented was replaced by an expanding youth justice system in which the emphasis was increasingly on 'justice' or punishment. There was a significant backlash against welfarism across criminal justice and penal policy in the 1970s, and the criticisms came from all parts of the political spectrum. Those on the right were critical of what they took to be the insufficiently tough approach characteristic of contemporary juvenile justice. Those on the left argued that behind all the talk of 'treatment', restrictive and potentially punitive forms of intervention were on the increase. The 1970s witnessed a doubling in the use of custody for juveniles with a concomitant decline in the use of community-based alternatives, albeit the use of cautions increased substantially. The latter trend continued during the 1980s which, paradoxically given the tough Thatcherite 'law and order' rhetoric (which included the introduction of the 'short, sharp shock' detention centre regimes), witnessed a significant and sustained decline in the numbers of young people being processed by the courts and sentenced to custody.

Several factors accounted for this fall. There was a significant drop in the number of 14–16-year-old males. The Criminal Justice Act 1982 contained restrictions on the use of custody and introduced a range of non-custodial penalties, several of which came to be used as high-tariff options. The number of intensive intermediate treatment schemes was increased: these appear to have served as an alternative to custody. Finally, there was diversion from court. This was central to the significant decline in the number of juveniles prosecuted in the latter half of the 1980s (Farrington 1992). Indeed, so successful was the general cautioning policy in relation to juveniles believed to be that, as early as the 1988 Green Paper, *Punishment, Custody and the Community*, the Home Office signalled its intention to transfer the lessons learnt in juvenile justice to policies for offenders generally (Home Office 1988: para.s 2.17–2.19). In the same period, two major pieces of legislation affecting young offenders came into force. The Children Act 1989 finally removed all civil care proceedings from the juvenile court, and the Criminal Justice Act 1991 changed the name of the juvenile court to the youth court and extended its jurisdiction to include 17-year-olds. Henceforth, unlike the practice in Scotland (see McAra 2002; Bottoms and Dignan 2004) and many other jurisdictions, care or family preceedings relating to children and young people were institutionally entirely separated from criminal proceedings.

The 1991 Act reduced the maximum term of detention in a young offender institution (YOI) to 12 months. YOIs had been introduced in 1988, superseding the youth custody centres that had themselves replaced borstals in 1982. The 1991 Act also signalled the importance of inter-agency and joint working. It gave Chief Probation Officers and Directors of Social Services joint responsibility for making local arrangements ('action plans') for dealing with young offenders, and more generally for providing services to the youth court. This was the final nail in the coffin of the 'welfare' model, and further reinforced, though temporarily, the pre-eminence of the 'justice' model in juvenile justice. Yet at least one commentator argued that it no longer made sense to talk in terms of welfare *or* justice. Rather, Pratt (1989) argued, what was emerging in English juvenile justice was a form of 'corporatism'. Centralised authority and bureaucratic control over decision-making was driving a system increasingly characterised by multi-agency working, in which the aims of 'economy' and 'efficiency' were of growing importance in the management of those caught up in the system (see below).

The early 1990s also witnessed a dramatic change in the tenor of official comment about juvenile offending. Concerns were fuelled by a number of events, including the well-publicised urban disturbances of 1991 (Campbell 1993) and a moral panic about 'persistent young offenders' (Hagell and Newburn 1994). In March 1993, the Government announced that it proposed introducing a new disposal, the secure training order (STO), aimed at 'that comparatively small group of very persistent juvenile offenders whose repeated offending makes them a menace to the community' (*Hansard*, 2 March 1993, col. 139). It was to apply to 12–15-year-olds (later amended to 12–14-year-olds) who had been convicted of three imprisonable offences and who had proved 'unwilling or unable to comply with the requirements of supervision in the community while on remand or under sentence'.

Public and political concern might not have reached the pitch it did were it not for the tragic abduction in February 1993 of two-year-old James Bulger from a shopping centre in Bootle, Liverpool and the repeated broadcasting of CCTV images of the toddler being led away. The subsequent arrest and charging of two 10-year-old boys 'inspired a kind of national collective agony' (Young 1996: 113). The trial of the two youngsters accused of James Bulger's murder was accompanied by massive national and international media coverage which, despite the age of the offenders, was unforgivingly punitive. Leading politicians from both main parties used the opportunity to air their tough-on-crime credentials. Tony Blair, then Shadow Home Secretary, delivered what one biographer (Sopel 1995: 155) described as a powerful 'speech-cum-sermon':

> The news bulletins of the last week have been like hammer blows struck against the sleeping conscience of the country, urging us to wake up and look unflinchingly at what we see. We hear of crimes so horrific they provoke anger and disbelief in equal proportions ... These are the ugly manifestations of a society that is becoming unworthy of that name.

The then Home Secretary, Michael Howard, responded by embracing a 'populist punitive' (Bottoms 1995) rhetoric and introducing a package of new measures, at the heart of which was the reassertion of the centrality of custody. Most famously, he announced that previous approaches which involved attempts to limit prison numbers were henceforward to be abandoned. The new package of measures would be likely to result in an increase in prison numbers, an increase which he appeared to welcome because '*Prison works. It ensures that we are protected from murderers, muggers and rapists – and it makes many who are tempted to commit crime think twice*' (quoted in Newburn 2003: 263, emphasis added).

The Criminal Justice and Public Order Act 1994 doubled the maximum sentence in a YOI for 15–17-year-olds to two years. The Act introduced the possibility that parents of young offenders be bound over to ensure that their children carried out their community sentences, and provided for the introduction of STOs for 12–14-year-olds. Five secure training centres (STCs) were to be built, each housing approximately 40 inmates. The new sentences would be determinate, of a maximum of two years, half of which would be served in custody and half under supervision in the community. Outside Parliament there was widespread criticism of the new provisions and Home Office-funded research cast doubt on the likely efficacy of such a policy (Hagell and Newburn 1994). But the STO met with relatively little political hostility with New Labour seeking to outflank the Conservatives over 'law and order' (Downes and Morgan 2007). The predictable consequence was a rise in the use of youth custody. The number of 15–17-year-olds given custodial sentences rose by almost four-fifths between 1992 and 1998. The number of young people serving custodial sentences rose by 122 per cent between 1993 and 1999 (Morgan and Leibling 2007; Morgan and Newburn 2007).

These events took place against a background in which all public services were being subjected to the scrutiny of the Audit Comission, established to promote the three 'Es' of economy, efficiency and effectiveness. In the mid-1990s the Commission turned its attention to the youth justice system and added its voice to the growing roll-call of commentators calling for increased emphasis on 'criminality prevention' (*inter alia* Utting *et al.* 1993; Farrington 1996). The Opposition Home Affairs team was simultaneously preparing their proposals for youth justice reform. The parallels between New Labour's pre-election consultation document, *Tackling Youth Crime: Reforming Youth Justice* (Labour Party 1996), and the Audit Commission's hugely influential report, *Misspent Youth* (Audit Commission 1996), were striking – both in terms of the issues covered and the proposals contained.

The Audit Commission had little of a positive nature to say about the youth justice system and a number of biting criticisms. Its view was that the system in England and Wales failed all three 'E' tests. The Commission was critical of the cautioning system, and particularly of 'repeat cautioning'. It argued that first-time cautions were reasonably effective, but that subsequent use became progressively less effective and ran the risk of bringing the youth justice system into disrepute. The Commission was critical of the lack of programmes directed at offending behaviour and dismayed by what it saw as the absence of coordinated working: 'The agencies dealing with young offenders have different views about what they are trying to achieve ... these different approaches need to be reconciled if agencies are to work together and fulfil their different responsibilities' (Audit Commission 1996: para. 21). According to the Commission, it was not just the approach of youth justice teams that was problematic. The whole court system, it suggested, was becoming less and less efficient: 'Overall, less is done now than a decade ago to address offending by young people. Fewer young people are now convicted by the courts, even allowing for the fall in the number of people aged 10–17 years, and an increasing proportion of those who are found guilty are discharged' (Audit Commission 1996: para. 69). The system, the Commission argued, needed to be streamlined, speeded up and greater attention given to early preventive work. Its approach was heavily influenced by the results of longitudinal criminological research that identified the 'risk factors' associated with offending by juveniles. These factors may be used to target areas where young people are at particular risk and help identify approaches that may reduce the risks.

The Commission's analysis and proposals and the subsequent legislation – the Crime and Disorder Act 1998 – were heavily managerialist in approach, emphasising inter-agency cooperation, the necessity of an overall strategic plan, the creation of key performance indicators and active monitoring of aggregate information about the system and its functioning. To a youth justice system that had been the site of competing philosophies, approaches and ideologies – notably welfarism, punitiveness and systems management – New Labour added a further dose of managerialism, together with its own potent blend of communitarianism and populism (Newburn 1998). The consequence of this blend, for some commentators, has been the emergence of 'new youth justice' (Goldson, 2000).

From their inception at the beginning of the twentieth century probation officers had as servants of the court given advice to sentencers about defendants' characteristics and their suitability for and likely response to different sanctions. Written reports for these purposes were first used systematically in the 1930s in the juvenile court, where they were initially called 'home circumstances reports' (see Haines and Morgan, this volume). Since then probation officers and services had been involved with both juvenile – mostly older adolescents – and adult offenders, as report-writers and supervisors of community sentences and releases on licence. It was logical, therefore, that the reformed youth justice system, at the heart of which is inter-agency working, should directly involve probation staff.

New Labour's new youth justice system

The 1998 Act: responsibilities and structures

Though, following the election, New Labour published a series of consultation documents regarding youth crime and justice, their approach was expressed in the title of a White Paper, *No More Excuses* (Home Office 1997a). The major proposals eventually found their way, largely unchanged, into the government's flagship legislation, the Crime and Disorder Act 1998. This Act, though followed by others, contains the key elements of Labour's 'new youth justice': the establishment of the Youth Justice Board (YJB), the creation of local authority youth offending teams (YOTs) and the restructuring of the non-custodial penalties available to the youth court. In *No More Excuses*, the government had identified:

> confusion about the purpose of the youth justice system and the principles that should govern the way in which young people are dealt with by youth justice agencies. Concerns about the welfare of young people have too often been seen as in conflict with the aims of protecting the public, punishing offences and preventing offending ...

The Government does not accept that there is any conflict between protecting the welfare of a young offender and preventing that individual from offending again. Preventing offending promotes the welfare of the individual young offender and protects the public. (Home Office 1997a: para. 2.1–2)

The Crime and Disorder Act 1998 s.37 established that: 'It shall be the principal aim of the youth justice system to prevent offending by children and young persons'. Five aims for were set out for the new system: a clear strategy to prevent offending and reoffending; offenders, and their parents, to face up to their offending behaviour and take responsibility for it; earlier, more effective intervention when young people first offend; faster, more efficient procedures from arrest to sentence; partnership between all youth justice agencies to deliver more effective interventions.

Juvenile justice has historically varied a good deal in terms of service delivery locally. Inspired by the criticisms by the Audit Commission (1996), New Labour sought to impose order from the centre. A Youth Justice Task Force was established, chaired by Norman (subsequently Lord) Warner, who had been adviser to Home Secretary, Jack Straw, in Opposition. Its secretary was Mark Perfect, co-author of the 1996 Audit Commission report. When, following s. 41 of the Crime and Disorder Act 1998, the YJB was created, a non-departmental public body sponsored by the Home Office, these two became its first Chair and Chief Executive respectively.

The YJB's principal functions are to establish appropriate performance measures, monitor the operation of the youth justice system in the light of national standards, conduct research, promulgate good practice and advise ministers. The 1998 Act provided for the Home Secretary to expand the Board's role and, in April 2000, he did so by making it the commissioning body for all placements of under 18s in secure establishments on remand or sentence from a criminal court. The Comprehensive Spending Review of the secure estate had concluded that there was 'little positive to say about the current arrangements … Regime standards are inconsistent and often poor. Costs vary considerably. There is no effective oversight or long-term planning' (Home Office, 1998). Since 2000, therefore, the YJB has had the responsibility of purchasing sufficient places from the Prison Service, from commercial contractors and from the local authorities to cater for all children and young persons who the courts determine shall be in custody.

If New Labour's commitment to the core elements of 'systemic managerialism' (Bottoms 1995) was reflected in the creation of the YJB, then the establishment of YOTs, the embodiment of partnership working, was the most significant reform introduced by the 1998 Act. Prior to 1998, youth justice teams, comprising mainly social workers, had primary responsibility for working with young offenders subject to non-custodial penalties, and for liaising with other criminal justice and treatment agencies in connection with that work. Stimulated by a concern with efficiency and consistency on the one hand and a pragmatic belief in multi-agency working on the other, YOTs *must* include representatives of both criminal justice and welfare agencies – social services, the police, probation, education and health are all stipulated

(s. 39(5)). Whether local authorities cooperate to form a YOT or provide their own is a matter for them. Arrangements, as a consequence, vary from one area to another. There are currently 156 YOTs in England and Wales with great variation between them in size, composition, funding and line management arrangements. YOTs are generally co-located, most have in the range of 20–60 full-time equivalent staff (though the largest, Birmingham, has 359 staff and six have fewer than 20 staff) and, though they are discrete entities, their managers are generally line managed from either within social services (or combined children's services departments) or chief executives' departments.

The staff making up the YOTs were initially mostly secondees, principally from social services. Over time the proportion of secondees has diminished and the proportion of permanent staff grown. According to YOT returns to the YJB, just over 300 seconded probation officers remain in YOT posts and a significant proportion of YOT managers are ex-probation.

The precise method of funding YOTs is unclear in the 1998 Act. Local authorities, chief officers of police and probation committees (as they then were) are empowered to make payments towards such expenditure or to contribute to a fund for this purpose (s. 39(4)). In the case of probation the contribution has so far been negotiated nationally and accounts for 8 per cent of the YOTs' aggregate income compared to 42 per cent from social services, 18 per cent from the YJB, 11 per cent from local authority chief executives, 10 per cent from the police and 6 and 5 per cent respectively from education and health (YJB 2005a: 17).

As Pitts (2001) notes, the constitution of the YOTs mirrors the Multi-Agency Diversion Panels of the 1980s and, in particular, the Northampton Diversion Scheme, the latter having been given a particularly good press by the Audit Commission (1996). However, whereas the diversion schemes were the product of an earlier era, YOTs have been established not to divert but to target and intervene. The primary functions of YOTs are to coordinate the provision of youth justice services for all those in the local authority's area who need them, and to carry out such functions as are assigned to the team in the youth justice plan formulated by the local authority.

Local youth justice plans are heavily influenced by the performance framework which has been developed by the YJB. This, in turn, has reflected the performance framework developed by the Home Office which provides the bulk of the YJB's budget, and the inter-departmental Office for Criminal Justice Reform (OCJR), a trilateral centre (Home Office, Department for Constitutional Affairs and Attorney General's Department) which reports monthly to a National Criminal Justice Board, which in turn oversees the 42 Local Criminal Justice Boards (LCJBs) on which all the key criminal justice agencies, including the YOTs, are represented (HM Government 2004). The nature and extent of this reporting system is an indication of just how significant the managerialist reforms to youth justice have been in the past decade.

The only specific pledge concerning crime which New Labour offered in its victorious 1997 election campaign concerned young offenders. The famous slogan: 'Tough on crime and tough on the causes of crime', first used by Tony Blair in 1993, was illustrated with the undertaking to 'halve the time it takes persistent juvenile crime to come to court' (Labour Party 1997). Achievement of this pledge is regularly reported in the annual reports of the YJB – the 142 days of 1996 having been reduced to 76 by the time of the 2001 election and to 66 in 2005 (YJB 2005a: 8). To this quantitative target the YJB had by 2005 added others, for example:

- to reduce the number of first-time entrants to the youth justice system by 5 per cent by March 2008 compared to the 2005 baseline;
- to reduce reoffending by young offenders by 5 per cent, relative to a 2000 baseline, by March 2006;
- to reduce, between 31 March 2005 and 31 March 2008, the number of under 18s in custody by 10 per cent. (YJB 2005a: 8–11 and YJB 2005b: 18–25)

These three targets illustrate the principal foci of the YJB and the performance management system the Board has put in place for the YOTs and the closed estate – prevention, and programmes which will reduce reoffending, delivered to the greatest extent possible without resort to custody.

The 1998 Act: powers and procedures

New Labour promised increased, earlier interventions in the lives of young offenders and those 'at risk' of becoming young offenders. One of the clearest illustrations of the influence of the Audit Commission was New Labour's reform of the cautioning system. The 1998 Act scrapped the caution (informal and formal) and replaced it with a reprimand (for less serious offences) and a final warning. The final warning may be used only once, unless there is a lapse of two years. Further, all young offenders receiving a final warning should be referred to a YOT and expected, unless it is inappropriate, to participate in an intervention. The Criminal Justice and Court Services Act 2000 removed the requirement that a police reprimand or final warning be given to a young offender only at a police station. This introduced the possibility of 'conferences' at which parents, victims and other adults could be present.

The new cautioning system stipulates 'two strikes and then you're out'. But there are other measures, both upstream and downstream of reprimands and final warnings, designed to prevent responses moving up-tariff. Responding to research evidence highlighting the link between early and frequent offending and later, extended criminal careers, the YJB has developed several early prevention schemes whose purpose is to mitigate crime and anti-social behaviour and prevent offending and criminalisation. The YJB has encouraged the development within YOTs of the following:

- *Youth Inclusion and Support Panels (YISPs)*. These comprise representatives of the key agencies (police, education, health, social services and the YOT) to work voluntarily with 8 to 13-year-olds identified as at risk of offending. The aim is to support the young people and their families in accessing mainstream services with a view to addressing the factors in their lives that put them at risk of offending.

- *Youth Inclusion Programmes (YIPs)*. These aim to engage, voluntarily, the 50 young people in an area who the key agencies identify as most at risk of offending. Again the aim is to address the factors in their lives that place them at risk through positive activities, offending behaviour programmes and improved access to services, particularly education.

- *Parenting programmes*. These are mostly voluntary, often as an adjunct to YISPs and YIPs, but in a minority of cases through Parenting Contracts or Parenting Orders, the latter being provided for by s. 8 of the 1998 Act. These programmes will become more important subsequent to the Government's 'Respect' initiative announced by Prime Minister Blair in early 2006 (Home Office 2006).

- *Safer Schools Partnerships (SSPs)*. Under these schemes, on the grounds that not attending school or being engaged in education greatly increases the risk that children and young people will offend, police officers are more or less intensively attached to schools with a view to reducing crime and victimisation, making the school and its environment more safe and secure and reducing truancy and exclusions.

None of these initiatives is without controversy on the grounds that they represent an expansion of the criminal justice orbit and risk stigmatising environments, children and their families with potentially net-widening and criminogenic consequences (see McAra 2006). There is no evidence of such consequences, however, and most YOTs now have a number of early prevention schemes (delivery of some of them contracted out to organisations like NACRO or Crime Concern) in their most deprived neighbourhoods or schools, with further expansion planned.

If the 1998 Act provided the basis for earlier interventions in the lives of young offenders and their parents (thereby adopting the 'what works' paradigm and employing the language of 'risk'), it also moved into the even more ambiguous territory of anti-social behaviour (ASB). It contained a range of orders – the child safety order, the anti-social behaviour order (ASBO), the local child curfew and the sex offender order – where there is no necessity for either the prosecution or the commission of a criminal offence. These, together with the abolition of *doli incapax* – the rebuttable common law presumption that a child aged 10–13 does not know the difference between right and wrong and therefore cannot be convicted – represent the most controversial aspects of the 'new youth justice'.

Abolishing *doli incapax* puts England and Wales further out of step with most jurisdictions in the rest of Europe, where the age of criminal responsibility is 12–15 (Tonry and Doob 2004). The measure drew sustained criticism when first mooted and has attracted condemnation both internationally and domestically (Commissioner for Human Rights 2005 paras 105–6; Commission on Families and the Wellbeing of Children 2005: 33–7).

New Labour has been much influenced by the 'broken windows' thesis (Wilson and Kelling 1982) and has introduced a range of measures enabling local agencies to tackle 'low-level disorder' or ASB. One of these new measures, the child safety order, relates to children under 10 and thus not criminally responsible. The order, made in a family proceedings court, is aimed at controlling ASB rather than protecting a child's welfare. It involves placing a child under supervision usually for a period of three months, up to a maximum of 12 months. Though the child safety order was subject to criticism in some quarters (Family Policy Studies Centre 1998) it was the ASBO which was and is most controversial.

ASBOs were designed to tackle ASB defined as: 'a matter that caused or was likely to cause harassment, alarm or distress to one or more persons not of the same household'. Prior to the 1998 Act much of this behaviour had been dealt with by noise, environmental protection and harassment legislation. However, proceedings against juveniles were often problematic under such legislation (Nixon *et al.* 1999) and the ASBO was designed, *inter alia*, with juvenile ASB in mind.

ASBOs have morphed. As a result of legislation since 1998, applications for orders can be made by social landlords as well as the police and local authorities. Orders are formally civil, requiring a civil burden of proof, but, following the Police Reform Act 2002, they can also be made on conviction (colloquially known as CRASBOs) and the evidence suggests that the subjects of such orders often have many and serious prior convictions. ASBOs, which are for a minimum of two years, comprise prohibitions deemed necessary to protect people within the area from further ASB. What is most controversial, however, is that non-compliance is a criminal matter, triable either way and carrying a maximum sentence of five years' imprisonment.

Many local authorities were initially reluctant to seek ASBOs. But Prime Minister Blair and successive Home Secretaries repeatedly kickstarted the initiative. In 2003 a unit (the ASBU) was created within the Home Office to promote local activism, and further legislation (the Criminal Justice and Court Services Act 2000, the Criminal Justice and Police Act 2001, the Police Reform Act 2002 and, in particular, the Anti-Social Behaviour Act 2003) added a raft of additional powers which the courts, police and local authorities were encouraged to use. If the number of ASBOs, and adoption of the term as a colloquialism, are the criteria, the Government's campaign was brilliantly successful. The number of orders imposed nationally ran at around 100 per quarter until the end of 2002 but by the end of 2004 the rate was over 500 rising to 600 per quarter in 2005, juveniles being the subjects of 45 per cent of them. Great pressure from above was exerted on decision-makers in areas without ASBOs in place (Morgan 2006a).

The ASB policy has been criticised by authorities international and domestic. The Council of Europe Commissioner for Human Rights observed:

> The ease of obtaining such orders, the broad range of prohibited behaviour, the publicity surrounding their imposition and the serious consequences of breach all give rise to concerns ... the orders are intended to protect not just specific individuals, but entire communities. This inevitably results in a very broad, and occasionally excessive, range of behaviour falling within their scope as the determination of what constitutes anti-social behaviour becomes conditional on the subjective views of any given collective ... such orders look rather

like personalised penal codes, where non-criminal behaviour becomes criminal for individuals who have incurred the wrath of the community …I question the appropriateness of empowering local residents to take such matters into their own hands. This feature would, however, appear to be the main selling point of ASBOs in the eyes of the executive. One cannot help but wonder … whether their purpose is not more to reassure the public that something is being done – and, better still, by residents themselves – than the actual prevention of anti-social behaviour itself. (Commissioner for Human Rights 2005: paras 109–11; see also Simester and Von Hirsch 2006)

An independent evaluation came to similar conclusions, pointing out that the Government's ASB campaign reinforced a 'declining standards' narrative, negatively focused on young people (Millie *et al.* 2005).

By 2005 concerns were being expressed regarding the impact of ASBOs on children and young people:

- first, that the minimum order was so long and the number of prohibitions imposed so often excessive, that breach was made likely;
- secondly, despite guidance being issued emphasising the need for full consultation with the relevant YOT prior to an order being sought (YJB *et al.* 2005), evidence that in some parts of the country the YOTs – and thus the partnership spirit of the 1998 reforms – were effectively being circumvented and ASBO applications were normally being heard in adult courts not covered by YOT representatives;
- thirdly, that in some areas ASBOs were being sought and granted without the recommended (YJB *et al.* 2005) lower tier measures (home visits, warning letters and acceptable behaviour contracts (ABCs)) first being tried;
- fourthly, that ASBOs, following breach, were dragging into custody some young people who would not previously have got there or, possibly more commonly, were providing an evidential short cut for the police to fast-track persistent young offenders into custody (see the evidence to and report of the Home Affairs Committee 2005).

These criticisms led to the introduction, at the end of 2005 and early 2006, of ASBO reviews after 12 months and a practice direction that ASBO applications relating to juveniles be heard, whenever possible, by youth court magistrates.

Opposition was also aimed at the provisions in the Crime and Disorder Act permitting local authorities to introduce 'local child curfew schemes'. The introduction of curfews in the UK had been foreshadowed by proposals in the consultation paper, *Tackling Youth Crime* (Home Office 1997b) and the White Paper, *No More Excuses* (Home Office 1997a). The former described the problem thus: 'Unsupervised children gathered in public places can cause real alarm and misery to local communities and can encourage one another into anti-social and criminal habits' (1997b: para. 114). The provisions in the 1998 Act enabled local authorities, after consultation with the police and with support of the Home Secretary, to introduce a ban on children of specified ages (though under 10) in specified places for a period of up to 90 days. Children breaking the curfew were to be taken home by the police, and breach of the curfew constitutes sufficient grounds for the imposition of a child safety order. In practice, there has been reluctance to use such powers, yet the Government remains keen on the idea. Armed with what appeared to be some positive results from an evaluation of a scheme in Hamilton, Scotland (McGallagly *et al.* 1998), new legislation was introduced to extend the reach of curfew powers. The Criminal Justice and Police Act 2001 extends the maximum age at which children can be subject to a curfew from 10 to 'under 16', and also makes provision for a local authority or the police to make a curfew on an area and not just an individual.

Critics of New Labour's youth justice policies have also pointed to its perceived failure to tackle the problem of increasing use of custodial sentences for young offenders. In its first term, Labour continued with the previous administration's STC building programme and introduced a new, generic custodial sentence: the detention and training order (DTO). Available to the courts from April 2000, DTOs are from six to 24 months, half the sentence being served in custody and half in the community. The DTO replaces both the Secure Training Order (for 12–14 year olds) and detention in a YOI (for 15–17 year olds). DTOs, available to the youth court, sit alongside continued provisions whereby grave offences – in the case of murder, mandatorily - are committed to the Crown Court and liable to 'long-term detention' for which the maximum period is the same as if the child or young person were an adult. These long-term detention cases are known as section 90 or 91 cases (Powers of the Criminal Courts (Sentencing) Act 2000, formerly s. 53 of the Children and Young Persons Act 1933).

The DTO represented an increase in the powers of the youth court to impose custodial sentences. Whereas the maximum period of detention in a YOI for 15–17-year-olds had been six months for a single offence, the DTO has a maximum of two years. Further, though the STO for 12–14-year-olds already provided for a two-year maximum, New Labour replaced the strict criteria for offenders under 15 relating to 'persistence' with the provision that the sentence be available where the court 'is of the *opinion* that he is a persistent offender'. The courts, including the Court of Appeal, have interpreted this power rather broadly (see Ball *et al.* 2001).

Yet the Government has also given greater emphasis to reparation and restorative justice, building on the experimental practice of restorative cautioning in Thames Valley (Young and Goold 1999). The reformed cautioning system, action plan, reparation and, following the Youth Justice and Criminal Evidence Act 1999, referral orders all promoted the idea of reparation and, wherever possible, victim involvement.

The action plan order was designed to be the first option for young offenders whose offending is serious enough to warrant a community sentence. *No More Excuses* described the order as 'a short, intensive programme of community intervention combining punishment, rehabilitation and reparation to change offending behaviour and prevent further crime' (Home Office 1997a). Reparation orders require reparation to either a specified person or persons or 'to the community at large'. Following the implementation of the 1998 Act, the YJB also committed considerable funds to the stimulation of restorative justice projects for young offenders and, together with Crime Concern, issued guidance on the establishment of victim–offender mediation and family group conferencing programmes. Of all New Labour's restorative youth justice initiatives, however, the most significant has been the creation of referral orders as part of the Youth Justice and Criminal Evidence Act 1999.

The referral order is available in the youth court and may be made for a minimum of three and a maximum of 12 months depending on the seriousness of the crime (as determined by the court). The order is mandatory for 10–17-year-olds pleading guilty to an imprisonable offence and convicted for the first time by the courts, unless the crime is serious enough to warrant custody or the court orders an absolute discharge. The disposal involves referring the young offender to a youth offender panel (YOP). The order constitutes the entire sentence for the offence (though it can be combined with certain ancillary orders, including those for costs) and, as such, substitutes for action plan orders, reparation orders and supervision orders.

The Act extends the statutory responsibility of YOTs to include the recruitment and training of YOP volunteers, administering panel meetings and implementing referral orders. Panels comprise one YOT member and at least two community panel members, one of whom leads the panel. Parents of all offenders aged under 16 are expected to attend all panel meetings. The offender can also nominate an adult to support them, but it is not intended that legal representatives participate. To encourage the restorative nature of the process a variety of other people, particularly victims, may be encouraged voluntarily to attend given panel meetings. The aim of the initial panel meeting is to devise a 'contract' and, where the victim chooses to attend, for them to meet and talk about the offence with the offender. The contract should always include reparation to the victim or wider community and a programme of activity designed primarily to prevent further offending.

Youth justice in England and Wales, then, has undergone a series of significant changes both in terms of its organisation, the instruments it uses and, to a degree, the philosophy that underpins it.

The reformed system in practice

The prevailing view within Whitehall is that the restructured youth justice system in England and Wales is a success (see Carter 2003; Home Office 2002: para. 1.11; HM Government 2006: para. 1.11). The Audit Commission (2004) found that: the new arrangements were a significant improvement and represented a good model for delivering public services; juvenile offenders were now more likely to receive an intervention, were dealt with more quickly and were more likely to make amends for their wrong-doing; magistrates were generally very satisfied with the service received from YOTs; and reconviction rates for young offenders had fallen.

The National Audit Office review (2004) was more reserved. It acknowledged that the YJB had developed the additional range of community penalties within a 'comparatively short time' and introduced 'improvements to the arrangements for assessing offenders' needs at the start of a sentence' (the YJB has developed its own assessment tool, ASSET, for use by YOTs). In addition, a raft of inspectorate reports have noted improvements in standards met and offered evidence of good joint working and improving delivery of community programmes (see, for example, HMI Probation 2004, 2005).

But official bodies have also voiced criticisms. The Audit Commission found that: too many minor offenders are appearing before the courts; the amount of contact time with offenders subject to supervision orders has not increased; public confidence in the youth justice system remains low; and black, minority ethnic and mixed race offenders remain substantially overrepresented among the stubbornly high custodial population. Further, the inspectorates have found serious fault with the performance of individual YOTs and custodial establishments and identified general shortcomings in both the delivery of community-based provision and the operation of the custodial system. For example, the YOTs generally fail to pay sufficient attention to public protection issues (HMI Probation 2005: 3 and 20–1) and young offenders in custody are too often housed in unsuitably large accommodation wings and, probably a related condition, too often feel unsafe (HMI Prisons/YJB 2005: 11–16).

These Whitehall criticisms coincide with those from some independent, penal pressure groups (see, for example, the Carlile Report (2006) on the excessive use of physical restraint and other control measures on children and young people in custody). Some academic commentators have lamented the diminished rights of childen and young persons, the growth of punitive interventions, the penetration of mainstream social policy by the criminal justice system and the unequal treatment of different ethnic groups (see, for example, Smith 2003; Pitts 2001; Bateman and Pitts 2005). Some other commentators, moreover, have criticised the YJB for not having developed accredited programmes for offenders along the line pursued by the National Probation Service.

These criticisms demand closer analysis of youth justice trends and programmes. Volume crime has fallen by more than two-fifths since the mid 1990s (Maguire 2007) and the survey evidence indicates that youth crime rates have not increased (see Newburn 2007). However, since most crime, whether committed by youth or adults, goes undetected, there is no straightforward relationship between rates of offending and criminalisation. What then has been the impact of the 1998 reforms on the criminalisation of children and young people?

The years immediately preceding and following the 1998 reforms exhibit continuity and change. If pre-court cautions and court sentences are aggregated there has been little change in the overall number of children and young people drawn into the system – only 6 per cent more in 2004 compared to 1994. However, whereas two-thirds of cases were dealt with pre-court in 1994, only around half are today. Children and young people who offend and are apprehended are now very much more likely to be prosecuted than was formerly the case. This outcome is to a large extent the logical outcome of the 1998 reforms and to that extent was intended. But it has led to the complaint that too many minor cases are now being unnecessarily brought before the youth court (Audit Commission 2004: 3). Since repeat cautions beyond two were relatively uncommon prior to 1998 (see Bottoms and Dignan 2004: 80) what other factors may have driven the process? We can identify four contributory factors.

First, police forces have been set targets for the number of offences brought to justice (OBTJs). As informal warnings do not count as OBTJs more children and young people are being acted against for offences that it is relatively easy for the police to process: that is, young people, whose offending typically takes place in groups in public places, represent a relatively soft police touch. Secondly, the development of inter-agency information exchange and application of the police intelligence model has meant that the police have become more effective at targeting persistent young offenders, a hypothesis supported by the fact that an increased proportion of sentenced young offenders have prior convictions, often many (see Home Office 2005a: chapter 6). Thirdly, the Government, as we have seen, has explicitly targeted the behaviour of young people through the ASB and 'Respect' campaigns (Morgan 2006a), both of which are likely to draw young people into the justice system. Fourthly, it is widely argued that the effectiveness of informal controls (in many neighbourhoods, families, schools, care homes, etc.) has declined such that the police are now more frequently called on to intervene in settings that used typically to consume their own smoke (that is, deal informally with such troubles *in situ*).

What is happening to the increased number of children brought before the courts? Table 10.1 demonstrates that the changes have been considerable. Most notable has been the introduction of the referral order, which now accounts for more than one quarter of all sentences and which has drawn candidates from across the complete range of alternatives, from discharges and fines (the proportionate uses of which have declined substantially), community penalties (which have likewise declined) and custody (the number of which sentences has modestly declined both absolutely and proportionately from the highpoint period of 1999–2002). When offences are imprisonable and the offender is appearing before the youth court for the first time, sentencers have no option but to impose a referral order unless they consider the case warrants a custodial sentence. It is clear that in some instances, where they would formerly have resorted to custody, sentencers are imposing referral orders, which can be made onerous and where failure to comply results in the offender being returned to court for resentencing.

The trend is clear. Young offenders are today more likely to be criminalised and subject to a greater level of intervention. If dealt with pre-court their warning is more likely to be accompanied by an intervention. They are more likely to be prosecuted. If convicted they are less likely to receive a discharge or fine. If subject to a community sentence it is more likely to be onerous. And last but not least, despite the relative *proportionate* decline in custodial sentences since 2002, the *number* of children and young people sentenced to custody is still 35 per higher than a few years before the 1998 Act (see Table 10.1).

Has the trend towards greater intervention served to reduce reoffending rates? In 1999 the YJB was set a target by the Home Office of reducing

Table 10.1 Proportionate use of different sentences (%), 1994–2004

	1994	1999	2004
Discharge	34	30	13
Fine	21	23	16
Referral order	0	0	27
Community penalty (excl. referral orders)	34	34	32
Custody	8	8	7
Other	2	4	5
Total sentenced	61,991	90,160	96,188

Table 10.2 Juvenile reconviction rates (2000 baseline)

Year	Actual reconviction rate	Predicted reconviction rate	Difference between predicted and actual reconviction rate
2003	36.9	37.8	–2.4%
2002	36.5	37.9	–3.6%
2001	35.3	37.0	–4.5%
2000	36.8	–	–

Source: Home Office (2005b: Table 2.1).

reoffending by young offenders by 5 per cent by 2004. The initial findings were very positive and a comparison of reconviction rates in 1997 and 2000 showed significant reductions across practically all offence categories. By 2001 the Home Office estimated that there had been a reduction in overall reoffending of 22.5 per cent. The Prime Minister congratulated the YJB on the startling success of the new youth justice reforms (see YJB 2003: 2–3). However, on closer inspection the estimates were found to have excluded a large number of cases, predominantly more serious cases, and the estimated reduction in reoffending was revised down to 7 per cent. More recent figures, using 2000 as the baseline, are more modest still (see Table 10.2).

Consideration of the actual against the expected reconviction rates for different disposals (Table 10.3) shows that the most significant reductions have been achieved with the lower-tier penalties. These gains, however, have been substantially mitigated by the less than impressive results from higher-tier penalties where reconviction rates have generally deteriorated from an already poor baseline. All of this suggests that were the current trend reversed – that is, a higher proportion of cases dealt with pre-court or by means of discharges, fines, referral and reparation orders post-court – the system would be as effective, and possibly more so, in achieving its stated aim.

Table 10.3 Reconviction rates by disposal (2000 baseline)

	% difference 2003	% difference 2002	% difference 2001
Pre-court disposal	+0.2	**–5.3**	**–6.5**
First-tier penalty			
Discharge	**–6.1**	**–7.2**	**–3.2**
Fine	**–7.8**	**–6.4**	**–7.1**
Referral order	**–6.5**	–3.8	–0.4
Reparation order	–1.2	–2.0	**–5.2**
Community penalty			
Attendance centre order	+0.6	–4.6	**–5.4**
Supervision order	–0.1	–0.8	**–1.3**
Action plan order	**+5.1**	+2.5	+0.6
CRO	+0.9	**+11.2**	**+8.2**
CPO	–1.8	–4.3	–4.8
Curfew order	**+6.2**	**+11.9**	**+7.0**
Custody	+4.4	+1.1	+3.2
All offenders	**–2.4**	**–3.6**	**–4.5**

Figures in bold denote a significant difference between the actual and the expected rate at the 0.05 level.
Source: Home Office (2005b: table x.x).

Prevention and community programmes

The YJB's stated aim is to build confidence in early prevention schemes designed to reduce the risk of offending and, when offending occurs, increase the use of effective pre-court and community-based measures. The evidence indicates overwhelmingly that these approaches better reduce offending than resort to custody, provided they are combined with improved engagement by the young people concerned with mainstream services. That is, preventing youth crime is not a project for the criminal justice system alone: it relies as much, if not more so, on such outcomes as educational engagement and attainment. If the proportion of young people leaving school ill-equipped to find a satisfying place in the labour market continues to be as high as is currently the case, the prospects for the incidence of youth crime are poor. Britain currently compares very unfavourably in all the international surveys of economic inequality, social exclusion and high-risk youth behaviour (teenage pregnancy, smoking, use of alcohol and illegal drugs, etc. – see Social Exclusion Unit 2001; WHO 2004) and, despite substantial expenditure and several initiatives designed to combat absenteeism and exclusions from school, the picture in recent years has not improved (see New Philanthropy Capital 2005; Commission on Families and the Wellbeing of Children 2005). This is the backcloth to the early prevention schemes which the YJB is promoting by providing YOTs with ring-fenced funding to build their development.

YIPs and YISPs

All YOTs now have one or more YIPs or YISPs. YIPs were the early subject of a YJB commissioned evaluation (Morgan Harris Burrows 2003) which identified some encouraging outcomes as well as some concerns. First, 73 per cent of the targeted high-risk children (50 per scheme) were being engaged, though few (8 per cent) at the aimed-for level of 10 hours per week. Moreover the schemes, all of them in deprived neighbourhoods, were engaging over 18,000 children not identified as high risk in various activities (sport, arts projects, education-related, etc.) of which sport was the most common. There was a significant reduction in the number of arrests and the seriousness of the offences for which the young people were arrested for those of the targeted children engaged from the beginning. The school-related data the evaluators were able to collect were seriously incomplete – itself an important finding. But the limited evidence suggested that though there was a modest reduction in the number of permanent school exclusions, school attendance among the participating target group marginally deteriorated. This outcome points to a concern about YOTs. Namely, that their existence may serve to displace the statutory attentions of the mainstream agencies from which YOT staff were originally recruited.

Safer School Partnerships

There are approaching 500 SSPs throughout England and Wales (only a handful of them funded by the YJB), though there is wide variation in the degree of police and youth service personnel investment in individual schools. An initial evaluation of a small controlled sample of SSPs, found evidence of reduced exclusions, truancy and authorised absenteeism and improved exam pass rates – though the available data did not permit estimation of offending behaviour both within and in the environs of the schools (Bowles *et al.* 2005). The sample was small and the results were not statistically significant. However, more recent work on a larger sample of schools has found the same positive results, all of them statistically significant (Bowles *et al.* 2006). Given that *not* attending school is a major criminogenic risk factor, these results are important.

Mentoring

Of the community-based initiatives adopted by New Labour, mentoring quickly became one of the most popular. The range of locations in which mentoring was adopted was extremely broad – one of the most significant being the New Deal initiative focused on unemployed young people aged 18 and over. The YJB issued guidelines for mentoring with young offenders and subsequently used its financial muscle to stimulate considerable activity. Between 2001 and 2004 the YJB was supporting at least 80 separate mentoring schemes. Recently published evidence from a substantial YJB-commissioned evaluation (St James Roberts *et al.* 2006) found relatively little evidence of improvements in behaviour, literacy or numeracy and, even more disappointingly, found no appreciable impact on reoffending within a year of the end of the programme. However, a separate evaluation which focused on more disaffected young people in non-YJB mentoring programmes, though again finding little impact on offending behaviour, uncovered evidence of a substantial impact on the young people's engagement with education, training and work (Newburn and Shiner 2005). Both studies indicate that mentoring holds promise: effectiveness likely lies in operational differences between schemes masked by aggregating data.

Referral orders and restorative justice

The referral order is arguably the emerging jewel in the crown of the reformed system, though the available research data (Newburn *et al.* 2002; Crawford and Newburn 2003) are mostly derived from the introductory phase rather than contemporary practice. The order now accounts for more than one quarter of all youth court sentences and is more effective in terms of reoffending than the characteristics of the offenders subject to it lead one to expect. Further, though some YOTs fail to convene initial panel meetings (usually because of empanelling difficulties) within the 15 working days which the YJB has laid down as the standard, most have now managed to recruit a healthy list of YOP volunteer members and no longer need to advertise. Further, in most YOTs the composition of the 5,000 plus YOP volunteers is increasingly diverse in terms of sex, age and ethnicity. This achievement bears out the results from a YJB-commissioned 2004 MORI survey of the public which revealed that large numbers of people would be *very* interested in undertaking voluntary work with young offenders, in particular assisting them with basic literacy and numeracy needs (YJB 2004b).

Reparation is the essence of the referral order and the independent evaluation of its introduction reported encouraging results (Newburn *et al.* 2002), an assessment borne out by the Home Office reconviction data (see Table 10.3 above). The evidence suggests that referral order outcomes would be even more favourable were YOTs more successfully to engage victims in the process. In the pilot sites victims personally participated in only 13 per cent of referral order cases by attending one or more YOP sessions. There was considerable variation in the rate from one YOT to another, largely as a result of the skill and effort devoted to cultivating victim participation (Newburn *et al.* 2002: 41–8). The YJB evidence suggests that the direct participation of victims continues to vary greatly from one YOT to another and that the overall rate of involvement remains at a relatively low level.

Intensive supervision and surveillance programmes

The YJB has invested considerable resources in intensive supervision and surveillance programme (ISSP) as the principal alternative to custodial remands and sentences in cases where that outcome is likely. The ISSP can be used as a condition of bail or as an adjunct to a community or custodial sentence for serious offenders or persistent young offenders who at the time of appearing in court have previously been charged, warned or convicted on four or more separate occasions in the preceding 12 months and have previously received at least one community or custodial sentence. An ISSP runs for a maximum of six months with intensive supervision (including electronic tagging or tracking) and engagement (education or vocational training, offending behaviour programmes, recreational activities, etc.) for 25 hours a week for the first three months. The ISSP was launched by the YJB in July 2001 and extended to all areas in October 2003. The programme has independently been evaluated, an early cohort having been followed up for two years (Moore *et al.* 2004; Gray *et al.* 2005).

The research shows that the ISSP is being targeted at relatively serious and persistent offenders (burglary and robbery being the most common index offences, with on average 12 offences in the preceding two years), a high proportion of whom would likely have received a custodial sentence had the ISSP not been an option. It is conceded that there has been some net-widening effect. Though the headline two-year reconviction rate of 91 per cent is very high, the rate for offenders with as many pre-convictions released from custodial sentences is at 95 per cent (Home Office 2005b: table 11.8), even higher still. Arguably more important, however, are the gains masked by the headline reconviction rate. The frequency of reoffending is down by 40 per cent and the seriousness of those further offences down 13 per cent. Further, the research shows that substantial engagement in education and other positive activities is being achieved and offenders' multiple practical problems are being addressed. Yet the evaluation also shows that a comparison group of offenders eligible for the ISSP but not receiving it (refused bail, placed on a community order or sentenced to a DTO) did just as well in terms of reoffending, a finding which has led some critics (Green 2004) to suggest that investment in ISSP is not worthwhile. It is more than likely, however, that the intensity of ISSP surveillance means that the further offences of the young people subject to the programme are more likely to be detected. Furthermore, although the initial availability of the ISSP did not lead to any greater reduction in the use of custody than was true in areas without it, the fact that the ISSP is generally being targeted at offenders at high risk of custody, and given that sentencers reportedly have confidence in the programme, it is also possible that the proportionate use of custody would be greater than it is were it not for the existence of the ISSP.

Diversity issues: sex and ethnicity

There has been a noteworthy increase in the number of girls being drawn into the youth justice system at all levels relative to boys (Heidensohn and Gelsthorpe 2007). This trend should not be overstated. But it does signal either a significant shift in the offending behaviour of girls or a change of attitude towards girls on the part of the police and the courts, or most likely both. At the deepest level of the system, the change also poses a dilemma for the YJB. Though girls remain a small proportion of children and young people in custody (7 per cent) the proportionate increase in their number (272 per cent) in the last decade has greatly outstripped the increase in the number of boys (40 per cent).

As with adults in the criminal justice system generally (see Bowling and

Phillips 2007) some of the minority ethnic groups, particularly the black communities, are significantly over-represented in the youth justice system, a feature commented on critically by the Audit Commission (2004: para. 73) and responded to by the YJB in 2005 by requiring all YOTs to audit their practice and develop action plans to improve equal treatment (YJB 2005a: 8). This initiative followed an in-depth study (Feilzer and Hood 2004). According to the most recent YJB statistics, 12 per cent of all the children and young people drawn into the system and whose ethnicity was recorded were from the minority ethnic groups. Half of these young people, that is 6 per cent, were black (YJB 2005d: 25).

The Feilzer and Hood study was based on a small sample of YOTs and a large number of cases dealt with by them. Regression analysis was employed to explore the degree to which different ethnic groups are more or less likely to be differentially treated at different decision-making points in the system for reasons apparently not legally legitimate (seriousness of offence, prior convictions, no early plea of guilty, etc.). The results from the study were complicated. Mixed race youths were significantly more likely to be prosecuted as opposed to being dealt with pre-court than their case characteristics suggested was justified. Black and mixed race youths were significantly more likely to be remanded in custody and then not convicted. Further, though black and mixed race offenders were no more likely to receive a custodial sentence, they were more likely to receive a longer sentence, either in the community or in custody. Asian youths, however, were more likely to be sentenced to custody than white youths with the same characteristics, a finding which points to the fallacy of assuming that the absence of over-representation of a minority ethnic group within a particular category is the equivalent of showing that there is no differential treatment.

Children and young people in custody

There are three groups of providers of youth custodial services – the Prison Service or commercially managed YOIs, the commercially run STCs and the local authority or commercially run secure homes (LASHs). Table 10.4 shows the number of children and young people in custody since 1991. Though the number has risen since the 1998 reforms, that increase has been modest compared to the very substantial rise prior to 1998 and, further, the custodial population has largely stabilised since 2000–1.

Table 10.4 Children and young persons in penal custody, June 1991–2005

	1991	1997	1999	2005
LASHs	70	95	90	238
STCs	–	–	55	248
Prison service accommodation	1,345	2,479	2,422	2,339
Total	1,415	2,574	2,567	2,825

Source: Youth Justice Board (unpublished).

The YJB currently purchases a total of 3,293 beds in three categories of establishment: 2,784 beds for males in 13 YOIs, all but two of which are managed by the Prison Service, plus four Prison Service units for 17-year-old girls; 274 beds in four STCs, all commercially managed; and 235 beds in 15 secure homes, all but one of which are managed by local authorities. Older adolescents aged 15–17 are mostly held in the YOIs and younger children, under 15, in the LASHs. The STCs mostly accommodate adolescents aged 15–16, though both they and the LASHs house a minority of older adolescents for whom, for one reason or another, the YOIs are considered unsuitable. Over 90 per cent of juveniles in custody are aged 15–17.

All but five of the YOIs are split-site establishments (juveniles in one section and young adults in another, more or less separated and self-sufficient) and typically provide large (60–80 bed) accommodation blocks of a traditional penal design. By contrast the LASHs are typically small establishments of 10–25 beds and are further subdivided into 6–8 bed living units. The STCs are larger but, like the LASHs, are also broken down into 6–8 bed living units.

Though the YJB plans for some flexibility in the number of places it purchases (the existing infrastructure is not geographically well distributed and beds are always out of commission for repair and refurbishment), this is often offset by the fact that young offenders who become 18 during the custodial portion of their DTOs are normally not transferred to adult establishments. At the time of writing (May 2006) the system is close to full. This means that the YJB's aim of holding inmates within 50 miles of home is satisfied in approximately only two-thirds of cases. In these circumstances, and given the characteristics of the children and young people in custody, it is perhaps not surprising that tragedies within the system are a regular occurrence. Fourteen children and young persons have died in custody since 1997, 13 by suicide and one while being restrained, two in STCs and 12 in YOIs (see Coles and Goldson 2005).

The children and young people in custody are overwhelmingly needy and troubled (see Morgan 2006b). Histories of self-harm are relatively common. Almost one-third have identifiable mental health problems and over half have significant or borderline learning difficulties (Harrington and Bailey 2005). It is difficult to say to what extent the latter finding reflects intrinsic learning difficulties or an absence of intellectual stimulation. Two-thirds of DTO detainees have been excluded from education, four in ten have at some stage been in the care of a local authority and 17 per cent have been on a child protection register (Hazell *et al.* 2002; see also HMI Prisons 2005). Literacy and numeracy ages are typically some four to five years below chronological ages. These problems are often compounded by substance abuse with around one-third reporting that they have taken drugs not to get high but just to 'feel normal' or to 'forget everything' or 'blot everything out' (Galahad SMS Ltd 2004) – i.e. as a form of self-medication.

Unsurprisingly, therefore, the YJB estimates that some 200–300 older boys 'require more intensive support than can currently be provided in YOIs' (YJB 2005c: para. 16). The more overcrowded the system the more likely it is that further tragedies will occur. Further, that risk will not be reduced if staff are not trained to deal with young people whose behaviour is sometimes very difficult. The Carlile Report (2006: para. 57) observed that:

In some cases there appeared to be a culture where dissent was not tolerated and that physical restraint was used to secure conformity … Over-reaction, especially if capricious and sudden, can be counter-productive and even dangerous.

There remains, as the YJB has acknowledged, 'a long way to go' (2005: 5).

Conclusion: the future of youth justice

Youth justice has always been characterised by competing aims, objectives and penal philosophies. *Punishment* and *welfare* sit uncomfortably together and New Labour's assertion in *No More Excuses* that there is no conflict between the measures being taken to prevent reoffending and promoting the welfare of individual offenders is questionable. Other tensions can be identified in the current system: between measures socially inclusive and exclusive; between reparation and retribution; between managerialism – the emphasis on speed of process, target setting and centrally fixed budgets – and the communitarian aim of engaging the public; between the Whitehall determination of policy (illustrated, currently, in the decision to establish NOMS) and the alleged 'localism' of delegating decision-making to local authorities, trusts or service managers; between the emphasis on choice and the deregulation of markets and extending the remit of state controls and policing into the home, the neighbourhood and the school. New Labour's youth justice system is, as Muncie (2001) has observed, a *mélange* of policies and practices, though it is also better funded than that which went before and therefore *potentially* better placed to deliver necessary services.

It is precisely because the new system is a *mélange* that it is difficult to predict its future course. Because youth crime and justice is so highly charged politically, it can easily be knocked off course by rare but outrageous events – as was the case with the Bulger murder in 1992. Further, the landscape within which youth justice operates is undergoing seismic shifts. These changes include the following:

- The amalgamation of police forces has been proposed, the first tranche of which was announced in spring 2006. It is unclear, given the twin rationale of creating increased regional capacity to deal with serious crime yet devolve to BCU commanders greater capacity to determine local priorities, how amalgamations, if and when they occur, will impact on police contributions to early prevention schemes and YOT budgets. Greater variation than already exists could destabilise the willingness of other agency partners to contribute to the extent that they currently do.

- The same issues arise from the creation of NOMS. How is the contribution of local Probation Services (in terms of finance, personnel and operational experience) in future to be determined if, as is envisaged, the planned probation trusts fail to secure contracts in the burgeoning mixed market for delivering Probation Services? Is the probation budget centrally to be top-sliced and channelled through the YJB to the YOTs, or are contributions to be negotiated locally? Quite apart from the uncertainties that may result from the latter prospect, how are synergies in joint planning and commissioning to be secured (see Morgan, this volume)?

- Following the publication of *Every Child Matters* (HM Treasury 2003) and the passage of the Children Act 2004 every local authority must establish a children's trust by 2008, bringing together the key child-related services within a *virtual* though not a *legal* entity, of which the YOTs will optionally, depending on local decision, become a part. Such is the uncertainty about the form and operation of children's trusts that the YJB has declined to offer YOT managers blueprint advice as to whether, ideally, they should be *within* or *without*. If they are within they are advised they must retain a strong separate steering group to maintain close relationships with criminal justice partners. If they are without, they must work in close partnership with their children's trust so as to secure good quality access to mainstream child-related services for their clients (YJB 2004).

- Other Children's Act and local authority changes have significant implications for YOTs. How will Asset, the YOTs' assessment tool, fit with the Common Assessment Framework (CAF) being developed for children generally? How compatible will the YJB's targets and performance indicators be with those developed by the Audit Commission's Common Performance Assessment (CPA) for inspecting local authorities' performance? Will the local area agreements (LAAs) being arrived at in local authorities cut across the YJB's regime?

There are many other developments. At the time of writing, for example, an Education Bill (DfES 2005) is being considered by Parliament which will create education trust schools giving parents greater voice regarding aspects of school management. What will be the implication for the inclusion in good-quality educational provision of the disengaged, under-achieving and frankly difficult children and young people who are prominent among YOT caseloads? A Green Paper, *Youth Matters*, sets out proposals for positive provision for young people and suggests they be provided with 'opportunity cards'. However, it is also suggested, negatively, that opportunities be denied offenders. Will these proposals come to fruition and with what impact?

As for the overall shape of youth justice, there seem to us to be some fairly clear priorities for youth justice in the next few years. First, it should be a central priority to reduce the number of young people in custody, a prospect to which the YJB is committed and which appears to have been given some recent, limited encouragement by the Government (HM Government 2006: para. 3.31). Secondly, it is important to reverse the trend whereby the proportion and numbers of young people dealt with informally is decreasing while the numbers prosecuted increases. There are a number of barriers to achieving this. One is the concern that increasing pre-court disposals will lead inevitably to the re-creation of the type of problem the Audit Commission identified in relation to repeat cautioning in the mid-1990s. Another is the difficulty that, as things stand, informal action pre-court does not count toward OBTJ targets. Thus a first and simple reform would be to amend the counting rules so that the police are administratively rewarded for engaging in restorative justice and other forms of conflict-resolution and preventative work in homes, schools and residential institutions and neighbourhoods.

The available evidence suggests that increasing the proportion of cases dealt with pre-court would in itself be an effective measure, but might well also ensure that an increased proportion of cases brought before the courts were dealt with in a more risk-proportionate manner by way of discharges, fines, referral and reparation orders. This, in turn, might allow greater confidence to be shown in taking a similarly risk-proportionate approach by supervising YOTs in relation to medium- and high-risk cases, thereby enabling custodial sentences to be used more sparingly. Finally, a reduced juvenile prison population would also open up the possibility that the YJB could restructure the custodial estate in order to meet its aim of making it more dedicated and child-centred. On many occasions in the recent past such proposals would have felt very much out of line with government policy and rhetoric. However, the recently unveiled Home Office five-year strategy *Protecting the Public and Reducing Re-offending* (Home Office 2006b) provides at least some encouragement for these aspirations.

Further reading

Roger Smith's (2003) *Youth Justice: Ideas, Policy, Practice* provides a balanced account of the developments leading to the youth justice reforms of 1998 and their subsequent shape. The Audit Commission's 1996 Report *Misspent Youth: Young People and Crime* and the New Labour government's response *No More Excuses* (Home Office 1997a) are critical to understanding the rhetoric and evidence on which the new system is based. Two recent books by Barry Goldson and John Muncie, *Youth Justice* and *Comparative Youth Justice* (both 2006), provide up-to-date, critical and comparative material on both policy and practice. For information about how the system is working there is no real substitute to using the Youth Justice Board's website (http://www.youth-justice-board.gov.uk) which provides access to the Board's annual reports and statistics and a growing corpus of commissioned evaluation reports on particular youth justice sentences and programmes. The Audit Commission's recent (2004) evaluation, *Youth Justice 2004: A Review of the Reformed Youth Justice System*, provides a more distanced overview.

References

Audit Commission (1996) *Misspent Youth: Young People and Crime.* London: Audit Commission.

Audit Commission (2004) *Youth Justice 2004: A Review of the Reformed Youth Justice System.* London: Audit Commission.

Ball, C., McCormac, K. and Stone, N. (2001) *Young Offenders: Law, Policy and Practice,* 2nd edn. London: Sweet & Maxwell.

Bateman, T. and Pitts, J. (2005) *The RHP Companion to Youth Justice.* Lyme Regis: Russell House.

Bottoms, A. E. (1995) 'The philosophy and politics of punishment and sentencing', in C.M.V. Clarkson and R. Morgan (eds), *The Politics of Sentencing Reform.* Oxford: Oxford University Press.

Bottoms, A.E. and Dignan, J. (2004) 'Youth justice in Great Britain', in M. Tonry and A.N. Doob (eds), *Youth Crime and Youth Justice: Comparative and Cross-National Perspectives*. Chicago: University of Chicago Press.

Bowles, R., Reyes, M.G. and Pradiptyo, R. (2005) *Monitoring and Evaluating the Safer School Partnerships (SSP) Programme*. London: YJB.

Bowles, R., Reyes, M.G. and Pradiptyo, R. (2006) *Estimating the Impact of the Safer School Partnerships Programme*. York: University of York, Centre for Criminal Justice Economics and Psychology.

Campbell, B. (1993) *Goliath: Britain's Dangerous Places*. London: Methuen.

Carlile, Lord (2006) *An Independent Inquiry into the Use of Physical Restraint, Solitary Confinement and Forcible Strip Searching of Children in Prisons, Secure Training Centres and Local Authority Secure Children's Homes*. London: Howard League for Penal Reform.

Carter, P. (2003) *Managing Offenders, Reducing Crime: A New Approach*. London: Home Office.

Coles, D. and Goldson, D. (2005) *In the Care of the State? Child Deaths in Penal Custody*. London: Inquest.

Commission on Families and the Wellbeing of Children (2005) *Families and the State: Two-way Support and Responsibilities – An Inquiry into the Relationship between the State and the Family in the Upbringing of Children*. Bristol: Policy Press.

Commissioner for Human Rights (2005) *Report by Mr Alvaro Gil-Robles, Commissioner for Human Rights, on his Visit to the United Kingdom, 4–12 November 2004*. Strasbourg: Council of Europe.

Crawford, A. and Newburn, T. (2003) *Youth Offending and Restorative Justice: Implementing Reform in Youth Justice*. Cullompton: Willan.

Department for Education and Skills (2005) *Youth Matters*. London: DfES.

Downes, D. and Morgan, R. (2007) 'No turning back: the politics of law and order into the millenium', in M. Maguire, R. Morgan and R. Reiner (eds), *The Oxford Handbook of Criminology*, 4th edn. Oxford: Oxford University Press.

Family Policy Studies Centre (1998) *The Crime and Disorder Bill and the Family*. London: Family Policy Studies Centre.

Farrington, D.P. (1992) 'Trends in English juvenile delinquency and their explanation', *International Journal of Comparative and Applied Criminal Justice*, 16 (2): 151–63.

Farrington, D.P. (1996) *Understanding and Preventing Youth Crime*. York: Joseph Rowntree Foundation.

Feilzer, M. and Hood, R. (2004) *Differences or Discrimination: Minority Ethnic Young People in the Youth Justice System*. London: YJB.

Galahad SMS Ltd (2004) *Substance Misuse and the Juvenile Secure Estate*. London: YJB.

Goldson, B. (ed.) (2000) *The New Youth Justice*. Lyme Regis: Russell House.

Goldson, B. and Muncie, J. (2006) *Youth, Crime and Justice*. London: Sage.

Gray, E., Taylor, E., Roberts, C., Merrington, S., Fernandez, R., and Moore, R. (2005) *ISSP: The Final Report*. London: YJB.

Green, D. (2004) *The Intensive Supervision and Surveillance Programme*. London: Civitas. Available at: http://www.civitas.org.uk/pdf/issp.pdf

Hagell, A. and Newburn, T. (1994) *Persistent Young Offenders*. London: Policy Studies Institute.

Harrington, R. and Bailey, S. (2005) *Mental Health Needs and Effectiveness of Provision for Young Offenders in Custody and in the Community*. London: YJB.

Hazell, N., Hagell, A., Liddle, M., Archer, D., Grimshaw, R. and King, J. (2002) *Detention and Training: Assessment of the Detention and Training Order and Its Impact on the Secure Estate across England and Wales*. London: YJB.

Heidensohn, F. and Gelsthorpe L. (2007) 'Gender and crime', in M. Maguire, R. Morgan and R. Reiner (eds), *The Oxford Handbook of Criminology*, 4th edn. Oxford: Oxford University Press.

HM Government (2004) *Cutting Crime, Delivering Justice: A Strategic Plan for Criminal Justice 2004–08*, Criminal Justice System. London: TSO.

HM Government (2006) *A Five Year Strategy for Protecting the Public and Reducing Re-offending*. London: TSO.

HM Inspectorate of Prisons (2002) *Annual Report 2001–2*. London: HMIP.

HM Inspectorate of Prisons (2004) *Annual Report 2002–3*. London: HMIP.

HM Inspectorate of Prisons (2005) *Annual Report 2003–4*. London: HMIP.

HM Inspectorate of Prisons/YJB (2005) *Juveniles in Custody 2003–4: An Analysis of Children's Experiences of Prisons*. London: HMIP/YJB.

HM Inspectorate of Probation (2004) *Annual Report: Youth Offending Teams*. London: HMI Probation.

HM Inspectorate of Probation (2005) *Joint Inspection of Youth Offending Teams: Annual Report 2004/2005*. London: HMIP.

HM Treasury (2003) *Every Child Matters*, Cm 5860. London: TSO.

Home Affairs Committee (2005) *Anti-Social Behaviour*, Fifth Report. London: Stationery Office.

Home Office (1988) *Punishment, Custody and the Community*, Cm 424. London: HMSO.

Home Office (1997a) *No More Excuses – A New Approach to Tackling Youth Crime in England and Wales*, Cm 3809. London: Home Office.

Home Office (1997b) *Tackling Youth Crime*. London: Home Office.

Home Office (1998) *Summary of the Response to the Comprehensive Spending Review of Secure Accommodation for Remanded and Sentenced Juveniles*. London: Home Office.

Home Office (2002) *Justice for All*, Cm 5563. London: TSO.

Home Office (2005a) *Offender Management Caseload Statistics 2004*, Statistical Bulletin 17/05. London: Home Office.

Home Office (2005b) *Juvenile Reconviction: Results from the 2003 Cohort*, Home Office Online Report 08/05 London: Home Office.

Home Office (2006a) *Respect Action Plan*. London: Home Office/COI.

Home Office (2006b) *Protecting the Public and Reducing Reoffending*. London: TSO.

Labour Party (1996) *Tackling Youth Crime: Reforming Youth Justice*. London: Labour Party.

Labour Party (1997) *New Labour – Because Britain Deserves Better*. London: Labour Party.

McAra, L. (2002) 'The Scottish juvenile justice system: policy and practice', in J. Winterdyk (ed.), *Juvenile Justice Systems: International Perspectives*. Toronto: Canadian Scholars Press.

McAra, L. and McVie, S. (2006) 'The usual suspects: street life, young people and the police', *Criminal Justice*, 5 (1): 5–36

McGallagly, J., Power, K., Littlewood, P. and Meikle, J. (1998), *Evaluation of the Hamilton Child Safety Initiative*, Crime and Criminal Justice Research Findings No. 24. Edinburgh: Scottish Office.

Maguire, M. (2007) 'Crime, data and criminal statistics', in M. Maguire, R. Morgan and R. Reiner (eds), *The Oxford Handbook of Criminology*, 4th edn. Oxford: Oxford University Press.

Millie, A., Jacobson, J., Mcdonald, E. and Hough, M. (2005) *Anti-Social Behaviour Strategies: Finding a Balance*. Bristol: Policy Press and Joseph Rowntree Foundation.

Moore, R., Gray, E., Roberts, C., Merrington, S., Waters, I., Fernandez, R., Hayward, G. and Rogers, R. (2004) *ISSP: The Initial Report*. London: YJB.

Morgan Harris Burrows (2003) *Youth Inclusion*. London: Youth Justice Board.

Morgan, R. (2006a) 'With respect to order, the rules of the game have changed: New Labour's dominance of the 'law and order' agenda', in T. Newburn and P. Rock (eds), *The Politics of Law and Order: Essays in Honour of David Downes*. Oxford: Clarendon Press.

Morgan, R. (2006b) 'Improving provision for children who offend', in *Young People and Crime: Improving Provision for Young People Who Offend – The Donald Winnicott Memorial Lecture*. London: Karnac.

Morgan, R. and Liebling, A. (2007) 'Imprisonment: an expanding scene', in M. Maguire, R. Morgan and R. Reiner (eds), *The Oxford Handbook of Criminology*, 4th edn. Oxford: Oxford University Press.

Morgan, R. and Newburn, T. (2007) 'Youth justice', in M. Maguire, R. Morgan and R. Reiner (eds), *The Oxford Handbook of Criminology*, 4th edn. Oxford: Oxford University Press.

Muncie, J. (2001) 'A new deal for youth? Early intervention and correctionalism', in G. Hughes, J. Muncie and E. McLaughlin (eds), *Crime Prevention and Community Safety: New Directions*. London: Sage.

Muncie, J. and Goldson, B. (2006) *Comparative Youth Justice*. London: Sage.

National Audit Office (2004) *Youth Offending: The Delivery of Community and Custodial Sentences*, HC 190. London: NAO.

New Philanthropy Capital (2005) *School's Out? Truancy and Exclusion – A Guide for Donors and Funders*. London: New Philanthropy Capital.

Newburn, T. (1998) 'Young offenders, drugs and prevention', *Drugs, Education, Prevention and Policy*, 5 (3): 233–43.

Newburn, T. (2003) *Crime and Criminal Justice Policy*, 2nd edn. Harlow: Longman.

Newburn, T. (2007) 'Youth crime and youth culture', in M. Maguire, R. Morgan and R. Reiner (eds), *The Oxford Handbook of Criminology*, 4th edn. Oxford: Oxford University Press.

Newburn, T. and Shiner, M. (2005) *Young People, Mentoring and Social Exclusion*. Cullompton: Willan.

Newburn, T., Crawford, A., Earle, R., Goldie, S., Hale, C., Masters, G., Netten, A., Saunders, R., Hallam, A., Sharpe, K. and Uglow, S. (2002) *The Introduction of Referral Orders into the Youth Justice System: Final Report*, Home Office Research Study No. 242. London: Home Office.

Nixon, J., Hunter, H. and Shayer, S. (1999) *The Use of Legal Remedies by Social Landlords to Deal with Neighbourhood Nuisance: Survey Report*, Centre for Regional Economic and Social Research Paper No. H8. Sheffield: Sheffield Hallam University.

Phillips, C. and Bowling, B. (2007) 'Ethnicities, racism, crime and criminal justice', in M. Maguire, R. Morgan and R. Reiner (eds), *The Oxford Handbook of Criminology*, 4th edn. Oxford: Oxford University Press.

Pitts, J. (2001) 'The new correctionalism: young people, youth justice and New Labour', in R. Matthews and J. Pitts (eds), *Crime, Disorder and Community Safety*. London: Routledge.

Pratt, J. (1989) 'Corporatism: the third model of juvenile justice', *British Journal of Criminology*, 29 (3): 236–54.

Rutherford, A. (1986a) *Growing Out of Crime: Society and Young People in Trouble*. Harmondsworth: Penguin.

St James Roberts, I., Greenlaw, G., Simon, A. and Hury, J. (2006) *National Evaluation of Youth Justice Board Mentoring Schemes, 2001–2004*. London: YJB.

Simester, A. P. and von Hirsch, A. (2006) 'Regulating offensive conduct through two-step prohibitions', in A. von Hirsch and A.P. Simester (eds), *Incivilities: Regulating Offensive Behaviour*. Oxford: Hart Publishing.

Smith, R. (2003) *Youth Justice: Ideas, Policy, Practice.* Cullompton: Willan.

Social Exclusion Unit (2001) *Preventing Social Exclusion.* London: SEU.

Thorpe, D., Smith, D., Green, C. and Paley, J. (1980) *Out of Care: The Community Support of Juvenile Offenders.* London: George Allen & Unwin.

Tonry, M. and Doob, A. N. (eds) (2004) *Youth Crime and Youth Justice, Comparative and Cross-National Perspectives – Crime and Justice: A Review of Research*, Vol. 31. Chicago: University of Chicago Press.

Utting, D., Bright, J. and Henricson, C. (1993) *Crime and the Family.* London: Family Policy Studies Centre.

Wilson, J.Q. and Kelling, G. (1982) 'Broken windows', *Atlantic Monthly*, March: 29–38.

World Health Organisation (2004) *Young People's Health in Context: Health Behaviour in School-aged Children (HBSC) Study: International Report from the 2001/2002 Survey.* Copenhagen: WHO Europe.

Young, A. (1996) *Imagining Crime: Textual Outlaws and Criminal Conversations.* London: Sage.

Young, R. and Goold, B. (1999) 'Restorative police cautioning in Aylesbury – from degrading to reintegrative shaming ceremonies?', *Criminal Law Review*, pp. 126–38.

Youth Justice Board (2003) *Gaining Ground in the Community: Annual Review 2002/03.* London: Youth Justice Board.

Youth Justice Board (2004a) *Sustaining the Success: Extending the Guidance Establishing Youth Offending Teams.* London: YJB.

Youth Justice Board (2004b) 'YJB Volunteering Strategy – Potential Public Interest in Working with Young People Who Offend'. London: YJB, unpublished.

Youth Justice Board (2005a) *Annual Report and Accounts 2004/05.* London: Youth Justice Board.

Youth Justice Board (2005b) *Corporate and Business Plan 2005/06 to 2007/08.* London: Youth Justice Board.

Youth Justice Board (2005c) *Strategy for the Secure Estate for Children and Young People.* London: Youth Justice Board.

Youth Justice Board (2005d) *Youth Justice Annual Statistics 2004/05.* London: Youth Justice Board.

Youth Justice Board/ACPO/Home Office (2005) *Anti-Social Behaviour: A Guide to the Role of Youth Offending Teams in Dealing with Anti-Social Behaviour.* London: YJB.

Chapter 11

Difference and diversity in probation

Loraine Gelsthorpe and Gill McIvor

Introduction

In this chapter we focus on the issue of offenders' different needs and whether or not it is appropriate to distinguish between them. The issues are central to conceptions of fairness, justice and discrimination. Following some preliminary discussion of what might be meant by diversity and what is known about different groups of offenders' needs and treatment, we then look at ways in which the Probation Service has sought to recognise diversity in both past and current policies and practices – particularly with regard to the notion of 'criminogenic needs'.

Our critical theme is what might be termed 'legitimate differentiation', thus broad consideration is given to the degree to which the Service should make differentiated provision in response to race/ethnicity, gender, sexual orientation, religion, disabilities and mental health factors. In other words, how should probation best aim to do justice to difference?

Concepts of difference and diversity

The organisation of material and themes for this chapter has presented a significant challenge given the interrelatedness of many of the issues; there are also limitations which reflect a paucity of data on social or cultural differences beyond race and gender. Human diversity, according to Sen (1992), arises from a range of factors: personal characteristics such as physical or mental health or abilities, age and gender; external factors such as family circumstances (wealth, culture, religion) and physical environment; and a person's capacity to achieve various 'functionings', which form a valued part of life and are critical to well-being, through the exercise of freedoms and choices. The Government views things rather more prosaically. In a report prepared by the Comptroller and Auditor General (NAO 2004) six key strands of diversity in the population are identified, namely race, disability, gender, sexual orientation, age and religion/belief. The Government also recognises and aims to attend to other ways in which society is diverse, such as people with a primary language other than English and those with low incomes (NAO 2004: para. 1.6). Further difficulties arise from the fact that while people rarely fall neatly into one single category, they are categorised as such. While dyslexia is disabling in the context of education and employment, it would not disadvantage an offender sentenced to a community order with unpaid work, for example. We are all rarely just men or women, black or Asian or white, but rather situate ourselves on a number of social and cultural planes. How well do criminal justice data systems capture these complexities? Moreover, there is little recognition of new ethnicities or cultural pluralism within criminal justice monitoring (see, for example, Home Office 2005b; Modood *et al.* 1994). Even within the two main areas in probation policy and practice where there has been a focus on difference – race and gender – it is difficult to find data which cut across the categories so as to be able to identify how one difference might mediate the other (Gelsthorpe 2006).

Turning to age differences, the common practice is now for the Probation Service to deal with offenders *from* the age of 18, and for Youth Offender Teams to deal with those *under* the age of 18. Indeed, 'youth' and 'young offenders' are dominant themes within current discourses on crime and criminal justice. But at the other end of the scale, attention to elderly offenders is sparse. Much of the available material is based on findings from the US and there are obvious questions as to the applicability of that material given the different context (Bramhall 2006). The lack of attention to older offenders and community penalties which fall under the auspices of probation is perhaps surprising – especially given the increasing recognition that both the general population (Midwinter 2005) and the offender population (Codd 1994; Wahidin 2004) are ageing.

Bramhall (2006) suggests that older offenders might be perceived as 'bad risks' for community penalties. Relationship breakdowns, redundancies, ill-health and unemployment, for example, may all be relevant here and rather challenge the popular idea that 'middle life' automatically means settled ties and commitments. However, it may be that precisely because we are not accustomed to thinking of this age group as offenders that sentencers see them as bad risks; after all, any assessment of dynamic and static 'risk' factors may be clouded by subjective judgments of offenders. Moreover, we can easily imagine how older offenders might be seen as more culpable or blameworthy due to their life experiences. But the older the offender, the more likely it is that they will be seen as 'infirm' and 'incapable' and perhaps 'unsuitable' for both cognitive behavioural interventions (on grounds that they are less malleable and adaptable) and unpaid work (on grounds that it will be too strenuous).[1] The traditional view has been that there are good reasons for distinguishing provision for offenders by age group, with the young being perceived as 'less responsible' and 'more reformable' (see Chapter 10, this volume), but even this distinction breaks down if we contrast the persistent 15-year-old violent offender and the first-time shoplifter in his or her mid-thirties. The issues regarding age are thus complex and at present there is little research information on offenders' 'age-related' needs or treatment in probation practice. We do know from caseload statistics that the age profile of those under different forms of supervision reveals that a quarter of those commencing community penalties tend to be over 35, a good third of both men and women starting CROs (now equating to supervision plus other requirements) were 21–29 and about a third 30–39 for instance, whereas the age profile of those commencing CPOs (now equating to unpaid work) has been more widely distributed (Home Office 2004b). But we do not know how far, if at all, age has shaped perceptions of offenders and subsequent provision. We know nothing about the way in which age itself might impact on desistance following specific community penalties (cf. May 1999) or on ways in which the age of offenders might have affected decision-making in relation to breach for example. Thus it seems that we do not really know if any of the differences in treatment in sentencing and in probation practice are based on popular myths, stereotypes and prejudice regarding age. At its most basic, information on age raises questions about the appropriateness of shared or mixed interventions, although there are limitations as to how different such interventions *can* be in terms of economy and feasibility, as well as real challenges with regard to how far they *should* be in terms of justice and equitable treatment. We have already drawn attention to the fact that the research lens often tends to be a single lens and not one which captures the way in which one difference (age) might mediate another (gender or ethnicity for example). This whole area in probation is ripe for further research.

Another dimension of diversity concerns religion and belief, factors which might serve to differentiate needs (on grounds of cultural or religious practices – work on the Sabbath or other 'holy days' and mixed-sex group work are two areas which immediately spring to mind where such issues might be relevant in probation practice), although the issue of what should be included as essential elements in any definition of religion is obviously a difficult one (Hepple and Choudhury 2001). What do we know about practice so far?

A Home Office-sponsored survey of some 1,830 religious organisations in England and Wales covering 20 distinct faith groups and designed to find out about discrimination produced only a 34 per cent response rate (Weller *et al.* 2001). However, some of the findings are relevant to an understanding of perceptions of unfair treatment. Muslim organisations consistently reported a higher level of unfair treatment than other organisations – in frequency as well as in terms of numbers – in every aspect of education, employment, housing, law and order, and in all local government services covered by the questionnaire (Weller *et al.* 2001). Interestingly, in most religious traditions the organisations which were able to answer questions about experiences of the Probation Service were less likely to indicate unfair treatment than was the case for other agencies in the criminal justice system. However, this was not so for Muslim organisations, with a higher proportion indicating unfair treatment from the Probation Service (around two in every three) than from lawyers and the courts (around one in three) (Weller *et al.* 2001). The authors' direct observations and discussions with probation staff suggest that where distinctive needs based on religion and belief are discerned they are dealt with on an individual basis, but perceptions of discrimination here point to the need for a more systematic review of how religion and belief can be accommodated. Notwithstanding the difficulties in defining religion and belief, the right to religious freedom is a fundamental human right, and manifestation of this is subject only to limitations concerning health and safety or 'for the protection of public order, health or morals, or for the protection of the rights and freedoms of others' (Article 9, Human Rights Act 1998, cited in Smiljanic 2002).

We perhaps know even less about sexual orientation and how this is or might be accommodated within probation. Certainly it has been an issue within prisons in relation to transgendered prisoners (HM Prison Service Directorate of Healthcare 1999) and we might expect the same to apply in group-work programmes and in unpaid working parties, for example.

Another area which deserves particular attention concerns mental health. This is obviously a difficult area, not least because definitions of mental health and ill-health elude precision; the high number and range of mental health problems experienced by those in prison (Bridgewood and Malbon 1995; Peay 2002; Fawcett Society 2004) is telling of the extent of definitional and practical difficulties in dealing with such offenders. Indeed, a good number of offenders experience significant problems in this area, but not in a way that means that they will be dealt with within the remit of Mental Health Act 1983. However, while there have been some attempts to measure the prevalence of mental ill-health among offenders in prison (Singleton *et al.* 1998) there is relatively little comparative information on offenders in the community (cf. Clarke *et al.* 2002, on community rehabilitation orders with additional requirements of psychiatric treatment; Nadkarni *et al.* 2000, on community forensic psychiatric involvement with probation hostels; Canton 2005, on risk assessment and compliance). General surveys suggest that one in six adults in Britain has a neurotic disorder (anxiety and depression), while one in seven has considered suicide at some point in their lives according to an ONS survey (ONS 2006b). Further, one in 200 has had a psychotic disorder such as psychosis and schizophrenia (ONS 2006b). Focusing on offenders themselves, Mair and May's (1997) study indicated that almost half (49 per cent) of a sample of nearly 2,000 probationers from across England and Wales said that they had experienced some form of long-standing illness or disability (compared with 48 per cent of prisoners and 26 per cent of the population as a whole). These pointers regarding the extent of the ill-health of probationers include 17 per cent of men and 33 per cent of women who mentioned mental disorders or depression. In a NAPO (2003) survey of psychiatric assessments in about half the probation areas in England and Wales, there was a suggestion that 27 per cent of those on probation caseloads were defined by staff as having a mental disorder. Most critically, although there are no published data on the issue, the OASys Data Evaluation and Analysis Team in NOMS[2] have indicated that within a sample of about 203,000 offenders (NPS 2005–2006 data), 13 per cent were recorded as having *significant psychological problems/ depression* and 22 per cent were recorded as having *some problems*. A further 6 per cent were recorded as having *significant psychiatric problems*, with a further 9 per cent *some problems*.[3] But despite encouragement from the Royal College of Psychiatrists for England and Wales to utilise treatment conditions more in sentencing offenders to community orders (specifically those which come under the auspices of the Probation Service) it is generally perceived that there has been a lack of attention to health needs.

We can contrast the high levels of need with the low number of mental health treatment requirements imposed. Whether it is due to changing perceptions, definitions or community provision in regard to mental health, the number of offenders starting court order supervision where an additional mental treatment requirement has been attached to a CRO declined between 1994 and 2004 (from 323 to 138).

With the Criminal Justice Act 2003 in place, the number of mental health requirements specified in commencements of supervision in CJA 2003 sentences between April and December 2005 was 253 in community orders and 37 in suspended sentences (NOMS 2005). Kemshall *et al.* suggest that the low use of treatment conditions may reflect poor liaison between probation and community psychiatric services. Informal observations from both forensic psychiatrists and probation officers would indicate that this is not so much a matter of poor liaison but one of extremely limited resources. Moreover, preoccupations with risk (see Chapter 13, this volume) and high-profile cases can rather obscure what is known about probationees and their mental health needs. O'Malley (2001), among others, pushes this further by arguing that those who are already socially excluded by virtue of their special needs (including health needs) have experienced the brunt of the risk-based penalty which has emerged over the past 20 years and have been subject to ever more tighter degrees of control. If chaotic lifestyle, volatility and unpredictability are thought to be among the attributes of those who are mentally disordered, then one can immediately see how new penal practice based on risk and enforcement will impact on these offenders. As forensic psychiatrist Adrian Grounds (1995) has indicated, supervision for mentally disordered offenders should not be primarily a surveillance and crime control process, but a framework of support (see Buchanan 2002 on issues concerning the care of the mentally disordered offender in the community).

There are clear concerns about mental health discrimination within the criminal justice system (Social Exclusion Unit 2004), ranging from the need for more mental health awareness training among the police to the paucity of mental health resources for offenders. There is scope for more research on the health needs of offenders in the community (looking at the intersections of gender, age and ethnicity among other things). Moreover, there is particular need to examine how offenders' needs are met in current probation provision and to explore the impact of 'new rehabilitationism' with its emphasis on tough community penalties, 'correction', cognitive deficits and enforcement on current attempts to meet the needs of offenders who experience mental health issues.

To give an outline of such a broad range of diverse groups in this way serves mainly to highlight that, at one level, there are no limits to considerations of difference and diversity in Probation Service practice. The key questions revolve around what level of differentiation is desirable (on the basis of research evidence on needs and effectiveness), what is permissible (in terms of the law), what is practicable (in terms of probation practice) and then what is legitimate (in terms of public perceptions of justice). But while there has been legislative impetus to address diversity from all the attention given to equality and equal rights in the last decade (through the Equal Opportunities Commission, the Commission for Racial Equality, the Disability Rights Commission and the Human Rights Act 1998, for example) and while the established race equality duty and the disability equality duty have already been enshrined in probation policy in the National Probation Service's Diversity Strategy (NPS 2003), there is arguably further work to do to consider properly the extent to which diversity should and can be acknowledged. The two areas where there has been a good deal of research and developmental work in probation then, race and gender, are especially instructive.

General background: race and gender

To give some context for our focus on race and gender differences within the criminal justice system, the 2001 UK Census showed that nationally 2.8 per cent of the general population were black, 4.7 per cent Asian and 1.2 per cent 'other' minority ethnic group, with the majority of the population being white. A more recent estimate of the non-white British population of England and Wales is 7.1 million, an increase of over 500,000 since mid-2001 (ONS 2006a). (By comparison, analysis of the 2001 Census indicated that only 2.1 per cent of the Scottish population belonged to a black and minority ethic (BME) group (Scottish Executive 2004).)

In terms of gender differences, while there are around 20,000 more boys than girls at each age from birth through to late teens, by age 22 the number of young women exceeds the number of young men. This is partly a reflection of higher net in-migration among women than men in recent years, but also death rates from suicide and accidents are higher for young men than young women. The difference between men and women increases through the 20s and 30s age groups, but is smaller again for those in their 40s (this reflects higher net in-migration among older men). From the late 50s, the difference between the sexes increases, as the death rates are greater among men than women. The ratio of men to women varies across different ethnic groups; for example, there are more women than men in the white, black and Indian groups in England and Wales. In contrast, there are more men than women in the Pakistani, Bangladeshi, Chinese and other groups (ONS 2004).

National figures in relation to crime suggest that four in every five offenders are male. Men outnumber women in all major crime categories. Indeed, between 85 and 95 per cent of offenders found guilty of burglary, robbery, drugs offences, criminal damage or violence against the person are male. Where women do offend, they are more likely to commit property-related offences than anything else, although there have been slight increases in lower-level violence (around pubs and clubs) in the last few years and increases in drugs-related offences (as for males) (Home Office 2006b). Broadly, women commit less serious crimes and they are less likely to persist in crime than males (McIvor 2004; Fawcett Society 2004). In 2005, the peak age of offending was 18 for males and 15 for females (Home Office 2006b).

327

Sentencing patterns and evidence of discrimination: ethnicity

Studies of the treatment of minority ethnic offenders within the criminal justice system have mostly focused on the disproportionate number of offenders in prison compared with the numbers in the general population. For instance, while minority ethnic groups represent 7.9 per cent of the overall population (4.6 million according to Labour Force Survey estimates), the minority ethnic population in prisons has been in the region of 24 per cent for men and in the region of 30 per cent for women (Home Office CJS 2005). There is a particularly high number of black and other minority ethnic (BME) group women who are imprisoned for drug importation offences – as 'drug mules' – but even if we take out foreign nationals from the analysis for both women and men, there is still concern about over-representation in prisons. According to self-report studies of criminal behaviour, there is no evidence to suggest BME groups commit more crime (Graham and Bowling 1995; Flood-Page *et al*. 2000). More recently, findings from the Crime and Justice Survey (Home Office 2005b) suggest that black or black British people between 10 and 25 are no more or less likely to commit crime than their white counterparts.

The demographic profile of the BME population may contribute to the high representation in the sense that the population (particularly the black African Caribbean population) is a 'young' population with about half (48 per cent) of BME groups being under 24 years compared with 31 per cent in the white population (ONS Social Trends 2000). Given that a high percentage of crime is committed by young people (of the estimated 1.8 million offenders found guilty or cautioned in 2005, about 11 per cent were aged 17 or under) (Home Office 2006b), we can reason that one might expect to see proportionately more BME young people within the criminal justice system than white. Concomitantly, unemployment rates are higher among BME groups (19 per cent for the black population compared with 6 per cent of the white population) (ONS Social Trends 2000), and other social criteria relating to school performance and school exclusion feature black groups as performing less well and subject to greater rates of exclusion (ONS Social Trends 2000; Barn 2001). While we do not know the precise relationship between these factors and crime, they may well contribute to an understanding of why there might be an over-representation of BME people within prisons. But perhaps more important than these contextual points is the evidence of discrimination ranging from a high rate of stops and arrests to high rates of remands in custody compared with white offenders and longer custodial sentences (Home Office 2006a). Hood's (1992) study of sentencing in the Crown Court showed a greater risk of custody for black than for white men with the same characteristics (in terms of offence seriousness, previous convictions and so on). The study showed also both the cumulative effect of discriminatory decisions and the discriminatory effects of social factors such as unemployment – which can affect decisions to remand people in custody and thereby create a 'custodial momentum'. Further, a recent study by Shute *et al*. (2005) found that one in ten black defendants in the Crown Court and one in five in the magistrates' courts believed that they had experienced unfair treatment by being given a more severe sentence than white counterparts.

Overall, while there are competing interpretations of some of the evidence on the over-representation of BME groups in the criminal justice system (see, for example, Smith 1997), there is now a substantial body of evidence to suggest that social and legal factors can interact in a way that will disadvantage BME offenders (Hood 1992; Bowling and Phillips 2002) and that biased decisions at each stage of the criminal justice process, even if small in themselves, may have a large cumulative impact.

Race issues and probation

Turning to probation, there is a suggestion that race issues were given recognition rather late in the day. According to Denney (1992), it was not until 1977 that the Home Office requested that probation areas with a significant African, Caribbean or Asian population should appoint a specialist probation officer to develop services for BME offenders. In practice, this proved to be a patchy and problematic provision (Mavunga 1993). The need for a more general approach to anti-racist probation practice was recognised only later (Bowling and Phillips 2002). A particular impetus here concerned the Brixton riots of 1981 – urban riots involving young black people – which forced Probation Services to recognise and respond to institutional racism (as defined by Sir William Macpherson in his report reflecting the Stephen Lawrence Inquiry 1999) as the 'collective failure of an organisation to provide an appropriate and professional service to people because of their colour, culture, or ethnic origin' (para. 34) and essentially meaning unreflective attitudes and practice. Most of the 54 local, more or less autonomous, Probation Services introduced some form of anti-racist training at this time.

A Probation Inspectorate thematic report on race equality followed (HMIP 2000) which highlighted concerns about pre-sentence reports and generally found that 'for many staff, the completion of race and ethnic monitoring forms was a mechanistic exercise with little meaning'. Some early research on possible bias within court reports had pointed to discrimination (Whitehouse 1983; Hudson 1989; Shallice and Gordon 1990) while other researchers were more equivocal on the issue (e.g. Mair 1986). Green (1989) argued that probation officers adopted a 'colour blind' approach where the organisational response was to treat all offenders in the same way and thus be neglectful of BME offenders' needs. Denney (1992) found evidence of derogatory comments on BME offenders – who were often perceived to be 'threatening' and 'intransigent' while white offenders were more likely to be perceived as victims of difficult circumstances. The probation discourse in relation to black offenders was thought to be more 'correctional' than 'appreciative'. Gelsthorpe's (1992) analysis of 1,152 court reports in respect of both race and gender issues found that the contrast between reports for males and females was much greater than between different ethnic groups, but she concluded that this did not at all diminish the need to look at organisational ideologies and practices with regard to race. Interestingly, this research was published at the time that national standards were coming into play in forceful manner –

stressing anti-discriminatory practice – although this stance was not sustained throughout the 1990s in a consistent way.

The Probation Inspectorate's thematic review of race equality in 2000 therefore served as a 'wake-up call' to some extent and there has been much activity to enhance recording practices and to develop appropriate responses to BME offenders within probation practice since. First, the National Probation Directorate's report (2001) *A New Choreography* established 'diversity' as a key business objective for the National Probation Service (NPS). The subsequent publication of *The Heart of the Dance* by the NPS (2003) translated the objectives into priority actions to guide probation practice on the ground and to ensure that the culture of probation is one which recognises appropriate service delivery.

Secondly, there have been huge efforts to address the key questions as to what works with BME offenders and whether or not there should be differentiated practice for black and white offenders. While there was relatively little research on BME offenders' needs and on what might 'work' for them prior to the 1990s, the enthusiasm of a few committed probation practitioners during the 1990s led to the production of resource packs and training manuals on such issues (see, for example, Kett *et al*. 1992; De Gale *et al*. 1993; Durrance *et al*. 2001), but these local initiatives did not have national impact. There have been a number of significant developments in efforts to address perceptions of inequality in provision and to establish more clearly what BME offenders' needs and experiences might be since 2000, however. One such development involved a survey of Probation Service provision (group-work programmes and so on) specifically targeting black and Asian offenders (Powis and Walmsley 2002). They identified 13 programmes that had run at some point during the previous ten years, but only five of which were extant. None of the programmes had an adequate evidence base to meet the criteria for accreditation, however. Moreover, while some staff showed a preference for running separate programmes for BME offenders, others advocated mixed group-work provision and there was little empirical evidence (in terms of effectiveness) to substantiate either position. Unfortunately the research did not include a focus on offenders' views, but the researchers could see that there might be plausible reasons to promote separate provision – not least on grounds that this might help BME offenders in terms of confidence levels. This is a point which Durrance and Williams (2003) take up in their critique regarding the narrow focus of Pathfinder programmes (revolving around problem-solving approaches and cognitive deficits for instance), arguing instead that programme material which explicitly addresses the social and cultural context within which offending occurs might better engage black and Asian offenders. (See also Rex *et al*. 2003 in relation the increasing awareness of the need to acknowledge diversity issues in the accreditation process.)

In contrast to Powis and Walmsley's (2002) research, another major study involved interviews with nearly 500 BME offenders under supervision by the Probation Service in order to produce some evidence on their 'criminogenic needs' and to inform decisions about the best form of provision for them (Calverley *et al*. 2004). The offenders in the sample were drawn from 17 probation areas, covering all parts of the country, including urban and rural areas, and areas with varying proportions of BME people within the population. The process of doing the research was itself instructive, not least because of challenges in meeting sample targets in different areas. Areas with large minority ethnic populations were revealed to be much better at identifying and keeping track of black, Asian and mixed heritage offenders.

Turning to the recurring theme of 'what works' and what is needed for BME offenders, the researchers remind us that instruments designed to capture and quantify criminogenic needs are 'social constructs' and the product of 'social processes'. Indeed, it is suggested that actuarial tools, in particular, can further discriminate against already marginalised and stigmatised groups (Silver and Miller 2002). Bhui (1999), for example, has argued that because risk assessments are based on data (such as police data) that reflect discriminatory processes in wider society, they can disadvantage black offenders. But Raynor and Lewis (2006) also remind us that such instruments can be useful in helping to determine individual characteristics and needs if proper consideration is given to possible biases and other limitations.

The key findings from the Calverley et al. study (2004) include the fact that black, Asian and mixed heritage offenders showed less evidence of crime-prone attitudes and beliefs, and lower levels of self-reported problems than white counterparts, although there was a high rate of unemployment among the interviewees (nearly 66 per cent indicated that they were unemployed – with just over 9 per cent recording that they were unavailable for work because of health or other reasons) (Raynor and Lewis 2006). Just over 69 per cent were dependent on state benefits and many interviewees attributed their unemployment to racist discrimination in the job market. The proportion of offenders who had no qualifications was, at 37 per cent, slightly lower than the 41 per cent identified by Mair and May (1997) in their analysis of (predominantly white) probationers, but as Calverley et al. (2004) point out, this disguises the fact that many of them had gained qualifications through adult education, some even in prison. Tellingly, those who reported most experiences of discrimination had significantly higher scores on the CRIME-PICS II P (problem) scale[4] than those who reported the fewest experiences of discrimination.

In sum, the researchers found that the criminogenic needs of minority ethnic offenders on probation were, on average, lower than for others. This suggests that there may have been differential sentencing. At the very least, the findings open up the possibility that some comparable white offenders were receiving less severe sentences than BME offenders, and that some BME offenders were being given sentences above the normal range of sentences for their level of offence seriousness. Both possibilities highlight the need for a continuing critical focus on sentencing processes. At the same time, notwithstanding difficulties in measuring criminogenic needs, the evidence points to the case for BME offenders to be offered opportunities to address problems and disadvantages which they face (Raynor and Lewis 2006).

On the specific issue of whether differentiated provision is necessary, it is certainly the case that some BME offenders feel that their distinctive cultural needs have been neglected. Lewis (2006), elaborating upon some of the findings outlined in Calverley et al. (2004), suggests that BME offenders generally have favourable experiences of supervision plans, supervision orders and specific programmes – on a par with white offenders. But at the same time, she highlights cause for concern in light of the responsivity principle which suggests that supervisors should make every effort to understand offenders' distinctive needs and experiences, including those pertaining to ethnicity, so as to facilitate positive engagement and a positive intervention outcome.

Interestingly, however, Calverley *et al*. (2004) found that only a third of the offenders wanted to be supervised by someone from the same ethnic group; most thought that it would make no difference (see also Lewis 2006). But this is nevertheless a substantial minority (35 per cent); some of those who found themselves the only black or Asian member of an otherwise white group felt isolated and uncomfortable. However, there was very limited support for programmes for members from ethnic minority groups only. Indeed, the findings tend to support the idea of ethnically mixed provision – without forgetting that BME offenders who find themselves as the only non-white members of programmes may well have distinctive needs. The overall message from the research appears to be that while practice needs to be informed by awareness of diversity, there is a need to avoid unwarranted assumptions about what diversity implies in terms of differentiated treatment.

Importantly, at the same time as the research by Calverley *et al*. (2004) was being undertaken, the NPD also piloted a number of Pathfinder projects for black and Asian offenders (not as part of its suite of nationally accredited interventions but alongside them). The NPD introduced the Pathfinders for black and Asian offenders as 'add ons' to the regular programmes – in relation to the Drink Impaired Drivers Programme and Think First, for example – or introduced responsive modes of delivery so as to try and maximise the impact of the group work. National project group meetings drew upon the experiences and wisdom of several of the practitioners and managers who had been involved in earlier local initiatives concerning black and Asian offenders and revealed a number of innovative activities where separate group work was not a practical option: mentoring schemes, and a Preparation or 'Empowerment Module' for instance, designed to assist participants in the group work programmes (Williams 2006). In the event, there were some implementation problems (especially where Asian and other suitably qualified staff were in short supply). More particularly, the relatively small numbers on each of the special Pathfinder programmes meant that systematic analysis of comparative outcomes was thwarted (Walmsley and Stephens 2006).

Policy and practice developments

If more recent policy and recent research studies suggest a more nuanced understanding and will to respond to the ethnically diverse offenders for whom the Probation Service is responsible than hitherto, it is salutary to note that the follow-up inspection report to the 2000 report published by the Probation Inspectorate (HMIP 2004) made rather depressing reading. The findings were that there were still significant delays in the analysis of data on ethnicity, the national database had not been adapted to accommodate the new 16 nationally agreed ethnic monitoring categories and the NPS had not sought to differentiate their database on enforcement by race or gender variables. The review concluded that none of the recommendations on ethnic monitoring made by the 2000 review had been met. It is suggested that much progress has been made particularly with regard to IT systems and their capacity to record ethnicity (Home Office 2006a), but the proportion of ethnic data missing in a small number of areas for those starting pre- or post-release supervision still renders the publication of figures for those areas impossible – and hence the national picture may be skewed somewhat by the focus on those areas with publishable data.

Nevertheless, the picture is clear enough for there to be continuing concern about differential access to community penalties for BME adults and young offenders (Bowling and Phillips 2002; Feilzer and Hood 2004). Indeed, there is now broad agreement that African Caribbean offenders in particular are less likely to be given community sentences than others, although there are competing explanations for this in terms of the seriousness of offences committed and the impact of not guilty pleas for example. There are also a number of forceful accounts that BME offenders have experienced considerable social exclusion and that the particularities of the disadvantages that they have experienced are captured neither by risk assessment instruments nor by the caring or controlling gaze of probation officers (Cole and Wardak 2006; Raynor and Lewis 2006). Additionally, while there is now more awareness of what BME offenders' experiences have been and what their needs are, there is still much work to do to tease out the needs of hybrid groups and identities (those who are black British, British Asian and so on, as opposed to 'African Caribbean' or 'Asian' for instance). The collection of essays edited by Lewis *et al.* (2006), drawing in part on the earlier work of Calverley *et al.* (2004), goes some way towards remedying the previous paucity of substantive information on BME offenders' needs, but even now it is far from clear that probation practice has got things right in terms of addressing distinctive needs.

The 'wake-up call' from the Chief Inspector of Probation (HMIP 2000) has clearly been important in directing attention to problems of discrimination and the needs of BME offenders, but key questions are how far anti-racist practice has become embedded within the Service and how far it has succeeded in addressing perceptions of inequality of treatment.

Sentencing patterns and evidence of discrimination: gender

Studies of gender differences in criminal justice have most often focused upon the differential treatment of men and women in the sentencing process. This issue has been fiercely debated but not entirely resolved. It is clear, however, that they are treated *differently* (e.g. Mawby 1977; Worrall 1990; Gelsthorpe 1987, 2001; Mair and Brockington 1988; Hedderman and Gelsthorpe 1997). In the probation arena the way in which report-writing practices may contribute to differential court outcomes for women and men has been a recurring concern. Eaton (1993) for example, in observing cases in the magistrates' court and examining what were then called social inquiry reports, concluded that women assessed negatively were likely to be dealt with more severely than others. In similar vein, Stephen (1993), writing ten years later, argued that the differential treatment of men and women by the courts was likely to be influenced by the way in which they are represented in pre-sentence reports; probation officers frequently provided explanations which highlighted personal traits in the case of male offenders and underlying emotional problems in the case of women. Indeed, there is substantial evidence that both the types of problems experienced and the motivations for offending are perceived by probation officers as being different for women and men and that this is reflected in report-writing practices (McIvor and Barry 1998; Horn and Evans 2000).

In terms of perceptions of behaviour, women's offending is frequently thought to be rooted in poverty and financial dependence (Cook 1997; Hedderman 2004). Financial penalties are often, therefore, inappropriate sanctions for women who offend. A Home Office study suggested that courts in England and Wales were reluctant to impose fines upon female offenders (Dowds and Hedderman 1997). In some cases this appeared to result in a more lenient response, in comparison with male offenders, by way of a discharge. In other cases it appeared that women may have been escalated up the sentencing tariff through the imposition of a community sentence – probation or community service – in lieu of a fine.

Further, various studies in different parts of the UK (Hine 1993; McIvor 1998) have found women to be under-represented in community service (now unpaid work in England and Wales), though there is also some evidence that when age, current offence and criminal history are controlled for women are as likely to receive community service as men (Mair and Brockington 1988). There are, moreover, clear differences in the characteristics of men and women sentenced to community service. Women on community service are more likely than men to be first offenders (Hine 1993; McIvor 1992) and there is some evidence that there is less consistency (in terms of criminal history and current offence) in the use of community service with women (Hine 1993; HMIP 1996). Indeed, in a thematic review of provision for women in 1996, Her Majesty's Inspectorate of Probation found that probation officers preparing PSRs often rejected community service orders as a viable option for women with childcare responsibilities and were unaware of the funds available for such provision. Moreover, there was a perception that women pose a higher breach risk on such orders, due to family responsibilities (despite evidence to suggest that women have more successful completions (Home Office 2005a; Scottish Executive 2006)). Ironically, too, in a more recent study of community service, women appear to gain rather more from the orders than men. In a study of some 1,851 offenders on community service, 148 of them being women, Gelsthorpe and Rex (2004) reported that from offenders' own assessments of what they gained, 49 per cent of the women indicated that they had improved their skills either a lot or quite a lot – compared with 35 per cent of the men. Further, over 50 per cent of the women indicated that they were either very likely or quite likely to do more training as a result of the community service or that it had at least improved their chances of getting a job (compared with under 40 per cent of the men).

Probation (now supervision as a requirement of a community order under the Criminal Justice Act 2003 in England and Wales), on the other hand, has traditionally been used more with women than with men though there is evidence that women are given probation at a lower point on the sentencing tariff. McIvor and Barry (1998), for instance, found that women who were subject to probation supervision in Scotland had fewer previous convictions and were more likely to be first offenders than men. The fact that women tend to have less extensive criminal histories than men may account at least partly for the common finding that female probationers are more likely to succeed on probation than men (e.g. Davies 1964; Wisconsin Corrections Division 1972; Frease 1964; Morgan 1994; McIvor and Barry 1998).

One of the most striking trends in sentencing across western jurisdictions – including the UK – in the last decade or so is the marked rise in female prison populations, which has far outstripped a smaller proportionate increase in the populations of imprisoned men. Higher female prison populations appear to reflect both increases in the numbers of women given custodial sentences and higher average sentence lengths (Gelsthorpe and Morris 2002; Deakin and Spencer 2003; Hedderman 2004). This trend is particularly concerning in view of the relatively minor offences in respect of which women are imprisoned and the vulnerability of many women who receive custodial sentences (Prison Reform Trust 2000; Fawcett Society 2004). Studies of imprisoned women conducted in the United States (Owen and Bloom 1995), Canada (Shaw 1994), Australia (Edwards 1995) England and Wales (Morris *et al.* 1995; Caddle and Crisp 1997) and Scotland (Loucks 1998) lend support to a general conclusion that imprisoned women are usually 'marginalised women' (Bloom *et al.* 1995) (as is the case with men we might add, although the view that the prison system has not accommodated women's particular needs and that their imprisonment may damage their children adds potency and poignancy to concerns about the number of women imprisoned).

Gender issues and probation

Various studies have suggested that the focus and content of probation practice with women has differed from that with men. For example, Stewart *et al.*'s (1994) analysis of probation officers' work with young offenders revealed that women's offending was more often explained as 'self-expressive' or 'coping' and probation officers' responses typically involved supportive counselling aimed at improving self-esteem or self-image and work on the problems arising from poverty and its associated stresses. In Scotland, McIvor and Barry (1998) found that the supervision of women offenders continued to approximate more to a traditional welfare model (dealing with practical problems and offering emotional support) while the supervision of male offenders was more directly focused upon offending behaviour and related issues. Empowerment was a key theme, with most women describing the process by which they had been enabled through probation to become more assertive in their personal relationships, to pay more attention to meeting their own needs and to begin making decisions for themselves (McIvor 1997).

As noted in Chapter 16, this volume, probation practice in the UK has increasingly been driven by a concern with 'evidence-based practice' and the 'what works' agenda. However, concern has been expressed that this agenda and the practices that it advocates may be less appropriate as a means of responding effectively to women who offend (McIvor 1999; Shaw and Hannah-Moffat 2000; Hollin and Palmer 2006). While Dowden and Andrews (1999) concluded from a meta-analysis of interventions with female offenders that interventions were more effective if they addressed women's criminogenic needs, they also acknowledged that further research is required to identify the relationship between particular problems (such as past victimisation and self-esteem) and offending by women. Andrews *et al.* (1990) have also acknowledged that gender may be an important factor in determining the effectiveness of different methods of intervention but this remains an issue which has largely been ignored.

Although women's offending tends to be under-explored and less well understood than offending by men, it is now recognised that women are likely to have different 'criminogenic needs' (Hedderman 2004) because their routes into offending and reasons for offending are often different from those of men (Jamieson *et al.* 1999). Research evidence indicates that some needs may indeed be similar (for example, criminal history, unemployment, substance misuse), though how they have come about and how they contribute to offending may be different for men and women and there are others which appear to be more specific to women, such as physical and sexual abuse (Hollin and Palmer 2006). This clearly has implications for the focus and content of probation practice, though both custodial and non-custodial interventions designed to address criminogenic need, and thereby reduce the risk of reoffending, tend to be based on the needs of male offenders. As Hedderman (2004: 241) concludes from her analysis of research on men's and women's criminogenic needs:

> ... overall the available evidence suggests that programmes which focus on male criminogenic factors are unlikely to be as effective in reducing reconviction among women offenders as they are for men. This is not only because they focus on factors which are less relevant to or operate differently for women, but also because they fail to address factors which are unique to, or more relevant for, women who offend.

A focus on criminogenic needs has been driven by, and, in turn, has driven, the use of structured assessment tools in probation practice, with tools such as OASys and LSI-R widely used across the UK. The use of structured assessment tools can be regarded as a manifestation of managerialism in probation which informs resource allocation or resource management and which may encourage assessments that are resource-led rather than needs-led (Maurutto and Hannah-Moffat 2006). While it is not appropriate to rehearse the benefits and disadvantages of structured approaches to risk assessment (see Chapter 8, this volume), it has also been argued that risk and needs assessments are likely to be highly gendered because the factors that they incorporate are drawn predominantly from studies of men (Shaw and Hannah-Moffat 2000,

2004). Practitioners have also expressed concern about the applicability of structured risk assessment tools with particular groups of offenders, such as women, BME offenders, those with mental health problems or perpetrators of domestic abuse (Gibbs 1999; Aye Maung and Hammond 2000; McIvor and Kemshall 2002).

Policy and practice developments

Concerns about the treatment of women have been taken up by academics, policy-makers and practitioners alike. Certainly there have been challenges to mainstream criminological theory since existing theories have largely been unable to account for differences in men and women's involvement in crime. Instead of attempting to accommodate female offending within existing theoretical frameworks, alternative theoretical perspectives have been developed which locate women's offending within paternalistic power relations, poverty and distress (e.g. Chesney-Lind 1997; Gelsthorpe 2004). Feminist theories of psychological development have also highlighted important differences in developmental processes between women and men (e.g. Gilligan 1982) which have implications for the type of interventions which are likely to engage women effectively in the process of change. Similarly, educationalists such as Belenky et al. (1986) have argued that women's learning differs from men's learning both in terms of its developmental sequence and in terms of its underlying theory (see also Covington 1998). The researchers argue that women view knowledge more as a set of connections than a set of distinctions, and that most women prefer to learn in collaborative, rather than competitive, settings. Further, women most often take a 'believing approach' in engaging and discussing new ideas, attempting to empathise with the speaker and cooperatively assimilate the truth. Set alongside evidence which suggests that women-only environments facilitate growth and development (Zaplin 1998), these theoretical insights point to a need for work with women in non-authoritarian cooperative settings, where women are empowered to engage in social and personal change. A sound analysis of the 'responsivity' principle conducted by Blanchette and Brown (2006) concerning *how* treatment should be delivered in different criminal justice settings emphasises not only the importance of matching treatment style to offender learning styles, but that alongside structured behavioural interventions case-specific factors should also be addressed. These include 'women-specific' factors such as healthcare, childcare and mental health. Certainly, substance abuse treatment effects are thought to be more robust when such factors are conceptualised as responsivity factors (Ashley et al. 2003).

A succession of reports which have attracted media attention (for example, Prison Reform Trust 2000; Fawcett Society 2004, 2006) combined with damning Prison and Probation Inspectorate Reports have served to promote a response at governmental levels. The Government's 'Women's Offending Reduction Programme' (WORP) was launched in 2004 to help coordinate departments and sensitise them to women's needs. It also aims to improve community-based provision for women offenders (WORP 2004–5) so that prison is used as a last resort. The approach has led to the setting up of multi-agency 'Women's Offending Action Teams' (WOATS), which might provide a floating service or could be placed in a 'one-stop shop' type provision from a women's centre which NOMS has tasked Regional Offender Managers to deliver in two pilot regions. In March 2005, Charles Clarke, then Home Secretary, announced the award of £9.15 million for these two pilots over a four-year period.

In Scotland, policy concern about the potentially damaging consequences of imprisoning women was triggered to a large extent by a number of suicides at Cornton Vale – the only dedicated Scottish female prison. A review of the use of custody and community disposals for female offenders in Scotland, commissioned by the Chief Inspectors of Social Work and Prisons and entitled *A Safer Way*, concluded that 'the backgrounds of women in prison are characterised by experiences of abuse, drug misuse, poor educational attainment, poverty, psychological distress and self harm' (Scottish Office 1998: 13). It made a number of recommendations including a review of the prison estate, the development of bail provision for women who have been accused of an offence, the increased use of supervised attendance orders for women who default on payment of their fines and the development of an inter-agency forum aimed at developing services for female offenders in Glasgow. Subsequent proposals put forward by the Inter-Agency Forum (established in 1999) included the possibility of establishing a daily court for women, providing additional resources to enable women to address their drug use, building upon and expanding existing diversion strategies at all stages in the system and the creation of 'Time Out' centres, to provide a wide range of residentially or non-residentially based support services for women. The work of the forum was subsequently taken forward by a ministerial group charged with turning the proposals into practical measures. The resulting report, entitled *A Better Way* (Scottish Executive 2002), recommended that greater emphasis should be placed upon alleviating the social circumstances that lead some women to offend, intervening early to ensure that women's needs can be met without recourse to imprisonment, promoting the use of the full range of community disposals (including the Time Out Centre advocated by the Inter-Agency Forum) and shifting the penal culture away from punishment and towards rehabilitation and 'treatment'. Importantly, *A Better Way* recognised the need to avoid the assumption that the 'what works' principles and programmes derived from men can appropriately and straightforwardly be applied to women.

The recognition that women who offend often have different needs from men and the growing awareness that female offenders frequently have histories of abuse prompted the initial development of group work programmes for women in some Probation Service areas in England and Wales (Mistry 1989; Jones *et al.* 1991). The development of these programmes was regarded as a means of ensuring that the particular needs of women were addressed in a safe and non-threatening environment that was conducive to the development of 'reciprocal relationships' (Eaton 1993; Worrall 1995) which appear to be central to women's growth and change. A similar rationale underpinned other innovative provision, such as the women's group-work programme developed by Hereford and Worcester (now West Mercia) which probationers indicated had provided them with considerable support (Rumgay 2000; Roberts 2002).[5] In addition to evidence from the Asha Centre which points to the need for multi-faceted programmes (Roberts 2002), Durrance and Ablitt (2001) explored the use of the Women's Probation Centre in Camden, which runs a wide-ranging programme for women and attributed the substantially lower reconviction rate among women (compared to predicted reconviction rates in the form of OGRS scores) to the creative and gender-specific programme. Although only a small-scale study involving 18 (7 BME, 11 white) women (ranging from 22 to 44 in years), the focus on service users by Rebecca Clarke, probation researcher, highlights some of the challenges that the two recently established community-based pilot initiatives for women in England and Wales face. Having interviewed the women to find out what they thought they needed to desist from offending and what they were able to access from the criminal justice system, Clarke suggests that there is a large disparity between their need for inter-agency cooperation (to address complex needs which cut across agencies) and the supply of this kind of service. Moreover, as one of Clarke's interviewees put it: 'If you're in an emotionally raw state it can be hard to get across what you need and then listen and take in what someone is telling you. Especially if you don't know them or trust them' (cited in Clarke 2004: 17).

As another service user observed, 'My experiences of these services, you know ... social services and probation ... [is not good] ... Even when you're meant to see them once or twice a month, you're lucky if they show up. Or it's someone else, someone new and you spend all the time explaining' (cited in Clarke 2004: 17). It is thus clear that the Home Secretary's two pilot centres face enormous challenges in galvanising local services to work together. While individual agencies may be willing to work with women, it is the coordination between agencies which may be significant. However, the development of the Asha Centre in Hereford and Worcestershire gives testament to the possibilities (Roberts 2002). There is also some cause to derive optimism from the experience of the 218 Time Out Centre that was established in Glasgow in December 2003 with funding from the Scottish Executive Justice Department (Loucks *et al.* 2006). 218 provides residential and non-residential services for women who are involved in the criminal justice system, adopting a 'holistic', gender-appropriate approach to women's needs. The evaluation suggested that women who had attended 218 are very positive about the service, believing that it had addressed their needs, and regarded the support they received in relation to problematic substance use to be a crucial aspect of the service. Most of the women who attended 218 reported reductions in drug and alcohol use, reductions in offending and improvements in health and well-being (Loucks *et al.* 2006). Costing no more than an alternative prison sentence, 218 has developed a model of intervention based on a recognition of the needs of women.

Despite developments in largely practitioner-led gender-appropriate programming in England and Wales (and, indeed, in other parts of the UK), provision for women under the National Offender Management Model (NOMM) is uncertain. As well as presenting different needs compared to male offenders, we have indicated that women generally present lower risk of harm and reconviction than men. The NOMM, however, allocates resources according to risk of harm or reconviction based on four tiers of service delivery (see Chapter 8, this volume). There is every suggestion that women will fall disproportionately into the first two tiers (made up of lower-risk offenders with fewer criminogenic needs) with the concomitant implication that women offenders may be more likely to be the subject of orders attracting fewer resources, supervised by less qualified and/or experienced offender managers, while men (particularly high-risk sexual and violent offenders) will receive much greater attention. This would apply to pre-sentence reports, with a high percentage of women being subject to fast-delivery reports (see Chapter 7, this volume).

Moreover, provision for women who fall into tier 3 of the new NOMS four-tier model (where interventions mostly consist of accredited programmes or drug rehabilitation requirements) is likely to be problematic, given that there is currently only one accredited programme for them at present (the 'Real Women Programme' which revolves around acquisitive offending; see Home Office 2004a). Roberts (2002) suggests that this is because the Joint Accreditation Panel who assess the effectiveness and viability of programmes has been dominated by forensic psychologists who favour cognitive-behavioural approaches which have been tested on men (as we have argued above). Moreover, in the face of evidence from programmes which have focused on women's needs, it is unlikely that accredited programmes alone will be sufficiently holistic in nature to address the complex needs of women.

Dealing with diversity: men's needs

This chapter would be incomplete without mentioning men's needs. It is a common observation that the maleness of crime is massively documented but relatively little theorised and certainly little considered in relation to probation practice. As Grosz (1987: 6) once asked: 'What is it about men, not as working class, not as migrant, not as underprivileged individuals, but *as men* that induces them to commit crime?' The literature on masculinity has increased markedly in the last few years, however (see Gelsthorpe 2002, for example, for a review of the literature). Moreover, there has been much developmental thinking around the concept of 'hegemonic masculinity' concerning the notion of a dominant array of traits or behaviours which are characterised as 'masculinity' and into which men are socialised and to which men are then expected to conform, thus rendering other kinds of 'masculine' behaviour as different, if not deviant (Connell 1987). But there are huge debates as to how far such a notion might mask the psychological complexity of men's behaviour (Collier 1998). Messerschmidt's (1993) analysis has been the most extensive attempt to apply Connell's thinking to the study of crime. He developed the idea of masculinity as a 'situational accomplishment' and of crime as a means of 'doing gender'. This is not without criticism either, because of the way in which ethnicity, age, disability and so on might mediate structures of 'gender' (Mac an Ghaill 1994) but it does bring us closer to the idea that there may be a crossover between the 'attractions of crime' that can be perceived as masculine elements of identity.

While there are many who would argue that probation practice has long reflected men's needs and 'male norms' (since they predominate in caseloads and since risk assessment instruments have been based on men, for example), recent attempts to theorise masculinity are arguably important. Certainly there have been local probation initiatives in this direction (particularly in relation to group programmes; see Jenkins 1994 for a review). The introduction of offence-specific programmes (e.g. anger management) in which the thinking behind the commission of particular violent offences is challenged and alternatives are offered suggest some consideration of *men's* behaviour, but in practice the methods utilised have varied a great deal; some have focused on the control of emotions in general rather than on masculinity for example. Moreover, these programmes have often been provided for all types of violent offenders and not just for men, although a focus on men and men's needs and problems is sometimes implicit in the design of the programmes (as we have discussed elsewhere in this chapter)

One question is whether there is scope or justification to enhance any 'gender awareness' elements of programmes. A number of researchers suggest that there is. Much of the work with sex offenders, for example, addresses cognitive distortions and heightens gender awareness (Scourfield 1998; see also Scourfield and Dobash 1999). There is nevertheless pressure to give even greater recognition to 'relations between men' and men's subjective experiences of masculinity in probation work. On the basis of research rooted and tested in probation practice Hearn and Whitehead (2006) argue that masculinity is generated through relations between men, and that attention to this might be critical to the effectiveness of programmes designed for men (particularly those aiming to address domestic violence for example). In other words, if a man's claim to be a man depends on his ability to display valued status features in relation to other men (imagined heroism, heroic courage, villainous deceit are all identified by Hearn and Whitehead) domestic violence can be understood as a way of achieving this and alternative ways of achieving identity can be presented to him.

Other recent work by Antony Whitehead points to the possibility that masculinity might be seen as a dynamic risk factor in offences of violence between men (1995, 2005). Defining masculinity as a common denominator of men, as men, across social divisions, he suggests that existing interventions into violence between men in prison, hospital and community settings may be enhanced by incorporating masculinity as a dynamic risk factor alongside other dynamic risk factors such as difficulties in anger management, social skills deficits or problems in moral reasoning. But this is developmental work and there is arguably some way to go before gender-specific activity in this direction is recognised and adopted.

Dealing with diversity, difference and justice

As we indicated in the introduction to this chapter, the material and themes that constitute its focus have presented a significant challenge, partly because of the inter-relatedness of issues, partly because of the relative dearth of literature in relation to certain dimensions of diversity and partly because conclusions that can be reached and the implications for policy and practice that flow from them differ according to the dimension of diversity that is being considered. But attending to and addressing diversity in probation practice is necessary to ensure that services and interventions provided can be as effective as possible. It is also critical as a means of meeting demands for equality of treatment that are now enshrined in law.

Public sector equality duties are developing apace. In Northern Ireland a duty to promote equality on nine separate grounds (including religion) was introduced in 1998. Following the enquiry into the murder of Stephen Lawrence, the law was changed in 2001 to place a duty on public bodies to promote race equality (in the Race Relations (Amendment) Act). A disability equality duty came into force in December 2006 (in the Disability Discrimination Act 2005). Another recent development concerns the introduction of the Equality Act 2006 indicating the establishment of a single Commission for Equality and Human Rights (replacing the separate commissions which have been in operation) and broadening provision in relation to sexual orientation, religion or belief. A key part of the Act is the 'gender duty' which brings equality issues concerning women in line with other public sector equality duties (race and disability). In particular, the legislation promotes the introduction of gender impact assessments (GIAs), a move which highlights the need to give further attention to what works for women and men in probation practice.

Our concluding argument, is that *equality* of treatment need not be equated with the *same* treatment. In other words, while it is important that negative discrimination is avoided, it is equally important that dimensions of diversity are appropriately accommodated as a means of promoting both *procedural* justice and *social* justice. Tyler (1990) identifies a number of factors that may enhance offenders' perceptions of procedural justice. These include ethicality, quality of decisions, efforts to be fair, correctability, honesty, representation and lack of bias. Tyler found that if people perceived themselves to be treated fairly, they were more likely to view criminal justice agencies as having legitimacy and the greater the perceived legitimacy of these agencies, the greater the level of compliance with their demands. He further contends that procedural justice 'is the key normative judgement influencing the impact of experience on legitimacy' (1990: 162). Perceiving criminal justice agencies as legitimate can, in turn, enhance intrinsic motivation to change as opposed to the extrinsic motivation that derives from punishment and deterrence and which dispels when the threat of sanction is removed. As Tyler and Huo (2002: 205) have argued, 'to the extent that people have willingly accepted authorities' decisions, their motivation to continue abiding by these decisions in the future is greater'.

With respect to difference and diversity, the concept of ethicality has, perhaps, the greatest resonance. Tyler defines ethicality as being demonstrated through politeness, respect and, importantly in this context, a demonstration of concern for individuals' needs. The latter implies attention to individual, social and cultural differences through which experiences and behaviours are mediated and which combine to constitute the offender as a human being. Failure to acknowledge and accommodate such diversity may not only mean that probation interventions are not appropriately tailored to the needs of the offenders to whom they are delivered. It may also, by this line of reasoning, undermine the perceived legitimacy of criminal justice agencies and the reasonableness of their expectations of behavioural change. Attention to these differences will also be an important prerequisite to promoting social justice, social inclusion and citizenship and the responsibilities and relationships which flow from them which may enhance offenders' reintegration and help promote their desistance from crime.

Attention to diversity issues in probation reflects, at best, local development and innovation, and leadership (through a national strategy *The Heart of the Dance* (NPS 2003)); at worst, it reflects unevenness in attention and reverses in practice (there is, after all, little attention to diversity in the Carter Report (Carter 2003) or the Government's response (Home Office 2004c)). There have been positive developments in relation to staffing (see the Home Office Section 95 reports),[6] at least insofar as ethnicity and gender are concerned, if not in regard to other forms of diversity. We have not addressed training strategies here, nor have we addressed victims and diversity, but we have tried to give a broad indication of key developments in relation to offenders thus far. In the steps towards the implementation of the framework of the National Offender Management Service it will be important to ensure that diversity issues remain at the forefront of practice, not simply in relation to managerialist concerns (Bhui 2006) and changing working cultures, but because of the need to do justice to difference.

Notes

1   Caseload statistics suggest that while 4 and 5 per cent of men and women (respectively) starting CROs in 2004 were over 50, fewer offenders over this age commence CPOs (Home Office 2004b).

2   We are grateful to Robin Moore in the NOMS OASys DEAT for these figures. It should be noted that although OASys is in widespread use it is not a requirement that it be used with all offenders; also, the sample was restricted to those assessments which met the approved standards of data collection.

3   A Youth Justice Board cross-sectional study of young offenders and mental health also shows a high degree of need in this area (Youth Justice Board 2005), all of which is suggestive of future needs within probation.

4   CRIME PICS II is commonly referred to as an Industry Standard interim outcome measure which, ideally, should be used in relation to later measures of reconviction. It has been used in the evaluation of the Straight Thinking on Probation (STOP) programme for example (see Chapter 2, this volume), and consists of two components: the first concerns attitudes to crime, the second concerns a problem inventory.

5   Gender-specific programming has also developed in North America where an array of programmes have emerged with slightly different foci but united by a common emphasis upon addressing female offenders' needs, using methods which are deemed appropriate for engaging effectively with damaged and vulnerable women (Bloom and Covington 1998; Covington and Bloom 1999).

6 Section 95 reports relating to race and gender are published by the Home Office and include statistics on BME and women staff within each of the key criminal justice system agencies. See: http://www.homeoffice.gov.uk/rds/index.htm

Further reading

For a general overview of issues relating to discrimination see Thompson (2003) *Promoting Equality. Challenging Discrimination and Oppression* and Thompson (2001) *Anti-Discriminatory Practice*. To go beyond this, and to look at some of the challenges presented by the claim that diversity should be celebrated, consult *Challenging Diversity. Rethinking Equality and the Value of Difference* by Davina Cooper (2005). Ben Bowling and Coretta Phillip's (2002) textbook entitled *Racism, Crime and Justice* gives a broad overview of issues and notes significant research and policy developments in relation to every criminal justice system agency (including probation).

On mental health issues see *Mental Disorder and Criminal Justice* edited by Brian Litttlechild and Debra Fearns (2005).

As well as consulting the Home Office series of Section 95 reports on race (http://www.homeoffice.gov.uk/rds/section951.html) (which give details of staff recruitment as well as facts and figures on prosecution, sentencing and imprisonment), see Lewis *et al.* (2006) *Race and Probation* for a comprehensive and up-to-date overview of issues.

As well as consulting the Home Office series of Section 95 reports on gender (http://www.homeoffice.gov.uk/rds/pdfs06/s95women0405.pdf) see McIvor (2004) *Women Who Offend*. See also Blanchette and Brown (2006) *The Assessment and Treatment of Women Offenders. An Integrated Perspective*. The authors systematically explore whether and how the assessment and treatment of women should differ from that of men.

References

Andrews, D. A., Bonta, J. and Hoge, R. D. (1990) 'Classification for effective rehabilitation: rediscovering psychology', *Criminal Justice and Behavior*, 17 (1): 19–52.

Ashley, O., Marsden, M. and Brady, T. (2003) 'Effectiveness of substance abuse treatment programming for women: a review', *American Journal of Drug and Alcohol Abuse*, 29: 19–53.

Aye Maung, N. and Hammond, N. (2000) *Risk of Re-offending and Needs Assessments: The User's Perspective*, Home Office Research Study No. 216. London: Home Office.

Barn, R. (2001) *Black Youth on the Margins. A Research Review*. York: Joseph Rowntree Foundation.

Belenky, M., Clinchy, B., Goldberger, N. and Tarule, J. (1986) *Women's Ways of Knowing*. New York: Basic Books.

Bhui, H. (1999) 'Race, racism and risk assessment: linking theory to practice with black mentally disordered offenders', *Probation Journal*, 46 (3): 171–81.

Bhui, H. (2006) 'Anti-racist practice in NOMS: reconciling managerialist and professional realities', *Howard Journal*, 45 (2): 171–90.

Blanchette, K. and Brown, S. (2006) *The Assessment and Treatment of Women Offenders. An Integrated Perspective*. Chichester: John Wiley & Sons.

Bloom, B. and Covington, S. (1998) *Gender-Specific Programming for Female Offenders: What Is It and Why Is It Important?* Paper presented at the Annual Meeting of the American Society of Criminology, Washington, DC.

Bloom, B., Immarigeon, R. and Owen, B. (1995) 'Editorial introduction', *Prison Journal*, 75 (2): 131–4.

Bowling, B. and Phillips, C. (2002) *Racism, Crime and Justice*. Harlow: Longman.

Bramhall, G. (2006) 'Older offenders and community penalties', in A. Wahidin and M. Cain (eds), *Ageing, Crime and Society*. Cullompton: Willan.

Bridgwood, A. and Malbon, G. (1995) *Survey of the Physical Health of Prisoners 1994*. London: Office of Population and Censuses and Surveys.

Buchanan, A. (2002) *Community Care of the Mentally Disordered Offender*. Oxford: Oxford University Press.

Caddle, D. and Crisp, D. (1997) *Imprisoned Women and Mothers*, Home Office Research Study No. 162. London: Home Office.

Calverley, A., Cole, B., Kaur, G., Lewis, S., Raynor, P., Sadeghi, S., Smith, D., Vanstone, M. and Wardak, A. (2004) *Black and Asian Offenders on Probation*, Home Office Research Study No. 277. London: Home Office.

Canton, R. (2005) 'Risk assessment and compliance in probation and mental health practice', in B. Littlechild and D. Fearns (eds), *Mental Disorder and Criminal Justice: Policy, Provision and Practice*. Lyme Regis: Russell House.

Carter, P. (2003) *Managing Offenders, Reducing Crime: A New Approach*. London: Home Office.

Chesney-Lind, M. (1997) *The Female Offender: Girls, Women and Crime*. London: Sage.

Clarke, R. (2004) *'What Works?' for Women Who Offend: A Service Users Perspective*, Research Paper 2004/04. London: Griffins Society. Available at: www.thegriffinssociety.org/Research_Paper_2004_04.pdf

Clarke, T., Kenney-Herbert, J. and Humphreys, M. (2002) 'Community rehabilitation orders with additional requirements of psychiatric treatment', *Advances in Psychiatric Treatment*, 8: 281–90.

Codd, H. (1994) 'White haired offenders', *New Law Journal*, 144 (6672): 1582–3.

Cole, B. and Wardak, A. (2006) 'Black and Asian men on probation: social exclusion, discrimination and experiences of criminal justice', in S. Lewis, P. Raynor, D. Smith and A. Wardak (eds), *Race and Probation*. Cullompton: Willan.

Collier, R. (1998) *Masculinities. Crime and Criminology*. London: Sage.

Connell, B. (1987) *Gender and Power*. Cambridge: Polity Press.

Cook, D. (1997) *Poverty, Crime and Punishment*. London: Child Poverty Action Group.

Cooper, D. (2005) *Challenging Diversity. Rethinking Equality and the Value of Difference*. Cambridge: Cambridge University Press.

Covington, S. (1998) 'The relational theory of women's psychological development: implications for the criminal justice system', in R. Zaplin (ed.), *Female Offenders: Critical Perspectives and Effective Intervention*. Gaithersburg, MD: Aspen Publishers.

Covington, S. and Bloom, B. (1999) *Gender-responsive Programming and Evaluation for Women in the Criminal Justice System: A Shift from What Works? To What Is the Work?* Paper presented at the Annual Meeting of the American Society of Criminology, Toronto, Canada.

Davies, G. (1964) 'A study of adult probation violation rates by means of the cohort approach', *Journal of Criminal Law, Criminology and Police Science*, 55: 70–85.

De Gale, H., Hanlon, P., Hubbard, M., Morgan, S. and Denney, D. (1993) *Improving Practice in the Criminal Justice System: A Training Manual*. Leeds: CCETSW.

Deakin, J. and Spencer, J. (2003) 'Women behind bars: explanations and implications', *Howard Journal*, 42: 123–36.

Denney, D. (1992) *Racism and Anti-Racism in Probation*. London: Routledge.

Dowden, C. and Andrews, D. A. (1999) 'What works for female offenders: a meta-analytic review', *Crime and Delinquency*, 45 (4): 438–52.

Dowds, L. and Hedderman, C. (1997) 'The sentencing of men and women', in C. Hedderman and L. Gelsthorpe (eds), *Understanding the Sentencing of Women*, Home Office Research Study No. 170. London: Home Office.

Durrance, P. and Ablitt, F. (2001) '"Creative solutions" to women's offending: an evaluation of the Women's Probation Centre', *Probation Journal*, 28 (4): 247–59.

Durrance, P. and Williams, P. (2003) 'Broadening the agenda around what works for black and Asian offenders', *Probation Journal*, 50 (3): 211–24.

Durrance, P., Higgett, C., Merone, L. and Asamoah, A. (2001) *The Greenwich and Lewisham Black and Self-Development and Educational Attainment Group Evaluation Report*. London: Inner London Probation Service.

Eaton, M. (1993) *Women After Prison*. Buckingham: Open University Press.

Edwards, A. (1995) *Women in Prison*. Sydney: New South Wales Bureau of Crime Statistics and Research.

Fawcett Society (2004) *Women and the Criminal Justice System. A Report of the Fawcett Society's Commission on Women and the Criminal Justice System*. London: Fawcett Society.

Feilzer, M. and Hood, R. (2004) *Differences or Discrimination?* London: Youth Justice Board.

Flood-Page, C., Campbell, S., Harrington, V., and Miller, J. (2000) *Youth Crime. Findings from the 1998/1999 Youth Lifestyles Survey*, Home Office Research Study No. 209. London: Home Office.

Frease, D. (1964) 'Factors relating to probation outcome', in *Board of Prison Terms and Parole*. Olympia, WA: Department of Institutions, Board of Prison Terms and Parole.

Gelsthorpe, L. (1987) 'The differential treatment of males and females in the criminal justice system', in G. Horobin (ed.), *Sex, Gender and Care Work: Research Highlights in Social Work 15*. London: Jessica Kingsley.

Gelsthorpe, L. (1992) *Social Inquiry Reports: Race and Gender Consideration*, Home Office Research Bulletin No. 32. London: HMSO.

Gelsthorpe, L. (2001) 'Critical decisions and processes in the criminal courts', in E. McLaughlin and J. Muncie (eds), *Controlling Crime*. London: Sage/Open University.

Gelsthorpe, L. (2002) 'Feminism and criminology', in M. Maguire, R. Morgan and R. Reiner (eds), *The Oxford Handbook of Criminology*, 3rd edn. Oxford: Oxford University Press.

Gelsthorpe, L. (2004) 'Female offending: a theoretical overview', in G. McIvor (ed.), *Women Who Offend*. London: Jessica Kingsley.

Gelsthorpe, L. (2006) 'The experiences of female ethnic minority offenders: the other "other"', in S. Lewis, P. Raynor, D. Smith and A. Wardak (eds), *Race and Probation*. Cullompton: Willan.

Gelsthorpe, L. and Morris, A. (2002) 'Women's imprisonment in England and Wales: a penal paradox', *Criminal Justice*, 2 (3): 277–301.

Gelsthorpe, L. and Rex, S. (2004) 'Community service as reintegration: exploring the potential', in G. Mair (ed.), *What Matters in Probation*. Cullompton: Willan.

Gibbs, A. (1999) 'The assessment, case management and evaluation system', *Probation Journal*, 46 (3): 182–6.

Gilligan, C. (1982) *In a Different Voice*. Cambridge, MA.: Harvard University Press.

Graham, J. and Bowling, B. (1995) *Young People and Crime*, London: Home Office Research Study No. 145. London: HMSO.

Green, R. (1989) 'Probation and the black offender', *New Community*, 16 (1): 81–91.

Grosz, E. (1987) 'Feminist theory and the challenge to knowledge', *Women's Studies International Forum*, 10 (5): 208–17.

Grounds, A. (1995) 'Risk assessment and management in clinical context', in J. Crichton (ed.), *Psychiatric Patient Violence: Risk and Relapse*. London: Duckworth.

Hearn, J. and Whitehead, A. (2006) 'Collateral damage: men's "domestic" violence to women seen through men's relations with men', *Probation Journal*, 53 (1): 38–56.

Hedderman, C. (2004) 'The "criminogenic" needs of women offenders', in G. McIvor (ed.), *Women Who Offend*. London: Jessica Kingsley.

Hedderman, C. and Gelsthorpe, L. (1997) *Understanding the Sentencing of Women*, Home Office Research Study No. 170. London: Home Office.

Hepple, B. and Choudhury, T. (2001) *Tackling Religious Discrimination: Practical Implications for Policy-Makers and Legislators*, Home Office Research Study No. 221. London: Home Office Research, Development and Statistics Directorate.

Hine, J. (1993) 'Access for women: flexible and friendly?', in D. Whitfield and D. Scott (eds), *Paying Back: Twenty Years of Community Service*. Winchester: Waterside Press.

HM Prison Service Directorate of Healthcare (1999) *Prison Service Guidelines on the Care, Management and Treatment of Prisoners with Gender Dysphoria*. London: HMPS.

HMIP (1996) *Report on Women Offenders and Probation Service Provision for Women Offenders*. London: Home Office.

HMIP (2000) *Towards Race Equality. A Thematic Inspection*. London: Home Office.

HMIP (2004) *Towards Race Equality: Follow-up Inspection Report*. London: Home Office.

Hollin, C. and Palmer, E. (2006) 'Criminogenic need and women offenders: a critique of the literature', *Legal and Criminological Psychology*, 11 (2): 179–95.

Home Office (2004a) *Focus on Female Offenders: The Real Women Programme – Probation Service Pilot*, Home Office Development and Practice Report No. 18. London: Research Development and Statistics Directorate.

Home Office (2004b) *Strength in Diversity: Towards a Community Cohesion and Race Equality Strategy*. London: Home Office.

Home Office (2004c) *Reducing Crime, Changing Lives*. London: Home Office.

Home Office (2005a) *Offender Management Caseload Statistics 2004: England and Wales*, Home Office Statistical Bulletin 15/05. London: RDS, NOMS.

Home Office (2005b) *Race and the Criminal Justice System: An Overview to the Complete Statistics 2003–2004: A Section 95 Report, Criminal Justice Act 2001*. London: Home Office.

Home Office (2006a) *Statistics on Race and the Criminal Justice System – 2005*. London: Home Office.

Home Office (2006b) *Criminal Statistics 2005 England and Wales*, Home Office Statistical Bulletin 19/06. London: Home Office. Available at: http://www.homeoffice.gov.uk/rds/pdfs06/hosb1906.pdf

Home Office (CJS) (2005) *Offending in England and Wales: First Results from the 2003 Crime and Justice Survey*, Home Office Research Study No. 275. London: Home Office Research, Development and Statistics Directorate.

Hood, R. (1992) *Race and Sentencing: A Study in the Crown Court*. Oxford: Oxford University Press.

Horn, R. and Evans, M. (2000) 'The effect of gender on pre-sentence reports', *Howard Journal*, 39 (2): 184–97.

Hudson, B. (1989) 'Discrimination and disparity: the influence of race on sentencing', *New Community*, 16 (1): 23–34.

Institute for Employment Studies (IES) (2002) *A Review of Training in Racism Awareness and Valuing Cultural Diversity*, RDS On-line Report 09/02. London: Home Office.

Inter-agency Forum on Women's Offending (2001) *Second Year Report*. Edinburgh: Scottish Executive Justice Department.

Jamieson, J., McIvor, G. and Murray, C. (1999) *Understanding Offending Among Young People*. Edinburgh: Stationery Office.

Jenkins, J. (1994) *Men, Masculinity and Offending: Groupwork Initiatives in Probation*. London: London Action Trust.

Jones, M., Mordecai, M., Rutter, F. and Thomas, L. (1991) 'The Miskin Model of groupwork with women offenders', *Groupwork*, 4: 215–30.

Kemshall, H., Canton, R. and Bailey, R. (2004) 'Dimensions of difference', in A. Bottoms, S. Rex and G. Robinson (eds), *Alternatives to Prison: Options for an Insecure Society*. Cullompton: Willan.

Kett, J., Collett, S., Barron, C., Hill, I. and Metherwell, D. (1992) *Managing and Developing Anti-racist Practice within Probation: A Resource Pack for Action*. Liverpool: Merseyside Probation Service.

Lewis, S. (2006) 'Minority ethnic experiences of probation supervision and programmes', in S. Lewis, P. Raynor, D. Smith and A. Wardak (eds), *Race and Probation*. Cullompton: Willan.

Lewis, S., Raynor, P., Smith, D. and Wardak, A. (eds) (2006) *Race and Probation*. Cullompton: Willan.

Littlechild, B. and Fearns, D. (eds) (2005) *Mental Disorder and Criminal Justice*. Lyme Regis: Russell House.

Loucks, N. (1998) *HMPI Cornton Vale: Research into Drugs and Alcohol, Violence and Bullying, Suicides and Self-Injury, and Backgrounds of Abuse*, SPS Occasional Paper 1/98. Edinburgh: Scottish Prison Service.

Loucks, N., Malloch, M., McIvor, G. and Gelsthorpe, L. (2006) *Evaluation of the 218 Centre*. Edinburgh: Scottish Executive Social Research.

Mac an Ghaill, M. (1994) *The Making of Men: Masculinities, Sexualities and Schooling*. Buckingham: Open University Press.

McIvor, G. (1992) *Sentenced to Serve: The Operation and Impact of Community Service*. Aldershot: Avebury.

McIvor, G. (1997) *Gender Differences in Probation Practice*. Paper presented at the British Criminology Conference, Queen's University, Belfast.

McIvor, G. (1998) 'Jobs for the boys? Gender differences in referral for community service', *Howard Journal of Criminal Justice*, 37: 280–90.

McIvor, G. (1999) 'Women, crime and criminal justice in Scotland', *Scottish Journal of Criminal Justice Studies*, 5 (1): 67–74.

McIvor, G. (ed.) (2004) *Women Who Offend: Research Highlights in Social Work 44*. London: Jessica Kingsley.

McIvor, G. and Barry, M. (1998) *Social Work and Criminal Justice Volume 6: Probation*. Edinburgh: Stationery Office.

McIvor, G. and Kemshall, H. (2002) *Serious Violent and Sexual Offenders: The Use of Risk Assessment Tools in Scotland*. Edinburgh: Scottish Executive Social Research.

Macpherson, W. (1999) *The Stephen Lawrence Inquiry: Report of an Inquiry by Sir William Macpherson of Cluny*, Cm. 4262-1. London: Home Office.

Mair, G. (1986) 'Ethnic minorities, probation and the magistrates' courts', *British Journal of Criminology*, 26 (2): 147–55.

Mair, G. and Brockington, N. (1988) 'Female offenders and the Probation Service', *Howard Journal*, 27 (2): 117–26.

Mair, G. and May, C. (1997). *Offenders on Probation*, Home Office Research Study No. 167. London: Home Office.

Maurutto, P. and Hannah-Moffat, K. (2006) 'Assembling risk and the restructuring of penal control', *British Journal of Criminology*, 46 (3): 438–54.

Mavunga, P. (1993) 'Probation: a basically racist service', in L. Gelsthorpe (ed.), *Minority Groups in the Criminal Justice System*. Cambridge: University of Cambridge Cropwood Series.

Mawby, R. I. (1977) 'Sexual discrimination and the law', *Probation Journal*, 24 (2): 38–43.

May, C. (1999) *Explaining Reconviction Rates Following a Community Sentence: The Role of Social Factors*, Home Office Research Study No. 192. London: Home Office.

Messerschmidt, J. (1993) *Masculinities and Crime: Critique and Reconceptualisation of Theory*. Lanham, MD: Rowman & Littlefield.

Midwinter, E. (2005) 'How many people are there in the Third Age?', *Ageing and Society*, 25: 9–18.

Mistry, T. (1989) 'Establishing a feminist model of groupwork in the Probation Service', *Groupwork*, 2: 145–58.

Modood, T., Beishon, S. and Virdee, S. (1994) *Changing Ethnic Identities*. London: Policy Studies Institute.

Morgan, K. (1994) 'Factors associated with probation outcome', *Journal of Criminal Justice*, 22 (4): 341–53.

Morris, A., Wilkinson, C., Tisi, A., Woodrow, J. and Rockley, A. (1995) *Managing the Needs of Female Prisoners*. London: Home Office.

Nadkarni, R., Chipchase, B. and Fraser, K. (2000) 'Partnership with probation hostels: a step forward in community forensic psychiatry', *Psychiatry Bulletin*, 24: 222–4.

NAPO (2003) *Mentally Disordered Offenders: A Briefing*. London: National Association of Probation Officers.

National Audit Office (2004) *Delivering Public Services to a Diverse Society*, Report of the Controller and Auditor General, HC 19-1 Sessions 2004–2005. London: TSO.

National Offender Management Service (2005) *Offender Management Caseload Statistics, England and Wales*. London: NOMS.

National Probation Directorate (2001) *A New Choreography: An Integrated Strategy for the National Probation Service for England and Wales*. London: National Probation Directorate.

National Probation Service (2003) *The Heart of the Dance. A Diversity Strategy for the National Probation Service for England and Wales 2002–2006*. London: Home Office.

O'Malley, P. (2001) 'Risk, crime and prudentialism revisited', in K. Stenson and R. Sullivan (eds), *Crime, Risk and Justice: The Politics of Crime Control in Liberal Democracies*. Cullompton: Willan.

Office for National Statistics (2000) *Social Trends*. London: ONS.

Office for National Statistics (2004) *Population: Focus on Gender*. London: ONS.

Office for National Statistics (2006a) *Population Estimates by Ethnic Group (Experimental)*. London: ONS.

Office for National Statistics (2006b) *Population: Focus on Health*. London: ONS.

Owen, B. and Bloom, B. (1995) 'Profiling women prisoners: findings from national surveys and a California sample', *Prison Journal*, 75 (2): 165–85.

Peay, J. (2002) 'Mentally disordered offenders, mental health and crime', in M. Maguire, R. Morgan and R. Reiner (eds), *The Oxford Handbook of Criminology*, 3rd edn. Oxford: Oxford University Press.

Powis, B. and Walmsley, R. (2002) *Programmes for Black and Asian Offenders on Probation: Lessons for Developing Practice*, Home Office Research Study No. 250. London: Home Office.

Prison Reform Trust (2000) *Justice for Women: The Need for Reform*, Report of the Committee on Women's Imprisonment, Chaired by Professor Dorothy Wedderburn. London: Prison Reform Trust.

Raynor, P. and Lewis, S. (2006) 'Black and Asian men on probation: who are they, and what are their criminogenic needs?', in S. Lewis, P. Raynor, D. Smith and A. Wardak (eds), *Race and Probation*. Cullompton: Willan.

Rex, S., Lieb, R., Bottoms, A. and Wilson, L. (2003) *Accrediting Offender Programmes: A Process-based Evaluation of the Joint Prison/Probation Services Accreditation Panel*, Home Office Research Study No. 273. London: Home Office Research, Development and Statistics Directorate.

Roberts, J. (2002) 'Women-centred: the West Mercia community-based programme for women offenders', in P. Carlen (ed.), *Women and Punishment. The Struggle for Justice*. Cullompton: Willan.

Rumgay, J. (2000) 'Policies of neglect: female offenders and the Probation Service', in H. Kemshall and R. Littlechild (eds), *Improving Participation and Involvement in Social Care Delivery*. London: Jessica Kingsley.

Runnymede Trust (1997) *Islamaphobia. A Challenge for Us All*. London: Runnymede Trust.

Scottish Executive (2001) *Criminal Justice Social Work Statistics 1999–2000*. Edinburgh: Scottish Executive.

Scottish Executive (2002) *A Better Way: The Report of the Ministerial Group on Women's Offending*. Edinburgh: Scottish Executive.

Scottish Executive (2004) *Analysis of Ethnicity in the 2001 Census: Summary Report*. Edinburgh: Office of the Chief Statistician.

Scottish Executive (2006) *Criminal Justice Social Work Statistics 2004–5*. Edinburgh: Scottish Executive.

Scottish Office (1998) *Women Offenders – A Safer Way: A Review of Community Disposals and the Use of Custody for Women in Scotland*. Edinburgh: Scottish Office.

Scourfield, J. (1998) 'Probation officers working with men', *British Journal of Social Work*, 28: 581–99.

Scourfield, J. and Dobash, R. (1999) 'Programmes for violent men: recent developments in the UK', *Howard Journal*, 38 (2): 128–43.

Sen, A. (1992) *Inequality Re-examined*. Oxford: Clarendon Press.

Shallice, A. and Gordon, P. (1990) *Black People, White Justice? Race and the Criminal Justice System*. London: Runnymede Trust.

Shaw, M. (1994) 'Women in prison: a literature review', *Forum on Corrections*, 6 (1) (Canadian Department of Corrections).

Shaw, M. and Hannah-Moffatt, K. (2000) 'Gender, diversity and risk assessment in Canadian corrections', *Probation Journal*, 47 (3): 163–72.

Shaw, M. and Hannah-Moffatt, K. (2004) 'How cognitive skills forgot about gender and diversity', in G. Mair (ed.), *What Matters in Probation*. Cullompton: Willan.

Shute, S., Hood, R. and Seemungle, F. (2005) *A Fair Hearing? Ethnic Minorities in the Criminal Courts*. Cullompton: Willan.

Silver, E. and Miller, L. L. (2002) 'A cautionary note on the use of actuarial risk assessment tools for social control', *Crime and Delinquency*, 48 (1): 136–61.

Singleton, N., Meltzer, H., Gatward, R., Coid, J. and Deasy, D. (1998) *Psychiatric Morbidity among Prisoners: Summary Report*. London: Government Statistical Service.

Smiljanic, N. (2002) 'Human rights and Muslims in Britain', in B. Spalek (ed.), *Islam, Crime and Criminal Justice*. Cullompton: Willan.

Smith, D. (1997) 'Ethnic origins, crime and criminal justice', in M. Maguire, R. Morgan and R. Reiner (eds), *Oxford Handbook of Criminology*, 2nd edn. Oxford: Oxford University Press.

Social Exclusion Unit (2004) *Mental Health and Social Exclusion*, Social Exclusion Unit Report. London: Office of the Deputy Prime Minister.

Stephen, J. (1993) *The Misrepresentation of Women Offenders*, Social Work Monograph No. 118. Norwich: University of East Anglia.

Stewart, J., Smith, D. and Stewart, G. (1994) *Understanding Offending Behaviour*. Harlow: Longman.

Thompson, N. (2001) *Anti-Discriminatory Practice*. Basingstoke: Palgrave.

Thompson, N. (2003) *Promoting Equality. Challenging Discrimination and Oppression*. Basingstoke: Palgrave/Macmillan.

Tyler, T. (1990) *Why People Obey the Law*. New Haven, CT: Yale University Press.

Tyler, T. and Huo, Y. T. (2002) *Trust in the Law: Encouraging Public Co-operation with the Police and Courts*. New York: Russell Sage Foundation.

Wahidin, A. (2004) *Older Women in the Criminal Justice System: Running Out of Time*. London: Jessica Kingsley.

Walmsley, R. K. and Stephens, K. (2006) 'What works with black and minority ethnic offenders: solution in search of a problem', in S. Lewis, P. Raynor, D. Smith and A. Wardak (eds), *Race and Probation*. Cullompton: Willan.

Weller, P., Feldman, A. and Purdam, K. (2001) *Religious Discrimination in England and Wales*, Home Office Research Study No. 220. London: Home Office Research, Development and Statistics Directorate.

Whitehead, A. (1995) *Men and Offending: 1A3 Programme Manual*. Sheffield: South Yorkshire Probation Service.

Whitehead, A. (2005) 'Man to man violence: how masculinity may work as a dynamic risk factor', *Howard Journal*, 44 (4): 411–22.

Whitehouse, P. (1983) 'Race, bias and social inquiry reports', *Probation Journal*, 30 (2): 43–9.

Williams, P. (2006) 'Designing and delivering programmes for minority ethnic offenders', in S. Lewis, P. Raynor, D. Smith and A. Wardak (eds), *Race and Probation*. Cullompton: Willan.

Wisconsin Corrections Division, Planning, Development and Research Bureau (1972) *1971 Probation and Parole Terminations*. Madison, WI: Wisconsin Corrections Division.

Women's Offending Reduction Programme (2004–5) *Annual Review*. Available at: http://www.homeoffice.gov.uk/documents/worp-annual-review-0405?view=Binary

Woods, P. (2005) 'Diversion from custody', in B. Littlechild and D. Fearns (eds), *Mental Disorder and Criminal Justice. Policy, Provision and Practice*. Lyme Regis: Russell House.

Worrall, A. (1990) *Offending Women: Female Lawbreakers and the Criminal Justice System*. London: Routledge.

Worrall, A. (1995) 'Gender, criminal justice and probation', in G. McIvor (ed.), *Working With Offenders: Research Highlights in Social Work 26*. London: Jessica Kingsley.

Youth Justice Board (2005) mental health needs and provision. London: Youth Justice Board.

Zaplin, R. (1998) *Female Offenders: Critical Perspectives and Effective Interventions*. Gaithersberg, MD: Aspen.

Chapter 12

Prolific/persistent offenders and desistance

Stephen Farrall, Rob C. Mawby and Anne Worrall[1]

Introduction

Our approach to this chapter will be one that sets projects for prolific or persistent adult offenders within the theoretical framework of recent literature on desistance. Our overarching argument will be that such projects, which combine intensive supervision with intensive surveillance, have so far focused solely on achieving 'crime reduction' through *either* rehabilitation *or* incapacitation/deterrence. Because of constraints of time and political pressure, existing evaluations have tended to reduce the complexities of the process whereby offenders stop committing crimes to simplistic measures of recidivism rates and the division of programme participants into 'successes' and 'failures'. (It will be noted that imprisoning a participant is not necessarily seen as a 'failure' for these projects, though it presumably has to be seen as a 'failure' for the participants.) In this chapter, we plan to explore the impact of such projects on participants using previously unpublished interview material and to set those experiences within a theoretical context. In particular, we want to explore the distinction between 'primary desistance' and 'secondary desistance' as discussed by Maruna and Farrall (2004). This distinction defines 'primary' desistance as 'any lull or crime-free gap', whereas 'secondary' desistance involves 'the assumption of a role or identity of a non-offender' – becoming a 'changed person'. Our tentative hypothesis is that prolific/persistent projects at their best buttress 'primary' desistance and prepare an offender for 'secondary' desistance, but that the latter will only occur when other personal, social and economic factors are favourable (see also Farrall 2002).

In this chapter we aim to do four things. First, we will provide a description of the development, organisation and existing evaluation research relating to current projects for adult prolific/persistent offenders. Next, we will explore the relationship between these projects and the literature on desistance, giving particular attention to issues of employment, personal relationships and motivation. We then discuss an emerging issue that requires further research and debate, namely the importance of place in efforts to desist (i.e. the locations that offenders inhabit and in which projects operate). Central to these issues is the challenge of managing a 'spoiled identity' as individuals track a 'zig-zag path of desistance' (Burnett 2004: 176; see also Piquero 2004). Finally, we consider the extent to which the principles underlying prolific/ persistent offender projects are compatible not only with those of desistance but also with those of the National Offender Management Service (NOMS).

Before proceeding further with the discussion, we need to acknowledge that the analysis that follows applies only, in our view, to prolific/persistent *male* offenders. There exist very few studies that might be termed specifically 'desistance' studies on women and there are very few women accommodated within prolific/persistent offender projects (Homes *et al.* 2005: 29–30). Women's criminal careers are, on average, much shorter than men's and their rates of reoffending, *regardless of sentence*, are traditionally lower – though the difference is now far less in relation to imprisonment (Carlen and Worrall 2004). Existing studies of young people (Graham and Bowling 1995; Jamieson *et al.* 1999) suggest that young women 'grow out of crime' earlier than young men. Nevertheless, without further extensive discussion, we remain somewhat uneasy about the significance of the term 'desistance' for women offenders (see also McIvor *et al.* 2004) and have excluded them from this chapter.

Intensive supervision and monitoring for prolific/persistent offenders

A recent joint inspectorates' report noted that, however defined, the 'habitual, persistent, prolific, recidivist or repeat offender' commits a disproportionate amount of all crime (Criminal Justice Chief Inspectors' Group 2004: 7). Indeed, Home Office research suggests that approximately 100,000 people (10 per cent of all offenders) are committing half of all crime in England and Wales at any point in time and a mere 5,000 people commit around 9 per cent of all crimes (Home Office 2003, 2004a).[2] Perhaps unsurprisingly, therefore, Labour governments since 1997 have shown a particular interest in targeting this 'hard to reach' group. Although intensive initiatives for persistent offenders are far from new, recent policy and legislative developments have led to a distinctive breed of intensive supervision and monitoring project, whose development and characteristics we have discussed elsewhere (Worrall *et al.* 2003; Mawby and Worrall 2004; Worrall and Mawby 2004; see also Criminal Justice Chief Inspectors' Group 2004 and Homes *et al.* 2005 for analyses of the 15 pilot 'Intensive Supervision and Monitoring' projects (ISMs) funded by the Government in 2002). Table 12.1 provides an overview of recent developments in the provision of projects for prolific and persistent offenders.

Overarching these projects that emerged in different locations to reflect local priorities and funded on a short-term basis by a wide variety of sources, the Government introduced in October 2002 the Persistent Offender Scheme (POS) as part of its Narrowing the Justice Gap programme. The POS focused on 'core persistent offenders', defined as those over 18 years old and convicted of six or more recordable offences in the last 12 months (Criminal Justice Chief Inspectors' Group 2004: 3). As the already existing prolific offender

Table 12.1 An overview of prolific/persistent offender schemes

Time period	Scheme	Target group	Funding	Evaluation
Post 1995	Mainly small-scale prolific offender projects (POPs) established to reflect local needs and priorities. Often inspired by the Dordrecht project.[3] Typically comprise a joint police-probation team working closely with offenders and coordinating their engagement with a range of other agencies. Examples include the Burnley/Dordrecht Initiative (Chenery and Pease 2000), the Hartlepool Dordrecht Initiative (Abbas et al. 2003), the Newcastle Initiative (Hope et al. 2001), the Stoke POP (Worrall et al. 2003) and the Bristol Prolific Offender Scheme (Vennard and Pearce 2004).	Locally defined prolific offenders, typically selected by crime type (acquisitive), volume and local intelligence.	Generally short term through either local sources, e.g. through CDRPs, police forces, or through regionally/nationally administrated funds, e.g. Safer Cities, SRB, the Crime Reduction Programme, the Neighbourhood Renewal Fund	Positive evaluations in terms of partnership working and short-term influence on offenders, but less conclusive in respect of cost-effectiveness and impact on overall crime reduction.
2002–	The Home Office funded 15 Intensive Supervision and Monitoring Projects (ISMs), incorporating some of the already existing prolific offender projects together with newly established ones. ISMs became a subsection of the POS (see below).	Defined by the Home Office as 'aged 18 or over with six or more offences in the last 12 months of liberty and OGRS scores of over 75'. The OGRS criterion was soon dropped and targeting was allowed by identifying local persistent offenders through police intelligence (Homes et al. 2005: 10).	Central (Home Office) short-term funding	The National Probation Directorate commissioned the Home Office RDS to undertake a process and outcome evaluation. One report has resulted, detailing similar findings to those above (Homes et al. 2005).

October 2002–September 2004	The Persistent Offender Scheme. This required all 43 police force areas in England and Wales to implement a scheme to identify and target adult persistent offenders.	'Core' persistent offenders, identified as those over 18 years old and convicted of six or more recordable offences in the previous 12 months.	Although centrally imposed, no additional central funding. Resourced through existing budgets of involved agencies.	No published overarching evaluation undertaken.
September 2004–	The Prolific and other Priority Offender Strategy. This replaced the POS. Each CDRP is required to implement the PPO strategy and it is included in the national business plans of the core agencies – the police, probation and prison services.	Local areas select offenders taking into account: (1) the nature and volume of their crimes; (2) the nature of the harm they cause; and (3) other local criteria influencing their impact on the community.	As POS	A Home Office PPO evaluation team issued a 'promising' preliminary report in October 2005 (Dawson 2005); the final report was due in late 2006.

projects, including ISMs, predated the POS, their absorption within it was not unproblematic. For example, some were working to different criteria in their definitions of 'prolific/persistent' which had implications for eligibility for inclusion. This led to some projects having to adapt their criteria to ensure compliance with the POS (Criminal Justice Chief Inspectors' Group 2004: 10).

In December 2003, Patrick Carter's review of correctional services in England and Wales was published, entitled *Managing Offenders, Reducing Crime: A New Approach* (Carter 2003). The Carter Report recommended targeted and rigorous sentences, specifying for 'persistent' offenders not only greater control and surveillance, but also help to reduce their offending. The Labour administration's enthusiastic response to the report suggested that intensive projects for prolific/persistent offenders were likely to maintain their high profile (Blunkett 2004). This was confirmed through the introduction of the Prolific and other Priority Offender Strategy (PPO) which replaced the Persistent Offender Scheme from September 2004. The PPO strategy has three strands: (1) Prevent and Deter; (2) Catch and Convict; and (3) Rehabilitate and Resettle (see Table 12.2). Under this strategy, intensive supervision and monitoring projects form part of the third strand, which focuses on 'working with identified prolific offenders to stop their offending by offering a range of supportive interventions. Offenders will be offered the opportunity for rehabilitation or face a very swift return to the courts' (source: http://www.crime-reduction.gov.uk/ppo (accessed 16 December 2005)).

The PPO strategy is led by Crime and Disorder Reduction Partnerships (CDRPs), with each CDRP in the country being responsible for implementing schemes at police basic command unit (BCU) level to address prolific offending. Recognising the challenges of facilitating multi-agency involvement, policy-makers determined that the framework for delivery of the strategy should be agreed by Local Criminal Justice Boards (LCJBs). By placing this authority in the LCJBs and responsibility for delivery in the CDRPs, the intention was to 'relieve' the burden of responsibility on the police and to provide the clout to 'encourage' the participation of a range of sometimes reluctant agencies. With regard to the targets of the strategy, local areas are guided to 'identify those individuals who are the most *prolific* offenders, the most *persistently anti-social* in their behaviour and those who pose the *greatest threat to the safety and*

Table 12.2 The three strands of the PPO strategy

1. Prevent and Deter	2. Catch and Convict	3. Rehabilitate and Resettle
Stopping people (overwhelmingly young people) from becoming prolific offenders	Catching and convicting those who are already prolific offenders	Offering real alternatives to those serving sentences – whether custodial or in the community – who are otherwise likely to resume their career as prolific offenders

Source: http://www.crimereduction.gov.uk/

confidence of their local communities' (source: http://www.crime-reduction. gov.uk/ppo (accessed 16 December 2005; original emphasis)). The criteria provided for identifying these individuals are: (1) the nature and volume of the crimes committed; (2) the nature and volume of other harm caused; and (3) other local criteria based on the impact of the individuals concerned on their local communities.

In terms of the numbers of prolific and other priority offenders to be targeted and managed, and remembering the Government's frequent references to a hard core of 5,000 prolific offenders that commit around one million crimes per year, JTrack[4] data recorded in November 2004 that there were 9,082 prolific and other priority offenders (PPOs) on programmes across England and Wales; by October 2005, this figure had increased to 10,597 (Home Office 2005).

At this point, it is worth briefly considering the question of definition. *Prolific* and *persistent* have been defined variously – as illustrated through the cases of the POS and PPO strategies. The recent joint Inspectorates' report accepted the official POS *persistent* definition, confirmed that there was no common agreement on the definition of a *prolific* offender and used the term to describe 'offenders prioritised or identified as requiring intensive or special treatment due to their offending patterns' (Criminal Justice Chief Inspectors' Group 2004: 11). Guidance on the transition of the POS into the PPO strategy acknowledged that different areas were using terms such as 'local persistent offender', 'priority offender' and 'prolific offender' to describe offenders who were likely to be included within the new strategy. Accordingly the PPO strategy allowed a flexible approach to defining prolific offenders to reflect local circumstances and requested that the new target group should be referred to as 'identified prolific and priority offenders' (Home Office 2004b: 2). Therefore, a *prolific* offender may be so defined on the basis of local intelligence. Although this chapter is concerned primarily with adult offenders, for completeness, a *persistent young offender* is a young person aged ten to 17 years inclusive who has been sentenced by any criminal court in the UK on three or more separate occasions for one or more recordable offences, and within three years of the last sentencing occasion is subsequently arrested or has information laid against him [sic] for a further recordable offence. All these definitions are contested and run the risk of net-widening (see Hagell and Newburn 1994; Soothill *et al*. 2003: 391–3).

With the advent of the POS and PPO strategies prolific/persistent offender projects in England and Wales are proliferating and they operate in a policy-driven context. Nevertheless, they represent a sophisticated amalgam of the theoretical underpinnings, policy objectives and multi-agency practices of previous generations of intensive supervision. They combine penal philosophies of deterrence, incapacitation and rehabilitation and seek to provide a mix of frequent contact, access to treatment (particularly drugs treatment) and community facilities, and constant monitoring. They also seek to demonstrate cost-effectiveness and increased public safety. While prolific offender projects for adult offenders were originally concerned with the reduction of volume property crime, predominantly theft and burglary, more recently projects have accepted offenders with some form of violence in their records.

The central feature of these projects has been the combination of intensive and combined attention from both the police and probation services. The other characteristics of the projects derive from this central feature. First, the project is staffed by designated police and probation personnel, and located in either police or probation premises. Secondly, participants in the project are required to meet local criteria that categorise them as 'prolific' – that is, among the most persistent offenders in the locality. Thirdly, they are subject to formal court orders of supervision or post-custodial licence. Fourthly, participants are subject to high levels of police monitoring and programmes of intensive probation supervision which seek to address their offending behaviour and other needs such as housing, substance misuse, leisure, education and employment. Fifthly, in order to achieve this, there has to be an agreed mechanism of information exchange between all participating agencies. Finally, there is an agreed procedure for swift enforcement in the event of non-compliance or further offending. (For fuller descriptions and analyses of the projects' characteristics, see Worrall *et al.* 2003; Mawby and Worrall 2004; Worrall and Mawby 2004; Homes *et al.* 2005.)

It is interesting, given the current commitment to addressing prolific/persistent offending, that the body of evaluation research on projects for prolific offenders is neither large nor conclusive. However, the number of studies is increasing, comprising a mixture of independent evaluations by academics, often on a limited budget (Chenery and Pease 2000; Hope *et al.* 2001; Tupman *et al.* 2001; Abbas *et al.* 2003; Worrall *et al.* 2003; Vennard and Pearce 2004) and the larger scale ISM evaluation undertaken by Home Office researchers (Homes *et al.* 2005). Evaluators have typically had to work with small sample sizes and, in some cases, without a matched comparison group. The resulting reports and their conclusions tend to be highly qualified in relation to reduced offending and cost-effectiveness. Nevertheless, many of the evaluations emerging in the UK have provided optimism that prolific offender projects can be effective in reducing the offending of the participant group (see, for example, Worrall *et al.* 2003; Vennard and Pearce 2004: 88). Most recently Homes *et al.* (2005: 36) reported from their study of 15 ISMs that their analysis indicated that for 192 offenders examined, ISM projects 'were associated with a reduction in offence rate'. Evaluations in the United States have been similarly tentative in their findings. Homes *et al.* in their brief review of the US literature note that Gendreau *et al.*'s (2001) meta-analysis of 'Intensive Supervision Programming' projects concluded that they had little effect on participants' future offending behaviour. (For a summary of the British and US evaluation literature see Homes *et al.* 2005: 3–4.)

However, prolific offender projects are complex in terms of their multi-agency nature and the needs of their clientele. Their value should be judged beyond crime rates and cost-effectiveness, though these are of course important. Other criteria which should be taken into account include, on the one hand, health, educational and social benefits for participants and, on the other hand, improved multi-agency working and information exchange between project partners and improved intelligence on prolific offenders. Projects working intensively with prolific offenders might be best regarded as being of a maintenance nature – of buttressing primary desistance – rather than a short sharp intervention that acts as a cure-all. Accordingly they should be assessed primarily on how well they maintain and motivate participants during the 'on project' period. The extent to which projects contribute to secondary desistance is a different but related issue and projects also need to be judged on how they affect participants over time – which might involve several relapses and returns to the project.

Persistence and desistance[5]

The topic of why people stop offending (or desist) has, of late, received sustained interest from criminologists. This was not always the case, however, and the work on desistance has grown in both stature and volume since the 1960s. Prior to this, the research into desistance was often small-scale, somewhat patchy and often conducted solely in the USA.

Research by criminologists such as Sheldon and Eleanor Glueck, Alfred Blumstein, Marvin Wolfgang and Thorsten Sellin in the USA and David Farrington in the UK has suggested that whether or not an individual participates in offending is closely associated with their age and a number of social and psychological variables. For example, Farrington (1992: 129) listed some of the variables found to be most strongly related to offending in the Cambridge Study in Delinquent Development – a follow-up study of over 400 boys originally living in London. Included were 'problematic' behaviours between age 8 and 14 years old (e.g. bullying and aggressiveness), teenage anti-social behaviours (e.g. heavy alcohol and tobacco use and gambling), impulsiveness, school problems (e.g. low school attainment and frequent truancy), family factors (e.g. poor relationship with parents), anti-social factors (e.g. convictions of other family members and friends) and socio-economic factors (low family income, poor housing and poor employment record). Several of these influences have also been found by other researchers to be associated with the onset of offending behaviours (see, for example, Graham and Bowling 1995: 33–43; Wolfgang *et al.* 1972; Sampson and Laub 1993; Elliott and Menard 1996). The data employed in studies of this nature have usually been derived from repeated interviews with members of cohorts, often followed from school age to adulthood. During these interviews, self-reported data on offending and various other topics have been collected from the cohort members. As noted, these data are often supplemented by official records and further interviews with partners, peers and teachers in order to gain these perspectives as well as to validate responses.[6]

A number of researchers have focused their attention specifically upon the later stages of offending careers, and in particular on the factors conducive to desistance from offending. Drawing on the insights of earlier work on criminal careers, they have pointed to a number of correlates of desistance. The literature on desistance is commonly based on criminal career data sets (e.g. Knight and West 1975; Loeber *et al.* 1991; Sampson and Laub 1993), or on one-off retrospective research (e.g. Shover 1983; Cusson and Pinsonneault 1986; Graham and Bowling 1995). In a few cases (e.g. Leibrich 1993; Burnett 1992) data have been collected by following the careers of persons after they have been made subject to criminal justice interventions. The research undertaken so far has shed light on the role of social and personal factors in desistance (see Adams 1997; Farrall 2000; Laub and Sampson 2001, and Farrall and Calverley 2006, for outlines of this body of work).

'Primary' and 'secondary' desistance[7]

Defining and operationalising desistance, like defining and operationalising many topics in social science, is not straightforward. The working definition most commonly used runs something like 'the voluntary termination of serious criminal participation' (Shover 1996: 121). The problem, of course, lies in defining something for measurement that is detectable only by its *continued absence*. This peculiarity has already been noted by Maruna (1998: 10–11) who likens these problems to what he describes as 'billiard-ball causality': 'Desistance is an unusual dependent variable for criminologists because it is *not an event that happens*, but rather the sustained absence of a certain type of event occurring. As such, desistance does not fit neatly into the linear, billiard-ball models of causality found most acceptable to criminologists' (emphasis added).

Maruna has not been alone in his recognition that desistance is not usually 'an event' but more akin to a 'process'. Chief among the theorists of desistance are Robert Sampson and John Laub, who provided convincing evidence that desistance was not abrupt but rather a 'gradual movement away from criminal offending' (Laub *et al.* 1998: 226). Laub and Sampson (2001: 11) went on to distinguish between what they call 'termination' (the outcome) and 'desistance' (the process) in their important review of work in this field. They wrote: 'Termination is the time at which criminal activity stops. Desistance ... is the causal process that supports the termination of offending'. Desistance, according to this approach, is the process that 'maintains the continued state of non-offending' (p. 11) beginning prior to termination but carrying on long after.

Maruna and Farrall (2004) suggest that this adds new confusion by conflating the causes of desistance with desistance itself. They note that the verb 'to desist' means to abstain from doing something. Likewise, in criminology, desistance is almost always used to mean 'the continued state of non-offending' rather than factors that lead to it. They propose, therefore, to return to 1940s criminology in order to redefine the issues at hand. Drawing on the work of Edwin Lemert (1948: 27), who introduced into the debates on the origins of deviance the terms 'primary' and 'secondary' deviation, they refer to 'primary' and 'secondary' desistance. Lemert wrote that 'Primary deviation involved the initial flirtation and experimentation with deviant behaviors'. Secondary deviation, on the other hand, is deviance that becomes 'incorporated as part of the "me" of the individual' (Lemert 1951: 76).

Primary desistance, Maruna and Farrall argue, represents desistance at its most basic and literal level: any lull or crime-free gap (see West 1982) in the course of a criminal career. Because we are interested – at both the theoretical levels and in terms of practice – most with desistance that results in the *total ending* of the criminal career, the focus of desistance research would be on secondary desistance. In other words, with the movement from the behaviour of non-offending to the assumption of a role or identity of a non-offender or 'changed person'. In secondary desistance, crime not only stops, but 'existing roles become disrupted' and a 'reorganization based upon a new role or roles will occur' (Lemert 1951: 76). Indeed, recent research (Giordano *et al.* 2002; Maruna 2001; Shover 1996) provides compelling evidence that long-term desistance does involve identifiable and measurable changes at the level of personal identity or 'the "me" of the individual' (Lemert 1951: 76).

This suggestion does not solve all of the problems with defining and operationalising desistance. However, this approach offers a new direction for work in this field. Maruna and Farrall suggest that 'Primary desistance, like primary deviation, could be expected to occur only sporadically, for short periods – a week here, two months there. Secondary desistance, on the other hand, involves a more sustained pattern of demonstrable conformity – a measurable, reflective and more self-conscious break with previous patterns of offending'. This definition of desistance might, however, get at the lived experience of desistance, which, as Maruna and Farrall note, is consistent with the colloquial understanding of desistance among ex-offenders. While ex-offenders do not describe themselves as 'desisting', they do talk about 'going straight', 'doing good' or 'going legit' (Irwin 1970). These phrases imply an ongoing work in progress. One goes legit. One does not talk about having turned legit or having become legit. The 'going' is the thing. As such, desistance is 'no end state where one can be; rather, it is a perpetual process of arrival' (Foote and Frank 1999: 179).

The factors associated with desistance[8]

A number of researchers (e.g. Uggen and Kruttschnitt 1998: 356) have provided evidence that desistance is associated with gaining employment, although the precise causal links between engaging in legitimate employment and desistance from offending have yet to be satisfactorily established. Mischkowitz (1994: 313) reported that 'erratic work patterns were substituted by more stable and reliable behaviour' among his sample of desisters. Meisenhelder (1977) noted that the acquisition of a good job provided the men in his sample with important social and economic resources, whilst Shover (1983: 214) reported how a job generated '... a pattern of routine activities – a daily agenda – which conflicted with and left little time for the daily activities associated with crime'.

Similar sentiments were expressed by Sampson and Laub (1993: 220–2) when they wrote that desisters were characterised as having '... good work habits and were frequently described as "hard workers"'. Farrington *et al.* (1986: 351) reporting on the Cambridge Study in Delinquent Development, wrote that 'proportionally more crimes were committed by ... youths during periods of unemployment than during periods of employment', a finding supported by the later work of Horney *et al.* (1995). However, as researchers such as Ditton (1977) and Henry (1978) have shown, full time employment does not preclude either the opportunities to offend nor actual offending. Graham and Bowling (1995: 56, table 5.2) found that for young males employment was not related to desistance, as did Rand (1987) when she investigated the impact of vocational training on criminal careers.

Getting a job was an often-voiced aspiration of the participants on the Stoke-on-Trent prolific offender project,[9] both as a means of earning money and also as a route into 'normal' society. One participant spoke of his long-term aim to run a sports gym, another talked about an opportunity to run a burger van. The project did help to prepare participants for work, e.g. through liaison with the Work Education Centre (WEC), but they faced several hurdles to overcome. The WEC worker commented that she had found the prolific offenders a difficult group – frequently they had little record of employment and they were often drug users. They had an image of the jobs they wanted. These were traditionally 'masculine' jobs – on building sites or driving and delivery jobs. They were reluctant to consider, for example, catering assistant jobs as they perceived these to be 'feminine'. Nevertheless, she had seen them progress towards being 'work ready', evidenced by improving their communication and social skills and adhering to a structure by turning up for appointments and conducting effective sessions. In addition, some participants found work. One obtained employment at a post office sorting office, but he was soon dismissed when his criminal record came to light. Another secured a job first in a factory and later in the building trade.

At the same time, however, some participants saw the project as a barrier to working. The project doctor frequently instructed participants not to seek work until they had stabilised their drugs use. He warned that if they applied for jobs, he would contact prospective employers and advise them against engaging the participants. (In doing this the doctor emphasised that he was acting in the interests both of the participants and also of public protection.)[10] The regime of intensive supervision was also seen as encroaching upon and invading the 'straight' world of work that the participants were trying to break into:

> Keeping the appointments with working was difficult. I was working in [a town thirty miles away] and didn't know what time I'd finish – and they don't like it, started bringing daft rules out like [the project's police officer] got to come out on site once a week and see that I'm still there – a wage slip wasn't good enough. Pathetic – they knew I was working but wanted to know where I was. I finished my job because of this course, because I was sick of all the rules. As well the doctor said my employer must be told if I was going on subutex – well I didn't want my employer to know I was on probation or anything like that cos I might have lost my job, so I've lost my job – I gave up the job because of this course – and I loved it. My main target was to get a job, that keeps me out of trouble – as soon as I got a job they weren't happy because they kept on bringing things up concerning contact with my employer. (Matt)

This participant was entrepreneurial and atypical in that he was adept at spotting job opportunities and taking them, even if the jobs were short lived and outside the tax system. The tension he expressed was recognised by the project team. One team member commented that if they had been probation officers in the field, they would just be happy that the offenders were working. In contrast, with their greater involvement in supervising and monitoring, they knew that offenders were not declaring their convictions, were working 'cash in hand' and still claiming benefits. Both probation and police officers faced the dilemma of whether to turn a blind eye as getting a job was a step towards respectability that gave the participants a sense of pride, kept them out of trouble and in money, or alternatively to tell them to work only on a legal basis. There was also the practical problem that if participants' benefits stopped as a result of getting a job, there was often a delay between finishing a short-lived job and resuming benefit payments. These funding gaps could be filled potentially through crime.

There was another unintended consequence for one participant who found work. His ability to obtain jobs and earn money increased his financial means. He then increased his drugs purchasing and intake, which in turn made him an unreliable employee, leading to dismissal, which led him back to offending to fund the level of drugs use he had built up to. In this cycle, paid work supported short-term primary desistance from crime, but fuelled drug use, leading to relapse and reoffending.

Another of the most common findings in the literature on desistance is that individuals cease to offend at about the same time that they start to form significant life partnerships (e.g. Farrall 2002). One of the clearest statements in support of this line of reasoning came from Shover (1983: 213), who wrote that 'The establishment of a mutually satisfying relationship with a woman was a common pattern ... [and] ... an important factor in the transformation of their career line'. Cusson and Pinsonneault (1986: 79–80) and Mischkowitz (1994: 319) followed West (1982: 101–4) in arguing that what was important (in terms of facilitating desistance) was not marriage *per se*, but rather the *quality* of the relationship and the offending career of the person whom the would-be desister married. The recent work of Laub *et al.* (1998) supports this contention – as marriages became stronger amongst the men in their sample, so these men's offending began to be curtailed. A number of studies have suggested that the experience of becoming a parent is also associated with desistance from offending (see, for example, Trasler 1979: 315; Irwin 1970: 203; Sampson and Laub 1993: 218; Caddle 1991: 37; Leibrich 1993: 59; Jamieson *et al.* 1999: 130, Uggen and Kruttschnitt 1998: 355; Hughes 1997 and 1998: 146; and Parker 1976: 41).

The Stoke prolific offender project's intention was to work not only with the participants, but also their families. Partners and parents were engaged by the project personnel. They were included in project activities and consulted concerning participants' progress and plans. Participants frequently mentioned their intention to improve their close relationships and cited the project as assisting them to do this:

It's helped me to rebuild relationships up with my daughter and my family which I didn't have before. They [the project team] come and they sit and they talk with me mum and they tell her what's going on and that reassures her and helps her and its better that way for me –

she understands what's going on now whereas before she didn't.
(Tom)

While relationships were an important part of supporting participants (see
also Farrall 2004), it was also clear that for a number of participants whose
relationships were volatile or strained, their partners were perceived by
project personnel as part of the problem. In such cases, they would try
and work with the partner, but there was no compulsion for the partner to
cooperate.

Despite the evidence suggesting that forming a life partnership may result
in desistance, some researchers have questioned this rather simple cause-and-
effect model.[11] Rand (1987: 137) tested the hypothesis that '... young men who
marry are less criminal than those who never marry' and found no support
for this in her data. Knight et al. (1977: 359) found no significant differences
(in terms of the number of subsequent convictions) between the married and
unmarried groups from the Cambridge Study in Delinquent Development.
Similarly, Mulvey and Aber (1988) reported finding no connection between
partnership and desistance, nor were they able to find any firm link between
parenthood and desistance. Rand (1987: 143) also found no support for the
idea that men who became fathers were less criminal than those who did
not.

However, at least some of these negative findings can be reassessed
following the findings of Uggen (2000) and Ouimet and Le Blanc (1996),
which suggest that the impact of various life events upon an individual's
offending is age-graded. For example, Ouimet and Le Blanc (1996: 92) suggest
that it is only from around the mid-20s that cohabitation with a woman was
associated with desistance for the males in their sample. In a similar vein,
Uggen (2000: 542) suggests that work appears to be a turning point in the
criminal careers of those offenders aged over 26, while it has a marginal
effect on the offending of younger offenders. When findings like these are
taken into consideration, the importance of structuring the enquiry by age is
made apparent. However, many of the earlier studies concerning the factors
associated with desistance were unaware of this caveat and as such their
findings that there was no impact of employment or partnership on desistance
must be treated accordingly.[12]

Various other factors have been identified which appear to be related
to desistance. Among members of the Cambridge Study in Delinquent
Development cohort, Osborn (1980) found that leaving London (where they
had grown up) was associated with reductions in subsequent offending
(both self-reported and official). Similar findings using alternative data sets
have been made by Sampson and Laub (1993: 217) and Jamieson et al. (1999:
133). The break-up of the peer group has been another and more commonly
cited factor. Knight and West (1975: 49) and Cromwell et al. (1991: 83) both
referred to cases in which peer group disintegration was related to subsequent
desistance (as did Warr 1998). Experiencing a shift in identity (Shover 1983:
210; Meisenhelder 1982; Maruna 1997 and 2000; Burnett 1992) and feeling
shame at one's past behaviours (Leibrich 1993: 204 and 1996) have also been
posited as processes associated with desistance.

An individual's motivation to avoid further offending is another key factor in accounting for desistance. Shover (1983), Shover and Thompson (1992), West (1978), Pezzin (1995), Moffitt (1993), Sommers *et al.* (1994) and Farrall (2002) have all pointed to a range of factors which motivated the desisters in their samples. Burnett (1992: 66 and 1994: 55–6) has suggested that those ex-prisoners who reported that they wanted to stop offending and, importantly, felt they were able to stop offending, were more likely to desist than those who said they were unsure if they wanted to stop offending. Participants in the Stoke prolific offender project illustrate the point:

> If you want to stay out of trouble, you can't fault the project, they'll give you any help you need. But you've got to want to stay out, to stop, yourself. (John)

John also vividly captured his lack of motivation when on the project for a second time:

> Nothing had changed from them [the project team], it was me, I just couldn't live on the money I was getting. There was the same number of appointments, they took us down the gym and I fucked that up ... I was just ... I don't think I had any intention ... I just couldn't live on what I was doing, so I knew I was going to go off ... I had to go to a [project] meeting or whatever and I knew as soon as I left there I was going out robbing, so I had no motivation to stay out, it was like I didn't give a fuck about anything, and that's through me not them. Nothing changed in the project […] the project couldn't have done anything more to stop me cos I didn't want to stop at the time.

Others have pointed to the influence of the criminal justice system on those repeatedly incarcerated. Cusson and Pinsonneault (1986), employing data drawn from in-depth interviews with ex-robbers, identified the following as influential factors in desisting: shock (such as being wounded in a bank raid); growing tired of doing time in prison; becoming aware of the possibility of longer prison terms and a reassessment of what was important to the individual. Similar findings have been made by other researchers. Leibrich (1993: 56–7), Shover (1983: 213) and Cromwell *et al.* (1991: 83) reported that desisters experienced a period of re-evaluation before coming to their decision to desist. Within a perspective heavily influenced by rational choice models, Shover and Thompson, wrote that '... the probability of desistance from criminal participation increases as expectations for achieving friends, money, autonomy and happiness via crime decrease' (1992: 97). Hughes' (1998) study of minority ethnic desisters living in the USA reported how fear of serious physical harm and/or death was cited by 16 of her 20 respondents. Similar fears were reported by those interviewed by Sommers *et al.* (1994) and Cusson and Pinsonneault (1986), and among Maruna's (1997) study of published autobiographies of desistance.

Work by Meisenhelder (1977: 323) and others (e.g. Shover 1983: 212; Hughes 1998: 147; Burnett 1992) has revealed that some of those repeatedly incarcerated say that they have become tired of prison and feel that they can no longer cope physically and emotionally with the experiences of prison life. In effect, some offenders reach a point in their lives when they can 'take no more' from the criminal justice system 'burn out' (Farrall 2002; Farrall and Calverley 2006).

Getting to grips with place[13]

Giddens (1984) puts great emphasis on the importance of places in the reproduction of social forms. Other commentators writing within the criminological arena have similarly noted how important specific places are in the production of criminal events generally (e.g. Sherman *et al.* and Reiss, quoted in Bottoms and Wiles 1992) and moreover as a central concept in structuration theory (Bottoms and Wiles 1992:19). Hagan's work (1997) suggested that there are certain meso-level social or community structures which influence individuals' desires, motivations and abilities to engage in, or refrain from, offending. A similar but often neglected dimension can be found in the work of Meisenhelder (1977), who refers to the spatial dimension of desistance. Not all 'places' (e.g. bars, snooker halls, railway stations, churches) are equal in terms of their ability to either facilitate or confirm a would-be desister's status as an 'ex-offender'. For example, some places (bars, gambling halls, snooker halls or certain street corners) have a negative effect, suggesting that an individual has not recanted their old ways and are still engaged in illegal or 'shady' activities. Other places are suggestive that an individual has made the break with crime, and these include churches, reputable employers, domestic family homes and other 'conventional' civic associations. Still other places may convey neither positive nor negative messages (for example, a large out-of-town supermarket or a railway station).[14]

The explanation given by the likes of Meisenhelder (1977 and 1982) and Goffman (1963) is that the places where an individual lives out his or her life communicates some element of 'who' they are and 'what' they do. Time spent in snooker halls or certain bars suggest a routine engagement with others who may themselves continue to be engaged in illegitimate endeavours. On the other hand, routinely spending time in stable employment, engaged in childcare duties, with other 'benevolent' bodies such as churches or civic groups, or engaged in some other 'constructive' use of one's leisure time can help to create (at least) the image of a reformed or reforming character. In this section we discuss how developing notions of place and what it means to the people who inhabit and act out their lives in these 'places' is of use in developing an understanding of desistance. As Bottoms and Wiles (1992) note, places are crucial in understanding patterns of offending, and in particular how places are important *generators* of actions and not merely *venues* in which actions are performed. This appeared to be true in the case of Niall (one of the ex-offenders followed up by Farrall and Calverley 2006), who described how he was now trusted by the authorities:

> My allotment's down there and they take their police cars down there
> to wash 'em through the car wash. Whenever I'm down there they'll

say, 'Oh, come on, Niall, let's have a look in your greenhouse then, what have you got growing?' 'cos, you know, they all know that I like a smoke [of cannabis]. And they all say 'Are you still at it then?' I'll say, 'Well I smoke, but I don't grow it any more.' 'All right then, can we have a look in your greenhouse?' Just having a laugh with me, you know, it's ... [Do they have a look in your greenhouse?] No. No, they don't, no. I always offer them some rhubarb. No, they wouldn't do. They just do it as a laugh 'cos I know them. Well I've known 'em for years, you know.

However, this was not always the case. Some of the Stoke prolific offenders felt 'branded' as 'career criminals' by the local police in the areas they lived in and resented being publicly shamed by the police near their homes, especially when they had committed themselves to an intensively supervised project. Luke, complained that he was repeatedly stopped, questioned and searched by local uniformed officers when he collected his daughter from primary school, in front of other children and their parents:

Just walking along the street made me paranoid [...] I kept getting stopped and harassed by the police in front of my daughter – wouldn't let me settle down and get on with life – got sick of it. (Luke)

Thus even his engagement in symbolic (if routine) activities associated with domesticity were negated by harassment – as he saw it – from the police. These participants, while trying to project themselves locally as reformed offenders, evidently felt that the location and their reputations would always prevent them rebuilding their spoiled characters.

The location of the Stoke project was also significant. The project was based in police premises, which impacted differently on the parties involved, not only the offenders but also the project staff. While the choice of a police station as the project base had some obvious advantages for team members, for example in terms of accessibility to police computer systems and for liaison with the police intelligence cell, it was, at least initially, a vaguely hostile setting in which to establish a project that was perceived as supporting 'public enemy number one' (see Mawby and Worrall 2004: 69; see also Homes *et al.* 2005: 10–12). The participants were divided on the police station base:

It's better here, it's central, it's as neutral as anywhere – it doesn't affect anyone coming here – it's no problem. (Peter)

However, some participants, with some justification, believed that they were being targeted as informers by other policing units, thereby setting up the possibility of conflict with others in their peer group. On the other hand, some felt the police station to be a safe meeting place and a secure project base, symbolically reinforcing its crime reduction objective.

In addition, the location of project activities was significant. Group activities were held at venues including the local YMCA, a local homelessness charity and a probation office. This did create situations where project members might come into contact with other offenders, such as drug testing and treatment order (DTTO) participants, and as an unintended consequence created a venue for the potential development of criminal networks:

> I came out clean, but it is tempting, back in the old area seeing the same people over and over, it's a vicious circle, but with the support of these it makes it easier to stay clean and not reoffend. (Tom)

Such ambivalence illustrates the problems identified by Clear's (2005: 182) argument that probation officers should be replacing 'caseloads' with 'placeloads', working increasingly in the locations inhabited by offenders. But, he asks of himself, 'who will watch the probationers to protect the community from them?' He then provides the 'simple answer … police should do it', thus leaving probation officers free to do what they are good at. Clear's analysis may appear at first sight to be unhelpful to the cause of prolific/ persistent offender schemes yet by highlighting the significance of place in the lives of offenders, he challenges the managerial trend towards increasing fragmentation and specialisation of provision.

Zig-zagging towards desistance?

In her study of desistance among convicted property offenders, Ros Burnett points to the ambivalence of offenders in their 'zig-zag' path towards desistance. She notes that 'behind the contrasting labels of "persister" and "desister", most property offenders are for a period in their criminal careers neither steadfastly one nor the other' (2004: 167). Similarly, Piquero (2004) discusses the 'intermittency' of many criminal careers, echoing the classic work of Matza (1964) on delinquency and 'drift'. This has implications for the existence, development and success measures for projects that work with prolific offenders.

At one level prolific offender projects have been branded as possible solutions to prolific offending through a win/win philosophy. On the one hand they will support the rehabilitation and resettlement of participants. If this succeeds the project records a success. On the other hand, if participants fail to respond to the support offered and/or return to offending then the project team will act swiftly to return them to prison and also judge this outcome as a success. As a recent Home Office report uncritically says, these projects are 'original in that reconviction and non-reconviction can both be counted as successful outcomes' (Homes *et al.* 2005: 2).

However, observation and interviews with the Stoke project practitioners and participants confirmed that the true situation is more complex and that projects provide support and enforcement, but principally fulfil a *maintenance* function while participants chart their 'zig-zag path of desistance' (Burnett 2004: 176) (see the case study of John below). Asked whether they had reoffended while on the project, those that were still participants (understandably) said they had not. Two participants were interviewed in prison and were more forthcoming. One commented:

There was that many things to do, meetings all the time. I had no time to go out robbing, I was still doing a bit, but it wasn't until I'd finished my licence that I actually got back in trouble again. (John)

The other confirmed that he reduced his offending:

… a hell of a lot. I don't normally last longer than three month, then I'm back in jail for two or three burglaries. I'm normally out every day committing burglaries. I'm glad they came and saw me, I think I did all right – the project's excellent. They do help you, you can talk to them, they'll come and see you. Look at my previous, I don't stay out long – this was the longest I've stayed out for ages. (Bob)

The project's police officer corroborated this:

Every offender is a success compared with where they would have been without the project. All have moved forward to some degree. For example, Bob was doing four–five burglaries per day, but while with TPI [the project] was doing one per month – he's back inside, but he's a massive success.

While the project's managers were aware of targets and performance and the need to secure extended funding, they too were aware of the importance of small gains for individuals. Interviewed towards the end of the evaluation, one of the probation managers was asked how such projects should be judged. She first mentioned the win/win scenario, but went on to say:

Look at the individuals – what impact has being on the project had on them, whether that individual is with the project for one month or twelve months? It is their most sustained period of being crime free, their most sustained period of being drug free, having structure to their day where previously there was none, a period where their main activity is not drugs or crime related.

Another probation manager commented:

The project is unusual in that offenders do come back. Most projects can't accommodate this. Some offenders need more interventions before they will desist. The Home Office want maximum throughput. My personal view is that prolific offenders take a lot of intervention to change. We're beginning to see the same with DTTOs, where a proportion succeed first time, but those who fail present the same need for continued intensive supervision. We've not convinced the Home Office of the wisdom that you must persist with these people to obtain the desired outcomes.

The maintenance view was also supported by the police manager:

I've no problem with people coming back. I'm more concerned with moving people on, we've not really sorted this out though we're aware of the 'drop-off' point post-order when offenders return to crime. You could put an argument forward for longer orders – all two years. If you can't rehabilitate these people, you may be able to maintain them. Increasing the maintenance can reduce their offending over a greater period of time.

These comments suggest the recognition through experience that intensive projects buttress primary desistance. The project doctor had interesting views on the place of these projects concerning working with prolific offenders with a range of issues and needs (beyond drug and alcohol misuse):

The key point and worry for me is 'Is the project a crutch in a crisis or a walking stick for life?' It can't be a walking stick, it must be the crutch, empowering people to be independent. I think it does that for those that go through it.

A case study of zig-zag desistance: John

John had been on the Stoke prolific offender project twice, prior to which he had not responded to community sentences or custodial penalties. At the time of first joining the project he was 32 years old and had been in and out of custody from the age of 14. Since 1982, he had amassed 116 convictions for offences including burglary, vehicle crime, theft, handling stolen property and assault. He also had a history of drugs and substance misuse, including glue sniffing as a young teenager, moving on to alcohol, then controlled drugs, including heroin and crack cocaine. Aged 34 at the time of the interview, John combines the complexities of desistance and persistence within his narrative as he talks about his two experiences of the project, ranging from pride in successfully completing his first period with the project to anger and despair during his second stint. Initially sceptical about the project, he used the support offered and valued the help with his drugs misuse, with finding accommodation and preparing him for a job. He initially had the motivation not to offend, he was supported by a relationship; then he lost motivation, the relationship ended and he returned to persistent acquisitive crime. Reflecting from prison, aged 34 and sharing a cell with a 21 year old, he felt he was now too old to continue offending and pinned his hopes on finding suitable courses and a place in a therapeutic prison. In the following extract, John initially speaks with pride of his first experience of the project:

They couldn't do anything more to help. They found me somewhere to live – my own place which I'd never had before, in my own name. They found me a job, which I didn't start. I got medication off the doctor to get me off the drugs, they did everything they could, they helped me stay out of trouble for six months. First time I'd completed my licence [...] it was the longest I've been out since I've been on the gear – six months – it's the longest I've been out in ten years.

John spoke with obvious pride in completing the prolific offender project successfully and talked about the certificate of completion he was presented with. He was also (justifiably) proud of completing his licence for the first time in a long offending career. This contrasts with his emotional stance during his second short-lived period with the project. One of us (Mawby) encountered John at a project meeting during this period and noted his obvious anger and frustration. When later reminded of this and asked about his second experience of the project, John commented:

> Well I'd packed in thieving when I first got out, but I was finding it hard, it's the first time I've ever been skint – I've never had a job in my life, but I've never been skint – I've always stolen for survival. I just couldn't get my act together being skint, get used to that way of life. Living on the dole, I just can't do it. That's what was getting me angry, in the end I just thought fuck it and I started going out robbing again. But when I go out robbing, I go out all day every day and I knew it was only a matter of time before I started getting followed again – that's what happened.

> *RM: What was so different about the second time, didn't you have as little money the first time?*

> I had no money but my girlfriend at the time was helping me a lot, but when I got out second time we'd split up, so I came out to no one. We got back together a couple of weeks before I got my '4' [four-year prison sentence] … but … I just couldn't … I was knocking around again with guys, the dealers and that and they've all got money – that made it even harder, everyone around having money – I was sponging off them all the time and I didn't have fuck all … Even now when I get out I know I can't live on the dole. If I can get a job great, hope I can get some training on this sentence – I've never worked in my life, I've got no training or anything.

At this point John was still struggling to overcome the emotional difficulties of managing and negotiating a spoiled identity (see also Farrall and Calverley 2006 on the emotional trajectories associated with desistance). The support of the project, during his first experience of it, had helped him to feel good about himself; for the first time in his life he had his own place, he was drug-free and he stayed out of prison for an unprecedented six months. During his second experience of the project, however, he was unable to re-establish the initial physical and emotional distance from his offending past or to re-create the 'normal' life that he had briefly glimpsed.

While in this chapter we have begun to explore the relationship between prolific offender projects and primary and secondary desistance drawing on qualitative data, we have also returned to the reconviction records of the participants of the Stoke-on-Trent prolific offender project. For our original evaluation of the project we compared the pre-, on- and post-project convictions of 22 participants with a matched sample of prolific offenders who did not participate in the project. Our analysis showed that:

- there was no significant difference in pre-project convictions between the participant and comparison groups;
- participants had a significantly lower number of convictions, on average, while participating on the project compared with the comparison group, who remained at large in the community;[15]

- There was no significant difference in the average number of convictions between the groups after the participants left the project.

To summarise, therefore, the quantitative analysis suggested that while on the project, some participants experienced crime-free gaps, namely periods of primary desistance (while others experienced periods of reduced offending). The analysis also suggested that this desistance was not necessarily sustained in the post-project period. To pursue further the question of desistance amongst our sample, in the summer of 2005 we revisited, through the Home Office Offenders Index, the reconviction records of the 22 participants, concentrating on the period since 30 September 2002 when we had last examined their conviction records through the PNC (Police National Computer). This exercise provides some indication of persistence/desistance in the period of approximately 2.5 years since we completed the project evaluation. Seventeen of the group had returned to prison for a variety of offences including fraud, burglary, robbery, assault, malicious wounding, breach of community order and multiple vehicle related offences. Four of the sample had been reconvicted and received non-custodial sentences including fines, curfew orders combined with an electronic tag, and drug treatment and testing orders (DTTOs). This leaves only one of the original participants who had not been reconvicted in this period. He was the oldest member of the sample (in his early 40s when he joined the project). Battling heroin addiction while a project participant and having amassed 89 convictions in an offending career that included dealing class A drugs, the project buttressed Peter's primary desistance (assisting him with drug treatment, preparation for work and reconciliation with his estranged family). Possibly, it also prepared him for secondary desistance at a time in his life when he was ready to change.

Prolific/persistent offenders, NOMS and 'interrupted' desistance

Persistent offenders and their desistance from offending are at the heart of the NOMS enterprise. Carter (2003: 28–9) asserts that 'persistent offenders need to know that they will be punished more' and that there will be a 'consistent approach to ensure that the liberty of persistent offenders is progressively restricted'. At the same time, 'they should have priority access to interventions to help reduce re-offending (in particular drug treatment)'. But if this fails to rehabilitate them, they must recognise custody as the 'ultimate sanction … reserved for the most serious, dangerous and highly persistent offenders'. The principles of seamless, 'end-to-end' management and the 'four C's of consistency, continuity, commitment and consolidation' (Raynor 2005) appear to sit well with the principles underlying prolific/persistent offender projects. In this sense, it might be argued that such projects anticipated many aspects of NOMS – intensive supervision and monitoring, multi-agency partnerships and a willingness to continue to work with offenders both in the community and in prison. But it should be remembered that these projects were originally intended to provide robust and 'credible' alternatives to imprisonment and it was only as it became increasingly obvious that persistent offenders were very unlikely to avoid imprisonment for any significant length of time that the 'win/win' ethos developed. It is questionable, however, whether it was ever intended that the 'revolving door' should become as embedded in projects as it has done.

It is at this point that the compatibility of prolific/persistent offender projects with either NOMS or the desistance literature has to be challenged. The relationship is complex and contradictory. NOMS is self-evidently not only, or even primarily, about rehabilitation. Rather, it is, *inter alia*, about compliance, enforcement and public protection – concepts that feature rarely in the literature on desistance. While many aspects of work with persistent offenders undoubtedly contribute to creating the circumstances within which offenders begin to desist – whether that is described as 'primary', 'temporary' or 'intermittent' desistance – this contribution may well be undermined by aspects of the projects that hasten a return to prison, which must surely rank as the ultimate 'place' for generating the offender identity (a point reinforced by Farrall and Calverley 2006). An additional concern is the NOMS principle of 'contestability', or the opening up of probation to competition. Prolific/persistent offender projects have been defined by their multi-agency partnerships and it is far from clear that this kind of work is not under threat from the introduction of a purchaser/provider split. Commissioning services for offenders from a number of different agencies will change the nature of the relationship between those agencies but not necessarily increase effectiveness (Fullwood 2005). As Malcolm Dean (2005) has asked, 'How is fragmenting probation provision between multiple providers going to help [integration]? It can't and it won't.'

Recent research on the relationship between probation officers/offender managers and offenders stresses the significance of continuity (Trotter 1999; Rex 1999; Partridge 2004; Robinson 2005). While one interpretation of this might be continuity of *offender management* both in custody and in the community, another interpretation might be that of continuity of relations, providing committed support while the offender 'zig-zags' their way to desistance. There is little evidence that the rhetoric of NOMS will accommodate a tolerance of 'zig-zagging'. Nevertheless, in reality, there is no alternative. If the custodial door is set to revolve, as it seems to be under current sentencing legislation and practice, then the only choice is whether or not we attempt to set in place sufficient support networks in the community to encourage offenders to remain 'out' for a little longer each time. Yet, while this war of attrition may eventually lead to criminal justice system 'burn out' for some persistent offenders, let us not pretend that returns to prison are anything other than setbacks or 'interruptions' on the path to desistance for many others.

Notes

1 The authors are listed alphabetically, having contributed equally to the writing of this chapter.
2 In a critical contribution to the persistent offender debate Garside (2004: 14–18) questions the accuracy of these figures and hence the wisdom of focusing scant

resources on identified convicted persistent offenders. He concludes (p. 18) that it 'stretches credibility to breaking point to claim that it is possible to achieve meaningful reductions in crime by targeting a few thousand of the usual suspects'.

3 The inspiration for a number of these projects has been the Dordrecht Project in Holland. This was established in 1992 and combined targeted policing with intensive supervision by probation officers. It reportedly reduced the number of domestic burglaries by one-third, but despite its high reputation, there is a dearth of authoritative information on the project. Buckland and Stevens (2001: 27) provide a brief overview.

4 In the absence of a joint criminal justice IT system, JTrack was developed as a means of tracking offenders from arrest to sentence to provide national and local management information for criminal justice agencies. Its development was criticised on the grounds of expense, utility and accuracy (see, for example, Criminal Justice Chief Inspectors' Group 2004: 16–17).

5 This section draws heavily upon Farrall (2002: ch. 1).

6 See Farrington (1997) for a more thorough summary of the literature and Blumstein et al. (1986) for discussions of the methodological sophistication of this field, its policy uses and other substantive issues.

7 This section draws heavily upon Maruna and Farrall (2004).

8 This section draws heavily upon Farrall (2002: ch. 1).

9 Interview material from the Stoke-on-Trent prolific offender project was collected by Rob Mawby in the course of evaluating the project in 2001/2 (Worrall et al. 2003; Mawby and Worrall 2004). We draw on interviews with six anonymised prolific offenders: Bob, John, Luke, Matt, Peter and Tom.

10 Whether the doctor would or should do this in practice is a moot point. During the period we observed the project, the participants never actually put him in the position of having to take this action; the most problematic drug users never got as far as securing a job.

11 There is also, of course, the issue of domestic violence, which clearly calls into question the observed association between partnership and desistance. For a discussion of findings relating to desistance from domestic violence, see Fagan (1989), Feld and Straus (1989, 1990), Tolman et al. (1996) and Quigley and Leonard (1996).

12 For example, some of the earliest investigations of the relationship between employment and desistance relied upon relatively young populations. For example, Rand's (1987) sample was under 26 years old, the members of Mulvey and La Rosa's (1986) sample were all between 15 and 20 years old with an average age of 18, and more recently, Graham and Bowling's (1995) sample were aged 17–25. Similarly, early investigations of the relationship between marriage and desistance were also based on relatively young populations: Mulvey and Aber's (1988) sample were aged between 16 and 19 years old; Pezzin's (1995) were between 14 and 22; Rand's (1987) were under 26; Knight et al.'s (1977) sample were all under 21 and the later extension of Knight et al.'s analyses (Osborn and West 1979) followed these men until they were 22–23.

13 This section draws upon Maruna and Farrall (2004). See also Farrall and Calverley (2006) for further discussions of the role of place in processes of desistance.

14 See also Goffman (1963: 102) on spaces.

15 The criterion used for judging the strength of these effects (i.e. differences before and after admission) was the t-test statistic, which has associated with it a statement of probability that the result is erroneous – e.g. a 'p' value. In this case p <.089. A 10 per cent level of significance was regarded as acceptable given the

small sample size. In interpreting this, it may be helpful to say that a difference of p <.089 means that the probability of getting this result by chance is 8.9 in 100 (for details of these statistics, see Worrall *et al.* 2003: 11).

Further reading

For further information on the background, development and evaluation of projects for prolific/persistent offenders, we would refer readers to Worrall and Mawby's chapter, 'Intensive projects for prolific/persistent offenders' in Bottoms *et al.* (2004) *Alternatives to Prison.* For those interested in the progress of recent projects, Homes *et al.* (2005) *Intensive Supervision and Monitoring Schemes for Persistent Offenders: Staff and Offender Perceptions* is an informative Home Office report. There are increasing numbers of books available on desistance. Farrall and Calverley (2006) is a recent summary of the field and a development of an earlier study in the same area. Ezell and Cohen's *Desisting from Crime* (2004) contains a very good summary of the main theoretical positions adopted to account for desistance. Maruna's *Making Good* (2001) is a must for those serious about understanding desistance. Farrall's 2000 edited collection reproduces many of the earlier texts, but this work, while often very good, is beginning to date somewhat. A more recent collection would be Maruna and Immarigeon (eds) *After Crime and Punishment: Pathways to Offender Reintegration* (2004). Mair's 2004 edited collection *What Matters in Probation* also provides essays which critique current developments in the field of corrections. Two recent special editions of journals (*The Howard Journal of Criminal Justice*, 43(4) and *Criminology and Criminal Justice*, 6(1)) include essays from many of those cited herein, but extend and refine their theoretical arguments.

References

Abbas, A., Harrison, J., MacDonald, R., Moore, R., Shildrick, T. and Simpson, M. (2003) *Dordrecht Project: First Report.* Middlesbrough: University of Teesside.

Adams, K. (1997) 'Developmental aspects of adult crime', in T. Thornberry (ed.), *Developmental Theories of Crime and Delinquency.* London: Transaction Press.

Blumstein, A., Cohen, J., Roth, J. A. and Visher, C. A. (eds) (1986) *Criminal Careers and 'Career Criminals'*, 2 vols. Washington, DC: National Academy Press.

Blunkett, D. (2004) *Reducing Crime – Changing Lives: The Government's Plans for Transforming the Management of Offenders.* London: Home Office.

Bottoms, A. and Wiles, P. (1992) 'Explanations of crime and place', in D.J. Evans, N.R. Fyfe and D.T. Herbert (eds), *Crime, Policing and Place.* London: Routledge.

Buckland, G. and Stevens, A. (2001) *Review of Effective Practice with Young Offenders in Mainland Europe.* University of Kent, European Institute of Social Services.

Burnett, R. (1992) *The Dynamics of Recidivism.* Oxford: Centre for Criminological Research, University of Oxford.

Burnett, R. (1994) 'The odds of going straight: offenders' own predictions', in *Sentencing, Quality and Risk: Proceedings of the 10th Annual Conference on Research and Information in the Probation Service.* Birmingham: University of Loughborough, Midlands Probation Training Consortium.

Burnett, R. (2004) 'To reoffend or not to reoffend? The ambivalence of convicted property offenders', in S. Maruna and R. Immarigeon (eds), *After Crime and Punishment: Pathways to Offender Reintegration.* Cullompton: Willan.

Caddle, D. (1991) *Parenthood Training for Young Offenders: An Evaluation of Courses in Young Offender Institutions*, Research and Planning Unit Paper 63. London: HMSO.

Carlen, P. and Worrall, A. (2004) *Analysing Women's Imprisonment*. Cullompton: Willan.

Carter, P. (2003) *Managing Offenders, Reducing Crime: A New Approach*. London: Home Office.

Chenery, S. and Pease, K. (2000) 'The Burnley/Dordrecht Initiative Final Report'. Burnley: University of Huddersfield/Safer Cities Partnership, unpublished.

Clear, T.R. (2005) 'Places not cases? Re-thinking the probation focus', *Howard Journal of Criminal Justice*, 44 (2): 172–84.

Criminal Justice Chief Inspectors' Group (2004) *Joint Inspection Report into Persistent and Prolific Offenders*. London: Home Office Communications Directorate.

Cromwell, P.F., Olson, J.N. and Avary, D.W. (1991) *Breaking and Entering*. London: Sage.

Cusson, M. and Pinsonneault, P. (1986) 'The decision to give up crime', in D.B. Cornish and R.V. Clarke (eds), *The Reasoning Criminal*. New York: Springer-Verlag.

Dawson, P. (2005) *Early Findings from the Prolific and Other Priority Offenders Evaluation*, RDS Home Office Development and Practice Report No. 46. London: Home Office.

Dean, M. (2005) 'Shame of Blair's market madness', *Guardian*, 14 December.

Ditton, J. (1977) *Part-time Crime: An Ethnography of Fiddling and Pilferage*. London: Macmillan.

Elliott, D. and Menard, S. (1996) 'Delinquent friends and delinquent behaviour: temporal and developmental patterns', in J.D. Hawkins (ed.), *Delinquency and Crime: Current Theories*. Cambridge: Cambridge University Press.

Ezell, M.E. and Cohen, L.E. (2004) *Desisting from Crime*. Oxford: Oxford University Press.

Fagan, J. (1989) 'Cessation of family violence: deterrence and dissuasion', in L. Ohlin and M. Tonry (eds), *Crime and Justice: An Annual Review of Research*, Vol. 11. Chicago: University of Chicago Press.

Farrall, S. (2000) 'Introduction', in S. Farrall (ed.), *The Termination of Criminal Careers*. Aldershot: Ashgate.

Farrall, S. (2002) *Rethinking What Works With Offenders*. Cullompton: Willan.

Farrall, S. (2004) 'Social capital and offender reintegration', in S. Maruna and R. Immarigeon (eds), *After Crime and Punishment: Pathways to Offender Integration*. Cullompton: Willan.

Farrall, S. and Calverley, A. (2006) *Understanding Desistance from Crime*. London: Open University Press.

Farrington, D.P. (1992) 'Juvenile delinquency', in J. Coleman (ed.), *The School Years*. London: Routledge.

Farrington, D.P. (1997) 'Human development and criminal careers', in M. Maguire, R. Morgan and R. Reiner (eds), *The Oxford Handbook of Criminology*, 2nd edn. Oxford: Clarendon Press.

Farrington, D.P., Gallagher, B., Morley, L., St Ledger, R.J. and West, D.J. (1986) 'Unemployment, school leaving and crime', *British Journal of Criminology*, 26 (4): 335–56.

Feld, S.L. and Straus, M.A. (1989) 'Escalation and desistance of wife assault', *Criminology*, 27: 141–61.

Feld, S.L. and Straus, M.A. (1990) 'Escalation and desistance of wife assault', in M.A. Straus and R.J. Gelles (eds), *Physical Violence in American Families: Risk Factors and Adaptations to Violence in 8,145 Families*. New Brunswick, NJ: Transaction Publishers.

Foote, C.E. and Frank, A.W. (1999) 'Foucault and therapy: the disciplining of grief', in A.S. Chambon, A. Irving and L. Epstein (eds), *Reading Foucault for Social Work*. New York: Columbia University Press.

Fullwood, C. (2005) 'The development of the National Offender Management Service: a "consumer" perspective', *VISTA*, 10 (1): 28–36.

Garside, R. (2004) *Crime, Persistent Offenders and the Justice Gap*. London: Crime and Society Foundation.

Gendreau, P., Goggin, C. and Fulton, B. (2001) 'Intensive supervision in probation and parole settings', in C. Hollin (ed.), *The Handbook of Offender Assessment and Treatment*. London: Wiley & Sons.

Giddens, A. (1984) *The Constitution of Society*. Cambridge: Polity Press.

Giordano, P.C., Cernkovich, S.A. and Rudolph, J.L. (2002) 'Gender, crime and desistance: toward a theory of cognitive transformation', *American Journal of Sociology*, 107: 990–1064.

Goffman, E. (1963) *Stigma*. London: Penguin Books.

Graham, J. and Bowling, B. (1995) *Young People and Crime*, Home Office Research Study No. 145. London: HMSO.

Hagan, J. (1997) 'Crime and capitalization: toward a developmental theory of street crime in America', in T. Thornberry (ed.), *Developmental Theories of Crime and Delinquency*. New Brunswick, NJ: Transaction Press.

Hagell, A. and Newburn, T. (1994) *Persistent Young Offenders*. London: Policy Studies Institute.

Henry, S. (1978) *The Hidden Economy: The Context and Control of Borderline Crime*. Oxford: Martin Robertson.

Home Office (2003) *Narrowing the Justice Gap and the Persistent Offender Scheme*, National Probation Service Briefing, Issue 14. London: Home Office.

Home Office (2004a) *Confident Communities in a Secure Britain: The Home Office Strategic Plan 2004–08*, Cm 6287. London, Home Office.

Home Office (2004b) *Transition of the Persistent Offender Scheme into the Prolific and other Priority Offender Strategy*, Letter to Chairs of the 42 LCJBs and CDRPs, 19 May. London: Home Office Criminal Justice Performance Directorate.

Home Office (2005) *The Prolific and other Priority Offender Performance Management Framework Headlines Measures Report for May 2005*. London: Home Office. PPO PMF Headline measures report for October 2005, available at http://www.crime-reduction.gov.uk/ppo (accessed on 15 July 2005).

Homes, A., Walmsley, R.K. and Debidin, M. (2005) *Intensive Supervision and Monitoring Schemes for Persistent Offenders: Staff and Offender Perceptions*, RDS Home Office Development and Practice Report 41. London: Home Office.

Hope, T., Worrall, A., Dunkerton, L. and Leacock, V. (2001) 'The Newcastle Prolific Offenders Project Final Evaluation Report'. Keele University/Staffordshire Probation Area, unpublished.

Horney, J., Osgood, D.W. and Haen Marshall, I. (1995) 'Criminal careers in the short term intra-individual variability in crime and its relation to local life circumstances', *American Sociological Review*, 60: 655–73.

Hughes, M. (1997) 'An exploratory study of young adult Black and Latino males and the factors facilitating their decisions to make positive behavioural changes', *Smith College Studies in Social Work*, 67 (3): 401–14.

Hughes, M. (1998) 'Turning points in the lives of young inner-city men forgoing destructive criminal behaviours: a qualitative study', *Social Work Research*, 22: 143–51.

Irwin, J. (1970) *The Felon.* Englewood Cliffs, NJ: Prentice Hall.

Jamieson, J., McIvor, G. and Murray, C. (1999) *Understanding Offending Among Young People.* Edinburgh: Stationery Office.

Knight, B.J. and West, D.J. (1975) 'Temporary and continuing delinquency', *British Journal of Criminology*, 15 (1): 43–50.

Knight, B.J., Osborn, S.G. and West, D.J. (1977) 'Early marriage and criminal tendency in males', *British Journal of Criminology*, 17 (4): 348–60.

Laub, J.H. and Sampson, R.J. (2001) 'Understanding desistance from crime', in M. Tonry (ed.), *Crime and Justice: An Annual Review of Research*, Vol. 26. Chicago: University of Chicago Press.

Laub, J., Nagin, D. and Sampson, R. (1998) 'Trajectories of change in criminal offending: good marriages and the desistance process', *American Sociological Review*, 63: 225–38.

Leibrich, J. (1993) *Straight to the Point: Angles on Giving up Crime.* Otago, New Zealand: University of Otago Press.

Leibrich, J. (1996) 'The role of shame in going straight: a study of former offenders', in B. Galaway and J. Hudson (eds), *Restorative Justice.* Monsey, NJ: Criminal Justice Press.

Lemert, E.M. (1948) 'Some aspects of a general theory of sociopathic behavior', in *Proceedings of the Pacific Sociological Society*, 16, pp. 23–9. State College of Washington Research Studies.

Lemert, E.M. (1951) *Social Pathology: Systematic Approaches to the Study of Sociopathic Behavior.* New York: McGraw-Hill.

Loeber, R., Stouthamer-Loeber, M., Van Kammen, W. and Farrington, D.P. (1991) 'Initiation, escalation and desistance in juvenile offending and their correlates', *Journal of Criminal Law and Criminology*, 82 (1): 36–82.

McIvor, G., Murray, C. and Jamieson, J. (2004) 'Desistance from crime: is it different for women and girls?', in S. Maruna and R. Immarigeon (eds), *After Crime and Punishment: Pathways to Offender Reintegration.* Cullompton: Willan.

Mair, G. (ed.) (2004) *What Matters in Probation.* Cullompton: Willan.

Maruna, S. (1997) 'Going straight: desistance from crime and life narratives of reform', *Narrative Study of Lives*, 5: 59–93.

Maruna, S. (1998) 'Redeeming One's Self'. PhD thesis. Evanston, IL: Northwestern University.

Maruna, S. (2000) 'Criminology, desistance and the psychology of the stranger', in D. Canter and L.J. Alison (eds), *Beyond Profiling: Developments in Investigative Psychology.* Aldershot: Dartmouth Books.

Maruna, S. (2001) *Making Good: How Ex-Convicts Reform and Rebuild Their Lives.* Washington, DC: American Psychological Association Books.

Maruna, S. and Farrall, S. (2004) 'Desistance from crime: a theoretical reformulation', *Kölner Zeitschrift für Soziologie und Sozialpsychologie*, 43: 171–94.

Maruna, S. and Immarigeon, R. (eds) *After Crime and Punishment: Pathways to Offender Reintegration.* Cullompton: Willan.

Matza, D.M. (1964) *Delinquency and Drift.* New York: Wiley.

Mawby, R.C. and Worrall, A. (2004) '"Polibation" revisited: policing, probation and prolific offender projects', *International Journal of Police Science and Management*, 6 (2): 63–73.

Meisenhelder, T. (1977) 'An exploratory study of exiting from criminal careers', *Criminology*, 15 (3): 319–34.

Meisenhelder, T. (1982) 'Becoming normal: certification as a stage in exiting from crime', *Deviant Behaviour*, 3: 137–53.

Mischkowitz, R. (1994) 'Desistance from a delinquent way of life?', in E.G.M. Weitekamp and H.J. Kerner (eds), *Cross-National Longitudinal Research on Human Development and Criminal Behaviour*. Dordrecht: Kluwer Academic.

Moffitt, T. (1993) '"Life-course persistent" and "adolescent-limited" antisocial behaviour: a developmental taxonomy', *Psychological Review*, 100: 674–701.

Mulvey, E.P. and Aber, M. (1988) 'Growing out of delinquency: development and desistance', in R.L. Jenkins and W.K. Brown (eds), *The Abandonment of Delinquent Behaviour: Promoting the Turnaround*. New York: Praeger.

Mulvey, E.P. and La Rosa, J.F. (1986) 'Delinquency cessation and adolescent development: preliminary data', *American Journal of Orthopsychiatry*, 56 (2): 212–24.

Osborn, S.G. (1980) 'Moving home, leaving London and delinquent trends', *British Journal of Criminology*, 20 (1): 54–61.

Osborn, S.G. and West, D.J. (1979) 'Marriage and delinquency: a postscript', *British Journal of Criminology*, 18 (3): 254–6.

Ouimet, M. and Le Blanc, M. (1996) 'The role of life experiences in the continuation of the adult criminal career', *Criminal Behaviour and Mental Health*, 6: 73–97.

Parker, H. (1976) 'Boys will be men: brief adolescence in a down-town neighbourhood', in G. Mungham and G. Pearson (eds), *Working Class Youth Culture*. London: Routledge.

Partridge, S. (2004) *Examining Case Management Models for Community Sentences*, Home Office Online Report 17/04. London: Home Office.

Pezzin, L.E. (1995) 'Earning prospects, matching effects and the decision to terminate a criminal career', *Journal of Quantitative Criminology*, 11 (1): 29–50.

Piquero, A.R. (2004) 'Somewhere between persistence and desistance: the intermittency of criminal careers', in S. Maruna and R. Immarigeon (eds), *After Crime and Punishment: Pathways to Offender Integration*. Cullompton: Willan.

Quigley, B.M. and Leonard, K.E. (1996) 'Desistance of husband aggression in the early years of marriage', *Violence and Victims*, 11: 355–70.

Rand, A. (1987) 'Transitional life events and desistance from delinquency and crime', in M.E. Wolfgang, T.P. Thornberry and R.M. Figlio (eds), *From Boy to Man, from Delinquency to Crime*. Chicago: University of Chicago Press.

Raynor, P. (2005) 'End-to-end Management: Will It Improve Effectiveness?' Unpublished Discussion Paper presented at NOMS Colloquium, London.

Rex, S. (1999) 'Desistance from offending: experiences of probation', *Howard Journal of Criminal Justice*, 38: 366–83.

Robinson, G. (2005) 'What works in offender management?', *Howard Journal of Criminal Justice*, 44 (3): 307–18.

Sampson, R.J. and Laub, J.H. (1993) *Crime in the Making: Pathways and Turning Points Through Life*. London: Harvard University Press.

Sherman, L.W., Gartin, P.R. and Buerger, M.E. (1989) 'Hot spots of predatory crime', *Criminology*, 27: 27–55.

Shover, N. (1983) 'The later stages of ordinary property offender careers', *Social Problems*, 31 (2): 208–18.

Shover, N. (1996) *Great Pretenders: Pursuits and Careers of Persistent Thieves*. Oxford: Westview.

Shover, N. and Thompson, C. (1992) 'Age, differential expectations and crime desistance', *Criminology*, 30 (1): 276–93.

Sommers, I., Baskin, D.R. and Fagan, J. (1994) 'Getting out of the life: crime desistance by female street offenders', *Deviant Behaviour*, 15 (2): 125–49.

Soothill, K., Ackerley, E. and Francis, B. (2003) 'The persistent offenders debate: a focus on temporal changes', *Criminal Justice*, 3 (4): 389–412.

Tolman, R.M., Edleson, J.L. and Fendrich, M. (1996) 'The applicability of the theory of planned behavior to abusive men's cessation of violent behavior', *Violence and Victims*, 1194: 341–54.

Trasler, G. (1979) 'Delinquency, recidivism and desistance', *British Journal of Criminology*, 19 (4): 314–22.

Trotter, C. (1999) *Working with Involuntary Clients: A Guide to Practice*. London: Sage.

Tupman, B., Chui, W.H. and Farlow, C. (2001) 'Evaluating the Effectiveness of Project ARC'. University of Exeter: unpublished report.

Uggen, C. (2000) 'Work as a turning point in the life course of criminals: a duration model of age, employment and recidivism', *American Sociological Review*, 67: 529–46.

Uggen, C. and Kruttschnitt, K. (1998) 'Crime in the breaking: gender differences in desistance', *Law and Society Review*, 32 (2): 339–66.

Vennard, J. and Pearce, J. (2004) *The Bristol Prolific Offender Scheme: An Evaluation*. Bristol: University of Bristol.

Warr, M. (1998) 'Life-course transitions and desistance from crime', *Criminology*, 36 (2): 183–215.

West, D.J. (1982) *Delinquency: Its Roots, Careers and Prospects*. London: Heinemann.

West, G.W. (1978) 'The short-term careers of serious thieves', *Canadian Journal of Criminology*, 20: 169–90.

Wolfgang, M.E., Figlio, R.M. and Sellin, T. (1972) *Delinquency in a Birth Cohort*. London: University of Chicago Press.

Worrall, A. and Mawby, R. C. (2004) 'Intensive projects for prolific/persistent offenders', in A. Bottoms, S. Rex and G. Robinson (eds), *Alternatives to Prison: Options for an Insecure Society*. Cullompton: Willan.

Worrall, A., Mawby, R.C., Heath, G. and Hope, T. (2003) *Intensive Supervision and Monitoring Projects*, Home Office Online Report 42/03. London: Home Office.

Chapter 13

High-risk offenders and public protection

Hazel Kemshall and Jason Wood

Introduction

Public protection is now a key aim of the National Probation Service (NPS), and in particular the effective community management of high-risk offenders. This chapter reviews the main legislative, policy and practice responses to these offenders, and how the NPS, in partnership with other agencies, is responding to this challenging area of work. Key developments such as the Multi-Agency Public Protection Arrangements (MAPPA) are explored as is the range of offenders covered by these new partnerships. The impact on probation is discussed, with specific attention to risk assessment and the main assessment tools. The chapter concludes by examining risk management and briefly contrasts the two main approaches of 'community protection' and the 'public health' model.

Recent developments

By the close of the twentieth century risk had come to preoccupy much of the Probation Service's agenda. This reflected increased policy, media and public concern with high-risk offenders, and most notably sex offenders, followed by a raft of legislation to deal more proactively with those deemed to present the highest risk of harm (Kemshall 2003a). As a result, policy trends and legislation had firmly enmeshed the Probation Service in a new penology of risk. Most notable has been legislation covering the surveillance and monitoring of sex offenders, in particular the creation of the sex offender register by the Sex Offender Act 1997 and the provision of the sex offender order in the Crime and Disorder Act 1998. Registration requirements have been strengthened by the Sexual Offences Act 2003 which also created three new orders: 'sexual offences prevention orders', 'foreign travel orders' and 'risk of sexual harm orders', and repealed the previous legislation above (see Shute 2004 for a full review; Home Office 2004d). Public protection panels were created by sections 67 and 68 of the Criminal Justice and Court Services Act 2000, with the Criminal Justice Act 2003 adding the Prison Service to police and probation as 'responsible authorities'. These acts in effect formalised the community management of high-risk offenders, and placed a duty on a range of agencies to cooperate in their assessment and management. MAPPA have been strengthened by subsequent Home Office guidance (Home Office 2003b, 2004a) and circulars on best practice (Home Office 2005c, 2005d; see also Kemshall *et al.* 2005).

Key legislation and statutory duties

Multi-agency work was given impetus throughout the 1990s by a number of key factors. Most notable was the 'discovery' of the predatory paedophile (Kitzenger 1999a, 1999b) and various studies that established the extent of the problem nationally and internationally (Grubin 1998; Cobley 2000). The prevalence of child sexual abuse has continued to attract concern (Kitzinger 1999a, 1999b) with research estimates that one in six children will be the victims of such abuse (Cawson *et al.* 2000). These developments were given added impetus by a number of high-profile cases that attracted intense media scrutiny and calls for a UK version of 'Megan's Law' (Sarah's Law) following the murder of Sarah Payne in 2000.[1] These cases have resulted in what some commentators have described as a 'moral panic' about organised abuse and paedophile rings (Kitzinger 1999a, 1999b; Thompson 1998). Perceived system and organisational failure in the management of high-risk offenders (e.g. Sydney Cooke) attracted media coverage and eroded public trust. As a result, public and media pressure grew for more restrictive and effective measures for the management of such offenders, particularly post release from prison. New Labour also emphasised joined-up criminal justice, for example in the Crime and Disorder Act 1998 and more recently in the Carter Report (2003), the creation of the National Offender Management Service and the creation of the Prison Service as a responsible authority in the Criminal Justice Act 2003.[2] MAPPA epitomise such a notion in practice. Connelly and Williamson (2000) characterise this approach to sexual and violent offenders as a 'community protection model' in which legislation prioritises public protection, partly through provisions for mandatory, indeterminate and preventative sentencing, and through intensive supervision methods in the community.

In addition to the increased attention to sex offenders (and in particular 'predatory paedophiles') both sentencing and penal policy throughout the 1990s was characterised by 'bifurcation' or a twin-track approach (Bottoms 1995). This approach attempts to base sentencing on risk, and adopts the idea of selective incapacitation for serious habitual recidivists and those considered as the most 'dangerous' (Greenwood and Abrahamse 1982; Greenwood and Turner 1987; Greenwood *et al.* 1996; Murray 1997).

Subsequent legislation has reinforced the emphasis upon public protection, most notably the Criminal Justice and Court Services Act 2000, sections 67 and 68 that placed a responsibility upon police and probation to:

establish arrangements for the purpose of assessing and managing risks posed in that area by –
(a) relevant sexual and violent offenders, and
(b) other persons who, by reason of offences committed by them (wherever committed), are considered by the responsible authority to be persons who may cause serious harm to the public. (s. 67(2), CJCS 2000)

The Act also requires the responsible authority to report on the activities of the public protection arrangements through an annual report (Home Office 2004b). The Criminal Justice Act 2003 strengthened these arrangements (see particularly ss. 325–7) and facilitates closer working between prisons, probation and police. It also places a 'duty to cooperate' upon agencies such as housing, social services, health authorities and youth offending teams. The Criminal Justice Act 2003 also introduced two new public protection sentences. The first is an indeterminate sentence that 'must be imposed if a sexual or violent offender is assessed by the court as posing a significant risk to the public and the offence committed carries a maximum penalty of ten years or more'. A tariff period will be set, and release is at the discretion of the Parole Board when the offender is deemed safe enough. A discretionary life sentence can still be made if the offence warrants it. An extended sentence can be imposed on the grounds of public protection on the same grounds but where the sexual or violent offence 'carries a penalty of less than ten years and where the sentence imposed is at least 12 months, the court must set a custodial period and an extended licence period ... The extended licence period may be up to 5 years for violent offenders and up to 8 years for sexual offenders' (Home Office 2003a: 3).

The Government's response to the Carter Review (see Home Office 2004c) reiterated that: 'public protection will always be the Government's first priority' (p. 10). In July 2004 there were 24,572 registered sex offenders in England and Wales (Home Office 2004b). This represented a 15 per cent increase on the preceding year. It should be noted that the cumulative effect of adding people to the register each year inevitably means that fewer are leaving the register than are joining it – resulting in predictably higher numbers. This figure is also partially due to the success of Operation Ore and other investigations into Internet paedophilia and pornography.[3] Of those offenders subject to MAPPA 26 committed a further serious sexual or violent offence, a fall of 46 per cent from the previous year. The overall numbers of offenders monitored by MAPPA fell by a quarter last year to 39,492 and the number of offenders subject to level 3 arrangements fell by 24 per cent to 2,152. These include violent as well as sexual offenders. The primary reason for the drop in numbers is that violent and sexual offenders in category 2 dropped by 57 per cent from 29,594 to 12,754 reflecting a change in counting practices to count only community-based offenders (not those in custody) bringing the recording of this category into line with registered sex offenders. Of those offenders referred to public protection panels (level 3) only 1 per cent were charged with a further offence. The workload projections arising from the Sexual Offences Act 2003 and the Criminal Justice Act 2003 have been estimated at a maximum of 100 sex offenders per year for the new sex offences; and 500 cases by 2006/7; 1,000 cases 2007/8; and 1,500 for 2008/9 for the dangerous offender sentences. There will be a cumulative effect on MAPPA as these offenders will remain on statutory supervision for long periods and many will remain at level 3 (National Probation Service 2004).

The new penology

These developments can be placed within a broader penal trend usually referred to as a 'new penology' of risk or actuarial justice (Feeley and Simon 1992, 1994; Feeley 2003), although the extent and nature of the new penology has been the subject of much debate (see, for example, O'Malley 2001a, 2001b; Rigakos and Hadden 2001; Kemshall 2002, 2003a). Despite this intense debate most commentators agree that the main precursors of actuarial justice are concerns with how best to manage the 'dangerous classes' and the 'habitual recidivists' (see Pratt 1997, 2000); economic pressures on crime management, particularly a burgeoning prison population at a time of declining resources (Flynn 1978; Garland 1990); and a decline in confidence in liberal crime management strategies resulting in an increased emphasis upon risk management rather than rehabilitation (Garland 1985, 1990, 2001).

Grand claims are made for the impact of the new penology at the theoretical level, with rather more mixed evidence arising from detailed empirical studies of risk practices (see, for example, Kemshall 1998; Kemshall and Maguire 2001; Robinson 2002). The latter studies indicate that in practice 'sea changes' take longer and are significantly mediated by the practices and values of staff and the culture of the organisation within which they are working. However, it is clear that at the start of the twenty-first century the Probation Service is a public protection agency tasked with the risk assessment of all offenders and the effective management of high-risk offenders in the community (NPS 2001; Criminal Justice and Court Services Act 2000).

Protection through partnership

A significant initiative in the community management of high-risk offenders has been the development of multi-agency partnership work. This development has been formalised by legislation establishing police, probation and prisons as 'responsible authorities' (i.e. those tasked with a statutory duty to 'make joint arrangements for the risk assessment and management of the risks posed by sexual and violent offenders, and other offenders who may cause serious harm to the public' (Home Office 2001a)) and further guidance from the Home Office in 2003 (and most recently in 2004) on MAPPA. This later guidance is concerned not only with the formal processes and structures of MAPPA, but also with best practice for risk assessment, the conduct of panel meetings and information exchange, and the effective management of high-risk offenders in the community. Partnership is seen as an important 'value-added' component to work with high-risk offenders, offering efficient and effective information exchange, quality risk assessment and additional resources for risk management.

The cumulative impact of policy and legislation from 1991 onwards has been an increased responsibility upon police and probation (and more recently prisons) to work together to identify, assess and manage high-risk offenders (Kemshall 2003a; Nash 1999). Extensive research for the Home Office (see Kemshall and Maguire 2001; Maguire *et al*. 2001) between November 1998 and October 1999 found varying degrees of formal cooperation, differing systems and processes, differing risk assessment tools in use and differing definitions of high-risk offenders. Risk management plans were also variable, and it was not always clear that risk management interventions were matched to the levels and types of risk identified. Subjective, 'professional' judgements often replaced actuarial tools, especially within the panel discussions, and as a consequence risk thresholds and categories were a moveable feast (see Maguire *et al*. 2001 for a full review).

These issues were addressed by subsequent legislation and guidance issued through the Home Office Public Protection and Courts Unit (PPCU) which sought to formalise systems, processes and working relationships, and also attempted to set criteria for the 'critical few' who were to be subject to panel scrutiny and more intensive management (Home Office 2001a, 2002). The critical few is an operational term and relates to very high-risk offenders (as defined by OASys) and those requiring very intensive risk management at level 3 of MAPPA.[4]

While there is much emphasis upon the critical few, the range of offenders covered in total by MAPPA is far wider. In brief, these are: Category 1: Registered sex offenders; Category 2: Violent and other sex offenders; Category 3: Other offenders (see Home Office 2003b: para.s 52–7). Given the numbers involved and the resources required for community management, it is essential that precious resources are targeted at the critical few, following the principle that 'cases should be managed at the lowest level consistent with providing a defensible risk management plan' (Home Office 2003b: para. 109). The 2003 guidance refines the definition and criteria for the critical few, recognising that inconsistency of definition had been a problem (see Department of Health 2002), and adds the following:

- Although not assessed as high or very high risk, the case is exceptional because the likelihood of media scrutiny and/or public interest in the management of the case is very high and there is a need to ensure that public confidence in the criminal justice system is sustained.

- An offender on discharge from detention under a hospital order.

- An offender returning from overseas (whether immediately following their release from custody or not).

- An offender having been managed as medium or even a low risk in the community ... comes to present a high or very high risk as the result of a significant change of circumstances.
  (Home Office 2003b, 2004a: para.s 116–17)

However, the consistent and reliable identification of the critical few remains a source of concern and has been the subject of further MAPPA evaluation

(Kemshall *et al.* 2005). This research (commissioned by the Home Office) carried out a national questionnaire survey of all the MAPPA areas supported by in-depth fieldwork in six areas (see Kemshall *et al.* 2005 for a full review of the methodology). The research examined key areas of MAPPA practice, processes and structures, and made recommendations for improving practice nationally – a number of which have been subsequently implemented. This research concluded that there is 'evidence of greater effectiveness and consistency across MAPPAs' (p. 2) and that the 'majority of areas considered they were "effective" or "very effective" at identifying the "critical few" offenders and in classifying them appropriately' (p. 22). This improved effectiveness rested upon improved referral processes to MAPPA, and more effective systems for risk assessment including the use of tools such as OASys and MATRIX 2000, and structured assessment discussions at panels.

The Carter Report (2003) and the subsequent creation of the National Offender Management Service (NOMS) has continued the commitment to partnership, and reinforced the role of the Prison Service as a responsible authority. While MAPPA is not significantly addressed by Carter, the notion of a seamless sentence and greater integration of prison and probation operations has implications for the management of high-risk offenders released from custody, in particular that release planning should take account specifically of risk issues and multi-agency resources can be mobilised for their effective community management.

The impact on probation

The 'risk business' has been a significant driver for change in the Probation Service, shifting the Service from a predominantly welfare orientation to a risk-based one (Kemshall 1998, 2002, 2003a). This has been paralleled by an increased emphasis upon changing criminal behaviours, usually through cognitive behavioural programmes targeted at risky behaviours and anti-social thinking, with effective programmes literally constituting a mechanism of moral engineering (Gibbs *et al.* 1992). Not only is the approach predicated on the adoption of proven techniques of intervention, it also relies on the correct identification and classification of offenders for 'treatment programmes' (Andrews *et al.* 1990), in effect those who can respond to the provision of 'skills, capacities and means' and those who cannot. This has resulted in a new bifurcation: not just between high risk and low risk (Bottoms 1977, 1995), but also between those who can be re-moralised and socially included, and those who cannot (Kemshall 2002). In this climate the Probation Service has been tasked with the assessment of risk in all cases, but this can mean different risks for different purposes. Much risk assessment is fairly routine, concerned with the appropriate targeting of offenders for programmes and uses the standard Offender Assessment System (OASys) for determining risk levels. This risk, however, is risk of reoffending and assists targeting on the 'risk-need' principle (Andrews and Bonta 1995). Such risk assessment is based upon the prevalence (or otherwise) of criminogenic factors – those factors most associated with reoffending – and is a statistically based assessment of probability, not necessarily a prediction of what will actually happen. Such assessments also attempt to provide the value-added of guiding assessors in problem definition, in essence identifying those areas for risk management and probation intervention (Ditchfield 1997; Raynor 1997a, 1997b). This type of risk assessment is not to be confused with the assessment of serious harm.

The assessment of harm (as opposed to general recidivism) has proved more problematic (Raynor *et al.* 2000; McIvor *et al.* 2001). However, it is the assessment of seriously harmful offending that most concerns criminal justice personnel and is the arena where public and media scrutiny is most often brought to bear. Prediction of such behaviours is, however, difficult and the credible assessment of those deemed to be 'dangerous' has been challenging (Walker 1996). Indeed the concept 'dangerousness' has proved so slippery that it has largely fallen into disuse, replaced with notions of serious harm most often associated with the offending of sexual and violent offenders (Kemshall 2001, 2003a). While OASys contains a risk of harm section, this has been less extensively tested and is the least actuarial in construction (Clark 2002), and is not intended to be used as a predictive tool but rather as a screening tool to sort out those offenders requiring further assessment around their potentially harmful offending. The concept of serious harm is also open to some interpretation, but serious harm is defined by the Criminal Justice Act 2003 as 'death or serious injury whether that is physical or psychological' and can, for example, encompass severe psychological trauma caused by offences of stalking or harassment. While this definition differs slightly from that in OASys, they are considered 'comparable' in the *National Guide for the New Criminal Justice Act 2003 Sentences for Public Protection* (NPS 2005a).

OASys attempts to capture the gradation of risk by using the following risk categories:

Low: no significant current indicators of risk of harm.
Medium: there are identifiable indicators of risk of harm. The offender has the potential to cause harm but is unlikely to do so unless there is a change in circumstances, for example failure to take medication, loss of accommodation, relationship breakdown, drug or alcohol misuse.
High: there are identifiable indicators of risk of serious harm. The potential event could happen at any time and the impact would be serious.
Very high: there is an imminent risk of serious harm. The potential event is more likely than not to happen imminently and the impact would be serious.
(From the Probation Service OASys tool, Home Office 2001b)

It is likely that offenders in the high and very high risk categories will be subject to further assessments using more specific tools like MATRIX 2000 for sex offenders and the HCR-20 for violent offenders (see Kemshall 2001 for a full review). These tools are tailored to both offence and offender type and use risk factors generated from these offender populations. Such tools combine both actuarial and dynamic factors and provide risk scores that can categorise offenders and can discriminate between low, medium and high risk. However, such tools can inadvertently generate more high-risk cases than available resources can manage (Kemshall and Maguire 2001) and categories can be revised by subjective judgements as both practitioners and managers pursue 'occupational survival' (Satyamurti 1981) in the face of high demand and low resource. Even the most formalised of risk tools are adapted 'on the job' by workforces seeking to manage potentially unlimited demands upon them (Maynard-Moody *et al.* 1990), and the time and resource taken to merely complete the assessment tools can itself be a bone of contention (e.g. NAPO's resistance to the time demands of OASys). The introduction of risk assessment tools into probation practice has had a chequered history extensively documented by Kemshall (1998) and Robinson (2002) in which professional values and occupational culture have played a key role. Tools can be circumvented, used without integrity and manipulated by assessors who ignore those risk factors that do not resonate with their own value base and practice held beliefs.

The challenge of risk assessment

Risk is an uncertain business and risk assessment attempts to reduce this uncertainty through techniques of prediction. Hacking has described this as an attempt to 'tame chance' through statistical methods of probability (1990). Throughout the twentieth century risk assessment techniques developed, based increasingly upon actuarial methods and meta-analysis. However, some significant difficulties remain, particularly for the assessment of harm. In brief, these are the lack of homogeneity of violent and sexual offenders that makes the development of an all-encompassing tool difficult. In addition, low base rates associated with violent and sexual offending have made the generation of risk factors difficult. In effect, the low frequency of these behaviours in the population at large makes their prediction difficult (Grubin and Wingate 1996). A common mistake by managers and staff is to mistake tools that merely screen out offenders who potentially present a high risk for tools that predict a high risk of serious harm (e.g. OASys). 'Triage' is thus mistaken for a full assessment. Risk assessment tools also have a limited transferability across groups and have often been based upon specific populations such as male offenders in institutional settings such as prisons, secure units and forensic hospitals. Risk assessment tools for female offenders have been particularly problematic (see Kemshall 2003b for a full review). Tools have general predictability, e.g. can predict the probable likelihood of a reconviction for a similar offence, but cannot predict either severity or imminence. The latter predictions are particularly important to those tasked with the risk management of high-risk offenders in the community and such assessments tend to rely heavily upon effective information exchange at MAPPA. This can be affected by lack of information, absence of key personnel and lack of time to thoroughly consider cases (Kemshall and Maguire 2001; Maguire *et al.* 2001).

Effective risk assessment, particularly of the critical few, requires at least the following: the use of the correct risk assessment tool appropriate for the offence and offender type. This requires tools relevant to the population being assessed and a more careful distinction between those tools that screen for potentially high risk of harm (OASys) and those that provide in-depth assessments and problem definition for interventions (e.g. HCR-20 for violent offenders or MATRIX 2000 for sex offenders). Reliable risk assessment is also dependent upon effective information exchange across relevant agencies with specific attention to at least the following information:

- Victims – who has been a victim in the past, who is likely to be in the future, how they are targeted and groomed, the circumstances under which the offender gains access, proximity and trust.

- Under what conditions and circumstances has this risk occurred in the past and under what conditions and circumstances might it occur in the future?

- Consideration of imminence – is there an opportunity, is an opportunity being created, is there a lack of internal controls on behaviour(s), or are external controls breaking down?

- Level of motivation to offend and level of motivation to comply with the risk management plan. What is the evidence of compliance and self-risk management? What is the offender's view of his/her risk?

- Are risks escalating? Is the/will the risk management plan be capable of containing the risk or not? What has worked in the past and what has failed in the past?

Choice of risk assessment tools

Work with high-risk offenders takes place in a climate of low public trust and harsh media scrutiny (Kemshall 2003a). In these circumstances it is essential that defensible decisions are made (Carson 1996; Kemshall 1998), that is decisions are grounded in the evidence, based on relevant information and using the most appropriate risk assessment tool. It is therefore imperative that risk tools are chosen with care and according to appropriate criteria. Without this, tools tend to be developed pragmatically to deal with local concerns, often by adapting or combining parts of existing tools or by using the practice experience of staff. These tools are rarely validated against the relevant population and can inadvertently give staff and managers a false sense of security about both the predictive nature of their risk assessments and of their defensibility. This can also result in inconsistency within and across agencies, and is open to ethical and legal challenges, not least under human rights legislation, particularly where such tools have been used to justify third-party disclosure or high levels of intrusion into people's lives.

Based upon an extensive review of existing research (Kemshall 2001) and a survey of risk tools in Scotland (McIvor and Kemshall 2002) it is possible to generate key criteria for the adaptation of risk assessment tools. In brief, this involves validation by at least one peer reviewed publication demonstrating the methodology used for validating the tool on a relevant population. Such tools should combine actuarial and dynamic risk factors well supported by research. These tools must be able to differentiate between low, medium and high risk with a degree of accuracy and consistency to ensure that risk thresholds are appropriate and interventions proportionate. Finally the tool(s) must have inter-rater/assessor reliability (that is, all assessors use the tool with the same result). It is also desirable that risk assessment tools are user-friendly, resource lean, 'easy' to train staff to use and their process of use is transparent and accountable (adapted from McIvor and Kemshall 2002: 51).

Risk management

Risk management should be understood as *harm reduction* either through the reduction of the likelihood of a risk occurring or the reduction of its impact should it occur (Laws 1996) and should not be understood as 'zero risk'. Risk management should also be proportionate and fair, afford reasonable protection to victims and public, and be subject to timely revision should risks change (either upward or downward). Current research indicates the most effective features of risk management (see Kemshall 2001 for a full review; and Kemshall and McIvor 2004 for sex offenders). In brief, cognitive-behavioural programmes have the most success but need to be combined with appropriate external controls (such as residence restriction) and the use of sanctions and enforcement for non-compliance (Beech and Fisher 2004; Matravers 2003; Vennard and Hedderman 1998). Such interventions should emphasise self-risk management and promote the use of internal controls over the longer term. There should be contingency plans in case of risk management failure, and rapid response arrangements to changing situations or deterioration in circumstances/behaviours. Supportive and integrative approaches should also be applied where risk assessments indicate their usefulness (e.g 'circles of support').

Risk management is potentially resource hungry as well as subject to harsh external scrutiny and accountability. In these circumstances it is essential that such work can be shown to be effective and value for money in an arena of finite resource. The absence of disaster is not enough as an evaluation strategy for success, and while some MAPPAs have already begun to monitor their work in order to meet the requirements of the annual report, it is important that this monitoring is extended into genuine evaluations of risk management work. This issue has been recognised by the NPS and the issue of PC 49/2005 (NPS 2005d) which addresses both quality issues in risk assessment and how to monitor risk assessments and subsequent case reviews.

SMART risk plans enable subsequent evaluation through sampling and audit of cases against the SMART criteria, that is plans should be

Specific
Measurable
Achievable
Realistic
Targeted (and timely). (Kemshall 2001, 2003c)

This enables the identification of 'drift' and ensures that the objectives set in individual cases are met. Audits by panel personnel of, say, 10 per cent of cases each year would assist reviews of practice standards, encourage consistency and help to identify system failures and resource gaps early. Corrective action can then be taken as a matter of course, integrated within the quality assurance function of MAPPA Strategic Management Boards. This best practice can then be evidenced and used in the annual report to reassure the public that risk management is being delivered with quality and integrity. This best practice approach has been emphasised by Probation Circular 10/2005 (Home Office 2005b) which presents a risk management framework and key headings for risk management plans.

Broadening risk management

Risk management can be divided into two basic approaches: the coercive and the integrative. The coercive relies upon the 'community protection model': conditions, restrictions, sanctions, enforcement and intrusive community measures (Connelly and Williamson 2000). This approach also recognises that some offenders will have high motivation to offend and low motivation to comply with treatment programmes. Such offenders may only be effectively contained in the community through high levels of surveillance and controls on behaviours (for example, through electronic tagging and exclusions from certain places such as schools and parks) and longer-term behaviour change may not be achievable.

Integrative approaches on the other hand emphasise inclusionary techniques, such as 'circles of support'. This initiative to combat such social isolation was originally imported from the USA via the Wolvercote specialist clinic for sex offender treatment. In brief, the initiative recognises that many sex offenders are social isolates and provides a 'circle' of supportive people to whom the offender can turn once released from either prison or a treatment centre. Such circles are made up of volunteers with whom the offender will have significant contact (for example, local church leaders, mentors, etc.). In addition to social support, the volunteers are trained to provide relapse prevention help and to identify 'warning signals' for risky behaviour. They will also inform the statutory authorities if the risky behaviour appears to warrant it. At present there are two pilot schemes in the UK and long-term evaluation of the programme here is awaited.

A further initiative is 'Stop it Now!', supported by an alliance of key voluntary and statutory agencies working with child sexual abuse. This initiative recognises that most child sexual abuse is not perpetrated by 'monsters' or strangers but by people children know. The initiative is a combination of education, public awareness raising and a Helpline to offer 'advice and support to people who suspect abuse and to those seeking help to stop their own abusive thoughts and behaviour' (Stop it Now! 2005). The Vermont Helpline in the USA has shown that abusers do come forward and benefit from treatment programmes, and that the awareness raising does result in more people able to recognise child sexual abuse (see http://www.stopitnow.org.uk; Tabachnick and Dawson 1999). In the UK approximately one-third of helpline callers are abusers or potential abusers, and the other main group of callers are partners of abusers seeking help (Kemshall *et al.* 2004).

These initiatives recognise that sex offenders (and other high-risk offenders) are present in communities (and always will be) and aim to broaden the responsibility for 'policing' them beyond the traditional boundaries of statutory agencies like police and probation and beyond the standard range of 'risk management' techniques of police visits and occasional covert surveillance. These initiatives can be understood as part of a broader approach that characterises both sexual and violent offending as a public health issue (Laws 1996, 2000). In brief, Laws argues that traditional, reactive responses to sexual and violent offending located within the criminal justice system have not proved effective (supported by growing crime rates and increased victimisation), and that perversely such approaches only serve to heighten public fears and the rejection of such offenders (especially sex offenders) (Laws 2000: 30). The Public Health Approach (PHA) is forward-looking, proactive and focused on prevention rather than punishment, exclusion or retribution. PHA operates on three levels:

> *The primary level:* at which the goal is prevention of sexually deviant behaviour before it starts, for example the identification and prevention of sexually deviant behaviour in children, and the long-term prevention of adults in engaging in sexual abuse.
>
> *The secondary level:* at which the goal is the prevention of first-time offenders from progressing, or the situationally specific or opportunistic offender from becoming a generalist.
>
> *The tertiary level:* at which the goal is effective work with persistent and more serious offenders. Specific goals are usually relapse prevention and effective treatment programmes.
>
> (see Laws 2000: 31)

Laws argues that as an alternative to (largely ineffective) incarceration increased efforts should be targeted at levels 1 and 2. This requires increased attention to 'prevention goals' of which the following are seen as the most important:

- *Public awareness and responsibility.* This involves informing the public of 'the magnitude and characteristics of sexual offending', including how sex offenders groom, but more importantly that sex offenders are part of the community. The emphasis is upon adult responsibility for responding to sex offending.

- *Public education.* This involves the demythologising of sex offenders and an emphasis upon treatment programmes that work. The message that something can be done and that treatment is worth investing in is a key one.

(adapted from Laws 2000)

This is supported by direct targeting of sex offenders encouraging both active and potential sex offenders/abusers to come forward for treatment. The emphasis is upon the prevention of those beginning to engage in abuse or thinking about it and relapse prevention for those with established behaviours. Harm reduction and risk minimisation are seen as key components of such a strategy. PHA is also being pioneered in the arena of violent offending and domestic violence (Laws 2000). These are important initiatives and are worthy of further evaluation. However, it is important to recognise that the transferability of largely US initiatives to the UK context is not without some difficulties. The UK has a less well developed public health approach to interpersonal violence and sexual abuse than in the USA, the UK does not have community notification (a Megan's Law) and treatment outside of the criminal justice system is virtually non-existent.

Conclusion

Public protection is now a key task for criminal justice agencies, including probation, within a largely risk-based penality. The focus thus far has been upon systems, processes and formal risk tools for the safe and credible assessment and management of risk. This has largely resulted in a coercive and community protection model of risk in which management of place, control, surveillance and exclusion/incarceration are major strategies. While these strategies may be necessary for the critical few, it is increasingly recognised that both probation and public protection panels will be tasked with the effective management of rather more level 1 and 2 offenders, where risk management is located either in single agencies (level 1) or in localised inter-agency arrangements (level 2),[5] and that reintegration and self-risk management are essential long-term objectives. This in itself requires a move from a 'zero risk' position to a position of acceptable risk, acknowledging that nothing is risk free and that the role of the Probation Service is to work with manageable risks in the community, *not* to manage risks away.

Acknowledgements

The authors gratefully acknowledge the support of Gill Mackenzie, Visiting Professor at De Montfort University, on two research projects cited in this chapter, and the support of Roy Bailey and Joe Yates in the MAPPA evaluation.

Notes

1 Megan's Law (named after 7-year-old Megan Kanka murdered in the USA by a known paedophile) allows the 'community notification' of details of sex offenders to members of the public. This can include the use of posters, distribution of flyers and access to sex offender registers via the Internet (Kanka 2000; Power 2003).
2 At time of writing the NOMs 'Guidance on the Management of High-risk Offenders' was still being drafted.

3 This is a contention made by senior police personnel. However, there is at present no research study to confirm or deny the impact of Operation Ore (or similar operations) on the sex offender register.

4 Level 1 management is carried out by a single agency; level 2 management is through local inter-agency arrangements but does not usually require the intensive management of the formal MAPPA procedures.

5 Given the introduction of both indeterminate and extended public protection sentences under the Criminal Justice Act 2003 most of the critical few will be in custody, with a small proportion under (possibly extended) licence or other forms of community supervision.

Further reading

Barbara Hudson's (2004) *Justice in the Risk Society* is a scholarly and in-depth examination of the relationship between risks and rights, placing risks within the broader neo-liberal preoccupation with governance. Hazel Kemshall (2003a), in *Understanding Risk in Criminal Justice*, provides an accessible examination of how risk is used by criminal justice agencies, particularly probation and police, and within crime prevention. The contemporary role of risk in criminal justice is explored in some detail, and the rise of risk is placed within broader penal and social policy. Finally, Nash's (2006) *Public Protection and the Criminal Justice Process* is an excellent review of current preoccupations with dangerousness and public protection. The book provides a critical examination of how public protection has driven the penal policy agenda and changed the work of key agencies such as police and probation.

References

Andrews, D.A. and Bonta, J. (1995) *The Level of Supervision Inventory-Revised*. Toronto: Multi-Health Systems.

Andrews, D.A., Bonta, J. and Hoge, R.D. (1990) 'Classification for effective rehabilitation', *Criminal Justice and Behaviour*, 17: 19–51.

Beech, A. and Fisher, D. (2004) 'Treatment of sex offenders in the UK prison and probation settings', in H. Kemshall and G. McIvor (eds), *Managing Sex Offender Risk*. London: Jessica Kingsley.

Bottoms, A. (1977) 'Reflections on the renaissance of dangerousness', *Howard Journal of Criminal Justice*, 16: 70–96.

Bottoms, A. (1995) 'The politics and philosophy of punishment and sentencing', in C. Clarkson and R. Morgan (eds), *The Politics of Sentencing Reform*. Oxford: Oxford University Press.

Carson, D. (1996) 'Risking legal repercussions', in H. Kemshall and J. Pritchard (eds), *Good Practice in Risk Assessment and Risk Management*, Vol. 1. London: Jessica Kingsley.

Carter, Patrick (2003) *Managing Offenders, Reducing Crime. A New Approach* (Carter Report). London: Home Office.

Cawson, P., Wattam, S. and Kelly, G. (2000) *Child Maltreatment in the United Kingdom: A Study of the Prevalence of Child Abuse and Neglect*. London: NSPCC.

Clark, D. (2002) *OASys – An Explanation*. Paper presented to Home Office 'Criminal Justice Conference: Using Risk Assessment in Effective Sentence Management'. Pendley Manor Hotel, Tring, 14–15 March.

Cobley, C. (2000) *Sex Offenders: Law, Policy and Practice*. Bristol: Jordans.

Connelly, C. and Williamson, S. (2000) *Review of the Research Literature on Serious Violent and Sexual Offenders*. Edinburgh: Scottish Executive Central Research Unit.

Department of Health (2002) *Safeguarding Children*. London: Department of Health.

Ditchfield, J. (1997) 'Actuarial prediction and risk assessment', *Prison Service Journal*, 113: 8–13.

Feeley, M. (2003) 'Crime, social order and the rise of neo-conservative politics', *Theoretical Criminology*, 7: 111–30.

Feeley, M. and Simon, J. (1992) 'The new penology: notes on the emerging strategy for corrections', *Criminology*, 30 (4): 449–75.

Feeley, M. and Simon, J. (1994) 'Actuarial justice: the emerging new criminal law', in D. Nelken (ed.), *The Futures of Criminology*. London: Sage.

Flynn, E. (1978) 'Classification for risk and supervision: a preliminary conceptualisation', in J. C. Freeman (ed.), *Prisons Past and Future*. London: Heinemann.

Garland, D. (1985) *Punishment and Welfare: A History of Penal Strategies*. Aldershot: Gower.

Garland, D. (1990) *Punishment and Modern Society: A Study in Social Theory*. Oxford: Clarendon Press.

Garland, D. (2001) *The Culture of Crime Control: Crime and Social Order in Contemporary Society*. Oxford: Clarendon Press.

Gibbs, J.C., Bassinger, K.C. and Fuller, D. (1992) *Moral Maturity: Measuring the Development of Sociomoral Reflection*. Hillsdale, NJ: Erlbaum.

Greenwood, P. and Abrahamse, A. (1982) *Selective Incapacitation*. Santa Monica, CA: Rand Corporation.

Greenwood, P. and Turner, S. (1987) *Selective Incapacitation: Why the High Rate Offenders are the Hardest to Predict*. Santa Monica, CA: Rand Corporation.

Greenwood, P., Rydell, C., Abrahamse, A., Caulkins, J., Chiesa, J., Model, K. and Klein, S. (1996) 'Estimated benefits and costs of California's new mandatory sentencing law', in D. Shichor and D. Sechrest (eds), *Three Strikes and You're Out: Vengeance as Public Policy*. Thousand Oaks, CA: Sage.

Grubin, D. (1998) *Sex Offending against Children: Understanding the Risk*. London: Home Office.

Grubin, D. and Wingate, S. (1996) 'Sexual offence recidivism: prediction versus understanding', *Criminal Behaviour and Mental Health*, 6: 349–59.

Hacking, I. (1990) *The Taming of Chance*. Cambridge: Cambridge University Press.

Home Office (2001a) *Initial Guidance to the Police and Probation Services on sections 67 and 68 of the Criminal Justice and Court Services Act 2000*. London: Home Office.

Home Office (2001b) *The Offender Assessment System: OASys*. London: Home Office.

Home Office (2002) *Further Guidance to the Police and Probation Services on sections 67 and 68 of the Criminal Justice and Court Services Act 2000*. London: Home Office.

Home Office (2003a) *Criminal Justice Act: A Briefing Paper*. London: Home Office.

Home Office (2003b) *MAPPA Guidance: Protection Through Partnership*. London: Home Office.

Home Office (2004a) *MAPPA Guidance: Protection Through Partnership (Version 1.2)*. London: Home Office.

Home Office (2004b) MAPPA *Annual Reports press release*. Available at: http://www.probation.homeoffice.gov.uk/output/Page241.asp

Home Office (2004c) *Reducing Crime, Changing Lives. The Government's Plans for Transforming the Management of Offenders*. London: Home Office.

Home Office (2004d) *Protecting the Public from Sexual Crime. Explaining the Criminal Justice Act 2000*. London: Home Office Communications Directorate.

Hudson, B. (2004) *Justice in the Risk Society*. London: Sage.

Kanka, M. (2000) *How Megan's Death Changed Us All: The Personal Story of a Mother and Anti-Crime Advocate*. The Megan Nicole Kanka Foundation. Available at: www. apbnews.com/safetycenter/family/kanka/sooo/03/28/kanka0328_0l.htm (accessed 28 March 2000).

Kemshall, H. (1998) *Risk in Probation Practice*. Aldershot: Avebury.

Kemshall, H. (2001) *Risk Assessment and Management of Known Sexual and Violent Offenders: A Review of Current Issues*. London: Home Office.

Kemshall, H. (2002) 'Effective practice in probation: an example of 'Advanced Liberal' responsibilisation', *Howard Journal of Criminal Justice*, 41: 41–58.

Kemshall, H. (2003a) *Understanding Risk in Criminal Justice*. Buckingham: Open University Press.

Kemshall, H. (2003b) 'Risk, dangerousness and female offenders', in G. McIvor (ed.), *Women Who Offend*. London: Jessica Kingsley.

Kemshall, H. (2003c) 'Community management of high risk offenders – a review of best practice for MAPPA', *Prison Service Journal*, March: 146.

Kemshall, H. and McIvor, G. (eds) (2004) *Sex Offenders: Managing the Risk*. London: Jessica Kingsley.

Kemshall, H. and Maguire, M. (2001) 'Public protection, partnership and risk penality: the multi-agency risk management of sexual and violent offenders', *Punishment and Society*, 3 (2): 237–64.

Kemshall, H., Mackenzie, G. and Wood, J. (2004) *Stop It Now! UK and Ireland. An Evaluation*. Leicester: De Montfort University/London: Stop It Now!

Kemshall, H., Mackenzie, G., Wood, J., Bailey, R. and Yates, J. (2005) *Strengthening the Multi-Agency Public Protection Arrangements*. London: Home Office.

Kitzinger, J. (1999a) 'Researching risk and the media', *Health, Risk and Society*, 1 (1): 55–70.

Kitzinger, J. (1999b) 'The ultimate neighbour from hell: media framing of paedophiles', in B. Franklin (ed.), *Social Policy, Media and Misrepresentation*. London: Routledge.

Laws, R.D. (1996) 'Relapse prevention or harm reduction?', *Sexual Abuse: A Journal of Research and Treatment*, 8: 243–7.

Laws, R.D. (2000) 'Sexual offending as public health problem: a North American perspective', *Journal of Sexual Aggression*, 5 (1): 30–44.

McIvor, G. and Kemshall, H. (2002) *Serious Violent and Sexual Offenders: The Use of Risk Assessment Tools in Scotland*. Edinburgh: Scottish Executive.

McIvor, G., Moodie, K. with Perrott, S. and Spencer, F. (2001) *The Relative Effectiveness of Risk Assessment Instruments*. Edinburgh: Scottish Executive Central Research Unit.

Maguire, M., Kemshall, H., Noaks, L. and Wincup, E. (2001) *Risk Management of Sexual and Violent Offenders: The Work of Public Protection Panels*, Police Research Paper 139. London: Home Office.

Matravers, A. (ed.) (2003) *Sex Offenders in the Community: Managing and Reducing the Risks*. Cullompton: Willan.

Maynard-Moody, S., Musheno, M. and Palumbo, D. (1990) 'Street-wise social policy: resolving the dilemma of street-level influence and successful implementation', *Western Political Quarterly*, 43: 831–48.

Murray, C. (1997) *Does Prison Work?* London: Institute for Economic Affairs.

Nash, M. (1999) *Police, Probation and Protecting the Public*. London: Blackstone Press.

Nash, M. (2006) *Public Protection and the Criminal Justice Process*. Oxford: Oxford University Press.

National Probation Service (2001) *A New Choreography: An Integrated Strategy for the National Probation Service for England and Wales. Strategic Framework 2001–2004*. London: Home Office.

National Probation Service (2004) *Sex Offender Strategy*. London: Home Office.

National Probation Service (2005a) *National Guide for the New Criminal Justice Act 2003 Sentences for Public Protection*. London: Home Office.

National Probation Service (2005b) *Public Protection Framework, Risk of Harm and MAPPA Thresholds*, Probation Circular 10/2005. London: National Probation Service.

National Probation Service (2005c) *MAPPA Consultation Paper*, Probation Circular 39/2005. London: National Probation Service.

National Probation Service (2005d) *Assessment and Management of Risk of Harm Action Plan*, Probation Circular 49/2005. London: National Probation Service.

O'Malley, P. (2001a) 'Discontinuity, government and risk', *Theoretical Criminology*, 5 (1): 85–92.

O'Malley, P. (2001b) 'Risk, crime and prudentialism revisited', in K. Stenson and R. Sullivan (eds), *Crime, Risk and Justice: The Politics of Crime Control in Liberal Democracies*. Cullompton: Willan.

Power, H. (2003) 'Disclosing information on sex offenders: the human rights implications', in A. Matravers (ed.), *Sex Offenders in the Community: Managing and Reducing the Risk*. Cullompton: Willan.

Pratt, J. (1997) *Governing the Dangerous*. Sydney: Federation Press.

Pratt, J. (2000) 'The return of the wheelbarrow men: or, the arrival of postmodern penality?', *British Journal of Criminology*, 40: 127–45.

Raynor, P. (1997a) *Implementing the 'Level of Service Inventory-Revised' (LSI-R) in Britain: Initial Results from Five Probation Areas*. Swansea: Cognitive Centre Foundation.

Raynor, P. (1997b) 'Some observations on rehabilitation and justice', *Howard Journal of Criminal Justice*, 36 (3): 248–62.

Raynor, P., Kynch, J., Roberts, C. and Merrington, S. (2000) *Risk and Need Assessment in the Probation Services: An Evaluation*. London: Home Office.

Rigakos, G. and Hadden, R.W. (2001) 'Crime, capitalism and the "risk society": towards the same olde modernity?', *Theoretical Criminology*, 5 (1): 61–84.

Robinson, G. (2002) 'A rationality of risk in the Probation Service: its evolution and contemporary profile', *Punishment and Society*, 4 (1): 5–25.

Satayamurti. C. (1981) *Occupational Survival*. Oxford: Blackwell.

Shute, S. (2004) 'The Sexual Offences Act 2003. The new civil preventative orders: sexual offences prevention orders; foreign travel orders; risk of sexual harm orders', *Criminal Law Review*, pp. 417–40.

Stop It Now! UK & Ireland (2005) *About Child Sexual Abuse*. Available at: http://www.stopitnow.org.uk/ch_sex_abuse.htm (accessed 18 February 2005).

Tabachnick, J. and Dawson, E. (1999) *Stop It Now! Vermont: Four Year Program Evaluation, 1995–1999*. Available from Stop It Now! USA.

Thompson, K. (1998) *Moral Panics*. London: Routledge.

Vennard, J. and Hedderman, C. (1998) 'Effective interventions with offenders', in P. Goldblatt and C. Lewis (eds), *Reducing Offending: An Assessment of Research Evidence on Ways of Dealing with Offending Behaviour*. London: Home Office.

Walker, N. (1996) *Dangerous People*. London: Blackstone Press.

Chapter 14

The resettlement of ex-prisoners

Mike Maguire

The Probation Service has a long tradition of working with offenders on their release from prison. This has ranged from offers of advice and support on a voluntary basis (including 'welfare' services such as help in finding accommodation) to the statutory supervision of prisoners granted early release, which includes the control function of ensuring that licence conditions are adhered to. At times, probation involvement with prisoners has been restricted mainly to post-release work, while at others probation officers have been encouraged to visit them in prison to build relationships and formulate release plans from an early point in their sentence. The related terminology has also changed over the years, reflecting shifts in policy and practice: thus the concept of 'after-care' has given way to 'throughcare' and more recently 'resettlement', while the term 'offender management' is now beginning to replace 'casework' or 'supervision' in official discourse. However, despite these variations, the basic problems and challenges surrounding release from custody have changed little. A high proportion of inmates enter prison with major social and personal problems (typically related to financial insecurity, lack of education, unemployment, substance abuse, social isolation or mental health) which face them again when they leave. Imprisonment itself often adds new problems and dislocates their lives still further: they may lose a house, a job or a relationship, and plans to improve their situation may be frustrated by difficulties in communicating with the outside world. They will have been exposed throughout their sentence to the negative influences and criminal attitudes of the inmate culture. And even if they fully intend to 'go straight', many will face distrust or rejection from ordinary members of the community, potential employers or service-providing agencies.

This chapter examines critically the main ways in which policy-makers, legislators, the Prison and Probation Services and other agencies have responded to these problems, which not only blight the lives of ex-prisoners but almost certainly increase the risk that they will reoffend. The central focus will be on developments in England and Wales over the last few years, which have seen a growth in central government's awareness of the importance of 'resettlement' to its aim of reducing reoffending. This has given rise to an agenda of major organisational and practice change built around the establishment of the National Offender Management Service (NOMS), the drawing up of national and regional resettlement strategies by multi-agency partnership boards and the promotion of concepts such as 'end to end' offender management and 'joined up' service provision 'through the gate'. The likely impact of these developments will be examined in the light of relevant theory and research. First, however, a brief overview will be given of earlier attempts to manage or ameliorate the transition from custody to community, highlighting the changing attitudes, approaches and levels of commitment to this kind of work shown by the Probation Service, as well as the important role played by other organisations (especially the voluntary sector).

History and background

From charitable aid to statutory supervision

The origins of 'resettlement' work lie in assistance to ex-prisoners provided by charitable organisations, notably the Discharged Prisoners' Aid Societies (DPAS), small groups of volunteers attached to county gaols, which date back to the early nineteenth century. Also important was the 'prison gate mission', which is regarded as one of the direct forerunners of the modern Probation Service. The mission was initially set up by churches in the 1870s to foster contacts between prisoners and clergymen from their home area or (as in Liverpool) simply to offer discharged prisoners a free breakfast in exchange for 'signing the pledge' to abstain from alcohol. However, the role soon expanded into assistance with problems such as accommodation or employment, and by 1894 help was being provided to over 15,000 ex-prisoners annually (for further discussion, see Jarvis 1972; Bochel 1976; Vanstone 2004).

During the first half of the twentieth century, both the DPAS and the new Probation Service continued to provide assistance to ex-prisoners on a voluntary basis. In the case of probation, this took the shape of 'voluntary after-care', a system whereby any prisoner could request assistance or support on release (see Maguire *et al.* 2000). However, the Probation Service also began to develop practice in the direction of more formal post-release supervision, first taking on the statutory 'after-care' of boys and young men released from Approved School and Borstal and then becoming officially responsible (under the Criminal Justice Act 1948) for the after-care of longer-term prisoners released from preventive detention and corrective training. Eventually, in the 1960s, it assumed primary responsibility for all after-care, both statutory and voluntary (effectively bringing to an end the long history of the DPAS). The new role was reflected in a change of name, to the Probation and After-Care Service. Probation officers also began to work inside prisons on a full-time basis in order to provide welfare services to inmates and help them prepare for release.

The culmination of this trend towards closer involvement with prisons and prisoners was the introduction of *parole* under the Criminal Justice Act

1968 (for general accounts of the development of parole, see Morgan 1983; Maguire 1992; Cavadino and Dignan 2002). This permitted the early release of medium- and long-term prisoners after serving at least one-third of their sentence (or 12 months, whichever was longer), on condition that they met regularly with a probation officer, did not reoffend and adhered to any other conditions or restrictions imposed: any behaviour giving rise to concern could lead to immediate recall to prison. Initially, only small numbers were granted parole, but the great majority of these completed their licence successfully, enhancing government and public confidence in the system. Consequently, the Parole Board adopted a much less cautious policy, and by 1980 around half of those eligible were being released early (Maguire 1992: 183). This placed an increasing burden on the Probation Service in terms of preparing for prisoners' release (for example, in visiting them in prison and checking the suitability of where they planned to live), facilitating their access to welfare services or employment opportunities, and enforcing attendance and compliance with conditions.

This workload was further increased in 1983 by the extension of parole to prisoners serving sentences as short as 13 months.[1] Partly because of this, and partly in response to the Government's wish to see the Probation Service concentrate less on 'welfare' and more on 'control' (especially of the more serious offenders), the tradition of offering voluntary after-care to ex-prisoners was rapidly eroded. In 1984, the Service's *Statement of National Objectives and Priorities* explicitly stated that lower priority should be attached to 'social work for offenders released from custody' (Home Office 1984). Over the next few years, too, a series of consultative papers (Home Office 1988a, 1988b, 1990) promulgated the concept of 'punishment in the community' and began to redefine the core tasks of the Probation Service, prioritising public protection, the prevention of reoffending and the strict enforcement of orders and licences.

The final nail was driven into the coffin of voluntary after-care in 1992, when the discretionary parole system was replaced by 'automatic conditional release' (ACR) at the half-way point of their sentence for *all* prisoners sentenced to between one and four years (Maguire *et al.* 1996; Maguire and Raynor 1997). This not only increased the probation workload yet further, but was accompanied by a set of National Standards (Home Office 1992) that emphasised enforcement procedures and sent a clear message that post-release supervision – which would now be compulsory for many prisoners who had neither 'earned' it nor voluntarily consented to it – was primarily about punishment, control and public protection rather than 'care'. By 1996, only 4,800 offenders were officially recorded as subject to voluntary supervision, compared with 26,700 in 1991 (Home Office 1997).

The biggest 'losers' from these changes were short-term prisoners (those sentenced to less than 12 months), who were not subject to statutory supervision and had constituted the bulk of those receiving voluntary after-care. As will be shown in the next section, the irony of this situation is that short-term prisoners – who form the majority of prison leavers – have both higher reconviction rates and higher levels of social need than almost any other category of offender. Yet for much of the 1990s they remained 'the forgotten majority' (NACRO 2000), largely neglected by Home Office policy-makers and the Probation Service alike.

The revival of the resettlement agenda

Despite the official neglect, the 'short termers' issue was kept alive through a series of reports by academics researchers (Hagell *et al.* 1995; Maguire *et al.* 1997, 1998), voluntary agencies (NACRO 1993, 2000) and inspection bodies (HM Inspectorates of Prisons and Probation 2001). These all pointed to similar conclusions, providing ample evidence of the need for reform.

First and foremost, they documented the high levels of social need to be found among short-term prisoners. For example, in broad terms:

- two-thirds were unemployed before going to prison;
- around a third had no long-term accommodation to return to after release;
- over half had almost no educational qualifications;
- well over half were involved in substance misuse.

Furthermore, many had complex and entrenched personal problems relating to mental health, family relationships or social skills. The problems were often multiple and interacted to create what Corden (1980, 1983) had earlier described as a 'cycle of disadvantage'. It was also demonstrated that women prisoners' resettlement problems and needs were often even greater than men's (Caddle and White 1994; NACRO 1996, 2001; Rumgay 2004; Gelsthorpe 2004a, 2004b); later research has similarly documented higher than average levels of need among ethnic minority offenders (NACRO 2002; Calverley *et al.* 2004). Little of this, it is emphasised, should have come as a major surprise to policy-makers: similar concerns had been raised many times in the past, particularly during the 1970s (e.g. Banks and Fairhead 1976; Corden *et al.* 1978, 1979, 1980; Fairhead 1981), though rarely with much impact on policy.

Secondly, they drew attention to how ex-prisoners' problems were often exacerbated by exclusionary attitudes on the part of service providers, including in some areas explicit policies to refuse them local authority housing or reluctance to accept them as patients for substance abuse treatment, as well as by unwillingness among employers to offer them jobs. Again, this is an issue documented many times in the past (see, for example, Martin and Webster 1971; Davies 1974).

Thirdly, they pointed out that, not only did short-termers receive little or no assistance after release, but as they were mainly held in overcrowded local prisons with limited facilities (in contrast to the better equipped training prisons for medium and long-termers) they also tended to be offered few opportunities in custody to take part in rehabilitative activities or make effective preparations for release.

Fourthly, they underlined the exceptionally high reoffending rates of short-term prisoners, pointing out that around 60 per cent were reconvicted within two years (compared with an overall prisoner reconviction rate of about 55 per cent), and that roughly half of these received a new prison sentence. Both rates have risen further in recent years, the reconviction rate for those serving under 12 months reaching 70 per cent for those released in 2003 (Shepherd and Whiting 2006: 9–10).

Although focusing on the particularly acute problems of short-termers, these reports – and others – also noted that all prisoners faced similar problems to some degree, and that many of those released on licence under probation supervision did not in reality receive services that addressed them effectively. This was especially true of medium-termers (those serving one to under four years), who were subject to automatic conditional release (ACR). The Probation Service was progressively 'swamped' with large numbers of such offenders, many of them on only a few months' licence, and many without understanding or experience of (or liking for) probation supervision. Budget and time restraints frequently prevented probation officers from visiting their future supervisees in prison, which made it difficult for them to build trusting relationships, while poor communication between prisons and probation meant that they often lacked knowledge about any planning or rehabilitative work that had been undertaken in custody and had to 'start again' after release. Moreover, managers' demands that they follow National Standards meant that much of officers' attention post-release was directed towards enforcement activities (especially attendance requirements). Consequently, the 'throughcare' ideal of coordination and continuity between pre- and post-release interventions was rarely realised in practice, and the supervision process became increasingly impersonal, rule-bound and bureaucratic.

Persuasive as these reports were, their direct influence on policy was limited. The real breakthrough in terms of directing serious government attention to the importance of resettlement – for short-term as well as longer-term prisoners – came through the combined impact of three official reports published between 2001 and 2003 which not only accepted many of the above points but produced concrete recommendations to address them through major policy and legislative change. Although focused on three different topics, they were linked by a common aim of finding more effective ways of reducing reoffending by ex-prisoners, which was becoming an increasingly important plank of the Government's broader 'what works' agenda (see later). These are known as the Halliday Report, the Social Exclusion Unit Report and the Carter Report.

The first, written by a senior civil servant, John Halliday (2001), entailed a wide-ranging review of sentencing policy. Halliday concluded that, while retaining the delivery of fair punishment as one of its core objectives, sentencing should be aimed more at the rehabilitation of offenders than was currently the case. Identifying the lack of post-release support to short-term prisoners as one of the main obstacles to achieving this, he proposed the introduction of a so-called 'seamless' sentence, which would be served partly in prison and partly in the community. Prison sentences of under 12 months, he recommended, should be replaced by a new sentence of 'Custody Plus', whereby a short period in custody (normally only a few weeks) would be followed by a much longer period under probation supervision. The period of imprisonment should be seen as preparation for the remainder of the sentence rather than as an end in itself. This idea was translated into legislation in the Criminal Justice Act 2003 and was due to be implemented in November 2006. However, it was deferred a few months before this, apparently because of concerns that the available resources would prove inadequate, and at the time of writing (December 2006) it is not clear when – indeed whether – it will eventually be introduced. In its absence, a significant hole remains in the strategy to improve resettlement. If implemented, the new sentence would serve as an essential framework for the development of 'through the gate' sentence planning and the 'joining up' of prison and community interventions for many recidivist offenders who would previously have had little access to rehabilitative work or services to meet their needs.

The second major report, entitled *Reducing Re-offending by Ex-Prisoners*, was published in 2002 by an influential cross-departmental government body, the Social Exclusion Unit (SEU), based in the Office of the Deputy Prime Minister (ODPM). The ODPM had earlier commissioned a piece of research by the Rough Sleepers Unit (2000) which had drawn particular attention to the problems of short-term prisoners, noting that:

> People who had been in prison before had frequently experienced the same problems each time they were released. Problems with accommodation, employment and substance misuse had not been resolved, possibly increasing the chances of them being imprisoned again. A number of people said that specific problems were faced by people on short sentences – an issue raised by the professionals and one that was to emerge again throughout the interviews with prisoners ... Few prisoners had adequate preparations for their release. Access to pre-release courses was patchy and many prisoners were discharged with little idea what was happening to them and with no access to support and advice.

The SEU report echoed many of these findings and those of the earlier mentioned reports, but went considerably further in terms of its vision for change. The crux of its argument was that addressing the problems posed by short-term prisoners was critical to Government's ambitions to bring about major reductions in crime and reoffending. Moreover, these problems were deep-rooted: many offenders were socially excluded and lacked the necessary education, skills or resources to build and sustain a crime-free life. They were therefore unlikely to be solved by piecemeal measures, such as attempts by voluntary groups to find accommodation, employment or drug treatment for individual offenders, which were time-consuming and frustrating and often ended in failure or only short-term success. Rather, a concerted, 'joined up' strategy was required, led by central government and involving commitment from all the relevant departments: this would identify the resettlement of ex-prisoners as a priority activity, which would be reflected in departments' and agencies' performance targets.

The location of the SEU within the Office of the Deputy Prime Minister not only enhanced the political influence of this report, but gave its authors the opportunity to adopt a cross-departmental approach in devising solutions:

for example, seeking to engage departments with responsibility for education, health and housing – which had previously regarded ex-prisoners as of low priority – at the core of its suggested strategy. Many of its recommendations were eventually translated into action in 2004 in the Reducing Re-Offending National Action Plan (see later).

Finally, the most controversial of the three, a broad review of the 'correctional services' by Patrick Carter (Home Office 2003), took as one of its main focuses the lack of coordination between the Prison and Probation Services in their delivery of rehabilitative and resettlement interventions. The report recommended major organisational changes to 'join up' the work and make it more meaningful and coherent from the offender's perspective. Carter also argued that the quality of interventions would be improved by introducing an element of commercial competition – what he called 'contestability' – and allowing other public sector, private or voluntary agencies to bid against probation and prisons for contracts to deliver them. These recommendations were immediately accepted by the Government and translated quickly into action (many would say too hastily – see, for example, Hough *et al.* 2006). Within a few months, the decision was taken to set up the new National Offender Management Service (NOMS), to become responsible for commissioning and overseeing the delivery of all interventions with offenders inside prison, in the community or 'through the gate'. In doing so, it would create a clear separation between 'offender management' (the planning and monitoring of each offender's 'journey' through his/her sentence, including the enforcement of conditions) and 'interventions' (individual rehabilitative, punitive or restorative activities within the sentence): either or both might eventually be subjected to 'contestability'. In addition, a 'National Offender Management Model' (NOMM) was designed, based on the notion of coherent, 'end-to-end' offender management (NOMS 2005; see also Raynor and Maguire 2006). As will be discussed later, these new arrangements, combined with the implementation of the Reducing Re-Offending National Action Plan, are already giving a new shape to resettlement practice in England and Wales.

Theories, aims and models

Before looking more closely at current and planned developments, it is helpful to consider some of the explicit and implicit theories, aims and assumptions behind different approaches to resettlement practice, as well as any research evidence as to which of these are most likely to be successful.

Definitions and models of resettlement

Although 'resettlement' has become a familiar word in recent years, it is important to remember that (a) it is a relatively new term in official language about work with prisoners and ex-prisoners, and (b) there is no clear consensus on what it entails (or should entail) in terms of its core aims or how these might be achieved.

The term was adopted by the Home Office only at the end of the 1990s, following a recommendation in a report on joint working by probation and prisons (Home Office 1998). The main reason given was that 'resettlement' would be better understood by the general public than 'throughcare', the word then most often used in official documents. However, Raynor (2004) suggests that it may also have been thought useful to remove the reference to 'care' in order to appear 'tough on crime'.

The new term was not precisely defined, reference being made simply to 'high quality sentence planning and successful resettlement in the community' (Home Office 1998: 9). This phrase 'resettlement in the community' trips easily off the tongue, perhaps conjuring up images of offenders returning from prison to take up their place within a stable and supportive network of law-abiding neighbours. However, once one begins to look at the reality of the situation, this image rapidly dissolves. Many offenders were not 'settled' within a 'community' before they went to prison, and have no such prospect before them on release. They may be socially isolated, with few supportive relatives or friends. They may have no home or job to return to, and if helped to find new accommodation or employment may lack the means and skills to keep them. Others have more resources and closer social ties, but the 'community' to which they return may be dominated by people with criminal attitudes, making it more difficult for them to avoid reoffending. Some, too, may have little desire or motivation to 'resettle' or 'go straight'. Immediately, difficult questions begin to be raised about what should be done, by whom, and for what reasons.

These kinds of questions have been answered differently at different times, often reflecting wider changes in penal philosophy and attitudes to offenders. Moreover, whatever the prevailing thinking, there has usually been – as there is now – a variety of approaches 'on the ground'. For example, interventions may to differing degrees:

- focus on the provision of 'welfare' services, or be built around measures to directly address offending behaviour;
- focus on providing practical assistance to offenders, or on enhancing their skills and motivation to solve problems for themselves;
- involve compulsion, or encourage voluntary participation by offenders;
- focus on short-term problem-solving or on sustainability;
- be delivered principally by voluntary/private or by state agencies;
- take place mainly in prison, begin after release, or operate 'through the gate'.

Different combinations can be found of all the above, and there are many overlaps. Nevertheless, they tend to coalesce into a small number of broad but fairly distinct 'models' of resettlement which will be described below. At the heart of most of the differences between these models are two fundamental dichotomies in the views and assumptions of those involved:

- a contrast between, on the one hand, those who see the primary (or even the sole) aim of resettlement as the prevention of reoffending and, on the other, those who place a high priority on other (non-criminal justice) goals such as helping vulnerable people in need, reducing social exclusion, repairing damage caused by imprisonment or spreading religious faith;

- a difference of views between those who locate the roots of crime mainly in structural factors (seeing offenders as largely helpless victims of social inequality and deprivation or other social problems), and those who place more emphasis on 'agency' (i.e. assuming that committing crime involves a strong element of choice and looking for explanations in offenders' thinking and attitudes). Of course, the view one takes of the reasons for offending is likely to influence one's views about the most effective ways of changing offenders' behaviour.

Again, these dichotomies are by no means rigid: many academics, policy-makers and practitioners recognise more than one resettlement aim and more than one explanation of crime. For example, those who pursue broader goals such as the reduction of social exclusion generally believe that achieving these will in the long run also lead to reductions in offending. Nevertheless, organisers of resettlement schemes have tended to prioritise one or other aim, and to favour one or other view about the core reasons for offending.

The basic model of resettlement that was practised throughout much of the twentieth century – what might be called the 'traditional' model – was characterised by:

- voluntary participation by the offender;
- responding to needs articulated by the offender;
- help and support with practical problems;
- brokering access to mainstream service providers;
- relatively little direct emphasis on offending behaviour.

The essence of this approach was captured in the Probation Service's original motto 'advise, assist, befriend', and embodied in its now almost defunct system of voluntary after-care. It has also long been associated with the work of the voluntary sector, where – despite much change and diversification – the tradition remains strong today. Raynor (2004: 222) refers to it as an 'opportunity deficit' model of resettlement, the label reflecting the implicit assumption that offenders commit crime 'because they have been deprived of resources and opportunities' and the consequent aim of 'putting them into contact with agencies which it is hoped will supply these'. In some of the more politically minded or campaigning organisations (including probation at some points in its history), the rationale for assisting ex-prisoners has included a belief that such deprivation is the result of unjust social policies, the assistance being regarded partly as an attempt to 'right the balance'. Others have been driven by religious motives or simply the wish to help people in need. In practice, these traditional approaches to resettlement have usually resulted in a focus on immediate problems (especially around accommodation and benefits) and contact and interventions have tended to be relatively short-term. However, many of those involved have recognised that longer-term support may be necessary if any lasting solution to such problems are to be found and have aimed to develop close continuing relationships with at least some 'clients'. In many cases, too, they have provided help to both offenders and non-offenders, making little or no distinction between them.

By contrast, in recent years the Probation Service (and latterly NOMS) has moved towards a resettlement model built around:

- a strong focus on offending behaviour and its reduction;
- systematic assessment of offenders' needs and risks by professional staff;
- a focus on those 'needs' thought to be 'criminogenic' or to heighten risk;
- a degree of compulsion to cooperate in rehabilitative activities;
- work on attitudes, thinking skills and/or motivation;
- increasingly strict enforcement of attendance requirements and other conditions of release.

This corresponds closely to what Raynor (2004: 233) calls an 'offender responsibility' model of resettlement, reflecting a view that offenders should be held responsible for their own actions and not treated as helpless victims of social or personal 'problems': rather, such problems should be treated as 'challenges or obstacles which confront offenders with choices about how to respond'. As he puts it:

> This is the model implied by phrases such as 'confronting offending' and 'challenging offenders' thinking', and it tends to place an emphasis on helping offenders to develop clear goals for the future, and the problem-solving resources and motivation to overcome some of the obstacles they will inevitably face. Such approaches may sometimes run the risk of underestimating the extreme difficulties many offenders face, but have the merit that they present further offending as avoidable, and offenders as capable of stopping.

While not necessarily denying the importance of addressing offenders' immediate practical needs, advocates of this kind of model argue that welfare provision alone is unlikely to prevent them from reoffending: it is equally, if not more, important to influence their mental processes and provide them with both the desire and the skills to make sustainable use of any opportunities that arise. Otherwise, for example, efforts made in finding them a job may be wasted when they leave after a few days, or their new accommodation may be lost when they fail to keep up the rent. There tends therefore to be a longer-term focus than in the first model. There are arguments as to whether offenders should be *compelled* to address problems which are thought to increase their risk of reoffending (so-called 'criminogenic needs') – for example, to undertake treatment for drug dependence, or to attend courses on basic skills or anger management – but there seems to be decreasing resistance to this idea in principle.

Two other, somewhat different 'models' also deserve mention, although they are less often articulated and, as yet, rarely found in practice. The first might be labelled a 'community-focused' model of resettlement. It reflects a view that while attention to individual problems or individual offending behaviour may be important, successful resettlement ultimately depends on offenders finding a place within (or being 'reintegrated' into) a local *law-abiding community*. A theoretical concept associated with this view is that of 'social capital' – a term which describes the kinds of social bonds, relationships, networks and connections that bring about a sense of belonging and give people a 'stake in society', as well as facilitating access to opportunities for self-advancement (see, for example, Maruna and Farrall 2004; Farrall 2004; Farrall and Sparks 2006: 11). In terms of claims about its potential for reducing reoffending, the idea can draw support from both control theory (which argues that people with strong social bonds tend to feel they have 'too much to lose' by engaging in crime: see Gottfredson and Hirschi 1990) and differential association theory (which asserts that the risk of offending is increased or decreased by the amount of time an individual spends with people with pro-criminal or anti-criminal attitudes: Sutherland and Cressey 1955; Erickson *et al.* 2000).

Advocates of community-focused resettlement include faith groups, who see joining a church or other faith community as a route for ex-offenders to achieve integration with a non-criminal circle of people. Another example is 'Circles of Support', a scheme aimed at providing sex offenders (who tend to be shunned by previous friends or family) with a specially created 'community' of volunteers who maintain contact with them and at the same time act as informal monitors of their behaviour (Kemshall and Maguire 2003; Kemshall and McIvor 2004).

The other model, which might be called 'desistance focused' resettlement, is still very much 'on the drawing board', but the theoretical ideas behind it are beginning to influence thinking about rehabilitation in general and could also be applied to 'through the gate' work with prisoners. 'Desistance' theory has been developed over the past few years by writers such as Maruna (2000), Farrall (2002, 2004) and Burnett (2004), with supporting evidence from qualitative studies based on interviews with offenders (for an overview, see Farrall and Calverley 2006). Its main focus is on the processes of personal change associated with offenders' attempts to desist from further criminal behaviour. Its basic tenets include the following:

1 *Agency is as important as – if not more important than – structure in promoting or inhibiting desistance from crime.* A frequently quoted finding is that of Zamble and Quinsey (1997), who concluded from a study of released prisoners in Ontario that 'factors in the social environment seem influential determinants of initial delinquency for a substantial proportion of offenders ... but habitual offending is better predicted by looking at an individual's acquired ways of reacting to common situations'. Maruna (2000) adds that these reactions are underpinned by offenders' individual understandings or accounts of their own situations and behaviour – what he calls their personal 'narratives' – some of which support continued offending and some of which support desistance. A key element of 'desistance narratives' is a belief that the offender has begun to take control of his or her own life.

2 *Individuals differ in their readiness to contemplate and begin the process of change.* This is to some extent simply a consequence of differences between individuals in mental processes (see point 3 below), but their readiness to

change can also be affected by a range of external factors, including age, major life events or 'transitions', physical and social circumstances, and social bonds. All of these, too, can interact and affect each other (Farrall and Bowling 1999; Farrall 2002; Ward *et al.* 2004).

3 *Generating and sustaining motivation is vital to the maintenance of processes of change.* This is a central point made by virtually all writers on desistance (see, for example, Maruna 2000; Farrall 2002; Maruna and Immarigeon 2004; Farrall and Calverley 2006). The concept of motivation is closely associated with Prochaska and DiClemente's (1984) well-known theory of change, in which the subject's mental readiness to embark upon each of a series of stages is considered critical. It has gained further prominence through Miller and Rollnick's (2002) advocacy of the value of 'motivational interviewing' (see below), and has also been linked with the notion of 'empowerment' of people with low self-esteem (Pollack 2000). It should, however, be noted that several psychologists have expressed concerns that in the treatment context the term has often been poorly defined and used in vague and ambiguous ways (see, for example, Drieschner *et al.* 2004).

4 *Desistance is a difficult and often lengthy process, not an 'event', and relapses are common.* For example, Burnett (2004) among others refers to a 'zigzag' rather than a linear process of change.

5 *While overcoming social problems is often insufficient on its own to promote desistance, it may be a necessary condition for further progress.* Burnett and Maruna (2004) argue that, however strong the motivation to change, it can be seriously undermined by, for example, persistent financial or accommodation problems.

6 *As people change they need new skills and capacities appropriate to their new lifestyle, and access to opportunities to use them.* This relates to the discussion above about the value of 'social capital': desistance theorists have stressed the importance of both social capital and 'human capital', the latter referring to a person's individual skills and resources (Farrall 2004; McNeill 2006).

McNeill (2006) discusses the implications of these propositions and findings for probation practice in general, arguing that the Service should move towards what he calls a 'desistance paradigm' in supervising offenders. Their implications specifically for resettlement practice have also been discussed in some detail by Maguire and Raynor (2006). In short, if the central intention of resettlement interventions is to reduce reoffending, they suggest a resettlement model in which:

- staff develop close relationships with offenders and try to understand and respond to their individual circumstances, levels of motivation and personal 'narratives', rather than applying a 'one size fits all' set of interventions;

- As far as possible, the focus is on a process of personal change led by the offender, the role of the penal professional being to support this process and help the offender maintain motivation in the face of setbacks;

- offenders are helped to acquire new skills which will allow them take better advantage of opportunities to improve their lifestyle;

- 'relapses' into prior patterns of behaviour are expected rather than taken to indicate that the desistance process has 'failed': as far as possible, 'knee-jerk' reactions such as automatic breaching and return to custody are avoided;

- social and practical problems are seen as obstacles to progress, and helping the offender to overcome them is part of the 'package'.

Lastly, brief mention should be made of a specific resettlement programme which has many affinities with the 'desistance' paradigm, although its designers do not make specific reference to desistance theory in their covering literature. Rather, they refer to it as a 'cognitive-motivational' programme (Fabiano and Porporino 2002). This is the 'FOR – A Change' programme, designed mainly for use with short-term prisoners in the weeks preceding release. 'FOR' consists of 12 group sessions which aim primarily to develop prisoners' motivation and help them set their own goals. It draws heavily on Miller and Rollnick's (2002) principles of 'motivational interviewing'. A key element of this is attempts by the programme's facilitators to 'develop discrepancy', that is to help offenders to see gaps between what they aspire to and their current reality, and thereby to become aware of the need to change. The programme then encourages offenders to set themselves clear achievable goals and make concrete plans for reaching them; it also attempts to prepare them for setbacks by boosting their motivation and resources to overcome them. The facilitators are trained to avoid lecturing or judging offenders, but rather to develop a 'working alliance', as far as possible helping prisoners towards 'self-efficacy'. In addition (and again similar to desistance theory), the programme recognises the importance of providing offenders with opportunities to address their practical and social problems. To this end, it includes a 'marketplace' session which is attended by representatives of agencies (such as providers of drug treatment, accommodation or employment training) which are likely to be of use to prisoners when they leave: this allows the offenders to make direct approaches to the providers to set up appointments. Finally, the programme includes continuing contact with programme staff or mentors post-release in order to help sustain motivation (for further discussion see Maguire and Raynor 2006; Clancy et al. 2006).

It must be stressed that the 'FOR' programme is exceptional in the resettlement field, in that it is based on clear aims and a coherent, theory-based 'model of change'. Generally speaking, however, the 'models' outlined above are 'ideal types' rather than being found in reality exactly as described. Indeed, many resettlement schemes are run without careful thought about their aims and underlying assumptions, or precisely how and why the methods chosen are expected to achieve them. They therefore tend to be quite eclectic, with many overlaps (and confusions) in discourses and working practices. However, as will be discussed more fully later, fundamental differences in aims, values and priorities do surface from time to time, causing real tensions between agencies involved in resettlement work. With the establishment of

NOMS and the growth of 'partnership' working, there are already signs that such tensions will increase. These can arise out of key questions about whose 'agenda' is to be the dominant one, what targets and performance indicators are set, how funding is distributed and controlled, and so on.

Finally, while they may differ on other issues, there is one aspect of resettlement practice on which there now seems to be strong agreement in principle among almost all stakeholders. This is that resettlement should be a 'joined up' process, in which prison and probation officers – in partnership with other agencies – work with offenders 'through the gate'. As noted earlier, the official term used by the Probation Service for many years was 'after-care', but this became replaced during the 1980s and 1990s by 'throughcare'. This reflected a gradual shift in probation thinking away from the traditional view of imprisonment as almost entirely a damaging experience and after-care as a means of repairing some of the damage: instead, it was increasingly accepted that work to deal with offenders' problems could be usefully begun in custody and continued after release. In other words, the transition from custody to community should be jointly planned and managed from early in the sentence, rather than simply a 'rescue job' left to the Probation Service or others after release (Maguire and Raynor 1997).

What works?

As pointed out earlier, 'resettlement' interventions need not necessarily be directly linked with the aim of reducing reoffending; they may be offered by voluntary groups purely in the spirit of charity to people in need, or may be regarded as part of the state's general responsibility to provide a social 'safety net' or to promote policies of social inclusion. However, while there are still those who take this view, resettlement has increasingly been seen as an integral element of the crime reduction (and 'what works') agenda, and whether it continues to receive funding from Government on a significant scale is likely to depend on evidence that it will benefit the wider public by reducing reoffending. This being the case, it becomes important to ask what kinds of intervention are most likely to achieve this, and in what kind of framework they should be delivered.

Despite this desire for knowledge about effectiveness, reliable research evidence in the area is so far limited. This is partly because records kept of post-release work are often poor, and it is difficult to determine what specifically has been done with whom. Moreover, offenders may receive treatment, services or assistance in relation to a wide range of problems from a wide range of providers, both inside prison and after release, and even if reliable information can be gleaned on what has been provided and by whom, it is very difficult to determine which of these, if any, have had any effect on their offending behaviour. (Similar problems, it should be noted, have dogged recent 'what works' research in many other areas of criminal justice and the penal system: see Maguire 2004; Tilley 2004.) It is increasingly being argued that the 'quasi-experimental' research methodology previously favoured by the Home Office – in essence, comparing the expected and actual reconviction rates of a group of offenders who have received one particular intervention with those of a group of offenders who have not – will not provide conclusive results in a world in which offenders are increasingly subject to multiple interventions. This is especially problematic where these span custodial and post-release activities: should one, for example, draw a distinction between – and try to measure separately the effects of – 'rehabilitative' interventions (such as cognitive-behavioural programmes) undertaken in custody and 'resettlement' work?[2] Instead, plans are being made to undertake more longitudinal studies, based on tracking cohorts of prisoners over a period of time as they pass through a number of different interventions, and looking at outcomes in relation to the overall path they have followed or the (hopefully) coordinated 'package' of activities and services they have experienced, rather than to one single intervention. This fits well with the NOMS principles of 'end-to-end' offender management and sentence planning based on holistic assessments of needs (see next section).

The quality of information available for research should also improve with the advent of the NOMS Offender Management Model and more systematic use of the national offender assessment tool OASys. In addition, the advent of targets and performance indicators for prisons (such as reducing the numbers of prisoners leaving with no accommodation or employment to go to) is leading to the collection of more data that can be used as 'proxy' measures of outcomes: improvements in such areas are seen as likely to 'translate' in the longer term into reductions in reoffending (although the evidence on this is also limited – much may depend on whether the accommodation or employment are sustained). Even so, it will be some time before any conclusive statements can be made about the effectiveness of different models of resettlement. In the meantime, perhaps the best evidence available is to be found in the qualitative, interview-based findings of Maruna (2000) and Farrall (2002), which provide some support to the potential effectiveness of a 'desistance' model, as well in the evaluations of the probation service's 'Resettlement Pathfinders', which in some areas included the 'FOR – A Change' programme (Lewis *et al.* 2003a, 2003b; Clancy *et al.* 2006; Raynor 2004; Maguire and Raynor 2006). The Pathfinder studies provide some encouragement for the development of models based around a combination of cognitive-motivational work, post-release mentoring and facilitating offenders' access to service agencies.[3]

Recent developments in policy and practice

The resettlement agenda has recently attracted far more serious attention and resources from many more agencies than ever before. The unprecedented level of importance attached to it derives mainly from three major policy initiatives, all mentioned earlier: (a) the planned (but now deferred) new sentence, 'Custody Plus'; (b) the establishment of the National Offender Management Service (NOMS); and (c) the launch of the *Reducing Re-Offending National Action Plan* (Home Office 2004a). These will be discussed briefly in turn.

Custody Plus

Although introduced under the Criminal Justice Act 2003, Custody Plus has not been implemented at the time of writing and relatively little will be said about it here.

The sentence of Custody Plus is intended to replace sentences of imprisonment of under 12 months. It will be served partly in custody (a minimum of two weeks and a maximum of 13 weeks) but mainly on licence in the community, where the minimum period of supervision will be six months (Home Office 2004b). Conditions may be attached to the licence either by the courts or by the prison governor, and any breach of conditions may result in recall to prison: recall will be an executive rather than a judicial decision.

From the resettlement viewpoint, the importance of the sentence – if it is implemented – lies in the fact that, for the first time, short-term prisoners would be subject to supervision after release, providing the potential for a major beneficial change in the level of official attention afforded to the problems of an exceptionally 'needy' group (as pointed out earlier, short-term prisoners tend to have higher needs and higher reconviction rates than almost any other). At the same time, concerns exist that (a) the Probation Service would be unable to cope with the flood of new ex-prisoners to supervise and would adopt little more than a 'tick box' approach to supervision (some estimates suggest that current probation caseloads would increase by 15–20 per cent, without any extra resources to handle them); (b) the application of strict National Standards to the enforcement of licence conditions for numerous offenders with 'chaotic lifestyles' (many of whom would previously have been deemed unsuitable for community supervision) would result in large numbers being breached and returned to prison; and (c) despite the legislative intention that Custody Plus is a replacement for current prison sentences, magistrates and judges would be tempted to give 'a short taste of prison' to offenders who would previously have received a non-custodial penalty, thus increasing prison numbers still further. Time will tell whether these fears are justified, but suffice it to say that there are at the moment some daunting challenges to overcome if this development is to realise the potential it undoubtedly holds for a significant improvement in criminal justice responses to the future equivalent of today's short-term prisoners.

NOMS, ROMs and the NOMM

As mentioned earlier, the Carter Report (Home Office 2003) led very quickly to the establishment of NOMS, a new organisation which has taken over control of many of the functions previously managed separately by the Prison and Probation Services (see Home Office 2006; Hough *et al.* 2006). Important aspects of this change (discussed elsewhere in this volume) included:

- the appointment of ten Regional Offender Managers (ROMs) with responsibility for the management of, and delivery of interventions to, offenders in custody or under community supervision in their region;[4]
- a formal separation between 'offender management' and 'interventions';

- plans for 'contestability' (whereby other public sector, private or voluntary agencies may bid to the ROMs to supply services currently provided by probation or prisons);
- implementation of the NOMS Offender Management Model (NOMM).

Where resettlement is concerned, the NOMM provides a framework for so-called 'end-to-end offender management' whereby – in theory, at least – the problems of lack of coordination between prison and probation will be overcome, each offender becoming the responsibility of one 'offender manager' throughout the whole of his or her sentence (NOMS 2005). The offender manager's role includes providing the court with a pre-sentence assessment of each individual's risk level and needs, based on the standardised Offender Assessment System (OASys) and formulating a sentence plan to address the risks and needs identified.[5] This plan, should continue 'through the gate' in the case of a prison sentence. It includes decisions to refer offenders to providers of specific 'interventions' such as education in basic skills, drug treatment or advice about accommodation.

Once the new NOMS arrangements are fully up and running, the cost of these interventions will normally have been 'pre-paid' by the ROM, who (under the contestability' principle recommended by Carter) will choose between competitive bids from the public, private or voluntary sectors to supply specific services for a maximum number of offenders serving custodial or community sentences over a given period. Under the conditions of the contract, offender managers will be able at short notice to 'draw down' services for individual offenders who have been identified by OASys as having a particular type of problem and/or who have special conditions attached to their sentence or licence.[6]

The establishment of NOMS has been highly controversial, particularly in relation to 'contestability', which some fear may have a devastating impact on the Probation Service and lead to greater privatisation of criminal justice (Rumgay 2005; Hough et al. 2006). There is wider support for some of the ideas behind the NOMS Offender Management Model, particularly those of bringing greater coordination into the planning and implementation of interventions 'through the gate', and identifying one person to whom the offender can relate ('end to end') throughout the whole of his or her sentence. However, there are also concerns that these aims may prove very difficult to achieve in practice. The separation between 'offender management' and 'interventions' can be somewhat artificial, and it could lead to a complex and bureaucratic system of referrals in which sight is lost of the 'whole person'. In theory, all service providers will be part of an 'offender management team' built around each individual (NOMS 2005), but as the members of this notional team are unlikely to meet as such, it is difficult to envisage it as an integrative system in practice (see Raynor and Maguire 2006). In addition, the emphasis upon strict enforcement of attendance rules may undermine the development of trusting relationships. Much will depend upon the skills of the offender manager in overcoming such obstacles, sustaining offenders' motivation and splicing together any benefits from disparate interventions.

The Reducing Re-offending Plan and its 'Pathways'

The Reducing Re-offending National Action Plan represented the Government's response to the Social Exclusion Unit's report on problems surrounding resettlement, especially in relation to short-term prisoners. The Action Plan required the production by April 2006 of 'Reducing Re-offending Strategies' and corresponding 'Action Plans' at regional level (i.e. in the nine English regions and in Wales). These plans are each divided into nine distinct 'Pathways': Accommodation; Education, Training and Employment (ETE); Mental and Physical Health; Drugs and Alcohol; Finance, Benefit and Debt; Children and Families of Offenders; Attitudes, Thinking and Behaviour; Public Protection; and Prolific Offenders. Their formulation and implementation is the responsibility of regional Reducing Re-offending Partnerships, made up of senior representatives from relevant agencies and coordinated by the ROMs. In addition, each Pathway has an identified lead agency at both national and regional level, and the delivery of its plans will be underpinned by performance targets and monitoring systems.

Although the two overlap, and both are led by the ROMs, the Pathways initiative is a separate development to the commissioning of specific services or interventions by ROMs to meet the statutory requirements of sentence or licence conditions. The Pathways have the broader purpose of contributing to the reduction of reoffending by increasing the amount and quality of service provision for ex-offenders in the region as a whole. It is expected that this will be paid for through the funding streams of a variety of partner agencies, depending on which needs are being addressed. For example, an ex-prisoner entering drug treatment which is not part of a court order could be paid for, like other citizens with similar needs, out of local health or social services budgets. He or she might self-refer, or be referred to the treatment provider by any of a number of other agencies (for example, CARATS, the prison-based drug advice service).

This system is a radical departure from previous practice, in that senior managers from agencies outside the criminal justice system are engaged in jointly planning services specifically for offenders – indeed, to some extent being asked to prioritise offenders over other groups who may have equally pressing needs for scarce resources such as social housing or drug treatment. To many people with a background in such areas, this is an alien idea. In normal circumstances, they would make decisions about provision based on assessments of individuals' levels of need and their suitability for the service in question: whether the person is an offender would be at most a secondary consideration (or sometimes even seen as a reason for placing them further down the queue). However, the message from Government – backed up by performance indicators and, to a much more limited extent, legislation (such as obligations on local authorities under the Homelessness Act 2002) – is that ex-prisoners constitute one of the vulnerable groups which require priority attention, the core rationale being that this will reduce reoffending and hence be to everyone's benefit.

Whether the system will 'work', in any of the three senses of changing the views of managers and staff in service agencies, delivering services to significant numbers of offenders or actually producing a reduction in reoffending, remains to be seen. There is clearly a long way to go in terms of changing attitudes, particularly in relation to perceptions of 'deserving' and 'undeserving' clients. Moreover, shifts in attitudes are only a first step. In several of the Pathways, the outcome is likely to depend above all on the levels of funding and resources available: for example, the Accommodation Pathway is severely handicapped by serious shortages of social housing in many parts of the country, and even the most committed managers are unable to facilitate a significant increase in provision (for offenders or anyone else).

Concluding comments

In comparison with the bleak situation of less than a decade ago, when the problems of people coming out of prison were virtually ignored (or, worse, ex-prisoners were deliberately excluded from services for people in need), the current prospects for resettlement are encouraging. The level of Government interest is unprecedented, as is the attention the issue is receiving from non-criminal justice agencies. Moreover, serious thought is being given to possible longer-term, 'sustainable' solutions, rather than simply applying what has often amounted simply to crisis intervention. However, the problems facing policy-makers and practitioners are deeply ingrained and there are no quick solutions. Current plans for change also contain inbuilt tensions and face major threats and challenges.

At the heart of the 'resettlement' problem is the sheer scale of the social and personal problems afflicting prisoners and ex-prisoners. Service providers in key fields such as health, housing and education are already operating on tight budgets, and access to suitable accommodation and drug treatment, in particular, is difficult for many other categories of vulnerable people in addition to ex-prisoners. If and when Custody Plus comes on stream, offender managers will be supervising greater numbers of ex-prisoners than ever before, many of them with chronic multiple needs. Major decisions will have to be made regarding priorities.

Where the management of offenders by NOMS is concerned, these decisions have already been made to some extent. The NOMM divides offenders under supervision into four tiers, based largely on the risk of harm they pose to others, their risk of reoffending and their 'criminogenic needs', as assessed by OASys. For those allocated to the lowest tier the focus is solely on delivering 'punishment', for those in tier 2 'punishment and help', for those in tier 3 'punishment, help and change', and for the high risk in tier 4 all the above plus 'control' (NOMS 2005: 16–19). Offender managers will be expected to 'draw down' only those (NOMS-commissioned and funded) services appropriate to the tier in which a particular offender is placed. In other words – unsurprisingly in a criminal justice organisation – virtually the sole priority is the reduction of reoffending, and resources are distributed accordingly. However, this leaves difficult questions about, for example, the extent of 'help' or 'change'-related services that should be offered to minor offenders who nevertheless have major long-term social problems, or to young people who do not yet pose a high risk but it is felt may do so in the future. It also raises questions about the continuation of services that are needed beyond the end of an ex-offender's licence period, when NOMS has no statutory obligation to continue paying for them.

Ideally, these kinds of questions should be addressed through the broader resettlement and rehabilitation agenda represented by the Pathways created under the Reducing Re-offending National Action Plan, which can call on a much wider pool of funding streams and service providers. Unfortunately, resource and prioritisation issues raise their head here to an even greater extent. However sympathetic they may be to the plight of ex-prisoners, or however convinced they may be by the argument that giving them greater access to services will reduce re-offending and prove to be a sound investment for society as a whole, those who control the budgets in key areas such as health and housing are faced by numerous competing claims for priority treatment from other vulnerable groups (the growing numbers of frail elderly people, people addicted to drugs or alcohol, people with mental health problems, homeless families, and so on). Moreover, for those with a background in areas of social policy other than criminal justice, the fact that somebody is an 'offender' or 'ex-prisoner' is only one consideration among many in assessing priorities. Indeed, a person's level of criminality or risk of reoffending is likely to be seen as less relevant to decisions about committing resources than, for example, his or her level of need judged by health criteria, or his or her likely response to the services offered. To take a concrete example, any region's Accommodation Pathway is likely to be dominated by people with a housing background, including members of local authorities and Supporting People commissioners, for whom the primary considerations in responding to people seeking accommodation tend to revolve around questions about sustainability, needs and suitability for particular types of accommodation or support services. They may also be guided by wider policies – for example, a general principle of spreading resources more thinly rather than concentrating them heavily on small groups of clients with high cost needs (this is currently found in moves in many areas to reduce the amount of accommodation-based support in favour of less intensive 'floating support' to cover many more people). This may result in commissioners of services using their funding in ways that do not fit well with the priorities of NOMS representatives (for example, neglecting the development of accommodation with intensive support suitable for prolific offenders or chaotic drug users). Similar issues may arise in decisions about the balance between residential and community-based treatment for substance abuse. Optimists would argue that there is a general trend towards pooling of funding and joint commissioning of services which will increase mutual understanding between agencies and foster more agreement about priorities, but at present such matters are anything but settled.

At 'ground level', too, there are a number of challenges around the practical and organisational arrangements involved in offender management. These mainly concern risks of fragmentation or duplication arising from the referral of one offender potentially to several different providers (a fear associated particularly with the plans for 'contestability' in relation to interventions).

This is of course, ironic, given that the central rationale for the establishment of NOMS was a need for more coherent and 'joined up' sentence planning and interventions. In addition, it may prove difficult for offender managers to develop the kinds of supportive and motivating personal relationships with offenders that research suggests are critical to maintaining their efforts to desist from crime (Maguire and Raynor 2006; Raynor and Maguire 2006). The NOMM encourages offender managers, using OASys, to identify a set of specific 'needs' for each offender and to respond to each of these by referring him or her to a specialist service provider. There is a risk that busy offender managers may begin to leave support and motivation to these providers, but at the same time, the latter may see their role purely as providing the specialist service, not as a surrogate supervisor, so that the general support role 'falls through the gap'. A somewhat different risk arises where 'intervention providers' undertake their own independent assessments and develop their own plans for offenders referred to them. For example, modern accommodation services frequently undertake thorough assessments which take into account a wide range of factors – including health and finance management – seen as affecting vulnerable people's ability to sustain a tenancy; they also create individual support plans and 'move-on' plans to deal with these. There is a danger that these may duplicate or cut across those of the offender manager. Such problems can be avoided by mutual understanding, good communication and clear agreements about where specific responsibilities lie, but this is much easier in theory than in practice.

Finally, in the longer term there are risks that the current keen political interest in resettlement will dissipate, or that there is a political backlash against what is seen as a set of policies which favour offenders over other 'more deserving' groups. As emphasised earlier, the Government has made it very clear that the core rationale behind recent policies in this field is the belief that they will lead to a significant reduction in reoffending, which will save money for mainstream agencies (e.g. health services will have to treat fewer assaulted people) and benefit potential victims and society in general. It is therefore critically important that the current initiatives are given the best chance possible of succeeding by maximising the quality of work with offenders. Perhaps the clearest messages to emerge from research about the most effective approaches are that the best results are most likely to be obtained by:

- 'continuity' of work 'through the gate', including regular post-release contact with people who have already developed a trusting relationship with offenders while they were in custody (there are some indications that volunteer mentors can play a valuable part in this: Clancy *et al.* 2006);

- attention to offenders' personal problems and 'welfare' needs (such as accommodation, financial problems or substance abuse), but equally to their mental processes, attitudes and levels of motivation to change: neither simply placing them on cognitive-behaviour programmes nor, alternatively, focusing only on finding them accommodation or employment is likely to be effective.

Despite the problems and controversies that have accompanied the establishment of NOMS, both these principles have informed the development of the NOMS Offender Management Model. They also underpin the 'FOR' programme which was used with considerable success in the Resettlement Pathfinders. The key question is whether they can be turned into effective practice for large numbers of prisoners.

Notes

1 This was achieved by cutting the minimum period to be served before release from 12 to six months. Before this change in the rules, the shortest sentence with eligibility for parole had been 20 months (which allowed just over one month – the minimum licence period – for supervision, starting at early release after 12 months and ending at the normal release date, which was then set at two-thirds of the sentence). Under the new rules, a prisoner serving 13 months could now be released on parole after six months (again allowing time for supervision before he or she reached the two-thirds point in the sentence). To reduce unfairness to shorter-term prisoners (who were not eligible for parole), from 1987 all those serving sentences of up to 12 months were automatically released without supervision at the half-way point in their sentence.

2 Particular problems arose in relation to Home Office evaluations of prison-based offending behaviour programmes (based on cognitive-behavioural methods), which were introduced in the late 1990s on a large scale following reviews of research in Canada and the USA indicating that they had reduced prisoners' reconviction rates by 10–15 per cent (Lipsey 1992; Andrews *et al.* 1990; for broader accounts see McGuire 1995, 2000; Raynor and Vanstone 2002). Early evaluations using a quasi-experimental methodology seemed to confirm a similar impact in England and Wales, but subsequent research found no significant differences between prisoners who had attended programmes and comparison groups who had not (Friendship *et al.* 2002; Cann *et al.* 2003). There are several possible explanations for these puzzling findings, but as it is unknown what other work was or was not done with offenders in either group, either inside prison or after release, it is impossible to come to any clear conclusions about them. For example, it is quite possible that the programmes had a temporary impact on some prisoners' thinking and intentions, but that this was later counteracted by the absence or poor quality of later 'resettlement' work.

3 In particular, regression analysis of data on participants in the first Pathfinders indicated that post-release contact with mentors was associated at a statistically significant level with lower than expected reconviction rates one year after release (Clancy *et al.* 2006).

4 In Wales, the equivalent of the ROM is the Director of Offender Management, Wales (DOMW).

5 For information on OASys, see: http://www.crimereduction.gov.uk/workingoffenders14.htm

6 At the time of writing, interventions are either provided by the Probation or Prison Services themselves, or commissioned locally by probation area boards or by prison governors. The scale of services commissioned from outside agencies is expected to increase substantially under NOMS.

Further reading

On the problems faced by people leaving prison, there are a number of important research-based reports, notably the Social Exclusion Unit's (2002) influential *Reducing Re-offending by Ex-Prisoners*, NACROS's (2000) *The Forgotten Majority: The Resettlement of Short-Term Prisoners* and the joint thematic review *Through the Prison Gate* published in 2001 by HM Inspectorates of Prison and Probation. A useful review of earlier literature is provided by Kevin Haines's (1990) *After-Care Services for Released Prisoners*. For discussions of the special problems faced by female prisoners, see NACRO's (2001) report *Women Behind Bars: A Positive Agenda for Women Prisoners' Resettlement*, and of ethnic minority prisoners, Calverley *et al.*'s (2004) report *Black and Asian Offenders on Probation*.

For findings from academic research on recent gaps and deficiencies in resettlement practice, see Maguire *et al.*'s (1997) report to the Home Office, *Voluntary After-Care*, the same authors' paper in the *Howard Journal* (2000), 'Voluntary after-care and the Probation Service: a case of diminishing responsibility', and that by Maguire and Raynor (1997) in the *British Journal of Criminology*, 'The revival of throughcare: rhetoric and reality in automatic conditional release'. There is also a useful Special Issue of *Criminal Justice Matters* (2004) which focuses on resettlement and includes short articles by important writers in the field.

To understand the thinking behind recent policy developments relating to resettlement, see Patrick Carter's review of the correctional services, *Managing Offenders, Reducing Crime – A New Approach* (Home Office 2003), particularly his ideas on 'end to end offender management'; John Halliday's (2001) *Making Punishments Work*, which recommended the introduction of Custody Plus; and the Social Exclusion Unit report mentioned above, which led to the Reducing Re-offending National Action Plan (http://www.homeoffice.gov.uk/docs3/5505reoffending.pdf). Details of the NOMS Offender Management Model can be found at http://www.probation2000.com/documents/NOMS%20Offender%20Management%20Model.pdf. For more critical comment on these developments, especially the direction being taken by NOMS, see the edited book by Hough *et al.* (2006) *Reshaping Probation and Prisons: The New Offender Management Framework*.

Finally, for theory and research concerning different 'models' of resettlement and their potential effectiveness in reducing reoffending, see Maguire and Raynor's (2006) paper in *Criminology and Criminal Justice*, 'How the resettlement of prisoners promotes desistance from crime: or does it?' This highlights the potential importance of desistance theory to resettlement issues: fuller accounts of desistance theory and its applications can be found in Maruna and Immarigeon's edited volume (2004) *After Crime and Punishment: Pathways to Offender Reintegration* and in Farrall and Calverley's (2006) textbook *Understanding Desistance from Crime: Theoretical Directions in Resettlement and Rehabilitation*. The most comprehensive recent piece of research on resettlement practice is described in Clancy *et al.*'s (2006) evaluation of the Probation Service's Resettlement Pathfinders, *Getting Out and Staying Out*.

References

Andrews, D., Zinger, I., Hoge, R., Bonta, J., Gendreau, P. and Cullen, F. (1990) 'Does correctional treatment work? A clinically relevant and psychologically informed meta-analysis', *Criminology*, 28: 369–404.

Audit Commission (2005) *Supporting People*. London: Audit Commission. Available at: http://www.audit-commission.gov.uk/reports

Banks, C. and Fairhead, S. (1976) *The Petty Short Term Prisoner*. London: Howard League for Penal Reform.

Bochel, D. (1976) *Probation and After-Care. Its Development in England and Wales.* Edinburgh: Scottish Academic Press.

Burnett, R. (2004) 'To reoffend or not to reoffend? The ambivalence of convicted property offenders', in S. Maruna and R. Immarigeon (eds), *After Crime and Punishment: Pathways to Offender Reintegration*. Cullompton: Willan.

Burnett, R. and Maruna, S. (2004) 'So prison works, does it? The criminal careers of 130 men released from prison under Home Secretary, Michael Howard', *Howard Journal*, 33 (4): 2000.

Caddle, D. and White, S. (1994) *The Welfare Needs of Unconvicted Prisoners*, Research and Planning Unit Paper No. 81. London: Home Office.

Calverley, A., Cole, B., Kaur, G., Lewis, S., Raynor, P., Sadeghi, S., Smith, D., Vanstone, M. and Wardak, A. (2004) *Black and Asian Offenders on Probation*, Home Office Research Study No. 277. London: Home Office.

Cann, J., Falshaw, L., Nugent, F. and Friendship, C. (2003) *Understanding What Works: Accredited Cognitive Skills Programmes for Adult Men and Young Offenders*, Home Office Research Findings 226. London: Home Office.

Cavadino, P. and Dignan, J. (2002) *The Penal System: An Introduction*, 3rd edn. London: Sage.

Clancy, A., Hudson, K., Maguire, M., Peake, R., Raynor, P., Vanstone, M. and Kynch, J. (2006) *Getting Out and Staying Out: Results of the Prisoner Resettlement Pathfinders*. Bristol: Policy Press.

Corden, J. (1983) 'Persistent petty offenders: problems and patterns of multiple disadvantage', *Howard Journal*, 22: 68–90.

Corden, J., Kuipers, J. and Wilson, K. (1978) *After Prison: A Study of Post-release Experiences of Discharged Prisoners*. York: Department of Social Administration and Social Work, University of York.

Corden, J., Kuipers, J. and Wilson, K. (1979) 'Accommodation and homelessness on release from prison', *British Journal of Social Work*, 9: 75–86.

Corden, J., Kuipers, J. and Wilson, K. (1980) 'Prison welfare and voluntary after-care', *British Journal of Social Work*, 10: 71–86.

Davies, M. (1974) *Prisoners of Society. Attitudes and After-Care*. London: Routledge & Kegan Paul.

Drieschner, K., Lammers, S. and Staak, C. (2004) 'Treatment motivation: an attempt for clarification of an ambiguous concept', *Clinical Psychology Review*, 23: 1115–37.

Erickson, K., Crosnoe, R. and Dornbusch, S. (2000) 'A social process model of adolescent deviance: combining social control and differential association perspectives', *Journal of Youth and Adolescence*, 29 (4): 395–425.

Fabiano, E. and Porporino, F. (2002) *Focus on Resettlement – A Change*. Canada: T3 Associates.

Fairhead, S. (1981) *Persistent Petty Offenders*, Home Office Research Study No. 66. London: HMSO.

Farrall, S. (2002) *Rethinking What Works with Offenders*. Cullompton: Willan.

Farrall, S. and Bowling, B. (1999) 'Structuration, human development and desistance from crime', *British Journal of Criminology*, 39 (2): 252–67.

Farrall, S. and Calverley, A. (2006) *Understanding Desistance from Crime: Theoretical Directions in Resettlement and Rehabilitation*. Maidenhead: Open University Press.

Farrall, S. and Sparks, R. (2006) 'Introduction', Special Issue, *Criminology and Criminal Justice*, 6 (1): 7–18.

Friendship, C., Blud, L., Erikson, M. and Travers, R. (2002) *An Evaluation of Cognitive Behavioural Treatment for Prisoners*, Home Office Research Findings 161. London: Home Office.

Gelsthorpe, L. (2004a) 'Making it on the out: the resettlement needs of women offenders', *Criminal Justice Matters*, 56: 34–5 (Special Issue on Resettlement).

Gelsthorpe, L. (2004b) 'Women and resettlement: trials and tribulations', *Safer Society*, October.

Goldblatt, P. and Lewis, C. (1998) *Reducing Offending*, Home Office Research Study No. 187. London: Home Office.

Gottfredson, M. and Hirschi, T. (1990) A *General Theory of Crime*. Stanford, CA: Stanford University Press.

Hagell, A., Newburn, T. and Rowlingson, K. (1995) *Financial Difficulties on Release from Prison*. London: Policy Studies Unit.

Haines, K. (1990) *After-Care Services for Released Prisoners: A Review of the Literature*. Cambridge: Institute of Criminology.

Halliday, J. (2001) *Making Punishments Work*. London: Home Office.

Her Majesty's Inspectorates of Prison and Probation (2001) *Through the Prison Gate: A Joint Thematic Review*. London: Home Office.

Home Office (1984) *Probation Service in England and Wales. Statement of National Objectives and Priorities*. London: Home Office.

Home Office (1988a) *Punishment, Custody and the Community*. London: HMSO.

Home Office (1988b) *Tackling Offending: An Action Plan*. London: Home Office.

Home Office (1990) *Partnership in Dealing with Offenders in the Community. A Discussion Paper*. London: Home Office.

Home Office (1992) *National Standards for the Supervision of Offenders in the Community*. London: HMSO.

Home Office (1997) *Probation Statistics Quarterly Monitor*, March. London: Home Office.

Home Office (1998) *Joining Forces to Protect the Public: Prisons-Probation*. London: Home Office.

Home Office (2003) *Managing Offenders, Reducing Crime – A New Approach: Correctional Services Review by Patrick Carter*. London: Prime Minister's Strategy Unit.

Home Office (2004a) *Reducing Re-Offending: National Action Plan*. London: Home Office. Available at: http://www.homeoffice.gov.uk/docs3/5505reoffending.pdf

Home Office (2004b) *Criminal Justice Act 2003: Briefing*. Available at: http://www.probation.homeoffice.gov.uk/files/pdf/NPD_Briefing_18.pdf

Home Office (2006) *Background to NOMS*. Available at: http://www.noms.homeoffice.gov.uk/background-to-noms/

Hough, M., Allen, R. and Padel, U. (eds) (2006) *Reshaping Probation and Prisons: The New Offender Management Framework*. Bristol: Policy Press.

Jarvis, F.V. (1972) *Advise, Assist and Befriend: The History of the Probation Service*. London: NAPO.

Kemshall, H. and McIvor, G. (ed.) (2004) *Managing Sex Offender Risk*. London: Jessica Kingsley.

Kemshall, H. and Maguire, M. (2003) 'Sex offenders, risk penality and the problem of disclosure to the community', in A. Matravers (ed.), *Managing Sex Offenders in the Community: Contexts, Challenges and Responses*. Cullompton: Willan.

Lewis, S., Maguire, M., Raynor, P., Vanstone, M., and Vennard, J. (2003a) *The Resettlement of Short-term Prisoners: An Evaluation of Seven Pathfinder Programmes*, Research Findings 200. London: Home Office.

Lewis, S., Vennard, J., Maguire, M., Raynor, P., Vanstone, M., Raybould, S. and Rix, A. (2003b) *The Resettlement of Short-term Prisoners: An Evaluation of Seven Pathfinders*, RDS Occasional Paper 83. London: Home Office.

Lipsey, M. (1992) 'Juvenile delinquency treatment: a meta-analytic enquiry into the variability of effects', in T. Cook, H. Cooper, D. Cordray, H. Hartmann, L. Hedges, R. Light, T. Louis and F. Mosteller (eds), *Meta-Analysis for Explanation: A Case-book*. New York: Russell Sage.

McGuire, J. (2000) *Cognitive-Behavioural Approaches*. London: Home Office.

McGuire, J. (ed.) (1995) *What Works: Reducing Reoffending*. Chichester: Wiley.

McNeill, F. (2006) 'A desistance paradigm for offender management', *Criminology and Criminal Justice*, 6 (1): 39–62.

Maguire, M. (1992) 'Parole', in E. Stockdale and S. Casale (ed.), *Criminal Justice Under Stress*. London: Blackstone Press.

Maguire, M. (2004) 'The Crime Reduction Programme: reflections on the vision and the reality', *Criminal Justice*, 4 (3): 213–37.

Maguire, M. and Raynor, P. (1997) 'The revival of throughcare: rhetoric and reality in automatic conditional release', *British Journal of Criminology*, 37 (1): 1–14.

Maguire, M. and Raynor, P. (2006) 'How the resettlement of prisoners promotes desistance from crime: or does it?', *Criminology and Criminal Justice*, 6 (1): 17–36.

Maguire, M., Perroud, B. and Raynor, P. (1996) *Automatic Conditional Release: The First Two Years*, Home Office Research Study No. 156. London: Home Office.

Maguire, M., Raynor, P., Vanstone, M. and Kynch, J. (1997) *Voluntary After-Care: Report to the Home Office*. London: Home Office.

Maguire, M., Raynor, P., Vanstone, M. and Kynch, J. (1998) *Voluntary After-Care*, Research Findings No. 73. London: Home Office.

Maguire, M., Raynor, P., Vanstone, M. and Kynch, J. (2000) 'Voluntary after-care and the Probation Service: a case of diminishing responsibility', *Howard Journal of Criminal Justice*, 39: 234–48.

Martin, J. and Webster, D. (1971) *The Social Consequences of Conviction*. London: Heinemann.

Maruna, S. (2000) *Making Good*. Washington, DC: American Psychological Association.

Maruna, S. and Farrall, S. (2004) 'Desistance from crime: a theoretical reformulation', *Kölner Zeitschrift für Soziologie und Sozialpsychologie*, 43: 171–94.

Maruna, S. and Immarigeon, R. (eds) (2004) *After Crime and Punishment: Pathways to Offender Reintegration*. Cullompton: Willan.

Miller, W. R. and Rollnick, S. (2002) *Motivational Interviewing. Preparing People for Change*, 2nd edn. New York: Guildford Press.

Morgan, N. (1983) 'The shaping of parole in England and Wales', *Criminal Law Review*, March: 137–51.

NACRO (1993) *Opening the Doors. The Resettlement of Prisoners in the Community*. London: National Association for the Care and Resettlement of Offenders.

NACRO (1996) *Women Prisoners: Towards a New Millennium*. London: National Association for the Care and Resettlement of Offenders.

NACRO (2000) *The Forgotten Majority: The Resettlement of Short-Term Prisoners*. London: National Association for the Care and Resettlement of Offenders.

NACRO (2001) *Women Behind Bars: A Positive Agenda for Women Prisoners' Resettlement*. London: National Association for the Care and Resettlement of Offenders.

NACRO (2002) *Resettling Prisoners from Black and Minority Ethnic Groups*. London: National Association for the Care and Resettlement of Offenders.

NOMS (2005) *The NOMS Offender Management Model*. London: National Offender Management Service. Available at: http://www.probation2000.com/documents/NOMS%20Offender%20Management%20Model.pdf

Pollack, S. (2000) 'Reconceptualising women's agency and empowerment: challenges to self-esteem discourse and women's lawbreaking', *Women and Criminal Justice*, 12 (1): 75–89.

Prochaska, J. and DiClemente, C. (1984) *The Transtheoretical Approach: Crossing Traditional Boundaries of Therapy*. Homewood, IL: Dow Jones-Irwin.

Raynor, P. (2004) 'Opportunity, motivation and change: some findings from research on resettlement', in R. Burnett and C. Roberts (eds), *What Works in Probation and Youth Justice*. Cullompton: Willan.

Raynor, P. and Maguire, M. (2006) 'End-to-end or end in tears? Prospects for the effectiveness of the National Offender Management Model', in M. Hough, R. Allen and U. Padel (eds), *Reshaping Probation and Prisons: The New Offender Management Framework*. Bristol: Policy Press.

Raynor, P. and Vanstone, M. (2002) *Understanding Community Penalties: Prison, Probation and Social Change*. Buckingham: Open University Press.

Rough Sleepers Unit (2000) *Blocking the Fast Track from Prison to Rough Sleeping*. London: Office of the Deputy Prime Minister. Summarised online at: http://www.odpm.gov. uk/index.asp?id=1150098

Rumgay, J. (2004) 'Scripts for safer survival: pathways out of female crime', *Howard Journal*, 43: 405–19.

Rumgay, J. (2005) 'NOMS bombs?', *Howard Journal*, 44 (2): 206–8.

Shepherd, A. and Whiting, E. (2006) *Re-offending of Adults: Results from the 2003 Cohort*, Statistical Bulletin. London: Home Office RDS-NOMS Reconviction Analysis Team. Available at: http://www.homeoffice.gov.uk/rds/pdfs06/hosb2006.pdf

Social Exclusion Unit (2002) *Reducing Re-offending by Ex-Prisoners*. London: Office of the Deputy Prime Minister.

Sutherland, E. and Cressey, D. (1955) *Principles of Criminology*. Chicago: Lippincott.

Tilley, N. (2004) 'Applying theory-driven evaluation to the British Crime Reduction Programme: the theories of the programme and of its evaluations', *Criminal Justice*, 4 (3): 255–76.

Vanstone, M. (2004) *Supervising Offenders in the Community: A History of Probation Theory and Practice*. Aldershot: Ashgate.

Ward, T., Day, A., Howells, K. and Birgden, A. (2004) 'The Multifactor Offender Readiness Model', *Aggression and Violent Behavior*, 9: 645–73.

Zamble, E. and Quinsey, V. (1997) *The Criminal Recidivism Process*. Cambridge: Cambridge University Press.

Part 3

What works in Probation?

As indicated in our earlier Introduction, Chapters 15–20 explore what is meant by effectiveness and what is known about it. This involves paying attention to values, victims, the interests of the public at large and the different voices of probation staff and the offenders with whom they work.

Politicians, policy-makers, practitioners and the public alike all want probation interventions to be 'more effective'. But the meaning of 'effectiveness' is often taken for granted. In Chapter 15 Simon Merrington and Stephen Stanley examine what is meant by 'effectiveness' by charting the different conceptions of evaluation in play through different probation 'periods', from the 'treatment' theme of the 1960s to mid-1970s to the more recent 'what works' and 'performance management' themes. They go on critically to discuss current prospects for measuring effectiveness. Their central argument is that it is important to utilise multi-modal forms of evaluation (and qualitative as well as quantitative measures) rather than use single or narrow measures (such as randomised controlled experiments) on their own.

Chapter 16 is concerned with the effectiveness of specific interventions. Here, Carol Hedderman rehearses recent developments relating to the effectiveness of sentencing and reviews the research findings regarding the impact of imprisonment, rehabilitations (probation orders), community punishment (community service orders) and fines. She also addresses the emerging evidence on newer sentences such as curfew orders and drug treatment and testing orders and discusses the crucial role that probation might play in working towards an improvement in effectiveness in relation to the new sentences introduced under the Criminal Justice Act 2003.

In Chapter 17 Loraine Gelsthorpe focuses on the challenges to the traditional value base in probation – encapsulated in the phrase that it was once the probation officer's role to 'advise, assist and befriend' offenders. Both the managerial revolution and the 'punitive turn' within criminal justice have had a huge impact on probation to the extent that there has been a search for a new value base. But whither that value base? Community justice, civil liberties, the diversity agenda or human rights, for example? The author sifts through the different possibilities, dwelling on the prospect of a human rights culture, but ultimately suggesting that while a legal framework of rights may be important, what is really required is a review of ethical practice so that probation staff can make informed and intelligent decisions on the ground.

The Government, we are told, is increasingly concerned with the law-abiding majority, those who are seen as potential victims. This emerges as both a concern to let victims speak out about the harms that they have experienced (through victim impact statements and the like) and to keep victims informed about proceedings, and to 'rebalance' justice so that victims' rights to lead their lives free from crime are protected. Chapter 18 thus revolves around victims of crime. Brian Williams and Hannah Goodman describe something of the apparent neglect of victims and recent attempts to place victims and witnesses centre-stage, charting the Probation Service's role in all of this in particular. Probation work with victims of crime has arguably come a very long way since the introduction of the Victim's Charter in 1990, but this has meant new demands and challenges for probation, some of which have been met with energy and imagination, especially in relation to work with Victim Support as one of the major voluntary agencies in this field. But there are a number of outstanding training and supervisory issues to address, if not the larger issue of where probation might play a role in governmental plans to emphasise the 'restorative' dimensions of criminal justice. Moreover, it is not yet clear how probation work with victims will continue under the NOMS.

Chapter 19 picks up the theme of the involvement of other agencies by looking at the concept and practice of 'partnerships'. Judith Rumgay outlines the varieties of partnership activity in which probation has engaged, and identifies and examines the ingredients for effective partnerships. She also speculates on the impact of post-Carter policy for probation, particularly the notion of 'contestability' and partnership practice within the NOMS. Future scenarios may include a proliferation of arrangements between probation and other organisations, consequential fragmentation and disarray, and tensions between professional integrity and situational opportunism. There may also be tension between commitment and capacity since 42 probation areas and boards (soon to be trusts) must deal with hundreds of administering authorities following the Government's partnership thrust. Although the provision for new partnerships may bring positive benefit to the effectiveness of interventions and work with offenders, the lessons from past practice are that the most productive partnership arrangements are those which allow agencies to play to their strengths; in this sense, the *quantity* and *variety* of partnership arrangements in the future may seriously undermine the *quality* of practice.

At the same time, the opening up of work with offenders to agencies beyond probation may serve to make the nature of work with offenders more transparent. Certainly there are concerns that the public do not know what probation officers do. Thus in Chapter 20 Rob Allen and Mike Hough turn our attention to media representations of probation work and to public opinion about community penalties more generally. The authors look at different ways of measuring public attitudes towards probation and community penalties as well as noting what those attitudes are: invariably more nuanced than the tabloid media would have us think, although there is a good deal of ignorance too, for the public typically overestimate crime rates and underestimate levels of sentencing. Having charted the complex terrain of public attitudes Allen and Hough consider what 'drives' public opinion and address the relationships between the public, the political decision-makers and the news media in particular. They also address various possibilities for increasing public confidence in community sentences via involvement (the public having a say in the identification of work projects for 'unpaid work' for example) and making the work more 'visible'. But again, the authors look to the future and potential impact of NOMS, to the development of trusts (to replace probation boards) and to the prospective changing cast of service providers in regard to the need to enhance confidence in community penalties.

Chapter 15

Effectiveness: who counts what?

Simon Merrington and Stephen Stanley

Introduction

Probation effectiveness has always been important, but what it means and how it is measured has varied over time. This chapter looks at the various ways effectiveness has been defined over the last 40 years, relating them in particular to their historical context. Our approach is not original and builds on the work of others, for example Raynor (1997).

Over time the perceived objectives and practice models of probation work with offenders have changed, and with them the methods for measuring success. The reasons for these changes have been partly to do with shifts in public and political attitudes to crime and treatment of offenders. But they have also been influenced by the results of effectiveness research, resulting in a two-way interaction between research and policy.

The sections are arranged thematically. Sometimes they correspond to separate time periods but often they overlap, as follows:

- the treatment era – 1960s to mid-1970s;
- diversion from custody – from the mid-1970s on;
- punishment in the community – from the late 1980s;
- public protection – from the early 1990s;
- what works – also from about 1990;
- performance management – from the late 1980s.

Evaluation in the treatment era

The development of measurement

The treatment model that became dominant in the post-War era was based on individualised modes of intervention developed from psychotherapy. The aim was to change individual offenders so that they led a life which conformed to the law. Intervention was built around casework with offenders, defined by the Morison Committee as: 'the creation and utilisation for the benefit of an individual who needs help with personal problems, of a relationship between himself and a trained social worker' (Home Office 1962).

There was a consensus that the success of the casework relationship should be assessed in terms of whether the offender was leading a law-abiding life. Davies (1969) used the argument that: 'The aim of everyone concerned in the sentencing process is that the individual placed on probation should not offend again, and the officer carries out his work with this ultimate purpose clearly in view' (Davies 1969: 1).

While the first national evaluation (Radzinowicz 1958) used successful completion as its (surrogate) indicator, the mainstream of work as exemplified in the Home Office Research Unit studies was to use reconviction as the indicator of success. The arguments for this were set out by Martin Davies (1969): 'Firstly probation research is a branch of criminology and this brings with it measurement of reconviction as a potential criterion of failure'. While this measure has its difficulties, other available outcome measures such as personal change, Davies argued, were more subjective or less reliable than the reconviction indicator.

This argument depends firstly on the perceived need of probation to stay solely within criminology as a discipline and secondly on a distinction, evident in the study on which Davies was reporting, between objective outcome measures and input or 'independent' factors such as level of stress in the social environment or relationship with a probation officer. While this has some analytic justification, the argument for allowing a lower standard of reliability and validity for measurement of inputs than of outcomes seems weak. Any associations observed between inputs and outcomes are likely to be spurious unless the two are defined and measured with the same degree of rigour.

Measuring reconviction proved problematic. Data from the Criminal Records Office (CRO) was hard to access and had several gaps. Davies and the parallel National Probation Study (see Simon 1971) were forced to rely also on local police or probation officers' records of conviction and the latter relied in part on offender self-reports (as there was no certain process of notifying convictions to the Probation Service). While it appears (Davies et al. 1974; Pease et al. 1977) that reliance on sources other than the CRO or (later) the Offenders' Index (see Philpotts and Lancucki 1979) produced more evidence of offending, it is less clear that this improved the reliability of the results. Data from different sources are subject to various forms of bias, not all in the same direction.

It also became clear (see Simon 1971 for a review of the literature) that any intervention was likely to be mediated by a range of social factors. To address this the Home Office Research Unit carried out work to study the links between probationers' social environments, their reoffending and the interventions of probation officers. This was based around an 'Index of Social Environment' (Davies 1973) which covered three dimensions: support at home; school or work; and 'crime contamination' (including previous convictions).

Each dimension was dichotomised so that there were eight different categories that offenders could fall into. The Index was intended to be used as a baseline, an assessment measure and an indicator of success. The final report (Davies *et al.* 1974) stressed the need for 'situational' intervention that addressed the social environment as well as individual pathology.

IMPACT – matching intervention and offender

This in turn led to the English apotheosis of the treatment approach to casework in the IMPACT experiment (Folkard *et al.* 1974, 1976). IMPACT (Intensive Matched Probation and After-Care Treatment) was an experimental study based on earlier research, including that of Davies. The hypothesis was that by reducing caseloads and allowing probation officers to work on intensive situational treatment, offenders' problems could successfully be addressed and 'failure rates' reduced (Folkard *et al.* 1974: 16). The theoretical background included typologies of treatment and of offenders. It was assumed that the treatment would be matched to offender type but the implementation of this was left to 'experimental' staff in the four participating areas.

The project was designed as a randomised control trial with qualifying offenders assigned randomly to experimental units or to ordinary probation teams. The intended target group was 'high-risk' offenders, who were defined mainly as males aged over 17 with more than one or two convictions since the age of 14.

The scope of the outcome measures used in the study was planned to cover situational and personality change as well as offending. The study notably canvassed probation officers' views on what should be counted in the evaluation. The researchers found that officers put more emphasis on measures of personal change and social situations and that while reconviction was the most frequently mentioned criterion it was given 'a low degree of importance' (Folkard *et al.* 1974: 45).

In practice the outcome measures actually published were a one-year reconviction rate and some 'soft' data based on probation officer ratings from three of the four areas and possibly subject to experimental bias. The authors concluded that the reconviction data showed no positive effect of the experimental treatment and no evidence that 'experimental treatment produced more beneficial results than control treatment' (Folkard *et al.* 1976: 17).

It is apparent that there were flaws in the implementation of the project. In particular the interventions lacked many of the characteristics (such as a developed theory base and consistent implementation) now thought to be essential for any successful programme (see the section below on What Works).

Nevertheless, the IMPACT results were interpreted more negatively than they merited. The extensive analysis produced some findings which, read in the light of the What Works literature, are helpful. But by showing effects usually in the 'wrong' direction, they were politically unpalatable both to the Probation Service (which had invested considerable belief that 'more is better' in IMPACT) and to the Home Office.

Task-centred casework – more structure, narrower focus

One flaw in interpreting IMPACT was undoubtedly the belief that there was a linear relationship between input and result in probation interventions. This assumption was already being challenged by Reid's work on short-term and task-centred casework (Reid and Shyne 1969; Reid and Epstein 1972). Task-centred casework was tested in England by the National Institute of Social Work (Goldberg and Stanley 1979, 1985; Goldberg *et al.* 1985).

This test comprised a series of single studies, without control groups, in a range of social work settings, including probation, to establish whether it was possible to implement task-centred casework and whether there was evidence that it reduced problems through achieving tasks (the dynamic of personal change that Reid theorised). The project was designed as a feasibility study preparatory to a full evaluation based on a controlled trial experiment. The probation contribution to the task-centred casework project was notable in that it was inspired at least as much by practitioners' dissatisfaction with existing models of intervention (including the approaches used in IMPACT) as by managers' belief in the effectiveness of the approach.

Because the project was concerned to test the model of task-centred casework its measurement was initially defined by that model. The main components were:

- analysis of probation officer inputs in terms of time, style and content (measured through self-reporting by officers and file reading by researchers);

- analysis of probation officer assessments of offenders' problems (within a typology developed by Reid), tasks to resolve these, their achievement and the reduction of problems;

- offender self-reports (to an independent interviewer) of their problems, tasks and the reduction of problems;

- reconviction rates within one year, using Offender Index data.

Although numbers were small (100 cases), the findings showed the learning that could come from a tightly designed and controlled project even when it did not use an experimental design.

In summary, evaluation in the 1960s and 1970s concentrated on studies of often diffuse and eclectic individualised work with offenders. The primary outcome was reconviction but the importance of social factors as mediating variables and outcome measures was recognised from an early stage. True random allocation designs were very rare. Nevertheless, the weaknesses were arguably more in the measurement and description of interventions and situational factors than in the research designs. Results, when set against expectations, were disappointing and so were not built on. They led to sights being set lower, on the provision of help or the reduction of problems rather than on reducing offending. The stage was therefore set for the ascendancy of alternatives to custody.

Diversion from custody

The collapse of the rehabilitative ideal in England and Wales was signalled by the 'disappointing' results from IMPACT, the publication of Martinson's findings in the United States and an equivalent review by Brody (1976) looking at the evidence from a UK perspective.

In Britain, as in America, this coincided with the growth of a movement for decarceration, not just in criminal justice but elsewhere. For example, in the 1970s the new social services departments and health authorities were encouraged to shift away from closed institutions for residential and psychiatric care to 'care in the community'. At least part of the drive for this shift was better value for money. Prisons and other closed settings were seen as expensive to build and maintain as well as morally wrong.

This set the scene for 'diversion from custody'. In the 1970s there was a strongly held view, from the Home Secretary downwards, that the prison population – then approaching 40,000 – was becoming 'intolerably' high. New sentences such as the suspended sentence and community service had been introduced with the express purpose of diverting offenders from custodial sentences. Other sentencing options such as day training centres (later probation centres) were coopted into offering more restrictive and intrusive alternatives to custody (Raynor 1997). The social inquiry report (SIR) promoted by the Streatfeild and Morison committees to advise courts on the prospects for treatment became the gatekeeper for the new alternatives and the probation order itself coopted as one of them.

The implication for evaluation was an implied shift from measuring outcomes of intervention with offenders (as IMPACT had attempted) to measuring the effect of process or procedural changes. Questions included how well the new sentences did their job, and how well the SIR helped the courts choose between them and custody. It should be noted that even now the orientation of probation evaluation was often individualistic; it looked at the impact of individual sentencing decisions. It did not generally consider system impact.

Diversion from custody was methodologically as hard a question to answer as effectiveness in reducing offending. How was it possible to know what would have happened if a particular alternative had not been chosen?

Evaluating the diversionary effect of community service

One significant attempt at addressing diversion was the evaluation of community service orders carried out by the Home Office Research and Planning Unit (Pease et al. 1977). Because the objectives of sentencing are never one-dimensional, the evaluation attempted to measure the effect of the sentence in reducing offending in addition to diversion from custody. For the latter the researchers used what they described as 'circumstantial' evidence. They attempted to collate judgements of the sentence likely to be imposed if community service orders were not made and evidence of sentences imposed for breach of community service, where courts asked for an assessment of suitability or where community service was proposed in a SIR. A high use of custody on each measure would indicate that the sentence was an effective alternative. Three of the four data sources gave diversion estimates of between 45 and 50 per cent but the one that did not was the (admittedly fragmentary) data from cases in the very early period of implementing community service where sentencers asked for assessments of suitability. The researchers accepted the estimate of 45–50 per cent, with a caveat that it might be an overstatement.

While one might criticise this approach and wonder why it was not possible to attempt the 'quasi-experimental' design outlined in the report (Pease *et al.* 1977: 3), the method used illustrates the practical difficulties of estimating diversion or displacement. The study illustrated two linked issues for the evaluation of diversion. It was difficult to show that a custodial sentence would have been imposed in the absence of the alternative, and the causal route towards diversion was difficult to establish. The difficulty of proof and the increased use of inferential arguments were shown also in a study in Hampshire that aimed to assess the potential for reducing the use of custody (Smith *et al.* 1984). This was based on evidence from interviews with sentencers and probation officers and an examination of sentencing statistics for Crown and magistrates' courts.

The Afan project and day centres

An evaluation of the diversionary effect of the Afan day centre – a project targeted at young offenders (Raynor 1988) – took a different approach. Two main measures of diversion were used: a measure of the use of custody in Afan and neighbouring magistrates' courts, and a comparison of the profiles of offenders at the day centre with those sentenced to custody and with those put on probation or community service. The findings from these two measures were that the use of custody reduced in Afan but subsequently also in neighbouring courts, and that project profiles were more like cases receiving custody than those on other community disposals. Both indicators were seen as evidence of a diversion effect, the size of which was difficult to measure. In common with the CSO assessment, data were collected about the rate of custodial sentencing for breach. In the Afan project only 20 per cent of breaches were sentenced to custody, which was interpreted as evidence of a commitment to keep offenders at the centre and thus reinforcing it as an alternative. This is at variance with Pease's use of the same statistic *as an indicator of the level of diversion.* It seems likely that sentencing after breach reflected the court's view of the breach as well as of the original offence and so the custody rate was not a reliable measure of diversion.

Predicting risk of custody

We have seen that while SIRs appeared to influence diversion from custody, it was difficult to measure the extent of diversion (see also Haines and Morgan, this volume). The problem remained to quantify the risk of a custodial sentence at the point of SIR preparation in order to target alternatives to custody appropriately.

One solution was the development of 'Risk of Custody' predictors of which the most widely used was developed by a working probation officer,

David Bale (1989). Such scales were based on the argument that a few key factors, such as remand status, type of court, offence type and seriousness, were particularly associated with the use of custodial sentences. The intention of those who developed the scales was to support gate-keeping processes whereby more intrusive proposals were concentrated on cases at higher risk of custody in an attempt to improve diversion from custody. Research work concentrated on improving the predictive ability of the scale rather than demonstrating how effective it was in diverting offenders from custody (see Mair 1989). In fact by the time they were fully developed and gaining wider acceptance the sentencing framework was changed by the 1991 Criminal Justice Act, which brought an end to 'alternatives to custody' (see section below on punishment in the community).

To summarise, 'diversion from custody' produced descriptive research and some evaluations. However, it proved no easier than with 'treatment' to demonstrate a significant effect at the level of the individual case. It was possible by triangulating different measures to infer (reliably or otherwise) a diversion rate from custodial to community service sentences. But it was not possible to establish how far this was affected by the simple availability of sentences, by the appeal of different sentence characteristics as promoted in SIRs, or by other processes. Likewise it was possible to show the viability of specific projects as alternatives to custody, but not to estimate reliably the diversion effect of these projects.

Punishment in the community

Probation has always involved some restriction to offenders' liberty, but it was the Government's Green Paper, *Punishment, Custody and the Community* (Home Office 1988), that first linked the Government's concern about the rising use of custody with the notion that probation must be strengthened as a punishment. The subsequent White Paper and 1991 Criminal Justice Act took up the concept of 'just deserts' (proportionate punishment) and defined probation and community service as intermediate penalties between fines and custody.

The Green and White Papers argued that the restriction of an offender's freedom while on probation or community service was a punishment, in the same sense that fines and custody were punishments. In relation to community orders the punishment might include attending regular supervision meetings, additional requirements such as participation in day centre programmes, alcohol or drugs treatment or doing unpaid work on a community service order. Offenders were also expected to cooperate in tackling the problems leading to their offending. Another aspect of punishment was the strict enforcement of orders, bringing offenders back to court for re-sentence if they failed to comply. 'Just deserts' required that the amount of punishment imposed in this way was proportionate to the seriousness of the offence. This theme has since been regularly revisited (for example, with the introduction of reparation and curfew orders) and 'proper punishment' was part of the vision in the National Probation Service's (NPS) *New Choreography* (National Probation Directorate 2001b: 7).

Effectiveness in this context involves measuring two objectives:

- ensuring that demanding requirements are imposed on offenders; and
- convincing sentencers and the public that probation is a 'tough' option.

National Standards

The main vehicle for imposing demanding requirements has been the National Standards, introduced in 1992. These are considered more generally in the section on performance management, but here we look at the aspects relevant to punishment. That punishment is a central objective is clear from the statement of aims in the 1995 edition: 'to strengthen the supervision of offenders in the community, providing punishment and a disciplined programme for offenders ...' (Home Office 1995: 2). The statement goes on to explain that this can be achieved 'by ensuring the public can have confidence that supervision in the community is an *effective punishment* and a means to help offenders become responsible members of the community'.

Table 15.1 illustrates the punishment aspects of the 1995 National Standards using the example of probation orders. Of these the latter two are more amenable to measurement, and have become the focus of effectiveness measures. Not all probation officers have been happy with having to enforce the standards strictly, but a survey found that staff thought them 'helpful in ensuring fair and consistent enforcement practice, and allowing them to use discretion where necessary' (Ellis *et al.* 1996: 54).

Enforcing compliance

Despite this consensus, attaining the latter two standards, especially the last one, proved difficult to achieve and became a political issue during the 1990s.

Table 15.1 Punishment aspects of the 1995 National Standards for Probation Orders

Objectives	Include confronting offending behaviour, challenging the offender to accept responsibility for their crime, making offenders aware of the impact of their crime on victims and ensuring that the supervision programme is demanding
Methods	To include planned and purposeful physical activities directed towards helping offenders to change attitudes and develop a greater sense of personal responsibility and discipline
Frequency of contact	First appointment within five working days of order start. Offender should attend a minimum of 12 appointments ... in the first three months of an order, six in the next three months and one a month thereafter
Enforcing compliance	Failure to comply with requirements of order (usually unacceptable absence) to be dealt with promptly. Breach proceedings to be initiated on or before the third failure within a 12-month period

By 1998 enforcing compliance had become a Key Performance Indicator, with a target of 90 per cent achievement. To make matters harder, the 2000 National Standards introduced by New Labour toughened the standard so that breach was expected on the second failure. Between 1999 and 2001 three audits were commissioned by the Association of Chief Officers of Probation to monitor achievement of the contact and enforcement standards. These showed gradual improvement (Hedderman and Hearnden 2001) and in the 2005–6 National Business Plan (see performance management section) specific targets continued to be set in relation to frequency of contact and enforcement of compliance.

Did this attention to the punitive aspects of probation result in the desired increase in public confidence? It is difficult to survey the public directly, because knowledge of probation work is so limited. However, a survey of judges and magistrates (Hough *et al.* 2003) found they were uniform in acknowledging and welcoming improvements in enforcement standards.

The 1995 National Standards maintained that 'the overall purpose of enforcement is to secure and maintain the offender's cooperation and compliance with the order in order to ensure successful completion …' (p. 22). But can it be shown that strict enforcement increases the chances of completion? It could be argued that setting clear rules and expectations increases the likelihood of compliance. By contrast, it seems likely that making the rules tougher increases the likelihood of failure, breach and non-completion. Perhaps surprisingly, Hedderman and Hearnden (2001) found that compliance improved between the second and third audits even though this coincided with stricter standards being introduced.

Another important effectiveness question is whether vigorous enforcement improves probation outcomes by reducing reconviction rates. It could be argued that allowing offenders *more* chance to complete their orders is likely to increase the prospect that they will benefit from a 'treatment effect' (a common finding in programme evaluations is that non-completers are more likely to be reconvicted than completers). This was examined by Hearnden and Millie (2004) using the same audit data. A comparison was made of reconviction rates in areas pursuing tough and lenient enforcement strategies, as defined by their breach rates. Although the tough areas had breach rates almost twice as high as lenient ones, there was no significant difference in their reconviction rates (49 and 47 per cent respectively). Though methodologically flawed (they did not examine how expected reconviction rates varied between the two groups), the study did not show that tougher enforcement necessarily leads to less crime.

If the aim is to achieve order completion then, as Hearnden and Millie argue, it may be better to emphasise securing compliance than dealing with non-compliance. In other words, the best strategy may be reward rather than punishment-based. National Standards enforcement emphasises the latter. But there is a long history of the former in probation, for example motivational work and early termination of orders in recognition of good progress. But is this consistent with the need to demonstrate the punishment aspects of probation?

Offender perceptions of punishment

Finally, we should consider the extent to which offenders themselves view their orders as punitive. If the purpose is to impose conditions which offenders *experience* as tough and demanding, then arguably this should be the best measure of effectiveness. Surprisingly, few studies have examined this. Qualitative studies show that offenders accept there is a degree of punishment involved in probation supervision, especially having to report at fixed times, give up one's time, work constructively and keep the officer informed as to one's movements. This is especially true of intensive programmes and 'punitive' requirements such as unpaid work or curfews. But even so, many offenders see punishment not as an end in itself but imposed by the court for their own good, as a way of helping them to stop offending (Moore *et al.* 2004; Merrington 1995). Further research is arguably needed into the subjective perceptions of punishment before it can be used as a metric for effectiveness.

There is no doubt that the last 20 years have seen a toughening of community sentences. But little progress has been made with measuring how much punishment is involved in community sentences and whether sentencing is tough enough to be 'proportionate'. The main effort has gone into making National Standards more demanding and dealing with non-compliance. The other aspect of effectiveness lies in convincing sentencers, politicians, the media and the public that probation is a tough option. This has not been particularly successful, with the consequence that custodial sentencing rates continue to rise despite tougher community sentences.

Public protection

In 1990, a new aim for probation was highlighted in the Government White Paper, *Crime, Justice and Protecting the Public* (Home Office 1990). Public protection has become increasingly important, to the point of becoming the first objective of the NPS in the Criminal Justice and Court Services Act 2000. But what exactly does it mean? It has much in common with the objective of reducing reoffending, which was discussed in the first section and will be returned to in the next. But public protection has a slightly different focus. It marks a shift of emphasis from offenders to victims, and links with other crime prevention activities. In particular, it refers to the Probation Service's duty, along with other agencies, to protect the public from risk of serious harm by potentially dangerous offenders. It is this aspect of effectiveness that we will explore here.

The task is not new. The Probation Service has been accountable for the protection of the public from serious offending ever since it took responsibility for the supervision of released prisoners in the 1960s. But during the 1990s there was increasing public concern about the supervision of dangerous offenders in the community. The Probation Inspectorate's thematic inspection on this subject (HM Inspectorate of Probation 1995) identified a need for better risk assessment and management, including maintaining registers and information sharing with other agencies, in respect of potentially dangerous offenders.

A further thematic inspection in relation to sex offenders (HM Inspectorate of Probation 1998) also emphasised victim issues and the importance of groupwork programmes, and contained a section on monitoring, evaluation and effectiveness.

Assessing risk of serious harm

The Home Office has put a lot of resources into improving procedures for assessing risk of serious harm, including seeking advice from academics (Kemshall 1996). Risk of harm assessment procedures have been introduced and these are now incorporated into the general assessment system, OASys. Risk indicators include a history or pattern of violent or sexual offending, aspects of the current offence (psychological or physical violence, a targeted victim, violence related to alcohol or drug abuse), psychiatric problems including self-harm, a history of assaulting staff or risks to children. The procedure involves a screening assessment for all offenders and a detailed assessment where necessary. Assessments are repeated at intervals to assess changes in risk level.

There are, however, some problems with assessing risk of harm accurately. Although OASys produces a statistical prediction of the risk of reconviction, there is no formal scoring system for quantifying the level of risk of serious harm. One reason for this is that risk of harm is multi-dimensional – it includes risk of harm to the public in general, a specific victim such as a partner, risk of self-harm and risk to probation staff. There is not necessarily a single factor underlying these types of behaviour. A second problem is that the kinds of violent behaviour being predicted are relatively rare, making prediction more difficult. It is hard to develop and validate predictors, such as those for general offending. Instead, the OASys-based risk assessment relies on a four-level classification from 'very high' to 'low' risk based on a judgement of the likelihood of serious harm *and* the seriousness of its impact. Separate judgements are required for each of the above victim categories.

How accurate and reliable are these assessments? A study of the reconviction of sex offenders (Hood *et al.* 2002) noted that the assessment approach of the parole board in deciding release on licence erred on the side of safety. There were few if any 'false negatives' – cases wrongly assessed as posing a low risk – but about 50 per cent of their sample were 'false positives' – cases assessed as posing a high risk who were not subsequently reconvicted. The impact of this bias, however necessary for public confidence, is that it makes casework inefficient: half of it is likely to be directed to cases that do not need a high level of control. Hood and his colleagues argued that the use of a more actuarially based predictor, classifying offences in more detail, would reduce the number of false positives.

As far as we are aware, this kind of retrospective study has not been undertaken in relation to the OASys-based risk of harm assessment, so it is not known whether assessments err on the side of caution. An alternative but less rigorous form of validation would be to repeat assessments by 'experts', but again we are not aware of any such studies. The main form of effectiveness monitoring is limited to examining the extent to which risk assessments are actually completed.

Effectiveness of risk management procedures

In 2001 new Multi-Agency Public Protection Arrangements (MAPPA), building on existing arrangements, were set up requiring each probation area to work with the police and other agencies on local panels to review cases and coordinate arrangements for their surveillance. In this, the NPS has tried to place MAPPA within the same contextual framework as accredited programmes, particularly those concerned with sexual offences or domestic violence.

The main components of the new approach to public protection can be summarised as follows:

- structured analysis and identification of risks from the offender from PSR through the course of the sentence;

- close work with the police and other agencies in surveillance and control, set out in the MAPPA;

- the use of interventions to reduce offenders' propensity to commit harmful crimes – such as the Sex Offender Treatment Programme – or to contain them – such as residence in approved premises (formerly probation hostels);

- speedy recall to custody when the conditions of licences are breached or offenders' behaviour gives rise to concern.

The effectiveness of these arrangements has been evaluated by a process review of MAPPA (Kemshall *et al.* 2005). The study was based on questionnaires to all MAPPA areas together with a case study of six areas. This focus on process is arguably a necessary first step as the study found instances where processes did not work consistently and cases were misallocated, as well as exemplars of good practice. Effective management of risk was thus defined in terms of procedures.

Effectiveness of risk management outcomes

What matters for public protection is not just that appropriate procedures have been followed but that offenders do not cause serious harm to the public. The problem is that failures – i.e. serious reconvictions – are rare. This makes it hard to detect whether risk management has made a difference. One study (Cann *et al.* 2004) found, for example, that over two years only 10 per cent of sex offenders released from custody in 1979 had been reconvicted of a further sexual offence. Low base rates for reconviction make it hard to design an outcome study to show whether a particular risk management regime had better outcomes than a comparison group.

An alternative approach is the systematic review of Serious Further Offences (SFOs) committed by offenders under supervision. These concentrate on identifying gaps in provision and failures or weaknesses in procedures that mean that opportunities to prevent an offence have been neglected. Each SFO is followed by a review and the lessons are incorporated into local practice. However, reviews are based on existing standards, which may themselves be inadequate. Further, by concentrating on failures, reviews may fail to identify the strengths of existing practice, and lead to undesirable changes. Moreover, although reviews of individual cases may point to practice and organisational failings they cannot of themselves prove that the offence would not have been committed even if case management had been better.

A study carried out for Inner London Probation Service (Rhys 2001) brought together the findings from such reviews. Rhys identified three broad groups of cases: those where the offence could not be predicted by the record or behaviour of the offender; those where the offender was categorised as high risk but the measures taken were not (or could not be) adequate to prevent the crime; and a middle group where patterns of behaviour – generally an undercurrent of violence in offending – could have been identified and used to trigger appropriate intervention. Rhys was writing before the introduction of MAPPA and before OASys was in general use, but her findings have the merit of putting forward a testable hypothesis – that some, but not all, serious offences can be identified through assessment and perhaps prevented.

The problem is that, although rare, they can be very serious offences and attract a high level of adverse publicity. This tends to overwhelm arguments about their exceptional nature. In that situation, the only defence is that all reasonable procedures were followed and that the offence fell into Rhys's first group.

In summary, measuring the effectiveness of public protection work is hazardous, and to our knowledge has not been fully addressed. Methods for assessing risk of harm are not as fully developed as those for predicting risk of reconviction. Because risk of harm is a multi-dimensional concept, we cannot expect assessment tools of the same level of reliability and validity. If assessment is difficult it follows that effective risk management is also difficult, relying on practitioners' ability to identify and monitor risk factors. The key to good risk management is likely to be high levels of contact in high-risk cases and good inter-agency communication. Finally, outcomes are also difficult to measure because of the relative rarity of incidents involving serious harm.

'What Works' and the reduction of reoffending

'What Works' refers to the movement in the UK, from about 1990 onwards, which revived confidence in the belief that rehabilitation programmes for offenders could reduce their likelihood of reoffending. This idea was promulgated in the What Works conferences of the early 1990s, and James McGuire's seminal book *What Works: Reducing Reoffending* (1995).

What Works has a good deal in common with the treatment era. What made it different was the wide publicity given to some Canadian and American research reviews using meta-analysis, especially those by Andrews *et al.* (1990) and Lipsey (1992). Meta-analysis is a statistical method which allows the results of a large number of studies to be combined. Because the studies may individually be small, it can detect a 'treatment effect' which might not be significant if the studies were considered individually. Andrews and others found effects in the 8–10 per cent range, which might be considered small in traditional terms, but which they argued would be judged clinically useful in a medical context. Meta-analysis works at quite a general level, allowing outcomes of different types to be combined by using a standardised outcome measure known as 'mean effect size'. This allows varied outcome measures such as parole violation, misbehaviour in prison, rearrest and reconviction to be combined into a standard metric, meaning that studies in different contexts may be combined. While broad in one sense, meta-analysis is narrow in another – only some types of studies qualify for inclusion. To calculate effect size one needs to compare the outcome for the treatment group and a comparison group (discussed further below). This means that studies without comparison groups are omitted, and some meta-analyses are restricted to studies using random allocation. A consequence of this is a bias towards North American studies. Other biases arise from the fact that most studies are of young, male offenders, with few meta-analyses exploring treatment effects with female and ethnic minority offenders (McGuire 2002: 15).

Most importantly, meta-analysis has shed light on the types of intervention which have better than average treatment effects. This is measured by examining the statistical association between 'treatment' variables, such as whether the programme uses cognitive-behavioural methods, and mean effect size. It is important to remind ourselves that these are not necessarily causal connections, and further research may reveal other more fundamental factors. Moreover, the treatment variables described in each study are usually coded subjectively by the meta-analysts and therefore subject to bias. Nevertheless, when these variables are used in combination, meta-analysis has found positive treatment effects of up to 40 per cent. The effectiveness findings, as quoted by McGuire (1995: 14), include:

- programme intensiveness should be matched with offender risk level;
- to reduce offending, programmes should intervene in problem areas most related to or supportive of further offending;
- programmes should use methods most suited to the learning styles of offenders;
- most effective programmes are multi-modal (address a variety of problems), skills-oriented and use cognitive-behavioural methods;
- programmes should be delivered as planned, using appropriate methods, by skilled staff, and be properly monitored and evaluated.

What Works gave rise to a series of evaluations which paid attention to outcomes and whether the above effectiveness principles were met. An example in the UK is Raynor and Vanstone's evaluation of the Mid-Glamorgan STOP programme (1997) which covered:

- programme design, including theory base, documentation and staff training;
- whether the programme was delivered as intended ('programme integrity');
- programme completion;

- offenders' views of why they offended and the value of the programme;
- staff views on the programme and its effectiveness;
- intermediate outcomes: attitude change and self-reported problems (using the Crime-Pics scale);
- final outcomes: reconviction rates (actual and predicted) for STOP members and several comparison groups receiving other sentences.

Some of these are considered in more detail below.

Programme integrity

Paying attention to whether programmes are actually delivered as intended is an important feature of What Works. In the STOP experiment sessions were videoed and watched to ensure that staff delivered them as intended. In a similar way, probation areas delivering Accredited Programmes approved by the NPD also had to video a proportion of sessions and submit them for quality assurance.

Offender and staff feedback

Qualitative methods are useful in obtaining information about what works and how. In the case of STOP, offenders were asked at the end of the programme why they had offended, what they saw as the purpose of the programme, positive and negative aspects of the programme and how useful it had been, and how they rated their chances of staying out of trouble. But other Pathfinder evaluations, such as the one of cognitive skills programmes (Hollin et al. 2004), have not attempted to collect offender feedback (although staff views were sought as part of the process evaluation). The What Works era has tended to favour quantitative outcome data at the expense of qualitative measures of effectiveness.

Programme completion and compliance

As Underdown (1998) has argued, fulfilling the obligations imposed by a court order is clearly an important outcome for community supervision, and we discussed this in the section on punishment. But there is another reason for the importance of programme completion as an outcome measure. The 'treatment' benefits cannot be experienced if the offender does not attend and an offender who attends most of a programme should benefit more than an offender who attends only a little (the 'time in treatment' argument). Most studies show that programme completers are less likely to be reconvicted than non-completers, suggesting a treatment effect (for example Hollin et al. 2004). For this reason, completion of a programme or order is often used as a proxy outcome measure. But we should be cautious about the evidence of a causal link between completion and reconviction. Completers may well be the sort of people less likely to be reconvicted, regardless of the programme.

Psychometrics

The use of psychometric scales measuring attitudes and behaviours was important in the treatment era, and in the What Works era too scales have been used for assessment of suitability and as measures of outcome. For example, Crime-Pics (Frude *et al.* 1994) is a problem and attitude scale developed to help Mid-Glamorgan Probation Service evaluate the STOP programme. Offenders completed an assessment at the start and end of the programme, and the mean scores showed an improvement (Raynor and Vanstone 1997). More encouragingly still, subjects whose scores improved showed lower levels of reconviction than those whose scores deteriorated.

To be useful psychometric scales must measure the behaviour or attitude targeted by the intervention. For example, the NPD selected several scales to measure the impact of cognitive skills programmes such as Think First. They included: Crime-Pics, the Levenson locus of control scale and the Rosenberg self-esteem scale. All of these have shown significant pre-test to post-test changes in conjunction with such programmes (McGuire and Hatcher 2001). However, it is necessary to show that any improvements are linked to a reduced risk of reoffending. In the STOP study quoted above, this was the case. But in another study, offenders whose attitudes changed pro-socially were *more* likely to be reconvicted than those whose attitudes did not (Wilkinson 2005).

Other intermediate outcomes

Some interventions are intended to have other immediate outcomes. For example, relevant outcomes might be acquisition of basic skills, improvements in employment status, drug or alcohol usage, health, finances, family relationships or accommodation. Such changes in social circumstances have the advantage that they can often be measured in simple terms and a direct link made to the programme inputs. Of course it is still necessary to examine whether such improvements result in a lower risk of reoffending.

Final outcomes: reduction of re-offending

As we have seen, it is a primary assumption of What Works that the main measure of effectiveness is whether interventions reduce offending. The commonest way of measuring this in the UK is reconviction (Lloyd *et al.* 1995; Friendship *et al.* 2004). This has a number of well-known disadvantages: it is a substantial underestimate of reoffending, since only a minority of offences are reported, detected, prosecuted and result in a court sentence or formal warning. Nor is it necessarily a consistent underestimate, since crime detection can vary by type of offence, from place to place and over time. But it also has advantages: it is systematically recorded and accessible for research at a national level using two main databases – the Home Office Offender Index and the Police National Computer. While these are not 100 per cent in agreement, they appear to be more reliable and consistent than any other source.

The other possible measure of reoffending is offenders' self-reports. These have been used occasionally (for example, Bottoms 1995). They have the advantage of including undetected crimes and usually report higher frequencies than reconviction data. But they suffer from the disadvantage of not being recorded in a standardised way and are prone to unreliability due to concealment, poor memory and subjective interpretation. Nevertheless, in some instances, self-report is the best way to capture reoffending, for example in the evaluation of drugs programmes (levels of usage) and domestic violence programmes (partner reports). To summarise, self-reports have potential, but reconviction data remain the preferred method in the UK despite accuracy problems. But we should note the caution of Lloyd *et al.* (1995: 11) 'Reconviction rates cannot and should not be ignored, nor should they be accepted uncritically.'

The traditional measure of reconviction has been the proportion of subjects reconvicted at least once during a two-year follow-up period. This proportion can then be compared with that for a comparison group (see below). It has recently become more common to use a one-year follow-up as well, since some studies have found that treatment effects fade over time (for example, Farrington *et al.* 2002). Whatever the time period the headline reconviction measure is crude. The offender may be reconvicted, but the offence may be less serious than previously or there may be a reduction in the frequency of offending. Given these considerations, it is surprising how few studies have sought to measure reductions in offence frequency and seriousness which, particularly for studies of persistent offenders, would be a superior approach. An example is the evaluation of the Intensive Supervision and Surveillance Programme (ISSP) for persistent young offenders (Moore *et al.* 2004). Here offence frequency during the 12 months from the start of the order was compared with the previous 12 months. Offence seriousness was also compared between the two periods using an offence seriousness scale.

Having defined reconviction it remains to decide how to interpret the result. Knowing that 50 per cent of programme participants were reconvicted within two years does not shed light on whether the programme makes a difference. To make this assessment some kind of comparison is necessary, and the Home Office Research, Development and Statistics Directorate has recently been trying to raise the standard of research by improving the quality of these comparisons. Friendship *et al.* (2004) have adapted Sherman's Scientific Methods Scale as shown in Table 15.2.

Friendship *et al.* argue that it is not possible to draw conclusions about what works, or effectiveness, unless research reaches Levels 4 or 5. For example, they judge the STOP study described above as Level 3, on the grounds that the comparison groups were only 'weakly matched' and the sample size was small. By contrast, they rate a study of prison-based cognitive skills programmes by Cann *et al.* (2003) at Level 4, on the grounds that the comparison group were individually matched on key variables with the treatment group. It is worth noting that they rate no recent probation studies in England and Wales above Level 3!

At Level 4, there are various issues concerning the achievement of 'well-matched' status. The requirement is to pick the comparison group so that they are matched on variables likely to be predictive of reconviction. These are known as 'baseline' variables because they measure similarity at the start of treatment. Typical variables are age, gender, offence type and criminal history. A reconviction predictor called OGRS (Offender Group Reconviction Scale –

Table 15.2 Scientific Methods Scale adapted for reconviction studies

Quality level	Method of comparison	Features
Level 1	No comparison	Data on intervention group only
Level 2	Comparison with predicted rate	No comparison group. Actual and predicted rates compared for intervention group only
Level 3	Unmatched comparison group	Intervention and comparison groups compared. Similarity of two groups not demonstrated
Level 4	Well-matched comparison group	Intervention and comparison groups compared. Groups well-matched on relevant variables
Level 5	Random control trial (RCT)	Intervention and comparison groups compared. Offenders randomly assigned between groups

Taylor 1999) was developed using Offender Index data to incorporate these variables into a prediction score. If both groups have similar mean OGRS scores then it is likely that they are well matched. However, OGRS is limited to 'static' data, and it is known that 'dynamic' variables such as drug use, employment status and motivation also influence likelihood of reconviction. Ideally these should be similar as well, but data are not often available. Then there are two ways of matching: group and individual. In the latter, pairs of individuals are matched by selecting the comparison group from a larger pool (the Cann study was done this way using the Offender Index). In the former, a comparison group is selected and then averages of the key variables are compared between the two groups. If they are similar, the groups are considered well-matched. If they are not similar, statistical methods can be employed to control for these differences while the reconviction rates of the two groups are compared. The most common method used is logistic regression, as in the cognitive skills programmes evaluation (Hollin *et al.* 2004). Much more attention is now given to the question of how well-matched comparison groups are, and whether other independent variables could explain an apparent 'treatment effect'.

The importance of having a comparison group is illustrated by the ISSP study (Moore *et al.* 2004). The persistent offenders attending ISSP showed a marked reduction in the frequency of their offending, by 43 per cent. But the comparison group showed a similar reduction – 46 per cent – over a similar period. The authors concluded that the reduction in both cases was influenced by a statistical phenomenon, regression to the mean. This occurs if the phenomenon being studied (in this case frequency of offending) fluctuates over time, and if people are selected for treatment because of abnormally high levels in the recent past – as in ISSP. In the follow-up period frequency of offending can be expected to revert to a more average level. In such cases effectiveness must be measured by whether the ISSP group outperforms the comparison group.

Random control trials (Level 5) provide, in theory at least, a way of ensuring that comparison groups are highly similar in all respects. It is perhaps surprising, therefore, that they have only been used rarely in this country (but see the IMPACT study above). The Home Office is currently commissioning some RCTs to rectify this situation. But we should be aware that using RCT in criminal justice is not as straightforward as in medicine and faces several practical and theoretical problems. There are practical and ethical problems if the experiment involves persuading sentencers to randomly assign people to different sentences. There is also a problem if sample sizes are small: random assignment cannot be relied on to produce two similar groups. Then there is a threat to validity if attrition is high. It is common for programme dropout to reach 20–30 per cent, so one is no longer comparing the effect of the intervention with that of the control condition. If drop-outs are excluded, then there is a risk of the two groups no longer being similar (as well as reducing sample size). Finally, an important aspect of medical RCTs is the *double blind*: neither the person administering the treatment, nor the patient, know whether the patient is in the treatment or control group. It is not possible to conceal this in criminal justice interventions, so it is possible that staff and offender responses are affected by this knowledge. The problems of using RCTs in criminal justice have been understood for some time (Clarke and Cornish 1972). Pawson and Tilley (1997) go further and argue that in criminal justice they are not a useful way of exploring causality, and advocate instead a process of 'realistic evaluation' which dispenses with a control group and focuses instead on understanding the mechanism of the intervention itself and the context in which it operates, and on differences in outcomes within the treatment group, in order to identify what works, with whom, under what circumstances.

Effective case management

Until recently most of the Government's What Works effort was concerned with delivery of effective programmes, mostly, but not always, groupwork programmes. But as early as 1997 Underdown emphasised the importance of case management as part of What Works. For him, case management was mainly about guiding and supporting programme work, by good assessment, planning, motivational work and relapse prevention. Since then some researchers have gone further, and asserted the importance of good casework, rather than programmes, for effective interventions. Central to this is the officer–offender relationship (see, for example, Burnett and McNeill 2005).

The literature on effective casework relationships goes back to the treatment era. For example, Truax and Carkhuff (1967) highlighted the importance of empathy, positive regard or concern, 'genuineness', and a concrete and specific approach to goals. This was reinforced by research from Miller and Rollnick (1992) on the value of motivational interviewing, and by Trotter (1993) on the impact of pro-social modelling by the supervising officer on reconviction rates. More recently a meta-analysis by Dowden and Andrews (2004) identified particular staff skills which contributed to effective rehabilitative work with offenders. These were effective use of authority, appropriate modelling and reinforcement, the use of a problem-solving approach and the development of relationships characterised by openness, warmth, empathy, enthusiasm, directiveness and structure.

It appears, therefore, that measuring the effectiveness of case management involves at least two dimensions: the effectiveness of the case management process/organisation and the effectiveness of the casework relationship. Further research is needed to explore the relative influence of casework and programmes on overall outcomes such as reoffending.

To summarise, What Works has revived the reduction of reoffending as a central objective of probation. But it has done more that that. It has emphasised the importance of rigour in research design so that findings are robust. It has also widened the scope of effectiveness measures to include the design, targeting and implementation of interventions, and drawn attention to the importance of intermediate outcomes as well as reoffending itself. Table 15.3, adapted from Underdown (1998), summarises this broader picture.

This spread of measures includes qualitative and quantitative approaches to triangulate findings and reach more robust conclusions. In particular, What Works has given renewed emphasis to quasi-experimental and experimental research designs using well-matched comparison groups or RCT.

Table 15.3 What Works effectiveness measures

Topic	Measures
1. Programme or intervention design	Design features such as theory base, appropriateness of methods, documentation
2. Targeting	Whether participants have appropriate risk level and criminogenic needs
3. Programme delivery	Whether programme is delivered effectively and as planned
4. Completion and compliance	Whether participants complete the programme and comply with its requirements
5. Stakeholder feedback	Feedback from offenders, staff, external providers and sentencers on effectiveness
6. Attitude and behaviour change	Change in appropriate attitudes/behaviour such as thinking skills, victim awareness, aggression
7. Other intermediate outcomes	Change in appropriate areas such as Basic Skills, job training, family relationships
8. Reoffending	Reduction in level of offending, including frequency and seriousness
9. Case management context	Quality of assessment, planning, referral to appropriate interventions and ongoing support
10. Casework skills	Effectiveness of working relationships between staff and offenders

Performance management

The last 20 years have seen an increase in the central prescription of probation objectives and practice methods, reducing the traditional autonomy of probation officers. Starting with the *Statement of National Objectives and Priorities* (SNOP) (Home Office 1984), this has involved the drawing up of national plans and priorities, National Standards, performance targets and measures of effectiveness and efficiency. To some extent this topic is different from the others discussed above in that the objectives emphasised at any one period will reflect some themes already mentioned. What performance management particularly does is *operationalise* the Government's priorities by defining effectiveness in very specific ways which are likely to influence probation practice.

Audit Commission report

Probably the most influential report in defining probation effectiveness and efficiency in the 1980s was the Audit Commission's study *The Probation Service: Promoting Value for Money* (Audit Commission 1989). This reviewed the whole role of probation in the light of the current overarching objectives of reducing the use of custody and rehabilitating offenders. It argued that value for money would be achieved by:

- targeting SIRs on serious offenders and not wasting money on minor offenders likely to receive fines and discharges;
- targeting probation/community service orders on more serious offenders and those at risk of custody, thus making cost savings;
- developing supervision methods which effectively challenge offending behaviour, thus saving money through a reduction in crime;
- developing partnership arrangements with other agencies to achieve better value for money;
- developing better management and information systems, for example local target setting.

The report highlighted examples of good practice, for example risk of custody scales to target SIR recommendations and day training centres for offenders at risk of custody. Current national developments, such as performance indicators and a financial management information system (see below), were also favourably reviewed.

National Standards, performance indicators and RMIS

National Standards for probation practice were mentioned in the section on punishment in the community, but they have a longer history. Intended to set a framework for professional standards and accountability, they replaced the earlier Probation Rules and local Good Practice Guidelines developed during the 1980s. They covered court work and pre-sentence reports, the supervision of community orders, supervision of custodial sentences pre- and post-release, hostels and bail schemes. The first National Standards were introduced in 1992, soon after the appearance of the Audit Commission report. A shorter, tougher version appeared in 1995 (Home Office 1995), and a further version in 2000. Examples of the Standards set are quoted in the section on punishment in the Community. The influence of these Standards on definitions of effectiveness has been considerable. One example, discussed below, is the role they have played in inspections by the Probation Inspectorate.

A linked development has been introduction of performance indicators. Following an efficiency scrutiny of the Probation Inspectorate in 1986, it was proposed that a set of key performance indicators (KPIs) be developed to assist in the promotion of efficiency and effectiveness. The first KPIs were published by the Home Office in 1994 and have grown in importance since then. Although selective, they cover the full range of probation work. Aspects measured include National Standards (i.e. professional practice), unit costs and outcomes such as stakeholder satisfaction, order completion and reconviction rates. At first they were used in HMIP inspections, but later, as we shall see, they became the basis of performance targets.

Effectiveness has received more attention than efficiency. An attempt to correct this has been the Resource Management Information System (RMIS). Starting in 1986, this aimed initially to measure both cost and effectiveness for probation activities. Later a more modest target was adopted, to measure probation unit costs. Two obstacles to achieving this locally were the lack of a reliable and up-to-date measure of time spent on each activity (not achieved until the activity sampling exercise in 1997) and the correct attribution of costs to activities across a range of work settings (never fully resolved). Despite these problems area level unit costs were published as part of the KPIs from the late 1990s. However, an HMIP inspection on use of information (HM Inspectorate of Probation 2000a) found that the burden of running RMIS outweighed the benefits and its use was discontinued. The RMIS episode was disappointing, marred by over-ambitious plans, poor cooperation with the unions, very slow progress, a high work burden and results of limited reliability.

HMIP inspections of effectiveness and efficiency

The Probation Inspectorate has had an increasingly sophisticated role in the assessment of probation efficiency and effectiveness since the late 1980s. The earliest inspections on this topic were known as Effectiveness and Efficiency (E&E) inspections, and took place between 1989 and 1993. Data were gathered from the usual local sources (reports, interviews and file inspection), but supplemented by KPIs. The second round were known as Quality and Effectiveness (Q&E) inspections, and the third round as Performance Inspection Programme (PIP) inspections. Space does not permit this evolution to be traced, but as an example, Table 15.4 shows the aspects of probation order effectiveness that were examined in the PIP inspection (HM Inspectorate of Probation 2000b).

The main thing that strikes one is the variety of ways effectiveness is defined: in terms of service provision, of compliance with practice standards, of quality of casework content, of consumer satisfaction, of outcome and

Table 15.4 Aspects of probation order effectiveness examined during PIP inspection of 2000

Aspect	Measured by
Key Performance Indicators: • reconviction rates (KPI 1)	• HO data on actual and predicted reconviction rates
• order completion (KPI 2)	• Service data provided to HO
• breach action (KPI 3)	• Service data provided to HO
• unit costs (KPI 7)	• Service data provided to HO using RMIS program
Compliance with national standards	Case files to ascertain compliance with contact and enforcement requirements, supervision plan quality and whether problems have been addressed
Observation of practice	Observation to judge quality of one-to-one casework
Sentencer satisfaction	Survey of sentencer views on service offered and how well offenders supervised
Group-work programmes	Review of group-work provision and What Works initiatives
Accommodation	Review of adequacy of accommodation provision
Drug misuse	Review of drug treatment provision
Employment, training and education (ETE)	Review of ETE provision
Equal opportunities	Review of equal opportunities policy and provision

value for money. In addition, there is a richness of qualitative and quantitative inspection methods. One interesting aspect of this inspection approach was the attempt to measure value for money by plotting cost against performance. For example, the average unit cost of probation orders in an area was compared with a quantitative performance rating (based on combining KPIs and other National Standards data). The areas giving best value for money had above average performance but below average cost.

Three-year plans, annual business plans and targets

The Home Office started issuing three-year plans including KPIs and specific targets in the mid-1990s. There is not space to trace the evolution of these plans. A recent refinement has been the linking of targets with area budgets. A small proportion of probation budgets (about 3 per cent in 2005/6) is allocated according to how far areas achieve a defined subset of their performance targets. This is known as the 'performance link' or 'weighted scorecard'.

Table 15.5 contains an extract from the NPS Business Plan for 2005–6 (NPD 2005). It illustrates how the definition of priorities and selection of performance targets reflects current views of effectiveness. It is structured under the key priorities for that year, and only measures contributing to the weighted scorecard (arguably the most important ones) are quoted.

Several points can be made about how effectiveness is measured. Some of the measures are very selective, even marginal (e.g. in relation to Priority 1). Much of the emphasis is on timeliness of practitioner actions, deriving from National Standards. Some measure offender response (e.g. attendance at appointments). Several measure achievement of volume targets for getting offenders through programmes or orders. There is little emphasis on the quality of probation work or the achievement of outcomes such as reduced use of custody or reoffending. Value for money does not feature among the targets. Overall, the picture does not seem as balanced as in the PIP example above.

Table 15.5 Selected performance measures taken from the National Probation Service Business Plan for 2005–6 (Annex B)

Priority	Performance measure used to set target
1. Contribute to building an excellent NOMS	Completion of race/ethnic monitoring data
2. Protecting the public from harm	Completion of risk of harm assessments, risk management plans and OASys sentence plans on high-risk offenders within five working days
3. Protecting the public from prolific offenders	Completion of risk of harm assessments and OASys sentence plans on prolific and other priority offenders within five working days
4. Implementing the 2003 Criminal Justice Act	Reports provided within timescale required by court Breach proceedings initiated in accordance with National Standards within ten working days Offender compliance with requirements of order/licence Appointments arranged in accordance with National Standards Appointments attended in accordance with National Standards Number of successful completions of enhanced community punishment orders
5. Implementing the National Action Plan on reducing reoffending	Number of Basic Skills awards Number of Drug Treatment and Testing Order completions Number of accredited programme completions

The European Foundation for Quality Management Model (EFQM)

In contrast to the top-down approach of HMIP inspections and three-year plans, the EFQM is a bottom-up approach to improving effectiveness. It is an organisational improvement tool which was introduced in the Probation Service in 2001 (NPD 2001a), though the requirement on areas to use it ceased in 2004. It is a general approach applicable to both public and private sectors, based on self-assessment by members of staff. It focuses not only on results, but also on the way the organisation does things (the enablers). The model is broken into nine criteria, as shown in Table 15.6.

Probation areas carried out the self-assessment process every autumn, which involved collecting evidence, scoring, and identifying strengths and areas for improvement. The latter were built into areas' annual plans. What effect has EFQM had on definitions of effectiveness? The main contrast with the business plan approach is that the model is not prescriptive about *how* effectiveness is measured. Instead it encourages assessment teams to focus on the elements of the excellence model, and what types of evidence might be available or collected in future. It encourages innovation, improvement and a mix of qualitative and quantitative methods. One significant effect has been the increased use of stakeholder satisfaction surveys which include sentencers, offenders, victims, staff and partnership organisations.

Table 15.6 The EFQM Model as used in probation

Enablers	Criterion	Description
	1. Leadership	How leaders set direction and motivate employees
	2. Policy and strategy	How policy is reviewed, developed and communicated
	3. People	How the organisation manages people
	4. Partnership and resources	Use of external partnerships and internal resources
	5. Processes	How the organisation manages its processes
Results	6. Customer results	Results achieved for external customers
	7. People results	Results achieved for its own people
	8. Society results	Results achieved for society generally
	9. Key performance	Results in relation to planned performance

In summary, performance management has had a strong influence on how effectiveness and efficiency have come to be defined in probation. The current NPD and area business plans are a world away from the tentative first steps of SNOP. The performance management approach does not of itself specify the nature of the objectives to be pursued nor how they will be measured. However, a number of characteristics emerge:

- greater use of targets and monitoring than of research to measure effectiveness;
- an emphasis on measurable items which can be monitored;

- a greater emphasis on activities than outcomes, possibly because they are easier to measure;
- particular emphasis on timeliness of activities, rather than content or quality;
- within outcomes too, the more easily measured items, such as order completion and stakeholder feedback, have been preferred to more difficult ones such as reconviction and reduction in factors underlying offending.

Overall, performance management has led to a rather selective, superficial and fragmented definition of effectiveness, and one subject to changes in emphasis as methods like RMIS and EFQM come and go.

Current prospects for measuring effectiveness

In this chapter we have shown how the emphasis of probation policy and practice has changed over the last 40 years, and how this has influenced the ways that effectiveness has been measured. Table 15.7 summarises our argument.

Which of these approaches remain relevant in the present, at a time when the NPS is about to be merged with the Prison Service and become the National Offender Management Service? The first thing that strikes us is that all the themes have useful aspects, even though those of the treatment era can be subsumed within What Works. Protection of the public, reduction of reoffending, diversion from custody and ensuring 'proper punishment' remain important objectives. Performance management as an approach will surely become even more important under NOMS, as areas of work are opened up to contestability and competition. This will apply especially to the question of efficiency and value-for-money, which has tended to take second place to effectiveness hitherto.

Finally, we return to the question of how effectiveness is measured and what counts as evidence. Over the last 40 years various methodologies have been used, ranging from large-scale research experiments such as IMPACT to quite simple monitoring of key indicators. All of these have their valid place, depending on what is being measured. But as researchers we are concerned that evidence should reach an appropriate level of rigour. For example, if the objective is diversion from custody we should expect a research study which compares custody trends in pilot areas and matched comparison areas. As noted in the What Works section, the Home Office is currently advocating greater use of RCTs. We have expressed our reservations about RCT, and would remind readers that it has not so far produced clear and useful results in a UK context. Instead, we would favour approaches along the lines of the PIP inspections, the EFQM Model and the STOP evaluation, which employ several methods, qualitative and quantitative, to ensure robustness of findings and explore the perspectives of different participants on what is effective.

Table 15.7 The changing emphasis of probation policy and measurement of effectiveness

Phase	Policy emphasis	Measurement of effectiveness
Treatment era	Reducing offending Rehabilitating offenders	Impact on offending Personal/social change Order completion
Diversion from custody	Providing community sentences which are alternatives to custody	Impact on custodial sentencing Profile comparison with custodials Use of custody on breach Risk of custody predictors
Punishment in the community	Ensuring that community sentences are tough and demanding	Are demanding standards enforced? Do they improve compliance? Are sentencers/the public convinced? Do offenders find them tough?
Public protection	Focus on victims Protecting public against dangerous offenders	Is assessment effective? Are risk management procedures thorough? Is serious harm prevented? Analysis of failures
What Works	Reducing reoffending Designing programmes that target crimino-genic needs Delivering programmes as planned Commitment to evaluation Evidence-based policy/ practice	Impact on offending Quality of programme design/delivery Programme completion Intermediate outcomes (attitudes etc.) Supportive case management? Qualitative and quantitative methods
Performance management	Management systems Target setting and monitoring Effectiveness and efficiency Flexible policy focus	National standards/ good practice Monitoring/audit rather than research Process rather than outcomes Focus on key targets/ indicators

Further reading

There is a fairly substantial literature on the methods available for evaluating the effectiveness of probation work with offenders. Often the books and articles combine a discussion of the methodology with a discussion of the results obtained. A valuable historical overview taking a similar approach to our own is that of Raynor (1997). Raynor has also updated and expanded his thinking in an as yet unpublished paper given at a Home Office research symposium in Cambridge in March 2006 (Raynor, forthcoming). This paper focuses particularly on the What Works phase and what may succeed it.

Of the various publications relating to the treatment era, perhaps the most comprehensive, and also contemporaneous, is Brody's review, *The Effectiveness of Sentencing* (Brody 1976). This includes a substantial discussion of the limitations of research methodology, including random control trials, showing that the debate as to their value is by no means new. In relation to diversion from custody, two publications illustrate well the approach of the period: one in relation to community service (Pease *et al.* 1977) and one in relation to probation centres (Raynor 1988). Readings on the effectiveness of probation as punishment are less easy to find, and mainly concentrate on the strictness of enforcement and its relationship with compliance and reconviction (see, for example, Hearnden and Millie 2004). Studies on the effectiveness of probation in reducing risk of serious harm tend to concentrate on process aspects (for example, Kemshall *et al.* 2005), but Cann *et al.* (2004) provide an example of an outcome study. By contrast, there is a large choice of readings in relation to What Works. Friendship *et al.* (2004) include a discussion of the drawbacks and advantages of reconviction studies and argue in favour of random control trials. Pawson and Tilley (1997) argue against the value of RCTs in criminal justice and advocate 'realistic evaluation' instead. Several authors argue for pluralistic evaluation methods, combining process and outcome evaluation, using qualitative and quantitative methods. These include Underdown (1998), McIvor (1997) and Friendship *et al.* (2004) too. Farrall and Calverley (2006) (a recent publication not discussed in this chapter) caution against relying on two-year reconviction rates and argue for longer follow-up periods to assess the impact of probation on desistance. A useful example of pluralistic evaluation is provided by Raynor and Vanstone (1997).

References

Andrews, D.A., Zinger, I., Hoge, R., Bonta, J., Gendreau, P. and Cullen, F.T. (1990) 'Does correctional treatment work? A clinically relevant and psychologically informed meta-analysis', *Criminology*, 28: 369–404.

Audit Commission (1989) *The Probation Service: Promoting Value for Money*. London: HMSO.

Bale, D. (1989) 'The Cambridgeshire Risk of Custody Scale', in G. Mair (ed.), *Risk Prediction and Probation: Papers from a Research and Planning Unit Workshop*, Research and Planning Unit Paper 56. London: Home Office.

Bottoms, A.E. (1995) *Intensive Community Supervision for Young Offenders: Outcomes, Process and Cost*. Cambridge: Institute of Criminology.

Brody, S.R. (1976) *The Effectiveness of Sentencing: A Review of the Literature*, Home Office Research Study 35. London: HMSO.

Burnett, R. and McNeill, F. (2005) 'The place of the officer–offender relationship in assisting offenders to desist from crime', *Probation Journal*, 52 (3): 221–42.

Cann, J., Falshaw, L. and Friendship, C. (2004) 'Sexual offenders discharged from prison in England and Wales: a 21-year reconviction study', *Legal and Criminal Psychology*, 9: 1–10.

Cann, J., Falshaw, L., Nugent, F. and Friendship, C. (2003) *Understanding What Works: Accredited Skills Programmes for Adult Men and Young Offenders*, Home Office Research Findings 226. London: Home Office.

Clarke, R.V.G. and Cornish, D.B. (1972) *The Controlled Trial in Institutional Research: Paradigm or Pitfall for Penal Evaluators?*, Home Office Research Study 15. London: Home Office.

Davies, M. (1969) *Probationers in Their Social Environment*, Home Office Research Study No. 2. London: HMSO.

Davies, M. (1973) *An Index of Social Environment*, Home Office Research Study No. 17. London: HMSO.

Davies, M., Rayfield, M., Calder, A. and Fowles, T. (1974) *Social Work in the Environment*, Home Office Research Study No. 21. London: HMSO.

Dowden, C. and Andrews, D. (2004) 'The importance of staff practice in delivering effective correctional treatment: a meta-analysis', *International Journal of Offender Therapy and Comparative Criminology*, 48: 203–14.

Ellis, T., Hedderman, C. and Mortimer, E. (1996) *Enforcing Community Sentences*, Home Office Research Study No. 158. London: Home Office.

Farrall, S. and Calverley, A. (2006) *Understanding Desistance from Crime*. Maidenhead: Open University Press.

Farrington, D.P., Ditchfield, J., Howard, P. and Jolliffe, D. (2002) *Two Intensive Regimes for Young Offenders: A Follow-up Evaluation*, Home Office Research Findings 163. London: Home Office.

Folkard, M.S., Smith, D.E. and Smith, D.D. (1976) *IMPACT: Intensive Matched Probation and After-Care Treatment. Volume 2. The Results of the Experiment*, Home Office Research Study No. 36. London: HMSO.

Folkard, M.S., Fowles, A.J., McWilliams, B.C., McWilliams, W., Smith, D.D., Smith, D.E. and Walmsley, G.R. (1974) *IMPACT: Intensive Matched Probation and After-Care Treatment. Volume I. The Design of the Probation Experiment and an Interim Evaluation*, Home Office Research Study No. 24. London: HMSO.

Friendship, C., Street, R., Cann, J. and Harper, G. (2004) 'Introduction: the policy context and assessing the evidence', in G. Harper and C. Chitty (eds), *The Impact of Corrections on Re-offending: A Review of 'What Works'*, Home Office Research Study No. 291. London: Home Office.

Frude, N., Honess, T. and Maguire, M. (1994) *CRIME-PICS II Manual*. Cardiff: Michael & Associates.

Goldberg, E.M. and Stanley, S.J. (1979) 'A task-centred approach to probation', in J.F.S. King (ed.), *Pressures and Change in the Probation Service*, Cambridge Institute of Criminology, Cropwood Conference Series No. 11. Cambridge: University of Cambridge Institute of Criminology.

Goldberg, E.M. and Stanley, S.J. (1985) 'Task centred casework in a probation setting', in E. M. Goldberg, J. Gibbons and I. Sinclair (eds), *Problems, Tasks and Outcomes*. London: Allen & Unwin.

Goldberg, E.M., Gibbons, J. and Sinclair, I. (eds) (1985) *Problems, Tasks and Outcomes*. London: Allen & Unwin.

Hearnden, I. and Millie, A. (2004) 'Does tougher enforcement lead to lower reconviction?', *Probation Journal*, 51 (1): 48–58.

Hedderman, C. and Hearnden, I. (2001) *Setting New Standards for Enforcement: The Third ACOP Enforcement Audit*. London: Association of Chief Officers of Probation.

HM Inspectorate of Probation (1995) *Dealing with Dangerous People: The Probation Service and Public Protection, Report of a Thematic Inspection*. London: Home Office.

HM Inspectorate of Probation (1998) *Exercising Constant Vigilance: The Role of the Probation Service in Protecting the Public from Sex Offenders, Report of a Thematic Inspection*. London: Home Office.

HM Inspectorate of Probation (2000a) *The Use of Information by Probation Services: A Thematic Inspection in 4 Parts. Part 2: The Deployment of Resources: A Study by HMIP*. London: Home Office.

HM Inspectorate of Probation (2000b) *Performance Inspection Programme – Eastern Region*. London: Home Office.

Hollin, C., Palmer, E., McGuire, J., Hounsome, J., Hatcher, R., Bilby, C. and Clark, C. (2004) *Pathfinder Programmes in the Probation Service: A Retrospective Analysis*, Home Office Online Report 66/04. London: Home Office.

Home Office (1962) *Report of the Departmental Committee on the Probation Service* (The Morison Report). London: HMSO.

Home Office (1984) *Probation Service in England and Wales: Statement of National Objectives and Priorities*. London: Home Office.

Home Office (1988) *Punishment, Custody and the Community*, Cmd 424. London: Home Office.

Home Office (1990) *Crime, Justice and Protecting the Public*, Cmd 965. London: Home Office.

Home Office (1995) *National Standards for the Supervision of Offenders in the Community*. London: Home Office.

Hood, R., Shute, S., Feilzer, M. and Wilcox, A. (2002) 'Sex offenders emerging from long-term imprisonment: a study of their long-term reconviction rates and of parole board members' judgements of their risk', *British Journal of Criminology*, 42 (2): 371–94.

Hough, M., Jacobson, J. and Millie, A. (2003) *The Decision to Imprison: Sentencing and the Prison Population*. London: Prison Reform Trust.

Kemshall, H. (1996) *Good Practice in Risk Assessment and Risk Management*. London: Jessica Kingsley.

Kemshall, H., Mackenzie, G., Wood, J., Bailey, R. and Yates, J. (2005) *Strengthening Multi-Agency Public Protection Arrangements (MAPPAs)*, Home Office Development and Practice Report 45. London: Home Office.

Lipsey, M. (1992) 'Juvenile delinquency treatment: a meta-analytic enquiry into the variability of effects', in T. Cook, H. Cooper, D.S. Cordray, H. Hartman, L.V. Hedges, R.L. Light, T.A. Louis and F. Mosteller (eds), *Meta-analysis for Explanation: A Casebook*. New York: Russell Sage.

Lloyd, C., Mair, G. and Hough, M. (1995) *Explaining Reconviction Rates: A Critical Analysis*, Home Office Research Study No. 136. London: HMSO.

Mair, G. (ed.) (1989) *Risk Prediction and Probation: Papers from a Research and Planning Unit Workshop*, Research and Planning Unit Paper 56. London: Home Office.

McGuire, J. (ed.) (1995) *What Works: Reducing Reoffending*. Chichester: Wiley.

McGuire, J. (2002) 'Integrating findings from research reviews', in J. McGuire (ed.), *Offender Rehabilitation and Treatment: Effective Programmes and Policies to Reduce Re-offending*. Chichester: Wiley.

McGuire, J. and Hatcher, R. (2001) 'Offense-focused problem solving', *Criminal Justice and Behaviour*, 28 (5): 564–87.

McIvor, G. (1997) 'Evaluative research in probation: progress and prospects', in G. Mair (ed.), *Evaluating the Effectiveness of Community Penalties*. Aldershot: Avebury.

Merrington, S. (1995) *Offenders on Probation*. Cambridge: Cambridgeshire Probation Service.

Miller, W.R. and Rollnick, S. (eds) (1992) *Motivational Interviewing: Preparing People to Change Addictive Behaviour*. New York: Guilford Press.

Moore, R., Gray, E., Roberts, C., Merrington, S., Waters, I., Fernandez, R., Hayward, G. and Rogers, R. (2004) *ISSP: The Initial Report*. London: Youth Justice Board.

National Probation Directorate (2001a) *The EFQM Excellence Model: A Guide to the Use of the EFQM Excellence Model in the National Probation Service of England and Wales*. London: Home Office.

National Probation Directorate (2001b) *A New Choreography: An Integrated Strategy for the National Probation Service for England and Wales*. London: Home Office.

National Probation Directorate (2005) *National Probation Service Business Plan 2005–6*, Probation Circular 24/2005. London: Home Office.

Pawson, R. and Tilley, N. (1997) *Realistic Evaluation*. London: Sage.

Pease, K., Billingham, S. and Earnshaw, I. (1977) *Community Service Assessed in 1976*, Home Office Research Study 39. London: HMSO.

Philpotts, G.J.O. and Lancucki, L.B. (1979) *Previous Convictions, Sentence and Reconviction*, Home Office Research Study No. 53. London: HMSO.

Radzinowicz, L. (ed.) (1958) *The Results of Probation, English Studies in Criminal Science*. London: Macmillan.

Raynor, P. (1988) *Probation as an Alternative to Custody*. Aldershot: Avebury.

Raynor, P. (1997) 'Evaluating probation: a moving target', in G. Mair (ed.), *Evaluating the Effectiveness of Community Penalties*. Aldershot: Avebury.

Raynor, P. (forthcoming) 'Community penalties and Home Office research: on the way back to "Nothing Works"?', *Criminology and Criminal Justice*. The author may be contacted at P.Raynor@swansea.ac.uk

Raynor, P. and Vanstone, M. (1997) *Straight Thinking on Probation (STOP): The Mid-Glamorgan Experiment*, Probation Studies Unit Report No. 4. Oxford: University of Oxford Probation Studies Unit.

Reid, W.J. and Epstein, L. (1972) *Task Centred Casework*. New York: Columbia University Press.

Reid, W.J. and Shyne, A. W. (1969) *Brief and Extended Casework*. New York: Columbia University Press.

Rhys, M.T. (2001) *Reports of Serious Incidents 1995–2000*. London: London Probation Area/London Action Trust.

Simon, F.H. (1971) *Prediction Methods in Criminology*, Home Office Research Study No. 7. London: HMSO.

Smith, D., Sheppard, B., Mair, G. and Williams, K. (1984) *Reducing the Prison Population*, Home Office Research and Planning Unit Paper 23. London: HMSO.

Taylor, R. (1999) *Predicting Reconvictions for Sexual and Violent Offences Using the Revised Offender Group Reconviction Scale*, Home Office Research Findings 104. London: Home Office.

Trotter, C. (1993) *The Supervision of Offenders: What Works*. Melbourne: Victoria Office of Corrections.

Truax, C. and Carkhuff, R. (1967) *Towards Effective Counselling and Psychotherapy*. Chicago: Aldine.

Underdown, A. (1998) *Strategies for Effective Offender Supervision*, Report of the HMIP What Works Project. London: Home Office.

Wilkinson, J. (2005) 'Evaluating evidence for the effectiveness of the Reasoning and Rehabilitation Programme', *Howard Journal*, 44 (1): 70–85.

Chapter 16

Past, present and future sentences: what do we know about their effectiveness?

Carol Hedderman

Effectiveness: the historical picture

The punishment of offenders by the state may be justified philosophically in two ways: as an expression of public disapproval for what has happened (retributivism); or as a mechanism for reducing the chances of such an act being committed by the same or another offender (utilitarianism).

For a sentence to be deemed appropriate from a retributivist perspective it must be deserved in some way by the offender. As a minimum the offender should admit to being, or be proved, guilty. However, the implications of the sentence for the future behaviour of that offender, or others, are deemed to be irrelevant. In other words, retributivism looks back to the offence rather than forward to the impact of the sentence in considering the appropriate penalty.

Even in its oldest form – the biblical 'eye-for-an-eye' – retributivism may be said to include some notion of proportionality. This aspect has been made explicit by writers such as Honderich (1984) and von Hirsch (1976). Reflecting concerns that excessive levels of intervention were being justified on the grounds that they constituted helpful treatment, they argue that the magnitude of a sentence should be limited by proportionality to the crime committed ('just deserts'). It follows from this that assessing sentencing from a retributivist perspective involves measuring the degree to which the guilty are punished and proportionality is achieved, or seen to be achieved,[1] but the notion of effectiveness in terms of how sentencing affects future offending is meaningless. For this reason, the chapter focuses on the 'utilitarian' aims of sentencing.[2]

Until the middle of the eighteenth century, state systems for punishing those who transgressed criminal laws may have incorporated some notion of seeking to save an offender's soul, but from the Industrial Revolution to the early 1970s, state systems for punishing offenders in westernised democracies became increasingly concerned with transforming law-breakers into reliable members of the workforce. This was to be accomplished by reincorporating

459

them into society after treating their offending through psychological and social interventions during a period in which their rights to liberty were suspended (Hudson 2003). Based on the work of writers such as Beccaria (1767) and Bentham (1789), the main aim of sentencing from a utilitarian perspective is a reduction in future offending. This may be achieved through deterrence of the offender or others, incapacitation or rehabilitation.

Despite the lengthy history of debates about whether sentencing should be primarily determined by retributivist or utilitarian objectives, it was only in the late 1960s and early 1970s that researchers began to systematically assess how far sentencing achieved any of its utilitarian objectives.

What can be said about effectiveness?

It is tempting to assume that one can assess the extent to which any given sentence, or intervention within a sentence, has reduced reoffending by measuring offending before and after a sentence has been imposed. But that is an impractical plan for a number of reasons. First, it assumes that nothing else has influenced the change. Second, it assumes that an offender would otherwise have maintained a steady rate of offending. Third, it is clearly not reasonable to compare the impact of a two-year period in custody with two years on a community order from the day both sentences were imposed, as the periods 'at risk' of further offending differ.[3] Fourth, as Chapter 15 documents, we cannot measure reoffending directly, but use proxies such as rearrest and reconviction or self-reported offending which all distort the underlying picture in some way.

Mair *et al.* (1997) even question whether it is acceptable to measure the impact of a sentence or intervention in terms of aims it was not imposed to achieve, or to measure its success in relation to only one aim when it was imposed to achieve several. In practice, even when an outcome study is accompanied by a well-conducted process evaluation (which includes asking practitioners and offenders what they think as well as collecting input and output data), researchers can only speculate on precisely *how* a reduction in reconviction was achieved. Generally, however, it is simply assumed that penalties which are intended to be rehabilitative and which can be shown to contain potentially rehabilitative elements such as counselling or help in finding a job, have *primarily* worked by fostering rehabilitation. Sentences which are intended to be severe and are imposed with the intention of deterring the offender and/or other potential offenders are assumed to have had a *primarily* deterrent effect. As discussed further below, given that the new sentences available under the Criminal Justice Act 2003 (CJA 2003) mix and match sentencing aims and sentencing options, the prospect of establishing a one-to-one match between a sentencing aim and behavioural outcome seems even more remote.

The lack of agreed and objective measures of incapacitation or general deterrence (Moxon 1998) also tends to limit most discussions of sentencing effectiveness. For example, while a recent review of the correctional services (Carter 2003) concluded that the increased use of custody probably made a modest contribution to crime reduction during the 1990s, this conclusion relied on (unpublished) statistical modelling rather than direct observation.

Despite the considerable conceptual differences in how incapacitation and deterrence are expected to operate, the lack of adequate or agreed measures of either means that reviews tend to conclude that their effects are not distinguishable from one another (Nagin 1998; von Hirsch *et al.* 1999; Carter 2003; Bottoms 2004). Another common conclusion is that while there may be some additional incapacitative or marginal deterrence effect from increasing the use of imprisonment, increasing the actual and perceived risk of being caught is a more effective, and more cost-effective, way of securing crime reduction (von Hirsch *et al.* 1999).

In this context, it is hard to disagree with Friendship *et al.*'s (2005: 10) conclusion that: '... as an outcome measure, the value of reconviction is not in dispute because it represents the *only* readily accessible measure of reoffending' (emphasis added).

Consequently, reconviction will form the main, but not the only, measure of effectiveness in this chapter.

The effectiveness of different types of sentence

Prior to the Criminal Justice Act 2003, the main forms of community sentences for adults were discharges, fines, community rehabilitation orders (formerly probation orders), community punishment orders (formerly community service orders) and community punishment and rehabilitation orders (formerly combination orders). Most of the studies which have compared the effectiveness of different forms of sentence have focused on this range.

Of the 1.5 million offenders dealt with in England and Wales for indictable and summary offences in 2004, 70 per cent were fined, 13 per cent received a community sentence which involved some form of supervision in the community and 7 per cent were sentenced to custody. The remainder received other sentences including discharges. Limiting this breakdown to the 338,000 offenders dealt with for indictable offences, 21 per cent were fined, 33 per cent given a community sentence, 24 per cent were sentenced to custody and the remainder received other sentences (Home Office 2005a; 2005b).

It is inappropriate to compare the raw reconviction rates for different types of sentence. The courts use different sentences for different sorts of offenders – with different risks of reconviction – and, as noted above, to achieve a range of different objectives. The sorts of offenders who are typically fined are therefore expected to be *inherently* less likely to reoffend than those given intensive probation supervision. Consequently, their lower reconviction rates, in isolation, reveal nothing about the effectiveness of the two disposals in preventing further offending. An examination of trends over time in 'raw' reconviction rates can tell us something about impact, however.

Between 1993 and 2001, when the number of sentenced prisoners in England and Wales rose from 28,000 to 46,000 and the prison population as a whole rose from 44,000 to 74,000, the raw two-year reconviction rate rose from 53 per cent (Kershaw and Renshaw 1997a) to 61 per cent (Home Office 2004a;

2005c).[4] Some of the rise in reconviction rates is explained by the inclusion of additional offences into the 'Standard List' used in calculating reconviction rates (Home Office 2003). However, this is not a complete explanation. The increase in reconviction over time suggests either that the nature of the offenders received into prison had changed significantly or that prison is becoming less effective even as its use increases.

Between 1993 and 1999, reconviction rates for community penalties remained relatively stable at 56–57 per cent (Home Office 2004b). However, more recent figures (Home Office 2004a; 2005c) show a raw reconviction rate of 59 per cent for 2001. Over the same eight-year period, the Probation Service's court order caseload rose from 97,000 to 120,000 and its entire criminal supervision caseload, including those supervised on release from prison, rose from 145,000 to 207,000 (Home Office 2004a).

It is possible to conduct special analyses which allow both for differences in the types of offenders receiving different sentences and for 'pseudo-reconvictions'.[5] However, the range of information that can practically be collated on offenders centrally is limited. This means that even when such modelling is carried out, it is not clear whether differences in reconviction rates reflect differences in sentence efficacy or reflect a level of variation between offenders (e.g. in their level of drug use) which was not considered. This is most obviously true when studies compare probation orders with and without conditions (Home Office 1993; Oldfield 1997). Clearly, for all such cases the courts concluded that that probation was a more suitable sentence than any other which indicates that the offenders are broadly comparable. However, as the Home Office (1993) acknowledged, those on orders with conditions tend to be higher risk when criminal history variables are allowed for, and they are likely to have more personal problems. Such offenders will have been given conditions such as attending a drug rehabilitation centre for a reason.

A Home Office study published in 1997 showed that the two-year reconviction rates for offenders sentenced in 1993 were 60 per cent for probation, 52 per cent for community service and 61 per cent for orders which combined probation and community service (Kershaw and Renshaw 1997b). The average reconviction rate for these orders was 57 per cent. However, controlling for pseudo-reconvictions brought this down to 53 per cent which is identical to the rate for those discharged from prison in the same year (Kershaw and Renshaw 1997a).

Another study (Moxon 1998) was able to examine the effectiveness of non-custodial sentences by comparing actual reconviction rates with those expected on the basis of age, sex and criminal history for those given such disposals. Using the same data as Kershaw and Renshaw (1997b), he found the actual two-year reconviction rates of those given conditional discharges (39 per cent) or fines (43 per cent) were one percentage point lower than expected. The reconviction rates for those given community service (48 per cent) and probation (55 per cent) were respectively two and three percentage points lower than expected. However, these results were not corrected for pseudo-reconvictions and no comparison with a prison sample was included.

Two, more recent, Home Office publications have provided information on reconviction rates by sentence for adults released from prison or commencing a community sentence. In the first, Spicer and Glicksman (2004) modelled actual reconviction rates against a predicted rate for a 2001 cohort. Unlike Moxon (1998) they were able to allow for a change in the 'case mix' over time. However, once again, pseudo-reconvictions were not allowed for because the date of offence was not available. As community penalty reconviction rates include more pseudo-reconvictions than custodial rates do (Kershaw and Renshaw 1997b), this is an important limitation.

With that proviso in mind, the analysis showed an *actual* reconviction rate for those released from custody of 58.2 per cent compared to a *predicted* rate of 60.1 per cent. The difference was statistically significant at $p \leq 0.05$ which means that the chances of the result happening by chance are less than one in 20. For those commencing community penalties the *actual* reconviction rate was 51.2 per cent compared with a *predicted* rate of 51.7 per cent. This difference was not statistically significant. The cautious conclusion to draw from this – bearing in mind the point about pseudo-reconvictions – is that there is currently little to choose between imprisonment and community penalties in preventing reoffending. Given this, the rise in raw reconviction rates on release from prisons is a particular source of concern as it suggests sentencers are becoming less adept at targeting sentences appropriately.

Another recent Home Office study (Cuppleditch and Evans 2005) was able to control precisely for pseudo-reconvictions in comparing reconviction rates for a sample of those released from custody or receiving a community sentence in 2002. Unlike most previous studies, which either ignore pseudo-reconvictions or make simple percentage corrections to allow for them, this study was able to actually identify pseudo reconvictions. This is because their analysis used Police National Computer (PNC) data which includes date of offence, rather than the Offenders Index which does not. The raw reconviction rate for those sentenced to community sentences (comprising community rehabilitation orders, community punishment orders, community rehabilitation and punishment orders and drug treatment and testing orders) was 53 per cent. For those released from prison the raw reconviction rate was 67 per cent. These figures do not, of course, allow for changes in the characteristics of those receiving each sentence. Nevertheless, as has been argued elsewhere (Hedderman 2006), there are good reasons to think that the increased use of imprisonment – which has led to a change in the types of offenders in prison, overcrowding and overstretched resources – has been counterproductive in terms of reducing reoffending.

One of the few random allocation studies to compare the impact of a short custodial sentence (14 days) and community service was conducted by Killias *et al.* (2000) in Switzerland. It is also unusual in that it took social factors into account and assessed outcome in terms of factors such as employment and home circumstances as well as recidivism (reconviction and rearrest). The results, based on a sample of 123 offenders, showed that those imprisoned developed antagonistic feelings towards prison and the criminal justice system. They were also more frequently arrested than those allocated to community service, although there were no outcome differences in terms of overall reconviction levels or on the social indicators.

One of the few UK studies to include information on some social factors as well as criminal history, age and sex was that conducted by May (1999). Based on a sample of more than 7,000 cases from six probation areas sentenced in 1993, this showed that social factors played a greater role in determining sentencers' choices between community penalties (community service, probation and combination orders) than criminal history. For example, males who had no social problems recorded were more likely to be sentenced to community service than other offenders. However, this did not entirely explain the better reconviction rates for this sentence. As the author concluded, the sentence itself may have had a positive effect on reconviction. Possible reasons for this are suggested by McIvor (1992) whose earlier study of community service in Scotland found that a high proportion of the offenders felt that they acquired new skills and/or a sense of satisfaction and increased self-confidence from the jobs they completed. Those who expressed the most positive views were the least likely to be reconvicted.

Overall, research studies and statistical analyses examining differences in the effectiveness of broad sentence types have usually taken variations in criminal history into account. However, as mentioned above, few studies have corrected for pseudo-reconvictions or allowed for the influence of social factors like homelessness, poor education and substance misuse. When the limits of these studies are considered alongside variations between courts, and over time, in the content and delivery of community orders and the offenders made subject to them, claims about the greater effectiveness of any particular sentence appear to be on very shaky ground. Arguably, considering the relative effectiveness of different types of community sentence will be of less relevance – and certainly harder to assess – now that the courts may impose a single 'generic' order in which the elements of previous community alternatives can be combined. The introduction of 'custody minus' option, which enables courts to combine the same wide range of community options with short spells in custody, makes comparing the effectiveness of short spells in custody with community supervision equally moot.

The effectiveness of 'new' sentences

Two major new community sentences were introduced in 1998 and 2000. The Powers of Criminal Courts (Sentencing) Act 2000 enabled courts to impose curfew orders, which require offenders to remain indoors for certain parts of the day with compliance being monitored by means of an electronic tag. The Crime and Disorder Act of 1998 empowered the courts to impose drug treatment and testing orders (DTTOs) on offenders with severe drug habits who are at risk of imprisonment.

Curfew orders

The impact of curfew orders with electronic monitoring in three pilot areas was examined by Sugg et al. (2001). The sample comprised 261 of the 375 given curfew orders in 12 months spanning 1996 and 1997 whose orders were not rescinded and who could be traced in central records. Sixty-one per cent (N = 160) of those on curfew orders were also made subject to other community sentences.

The expected two-year reconviction rate for those on curfew orders (based on actuarial modelling) was 67 per cent. Their actual reconviction rate was 73 per cent which suggests that they did worse than expected. However, this was similar to the reconviction rate for a comparison group of offenders on straight probation whose reconviction rates were also higher than predicted. Sugg *et al.* suggest that the most likely explanation for this is that the algorithm used to calculate an expected rate is based on national data and does not take into account local factors such as the police clear-up rate.

When the two-year reconviction results for 160 offenders on joint orders were compared with the 101 offenders on stand-alone curfew orders, the former were at a higher risk of being reconvicted (70 per cent *v* 62 per cent) and more of them were convicted (exact figures not reported).

In a recent review of what he terms 'community custody', Roberts (2004) examines the value of curfew orders and similar sentences from a number of perspectives using evidence (mainly) from the UK, North America and Australia. The review repeats the conclusions of an earlier US review (Rogers and Jolin 1989) that there is little difference between recidivism rates for electronically monitored and imprisoned offenders but also notes that curfew orders have at least two other benefits. First, while noting deficiencies in the quality and number of interview studies with offenders, Roberts reports that offenders, and their families, tended to find the experience of community custody much more restrictive than they had anticipated, but also less damaging: 'Many (but by no means all) recognise that community custody creates opportunities for them to change their lifestyle, and to preserve social relationships that would otherwise be threatened or disrupted by incarceration' (Roberts 2004: 115).

Second, Roberts presents statistical evidence to show that while the introduction of curfew orders seems to have had little impact on the decision to use custody in Britain, in a number of other countries (but especially Canada and Finland) the numbers being sent to prison reduced relatively quickly. This is not simply because the British public are less tolerant of the concept of offenders 'escaping' imprisonment, but because other jurisdictions have implemented community custody differently and presented it differently to sentencers, victims and the wider public. Roberts concludes by outlining improvements which might be made in all jurisdictions wishing to increase uptake including: locating the sanction on a scale of severity and not trying to introduce it for all forms of offending (at least initially); presenting it to the offender and the public as a form of suspended custody and ensuring that it is enforceable; distinguishing it from other forms of existing community provision; taking account of the offender's and the victim's circumstances when considering the suitability of the disposal; avoiding overloading it with conditions; allowing the sentence to be varied in line with the offender's performance and circumstances; and resourcing supervision sufficiently. Looking at this list, it is perhaps obvious why curfew orders have not been an unqualified success in England and Wales.

DTTOs

Drug treatment and testing orders are designed for offenders on the cusp of custody. It is therefore unsurprising that the results of the pilot study (Hough *et al.* 2003; Turnbull *et al.* 2000) found that 80 per cent of the 174 offenders on whom data are available had been reconvicted within two years. This figure was eight percentage points higher than the rate of reconviction for all offenders with demographic and criminal profiles comparable to the DTTO group. This partly reflects limitations in the methods of calculating expected rates which cannot allow for key predictive factors such as dependent drug use. But equally important, the divergence could be largely attributed to the very large gap of 15 percentage points between observed and expected rates in one of the three pilot sites. The authors conclude that these results highlight the importance of implementation factors in determining the success or otherwise of an intervention.

The DTTO study also showed low completion rates: only 30 per cent of the sample finished their order successfully. There were also very marked differences in reconviction rates between those who completed orders (53 per cent reconvicted) and those whose orders were revoked (91 per cent reconvicted). McIvor's (2004) evaluation of the Scottish DTTO pilot showed a much higher completion rate (48 per cent), and a much lower overall reconviction rate (66 per cent). Meanwhile a further – and larger – reconviction study of DTTOs in England and Wales shows that at a time when probation areas were under pressure to meet DTTO commencement targets, reconviction rates rose to 90 per cent (Home Office 2004b). Taken together these findings suggest that schemes may be able to minimise reconviction rates by maximising retention rates. However, incentives to maximise the number of commencements will probably drive up reconviction rates (Hedderman and Hough 2005).

The Criminal Justice Act 2003

The Criminal Justice Act 2003 lays out the aims of sentencing as being the

- punishment of offenders;
- reduction of crime (including its reduction by deterrence);
- reform and rehabilitation of offenders;
- protection of the public; and
- making of reparation by offenders to persons affected by their offence.

Influenced by the recommendations of the Halliday Review (Home Office 2001) this list differs slightly from the traditional sentencing principles of punishment, general or individual deterrence, incapacitation and rehabilitation which have been generally understood to underlie sentencing decisions (Thomas 1979). This is an important shift for three reasons. First, it introduces a specific acknowledgement of the victim's perspective by according reparation equivalent status to other sentencing aims. Second, the legislation focuses on the impact of sentences in terms of crime reduction and public protection. Arguably these effects are more easily distinguished than incapacitation and deterrence, although identifying a direct causal link between sentencing and these aims is no more straightforward. Third, and perhaps most importantly, for the first time sentencing aims have been given statutory status. Previously sentencing aims in an individual case might be no more than the implicit or explicit aspirations of the sentencer which might or might not be shared by the offender, the victim, the supervising service or the wider public.

It is too early to assess what impact the CJA 2003 has had in practice, but the legislation alone raises concerns. The most obvious difficulty is that the different aims of sentencing are not necessarily compatible in individual cases and may even conflict with each other. Arguably, matters might have been more straightforward if the CJA 2003 had brought in a direct correspondence between a sentencing aim and a sentence (for example, community punishment and prison punish, probation reforms, compensation compensates). Instead there has been an increasing tendency to advertise all sentence types as being capable of meeting all sentencing aims. Community punishment, for example, is now expected to punish and to reform and even to provide a form of generalised reparation. But this presents sentencers with a dilemma. If community service is a bit rehabilitative and a bit punitive, should they be adding a bit of probation supervision and a bit of custody to ensure a proper measure of each? The history of the combination order shows that the temptation to overload is considerable and it is not obvious how it will be avoided as sentencers decide which of the many parts of a generic community sentence they should impose.

Although sentences might be overloaded by seeking to punish through community punishment, reform through a cognitive behavioural programme and protect through tagging, at least the decision-making process would be transparent. But given that the 'custody plus' sentence is expected to do all three, why not choose that? Perhaps of most concern is that overloading offenders with conditions may result in many offenders going to prison for failing to comply, although their original offences did not merit custody, because the CJA 2003 makes custody a much more likely outcome when an order is breached. More worrying still, the Act's potential to increase the population through increased custodial sentencing and breach seems, initially, to have been ignored. Even the highest scenario shown in the prison projections published in 2005 (de Silva *et al*. 2005) assumed that, at worst, the CJA 2003 would not affect the prison population. Otherwise it was expected to bring about a small *decrease*. The phrasing of the latest projections (de Silva *et al*. 2006) is more opaque about the effects of the CJA, but acknowledges that estimates have been revised to take into account the experience of implementing some of its provisions. Partly as a consequence, the high scenario projected for the prison population for 2010 published in 2006 is 94,020 rather than the 87,840 figure published a year earlier.

Perhaps one of the best ways of combating both sentencing and breach inflation is to provide stronger evidence about which sentencing elements are most effective at least in terms of reducing reoffending and (thereby) protecting the public and possibly even contributing to crime reduction, and also in terms of providing some reparation to victims or to society in general.

The effectiveness of interventions delivered as part of a sentence

In the mid-1960s, faced with mounting scepticism about whether prison reformed as well as punished offenders, the New York State prison service commissioned a research review to examine the rehabilitative impact of interventions in institutional and non-institutional settings. The review, conducted by Robert Martinson (1974), examined over 200 studies published over 22 years. Martinson's report supported the sceptics' perspective in that he found little evidence of interventions significantly reducing offending. Although Martinson pointed out that the result was not clear cut, because of the methodological shortcomings of some of the studies, the overall message was taken to be that 'Nothing Works'. Similar overall conclusions were reached in the UK by Brody (1976) and Folkard *et al.* (1976).

Of course, then, as now, research results were not received in a political vacuum. Raynor (2003) has suggested that one reason Martinson's caveats, and the methodological limitations of the UK studies,[6] were ignored was that 'Nothing Works' was what the US and UK governments of the day wished to hear. While a Canadian review, which was restricted to studies of a higher methodological standard, found evidence that some interventions were effective (Gendreau and Ross 1979), this was ignored in the US and the UK during the 1980s and early 1990s. The 'Nothing Works' conclusion legitimated the increasingly right-wing Conservative governments in both countries limiting public expenditure on prisons to that needed to contain and punish offenders. Public expenditure on the supervision of offenders on community sentences and post-release supervision to 'advise, assist and befriend' could no longer be justified. But probation supervision could be justified on cost grounds as an 'alternative to custody'. This shift in the purpose of probation resulted in over a decade of probation research which was almost exclusively devoted to studying how effectively it diverted offenders from custody rather than its impact on offending behaviour (Raynor 2004).[7]

A few small-scale outcome studies were conducted during this period. For example, Raynor and Vanstone (1996) found that the STOP cognitive behavioural programme was effective after one year. However, by the second year no differences were apparent in the treatment group and comparison group reconviction rates.

The resurgence of confidence that some interventions with offenders did help to reduce reoffending reflects the fact that many of those working with offenders and designing interventions for them in the UK were aware of the countervailing evidence and never lost confidence in the idea that some interventions were effective (Raynor 2003). It has also been suggested (Raynor 2004) that senior members of the Probation Inspectorate, the Home Office and the Probation Service were a receptive audience for such findings in the mid-1990s because they saw 'What Works?' as a defence against the then Home Secretary (Michael Howard) who believed that (only) 'Prison Works'.

During the late 1990s, a new role for probation was outlined in which its purpose was to reduce the reoffending of those under its supervision and to protect the public (Home Office 2001). At the very least this created a receptive context for reviews such as that by Hollin (1990) and further rigorously controlled Canadian meta-analyses (e.g. Andrews *et al.* 1990; Lipsey 1992), which showed that some interventions could be effective with some offenders in some circumstances. Taken together with the publication of McGuire's (1995) edited volume, the evidence was sufficient for both reviews of the literature and of current probation practice to be initiated by the Home Office (Vennard *et al.* 1997) and the Probation Inspectorate (Underdown 1998).

Although different authors came up with slightly different lists, the 'What Works?' literature identifies some common elements which tend to be present when interventions reduce recidivism. These are summarised in Table 16.1 (taken from Vennard *et al.* 1997). The same study found that by 1996 at least 39 of the then 54 probation areas in England and Wales reported running programmes which employed cognitive behavioural techniques, although their commitment to the full 'What Works?' agenda was questioned because of the general absence of elements such as programme integrity and adequate staff training.

In fact there were major practical difficulties to be faced in translating these findings into practice. Having been derived from meta-analyses it was rarely possible to point to a start-to-finish example of offender supervision which could be imported. Faced with a massive design and development task, the prison and probation services succumbed to the temptation of importing some stand-alone programmes. The North American 'Reasoning and Rehabilitation' programme was known to have positive effects in several other countries and a few probation areas had developed programmes to deal with special groups themselves (e.g. the Thames Valley sex offender programme). The programme

Table 16.1 Common elements identified in programmes which were successful in reducing recidivism

More intensive programmes should be targeted at high-risk offenders, those of lower risk should receive minimal intervention.	Treatment should be 'multi-modal' and designed to impart skills such as improving problem-solving through techniques including (but not limited to) those based on cognitive behavioural and social learning theories.
Interventions should focus on those factors which contribute directly to criminal behaviour, such as anti-social attitudes, drug dependency, limited cognitive skills.	Programmes which take account of risk, criminogenic need and responsiveness can work in any treatment setting, but generally work better in the community than in prison.
Teaching styles must fit offenders' learning styles. Generally this is active and participatory. Client-centred counselling is not generally successful.	Interventions should be delivered consistently over time and not allowed to drift in terms of the content or mode of delivery. This requires that those delivering the intervention are well-trained in it.

Source: Derived from Vennard *et al.* (1997).

designed by James Maguire, from which 'Think First' has been developed, had also been adopted in a number of probation areas (although its operation varied somewhat from one site to another). Areas were then invited to nominate other programmes which might be evaluated (Hedderman 2004).

It is also important to remember that, while 'What Works?' had become the dominant philosophy during this period, there have continued to be dissenting voices who query the evidence base (e.g. Mair 2004a), who express concerns about putting too much reliance on one approach (Bottoms *et al.* 2001) and who criticise the 'What Works' evidence base and the unthinking implementation of its principles for being blind to issues of ethnicity and gender (Shaw and Hannah-Moffat 2004).

Some senior probation practitioners, whose training emphasised sociological rather than individual theories of offending which dominated North American penology, also seemed uncomfortable with the primacy given to cognitive behavioural therapy which requires offenders to see themselves as responsible for their actions, regardless of how their social circumstances and life chances may have contributed to their offending (Mair 2004b). More frequently, however, their comments reflect reservations about putting all the Probation Service's eggs in the cognitive behavioural basket, together with concerns about the pace of change required. This view is shared by a number of psychologists, who express concerns about the way somewhat fluid psychological concepts, such as the notion of 'criminogenic' factors, and sometimes tentative findings about 'What Works?' have created a practice straightjacket which limits innovation and development. As Thomas-Peters (2006: 33) laments: 'Somewhere during the 1990s the question mark was lost from the expression "What Works?"; and with it has gone some tolerance and perspective'.

Even those who accept the broad thrust of the What Works message expressed concerns about the validity of some of the evidence base and warned against generalising too broadly from it (e.g. Vennard *et al.* 1997; Raynor and Vanstone 2002) as a careful reading of the research showed that practitioners were right to be sceptical of cognitive behavioural interventions alone securing change or that they were a panacea. For example, while noting that some studies of programmes employing such techniques showed large reductions in reoffending, Vennard *et al.* conclude:

> ... the research literature does not demonstrate that cognitive behavioural approaches, or indeed any other type of approach, routinely produce major reductions in reoffending among a mixed population of offenders ... it is not possible to identify any all-purpose methods or forms of intervention as being reliably and consistently better than standard or traditional programmes with offenders. (Vennard *et al.* 1997: 33–4)

Ignoring these reservations, the incoming Labour government focused instead on the more positive element of the same paragraph that 'Among mixed populations of offenders, programmes *might* achieve a reduction in recidivism of some 10–15 per cent ...' (p. 34, emphasis added).

Taking this optimistic estimate, and encouraged by the then Chief Inspector of Probation, Sir Graham Smith, the new Government created the Effective Practice Initiative. A highly influential Probation Inspectorate report (Underdown 1998) not only played a part in this decision, but also indicated that leaving implementation to individual areas would perpetuate inconsistent practices. This threat, together with the Government's preference for New Public Management[8] modes of working, led to the creation of the National Probation Service in 2001. At that time, the National Probation Directorate took charge of the Effective Practice Initiative, which had been driven by the Inspectorate.

A key part of the implementation of the Effective Practice Initiative involved using money from the multi-million pound Crime Reduction Programme to create a series of 'Pathfinder' projects which were intended to turn 'What Works' principles into practice. The resulting lessons would then be rolled out to other areas. Use of the term 'Pathfinder' rather than 'Pilot' is important as, while the latter acknowledges the possibility of failure, the former implies that the exercise is merely one of exemplification rather than proof. As a Cabinet Office publication (Jowell 2003: 10) warns 'By creating unrealistic expectations, they tend to make neutral evaluation more difficult'. Arguably, if trailed as pilots, the mixed results which various 'Pathfinders' have produced might have been greeted with less surprise and dismay. But, as indicated by both the nomenclature and the fact Pathfinders were funded initially for a maximum of three years, the National Probation Service was not engaged in a neutral experiment but was under pressure to succeed and to do so very quickly. This in itself may even help to explain some negative results as compressing timescales can lead to impact assessments being adversely affected by teething problems (Jowell 2003; Hedderman 2004).

Over the last two years, a number of reports about the way Effective Practice Initiative (EPI) Pathfinders were implemented and operated have been published. Many show little sign that the lessons from previous research about managing implementation effectively (e.g. Sarno *et al.* 2000) had been taken into account. Indeed the level of implementation failure in some cases has been so great that reconviction studies have only been conducted in some instances. Of those an even smaller number have so far been published, although the results have been with the Home Office for more than a year,[9] raising concerns that they may never see the light of day.

This section focuses on three sets of results from the EPI: those concerning cognitive behavioural programmes which seek to alter offenders' attitudes to offending and their offending behaviour; those designed to enhance offenders' chances of obtaining employment through education, training and employment (ETE) initiatives; and restorative justice schemes which are intended to reintegrate offenders into the community as well as, as the name implies, to help victims overcome the experience of victimisation.

Cognitive-behavioural programmes

The first prison-based results looked promising, with Friendship *et al.* (2002) reporting an 11–14 percentage point reduction for those classified as being at medium risk who were referred to two types of cognitive skills programmes. However, in both of the studies which examined accredited versions of the same programmes (Falshaw *et al.* 2003 and Cann *et al.* 2003), the comparison group appeared to outperform the treatment groups. A rare study on female offenders found similar results (Cann 2006). While the authors suggest the later results may also be a consequence of measurement failure or theory failure the most likely explanation for disappointing post-accreditation results is that some aspect of delivery was lost, with adverse consequences, as small well-implemented pilots were rolled out.

The first EPI study to report on the impact of cognitive-behavioural programmes in the community run prior to accreditation found that the treatment group had reconviction rates 22.5 percentage points higher than the comparison group (Ong *et al.* 2003). While Debidin and Lovbakke (2005) legitimately question the value of these results because the comparison group was not well matched to the treatment group, another possible explanation is that the treatment group results include those who were referred to the programme but who did not attend it. This approach accords with analytic conventions, as taking out the non-attenders is regarded as distorting the results so that only those who are most likely to change (as evidenced by their attendance patterns) are retained in the treatment group. However, it is clearly implausible that someone who does not attend a programme will be affected by it. It is also unlikely that all of those who are retained in treatment would have changed without any assistance. For this reason, the most comprehensive and recent evaluation of accredited general offending and substance abuse programmes which assessed their impact across 24 probation areas between 2000 and 2001 has reported the results as a two-way analysis (treated versus comparison group) and three-way analysis, with the treatment group divided into completers and non-completers. In the first analysis 69.9 per cent of those referred to the programmes were reconvicted after 18 months compared to 57.9 per cent of the comparison group. Splitting those referred to the programmes into those who completed and those who did not showed that only 54.5 per cent of the former were reconvicted compared to 77.6 per cent of the latter. While this is clearly not proof of effectiveness, it does highlight the need for further studies and raises questions about what the results might have looked like if some of the non-completers could have been retained.

ETE

Over half (55 per cent) of offenders subject to community sentences are unemployed at the start of their orders and three-quarters of prisoners do not have paid employment to go to on release from custody (Home Office 2004c). Unemployed offenders are significantly more likely to be reconvicted than those who are in employment (Crow *et al.* 1989; Simon and Corbett 1996; May 1999). A consistent message from the literature is that offenders are handicapped in their efforts to obtain employment by a number of major social and personal difficulties and that it is common for them to have more than one of the following problems (Fletcher *et al.* 1998; Metcalf *et al.* 2001; Lewis *et al.* 2003):

- poor literacy and numeracy skills (or 'basic skills');
- lack of, or low-level, qualifications;
- little experience of legitimate or sustained employment;
- low self-esteem, confidence and motivation to find employment;
- poor health;
- drug misuse and problem drinking;
- poverty and debt;
- homelessness/unstable housing.

It follows that any successful intervention will involve dealing with the range of an offender's problems not just one element, a point which is also supported by previous research (e.g. Gaes *et al.* 1999; Webster *et al.* 2001).

Unfortunately, the first Basic Skills and Employment Pathfinders funded under the Crime Reduction Programme were only comprehensive in their approach to ETE. Reading the evaluations report on the Basic Skills (McMahon *et al.* 2004) and Employment (Haslewood-Pocsik *et al.* 2004) Pathfinders, it also seems that those responsible for implementing both schemes did so in ignorance of the implementation problems which have undermined the effectiveness of previous schemes (e.g. Roberts *et al.* 1997; Sarno *et al.* 2000). The result was that of the 1,003 offenders assessed as probably having basic skills deficits, 155 were subject to an in-depth assessment and 20 were available for interview having completed relevant training. Twenty-two offenders completed the Employment Pathfinder of the 400 anticipated. In both cases, it was impossible to examine outcomes in terms of reconviction. This was particularly unfortunate as a previous study of two employment schemes for offenders on community supervision had given grounds for cautious optimism. Sarno *et al.* (2001) report a one-year reconviction rate of 43 per cent among 16–25 year olds who attended the London-based programme, compared to 56 per cent of those who were referred but did not attend (Sarno *et al.* 2001). Those who completed the programme were also slower to reoffend. For the reasons explained above selection effects cannot be ruled out when comparing completers and non-completers, but the results suggest that employment schemes might have some impact on recidivism, at least in the short-term.

Restorative justice

The first schemes which included elements of 'restorative justice' appear to have developed in the US in the early 1970s (Marshall 1999). By the mid-1980s, several small-scale projects were running in the UK. Then, as now, such schemes varied, in this country and elsewhere, in the ways they operated (Miers 2001; Miers *et al.* 2001). Some are an entirely pre-sentence option, others use restorative justice measures in place of a sentence or as part of a sentence. The extent of direct mediation between the victims and offenders also varies, as does whether the mediation is restricted to the victim and offender or extended to include supporters of both parties or even of the wider community.

As Crawford and Newburn (2003: 21) point out, variation in restorative justice schemes is not simply operational, but conceptual:

... is notoriously difficult to define ... restorative justice emerged as a critique of traditional forms of justice and, as such, is often defined in terms of what it is not rather than in terms of what it is.

Nevertheless, they are able to identify three key features which characterise a restorative justice approach. First, it recognises that a crime is more than an offence against the state and that those most affected by it should have a say in the society's response. Second, the decision-making processes must be deliberative and participatory with the aim of building consensus while restoring control to the parties most affected. Third, the ultimate aim of restorative justice should be to repair the harm done.

Given these features, it is unsurprising that most previous evaluations tended to concentrate on which forms of restorative justice achieved the highest satisfaction levels of participants. As noted above, some authors have questioned the legitimacy of assessing any intervention in relation to aims it was not explicitly intended to achieve. Arguably, reducing the likelihood of the offender repeating a similar offence is neither an essential, nor inevitable, aim of restorative justice in all cases. Nevertheless, some reconviction studies do exist, as it is reasonable to assume that if the offender is genuinely remorseful, he or she may be expected to be less likely to commit further transgressions. One of the best known was conducted in Canberra Australia (Sherman *et al*. 2000). This compared the recidivism of offenders assigned to the Canberra Reintegrative Shaming Experiments (RISE) diversionary conferences compared with others assigned to standard court processing. The overall sample size was just under 1,400. The cases involved four types of offending: drink driving by adults, shoplifting by juveniles, other property offending by juveniles and violent crimes involving offenders aged under 30. A 38 per cent decrease was reported in the one-year follow-up among the violent offenders assigned to conferences. This was not true for the other three offence groups. Detected reoffending even increased for the drink-drivers by 6 per cent. The authors recommend repeating the experiment in other venues and breaking 'violence' down into more specific categories such as assault, grievous bodily harm and robbery. However, this may be hard to operationalise successfully and ethically as the victims of at least some of these offences may be the most fearful of having direct contact with their attackers and least willing to agree to a conference.

In the first phase of the UK's Crime Reduction Programme, the Government commissioned a review of existing restorative justice schemes. Having reviewed seven schemes, Miers *et al*. (2001) concluded that, while victims' and offenders' satisfaction levels were generally high, a minority of victims expressed concerns about the offenders' motives for agreeing to participate. This was one of the few British studies of restorative justice to examine reconviction. It found that only one scheme had a significant effect on reconviction. Forty-four per cent of the 153 adult offenders who took part in direct or indirect mediation in the West Yorkshire scheme were reconvicted in contrast to 56 per cent of a comparable control group (N = 79) drawn from referrals where the scheme did not provide an intervention. These rates did not allow for differences in the profile of the two groups, but doing so was said to widen rather than narrow the reconviction gap.

A subsequent independent evaluation of three restorative justice schemes funded under the Crime Reduction Programme is due to be completed by the end of 2006. In one of the schemes (covering sites in London, Northumbria and Thames Valley) suitable cases are being randomly allocated to restorative justice or other disposals so that the differences in outcome can be rigorously assessed (Shapland *et al.* 2006).

A meta-analysis of the international literature by Bonta *et al.* (2002) found a reduction in reconviction of between 2 and 8 per cent for offenders involved in restorative justice programmes; however, the studies reviewed were methodologically flawed. None used random assignment or adequately matched control groups, leading the authors to conclude that the reconviction rates might be a consequence of siphoning those least likely to reoffend into the restorative option. Similar conclusions were reached by a more recent meta-analytic review (Latimer *et al.* 2005).

UK studies of restorative cautioning for juveniles have indicated that this has little, if any, effect on reconviction. Wilcox and Hoyle's review (2004) of the reconviction rates of 728 offenders on 34 projects who could be tracked, compared with a matched national sample weighted to allow for the fact that those on the projects were far less likely to have previous convictions (23 per cent *v* 60 per cent), found no significant difference in their 12 months reconviction rates (31 per cent *v* 33 per cent). A more recent study focused on the well-known Thames Valley scheme compared to the use of traditional cautions in two other areas also found little difference in overall reconviction rates or the frequency and seriousness of their reoffending (Wilcox *et al.* 2004).

Conclusion: making sentences and interventions more effective

Evidence about the effectiveness of different types of sentence in reducing reoffending is lamentably thin. All we can say with certainty is that the reconviction rate differences between sentence types are marginal, after taking account of demographics and criminal histories. This does not mean that reductions in reconviction rates achieved by altering sentencing practice are not worth striving for. Even if one is talking only about a percentage point shift in low single figures, this is important in both human and financial terms. As a recent government Green Paper (DfES 2005: 10) notes:

A former prisoner who re-offends costs the criminal justice system an average of £65,000 up to the point of re-imprisonment, and, after that, as much as £37,500 each year in prison … As well as this – and often unquantifiable – are the personal costs of crime, especially the impact on victims. The families of offenders are also likely to be faced with considerable financial and personal consequences … Each year around 125,000 children see one of their parents sent to prison.

Friendship *et al.*'s (2005) quasi-systematic review concludes that the current quasi-experimental methods which are most commonly used to examine the outcome of interventions delivered as part of a sentence are unsatisfactory. Where formal control groups are selected and compared, there are always going to be questions about the comparability of the groups. Randomised controlled trials (RCTs) are very rarely conducted into sentencing in England and Wales for ethical and practical reasons, with practitioner resistance being the most difficult obstacle to overcome (Hedderman and Hough 2005). Given the range of potential custody/community sentencing mixes which the CJA 2003 may encourage, the practicality and even the value of a sentencing RCT seems questionable.

In the medium term, the most practical research strategy for assessing the impact of entire sentences and interventions delivered as part of a sentence is probably to continue the current practice of constructing 'virtual' control groups, whereby statistical modelling techniques are used to calculate expected reconviction rates for offender groups of any given demographic and criminal profile. However, such studies should ideally control for pseudo-reconvictions and include outcome measures such as time to further offence and seriousness of subsequent offending. As date of offence is held only on the Police National Computer (PNC), the speed with which the Home Office pursues plans to merge its own (Offenders Index) reconviction database with that of the PNC will largely determine how quickly and how often this can be done.

In one of the few British random control trials of probation, Deering *et al.* (1996) allocated offenders to normal supervision or supervision with additional cognitive behavioural elements once a probation order had been imposed. There were only 60 offenders in the original pool and a third of the 30 given additional 'treatment' had to be excluded from the final analysis because they failed to complete.[10] This approach may in the longer term offer a way forward in assessing the impact of interventions delivered as part of a sentence. However, given that the completion problem it identified seems to persist and that 'going to scale' also seems to be an issue, it seems that there are more urgent problems to deal with first.

It is also worth reminding ourselves of a fundamental tenet in undertaking any research project – the nature of the question determines the nature of the methods which should be employed to address it. RCTs may be a methodologically superior way of assessing the outcome of a single intervention, but such studies, in themselves, do not tell us *why* something works. RCTs work best in laboratories where delivery is uniform and other potentially influential factors can be held constant (high internal validity), but when something works in such a falsely constrained environment it may not work in the real world (low external validity). Not only is high internal validity not achievable in the probation context, its desirability is also doubtful. It is likely that different combinations of interventions, and variations in their amounts and sequencing, may yield different outcomes according the nature of the offender and their experience of previous interventions. In seeking to simplify and control other potentially influential factors we may miss out on discovering 'what works best, for whom and in what circumstances'. This is especially true if, as it has also been suggested, the very relationship between the supervisor and offender may be a critical success factor (Partridge 2004). In this context, it would be unwise to restrict our understanding of what works to the few studies which score very highly on Friendship et al.'s (2005) review.

It was understandable to begin the Effective Practice Initiative with cognitive behavioural programmes, as reviews of the literature up to that point show them to be a common factor in many studies of effectiveness (see McGuire 1995 and Vennard and Hedderman 1998 for reviews). However, some of the other equally important messages contained in the literature were given less attention (Hedderman 2004). This includes recognising that as offenders commonly have more than one problem, they need more than one form of assistance; that motivational work before, and follow-up work after, attending a programme can be essential elements; that no intervention works for every one and that selection criteria should therefore be adhered to closely; that there is a balance to be struck between programme integrity and matching delivery to offenders' learning styles (responsivity); and that programmes should be delivered by well-trained and well-resourced staff.

Early reconviction results from evaluations of cognitive behavioural programmes in prison and in the community suggest that cognitive behavioural programmes have had limited impact in this country, and that this is at least partly because these other 'What Works?' principles have not been been given enough attention (Falshaw et al. 2003; Clarke et al. 2004; Hollin et al. 2004).

It is self-evident that for a sentence to stand a chance of being effective an offender must actually undergo it. This is not usually a problem in relation to prison as escape levels are low. However, only around half of those on probation and community service orders in three studies conducted in 1999 and 2000 attended all appointments without any unacceptable absences (Hedderman and Hearnden 2001). For some of the EPI interventions discussed above, attendance rates of 50 per cent would be a significant improvement.[11] The best answer to the question of whether differences in the reconviction results of programme completers and non-completers are real or result from selection effects is to ensure that the majority of offenders who are allocated to interventions complete them.

Ever tougher enforcement procedures are not the way to achieve higher completion rates. Ultimately this will lead to supervision being limited to those who do not need it because they are the only ones who never miss an appointment or fail to turn up for their weekend spells of custody. It is ironic that political pressure to be seen as tough on offenders has created so overzealous an enforcement system that it is undermining the very thing National Standards were originally intended to do, which is to foster compliance (Hedderman and Hough 2004). If the breach provisions in the 2003 Criminal Justice Act are fully operationalised, they are likely to undermine effective practice by further limiting what probation officers can do to encourage and insist on compliance.

The biggest challenge for both researchers and practitioners who want to know what works in reducing reoffending is to move away from examining the impact of discrete interventions to offender-focused evaluations. Although programmes are important, they are only part of the 'What Works' message – they are not the message in themselves. Moreover, to be effective, all the well-established elements of 'What Works' need to be incorporated into the supervision process, not just into the programme elements.

Finally, while important, the 'What works in reducing reoffending?' question is not the only one we should be asking. As Peter Raynor (this volume; Chapter 2) notes, the heavy focus on this aspect of work with offenders has led to the 'alternative to custody' debate disappearing from the political landscape. This is so despite the evidence that the increased use of custody is neither a response to rising crime nor an antidote to it (Hedderman 2006).

I was reminded of another somewhat unfashionable reason for continuing to work with offenders by a senior member of the Prison Service recently who remarked: 'Even if research showed that education and training and resettlement work were entirely ineffective, I hope that we would still be allowed to do it, because it's the right thing to do.' I hope she is right.

Evaluations of restorative justice indicate that there are other ways in which the merits of our responses to offending can be judged. Restorative justice schemes clearly have important non-reconviction benefits. The future of such schemes looks relatively secure because of those benefits and despite the equivocal evidence of their effect on reoffending. It is equally important to consider the non-reconviction benefits of other interventions. Working with offenders to understand the consequences of their offending for themselves or others, improving their basic skills and helping them into employment may not result in all or most of them stopping offending entirely or immediately, but it may reduce the rate of their reoffending. It may also promote desistence through the maintenance of positive social relationships, creating the opportunity to make a positive contribution to society and enabling those who commit crime to become much more than simply 'ex-offenders'.

Notes

1 Examples of this sort of work include Hedderman and Gelsthorpe's (1997) examination of whether men and women convicted of the same types of offence received comparable sentences; and Hough and Roberts's (1998) discussion of how far actual sentencing severity accords with public expectations of it.

2 See Easton and Piper (2005) for a fuller discussion of both philosophical positions and a consideration of how far each has influenced current sentencing policy and legislation.

3 Even taking acts against other inmates into consideration would not resolve this problem as the prison environment clearly limits the inmate's ability to commit specific types of offence (child abuse and car theft being among the most obvious).

4 In a break with convention, the volume of Offender Management Statistics published in 2005 merely repeated the 2001 reconviction figures published in the 2004 volume rather than updating them to relate to those made subject to a community sentence or released from custody in 2002.

5 Pseudo-reconvictions are convictions which occur during the follow-up period but which result from offences committed prior to the sentence of interest. They are

excluded from reconviction studies because they are not a measure of the current sentence's effectiveness. See Chapter 15 for a detailed discussion.

6 See Chapter 15 for a discussion.

7 Bizarrely, as Raynor and Vanstone (this volume, Chapter 2) point out, the idea of 'alternatives to prison' is now itself so neglected that the term has almost entirely disappeared, at least from political debate.

8 See Clarke *et al.* (2000) for a general discussion of New Public Management, and Gelthorpe and Morgan's introduction to this volume for the way this approach has affected probation.

9 For example, those relating to Rex *et al.*'s (2004) study of community service.

10 The handling of 'drop-outs' in an analysis of this sort is of critical importance to the outcome, of course.

11 More recent figures published by NOMS on the Internet (undated) suggest that completion rates have improved but the figures are hard to interpret as no information is provided on how they are derived.

Further reading

Easton and Piper (2005) provide a highly accessible account of developments in sentencing and punishment theories, policy and practice. Sentencing effectiveness is most frequently measured by examining reconviction rates. Mair *et al.* (1997) consider how reconviction rates are calculated and the important limits this places on what differences in reconviction rates may be said to mean.

Zamble and Quinsey's book (1997) has helped to shape recent thinking about the prediction of reoffending in terms of preventive intervention, risk assessment and management, release policies and post-release supervision. Hollin and Palmer's recent work (2006) explores the theories and research underlying offending behaviour programmes, design and implementation issues and how best the impact of such programmes might be evaluated.

References

Andrews, D.A., Zinger, I., Hoge, R.D., Bonta, J., Gendreau, P. and Cullen, F.T. (1990) 'Does correctional treatment work? A clinically relevant and psychologically informed meta-analysis', *Criminology*, 28: 369–404.

Beccaria, C. (1995 [1767]) *On Crimes and Punishments and Other Writings*. Cambridge: Cambridge University Press.

Bentham, J. (1970 [1789]) *An Introduction to the Principles of Morals and Legislation*. London: Athlone Press.

Bonta, J., Wallace-Capretta, S., Rooney, J. and McAnoy, K. (2002) 'An outcome evaluation of a restorative justice alternative to incarceration', *Contemporary Justice Review*, 5: 319–38.

Bottoms, A.E. (2004) 'Empirical research relevant to sentencing frameworks', in A. Bottoms, S. Rex and G. Robinson (eds), *Alternatives to Prison: Options for an Insecure Society*. Cullompton: Willan.

Bottoms, A.E., Gelsthorpe, L. and Rex, S. (eds) (2001) *Community Penalties: Change and Challenges*. Cullompton: Willan.

Brody, S.R. (1976) *The Effectiveness of Sentencing: A Review of the Literature*, Home Office Research Study No. 35. London: HMSO.

Cann, J. (2006) *Cognitive Skills Programmes: Impact on Reducing Reconviction Among a Sample of Female Prisoners*, Findings No. 276. London: Home Office.

Cann, J., Falshaw, L., Nugent, F. and Friendship, C. (2003) *Understanding What Works: Accredited Cognitive Skills Programmes for Adult Men and Young Offenders*, Home Office Research Findings No. 226. London: Home Office.

Carter, P. (2003) *Managing Offenders, Changing Lives: A New Approach*. London: Home Office.

Clarke, A., Simonds, R. and Wydall, S. (2004) *Delivering Cognitive Skills Programmes in Prison: A Qualitative Study*, Online Report 27/04. London: Home Office.

Clarke, J., Gerwitz, S. and McLauglin, E. (eds) (2000) *New Managerialism, New Welfare?* London: Sage.

Crawford, A. and Newburn, T. (2003) *Youth Offending and Restorative Justice: Implementing Reform in Youth Justice*. Cullompton: Willan.

Crow, I., Richardson, P., Riddington, C. and Simon, F. (1989) *Unemployment, Crime and Offenders*. London: Routledge.

Cuppleditch, L. and Evans, W. (2005) *Re-offending of Adults: Results from the 2002 Cohort*, Home Office Statistical Bulletin 25/05. London: Home Office.

De Silva, N., Cowell, P. and Chow, T. (2005) *Updated and Revised Prison Population Projections, 2005–2011, England and Wales* (July), Home Office Statistical Bulletin 10/05. London: Home Office.

De Silva, N., Cowell, P. and Chow, T. (2006) *Prison Population Projection 2006–2013, England and Wales* (July), Home Office Statistical Bulletin 11/06. London: Home Office.

Debidin, M. and Lovbakke, J. (2005) 'Offending behaviour programmes in prison and probation', in G. Harper and C. Chitty (eds), *The Impact of Corrections on Re-offending: A Review of 'What Works'*, Home Office Research Study No. 291, 2nd edition. London: Home Office.

Deering, J., Thurstone, R. and Vanstone, M. (1996) 'Individual supervision: an experimental programme in Pontypridd', *Probation Journal*, 43 (2): 70–6.

DfES (2005) *Reducing Re-Offending Through Skills and Employment*, Cm 6702. London: DfES.

Easton, S. and Piper, C. (2005) *Sentencing and Punishment: The Quest for Justice*. Oxford: Oxford University Press.

Falshaw, L., Friendship, C., Travers, R. and Nugent, F. (2003) *Searching for 'What Works': An Evaluation of Cognitive Skills Programmes*, Findings No. 206. London: Home Office.

Fletcher, D., Woodhill, D. and Herrington, A. (1998) *Building Bridges into Employment and Training for Ex-Offenders*. York: Rowntree Trust.

Folkard, M. S., Smith D. D. and Smith D. E. (1976) *IMPACT Volume II: The Results of the Experiment*, Home Office Research Study No. 36. London: HMSO.

Friendship, C., Blud, L. Erikson, M. and Travers, R. (2002) *An Evaluation of Cognitive Behavioural Treatment for Prisoners*, Research Findings No. 161. London: Home Office.

Friendship, C., Street, R., Cann, J. and Harper, G. (2005) 'Introduction: the policy context and assessing the evidence', in G. Harper and C. Chitty (eds), *The Impact of Corrections on Re-offending: A Review of 'What Works'*, Home Office Research Study No. 291, 2nd edition. London: Home Office.

Gaes, G. G., Flanagan, T. J., Motiuk, L. and Stewart, L. (1999) 'Adult correctional treatment', in M. Tonry and J. Petersilia (eds), *Crime and Justice: A Review of Research*, 26: 361–426.

Gendreau, P. and Ross, R. R. (1979) 'Effective correctional treatment: bibliotherapy for cynics', *Crime and Delinquency*, 25: 463–89.

Haslewood-Pocsik, I., Merone, L. and Roberts, C. (2004) *The Evaluation of the Employment Pathfinder: Lessons from Phase I and a Survey from Phase 2*, Online Report 22/04. London: Home Office.

Hedderman, C. (2004) 'Testing times: how the policy and practice environment shaped the creation of the What Works evidence-base', *VISTA*, 8: 182–8.

Hedderman, C. (2006) 'Keeping the lid on the prison population: will it work?', in M. Hough, R. Allen and U. Padel (eds), *Reshaping Probation and Prisons: The New Offender Management Framework*. London: Polity Press.

Hedderman, C. and Gelsthorpe, L. (1997) *Understanding the Sentencing of Women*, Home Office Research Study 170. London: HMSO.

Hedderman, C. and Hearnden, I. (2001) 'To discipline or punish? Enforcement under National Standards 2000', *VISTA*, 6 (3): 215–24.

Hedderman, C. and Hough, M. (2004) 'Getting tough or being effective: what matters?', in G. Mair (ed.), *What Matters in Probation*. Cullompton: Willan.

Hedderman, C. and Hough, M. (2005) 'Diversion from prosecution at court and effective sentencing', in A.E. Perry, C. McDougall and D.P. Farrington (eds), *Reducing Crime: The Effectiveness of Criminal Justice Interventions*. Chichester: Wiley.

Hedderman, C. and Sugg, D. (1997) 'The influence of cognitive behavioural approaches: a survey of probation programmes', in *Changing Offenders' Attitudes and Behaviour: What Works?*, Home Office Research Study No. 171. London: Home Office.

Hollin, C.R. (1990) *Cognitive-Behavioral Interventions with Young Offenders*. New York: Pergamon.

Hollin, C.R. and Palmer, E.J. (2006) *Offending Behaviour Programmes: Development, Application and Controversies*. Chichester: Wiley.

Hollin, C., Palmer, E., McGuire, J., Hounsome, J., Hatcher, R., Bilby, C. and Clark, C. (2004) *Pathfinder Programmes in the Probation Service: A Retrospective Analysis*, Online Report 66/04. London: Home Office.

Home Office (1993) *Reconvictions of Those Given Probation and Community Service Orders in 1987*, Statistical Bulletin 18/93. London: Home Office.

Home Office (1995) *National Standards for the Supervision of Offenders in the Community 2000*. London: Home Office.

Home Office (2001) *Making Punishments Work: Report of a Review of the Sentencing Framework for England and Wales* (The Halliday Review). London: Home Office.

Home Office (2003) *Prison Statistics, England and Wales, 2001*, Cm 5743 London: HMSO.

Home Office (2004a) *Offender Management Caseload Statistics 2003 England and Wales*, Home Office Statistical Bulletin 15/04, London: Home Office.

Home Office (2004b) *Probation Statistics, England and Wales, 2002*. London: Home Office.

Home Office (2004c) *Reducing Reoffending: National Action Plan*. London: Home Office.

Home Office (2005a) *Sentencing Statistics 2004, England and Wales*, Home Office Statistical Bulletin 15/05. London: Home Office.

Home Office (2005b) *Criminal Statistics, England and Wales, 2004*, Home Office Statistical Bulletin 19/05. London: Home Office.

Home Office (2005c) *Offender Management Caseload Statistics 2004 England and Wales*, Home Office Statistical Bulletin 17/05. London: Home Office.

Honderich, T. (1984) *Punishment: The Supposed Justifications*. Harmondsworth: Penguin.

Hough, M. and Roberts, J. V. (1998) *Attitudes to Punishment: Findings from the British Crime Survey*, Home Office Study No. 179. London: HMSO.

Hough, M., Clancy, A., Turnbull, P.J. and McSweeney, T. (2003) *The Impact of Drug Treatment and Testing Orders on Offending: Two-Year Reconviction Results*, Findings No. 184. London: Home Office.

Hudson, B. (2003) *Understanding Justice: An Introduction to Ideas, Perspectives and Controversies in Modern Penal Theory*, 2nd edn. Maidenhead: Open University Press.

Jowell, R. (2003) *Trying It Out – The Role of 'Pilots' in Policy-making. Report of a Review of Government Pilots.* London: Cabinet Office.

Kershaw, C. and Renshaw, G. (1997a) *Reconvictions of Prisoners Discharged from Prison in 1993, England and Wales*, Statistical Bulletin 5/97. London: Home Office.

Kershaw, C. and Renshaw, G. (1997b) *Reconvictions of Those Commencing Community Penalties in 1993, England and Wales*, Statistical Bulletin 6/97. London: Home Office.

Killias, M., Aebi, M. and Ribeaud, D. (2000) 'Does community service rehabilitate better than short-term imprisonment? Results of a controlled experiment', *Howard Journal*, 39 (1): 40–57.

Langan, P. and Farrington, D. P. (1998) *Crime and Justice in the United States and in England and Wales 1981–1996*. Washington, DC: Bureau of Justice Statistics.

Latimer, J., Dowden, C. and Muise, D. (2005) 'The effectiveness of restorative justice practices: a meta-analysis', *Prison Journal*, 85 (2): 127–44.

Lewis, S., Vennard, J., Raynor, P., Vanstone, M., Raybould, S. and Rix, A. (2003) *The Resettlement of Short-term Prisoners: An Evaluation of Seven Pathfinders*. RDS Occasional Paper No. 83. London: Home Office.

Lipsey, M. W. (1992) 'The effect of treatment on juvenile delinquents: results from meta-analysis', in F. Losel, T. Bliesener and D. Bender (eds), *Psychology and Law: International Perspectives*. Berlin: de Gruyter.

Lloyd, C., Mair, G. and Hough, M. (1994) *Explaining Reconviction Rates: A Critical Analysis*, Home Office Research Study No. 136. London: Home Office.

McGuire, J. (ed.) (1995) *What Works: Reducing Reoffending*. Chichester: Wiley.

McIvor, G. (1992) *Sentenced to Serve: The Operation and Impact of Community Service by Offenders*. Aldershot: Avebury.

McIvor, G. (2004) *Reconviction Following Drug Treatment and Testing Orders*. Edinburgh: Scottish Executive.

McMahon, G., Hall, A., Hayward, G., Hudson, C. and Roberts, C. (2004) *Basic Skills Programmes in the Probation Service: An Evaluation of the Basic Skills Pathfinder*, Findings No. 203. London: Home Office.

Mair, G. (1995) 'Evaluating the impact of community penalties', *University of Chicago Law School Roundtable*, 2 (2): 455–74.

Mair, G. (2004a) 'The origins of What Works in England and Wales: a house built on sand?', in G. Mair (ed.), *What Matters in Probation*. Cullompton: Willan.

Mair, G. (2004b) 'What Works: a view from the chiefs', in G. Mair (ed.), *What Matters in Probation*. Cullompton: Willan.

Mair, G., Lloyd, C. and Hough, M. (1997) 'The limitations of reconviction rates', in G. Mair (ed.), *Evaluating the Effectiveness of Community Penalties*. Aldershot: Avebury.

Marshall, T. (1999) *Restorative Justice: An Overview*. London: Home Office.

Martinson, R. (1974) 'What works? Questions and answers about prison reform', *Public Interest*, 10: 22–54.

May, C. (1999) *Explaining Reconviction Following a Community Sentence: The Role of Social Factors*, Home Office Research Study No. 192. London: Home Office.

May, C. and Wadwell, J. (2001) *Enforcing Community Penalties: The Relationship between Enforcement and Reconviction*, Findings No. 155. London: Home Office.

Metcalf, H., Anderson, T. and Rolfe, H. (2001) *Barriers to Employment for Offenders and Ex-offenders*, Department for Work and Pensions Research Report No. 155. Leeds: CDS.

Miers, D. (2001) *An International Review of Restorative Justice*, Crime Reduction Research Series Paper 10. London: Home Office.

Miers, D., Maguire, M., Goldie, S., Sharpe, K., Hale, C., Netten, A., Uglow, S., Doolin, K., Hallam, A., Newburn, T. and Enterkin, J. (2001) *An Exploratory Evaluation of Restorative Justice Schemes*, Crime Reduction Research Series Paper 9. London: Home Office.

Moxon, D. (1998) 'The role of sentencing policy', in P. Goldblatt and C. Lewis (eds), *Reducing Reoffending: An Assessment of Research Evidence on Ways of Dealing with Offending Behaviour*, Home Office Research Study No. 187. London: Home Office.

Nagin, D. S. (1998) 'Deterrence and incapacitation', in M. Tonry (ed.), *The Handbook of Crime and Punishment*. New York: Oxford University Press.

NOMS (undated) *Performance Report on Offender Management Targets July 2005 – September 2005*. See: http://www.noms.homeoffice.gov.uk/downloads/Perf_Rep_Offender_Man_Targs%2007-2005%20-%2009-2005.pdf

Oldfield, M. (1997) 'What worked? A five-year study of probation reconvictions', *Probation Journal*, 44 (1): 2–10.

Ong, G., Roberts, C., Al-Attar, Z. and Harsent, L. (2003) *Think First: An Accredited Community-Based Cognitive Behavioural Programme in England and Wales. Findings from the Prospective Evaluation in Three Probation Areas. Report Produced for National Probation Directorate by Probation Studies Unit*. Centre for Criminological Research, University of Oxford.

Partridge, S. (2004) *Examining Case Management Models for Community Sentences*, Home Office Online Report 17/04. London: Home Office.

Raynor, P. (2003) 'Research in probation: from "Nothing Works" to "What Works"', in W.H. Chui and M. Nellis (eds), *Moving Probation Forward: Evidence, Arguments and Practice*. Harlow: Pearson Education.

Raynor, P. (2004) 'Editor's introduction', *VISTA*, 8 (3): 127–9.

Raynor, P. and Vanstone, M. (1996) 'Reasoning and rehabilitation in Britain: the results of the Straight Thinking on Probation (STOP) programme', *International Journal of Offender Therapy and Comparative Criminology*, 40 (4): 272–84.

Raynor, P. and Vanstone, M. (2002) *Understanding Community Penalties: Probation, Policy and Social Change*. Buckingham: Open University Press.

Rex, S., Gelsthorpe, L., Roberts, C. and Jordan, P. (2004) *What's Promising in Community Service: Implementation of Seven Pathfinder Projects*, Findings No. 231. London: Home Office.

Roberts, J. V. (2004) *The Virtual Prison: Community Custody and the Evolution of Imprisonment*. Cambridge: Cambridge University Press.

Roberts, K., Barton, A., Buchanan, J. and Goldson, B. (1997) *Evaluation of a Home Office Initiative to Help Offenders into Employment*. London: Home Office.

Rogers, R. and Jolin, A. (1989) 'Electronic monitoring: a review of the empirical literature', *Journal of Contemporary Criminal Justice*, 5: 141–52.

Sarno, C., Hearnden, I. and Hedderman, C. (2001) *From Offending to Employment: A Study of Two Probation Schemes in Inner London and Surrey*, Home Office Research Findings No. 135. London: Home Office Research and Statistics Directorate.

Sarno, C., Hearnden, I., Hedderman, C., Hough, M., Nee, C. and Herrington, V. (2000) *Working Their Way Out of Offending: A Study of Two Probation Employment Schemes*, Home Office Research Study No. 218. London: Home Office Research and Statistics Directorate.

Shapland, J., Atkinson, A., Atkinson, H., Chapman, B., Colledge, E., Dignan, J., Howes, M., Johnstone, J., Robinson, G. and Sorsby, A. (2006) *Restorative Justice in Practice – Findings from the Second Phase of the Evaluation of Three Schemes*, Findings No. 274. London: Home Office.

Shaw, M. and Hannah-Moffat, K. (2004) 'How cognitive skills forgot about gender and diversity', in G. Mair (ed.), *What Matters in Probation*. Cullompton: Willan.

Sherman, L., Strang, H., Woods, D. (2000) *Recidivism Patterns in the Canberra Reintegrative Shaming Experiments (RISE)*. Canberra, ACT: Australian Institute of Criminology; see: http://www.aic.gov.au/rjustice/rise/recidivism

Simon, F. and Corbett, C. (1996) *An Evaluation of Prison Work and Training*. London: Home Office.

Spicer, K. and Glicksman, A. (2004) *Adult Reconviction: Results from the 2001 Cohort*, Online Report 59/04. London: Home Office.

Sugg, D., Moore, L. and Howard, P. (2001) *Electronic Monitoring and Offending Behaviour – Reconviction Results for the Second Year of Trials of Curfew Orders*, Findings No. 141. London: Home Office.

Thomas, D.A. (1979) *Principles of Sentencing*. London: Heinemann.

Thomas-Peters, B.A. (2006) 'The modern context of psychology in corrections: influences, limitations and values of "What Works?"', in G. Towl (ed.), *Psychological Research in Prisons*. Oxford: Blackwell.

Turnbull, P. J., McSweeney, T., Webster, R., Edmunds, M. and Hough, M. (2000) *Drug Treatment and Testing Orders: Evaluation Report*, Home Office Research Study No. 212. London: HMSO.

Underdown, A. (1998) *Strategies for Effective Offender Supervision: Report of the HMIP What Works Project*. London: Home Office.

Vennard, J. and Hedderman, C. (1998) 'Effective interventions with offenders', in *Reducing Offending: An Assessment of Research Evidence on Ways of Dealing with Offending Behaviour*, Home Office Research Study No. 187. London: Home Office.

Vennard, J., Sugg, D. and Hedderman, C. (1997) *Changing Offenders' Attitudes and Behaviour: 'What Works'*, Home Office Research Study No. 171. London: Home Office.

von Hirsch, A. (1976) *Doing Justice: The Choice of Punishments*. New York: Hill & Wang.

von Hirsch, A. and Roberts, J. V. (2004) 'Legislating sentencing principles: the provisions of the Criminal Justice Act 2003 relating to sentencing purposes and the role of previous convictions', *Criminal Law Review*, August: 639–52.

von Hirsch, A., Bottoms, A., Burney, E. and Wikström, P.-O. (1999) *Criminal Deterrence and Sentence Severity: An Analysis of Recent Research*. Oxford: Hart.

Webster, R., Hedderman, C., Turnbull, P. J. and May, T. (2001) *Building Bridges to Employment for Prisoners*, Home Office Research Study No. 226. London: Home Office.

Wilcox, A. and Hoyle, C. (2004) *The National Evaluation of the Youth Justice Board's Restorative Justice Projects*. London: Youth Justice Board.

Wilcox, A., Young, R. and Hoyle, C. (2004) *An Evaluation of the Impact of Restorative Cautioning: Findings From a Reconviction Study*, Research Findings No. 255. London: Home Office.

Chapter 17

Probation values and human rights

Loraine Gelsthorpe[1]

Introduction

In his first speech as Prime Minister to the Labour Party Conference, on 30 September 1997, Tony Blair pronounced that 'Our new society will have the same values as ever. It should be a compassionate society, but it is compassion with a hard edge.' It is arguable that this notion of a hard edge now dominates within probation practice and this leads us to pose some questions about values and rights.

Penal practices, values and sensibilities have undergone enormous transformation since the early 1990s and it follows that we should ask some searching questions about the moral dimensions of what probation officers now do in their everyday practice with offenders and victims, and more particularly what they are guided to do by national directives. It is also important to raise some questions about the normative values and human rights which should inform probation practice. In contrast to the Prison Service, which has been frequently challenged to display its humanitarian and civilised values (Liebling and Arnold 2004), the Probation Service itself has perhaps symbolised a particular humanitarian value base revolving around social work. As Nellis (Chapter 1, this volume) describes, from its inception the Probation Service has epitomised 'care' for offenders. The popular story is that the Probation Service's roots lay in the activities of police court missionaries who would offer 'five bob' and a Bible to miscreants identified by the court. Nellis offers a detailed revisionist history to show that while politicians, policy-makers, practitioners and academic commentators alike recognised the importance of the introduction of probation in 1907, they did not all do so from the same perspective. Indeed, the story is altogether a complicated one. Certainly, the roots of probation practice lie as much in established judicial practice and in penal reform initiatives as in activity by the Church of England Temperance Society and police court missionaries. Thus the aim was to both 'toughen up' established mechanisms to impose recognisances on offenders (convicted and unconvicted offenders alike if the courts so chose) by creating a condition that they be supervised by a person named in a probation order, and at the same time emphasise the non-punitive nature of the order through the notion that such a person might serve to 'advise, assist and befriend' the offender. It was clearly intended that probation practice would be a means of using imprisonment less; it wasn't a soft option, but it would be a way of remoralising 'probationers' as they were then called. The importance of 'social work' values to the enterprise perhaps has been privileged in popular accounts of the history of the Service precisely because its development was entwined with the early days of the Church of England Temperance Society. It took some time to disentangle proper probation from missionary work and denominational ties. It is perhaps for this reason that 'treatment' or 'social work' values continued to be the dominant currency.

But if the history of probation is more complicated than has been presupposed, it is fair to say that the value base for probation is arguably even less clear now than it was then, a hundred years ago. The notion that probation officers might serve to 'advise, assist and befriend' offenders no longer has currency at all – even if it was never entirely straightforward in the first place. The *broad* social values relating to the 'humanisation' of the individual offender and his or her treatment, to which the Probation Service laid claim from its inception in 1907 right through to the Criminal Justice Act 1991, seem to have disappeared. There is now a *lacuna* in the value base. As other chapters in this volume describe (see Chapters 8 and 13 in particular), the National Probation Service's strapline now revolves around 'enforcement, rehabilitation and public protection'. These three themes do not easily meld into a single value position in relation to offenders – the key clientele of the probation service (see Chapter 18 on victims as key clientele also). One general impression that has emerged from round-robin responses to policy diktats is that by the late 1990s probation officers had been made into 'screws on wheels', that is mobile prison officers and enforcers. In November 2006 Home Secretary John Reid appeared to endorse this by suggesting that probation officers should concentrate on enforcement and let voluntary agencies and others deliver drug treatment and other interventions.[2] The reality is undoubtedly more complex and nuanced than this. However, there is evident consternation about the ever-sharper 'hard edge'.[3]

There have been a number of attempts to address the changing values which inform probation practice – including the diversity agenda, civil liberties, restorative justice and community justice – along the way towards 'probation as enforcement'. A key purpose of this chapter is to outline some of these attempts and then to dwell on the potential for imbuing criminal justice, and thus probation practice, with both a human rights discourse – as established in the legislative changes of the Human Rights Act of 1998 – *and* a new normative discourse. The latter revolves around the idea of probation *facilitating* compliance rather than serving chiefly to *enforce* compliance.

The chapter is divided into four main sections. Notwithstanding the fact that the social work values which are taken to be the foundation of probation practice have a complicated history, I first sketch out the changing value base and refer to the impact of new public management on values in probation practice. The second section revolves around alternative value systems which have been put forward. The third section sets out arguments for a culture of rights. In the fourth and final section I turn to the prospects for a new value base which concerns 'decent' probation practice and the 'responsible offender', but at the same time look at interpretative practices on the ground and the exercise of professional discretion and judgement. I do so because values cannot be 'parachuted' in or superimposed on practice unless they carry legitimacy.

Values in probation: from social work to management and enforcement

The foundational platform of social work values in probation practice has never been as straightforward as imagined in popular history. Nevertheless it endured until the late 1980s. (See Chapters 1 and 2 for detailed discussion; I rehearse only significant developments here.) Certainly, there was recourse to the rhetoric of 'social work values' to help ward off the perceived threat of the Government's 'punishment in the community' strategy (Allan 1990) which culminated in the Criminal Justice Act 1991 and ultimately in the introduction of National Standards. Nellis (1995a) suggests that managers may have been wary of the 'social work' discourse at this stage, but basic grade officers generally still talked the 'social work' talk. The 1991 Criminal Justice Act emphasised a deserts-based philosophy (proportionality in sentencing so that the seriousness of the offence would be matched by the severity of sentencing).[4] More particularly in this context, it redefined alternatives to custody as community penalties, placed protection of the public and the prevention of reoffending on a par with rehabilitation as an aim of the probation order, and introduced the combination order (a mixture of community service and probation). As indicated, this new orientation led to popular claims within the service that probation officers were becoming 'screws on wheels', that the Service was experiencing a 'coercive tilt' and that altogether the dawning era was one of 'control in a cold climate'. Ironically, it has to be said, the police, judiciary and magistracy, among others, all saw the 1991 Act as 'liberal and lenient', largely because of the new focus on community penalties and the new restrictions on the use of custody (Easton and Piper 2005). As Nellis (1995a) describes, the most radical proposals in the 'punishment in the community' strategy were not implemented (a fully nationalised service and electronic monitoring), but the Service nevertheless experienced a seismic shock. The Home Office line was that the Probation Service had been too preoccupied with the 'identity and values' of the past and that it should have moved on from the days when social work skills and values embodied its sole purpose. In any case, a common purpose and common objectives were envisioned in the intentions to create an integrated and coordinated criminal justice system (Faulkner 1989: 1–5).

But any optimism that the 1991 Act would at least serve to reduce imprisonment (with its clearly established criteria for custody), even at the cost of toughening up control in the community, was short-lived. Immediately following the implementation of key sections of the Act there followed a series of crises which led to a backlash against the legislation. Rising crime figures, public and police concern about youth crime (particularly following the murder of infant James Bulger by two ten-year-old children in Bootle, Liverpool (which itself led to national agonising about the state of the nation), combined with concerns about car crime and offending while on bail, all played their part in this. Almost at once, fuelled by sentencers' dislike of the legislation, the Government backtracked; within six months of the introducton of the Act, the restrictions on custodial sentencing were relaxed; within two years, the legislation had been revised. Michael Howard, then Home Secretary insisted that 'prison works' (in terms of incapacitation); a new prison building programme was started and there was a move to toughen regimes. (For a detailed history of prison policies and practices in this period see Liebling and Arnold (2004).)

At the same time a new three-year plan for probation was revealed. This referred not to 'values but to 'commitments' and 'responsibilities', and emphasised that the purpose of probation was broadly to be of 'service to the courts and the public by supervising offenders in the community, helping offenders to lead law-abiding lives and safeguarding the welfare of children in family proceedings' (Home Office 1992). The language of the plan was distinctly managerial.

> It will act as a benchmark against which the government will judge progress in the achievement of priorities. The plan is also designed to provide a framework within which local services can make decisions, set budgets and plan for the future … As … other management information becomes available future plans are likely to see a shift more towards quantified objectives of desired impact and away from those which relate to procedural issues within the service. Future plans will therefore reflect work now in hand to develop a high level of performance indicators. (Home Office 1992: 1)

Indeed, the tone of the document was to suggest that these were organisational requirements. There was nothing here to which a social work sensibility might take exception, and certainly nothing to suggest retribution in the community. But equally, there was nothing to indicate reaffirmation of social work values either. More generally, it perhaps reflected 'new managerialism'.

In the Introduction to this book the editors intimate how social transformations reflecting a shift from 'modernity' to 'late modernity' have engendered a culture of risk, a culture of individuality and a culture of litigation (at the extreme of a rights-based culture perhaps). Allied to these shifts in social, economic, political and legal cultures is the growth of managerialism: the movement towards managerial forms of organisational coordination. The managerialist movement, as such, has arguably been inextricably bound up in the reconstruction of public services in the UK from the 1980s onwards (Clarke et al. 2000), which has itself involved the development of processes designed to scrutinise, evaluate and regulate the performance of agencies and organisations involved in service provision. Many of the processes are internal to agencies and organisations themselves. But some have been embedded within external organisations. The list of such organisations is endless: OFSTED, OFTEL, OFGEM, the Audit Commission, the Prisons and Probation Inspectorates and so on (see Morgan, Chapter 3, this volume). Some existing organisations (e.g. the Social Services Inspectorate) have taken on the mantle of evaluation and inspection. The language of auditing, inspection and evaluation is not without difficulty (Power 1997; Hood *et al.* 1998), but is generally taken to mean setting, monitoring and enforcing rules and standards, surveillance and performance measurement.

The suggestion is that this new culture of auditing and accountability is at once obstructive and enabling of good practice (Strathern 2000). It is perhaps a place where the financial and the moral meet in the twinned precepts of economic efficiency and ethical practice. It is almost impossible to critique the principles inherent in new public management because they promulgate responsibility, openness of enquiry, transparent decision-making, efficiency and a whole host of other things that we might hold dear in the interests of 'development'. Yet at the same time there may be seemingly dire consequences for practice if target-setting, performance target-achieving and economies of scale reduce innovative and responsive work with offenders and victims.

As late as 1972 the Probation Service was still driven by a casework philosophy, and the Service's view of management was said to be 'largely ... an extension of supervision [and] ... and enabling function providing facilities for the main grade officers to perform their work satisfactorily' (Butterworth Report (1972), cited in McWilliams 1992: 11). But the Butterworth Report (1972) heralded the management era with its recognition of a need for increased planning and control. No doubt increased size and complexity in staffing and organisation, the increasing range of functions, increasing emphasis on centralised policy and planning and an early version of performance-related pay all played a part in this move also (Haxby 1978; May 1991). The central imperative in probation (and the balance of government/local activity) is outlined in Chapter 3 (this volume). The point here is to question how far traditional probation values have become submerged in the discourse of new management.

In a prescient analysis of working credos *Criminal Justice and the Pursuit of Decency*, Andrew Rutherford (1993) set out senior practitioners' (senior probation officers, prison governors and others) 'beliefs and sentiments' and ideologies. He does this in a context of political, managerial and policy reform. Rutherford identifies three working credos: the punishment credo – which gives priority to the punitive degradation of offenders; the efficiency credo – which prioritises managerial change, pragmatism, efficiency and expedience; and then the 'caring' or 'humanity' credo which prioritises liberal and humanitarian values in relation to offenders (see Table 17.1).

We might quibble about the subcategorisation of the themes within these broad ideologies, but they nevertheless serve us well in thinking about probation practice in a changing context of governance, managerial reform and political intervention. The issue is how far Rutherford's credos might apply in the Probation Service today. Is one or more credo privileged? The answer might be that we can see a mixed menu of credos in operation, although in broad terms arguably rather more ingredients from one and two than three, the tough edge of compassion and the expedient managerialism

Table 17.1 Rutherford's three working credos

Credo 1: punishment	Credo 2: efficiency	Credo 3: care
Moral condemnation	Pragmatism	Liberal, humanitarian
Dislike of offenders	Management, system-based	Empathy with offenders
Degradation	Process oriented	Optimistic, enthusiastic
Unfettered discipline	Lack of correctional	Belief in constructive work
Expressive function	ideology	Open and accountable
of sanctions	Separation of action from	procedures
	beliefs or sentiments	Links with social policy

Source: Rutherford (1993: ch. 1).

showing through. The new preoccupations then appeared to be punishment, policy and planning and the humanitarian ideals thought to be inherent in the broad social work philosophy of probation were seen to be under attack.

Again, the story is a complicated one, for the defence of social work values at this time appeared to play into the hands of the Home Office who demanded to know more precisely what the social work values that were now being eroded actually were (Faulkner 1989). This is not the place to address the internecine debates about the differences between generic social work values and 'humanist' philosophy and between 'care' and 'control', although those debates are important to the overall story of probation practice (Christie 1982; Matheson 1992; Nellis 1995a). Suffice to say here that faced with a new criminal justice impetus which has emphasised punishment and control in the community the Probation Service has perhaps found itself floundering in attempts to re-establish clearly identifiable values which might be perceived as legitimate by government, practitioners and the public alike (leaving aside 'consumers' for the moment, although offenders' perceptions and experiences of probation work are not irrelevant to the task of identifying core values). The emerging managerial culture of the 1990s certainly does not square easily with all that had gone before in terms of 'probation values', however loosely or mistakenly conceived they have been.

One of the most recent attempts to reassert probation values came with the publication of *A New Choreography* (NPS 2001). In this document the 'values' of probation were identified by the National Probation Directorate (NPD) as:

- valuing NPS staff and partnership colleagues;
- victim awareness and empathy;
- paramountcy of public protection;
- law enforcement;
- rehabilitation of offenders;
- empiricism;
- continuous improvement;
- openness and transparency;
- responding and learning to work positively with difference;
- problem-solving;
- partnership;
- better quality services.

But as Hoy (2005/6) has noted, very few of these can really be described as 'values'. They read more like an operational methodology. As described in Nellis and Gelsthorpe (2003) *A New Choreography* failed to take thinking about values forward in a coherent fashion: 'It promoted an eclectic mix of moral commitments (victim awareness; rehabilitation of offenders), scientific aspirations (empiricism) and organisational imperatives (partnership; continuous improvement)' (2003: 230). The document includes the rather vague notion that the Probation Service should be 'responding and learning to work positively with difference in order to achieve diversity'. Our translation of this is helped by Stretch Objective seven within the document, 'valuing and achieving diversity in the NPS and in the services it provides' (NPS 2001: 33). In other words, no one is to be excluded by virtue of their gender, race or ethnicity, religion or sexual orientation, but the emphasis is very much on staffing and recruitment, the belief being that a diverse staff group will equal equality of provision on the ground for offenders and victims within these groups. One of the paradoxes here is that in the broad context of micro-managerialism (detailed policies, performance targets, recruitment targets, instructions and so on) requirements emanating from the diversity agenda can themselves seem oppressive. (See also Nellis (2001) for a more general critique of managerialism in this regard.)

If the traditional values of probation are seen to be under attack because of their seeming inability to respond to a changing conceptualisation of the criminal justice system and the associated policy agenda, and the NPS vision for probation revolves around an eclectic mix of the managerial and the moral with a strong tilt towards enforcement, what values *should* guide probation practice?

A Service in search of a new value base

Other ideologies or value systems that have been explored as possibilities have included anti-custodialism (Senior 1989), community safety (Nellis 1995a), community justice (Harding 2000), restorative justice (Nellis 1995a; 2001), relational justice/reintegrative shaming (Spencer 1995) and humanity and mercy (Glover 1999; Lacey 2002). But, taking each of these in turn, they are neither straightforward nor carry widespread favour. Abolitionism or an explicit anti-custodial stance has never been incorporated within the 'social work' values at the root of probation (Millard 1991; Christie 1993). It is true that within juvenile justice circles in the 1980s there were some inspired practitioner-led attempts to manage or 'control' the use of custody for young offenders (Rutherford 1989), but these attempts did not extend to probation. It is arguable that probation would lose all semblance of legitimacy if it were explicitly to oppose custodial sentences or denounce them as oppressive, although it is perfectly legitimate to enjoin those aims both within and without the Home Office who have argued for a reduction in the use of custody.

'Community safety' perhaps suggests important recognition that offenders and victims may be drawn from the same pool of poor, marginalised individuals and families. One implication of this is that welfarist social policies are needed to facilitate social and economic and structural changes. Moreover, the notion of community safety makes explicit a commitment to public protection. But the notion of using 'community safety' to spearhead probation values may be too vague and wide because of its associations with broader local authority-led initiatives to reduce opportunities for crime as well as responding to it. Nevertheless, John Harding (2000), among others, when Chief Probation Officer for the Inner London Probation Service, built on this notion by suggesting that best outcomes in relation to crime reduction are most likely to be achieved by a bridge-building effort between criminal justice professionals and the involvement of communities most at risk. Drawing on US experiments designed to facilitate the development of life skills among young offenders, he described a framework of interventions linking young offenders, their families and community support services (2000). The key aim was thus to promote community-based probation whereby probation officers develop partnerships with the police and community members to reduce reoffending by those in their midst.

The notion of partnership lies at the heart of probation practice of course, though arguably much less with the police than with mental health and voluntary agencies. Moreover, despite the new moves towards partnership via NOMS, it is not at all clear that this will necessarily enhance existing relationships with the police (as opposed to prisons and other agencies), and the managerial culture which has now been established could in any case mean that contestability will militate against effective partnerships. If we add to this the fact that efficiency drives within probation have led to shutting down many 'community'-based probation offices to maximise resources, then the prospects for team work between agencies within the communities which are most likely to produce offenders may be constrained. The idea of 'community justice' is clearly an important aspiration but creative partnerships between agencies may have to be 'grown locally' rather than imposed as a set of values. (See Liddle and Gelsthorpe (1994) on factors which promote community-based inter-agency work.)

As Nellis (1995a) has noted, probation officers have been involved in pioneering work in regard to mediation and reparation in neighbourhood disputes as forms of restorative justice (RJ), though they have probably been more active in relation to the former than the latter because of the potential for fostering personal responsibility in offenders. However, the evidence of crime reduction with regard to restorative justice has so far been mixed; as with other penal aims, perhaps the most we can say is that it is an approach which works sometimes, with some people, in some situations. Notwithstanding the difficulties in deciding *where* RJ should fit within the criminal justice system (as an alternative to a sentence, as a condition of another sentence, or as a penalty in its own right?) and *whose* needs should take priority – the offender's or the victim's – restorative justice, as a process, can be slow to put into effect, not least because it is resource intensive. Again, the ideals of RJ may be useful within probation practice, but as a set of values it is problematic.

As an offshoot of broad RJ approaches though, James (1995) has championed the notion of linking crime, shame and reintegration (drawing on Braithwaite 1989) and relational justice (drawing on Burnside and Baker 1994). The essence of the argument is that any punitive intervention should aim to shame offenders so as to bring home the consequences of wrong-doing. Shaming is most effective when it helps to reintegrate the offender into the community, but counter-productive when it leads to stigmatisation. Thus reintegrative shaming means punishment and shaming as a process within an ongoing relationship with the offender (condemn the sin and not the sinner, in other words). This means that there have to be people in the offender's life whom he or she respects. Relational justice perhaps brings these issues together by suggesting that crime affects not just victims and their families but the community at large, and that 'justice' has to seek to repair relationships damaged by crime – stressing the offender's responsibility for his or her actions. Punishment should not be an end in itself; rather it should serve to facilitate the reintegration of the offender back into the community. It is of course hard to question any of this: the proposition that offenders, victims *and* communities be considered seems entirely laudable. Importantly, David Faulkner (one of the key architects of criminal justice policy in the 1980s) very much sees this sort of approach as being related to the concepts of social responsibility and citizenship (Faulkner 1994, 2001, 2002). But again it is arguable that the positive evidence on reintegrative shaming is variable (see Dignan 2005) and that relational justice is too imprecise to guide the work of the Probation Service.

Thus the search for a transcendent justification for the Probation Service's activities, as Bill McWilliams (1987) once put it, goes on. 'Humanity' and 'mercy' (Glover 1999; Lacey 2002) have also appeared as possibilities for a new normative stance within probation. But it is arguable that these broad concepts would not give the Probation Service a distinctive public identity even if the concepts are to be embraced as ideals.

The 'What Works' movement might also be considered a new credo, although one of the limitations here is that unless there are explicit statements about the intended purposes or outcomes of probation practice, questions about 'what works' are arguably problematic, if not meaningless (Robinson and McNeill 2004). Moreover, commentators on the impact of 'what works' developments of the cognitive behavioural variety have noted resistance among probation staff. On the one hand this is perceived to revolve around a 'nostalgic mythology which argues … that it would be better not to change' (Raynor 2003: 335), or, on the other hand, the argument that such developments fail to take proper account of the individual offender and his/her complex needs (Atkinson 2004).

The diversity agenda – described in Probation Service documents *A New Choreography* and in *The Heart of the Dance* – to which such debates about the 'ideals' of justice have contributed might also be seen as an alternative value base to the traditional values in probation (see Chapter 11, this volume; also Nellis and Gelsthorpe 2003). However, this agenda has its limitations since it focuses on equal opportunities in relation to staff recruitment; whether this can translate into a better service and better justice for disadvantaged offenders remains open to question (there has been relatively little research to assess the impact of equal opportunities and anti-discriminatory practice on the culture and practice of the Probation Service). Moreover, we should be mindful of the fact that successive Probation Inspectorate reports have been critical of continued discriminatory practices, despite apparent advances in dealing with diversity (see Chapter 11, this volume).

So what might be the best way forward? Some commentators have suggested that the human rights discourse and the idea of a 'human rights culture' is a way of invigorating the early anti-discriminatory discourses and of facilitating a respect for difference (at the heart of diversity) and, importantly, a way of avoiding the worst excesses of managerialism (understood as an expression of state power). Moreover, a 'language of human rights' is shared across the criminal justice system, which the earlier probation 'social work' discourse was not. John Scott (2002), the Chief Officer of Probation most involved in charting the implications of the Human Rights Act 1998 for the Probation Service, has expressed enthusiasm for the transformative potential of the legislation. Building on some of former Chief Probation Officer Cedric Fullwood's (1999) foundational work on civil liberties and ways in which they should inform probation practice, Scott suggests that the human rights discourse can give impetus and legitimacy to existing forms of good practice. Community involvement, the recognition that offenders are citizens and partnerships with statutory and voluntary agencies as a bridge to helping offenders are all seen as ways of taking the human rights agenda forward. I give particular attention to the human rights framework here because it is arguable that probation in the twenty-first century might usefully be shaped by such a discourse.

Human rights: a new value-base for probation?

The late twentieth century may reasonably be described as the 'age of rights' (Bobbio 1995). Certainly a number of factors have conspired to put the concept of rights high on the social and political agenda. These range from human rights as an offspring of the post-War expansion of international conventions, human rights as part of the development of regional systems of protection, the emergence of human rights as a platform from which to resist some of the worst features of capitalist globalisation and human rights as new ideals of equality and justice (Freeman 2002; Turner 2006). To these perspectives we might add the notion of human rights as a solution to the problems of a fragmentary society. As Klug (2002) has put it, human rights might be seen as providing 'values for a godless age'.

Human rights may also be presented as resistance to the oppressive culture of control which Garland (2001), among others, has described. Thus there is an idea of 'human rights' as a new criminal justice discourse. Suffice it to say that whether or not human rights law can help us reconstruct a normative theory of crime control and justice is an extremely difficult question. There is the hard questions as to whether the Human Rights Act 1998 is necessarily limited to a constraining influence rather than serving as a normative one (Cheney et al. 1999; cf. Hudson 2001), but I will return to these questions in due course.

To set the scene, the Human Rights Act 1998 came into full effect across the UK in October 2000. Since then all UK laws have been required to be framed and interpreted in a way that is compatible with the European Convention of Human Rights. The Convention, of course, was inspired by the horrors and miseries of the Second World War, and derives from the Declaration of Human Rights which was adopted by the United Nations General Assembly in 1948. Once a state joined the Council of Europe[5] and submitted to the jurisdiction of its court in Strasbourg, its citizens could apply to that court if all other avenues in their home state had been exhausted. Failure to comply with the Convention can result in the 'offending state' being required to pay compensation to the citizen whose rights have been violated or, in exceptional cases, expulsion from the Council of Europe. In essence, the Convention establishes a mixture of basic civil and political rights (fundamental, judicial, social and personal) to all within the jurisdiction of a member state of the Council of Europe. The substance of the Convention can be found within its first 18 Articles and additional protocols. As Cheney *et al.* (1999) describe, the rights and freedoms the states each undertake to secure include the right:

- without discrimination, to life, liberty and security of the person;
- not to be subjected to torture, or to inhumane or degrading treatment or punishment;
- to a fair trial and the presumption of innocence;
- to respect for private life, home and correspondence;
- to freedom of expression, freedom of thought, conscience and religion;
- to freedom of assembly and association;
- to the peaceful enjoyment of personal possessions.

Article 3 of the European Convention, which guarantees protection against inhuman or degrading punishment, is of particular interest to probation. One can imagine that, if those undertaking unpaid work in the community as part of a community order under the Criminal Justice Act 2003 were required to wear leg-irons and humiliating clothing, this might be judged a breach of Article 3. Thus the Prison Reform Trust (1997) has taken a close interest in electronic monitoring and has collected relevant case studies, for example, the man who cut off his tag and threw it into a pond because he claimed that it made him feel like a dog, or the man wearing a tag who was assaulted by youths because they believed he was a sex offender. At the same time, there have been concerns that as a consequence of electronic monitoring of offenders there may be a breach of Article 8 which guarantees respect for private and family life. If an offender's life is disrupted to a sufficient degree and the family breaks down as a result, it is arguable that the punishment and control mechanism of electronic monitoring would breach Article 8. But the issues are complicated, not least by the fact that 'tagging' has been welcomed by some offenders, and particularly when it facilitates early release from prison for example (Mortimer and May 1997).

Towards 'a rights culture'

The Human Rights Act 1998 (HRA) 'domesticated' the European Convention on Human Rights by giving our domestic courts powers and responsibilities such that cases could be brought here without having to go to the European Court of Human Rights. As well as allowing for litigation in the courts, one of the effects of the HRA was that new legislation has to be accompanied by a declaration of 'compatibility' with the HRA. There are two approaches that could follow from the implementation of the HRA. The HRA could be used to give impetus to the development of a rights culture, making human rights the anchoring value of criminal justice, permeating policy and practice in a thoroughgoing way. Alternatively, the approach could be that of 'fire-watching', seeking to change policy and practice as little as possible, but making sure that any cases brought by offenders or victims against probation and other criminal justice agencies are unlikely to succeed. There are many probation and other criminal justice practitioners making strenuous and constant efforts to promote the first approach, developing a rights culture. John Scott (2002) as Chief Officer was one of the architects of the Probation Service's response to the HRA. He argued that the Act had tremendous transformative potential, certainly in terms of giving legitimacy to forms of good practice. However, there are also many sightings of the second and more limited 'fire-watching' approach.[6]

There are some difficulties in the way of establishing a rights culture. First, there is still some ambivalence in England and Wales about human rights conventions and acts, especially when they are seen as imported or imposed from 'abroad'. Bills of Rights in the UK and in the founding of the USA were concerned with establishing democratic forms of government rather than defending the rights of individual citizens against other citizens or against (democratic) governments. This explains, for example, why the death penalty persists in the USA: the death penalty is regarded as an expression of the will of the people rather than a denial of the rights of the person executed, and its abolition other than through a changed expression of the people would be seen as interference with the democratic process.[7] Although we no longer have the death penalty, the same sort of attitude to rights conventions is seen when the European Charter of Fundamental Rights and Freedoms is decried as Brussels encroaching on the sovereignty of Parliament.[8] The 'mainland' European notion of the citizen as possessor of a bundle of rights is not well established here. There are many cultural reasons for this difference in attitudes to rights legislation, but the experience of those European countries that suffered occupation by the Nazi regime in the Second World War has certainly taught them that people may well need protection against their own governments: governmental sovereignty needs to be balanced by individual human rights. In the UK, however, the distinction between 'fundamental rights and freedoms' and 'privileges of citizenship' is not clear-cut.

As well as cultural ambivalence or lack of commitment to the idea of fundamental rights and freedoms, there are additional impediments in the way of establishing offenders' rights. Although the most basic rights (to life, to freedom from torture, to freedom from loss of liberty without conviction) are generally regarded as non-derogable (i.e. they cannot be suspended by individual governments), what are sometimes known as 'second-' or 'third-tier' rights, or more commonly as civil and political rights as opposed to fundamental human rights, may be limited for a variety of reasons (Ashworth 2002). These include rights to privacy, rights to free speech and so on. Under Article 8 of the Convention, for example (the right to respect for private and family life), interference with the rights of offenders, whether in prison or under supervision in the community may be permitted where it is 'necessary' in a democratic society 'in the interests of national security, public safety or the economic well-being of the country, for the prevention of disorder or crime, for the protection of health or morals, or for the protection of the rights and freedoms of others'. Similarly, in relation to the right to free speech and so on (Article 10 – the right to freedom of expression), the Convention indicates that:

> the exercise of these freedoms, since it carries with it duties and responsibilities, may be subject to such formalities, conditions, restrictions or penalties as are presented by law and are necessary in a democratic society, in the interests of national security, territorial integrity or public safety, for the prevention of disorder or crime, for the protection of health or morals, for the protection of the reputation or rights of others, for preventing the disclosure of information received in confidence, or for maintaining the authority and impartiality of the judiciary.

The offenders' rights that are best established throughout Europe are the 'due process' rights concerning no loss of liberty or other rights without conviction, fair trials and procedures (Articles 5 and 6). These are arguably less contentious than other rights, for example the right to privacy, and are widely regarded as fundamental to the rule of law. However, in the controversies about the detention of suspected terrorists in Belmarsh prison, it is suggested that those rights have been infringed by the Government. Freedom from torture and fair trials have been judged by the European Court of Human Rights to have been withheld in dealing with Irish terrorists, and we see now that attitudes towards rights of terrorists have changed little, despite the assertions in most rights conventions that these rights are inviolable. Although different European countries have breached rights to greater or lesser degrees in response to their domestic terrorism threat (for example, Spain is said to have paid more regard to due process rights in response to ETA than the UK has in dealing with the IRA), post-September 11 fears and expectations of terror attacks may have weakened adherence to rule-of-law rights throughout the West (cf. Feldman (2006) who distinguishes between the government and judiciary and who highlights the notion of judicial deference in this regard).

The due process rights relevant to offenders and criminal justice agencies are more to do with trials and pre-trial detentions than they are to do with sentencing and the administration of punishment. In the case of Venables and Thompson, the ten-year-old boys convicted of the murder of two-year-old James Bulger in 1993, for example, the boys were successful in their challenge to the ECHR regarding the trial procedures and the rights of the judiciary and the Home Secretary in fixing sentencing tariffs, but not whether the sentences were 'excessive or damaging'.[9] The Convention does not interfere with countries' powers to set their own punishment schedules; signing up to the Convention is consistent with the existence of wide differences in the typical lengths of prison sentences, imprisonment rates and range of community penalties. After the right to freedom and not to be subjected to inhuman and degrading punishment, the rights that are most relevant for the actual administration of penalties are the civil, or third-tier rights, such as privacy, freedom of expression and the right to religious observance. These civil liberties are, in the UK, widely perceived as privileges of citizenship rather than as rights due to all persons. This means that while offenders' rights are poorly articulated in most countries (Braithwaite 1999), in the UK it is fairly difficult terrain on which to establish the idea that offenders have rights, as do all other persons, rights which should be respected and upheld during punishment.

Attitudes to offenders are saturated with the notion of *less eligibility* (Sparks 1996). This is the nineteenth-century principle that offenders' circumstances should always be worse than those of the least advantaged non-offenders. It is a concept originally developed under the Royal Commission on the Poor Law in 1832 and associated with the workhouse – that conditions should be worse than any non-indigent worker is likely to have to endure. Less eligibility acts as a brake on improvements in prison conditions, so that instead of making sure that conditions for offenders match the most civilised standards to which a society aspires, they correspond to the worst conditions that can be encountered within the society (Rusche and Kirchheimer 1968). Although members of the public are hardly likely to use the phrase 'less eligibility', the concept is reflected in populist views that prison shouldn't be 'soft' and offenders shouldn't have 'treats'. Mountaineering and canoeing as 'character-building' elements of young offender programmes have long been a popular target of letter writers to the tabloid press, so too the provision of accommodation or help to gain employment as elements of probation/community rehabilitation supervision. Although less eligibility has been particularly associated with the decline of rehabilitative probation and the 'austere regimes' policy in the 1980s, this idea is seldom absent from popular and political attitudes to offenders.

A contemporary communitarian idea has an impact similar to less eligibility and presents a further obstacle to the establishment of offenders' rights. This is the idea that rights must be coupled with responsibilities. Rights (at least at second- and third-tier levels) are said to be due only to those who accept the responsibilities of citizenship, those who behave responsibly. Offenders, by definition, have already failed the responsibility test. They can only regain rights by demonstrating responsibility. The first way in which they do this is by accepting responsibility for their offending, and then by behaving responsibly in prison or in the community: participating in programmes, keeping appointments, endeavouring to overcome alcohol or drug abuse, improving employment skills, engaging in pro-social rather than anti-social behaviour. Much contemporary penal practice is directed towards *responsibilisation* of offenders in and out of prison, during and after supervision (Hannah-Moffat 2000). I will return to the notion of the 'responsible offender' in due course, but for the moment, it is relevant to turn to the closely connected *zero-sum* equation of offenders' rights and victims' rights. According to this view, either victims' rights or offenders' rights can be protected and prioritised; what helps one must hurt the other. This view is often expressed by politicians when challenged about offenders' rights: 'what I care about is the rights of victims and members of the public', they say, as if respecting offenders' rights must necessarily undermine those of victims. But the logic of human rights is that persons have rights just by virtue of being human, they do not have to earn these rights by behaving responsibly. This is what is sometimes known as a *positive rights agenda*, and its adoption is the principal precondition of the development of a rights culture (Hudson 2001). The rights-and-responsibilities coupling is the very antithesis of the positive rights agenda: but it is arguable that human rights are not earned by good citizenship, nor are they to be forfeited by bad or irresponsible citizenship.

Challenges under human rights legislation demonstrate the tensions between these ideas of 'fundamental rights and freedoms' and the 'rights and privileges', 'rights and responsibilities' couplings. The UK is behind much of Europe (from the point of view of a positive rights agenda) in prisoners' rights such as rights to vote, receive conjugal visits, uncensored mail and privacy of visiting areas. It is also way behind some European countries in provision of standards of decency, lack of which may be construed as failure to guarantee freedom from degrading punishment.[10] There have been some interesting cases relating to offenders in the community over the last few years also. In *R* v. *NPS* ([2003] EWHC 2910, for example, a prisoner shortly due to be released challenged the decision of the National Probation Service to make it a condition of approving the accommodation in which he proposed to live that the manager be informed of his conviction for murder. The facts of the case included low OASys scores for further risk of offending but recognition of the potential serious consequences for victims with regard to risk of harm (given that he had killed his wife and his new accommodation might bring him into contact with women similarly aged to himself). Moreover, the risk assessment carried out by the probation officer indicated that he had not fully addressed his offending behaviour. The NPS argument was that there was a presumption in favour of disclosure to the manager of the accommodation complex. Utilising MAPPA guidance in a statement immediately prior to the hearing, the probation officer depicted the case as falling into level 1 (which in general circumstances relating to low and medium risk of harm means that a single agency might undertake the management of the case). It should be noted also that the Probation Service had opposed release but was overruled by the Parole Board. The focus of the offender's legal challenge was that disclosure was disproportionate; he recognised that offenders released on life licence should be supervised in order to protect the public, but felt that disclosure to the housing manager would go too far and affect the possibility of him establishing normal relationships and normal life; he felt that he would be shunned by other residents. Further details of the case need not detain us here; suffice it to say he won his case (under Article 8). The case raises important questions about the balance of rights: the perceived need for disclosure to protect the public and the potential harm that the offender anticipated would result from it. A constitutional right for offenders to experience rehabilitation would have made the offender's case even more compelling than it was. Another interesting Article 8 challenge is found in *R (Irving)* v. *London Probation Board* ([2005] EWHC 605) which also relates to an accommodation issue for a prisoner about to be released into the community and managed by the Probation Service.

In the context of developing more constructive and 'woman-wise' programmes in prison and in the community for female offenders, Pat Carlen has analysed the different prospects for penal reforms if they are introduced, alternatively, because of principle, in response to crises or in response to external pressures (Carlen 2002). She characterises the UK system as (usually) introducing reforms because of crises or external pressures. The 'Woolf moment' after the Strangeways riots in 1990 (Woolf and Tumim 1991) is an example of reform in response to crisis; greater concern for the less disruptive offenders' rights, such as rights to religious observance, in response to the HRA is an example of reform in response to external pressure (the approach characterised here as 'fire-watching'). Carlen (2002) demonstrates that where reforms are not introduced in response to principle – principle which is widely disseminated and becomes widely shared – there is usually a form of 'clawback'; that is, the reforms don't stick and previous practices are soon reasserted.

With regard to rights, the 'reform through principle' approach would be the development of a rights culture throughout the criminal justice system. If civil liberties are regarded as rights and not as privileges, then the duty of governments and all those who are involved in agencies – such as Probation – which have powers in relation to the lives and liberties of individuals and groups within the population is to protect the rights of all. The goal to be achieved is a 'rights balance': that rights of offenders and victims are balanced rather than the one sacrificed to the other. This means that criminal justice must seek to balance respect for the rights of offenders with adequate public protection and redress to victims.

Developing a 'rights culture' rather than 'rights fire-watching' is arguably consistent with probation values, and is contained in some of the best rationales and descriptions of 'What Works' programmes and of restorative justice projects. Both approaches stress that the offender is a person, not just the personification of a criminal act; both approaches stress the importance of treating offenders *and* victims with respect. Achieving a 'rights balance' is the goal of restorative justice, and it is also the goal of rehabilitative programmes which aim to enhance offenders' capacity to enjoy the rights and privileges of citizenship and at the same time to behave responsibly towards their communities. Adoption of a positive rights agenda and of the rights balance approach – the key elements of developing a rights culture – would help to protect the best of contemporary probation practice from 'clawback'.

Some general problems regarding human rights and criminal justice

It is also important to consider the context of recent changes in penal policy and the focus on risk and risk-assessment here. Sentences designed for public protection (rather than commensurate punishment or rehabilitation) present challenges to the idea of offenders' rights. Public protection sentences for offenders who pose a danger to the public have always existed, and they are a feature of most penal systems (Pratt 1996). Increasingly, they are confidently embedded at the core of penal systems both in prisons and in community punishment, and in community protection provisions and arrangements. Where governments were possibly once reluctant to provide preventive detention and prolonged supervision to deal with a small number of especially dangerous offenders, they now introduce and impose them more freely, arguably to demonstrate their populist credentials as well as their commitment to community safety. As Kemshall and Wood describe in Chapter 13 (this volume) the Probation Service is involved in the administration of public protection sentences at all stages: recommendations, risk assessments, working with offenders in prison and on release.

While the 1991 Criminal Justice Act provided a 'risk track' where more-than-proportionate sentences could be given on the grounds of danger to the public, this track was clearly intended for sexual and violent offences, and the danger to be protected against was 'clear and present danger' of physical injury. In successive legislation since 1991, this track has been expanded to include a wider range of offences, and to include *persistence* as well as *dangerousness*. (See the 1996 White Paper *Protecting the Public* (Home Office 1996) for example, as well as the Sex Offenders Act 1997, the Crime and Disorder Act 1998 and the Powers of the Criminal Courts (Sentencing) Act 2000.) As a result, there has been an increase in the population of longer than commensurate and discretionary life imprisonment. The Criminal Justice Act 2003 (CJA) maintains these provisions for dangerousness and for management of sexual offenders, and also carries forward the possibility of more-than-proportionate sentences for offenders who may be persistent but who do not necessarily pose risk of sexual or violent danger. The Sexual Offences Act 2003 includes greater specification of sexual offences and tries to close some loopholes such as 'grooming' as well as introducing some new protection orders, but it does not significantly alter the arrangements for managing dangerousness introduced by the Crime and Disorder Act 1998 and the Powers of the Criminal Courts (Sentencing) Act 2000. This is not the place to elaborate upon these points; suffice it to say here that the 2003 Act has increased the use of protective sentences. This is not without controversy (Easton and Piper 2005).

The custody-plus, custody-minus provisions in the Criminal Justice Act 2003 and the general acceptance in legislation and in sentencing practice of the Halliday Report's (2001) redefinition of proportionality from 'proportionality to current offence' to 'proportionality to current offence plus criminal record' add to the complexity of upholding values of proportionality and of balancing the rights of offenders, victims and the public in criminal justice policy and practice.[11]

Although the advice of the Sentencing Guidelines Council and the Court of Appeal is directed at sentencers rather than at probation officers, from a human rights perspective the Probation Service might be aware of proportionality in two senses. Firstly, if a sentence is more-than-commensurate then probation officers should keep in mind that the offender concerned has paid the proportionate retributive penalty and therefore ensure that impositions and work initiated and administered by the Probation Service are clearly linked to rehabilitation and the reduction of the likelihood of reoffending. In other words, the interventions should not contain elements which are punitive rather than rehabilitative and reintegrative. Secondly, probation officers should keep in mind the idea that control, surveillance and programmes designed to protect the public by reducing the risk posed by an offender should be proportionate to the degree of risk actually posed.

The European Convention does not specifically include a right to proportionate punishment. Nevertheless, there is a principle of proportionality contained in the Convention and similar ordinances. This decrees that there must be proportionality between the deleterious and salutary effects of measures which restrict rights and freedoms (Fordham and de la Mare 2001). Freedom-limiting rights and measures which are inflicted to prevent crime should, according to this principle, observe proportionality between the restrictions and the crimes that are expected to be prevented. This balance surely has to take into account the nature and seriousness of the crimes which an offender is thought likely to commit in the absence of any preventive measures, as well as the number of offences that might be committed. Crime prevention by incapacitative imprisonment strategies has been questioned because of the ethics of linking amounts of incarceration to numbers of crimes that might be 'saved' (Zimring and Hawkins 1995). Calculations of how many crimes may be saved by increased imprisonment rates (the ratio known as the 'lambda') provoke objections that punishment should be a matter of principle and morality rather than arithmetic. As well as the number of crimes that may be prevented, however, the human rights principle of proportionality suggests that the nature of the crime is relevant, and that, for example, extra imprisonment or very restrictive and intrusive community supervision would not be justified for the prevention of minor crimes, however many minor crimes might thereby be prevented.

It is suggested that other rights, such as the right to respect for private and family life, should be considered when imposing and carrying out measures for the sake of prevention of further crimes. Whether considered as part of the principle of proportionality, as freedom from degrading punishment or as rights in their own regard, respect for private and family life and religious freedom should arguably restrict the intrusiveness of probation supervision and programmes. Curfews, electronic tagging and attendance at treatment centres should be planned carefully to interfere as little as possible with family and intimate life, just as they should be planned so as not to restrict the right of religious observance.

Respecting the rights of offenders and balancing the rights of victims, offenders and the public commends the principle of *parsimony* in punishment. 'Parsimony' – the least amount of punishment likely to be effective – is a refinement of the principle of *limited retributivism* associated with Norval Morris (1992). This is the principle that proportionality to offence seriousness should set the limits of punishment, but within those limits the actual penalty should be able to be fixed according to crime prevention utility. Parsimony, Michael Tonry's preferred version, would mean that proportionality sets the upper but not the lower limit of allowable punishment. Tonry and Rex (2002) assess limited retributivism as being the key principle behind the Halliday Report, although they say that it is not adhered to perfectly. In their view, parsimony is adhered to only weakly. This is certainly true of the CJA 2003 that has resulted from the Halliday Report (2001): indeterminate sentences breach the principle of limited retributivism in its standard form, and the spirit of the Report and current legislation pays little regard to parsimony.

Probation might draw from the work on parsimony and limited retributivism in relation to sentencing. 'The least restrictive sanction'[12] likely to achieve the necessary crime prevention effects might be a suitable guide to programme planning and programme implementation concerning the demands made on offenders. It follows that different forms of intervention and support might be promoted. Projects like the Circles of Support in Canada, which provide a group of supporters to help sex offenders develop a social and community life, rather than concentrating on keeping the offender out of contact with the community, might be encouraged in this regard so that while 'formal interventions' are limited, support interventions are not (Petrunik 2002; Silverman and Wilson 2002).

Public protection is, of course, a legitimate task and provides the basic rationale for the criminal justice system in general, and especially for the Probation Service (see Chapter 13, this volume). But as Hudson (2001) has argued, the rights-balance approach suggests that what needs to be achieved is *risk management* rather than *risk elimination* (Clear and Cadora 2001).[13] Risk management is the strategy of trying to reduce risks by better assessments, better programming and better decision-making, for example about parole; risk elimination attempts to remove any possibility of the risked event occurring by removing the possibility of carrying out the action from the potential offender. Risk management tries to minimise bad events from occurring but nevertheless accepts that risked events cannot be eliminated altogether without unacceptable levels of restriction of liberty and other rights. Indeterminate sentences which disregard proportionality and community programmes where the deleterious effects on offenders' rights are disproportionate to the salutary effects on crime prevention and offender rehabilitation, are examples of risk control policies which approach the model of risk elimination. Achievement of a rights-balance rather than the zero-sum approach to rights is most likely if Probation keeps constantly in view the principles of proportionality, least intrusion and least restriction, so that gains in public protection will not be at the expense of offenders' human rights.

Towards a conclusion on the development of a rights culture within probation

Ideally, criminal justice systems should balance the aspirations to deal justly with offenders, to contribute to crime reduction and public safety and to provide redress and reassurance for victims. Although real, existing criminal justice systems must serve these different objectives and values, the balance between them changes from time to time. These criminal justice orientations have been described as *crime control* and *due process* models (Packer 1969), and although their objectives are necessarily combined in actual penal policy and practice, looking at them as conceptually separate models highlights the fact that there are tensions between the two sets of goals and values. In the UK and other western jurisdictions, we can observe pendulum swings between the two models.

The 1991 Criminal Justice Act might be seen to have marked the high tide of the due process approach given the criteria for custody which it includes, for example, and the emphasis on proportionate sentencing, coming as it did after a decade in which sentencing and penal policy reforms had all been in this direction. From the Criminal Justice Act 1982 and throughout the 1980s, the goals of reform involved the reduction of indeterminate sentences (for example care orders), greater consistency and proportionality of sentence to current offence seriousness. These reforms affected not only the courts. Probation adopted 'justice model' styles of report writing; gate-keeping was introduced to make sure that interventionist sentencing was not being recommended for minor crimes and that custody was not being encouraged because of unclear recommendations or an absence of recommendations; community penalties aimed to incorporate degrees of restriction of liberty commensurate with the offence for which they were imposed.

From 1993 up to and including the legislation in 2003, changes and reforms have been in the direction of crime control. This swing has involved probation as well as sentencing. The 'What Works' accredited programmes, involvement in inter-agency community safety policies and arrangements and risk assessment and risk management as the primary Service objectives are all moves to ensure the Probation Service's engagement and effectiveness in crime control. This swing is neither surprising nor regrettable. Commentators such as Anthony Bottoms (1995) have observed that the just deserts era saw reforms almost entirely concerned with values that were internal to the criminal justice system (consistency, proportionality, fairness), taking little notice of political and public concerns for crime reduction and public protection. What would make this latest pendulum swing deplorable, however, is if it meant sweeping aside all commitment to fairness to offenders. The Home Office document *Rebalancing the Criminal Justice System in Favour of the Law-abiding Majority* with its headline emphasis on the protection of the public (Home Office 2006) is certainly suggestive of this, although a more nuanced reading of this addition to the panoply of reforms proffered by the Labour government since taking power in 1997 might indicate that substantive changes in this direction have been exaggerated and that the document merely reiterates the pre-existing movement towards crime control and public protection.

There has been some pessimism about the impact of the HRA on sentencing and the administration of punishment (Henham 1998). Two provisions of the European Convention and the HRA in particular prompt this pessimism. One is the provision that rights (short of fundamental rights) can be limited for clearly defined purposes to do with, among other things, the prevention of crime and disorder. The other factor is the principle of *margin of appreciation*, which is that – fundamental rights again aside – each country can interpret rights and provisions according to its own political tradition and culture. Taken together, these two principles could mean that governments can engage in any penal purposes they see fit, and that rights can be defined as widely or as narrowly as governments see fit.

However, whatever the strengths and limitations of the HRA 1998 and convention/legislative approaches to rights in general, the idea of human rights is held to be a way of keeping the two criminal justice modes – crime control and due process – in balance (Ashworth 1995). Human rights means that criminal justice must pay attention to the rights of victims not to be re-victimised and the rights of the general public to live their lives in security and freedom from fear, but it also must care about the rights of offenders to have their liberty restricted only to the degree that is strictly and demonstrably necessary to prevent harm to others. Furthermore, restriction of liberty, however necessary, should not involve lack of care for offenders' rights to family life, freedom of religious observance, freedom from degrading treatment and participation in civil/political rights. One way of achieving this is to develop a criminal justice ethic in which crime control goals are pursued within due process restraints (Braithwaite and Pettit 1990). Whether seeing a rights culture in these terms, drawing on existing criminal justice models, or whether seeing it in terms of new concepts and models, adopting human rights as the value base for criminal justice means developing a rights culture, and, moreover, a rights-balance value commitment.

In practical terms, human rights protection should be built into probation practice at every level. New polices and practices should be subjected to a rights audit whenever and wherever they are introduced. This does not mean a bland, generalised statement of compliance; it means going through each innovation one by one, looking at whose rights might be augmented or curtailed, assessing which rights are strengthened or threatened, and to what degree. This rights audit approach might be an element of all practice and policy evaluation (Hudson 2001).

A body of UK judgements is beginning to emerge with regard to the protection of offenders' rights in the HRA era, although these judgements give rather mixed messages about the impact of the HRA on the administration of punishment. The Probation Service should not react to this with anxiety about the extent of practice change that may be demanded, or with either optimism or pessimism about the degree of cultural change that may be set in train, but arguably might develop a rights culture as a basic value for the management of offenders in the twenty-first century. As stated earlier, a human rights approach incorporates values of equality, respect for diversity and concern for community, victims and offenders. Prioritising rights entails managing risk, because it involves the duty of seeing that all are enabled to live their lives freely and securely. Risk control – overemphasising risk, dividing people into the risked and the risky – would leave the criminal justice system mired in the zero-sum approach. Although it might seem obvious that victims' and the public's rights to safety are more important than offenders' rights to as much liberty as possible and to respectful treatment, it would be a mistake to think that the former are everything and the latter are but nothing. If both sets of views and needs are 'rights', then they are the same category of thing and must be held in careful balance, rather than the one being everything and the other nothing (Dworkin 1986).

Synergising sensibilities

But it would be a mistake to pin *all* hopes and desires for a new system of values on human rights; while a rights culture provides a basis for probation activities, it does not itself provide the 'transparent statement of values' that might inspire probation practitioners. We have also to question whether the credibility of human rights depends on a prior sensibility which expresses why and how they matter, or whether the legislation itself creates and sustains the sensibility. We are urged to reflect on this issue by Michael Ignatieff, an internationally recognised commentator on human rights, among others. Important as it is, an abstract commitment to rights, is perhaps not enough to kindle and sustain respect, decency and a moral agenda within probation practice. Ignatieff suggests that we view the human rights discourse as something on the 'outermost arc of our obligations, but which are only as strong as our innermost commitments' in essence (2000: 41).

In this sense a culture of human rights might serve as much more than 'a dry enumeration of entitlements in constitutional codes ... and as more than a set of instruments that individuals use to defend themselves' as Ignatieff once put it (2000: 125). But it will not pay to be confident that the notion of a culture of human rights *alone* will be able to provide ethical salvation for the Probation Service; rather it can serve as a resource for sustaining ethical ideal and moral sensibilities. A 'rights culture' need not be the simple 'back-stop' that many have assumed it to be: it can also be a galvaniser of good practice. At the same time there is arguably need for another kind of 'viable post-managerialist vision' too, as McLaughlin (2001) has suggested, so that the dangers of managerialism in everyday probation practice can be attended to. (As discussed below, they *are* addressed in the exigencies of probation practice, through local discretion and 'resistance', but almost as unintended consequences of the managerial thrust rather than deliberate policy and practice.) A culture of human rights should arguably be accepted *sine qua non*, with the HRA welcomed as a legal lowest common denominator, but there needs to be professional practice and commitment which embodies more than the 'mechanistic' adherence to policy. Nellis and Gelsthorpe (2003) have framed this in terms of probation staff needing to be equipped to draw on 'overarching knowledge', to know *when* and *how* to exercise intelligent discretion is better than hidden discretion and discretion as resistance to the excesses of managerialism for example. There are clear implications here for training (see Chapter 4, this volume). It is important too, for those coming into the Probation Service to be aware of both the strengths and weaknesses of earlier value-based discourses, including the agenda outlined in *A New Choreography*. But the modern Probation Service arguably needs to make more transparent other values at work too.

The Probation Boards' Association (PBA 2005) survey of views on the values that should be at the heart of the service produced a wide range of responses including 'belief in a need to be inclusive', 'care for offenders', 'the promotion of citizenship' (the reintegration and rehabilitation of offenders), 'respecting the inherent dignity of the human person' (offenders included), 'humanity', a 'human touch', 'reform and restore', respect for the offender, 'tolerance and sympathy', and more besides. Some of these statements reflect values already addressed in the discussion above. In terms of the *aims* of work with offenders, the notion of 'responsibility' captures much of the intention of rehabilitating and reintegrating offenders; there appears to be a shared sense of purpose which revolves around encouraging the 'responsible offender' (working alongside offenders to identify their problems, promoting self-diagnosis, encouraging voluntary mentoring support, and so on). Indeed, one might view the central aims and values of probation as being to engage in problem-solving so as to *facilitate compliance*.

In terms of the *process* by which the aims might be achieved, Margalit (1996) usefully sets out the values of decency (interestingly, a language adopted within the Prison Service, but not obviously within the Probation Service), and it seems to me that much that is mentioned in the PBA debate can be encapsulated within the notion of 'decency'. Decency first appeared in Home Office parlance in the 1991 White Paper (Home Office 1991). Michael Howard, as Home Secretary, used the term to mean that prison conditions should be 'decent but austere', but, more positively, as Director General of the Prison Service in 1999 Martin Narey viewed 'decency' as meaning 'fair and humane' treatment. The term received official promotion following exposure of prison staff abuse of prisoners (HMCIP 2001).

The values inherent in what the Service is trying to achieve, in terms of public protection and *communicating* to different stakeholders (including offenders) what can be gained via community orders, are also critical here. There is great reliance on deterrence-based approaches for securing compliance with the requirements of community orders. Yet greater understanding of what motivates offenders to adopt law-abiding lifestyles might result in a more educative and communicative approach (using various forms of mediation, 'making amends' or restorative justice). Based on empirical analysis of the views and experiences of lay magistrates, probation staff, offenders and victims, Rex (2005) identifies the role of 'communication' as crucial for processes which address both victims' and offenders' needs.

Whatever else it does, probation training needs to offer a deeper, broader and more sophisticated understanding of values than are relayed via the managerialist agenda. As indicated, a culture of human rights can provide an important basis for probation practice, but probation values need also to be conceptualised and articulated as forward-looking normative statements to help those working within the Service to address contemporary penal challenges.

An addendum

For all the debates and attempts to capture critical values, it is important to question how values are placed or fixed at the heart of any organisational practice. There is an issue as to whether national policy is ever unfurled in local areas in precisely the way envisaged by those who inhabit central governmental offices. There are certainly claims that contemporary penal policy and practice is 'volatile and contradictory' and that state-sanctioned punishment lacks coherence and stability (O'Malley 1999; Simon and Feeley 1995; Garland 1996). As Garland has noted, 'the politics of penal modernism are deeply ambivalent. They depend on the ideological orientation of those who staff the institutions, and upon the political and legal context in which they operate' (Garland 1995: 188). Elsewhere, Garland (2001) has written about the culture of control and ways in which this has impacted on penal practice. However, critics have suggested that there has been more resistance and variation on the ground than he has acknowledged (see, for example, Matthews 2002; Gelsthorpe 2005).

Thus the juggernaut of 'control' that Garland has described in his account of the punitive turn within late modern society is certainly important in attempts to understand the links between national political-orientated penal strategies and local strategies. But there is arguably a need to think much more about ground-level practice (Gray and Salole 2006). Certainly what is intended, and what is experienced, may be very different. In their ethnography of a young offender establishment in Canada, Gray and Salole (2006) remind us that even the physical conditions of a building can shape experiences of punishment (the dingier the better according to some staff they interviewed – in terms of pressing home the punitive intentions of the regime). But more particularly we should remember that control and punishment are mediated by human agents. This leads me to mention discretion and resistance – we might question how far professional staff resist and adapt what they perceive to be the excesses of a new credo based on punishment and efficiency when the more traditional credo (based on social work values of understanding and care) are seemingly cast into the shadows. As Cheliotis (2006) has asked in an analysis of penal currents, 'how iron is the iron cage of new penology?'

As a lecturer within the university context I have been involved in teaching senior criminal justice managers over the past few years and there have been lively discussions with probation, prisons and police staff about the pros and cons of managerial reform, political intervention and the impact of these things on the exercise of professional discretion. On the one hand there are laments that discretion (mandated flexibility in decision-making about individuals) has been eroded to the point of being virtually non-existent. On the other hand various monitoring mechanisms now in place are thought to be a useful check against rampant discretion and discrimination. There is a tension here between the deprofessionalising tendencies of a management structure where probation officers cannot exercise professional judgement and the professionalising tendencies of that same structure which may serve to limit problematic decision-making (Loader and Sparks 2002).

Tellingly, in repeated classroom-based case study exercises designed to tease out some of the tensions, different cohorts of senior prison and probation practitioners have come to different decisions on the principles which should guide a probation officer in deciding if an explanation for a missing appointment is acceptable. They have all been aware of National Standards (especially probation officers) but their different perspectives have reflected different normative stances on what is appropriate, depending on local circumstances and what else is known about the offenders in each case. In the course of such discussions, senior staff have expressed dismay that new probation officers rely almost totally on policy documents and National Standards, appearing not to cultivate professional intuition and judgement.

In a presentation at a 2006 conference on parole, Helen Collins (2007), a senior probation officer, drew on personal research on decision-making in relation to the recall of offenders on licence to emphasise wide variation in the exercise of discretion. Using two hypothetical cases (one of which concerned an offender subject to a discretionary conditional release licence who was in breach for being charged with a further unrelated offence, and the other revolving around an offender subject to an automatic conditional release licence who was in breach for technical violations in the form of failing to attend appointments) she attempted to see if there would be any difference in her sample of 29 probation officers' decisions. In the first case only one officer initiated expedited recall, three initiated non-expedited recall, 16 initiated an assistant chief officer warning, seven initiated a formal warning and one initiated a home visit prior to any enforcement action being taken. The second case produced similar variation in response: seven officers initiated non-expedited recall, 11 an assistant chief officer warning, one a formal warning and nine officers a home visit. There are other interesting details concerning experience in service and decision-making patterns but this small piece of research mainly serves to suggest that probation officers are not interpreting Home Office or NPS guidelines in mechanistic fashion, but rather using professional judgement to determine appropriate action.

One key question that remains of course is how far this can be justified in view of ostensible organisational failures (namely the case of Anthony Rice: HMIP 2006). At the same time, there is arguably need for a balance between uniformity and individualisation of treatment. Discretion can be unwelcome when it leads to unjustifiable decisions (negative discrimination) and inconsistency (inappropriate disparity in treatment), but it can also be a force for good in that it provides a mechanism to show mercy which, even if defying precise definition, many would recognise as being necessary to the conception and delivery of justice. It allows justice to become 'humane' (Gelsthorpe and Padfield 2003). Thus one challenge is how far 'the exercise of professional judgement' (beyond rules and principles), representing humanitarian values, can be imbued and embedded within probation practice in a managerial context in which many probation officers presently feel deskilled and deprofessionalised (Eadie and Winwin Sein 2005/6). We do not know how far probation staff actually resist the long reach of increasing managerial control or other constraints on practice. The image of puppet-like adherence to managerial control is certainly not appropriate. We need more of a window on ordinary instances of everyday decision-making within a probation office to know what really goes on. But just as we know that prison officers choose between enforcing the letter of the law and tolerating rule-breaking behaviours on the part of prisoners because it makes good sense to do so in the broad context of maintaining order (Liebling and Price 2003), so also can we imagine that probation practice on the ground reflects a similar mix of personal values, idiosyncratic meanings, organisational dynamics and routines that mean that dictates from on high will be reinterpreted in everyday practice in order that probation practice is rendered meaningful. As Goffman

(1959) put it in an early analysis of the art of impression management, there are 'front-stage' and 'back-stage' performances in every organisation.

One of the most convincing stories of resistance from professional staff in the field to punitive and controlling policies, comes from Mona Lynch (1998, 2000) who conducted an ethnographic analysis of practice in a parole office of the Californian Department of Corrections. Given the state's efforts to systematise parole through actuarial classification and the aggregate management of risk, one might have expected mechanistic decision-making (and a sense of being deskilled and demoralised among the staff). However, Lynch shows how the staff circumvented management requirements (including rigid systems for scoring offenders based on case histories) and chose to preserve and prioritise 'an individualistic approach to the clientele and an intuitive approach to case management' (1998: 861–2). Similarly, Gwen Robinson (2002), analysing probation's risk-based approach to the management of offenders (including statistical predictors of reconviction), concluded that probation officers continued to rely upon 'rehabilitative impulses and clinical decision-making practices' in the two areas which she studied in England and Wales. As Robinson and McNeill (2004) have put it in their focus on two Scottish probation sites, diversity of purpose and approach is much in evidence beneath the master narratives emanating from the centre. Thus 'social inclusion' and 'anti-custodialism' were prominent alongside 'control' and 'public protection' (2004: 295).

What are the implications of this brief detour into discretion and resistance? I am not seeking to promote insurgency among the ranks. Nor do I wish to argue that there should be no constraints whatsoever on discretion (which can, after all, be a force for ill as well as good and there is need for balance between structure and human agency – see Gelsthorpe and Padfield 2003: ch. 1). My purpose here has been twofold. First, I want to suggest that excessive managerialism (calling probation officers to account with an overemphasis on regulation and performance indicators, for example) may well inhibit sound professional judgement and professional intuition. There is very real concern about the impact of managerialism on probation practice. As Onora O'Neill (2002) argued in one of her BBC Reith lectures, 'Plants don't flourish when we pull them up too often to check how their roots are growing: political, institutional and professional life too may not flourish if we constantly uproot it to demonstrate that everything is transparent and trustworthy' (2002: 19). Secondly, I want to draw attention to the fact that 'softer', 'decent' and humane objectives may well survive within systems which can appear to be irreversibly punitive and inhumane, though it is obviously better to try and cultivate these things rather than to rely on the vicissitudes of human endeavour! A key implication here is to suggest that the 'counter' to managerialism is to empower the individual probation practitioner to act ethically, not simply legally.

Finally, I would add that public opinion surveys of attitudes towards punishment consistently suggest that the public generally overestimate crime and underestimate levels of punishment. On close questioning, the public are not necessarily seeking vengeance in quite the way that some of the tabloid newspapers presuppose (Roberts and Hough 2002). Rather, they are seeking a reduction in crime. They wish to feel safe. Bottoms thus observes that, as well as the legitimacy of internal criminal justice agency policies and directions being important, 'the *external* legitimacy of penal policies *vis-à-vis* the wider audience of citizens at large' is also important (2003: 81). For example, despite the fact that prisons have seemingly embraced managerialism (with all its promises of good things), dehumanising moments have been identified and criticised by the public. Newspaper reports of a female prisoner giving birth to her baby in an outside hospital shackled to an officer drew sharp condemnation from the public, as did news of a man dying of cancer handcuffed to his bed (Coyle 2003). Community penalties have had a bad press for some years now. A lack of political will, the absence of an absolutely convincing platform of evidence regarding 'what works' and political messages that 'prison works' have all conspired to signify a lack of faith in community penalties. As indicated in the Introduction to this collection, recent cases such as that of Anthony Rice have served to compound a perceived lack of legitimacy in regard to community penalties, probation in particular. Thus the credos of punishment and efficiency are perhaps in the ascendancy, while 'care' as a normative value for probation practice is seemingly in decline. Whether or not we can envisage a moment when the public might think that probation interventions have become 'too harsh' or 'too controlling', or that attempts to enforce compliance rather than facilitate it, are not 'decent' enough, is hard to say. But there is evident public capacity to identify that which goes beyond legitimate punishment. Probation practitioners might take heart from this.

Notes

1 With thanks to Barbara Hudson, Professor of Law at the University of Central Lancashire, UK, for her contribution to this chapter in terms of the discussion on the development of a rights-based culture, elements of which she initially drafted. Barbara Hudson has championed the development of a rights-based culture within criminal justice circles and I am grateful to her for generous permission to draw on her work in this way. I am also grateful to Mike Nellis for kind permission to draw on a previously published chapter on probation values (Nellis and Gelsthorpe 2003) and to Rod Morgan and Nicky Padfield for their helpful comments during the preparation of this chapter.

2 Home Secretary's speech to prisoners and prison staff at HMP Wormwood Scrubs, 7 November 2006.

3 Probation work in Scotland survived within the remit of social work for much longer than in England and Wales, but as McIvor and McNeill show (Chapter 5, this volume) this situation is now changing.

4 See chapter 3 in Easton and Piper (2005) for a detailed account of the roots and meaning of 'just deserts'.

5 Note that the Council of Europe should not be confused with the European Union.

6 Barbara Hudson was present at a Probation HRA training conference where the participants were assured that if they followed Home Office guidelines and National Standards they would have nothing to worry about, and at a Prison Service conference where the audience of governor grades was told that there was 'nothing to fear' in the HRA.

7 It should be noted that although the Supreme Court has not held the death penalty to be unconstitutional *per se*, it has allowed successful rights-based challenges to the way it is used (for example, against juveniles), so it is not entirely removed from the rights-based scrutiny of the court.

8 This is, of course, a different document from the ECHR documents. The Charter, produced in December 2000, is a document containing human rights provisions 'solemnly proclaimed' by the European Parliament, the Council of the European Union and the European Commission; it is separate from the Strasbourg mechanisms. See: http://wwweuroparl.europa.eu/charter/docs/default_en.htm

9 See: http://alpha.bailii.org/eu/cases/ECHR/1999/171.html around para. 93.

10 'Slopping out' has largely been phased out but provision of flush toilets in shared cells scarcely assures freedom from degrading conditions (see, for example, *The Herald* (Glasgow), 6 November 2006). The right to vote is currently a controversial issue. The UK still deprives serving prisoners of the right to vote, but a European Court of Human Rights judgement in 2004 to which a serving prisoner applied upheld the petition, ruling that a blanket ban on prisoners was disproportionate to the legitimate aim being pursued and could be construed as an additional sanction. (See *Hirst v. United Kingdom* (74025/01) (unreported, 6 October 2005) ECHR (Grand Chamber).) As a result of this, in December 2006 the Government announced plans to review the situation and to engage in public consultation (*The Times*, 15 December 2006: 28).

11 For a range of views on the Halliday Report, see Rex and Tonry (2002).

12 This phrase expresses the same principle in UK thinking about probation and juvenile justice and is closely associated with the work of Andrew Rutherford in the 1980s.

13 Clear and Cadora use the term 'risk control' rather than risk elimination, but it is arguable that 'risk elimination' makes the distinction clearer (see Rutherford 1996).

Further reading

For an account of the modernisation of the Probation Service and the impact of this process on probation values see the quartet of articles produced by Bill McWilliams in the *Howard Journal of Criminal Justice*. These essays are seminal works on the changing value base within probation: (1983) 'The Mission to the English police courts – 1876–1936'; (1985) 'The Mission transformed: professionalisation of probation between the wars'; (1986) 'The English probation system and the diagnostic ideal'; (1987) 'Probation, pragmatism and policy'.

Brian Williams's (1995) edited collection of essays about *Probation Values* is important insofar as the contributors review some of the effects of the modernising processes within probation. Essentially, the contributors argue that some of the traditional values of the social work profession offer protection against the worst excesses of politically imposed change. They look at social work values within equal opportunities, training, court reports and throughcare for example, as well as at specific areas of practice in relation to alcohol, drugs and sexual offending.

Readers would do well to follow the later debates about values in the *Howard Journal of Criminal Justice* too since they move on from social work values to consider other possibilities: Nellis (1995a) 'Probation values for the 1990s'; James (1995) 'Probation values for the 1990s – and beyond?'; Spencer (1995) 'A response to Mike Nellis: probation values for the 1990s'; Nellis (1995b) 'The third way for probation: a reply to Spencer and James'.

Mike Nellis and Loraine Gelsthorpe explore 'Human rights and the probation values debate' in Chui and Nellis (2003) *Moving Probation Forward. Evidence, Arguments and Practice*. Although the present essay draws on this earlier one some elements of the argument are necessarily truncated while other points have been expanded and so it would be worth consulting the earlier essay too.

References

Allan, R. (1990) 'Punishment in the community', in P. Carter, T. Jeffs and M. Smith (eds), *Social Work and Social Welfare Yearbook 2*. Milton Keynes: Open University Press.

Ashworth, A. (1995) 'Principles, practice and criminal justice', in P. Birks (ed.), *Pressing Problems in the Law, Vol. 1: Criminal Justice and Human Rights*. Oxford: Oxford University Press.

Ashworth, A. (2002) *Human Rights, Serious Crime and Criminal Procedure*. London: Sweet & Maxwell.

Atkinson, D. (2004) 'The What Works debate: keeping a human perspective', *Probation Journal*, 5 (3): 248–52.

Auld, Lord Justice (2001) *Review of the Criminal Courts of England and Wales*. London: Stationery Office.

Bobbio, N. (1995) *The Age of Rights*. Cambridge: Polity Press.

Bottoms, A. (1995) 'The philosophy and politics of punishment and sentencing', in C.M.V. Clarkson and R. Morgan (eds), *The Politics of Sentencing Reform*. Oxford: Clarendon Press.

Bottoms, A.E. (2003) 'Restoration and retribution in international criminal justice: an exploratory analysis', in A. von Hirsch, J. Roberts, A. Bottoms, K. Roach and M. Schiff (eds), *Restorative Justice and Criminal Justice: Competing or Reconcilable Paradigms?* Oxford: Hart.

Braithwaite, J. (1989) *Crime, Shame and Integration*. Cambridge: Cambridge University Press.

Braithwaite, J. (1999) 'Restorative justice: assessing optimistic and pessimistic accounts', in M. Tonry (ed.), *Crime and Justice, A Review of Research, 25*. Chicago: University of Chicago Press.

Braithwaite, J. and Pettit, P. (1990) *Not Just Deserts: A Republican Theory of Criminal Justice*. Oxford: Oxford University Press.

Burnside, J. and Baker, N. (eds) (1994) *Relational Justice: Repairing the Breach*. Winchester: Waterside Press.

Butterworth Report (1972) *Report of the Butterworth Enquiry into the Work and Pay of Probation Officers and Social Workers*, Cmnd 5076. London: HMSO.

Carlen, P. (2002) 'Penal politics and the new vocabularies of expert and commonsense knowledge', in P. Carlen (ed.), *Women and Punishment: The Struggle for Justice*. Cullompton: Willan.

Cheliotis, L. (2006) 'How iron is the iron cage of new penology?', *Punishment and Society*, 8 (3): 313–40.

Cheney, D., Dickson, L., Fitzpatrick, J. and Uglow, S. (1999) *Criminal Justice and the Human Rights Act 1998*. Bristol: Jordan.

Christie, N. (1982) *Limits to Pain*. London: Martin Robertson.

Christie, N. (1993) *Crime Control as Industry*. London: Routledge.

Chui, W.H. and Nellis, M. (eds) (2003) *Moving Probation Forward. Evidence, Arguments and Practice*. Harlow: Pearson Longman.

Clarke, J., Gewirtz, S., Hughes, G. and Humphrey, J. (2000) 'Guarding the public interest? Auditing public services', in J. Clarke, S. Gewirtz, E. McLaughlin (eds), *New Managerialism. New Welfare?* London: Sage, in association with the Open University.

Clear, T. and Cadora, E. (2001) 'Risk and community practice', in K. Stenson and R.R. Sullivan (eds), *Crime, Risk and Justice: The Politics of Crime Control in Liberal Democracies.* Cullompton: Willan.

Collins, H. (2007) 'A consideration of discretion, offender attributes and the process of recall', in N. Padfield (ed.), *Who to Release? Parole, Fairness and Criminal Justice.* Cullompton: Willan.

Coyle, A. (2003) *Treating Prisoners with Humanity: Some Questions of Definition and Audit.* London: International Centre for Prison Studies.

Dignan, J. (2005) *Understanding Victims and Restorative Justice.* Maidenhead: Open University Press.

Dworkin, R. (1986) *A Matter of Principle.* Oxford: Clarendon Press.

Eadie, T. and Winwin Sein, S. (2005/6) 'When the going gets tough, will the tough get going? Retaining staff in challenging times', *VISTA*, 10 (3): 171–9.

Easton, S. and Piper, C. (2005) *Sentencing and Punishment. The Quest for Justice.* Oxford: Oxford University Press.

Faulkner, D. (1989) 'The future of the Probation Service: a view from government', in R. Shaw and K. Haines (eds), *The Criminal Justice System: A Central Role for the Probation Service.* Cambridge: University of Cambridge, Institute of Criminology.

Faulkner, D. (1994) 'Relational justice: a dynamic for reform', in J. Burnside and N. Baker (eds), *Relational Justice: Repairing the Breach.* Winchester: Waterside Press.

Faulkner, D. (2001) *Crime, State and Citizen.* Winchester: Waterside Press.

Faulkner, D. (2002) 'Probation, citizenship and public service', in D. Ward, J. Scott and M. Lacey (eds), *Probation: Working for Justice*, 2nd edn. Oxford: Oxford University Press.

Feldman, D. (2006) 'Human rights, terrorism and risk: the roles of politicians and judges', *Public Law*, pp. 364–84.

Fordham, M. and de la Mare, T. (2001) 'Identifying the principles of proportionality', in J. Jowell and J. Cooper (eds), *Understanding Human Rights Principles.* Oxford: Hart.

Freeman, M. (2002) *Human Rights: An Interdisciplinary Approach: Key Concepts.* Cambridge: Polity Press.

Fullwood, C. (1999) 'Civil liberties and social control in the community', *VISTA*, 5 (1): 4–14.

Garland, D. (1995) 'Penal modernism and postmodernism', in S. Cohen and D. Bloomberg (eds), *Punishment and Social Control.* New York: Aldine.

Garland, D. (1996) 'The limits of the sovereign state: strategies of crime control in contemporary society', *British Journal of Criminology*, 36 (4), 445–71.

Garland, D. (2001) *Culture of Control: Crime and Social Order in Contemporary Society.* Oxford: Clarendon Press.

Gelsthorpe, L. (2001) 'Accountability: difference and diversity in the delivery of community penalties', in A.E. Bottoms, L. Gelsthorpe and S. Rex (eds), *Community Penalties: Change and Challenges.* Cullompton: Willan.

Gelsthorpe, L. (2005) 'Back to basics in crime control: weaving in women', in M. Matravers (ed.), *Managing Modernity. Politics and the Culture of Control.* London: Routledge.

Gelsthorpe, L. and Padfield, N. (eds) (2003) 'Introduction', in *Exercising Discretion. Decision-Making in the Criminal Justice System and Beyond.* Cullompton: Willan.

Glover, J. (1999) *Humanity: A Moral History of the Twentieth Century.* London: Jonathan Cape.

Goffman, E. (1959) *The Presentation of Self in Everyday Life.* London: Penguin.

Gray, G. and Salole, A. (2006) 'The local culture of punishment: an ethnography of criminal justice worker discourse', *British Journal of Criminology*, 46 (4): 661–79.

Halliday Report (2001) *Making Punishments Work: Review of the Sentencing Framework for England and Wales*. London: Home Office.

Hannah-Moffat, K. (2000) 'Prisons that empower: neo-liberal governance in Canadian women's prisons', *British Journal of Criminology*, 40 (3): 510–31.

Harding, J. (2000) 'A community justice dimension to effective probation practice', *Howard Journal of Criminal Justice*, 39: 132–49.

Haxby, D. (1978) *Probation: A Changing Service*. London: Constable.

Henham, R. (1998) 'Human rights, due process and sentencing', *British Journal of Criminology*, 38 (4): 592–610.

Her Majesty's Chief Inspector of Prisons for England and Wales (2001) *Annual Report 1999–2000*. London: Home Office.

HMI Probation (2006) *An Independent Review of a Serious Further Offence Case: Anthony Rice*. London: HMIP.

Home Office (1991) *Custody, Care and Justice*, White Paper. London: HMSO.

Home Office (1992) *Three Year Plan for the Probation Service 1993–96*. London: HMSO.

Home Office (1996) *Protecting the Public: The Government's Strategy on Crime in England and Wales*. London: HMSO.

Home Office (2006) *Rebalancing the Criminal Justice System in Favour of the Law-abiding Majority*. London: HMSO.

Hood, C., Scott, C., James, O., Jones, G. and Travers, T. (1998) *Regulation Inside Government: Waste-Watchers, Quality Police and Sleaze Busters*. Oxford: Oxford University Press.

Hoy, C. (2005/6) 'Probation one hundred years on', *VISTA*, 10 (3): 138–45.

Hudson, B. (2001) 'Human rights, public safety and the Probation Service: defending justice in the risk society', *Howard Journal*, 40 (2): 103–13.

Ignatieff, M. (2000) *The Rights Revolution*. Toronto: House of Anansi Press.

James, A. (1995) 'Probation values for the 1990s – and beyond?', *Howard Journal of Criminal Justice*, 34 (4): 326–43.

Klug, F. (2002) 'Human rights: a common standard for all peoples?', in P. Griffith and M. Leonard (eds), *Reclaiming Britishness*. London: Foreign Policy Centre.

Lacey, M. (2002) 'Justice, humanity and mercy', in D. Ward, J. Scott and M. Lacey (eds), *Probation: Working for Justice*, 2nd edn. Oxford: Oxford University Press.

Liddle, M. and Gelsthorpe, L. (1994) *Organisational Arrangements for the Local Delivery of Crime Prevention*, Home Office Crime Prevention Series. London: Home Office.

Liebling, A. and Arnold, H. (2004) *Prisons and Their Moral Performance. A Study of Values, Quality and Prison Life*. Oxford: Oxford University Press.

Liebling, A. and Price, D. (2003) 'Prison officers and the use of discretion', in L. Gelsthorpe and N. Padfield (eds), *Exercising Discretion: Decision-Making in the Criminal Justice System and Beyond*. Cullompton: Willan.

Loader, I. and Sparks, R. (2002) 'Contemporary landscapes of crime, order, and control: governance, risk and globalisation', in M. Maguire, K. Morgan and R. Reiner (eds), *The Oxford Handbook of Criminology*, 3rd edn. Oxford: Oxford University Press.

Lynch, M. (1998) 'Waste managers? The new penology, crime fighting, and parole agent identity', *Law and Society Review*, 32 (4): 839–69.

Lynch, M. (2000) 'Rehabilitation as rhetoric: the ideal of reformation in contemporary parole discourse and practices', *Punishment and Society*, 2 (1): 40–65.

Margalit, H. (1996) *The Decent Society*. Cambridge, MA: Harvard University Press.

Matheson, D. (1992) 'The Probation Service', in E. Stockdale and S. Casale (eds), *Criminal Justice Under Stress*. London: Blackstone.

Matthews, R. (2002) 'Crime control in late modernity', *Theoretical Criminology*, 6 (2): 217–26.

May, T. (1991) *Probation: Politics, Policy and Practice*. Buckingham: Open University Press.

McLaughlin, E. (2001) 'Managerialism', in E. McLaughlin and J. Muncie (eds), *The Sage Dictionary of Criminology*. London: Sage.

McWilliams, W. (1983) 'The Mission to the English police courts – 1876–1936', *Howard Journal of Criminal Justice*, 22: 129–47.

McWilliams, W. (1985) 'The Mission transformed: professionalisation of probation between the wars', *Howard Journal of Criminal Justice*, 24: 257–74.

McWilliams, W. (1986) 'The English probation system and the diagnostic ideal', *Howard Journal of Criminal Justice*, 25: 41–60.

McWilliams, W. (1987) 'Probation, pragmatism and policy', *Howard Journal of Criminal Justice*, 26: 97–121.

McWilliams, W. (1992) 'The rise and development of management thought', in R. Statham and P. Whitehead (eds), *Managing the Probation Service*. Harlow: Longman.

Millard, D. (1991) 'Letters', *Probation Journal*, 38: 218.

Morris, N. (1992) 'Desert as a limiting principle', in A. von Hirsch and A. Ashworth (eds), *Principled Sentencing*. Edinburgh: Edinburgh University Press.

Mortimer, E. and May, C. (1997) *Electronic Monitoring in Practice: The Second Year of the Trials of Curfew Orders*, Home Office Research Study No. 177. London: Home Office.

National Probation Service (NPS) (2001) *A New Choreography*. London: National Probation Service.

Nellis, M. (1995a) 'Probation values for the 1990s', *Howard Journal of Criminal Justice*, 34 (1): 19–44.

Nellis, M. (1995b) 'The third way for probation: a reply to Spencer and James', *Howard Journal of Criminal Justice*, 34 (4): 350–3.

Nellis, M. (2001) 'Community values and community justice', *Probation Journal*, 48 (1): 34–8.

Nellis, M. and Gelsthorpe, L (2003) 'Human rights and the probation values debate', in W.H. Chui and M. Nellis (eds), *Moving Probation Forward. Evidence, Arguments and Practice*. Harlow: Pearson Education.

O'Malley, P. (1999) 'Volatile and contradictory punishment', *Theoretical Criminology*, 3: 175–96.

O'Neill, O. (2002) *A Question of Trust. The BBC Reith Lectures 2002*. Cambridge: Cambridge University Press (online at: http://www.bbc.co.uk/radio4/reith2002).

Packer, H. (1969) *The Limits of the Criminal Sanction*. Stanford, CA: Stanford University Press.

Petrunik, M.G. (2002) 'Managing unacceptable risk: sex offenders, community response and social policy in the United States and Canada', *International Journal of Offender Therapy and Comparative Criminology*, 46 (4): 483–511.

Power, M. (1997) *The Audit Society: Rituals of Verification*. Oxford: Oxford University Press.

Pratt, J. (1996) 'Governing the dangerous: an historical view of dangerous offender legislation', *Social and Legal Studies*, 5 (1): 21–36.

Prison Reform Trust (1997) *Electronic Tagging: Viable Option or Expensive Diversion?* London: Prison Reform Trust.

Probation Boards' Association (2005) *Value* (June) Survey: What values should be at the heart of a service that deals with offenders in today's society? See: http://www.probationboards.co.uk/dox/PBA%20value%20book%20V.2.pdf

Raynor, P. (2003) 'Evidence-based probation and its critics', *Probation Journal*, 50 (4): 334–45.

Rex, S. (2005) *Reforming Community Penalties*. Cullompton: Willan.

Rex, S. and Tonry, M. (2002) *Reform and Punishment: The Future of Sentencing*. Cullompton: Willan.

Roberts, J. and Hough, M. (2002) *Changing Attitudes to Punishment. Public Opinion, Crime and Justice*. Cullompton: Willan.

Robinson, G. (2002) 'Exploring risk management in probation practice: contemporary development in England and Wales', *Punishment and Society*, 4 (1): 5–25.

Robinson, G. and McNeill, F. (2004) 'Purposes matter: examining the "ends" of probation', in G. Mair (ed.), *What Matters in Probation*. Cullompton: Willan.

Rusche, G. and Kirchheimer, O. (1968) *Punishment and Social Structure*. New York: Russell & Russell.

Rutherford, A. (1989) 'The mood and temper of penal policy: curious happenings in England and Wales in the 1980s', *Youth and Policy*, 27: 27–31.

Rutherford, A. (1993) *Criminal Justice and the Pursuit of Decency*. Winchester: Waterside Press.

Rutherford, A. (1996) *Criminal Policy and the Eliminative Ideal*, Inaugural Lecture. Institute of Criminal Justice, University of Southampton.

Scott, J.R.M. (2002) 'Human rights: a challenge to culture and practice', in M. Lacey, J. Scott and D. Ward (eds), *Probation: Working for Justice*. Oxford: Oxford University Press.

Senior, P. (1989) 'Radical probation: surviving in a hostile climate', in M. Langan and P. Lee (eds), *Radical Social Work Now*. London: Unwin Hyman.

Sentencing Advisory Panel (October 2001) *The Use of Extended Sentences: Advice to the Court of Appeal*. London: Sentencing Advisory Panel.

Silverman, J. and Wilson, D. (2002) *Innocence Betrayed: Paedophilia, the Media and Society*. Oxford: Polity Press.

Simon, J. and Feeley, M. (1995) 'True crime: the new penology and public discourse on crime', in T. Bloomberg and S. Cohen (eds), *Punishment and Social Control*. New York: Aldine de Gruyter.

Sparks, R. (1996) 'Penal austerity: the doctrine of less eligibility reborn?', in R. Matthews and P. Francis (eds) *Prisons 2000*. Basingstoke: Macmillan.

Spencer, J. (1995) 'A response to Mike Nellis: probation values for the 1990s', *Howard Journal of Criminal Justice*, 34 (4): 344–9.

Strathern, M. (ed.) (2000) *Audit Cultures. Anthropological Studies in Accountability, Ethics and the Academy*. London: Routledge.

Tonry, M. and Rex, S. (2002) 'Reconsidering sentencing and punishment in England and Wales', in S. Rex and M. Tonry (eds), *Reform and Punishment: The Future of Sentencing*. Cullompton: Willan.

Turner, B. (2006) *Vulnerability and Human Rights*. University Park, PA: Pennsylvania State University Press.

Williams, B. (ed.) (1995) *Probation Values*. Birmingham: Venture Press.

Woolf, Rt Hon. Lord and Tumim, His Honour Judge Stephen (1991) *Prison Disturbances April 1990: Report of an Inquiry by the Rt Hon. Lord Justice Woolf (Parts I and II) and His Honour Judge Stephen Tumim (Part III)*, Cm. 1456. London: HMSO.

Zimring, F. E. and Hawkins, G. (1995) *Incapacitation: Penal Confinement and the Restraint of Crime*. New York: Oxford University Press.

Chapter 18

Working for and with victims of crime

Brian Williams and Hannah Goodman

Introduction

Early studies in the field of victimology began in the 1940s and concentrated on developing typologies of victim characteristics and behaviour, often emphasising the extent to which victims were seen as contributing to their own victimisation. This was challenged by the rise of the feminist movement in the 1970s which raised awareness of the treatment of victims of rape, child abuse and domestic violence within the criminal justice system and questioned the early victimologists' assumptions and methodology (see Williams 2005b). This period saw the creation of the first refuges for female victims of domestic violence. It also saw the creation of the Rape Crisis movement (Mawby and Walklate 1994).

An increased awareness of the effects that crime can have on victims also played a part in the creation of Victim Support in 1974. Victim Support is now a national charity that offers emotional support to victims and witnesses of crime across the UK and Ireland. Victim Support also campaigns to raise awareness of the needs of victims of crime.

The victims' movement began to gather impetus over the next few years and the standards of service that victims could hope to expect from criminal justice agencies and Victim Support were first drawn together by the Victim's Charter in 1990. The Charter, despite introducing the requirement for the Probation Service to work with victims of crime as well as offenders, introduced very few actual rights for victims (Williams 1999c). Concerns remained that victims were left feeling uninformed about the progress of their case and that the system was 'geared more to the needs of practitioners and offenders than to those of victims and witnesses' (Office for Criminal Justice Reform 2004: 4).

Recent years have again seen moves aimed to place victims and witnesses at the 'heart of the criminal justice system' (Jackson 2003). This has led to a number of developments such as the Domestic Violence, Crime and Victims Act 2004 and the Code of Practice for Victims of Crime introduced by it. This chapter will explore recent changes within the field of probation work and explore whether these have had a real impact on the experiences of victims of crime.

Probation work with victims

Probation work with victims of crime in England and Wales has come a long way since the introduction of the Victim's Charter in 1990. The requirements of the Charter made fairly substantial new demands upon the Probation Service at a difficult time without any extra resources being provided, and initially they were not fulfilled to a high standard in most areas. Having said that, it is important to add that in subsequent years, and certainly since the late 1990s, the service given by probation staff to those victims with whom they are required to work has become increasingly consistent, professional and highly valued. There is a continuing debate about what level of service can and should be provided, but the basic demands of the relevant legislation are being met throughout the National Probation Service, and legal requirements to provide a service have progressively increased as the number and types of victims covered by the law have been amended.

This chapter will discuss the issues in relation to probation work with victims in the same order as in this introduction, covering:

- victim contact work;
- victims and probation reports;
- offender supervision and group work;
- relationships between probation and the victims' organisations;
- restorative justice;
- staff training issues.

The main responsibility of the Probation Service in relation to victims concerns the sharing of information in cases where the offender is in prison or on licence or parole after release. The history of probation contact work with victims has been recounted elsewhere (Williams 1999; Crawford and Enterkin 2001; Tudor 2002), and it is summarised only briefly here. Suffice it to say that until the arrival of the Victim's Charter, most probation workers had only occasional contact with victims of crime and no policy framework within which to locate such work. The Charter required probation services to offer victims, their relatives and survivors of the victims of very serious offences (initially only those where the offender was sentenced to life imprisonment) the opportunity to receive and provide information about the offence, its effects upon them and their views and concerns about the offender. A revised Charter in 1996 made this service more widely available, covering the victims of violent and sexual offences where the perpetrator was sentenced to four years or more in prison. Combined with an upward drift in sentence lengths, this instantly changed the provision from one which affected only a few hundred people each year into a major new service to thousands of people who had been the victims of crime.

As mentioned above, implementation was initially inconsistent and patchy, but this could not continue once the arrangements were widened to apply to so many more cases. Circular instructions on the implementation of the provision were first issued in 1994, new National Standards covered victim issues for the first time in 1995, and the victim contact service was put on a statutory basis under the Criminal Justice and Court Services Act 2000 (which also reduced the minimum prison term covered to one year, considerably increasing the numbers of victims eligible for the service with effect from 2001). Meanwhile, the National Probation Inspectorate looked into the quality of the service being provided in a thematic inspection in 2000 (HMIP 2000) which was followed up by another similar piece of work three years later (HMIP 2003). The reports of these inspections made a powerful case for greater clarity and uniformity in service provision, and many of their recommendations were implemented by the Home Office and the National Probation Service. The second inspection report noted that staffing had increased appropriately in order to allow services to meet their new responsibilities but called for more and better staff training. It also reiterated the concern expressed in the previous report that the National Probation Service was not collecting race and ethnicity data on victims, which is required for fair and effective service delivery.

Alongside direct victim contact work, the Probation Service began to take victims into account in other aspects of its work. The 1995 National Standards (mentioned earlier) made it clear that reports for criminal courts should reflect the impact of offences upon victims and detailed guidance on implementing this requirement was subsequently issued. Individual and group work with offenders increasingly reflected the need both to protect victims of crime and to try and shift the offenders' attitudes towards them. Indeed, some group work programmes began to be designed in consultation with victims' organisations.

Since the mid-1970s, probation staff had been involved in the management of victims' organisations (this applied particularly to Victim Support, which made it a requirement for recognition of local schemes that the relevant criminal justice agencies be represented on their management committees, but also in some cases to Rape Crisis centres, women's refuges and other, smaller, campaigning and self-help victims' organisations). As well as sitting on committees, these links also sometimes involved probation representatives in the supervision of staff and in delivering volunteer training. In some cases, however, pressure of work and lack of clarity about their role and the priority it should be given reduced probation representatives to a passive or symbolic role, and contacts were not as strong as either organisation might have wished. They were strengthened again in many areas from the mid-1990s by the need to agree protocols on information exchange and to provide mutual support in delivering victim contact work, particularly in cases where voluntary agencies were already in contact with the victims with whom probation staff needed to work. There was a growing recognition on the part of the Probation Service that the victim agencies had an important part to play in helping it to make effective contact with the victims of serious crime and formal partnership agreements were made in a number of areas.

Probation staff representation was also built into the multi-agency youth offending teams (YOTs) established under the Crime and Disorder Act 2000. This meant that probation workers regained a central role in the supervision of offenders aged 10–17, a task which had been taken away from probation services in an earlier reorganisation of youth justice. In the process, probation officers working in and managing YOTs became responsible for delivering a range of new court orders, many of which included an element of reparation to victims. Thus the move towards restorative justice began to have an impact upon probation staff.[1] In 2003, the Home Office launched a consultation about the possible role of restorative justice in the adult criminal justice system and subsequently introduced a pilot project (discussed below) and new legislation in this area (Home Office 2003a; NPS 2003b).

Much of the new work was delivered by specialist staff, but generic probation officers increasingly had to deal with issues affecting victims of crime. For some, this was a difficult cultural change. Many probation officers traditionally saw themselves as social workers with offenders, and resisted working with victims at all. Newly qualified staff who had not trained as social workers were nevertheless ill-prepared for victim work by a training programme which still emphasised work with offenders and whose curriculum made only passing references to victims, mostly in the context of reducing the risk offenders pose to victims (see also Chapter 8, in this volume).[2]

The Victims' Code of Practice was released in 2005. The Probation Service is one of the agencies which have a statutory duty under this to provide a service to victims of crime. However, this states the duties of local probation boards and that the duties set out in the Criminal Justice and Court Services Act will be placed under the 'oversight of the Parliamentary Commissioner for Administration', also known as the Parliamentary Ombudsman (Cabinet Office website), and does not expand on the responsibilities that were laid out in the Act. The Ombudsman is responsible for investigating 'complaints that injustice has been caused by maladministration on the part of government departments or other public bodies' (Cabinet Office website) and so will be responsible for investigating when the requirements of the Code of Practice are not met.

Victim contact work

A number of aspects of victim contact work vary from one place to another. This is partly because at least two different models of how the work should be delivered grew up during the early days when no official guidance about how it might best be done had yet been issued (described by Crawford and Enterkin (1999: 47) as a 'policy vacuum'). As a result, victim contact work is undertaken by different levels of staff, sometimes by specialists but often by generic workers, and there is a wide range of views about how intensively probation staff should work with victims under these arrangements. Essentially, victim contact work involves making contact with victims soon after the offender is sentenced and offering continuing contact should the victims wish to be kept informed and to be consulted.

To begin with the range of *models of delivery,* the fundamental and unresolved question is whether victim contact work should be undertaken by the same worker who supervises the offender in the case, by another member of staff such as a court probation officer who also has other responsibilities involving work with offenders, or by someone who specialises in working with victims. Where specialists are employed, they are often Probation Service officers whose status makes it difficult for them (at least in the case of newer staff) to challenge qualified and senior colleagues' views and decisions. The first thematic inspection report (HMIP 2000: chapter 4) recognised these issues but took the view that there was insufficient evidence available for the Inspectorate to favour one approach over the others. Although the number of victims interviewed for the inspection was small, it is noteworthy that the research the inspectors undertook found that one approach did not yield higher levels of victim satisfaction than another. Similarly, Crawford and Enterkin (1999) found equally high levels of victim satisfaction in two areas operating different models.

Much depends upon how well the staff are trained and supervised (discussed in the penultimate section of this chapter below), how well the work is resourced and the associated issue of how broadly the victim contact task is interpreted within the agency. As far as the *intensity of contact* is concerned, practitioners need to be sensitive to the individual needs of victims. Victims in serious cases (and in some less serious cases where they have reacted badly to being victimised for one reason or another[3]) are likely to expect staff to spend long periods of time with them, which is easier to accommodate in some areas than in others, partly according to the managerial choices made about models of delivery of the work. Specialist staff may be more likely to appreciate the need to find time to become involved in emotionally demanding relationships with victims than officers who also have a relationship (often long-standing) with the offender in the case. A worker who is asked to view video footage of a murder victim by the person's surviving relatives, or to look at photograph albums and similar mementoes, can hardly walk away. The employment of specialist victim workers makes it more likely that staff will find time to meet such demands, and if they are well supervised, it is also less likely that they will over-identify with victims and experience role conflicts: as the inspection report dryly noted, 'some staff operating in the role of supervising officer and victim contact officer experienced problems in containing the demands inherent in the two roles' (HMIP 2000: 33).

In at least one area (Leicestershire and Rutland) a psychologist is brought in by the service to provide regular, independent clinical supervision of staff in the probation and police services who work directly with victims. Staff participation is mandatory but the content of the discussions is confidential. This is intended to help protect staff from stress, secondary victimisation or over-identification with the victims with whom they work.

What is clear is that the task is not a narrowly bureaucratic one: while it is mainly about providing victims with information and collecting information from them for use within the probation and other criminal justice services, it has an emotional content which makes a purely administrative approach unacceptable. In some areas, the work is undertaken by a senior probation officer, in others by main grade staff and elsewhere by probation service officers. The emotional intensity of some contacts raises questions about the appropriateness of employing (for example, as in one area) community service officers whose main experience involves supervising offenders undertaking unpaid work in the community to carry out the work with victims. It may not require a qualification in probation or social work, but it certainly requires sensitivity, understanding of the criminal justice system and specialised preparatory training. The inspection report in 2003 drew attention to the need to improve staff training in this area (HMIP 2003a). There is, however, a need for more research on victims' views of the different models, of the ability of staff to offer an appropriate service to victims and of how their needs can best be met. Some areas have sophisticated quality measurement arrangements in place, undertaking regular user satisfaction surveys and externally facilitated focus groups of victims of specific types of offence, while others do not.

In 2004 MORI was commissioned by the National Probation Service to undertake a study of victims' views of the Probation Victim Contact service. Of the 437 people interviewed, around half felt quite or very satisfied with the service that they had received. Overall, victims were satisfied with the service they had received from their victim contact officer, how easy it was to contact their officer and the information that they were given such as explaining prison sentences and parole decisions (NPS 2004). Participants did, however, express less satisfaction in other respects, feeling that they were not always kept informed at all stages of their offender's sentence (MORI 2004: 3). While only 46 per cent of participants were satisfied with the treatment that victims receive throughout the criminal justice system, 81 per cent were satisfied with the treatment they received from the Victim Contact Service (MORI 2004: 7).

Important issues in relation to equality of access to services still need to be addressed. Not all probation areas have strong links with voluntary sector victim agencies, but these are necessary if referrals are to be made in appropriate cases (HMIP 2000). The specific needs of gay and lesbian victims and victims of homophobic violence are not met in many areas, and practice needs to be improved in relation to ethnic minority victims and victims of racist hate crime (HMIP 2000; Knight and Chouhan 2002). Indeed, only a few innovative probation areas are experimenting with more effective responses to hate crimes and the relevant statistics are still not being collected by the National Probation Service despite the Inspectorate's recommendation that they should be (HMIP 2003a). However, a number of areas have widened the categories of victims for whom they offer to provide contact, to include all victims of imprisoned offenders in racially aggravated cases regardless of sentence length.

Victim contact work appears to offer an effective response to a number of the demands which victims of crime commonly make of the criminal justice system:

- to be heard, and treated with dignity, fairness and respect (see Williams 1999a; Wemmers 2002);

- to be provided with information about the criminal justice system and the outcome of their case, and protected from 'secondary victimisation' by criminal justice agencies (see for example Maguire and Kynch 2000);
- in certain cases, to be provided with or referred for counselling or support to address the emotional impact of the offence (Williams 1999a);
- to be protected from further victimisation, especially where there is concern that the same offender might revictimise them (Zedner 2002).

The victim contact arrangements have led to radical changes in the ways in which prisoners are dealt with, as well as improving the service provided to victims. The most obvious examples relate to parole and resettlement. Parole is now usually conditional upon satisfactory reports on victim contact in relevant cases (i.e. those where the victim wished to maintain contact with the Probation Service during the offender's sentence), and the conditions under which prisoners are released frequently include requirements derived from concerns expressed by victims when they are contacted by the Probation Service. Such conditions can include a requirement not to reside in or visit certain areas, or not to attempt to contact specified individuals. The days when victims and their families would move house because they wanted to avoid contact with the offender after release from prison have almost gone: victim contact arrangements mean that it should now normally be the offender's plans which must be changed in recognition of the victim's fears or wishes.[4] Clearly, this has implications for civil liberties: offenders' freedom of movement can be severely impaired (see below). One of the key issues for staff training is achieving an appropriate balance between the human rights of the parties concerned. Increasingly, staff need to be aware of the key legal judgements in this area. It is also important to recognise that there is no automatic trade-off, improving the rights of victims achieved by reducing the rights of offenders. In any event, the two groups are not discrete, but overlapping (Elias 1993; Williams 2005a; Rumgay 2004; Boswell 2000; Farrall and Maltby 2003).

Conditions imposed upon offenders after their release from prison must not be excessive and cannot infringe their human rights without due justification. For example, the case of a life sentenced prisoner who was originally released on condition that he did not visit his home city went to judicial review and the life licence was amended to exclude him from the area of the city in which the victim's parents lived, but allowed him to seek work in and visit his own family in the city. Thus the case law dictates that conditions need to be precise and justified, balancing the rights of the offender and those of the victims or survivors (Stone 2002; NPS 2003c).

Changes implemented following the introduction of the Domestic Violence, Crime and Victims Act 2004 increase the remit of Victim Contact workers. The Act contains provision for information to be passed on to a victim or their representative where their offender is convicted of a violent or sexual offence and a 'relevant sentence is imposed' (chapter 2, s. 35). For the first time provision is made to give information to the victims of mentally disordered offenders (previously omitted from the contact arrangements because of concerns about breaching medical confidentiality). The Act allows information to be given to victims where an offender has been convicted of a violent or sexual offence, and has been given a hospital order with a restriction order due to the person being found not guilty by reason of insanity.

The information that can be passed on to victims includes whether the person will have any conditions placed upon their release, including those regarding contact with the victim and their family, and information that the local probation board deems relevant to the case. In the cases of victims of mentally disordered offenders, they can be given information regarding conditions that would be put in place if their offender is released from hospital (2004 Act: chapter 2, s. 35). These provisions are detailed in the Probation Circular 42/2005; however, this service will not be available retrospectively to victims of mentally disordered offenders who were sentenced before 1 July 2005 (Probation Circular 42/2005: 3).

Additional changes to the work that is carried out with victims may come following the merger of the Prison and Probation Services into the National Offender Management Service. A statement made by Paul Goggins, the Minister for Probation and Prisons, stated that the introduction of NOMS would have a restorative justice element allowing for offenders to make reparation to their victims (Batty 2004). This may also be carried out by the payment of a surcharge by the offender, as introduced by the Domestic Violence, Crime and Victims Act 2004 (s. 161A).

Victims and probation reports

The requirement to address victim issues in Pre-Sentence Reports (PSRs) was mentioned earlier. There are also important issues relating to the incorporation of victim perspectives in reports on parole and other forms of early release from prison.

In relation to PSRs, the 1995 National Standards (the regulations which govern probation officers' work) introduced an important change. They made it clear for the first time that the section of court reports dealing with the analysis of the offence must assess its consequences 'including the impact on the victim', and provide 'an assessment of the offender's attitude to the victim and awareness of its consequences, drawing attention to any evidence of acceptance or minimisation of responsibility, remorse or guilt and any expressed desire to make amends' (Home Office 1995: 9–10). While these areas would have been discussed in many reports prior to 1995, the new National Standards requirement reinforced the importance of addressing victim perspectives and made doing so much more routine practice for probation staff preparing court reports. The subsequent (2000) edition of the National Standards repeated these requirements and also required details of any reparation undertaken by the offender to be added to reports. In the most recent (2005) edition of the Standards, these requirements are restated, and reference is also made to Victim Personal Statements (VPS) (of which more below).

Unfortunately, the Probation Service is dependent upon other agencies for objective information about the impact of offences upon victims,[5] and they do not always supply it in a timely or accessible way. An inspectorate report in 2000 found that information from the Crown Prosecution Service failed to reach report writers in time to be included in court reports in up to 50 per cent of cases, although work was in hand in some areas to improve communications (HMIP 2000). This remains a problem in many parts of the country. If neither the CPS file nor a VPS is available to report writers, they have to fall back on the offender's account, which is unlikely to be objective and in many cases will be inaccurate, unless probation officers go to the trouble of obtaining information directly from the police. Contact with the police is becoming more common, especially in the case of more serious offences and high-risk offenders (Dominey 2002). However, tracking down the officer concerned can be time-consuming and difficult, and this avenue is only likely to be explored in more serious and sensitive cases.

An area where the Probation Service's work with victims has come under fire has been in the field of 'domestic' violence. In 2004 a report was released which found that these victims were not receiving a good service in many cases. Only a fifth of cases reviewed by inspectors were rated as demonstrating 'good' practice, and none were rated higher than this. In approximately two-thirds of cases, the risk to the victim's safety was not being adequately considered. In some cases, information was not being stored securely which could allow for it to be 'accessed inappropriately' (HMIP 2004; *The Guardian* 2004; BBC News 2004).

The introduction of VPSs nationally in 2001 should have improved matters, but in practice they seem to be routinely passed on by the police to other criminal justice agencies only in a minority of areas.[6] Indeed, some probation practitioners have never seen such a report.[7] This is particularly unfortunate in view of the reference in the 2005 National Standards to the need to draw upon this source of information in appropriate cases when compiling PSRs (Home Office 2005). It is difficult to understand why police officers are routinely compiling these reports but they are then not being used for the purposes for which they are drawn up: it may be that a future thematic inspection will investigate this issue. It is particularly concerning in view of findings elsewhere that victims did not trust the criminal justice system to use such information in their interests (Erez and Rogers 1999): if it were widely known that VPSs are not being passed on to those agencies for which they are prepared, many more victims would be likely to withdraw their cooperation from the scheme. Nevertheless, probation workers writing reports do have access to the offenders' attitudes and the issues raised in the 1995 Standards remain pertinent. While there is little knowledge about how to measure empathy towards victims or what relationship it has to subsequent behaviour (Dominey 2002) it remains useful to discuss the consequences of an offence and the offender's personal responsibility for these, and to look out for evidence of minimisation, denial or the opposite.

There are also problems in obtaining relevant information when it comes to reports about prisoners. Unless victims covered by the contact arrangements discussed earlier have agreed to remain in contact with probation, it can be difficult (and it may not be appropriate to try) to trace them. This is complicated by data protection legislation and agency rules about information sharing

(Tudor 2002). At the other end of the scale, offenders sentenced to fewer than 12 months in custody, who may be eligible for early release with electronic tagging, may well be reported upon without access to victim information, although the report on which the decision is made is supposed to cover the proximity of the proposed release address to the victim and the potential for contact between victim and offender after release. In general, however, victim information does seem to be available to those preparing parole and other reports on prisoners, and it is clearly being acted upon. As noted earlier, a judicial review has meant that prisoners are frequently released subject to stringent conditions in relation to where they may live, places they may not visit and even specific activities in which they may not take part with a view to protecting previous or potential victims (see NPS 2003c).

Another recent development has been the introduction of Multi-Agency Public Protection Panels (MAPPPs). MAPPPs allow for agencies to share information on those offenders deemed to pose a high risk to society, and to work together to manage this risk. Goodey notes that as victims are now given the opportunity to make a 'contribution' to this process, victims themselves now have a corresponding responsibility towards community safety (2005: 135).

Victim issues in offender supervision and group work

Consultation with victims is a feature of some offender groups attended as a requirement of community supervision, and victim organisations are often consulted about the design or involved in the delivery of 'victim awareness' sessions. The most highly developed example of the first is in Scotland, where programmes for male 'domestic' violence offenders involve women partners in a number of ways. The Edinburgh Domestic Violence Probation Project (DVPP) works with male perpetrators referred by criminal justice social workers (the Scottish equivalent of probation officers – see Chapter 5). The process begins with an assessment in which contact is normally made with the man's partner or ex-partner who is invited to provide information in confidence which places the current offence in context. This information may be used in court reports, but will not usually be attributed. The liaison process continues if the man is sentenced to the groupwork programme:

> Following sentence, DVPP asks the partners of men who are required to attend the programme to act as consultants throughout the life of the order – whether or not they continue to live with the man. The men understand that this is a condition of their probation order. (Morran *et al.* 2002: 186)

Thus the individual victim's safety is monitored, the offender is held accountable and victims are given a voice in the supervision process. Clearly, these are sensitive situations and intensive work is usually required with both victims and offenders. The project has been running successfully since 1990 and over 400 women victims have been consulted during this period in a process designed with advice from Women's Aid. In England and Wales, an Integrated Domestic Abuse Programme (IDAP) was piloted in a number of areas and is now being implemented nationally. Like the Scottish projects, it involves contact with the known victims of the offenders taking part in the programme by women's safety workers. These may either be probation staff or (more commonly) employees of voluntary agencies such as 'domestic' violence or Victim Support schemes. This is an accredited programme, meaning that it has been validated by research as likely to be effective, and approved for national use, and involves 27 weekly sessions (Home Office 2003c). This programme was heavily influenced by the Duluth model, also drawn upon for the design of the DVPP, and it builds upon a range of previous group-work programmes in England and Wales (see Mullender 1996).

Another accredited programme has been developed in two men's prisons, based on groups run by the Correctional Service in Canada. Although similar to IDAP, it differs in that it was specifically designed for incarcerated offenders and is more intensive, involving 25 or 26 sessions delivered two or three times a week. In order to ensure continuity, work is now under way to adapt the programme so that it can be delivered in community settings, initially with a view to allowing men coming out of prison part way through it to complete the programme post-release. Ultimately, it may also become available as an alternative programme for serious offenders in the community.

Group work with offenders may involve specific sessions or exercises aimed at eliciting greater awareness of the impact of the offending upon victims. These are undertaken with a view to challenging offenders' denial or minimisation of the harm they have done to their victims, or indeed of the very individuality of the victim. In order to subject victims to the pain and indignity involved in many crimes, the offender shields himself or herself psychologically from this by using mental tactics such as dehumanising the victim, denying or minimising the harm done, denying personal responsibility or elevating their own needs above those of the victim.[8] Many attempts to change offenders' behaviour involve challenging these cognitive processes. Specific references to the victim experience are frequently employed as part of this approach, although less direct approaches are more common in many of the accredited cognitive-behavioural group-work programmes.

For example, programmes on Enhanced Thinking Skills and Drink Impaired Driving both emphasise offenders' moral and critical reasoning skills, the consequences of offending and the value of seeing the perspectives of others. These approaches are clearly relevant to victim awareness, but they bring victim issues to offenders' attention rather more subtly than victim awareness sessions as such. Similarly, many groups use a storyboard approach to offence analysis which encourages members to think about the implications of their actions for the other parties involved. Programmes such as Enhanced Thinking Skills also address stereotyping and its consequences, both in terms of the damage it can do to offenders and to victims. Anger management programmes tend to encourage participants to analyse not only the process of arousal and outburst, but also the effects and impacts of expressing anger in different ways. Indeed, accredited programmes will form an integral part of the work of the Probation Service as they are one of the 12 requirements that can form part of an order following the implementation of the Criminal Justice Act 2003 (Criminal Justice Act – New Community Orders website).

Treatment programmes for imprisoned sexual offenders typically involve selected inmates in group sessions which are structured to create opportunities for 'offenders to face up to their responsibilities, with other group members challenging what is being said' (Spencer 1999: 90). Thus, rather than colluding with offenders' rationalisations and excuses, a regular meeting is set up at which other offenders will join the therapists in challenging these and presenting alternative perspectives including effects upon victims and the ripple effect upon others affected by offences, such as the offender's family. Many such groups include 'homework' such as drafting (unsent) letters of apology to victims, the aim being to assess the extent to which the offender has become able to take responsibility, recognise the harm done and stop blaming others. Some victim advocacy groups have criticised this focusing of resources upon offenders, while others argue that nothing will change if offenders are not challenged and treated. Having said this, victims and offenders are far from being entirely discrete and separate groups, as noted above, and furthermore many offenders will also need help with issues arising from their own victimisation, often as children, and the unresolved rage arising from this which may well have contributed to their offending behaviour (Boswell 2000; Farrall and Maltby 2003; Rock 2002; Webb and Williams 2000; Rumgay 2004).

One experiment in implementing restorative justice within prisons included the provision of victim awareness training for inmates of a local prison in Bristol. A coordinator was appointed for one year to run victim impact groups and to prepare victims and prisoners for direct meetings. Because the project was based in a local prison, however, turnover was rapid and the coordinator decided to concentrate upon group work and following up individual group members to ensure that they had the opportunity to take part in any restorative initiatives being run in the prisons to which they were subsequently allocated. Referrals were received from the Probation Service's victim liaison workers and from Victim Support, as well as men applying to join groups in response to publicity within the institution. Other priorities prevented the worker from undertaking any staff training about the project and its aims (Wootton 2004).

Similarly, a voluntary agency runs mediation awareness sessions in a long-term adult prison, Moorland. Staff from the agency, Remedi, work with offenders in groups: suitable participants are identified by prison staff as part of the sentence planning process, and those assessed as good prospects for mediation are invited to join the group. In the few cases where inmates come from the local area, there is a data-sharing agreement with the police service, but in the majority of cases onward referrals have to be made to the Probation Service in the home area, which can then take forward the arrangements for mediation in appropriate cases. Often, letters of apology are prepared by the offender and forwarded to the outside probation officer or victim liaison worker. A few face-to-face mediations have been held at other prisons to which inmates have been sent after taking part in the group, and in the long term this option should become more widely available to victims in the community.

Another initiative in adult prisons involves the use of family group conferences. This brings sentenced offenders and victims together in carefully prepared, structured meetings which provide opportunities for reconciliation and resolution of conflicts. The project is experimental, providing an opportunity through action research to evaluate the effectiveness of this model, including any impact upon offender recidivism (Sutton 2002).

In remand prisons in London where inmates are awaiting trial, another experiment is under way. This involves family group conferences reaching agreements between victims and offenders who admit offences of burglary and robbery; the agreement is then sent by the project to the probation officer preparing the pre-sentence report, so that the court can take it into account. By the end of 2003, 250 cases had reached the stage of holding a family group conference, and a similar sized control group of offenders with whom the project has not worked is being used for comparative purposes.

In a number of other prisons (including Bristol, discussed above), restorative justice consultants have trained staff in restorative approaches with a view to developing not only victim-offender work but also new approaches to disciplinary procedures and disputes within the prison (Braithwaite 2002). Clearly, restorative justice in prisons is the subject of a number of pilot projects and of a series of attempts to evaluate its effectiveness, albeit not very systematic or well-resourced. These activities need coordinating if the impetus is to be sustained.

There is also a danger that group work aimed at eliciting empathy towards victims neglects to take account of the links between victimisation and offending. Some offenders may need to work through issues relating to their own victimisation before they can begin to contemplate putting themselves psychologically into the position of their own victims. In the current climate in which making such links is politically unpopular, the needs of some groups of offenders may be neglected, with future consequences for repeated offending and further victimisation (see Rumgay 2004).

Relationships between probation and victims' organisations

A number of authors have suggested that statutory criminal justice agencies and central government find it easier to deal with Victim Support than with the other, sometimes more militant, victims' organisations (Williams 1999a; Mawby 2003; Spalek 2003). The original version of the Victim's Charter listed a range of helping organisations to which victims might turn, but excluded any reference to Rape Crisis or Refuge. Neither was there any reference to local groups such as those assisting victims of racial harassment in a number of areas, or to organisations such as Support After Murder and Manslaughter (SAMM).[9] While this was subsequently corrected to some extent, it indicated a degree of official reticence about endorsing the work of self-help, often feminist-inspired or anti-racist agencies which have valuable services to offer. Only very recently has some (temporary) central government funding been made available to such services. On the ground, this distant relationship has been replicated in many areas in the Probation Service's attitude towards self-help victims' organisations. Although the probation inspectorate's second survey found 'evidence of good working practices with VSSs' (i.e. victim support schemes – HMIP 2003: 68), no reference is made to other victim support agencies, which suggests that these are regarded as, at best, less important than Victim Support itself. If the Probation Service does not take steps to correct this bias, it will remain open to accusations that it is interested only in doing business with what has been characterised as the 'respectable' end of the spectrum of victims' organisations (Mawby and Walklate 1994), leaving the more outspoken organisations out in the cold. In practice, the issues raised by campaigning victims' organisations may often prove helpful in ensuring that victims receive a better deal, and it might well be profitable to open channels of communication with agencies other than Victim Support. In at least one area, a network or federation of organisations working with victims has been formed to facilitate inter-agency contact (the Victims and Witnesses Action Group in Leicester: see Goodman 2004).

Probation Service relationships with Victim Support have been formalised in most areas by means of probation involvement in the management of local VSSs, and often, also, by written agreements or protocols between the agencies. In some cases, there are service-level agreements specifying the level of services to be provided by VSSs in return for funding from the Probation Service (HMIP 2003). These cover, for example, arrangements whereby Victim Support volunteers work alongside probation staff to deliver victim contact services (as in Northumbria – see Crawford and Enterkin 1999). There is a difficult balance to be struck between blurring the boundaries between state and non-governmental organisations, coopting independent voluntary organisations and developing trusting relationships where the expertise of the voluntary sector is recognised and rewarded (Crawford 2000). Victim Support nationally has discouraged the trend towards direct service provision on behalf of statutory agencies, arguing that this is not the responsibility of the voluntary sector and that victims should not be used in the service of offender rehabilitation (Reeves and Mulley 2000). It has also been suggested that Victim Support, as a charity, is prohibited by law from undertaking statutory functions of the Probation Service (Harris 2003). However, this does not prevent close collaboration in a number of areas such as:

- reciprocal or joint training initiatives, whereby staff, volunteers and individual victims participate in training on victim awareness in general or on specific aspects of service delivery, and organisations share training materials and resources;

- referral of offenders to Victim Support for help with their issues as victims of crime, including claiming compensation in appropriate cases;

- support by victim support agencies for victims taking part in family group conferences or other restorative interventions (see below). (Harris 2003)

Restorative justice

There has been a dramatic increase in interest in restorative justice (RJ) internationally in recent years. This was reflected in youth justice legislation in New Zealand in 1989 and subsequently in a number of other jurisdictions, eventually followed by more limited legal changes to the youth justice system in England and Wales in 1998 and 1999 (although these were seen by some as a major movement towards restorative methods of doing justice: for opposing views, see Crawford and Newburn 2003; Smith 2003; see also Chapter 10, in this volume). More recently, the Government has once again begun experimenting with restorative approaches within the adult criminal justice system.[10] This intention was clear from a consultation exercise about RJ undertaken in 2003, which was rapidly followed by the announcement of a pilot project on the use of RJ as a method of diversion for adult offenders from court using the 'conditional caution' procedures of the Criminal Justice Act 2003 (Home Office 2003d; Clothier 2003). There is, however, some ambiguity in the official documents about which agency might be responsible for taking the initiative in respect of restorative cautions: at present the police, rather than probation, are seen as the lead agency.

The youth justice changes have impacted upon the Probation Service directly, because each YOT consists of staff from a number of agencies including probation (and many probation staff have also taken management posts within YOTs). At a time when the workload of the Probation Service was growing, but it was difficult to recruit qualified staff (see Chapter 4, of this volume), the loss of these staff was keenly felt. However, apart from this parochial concern, the new youth justice arrangements are likely to have had an impact upon the ways in which probation staff undertake and conceptualise work with victims, so the most significant aspects of the new system will be briefly described here.

The Crime and Disorder Act 1998 created YOTs themselves, along with a range of new court orders including reparation orders. These require young offenders to make direct or indirect reparation to victims in cases where the latter express a willingness to become involved. Reparation orders, although initially popular with the courts, were all but superseded by the provisions of the Youth Justice and Criminal Evidence Act 1999. This required youth courts to send almost all first offenders to a Youth Offender Panel composed of a YOT member (who might be the probation member of the team) and two community representatives. These panels administer referral orders which are normally expected to include an element of reparation. In practice, only a minority of victims have, for one reason or another, taken up the opportunity to become involved in panel meetings or direct reparation (Crawford and Newburn 2003). Some observers have suggested that reparation has become rather mechanistic and that victims have been sidelined. Nevertheless, youth justice practitioners are working directly and indirectly with victims and issues of victimisation to an unprecedented extent, and this experience will no doubt find its way back into the Probation Service as staff seconded to serve as members of YOTs return to their posts in probation. This has been the experience in at least some probation areas as a result of staff moving from specialist victim contact duties back into fieldwork.

Immediately following the consultation on the role of restorative justice with adult offenders, the Home Office commissioned a 15-month action research project to test the use of direct and indirect victim-offender mediation and community reparation with adult offenders and their victims as a diversion from court. The main evaluation criteria for the experiment were reducing offending, increasing levels of victim satisfaction, efficiency and effectiveness (Home Office 2003d). Reconviction rates of the offenders taking part were monitored, along with those of a control group.

The implications of the pilot projects mentioned above are difficult to predict. It is clear that the possibility of using probation staff to implement RJ approaches to the conditional caution is under consideration, but there are practical problems with this approach. Not least of these is the problem of probation caseloads becoming 'silted up' with relatively minor offenders when it needs to concentrate its attention upon diverting offenders of medium seriousness from custody. However, restorative conferences are currently convened in a number of areas by the police rather than probation, so the probation role might appropriately be a relatively minor one (Morgan and Smith 2003). In future, though, there is considerable scope for increased involvement in restorative interventions with more serious offenders, perhaps along the lines of successful projects with long-term prisoners in North America (Umbreit et al. 1999). There have been several experimental projects in prisons in the UK, some involving bringing victims into the prison to meet the offender, others arranging meetings between incarcerated offenders and surrogate victims who discuss the impact of offences on their lives, and yet others training staff or prisoners about mediation and supporting inmates who decide to write letters of apology (see, for example, Gray 1994; the brief descriptions of projects earlier in this chapter and www.remediuk.org). This is an area of work which can be expected to increase, although as yet it has depended upon short-term funding from a variety of sources. Much will depend upon the findings of evaluative, longitudinal research being undertaken by a team at Sheffield University.

More recently, a Criminal Justice System guide has been released entitled *Restorative Justice: Helping to Meet Local Needs*. This includes guidance on introducing RJ, including having a strategic approach, hiring and training of specialist staff and 'building on existing resources' (CJS 2005b: 17). Although additional resources have not been allocated for the development of RJ practices, there is clearly an acceptance and wish for these to become more widespread.

Staff training

The training required for probation work with victims has been under discussion for a number of years. In the early stages of implementing victim contact work, the Home Office took the unusual step of providing 'cascade' training at a national level in order to ensure that staff had a common basis of understanding about the task (Home Office 1996; HMIP 2000). Those who attended the courses were expected to provide similar training for the colleagues who had been unable to do so, for which a manual was provided. This initiative does not seem to have been repeated, however, and the training manual was not updated in the light of subsequent changes.[11] In the absence of further such central initiatives, a number of probation areas set up professional networks which bring victim workers together periodically to discuss areas of common concern, and the Association of Chief Officers of Probation established a national working group with practitioner representatives which raised issues formally with the Home Office. Although the group made specific recommendations with respect to staff training, these do not appear to have been systematically implemented.

The ACOP group was superseded in 2001 by a 'Victim CLAN' (one of a number of Centrally Led Action Networks, in this case including representation from Victim Support as well as probation managers and practitioners) and the National Probation Service issued very detailed practice guidance in 2001 (NPS 2001[12]) – although this is no substitute for staff training and it did not address training issues. Some areas also incorporated victim issues into regular training courses on work with long-term prisoners and into new staff induction courses (Nettleton *et al.* 1997). In a small number of areas, specialised training programmes were developed for victim liaison staff. Nevertheless, the Inspectorate report in 2000 found that only a minority of probation areas had effectively addressed 'staff learning, development, supervision and support needs' in relation to victim work (HMIP 2000: 16). It drew attention to the 1998 report mentioned above and pointedly quoted its recommendations at some length (HMIP 2000: 84–6).

The second inspection report also drew attention to the inadequacies of staff training for work with victims, and specifically recommended the development of a national training strategy (HMIP 2003: 11). It found that most case managers' level of awareness of 'the importance of the victim perspective in work with offenders was woefully inadequate' (*ibid.*: 44) and that the provision of training for those undertaking direct work with victims was at best patchy. These critical findings and the recommendation stand out in what is a broadly positive report: the inspectors appear to have been exasperated at the neglect of their (and others') previous recommendations in this area. They call for a consistent, national approach to training, and explicitly reject the existing Level 3 Criminal Justice NVQ as inadequate for these purposes. The reason given is that the staff interviewed said 'it did not cover their role adequately as it lacked a substantial victim component' (*ibid.*: 44). This is in the process of being remedied: regional training consortia have developed a new NVQ in Working with Victims, Survivors and Witnesses which should ensure that Probation Service officers undertaking victim contact work do so on the basis of some standardised preparatory training.

As far as probation officers' initial professional training is concerned,[13] there have been calls over a long period for at least basic victim awareness material and information about the probation task in working with victims to be covered as part of the two-year qualifying course (Aubrey and Hossack 1994; Nettleton *et al.* 1997; Williams 1999a; Williams 2002; Tudor 2002). The curriculum is already very full, however, and trainees have to complete both a degree and an NVQ within a two-year period. A consultation exercise was undertaken in 2000 and although amendments were suggested, reflecting the concern that victim issues are not required to be addressed in any depth, neither the NVQ competences nor the wider curriculum was changed in response to this (Nellis 2003).

Ideally, in our opinion, staff working with victims should receive training in a number of areas:

- the experience of victimisation and how it is likely to affect people;
- victims' needs and the services available;
- how to address offenders' attitudes towards victims, and how to challenge denial and minimisation of offences and belittling of the victim;
- the recent history of probation work with victims and the policy context;
- the law and current national and local policies relating to work with victims;
- the relevance of restorative justice and its application within probation and youth justice (Nellis 2003);
- anti-oppressive practice with victims (for example in relation to hate crimes, human trafficking and the targeting of particular groups for victimisation) and wider issues of professional values;
- effective engagement with victims;
- planning for case closure and referral to other agencies;
- opportunities to practise the skills required, for example using role-play or dramatised scenarios. (Williams, 1999b)

Delivering such training at an introductory level takes at least several days, and given the rapidity of change in this area of work, regular 'refresher' courses are also likely to be required. Some degree of standardisation needs to be introduced in order to ensure that all staff working with victims have at least a basic understanding of the issues involved and the techniques they need to apply. There is some doubt about the effectiveness of the 'cascade' model of training in this area, whereby one member of staff undertakes direct training and is expected to relay the learning to colleagues – but it saves money.

Conclusion

The requirements of the Victim's Charter made new and challenging demands upon the Probation Service. Although there were problems in implementing it, over a period of years this was achieved largely successfully. In the process, the whole culture of the Probation Service changed to accommodate the victim perspective, if not to the extent that many specialist staff and their colleagues in the victims' movement would wish. An important aspect of this was the development of links between the Probation Service and specialist colleagues in the police service so that relevant information about victims and offenders can be exchanged and shared staff training can be facilitated.

Her Majesty's Inspectorate of Probation has played an important role in these changes. Its 2000 inspection took place long enough after the initial phase of victim contact work for things to have settled down somewhat, and the report was timely in calling for resources and recognition for this massive new area of work. A new performance indicator was introduced, monitoring probation work with victims, although it operates by penalising underperforming areas rather than rewarding those which exceed the minimum required standards. The subsequent inspection emphasised the need for greater consistency, better staff training and proper attention to equal opportunities issues.

Inconsistency has bedevilled the Probation Service's work with victims of crime from the beginning. As far as victim contact work is concerned, this is hardly surprising given the range of models of service delivery and the consequent variations in levels of resources allocated to the work, intensity of contact with victims and types of staff involved. While it may be appropriate for services to vary according to local needs, these differences would seem less rational and planned than that. A particular anomaly has in the past been the exclusion from the victim contact arrangements of the victims of offences committed by mentally disordered offenders; however, recent changes to the law bring these cases into the victim contact system.

The implementation of the victim personal statement scheme appears to have been highly problematic, and it has had a substantial effect upon the Probation Service's ability to prepare court reports which take a victim perspective fully into account. Indeed, the exchange of information about victims between the various agencies of the criminal justice system is generally problematic.

Ways are being found to involve victims and representatives of victims' organisations in work with offenders, and this is an imaginative approach which should help to improve mutual understanding. Local probation areas seem to have developed good relations with Victim Support, but in many cases not with the whole range of other organisations working with victims.

Training issues clearly need attention, both in relation to in-service training for probation staff preparing court reports and working with victims and offenders, and in relation to initial professional training. Moves to bring the professional training of prison staff closer to the model employed in training probation officers under the new National Offender Management Service may make this easier to achieve. Staff supervision also needs to be improved, along with some degree of standardisation of the level of staff involved in direct work with victims.

Restorative justice offers a range of challenges. At the time of writing, it seems unlikely that the Probation Service will be given a major role in restorative approaches to work with victims and offenders under conditional cautions, but it appears that a variety of local initiatives will ultimately need either to be brought under central direction (if resources can be found) or else they will die out, as previous such projects eventually did when their funding expired.

The National Offender Management Service has been created without much (if any) thought being given to its impact upon victims of crime. There appears to be an assumption that integrated services can only serve their interests better – but mergers of this kind take time to settle down, and the interests of relatively marginal groups such as victims and those who work with them can easily be overlooked in the anxiety to meet centrally defined targets. The achievements of the previous two decades in improving the ways that victims' needs are met by probation staff could easily be lost in the maelstrom of change.

Acknowledgement

We would like to record our gratitude to Loraine Gelsthorpe and Alan Gray, who read and commented on an earlier version of this chapter and provided us with a number of useful contacts. Thanks also to Pam Barber, Stephen Bradley, Lawrence Clossick and Lindy Wootton for their help with specific points.

Notes

1 This was not the first time probation staff had taken such a role. Experimental projects involving victim-offender mediation with adult offenders were established in the mid-1980s and subsequently integrated into the work of two probation areas (West Midlands and West Yorkshire). The remaining pilot projects did not survive after the initial funding ran out, but the models developed were influential when victim work became part of the probation role again (Tudor 2002).

2 There were exceptions. The qualifying training for probation officers at De Montfort University, for example, includes an optional module on 'Working with Victims' (but this is not a requirement of the national curriculum). There will shortly be a Level 3 NVQ on Working with Victims, Survivors and Witnesses but this is designed for probation services officers – what used to be called 'ancillary staff' but now a major workforce – rather than those qualified as probation officers.

3 A whole range of predisposing factors may lead victims to cope less well than others in similar cases. Victims may be more vulnerable, for example, where victimisation is repeated and/or part of a pattern – the obvious example being hate crime. Bereavement, depression and other extraneous factors can also aggravate the effect of crime on victims.

4 These statements are qualified ('usually', 'normally') because a good deal seems to depend upon the membership of particular panels making parole decisions and the extent to which victim issues are highlighted varies.

5 For example, medical reports of injuries to victims, verified statements of expenses incurred by victims, details of the cost of repairing criminal damage, and so on.

6 Victim personal statements are taken by the police at the time of the initial enquiry, and can be updated subsequently (prior to an offender appearing in court). They are meant to be made routinely available to other criminal justice agencies (specifically the prosecution, Probation and Prison Services, YOTs and courts) to assist decision-making (Home Office, undated but published 2002).

7 The first author makes it a practice, when undertaking training on victimology and work with victims, to ask students and practitioners whether they have ever seen a VPS. Until recently, only police officers and former police officers ever responded positively. Since 2004, it is more common, but still not very common, for workers from other agencies to have seen one.

8 For detailed examples see Spencer (1999: 88–90).

9 SAMM now receives some financial support from the Home Office through the Victim Support national office with which it shares premises. A wide range of organisations in addition to Victim Support became involved in consultations such as *Speaking Up for Justice* (Home Office 1998) and the *Review of the Victim's Charter* (Home Office 2001), thus opening up the debate at national level.

10 A number of experiments were undertaken by local probation services in the late 1980s: see note 1.

11 At the time, probation services were told that changes had to be introduced in a 'resource neutral' context, i.e. no additional resources would be provided.

12 This was subsequently revised to reflect legal judgements and advice (NPS 2003c).

13 See note 2.

Further reading

For a practitioner/campaigner account of the issues in relation to working with victims of crime, we would strongly recommend Reeves and Mulley (2000) 'The new status of victims in the UK: opportunities and threats'. For a more academic view from a writer with long experience in this field, we would encourage readers to look at Rock (2002) 'On becoming a victim'. An account by a practitioner who has been involved in practice and policy development since the 1980s can be found in Tudor (2002) 'Probation work with victims of crime'.

In relation specifically to youth justice, an excellent overview is contained in the research-based evaluation by Crawford and Newburn (2003) *Youth Offending and Restorative Justice: Implementing Reform in Youth Justice*.

For those with an interest in victimology, see Goodey (2005) *Victims and Victimology: Research, Policy and Practice* or Williams (2005a) *Victims of Crime and Community Justice*.

References

Batty, D. (2004) *More Criminals to Say 'Sorry'*. See: http://society.guardian.co.uk/crimeandpunishment/story/0,,1133189,00.html (accessed 10 December 2004).

BBC news (2004) *Probation Fails Domestic Victims*. See: http://newsvote.bbc.co.uk/mpapps/pagetools/print/news.bbc.co.uk/1/hi/uk/3935169.stm (accessed 10 December 2004).

Boswell, G. (ed.) (2000) *Violent Children and Adolescents: Asking the Question Why*. London: Whurr.

Braithwaite, S. (2002) 'Developing practice in prisons', in Thames Valley Partnership, *Restorative Justice in Prisons: Resource Book and Report*. Aylesbury: TVP.

Cabinet Office, Propriety and Ethics Team (undated) See: http://www.cabinetoffice.gov.uk/propriety_and_ethics/parliamentary_ombudsman (accessed 17 December 2004).

Clothier, D. (2003) E-mail communication to members of the Restorative Justice Consortium on Home Office invitation to tender for pilot project, 30 October.

Crawford, A. (2000) 'Salient themes towards a victim perspective and the limitations of restorative justice: some concluding comments', in A. Crawford and J. Enterkin (eds), *Integrating a Victim Perspective within Criminal Justice*. Dartmouth: Ashgate.

Crawford, A. and Enterkin, J. (1999) *Victim Contact Work and the Probation Service: A Study of Service Delivery and Impact*. Leeds: University of Leeds Centre for Criminal Justice Studies.

Crawford, A. and Enterkin, J. (2001) 'Victim contact work in the probation service: paradigm shift or Pandora's box?', *British Journal of Criminology*, 41 (4): 707–25.

Crawford, A. and Newburn, T. (2003) *Youth Offending and Restorative Justice: Implementing Reform in Youth Justice*. Cullompton: Willan.

Criminal Justice Act 2003: New Community Orders. See: http://www.no8chambers. co.uk/articles/Community%20Orders.htm (accessed 1 April 2005).

Criminal Justice System (2005a) 'Victims' Code of Practice: Consultation'. See: http://www.homeoffice.gov.uk/docs4/COI_Victims%20Code_final_1.pdf (accessed 1 April 2005).

Criminal Justice System (2005b) *Restorative Justice: Helping to Meet Local Needs*. Home Office Communications Directorate.

Domestic Violence, Crime and Victims Act 2004. See: http://www.hmso.gov.uk/acts/ acts2004/40028--e.htm#35 (accessed 9 December 2004) and http://www.legislation. hmso.gov.uk/acts/acts2004/40028--c.htm (accessed 16 December 2004).

Dominey, J. (2002) 'Addressing victim issues in Pre-Sentence Reports', in B. Williams (ed.), *Reparation and Victim-Focused Social Work*. London: Jessica Kingsley.

Elias, R. (1993) *Victims Still*. London: Sage.

Erez, E. and Rogers, L. (1999) 'The effects of victim impact statements on criminal justice outcomes and processes: the perspectives of legal professionals', *British Journal of Criminology*, 39 (2): 216–39.

Farrall, S. and Maltby, S. (2003) 'The victimisation of probationers', *Howard Journal of Criminal Justice*, 42 (1): 32–54.

Goodey, J. (2005) *Victims and Victimology: Research, Policy and Practice*. Harlow: Pearson, Longman Criminology Series.

Goodman, H. (2004) 'Working towards a seamless service for victims and witnesses of crime in Leicester', *Community Safety Journal*, 3 (2): 32–5.

Gray, A. (1994) 'Direct and indirect mediation – prisoners meet with victims', *On Probation: The Staff Newsletter of Leicestershire Probation Service*, 1 (August): 6.

Guardian, The (2004) 'Probation Service "fails domestic violence victims"'. See: http:// society.guardian.co.uk/crimeandpunishment/story/0,,1271885,00.html (accessed 10 December 2004).

Harris, M. (2003) 'NAPO and Victim Support', *NAPO News*, 153 (October): 13.

HM Inspectorate of Probation (2000) *The Victim Perspective: Ensuring the Victim Matters*. London: Home Office.

HM Inspectorate of Probation (2003) *Valuing the Victim*. London: Home Office.

HM Inspectorate of Probation (2004) *Reducing Domestic Violence: An Inspection of National Probation Service Work with Domestic Violence Perpetrators*. London: Home Office.

Home Office (1995) *National Standards for the Supervision of Offenders in the Community*. London: Home Office.

Home Office (1996) *Training Materials for Contact with Victims*, Probation Circular 21/96. London: Home Office.

Home Office (1998) *Speaking Up for Justice: Report of the Interdepartmental Working Group on the Treatment of Vulnerable or Intimidated Witnesses in the Criminal Justice System*. London: Home Office.

Home Office (2001) *A Review of the Victim's Charter*. London: Home Office Communication Directorate.

Home Office (2003a) *Restorative Justice: The Government's Strategy*. London: Home Office.

Home Office (2005) *National Standards for the Supervision of Offenders in the Community*. London: Home Office.

Home Office (2005a) *Domestic Violence Programmes*, Probation Circular 49/2003. London: Home Office.

Home Office (2005b) *Restorative Justice: The Diversion Pilot*. London: Home Office. See: http://www.homeoffice.gov.uk/justice/victims/restorative/diversionpilot.html

Home Office (2005c) *The Victims' Code of Practice: Indicative Draft*. London: Home Office. See: http://www.cjsonline.gov.uk/downloads/application/octet-stream/code_of_practic_draft.doc (accessed 9 December 2004).

Home Office (undated) *The Victim Personal Statement Scheme: A Guide for Investigators*. London: Home Office. See: http://www.homeoffice.gov.uk/docs/guideinvestig.pdf

Jackson, J.D. (2003) 'Justice for all: putting victims at the heart of criminal justice?', *Journal of Law and Society*, 30 (2): 309–26.

Knight, C. and Chouhan, K. (2002) 'Supporting victims of racist abuse and violence', in B. Williams (ed.), *Reparation and Victim-Focused Social Work*. London: Jessica Kingsley.

Maguire, M. and Kynch, J. (2000) *Public Perceptions and Victims' Experiences of Victim Support: Findings from the 1998 British Crime Survey*. London: Home Office Research, Development and Statistics Directorate.

Mawby, R. (2003) 'The provision of victim support and assistance programmes: a cross-national perspective', in P. Davies, P. Francis and V. Jupp (eds), *Victimisation: Theory, Research and Policy*. Basingstoke: Palgrave Macmillan.

Mawby, R. and Walklate, S. (1994) *Critical Victimology: International Perspectives*. London: Sage.

Morgan, R. and Smith, A. (2003) 'The Criminal Justice Bill 2002: the future role and workload of the National Probation Service', *British Journal of Community Justice*, 2 (2): 7–24.

MORI (2004) *Views of the Probation Victim Contact Scheme*. London: National Probation Service.

Morran, D., Andrew, M. and Macrae, R. (2002) 'Effective work with abusive men', in B. Williams (ed.), *Reparation and Victim-Focused Social Work*. London: Jessica Kingsley.

Mullender, A. (1996) *Rethinking Domestic Violence: The Social Work and Probation Response*. London: Routledge.

National Probation Service (2001) *Victim Contact Work: Guidance for Areas*, issued with Probation Circular 62/2001. London: NPS.

National Probation Service (2003a) *Victim Contact Work: Revised Sections 6 (Stage 2) and 9 of the Guidance to Areas*, Probation Circular 29/2003. London: NPS.

National Probation Service (2003b) *Criminal Justice Act 2003*, National Probation Service Briefing. London: NPS.

National Probation Service (2003c) *Victim Contact Work: Guidance on Recent Court Judgments*, Probation Circular 28/2003. London: NPS.

National Probation Service (2004) *Views of the Probation Victim Contact Scheme*, Briefing 20. London: NPS.

Nellis, M. (2003) 'Probation training and the community justice curriculum', *British Journal of Social Work*, 33 (7): 943–59.

Nettleton, H., Walklate, S. and Williams, B. (1997) *Probation Training with the Victim in Mind: Partnership, Values and Organisation*. Keele: Keele University Press.

Office for Criminal Justice Reform (2004) *Increasing Victim's and Witnesses' Satisfaction with the Criminal Justice System*. London: Home Office.

Probation Circular 42/2005, *Extension of Victim Contact Scheme to Victims of Mentally Disordered Offenders – The Domestic Violence, Crime and Victims Act 2004*. London: National Probation Directorate.

Reeves, H. and Mulley, K. (2000) 'The new status of victims in the UK: opportunities and threats', in A. Crawford and J. Enterkin (eds), *Integrating a Victim Perspective within Criminal Justice*. Dartmouth: Ashgate.

Rock, P. (2002) 'On becoming a victim', in C. Hoyle and R. Young (eds), *New Visions of Crime Victims*. Oxford: Hart.

Rumgay, J. (2004) *When Victims Become Offenders: In Search of Coherence in Policy and Practice*. London: Fawcett Society. See: http://www.fawcettsociety.org.uk/documents/When%20Victims%20Become%20Offenders%20Report.doc

Smith, R. (2003) *Youth Justice: Ideas, Policy, Practice*. Cullompton: Willan.

Spalek, B. (2003) 'Victim work in the Probation Service: perpetuating notions of an "ideal victim"', in W.H. Chui and M. Nellis (eds), *Moving Probation Forward: Evidence, Arguments and Practice*. Harlow: Pearson Longman.

Spencer, A. (1999) *Working with Sex Offenders in Prisons and through Release to the Community: A Handbook*, Forensic Focus 15. London: Jessica Kingsley.

Stone, N. (2002) 'In court', *Probation Journal*, 49 (1): 66–7.

Sutton, K. (2002) 'Setting the scene in the modern Prison Service', in Thames Valley Partnership, *Restorative Justice in Prisons: Resource Book and Report*. Aylesbury: TVP.

Tudor, B. (2002) 'Probation work with victims of crime', in B. Williams (ed.), *Reparation and Victim-Focused Social Work*. London: Jessica Kingsley.

Umbreit, M.S., Bradshaw, W. and Coates, R.B. (1999) 'Victims of severe violence meet the offender: restorative justice through dialogue', *International Review of Victimology*, 6 (4): 321–44.

Webb, D. and Williams, B. (2000) 'Violent men in prison: confronting offending behaviours without denying prior victimization', in H. Kemshall and J. Pritchard (eds), *Good Practice in Working with Victims of Violence*. London: Jessica Kingsley.

Wemmers, J.-A. (2002) 'Restorative justice: the choice between bilateral decision-making power and third party intervention', in B. Williams (ed.), *Reparation and Victim-Focused Social Work*. London: Jessica Kingsley.

Williams, B. (1999a) *Working with Victims of Crime: Policies, Politics and Practice*. London: Jessica Kingsley.

Williams, B. (1999b) 'Initial education and training for work with victims of crime', *Social Work Education*, 18 (3): 287–96.

Williams, B. (1999c) 'The Victim's Charter: citizens as consumers of criminal justice services', *Howard Journal*, 38 (4): 384–96.

Williams, B. (2002) 'Introduction', in B. Williams (ed.), *Reparation and Victim-Focused Social Work*. London: Jessica Kingsley.

Williams, B. (2005a) *Victims of Crime and Community Justice*. London: Jessica Kingsley.

Williams, B. (2005b) 'Victims', in C. Hale, K. Hayward, A. Wahidin and E. Wincup (eds), *Criminology*. Oxford: Oxford University Press.

Wootton, L. (2004) *The Restorative Justice Project at HMP Bristol 2003–2004: An Experiential Account of the Project from the Coordinator's Perspective*, available from the author at: lindy@woottoncane.freeserve.co.uk

Zedner, L. (2002) 'Victims', in M. Maguire, R. Morgan and R. Reiner (eds), *The Oxford Handbook of Criminology*, 3rd edn. Oxford: Oxford University Press.

Chapter 19

Partnerships in probation

Judith Rumgay

At the time of writing this chapter, amid the confusion that has infused the aftermath of Patrick Carter's (2003) review of correctional services (Rumgay 2005), one element of policy intentions concerning its implementation has remained constant and appears likely to remain so. That element concerns the introduction of 'contestability' into the provision of community-based services for offenders. In so far as this term signifies a full-throated policy of contracting discrete elements of probation tasks to organisations outside the service itself, which may be reduced to the status of competitor for the right to deliver services that it has hitherto largely monopolised, it represents the ultimate extension of a market approach that originated in the early 1990s. There are two notable differences, however. Firstly, the terminology favoured hitherto has been the language of 'partnership' between the Probation Service and non-statutory organisations, with its connotations of mutual cooperation and advantage. The terminology now preferred, of 'contestability', points to competition, not only between non-statutory organisations, but also between the Probation Service and those organisations, for the work of delivering community-based correctional services. Secondly, where the introduction of financially contracted 'partnerships' pursued a policy of delegation to local areas to develop arrangements according to need and opportunity, the formation of the National Offender Management Service (NOMS) anticipates an emphasis on centralised needs assessment and purchasing by Regional Offender Managers (ROMs).

This chapter will continue to use the term partnership, since, as we shall see, it is more suited than the narrowly focused language of market contestability to encompass the contemporary criminal justice and social policy worlds in which multi-agency collaboration in a variety of forms has proliferated in an age of 'joined-up government'. Indeed, to some extent, a clear appreciation of partnership activity has been obscured by the proliferation of different forms that it has taken. However, this review of partnership development and its characteristics will inevitably raise a serious question as to whether the recent shift in terminology reflects a real shift in the tenor of relationships between the Probation Service – or the future NOMS – and those statutory and non-statutory organisations to which it is allied.

The chapter begins by describing the varieties of partnership activity in which the Probation Service is now an active participant. It moves on to examine the ingredients of effective partnership and finally speculates on the impact of current, post-Carter policy for the Probation Service within NOMS.

Which partnership?

The Probation Service has long been proud of its cooperative relationships with both statutory and non-statutory organisations at local level. It is not suggested here that this pride is misplaced. Nevertheless, as we shall see, perhaps the most notable feature of its activity since the early 1990s, when central directive rather than local initiative became more influential in partnership development, is the extent to which it has been driven by government mandate rather than the Service's internal values. Despite its frequent appeals to evidence-led policy and practice, Government eagerness to embrace partnership as a solution to many social ills, among which crime and community safety have figured prominently, outpaced from the beginning the sum of knowledge as to its effectiveness as a strategy for promoting law abidance. Moreover, its confidence resonated with a widespread common-sense consensus that partnership between organisations with overlapping interests was self-evidently a positive mechanism for advancing their goals (Home Office Standing Conference on Crime Prevention 1991). As a principle upon which to base crime policy, therefore, the partnership agenda met with little opposition.

The result has been a proliferation of diverse activities with rather little attention paid to the relationships between them or to their differing goals. We begin, therefore, by examining the forms of partnership in which the Probation Service is currently involved. These forms can be categorised as contractual relationships, multi-agency crime prevention, targeted groups and social planning and provision.

Contractual relationships

When, after several years of undertaking 'to ensure that there will be room in the prison system for every person whom the judges and magistrates decide should go there' (Whitelaw 1982), the Conservative government concluded that the ensuing prison population crisis could not be resolved fast enough or cheaply enough by its burgeoning building and refurbishment programme, it looked with renewed interest to community-based sentences. During those years of central neglect, the Probation Service had invested considerable energy in revitalising the declining popularity of the probation order through establishing a range of intensive supervision programmes designed to compete for prison-bound defendants, with notable success in driving up the proportion of serious and recidivist offenders on its caseload. Home Office statistics demonstrate this in two ways: showing a decrease in the proportion of previously unconvicted offenders placed on probation from 23 per cent in 1981 to 11 per cent in 1991; and showing an increase in the proportion of offenders with prior custodial experience placed on probation from 24 per cent in 1981 to 38 per cent in 1991 (Home Office 1993a). Government policy-makers thus found fertile soil for colonisation by the seeds of its strategy for 'punishment in the community' (Home Office 1988a). Contrary to the Probation Service's approach of developing a suite of intensive 'in-house' programmes, however, central policy included an expanded role for what the Home Office (1990a, 1990b) chose to call the 'independent sector' in the delivery of supervision services.

For some reason, the Home Office never acknowledged the source of its inspiration for this aspect of its policy in the legislation of the NHS and Community Care Act 1990, under which health and social services were to be contracted out from the public sector. The Home Office preferred the term 'partnership' to 'contracting' for its vision. The declared intent of policy, however, clearly borrowed the new paradigm for the organisation and delivery of health and welfare services: a shift from 'in-house' monopoly of programme provision to contracted interventions coordinated through case management. The Home Office was explicit in this aim: 'Probation officers must see themselves less as exclusive providers of services and facilities, and more as managers of supervision programmes' (Home Office 1990a). Successive documents reiterated and elaborated this theme, insisting that 'elements of a supervision programme could and *would* be provided by organisations or individuals outside the Probation Service' (Home Office 1990b, emphasis added).

The process of partnership development was initiated through the Supervision Grants Scheme (commonly known as SUGS), through which funds were awarded directly from the Home Office for 'independent sector' programmes to be developed in partnership with local Probation Service areas. Assessing the potential strength of applications for SUGS funding within the centre, at a distance from the localities in which they were based, proved problematic: in practice, it appears that the declared relationships between local probation areas and their new 'partners' often tended more to the theoretical than the substantial, leading to poor integration of projects into the mainstream of service delivery. It was not long before the Home Office concluded that it was sensible to devolve responsibility for partnership development to local probation areas (Home Office 1992). To prevent the Probation Service from defaulting on its new obligation to deliver partnership policy on the ground, the Home Office required all local areas to submit their plans for expenditure of a minimum 5 per cent of their revenue budgets on initiatives based on financial contracts with the 'independent' sector (Home Office 1993b, 1993c). This sector turned out, in effect, to be composed entirely of voluntary organisations, at least as far as studies involving national surveys of partnership developments could ascertain (Nellis 1995; Rumgay 2000). Target partnership spending was subsequently raised to 7 per cent, to include arrangements for accommodation schemes, which, since 2003, have been superseded by the Supporting People programme of multi-agency planning, commissioning and provision of services to assist vulnerable people in independent living (see further below).

After a period in which Home Office interest appeared to wane in favour of promoting multi-agency collaborations between the statutory services (Rumgay 2001), the level of 5 per cent direct funding of partnerships from Probation Service budgets has recently been reiterated (Home Office 2006). In explaining that the money is to be spent on the delivery of services to offenders, new guidance explains that '[a]ll resources deployed to voluntary, community and private sector organisations ... including payments under contract, grants, and dedicated resources in kind such as seconded staff, or training are eligible against the target' (Home Office 2006). This appears to mark a relaxation of the earlier exclusion of 'resources in kind' from partnership expenditure, which threatened pre-existing and often long-standing arrangements such as secondments of probation officers into substance misuse agencies. However, it is also to be noted that many of these secondment arrangements concerned statutory organisations such as community drug and alcohol teams (DATs), which appear still to be excluded from permitted partnership expenditure.

Notwithstanding its aforementioned satisfaction with conventional co-operative relationships with alternative agencies, the Probation Service initially greeted this particular form of mandated partnership with deep ambivalence. A study conducted in the early years of partnership development combined analysis of area strategy documents with a national telephone survey and three detailed case studies (Rumgay 2000). Conducted during the period in which probation officers were highly sensitive to the perceived potential of the partnership enterprise to undermine their job security, the study revealed large differences in the quality of partnership activity between areas. While the initiative produced examples of excellent practice, the threat to professional autonomy perceived by many probation officers contributed to negative responses ranging from indifference to outright hostility. Moreover, the inexperience of senior managers in developing and supporting contracted services contributed to early difficulties in resolving tensions between practitioners at ground level.

Nevertheless, the Probation Service's ability to protect its professional territory was a remarkable characteristic of early partnership development. Partnership strategy documents revealed a broad spectrum of activities from Citizen's Advice Bureau surgeries to furniture removal, among which the only clearly common feature was the absence of Probation Service interest in providing such services in-house. The most successful partnership contracts owed much to the demonstration of complementarity, rather than competition, between the Service and its new collaborators in terms of the division of professional roles. Indeed, the insecurity of many probation officers following the introduction of contractual partnerships appears naively to have underestimated the Service's resourcefulness in preserving its boundaries – unless one views current, post-Carter policy as proof of a long-term conspiracy to deprive staff of their jobs through market testing. While such a conspiracy theory would retrospectively justify their sensitivity, it seems unlikely that a sustained, coherent policy of incremental privatisation has survived the past 15 years intact, given the unremitting flux of most other aspects of government policy and legislation for criminal justice in general and the Probation Service in particular, in which change has appeared to be the primary consistent feature. Nevertheless, it has been notable that, since the early 1990s, probation officers have felt sufficiently threatened for their future that they have been induced to embrace a range of new duties under the effective practice initiative (Mair 2004) as well as a broadening partnership mandate (Rumgay 2004) with considerably less overt antagonism.

Confidence in its ability to protect its boundaries, recognition that voluntary sector workers had little interest in taking over core Probation Service responsibilities and a diminution of central interest in this particular variety of partnership were perhaps strong factors in a relaxation of probation officers' preoccupation with this threat to their autonomy during the later 1990s. We will return to the contemporarily revitalised topic of contracted supervision services later, but our focus now turns to the proliferation of multi-agency collaborations that have dominated partnership policy and activity since the mid-1990s.

Crime prevention

Throughout the 1980s, interest grew in the potential for preventing crime rather than dealing with its results, assisted by new criminological paradigms that emphasised situational opportunism in offending behaviour (Mayhew *et al.* 1976) and rational choice in offender decision-making (Clarke and Cornish 1985). Emerging approaches to situational crime prevention (e.g. Clarke 1980) and control of public disorder (e.g. Homel and Clark 1994) suggested the likely benefits of multi-agency collaboration rather than reliance on policing alone to achieve maximum effectiveness. Home Office initiatives to explore and promote the potential for multi-agency partnerships in crime prevention included establishing its Standing Conference on Crime Prevention in 1985, disseminating good practice examples (e.g. Home Office 1990c), and launching a major, long-running action research project entitled the Safer Cities Programme (DETR 2000; Tilley 1992).

As in the case of contractual partnerships, the early approach of facilitation by the Home Office was followed by mandate. The Crime and Disorder Act 1998, s. 5, imposed a duty on local councils, in cooperation with police and other relevant agencies, including probation, to develop and implement a strategy for reducing crime and disorder in their localities. These collaborative Crime and Disorder Reduction Partnerships (CDRPs) were required to publish crime reduction strategies based on local crime audits and consultation with interested groups. Some of these collaborations resulted in a voluntary widening of their remit from crime and disorder to include broader issues of community safety, such as traffic control (Phillips *et al.* 2000), illustrating the intuitive, albeit unproven (Home Office Standing Conference on Crime Prevention 1991) attractiveness of the partnership principle.

Several studies testify to the public relations capital that the Probation Service has accrued through its involvement in these collaborations. After the police, the Probation Service has played the most prominent role in supplying information for local audits, typically providing demographic data on offenders (Phillips *et al.* 2000). The Service's participation presumably also contributed to the relatively high priorities set for offender rehabilitation alongside enforcement and other strategies for prevention (Phillips *et al.* 2000). Moreover, it has established a reputation as being 'enthusiastic about community safety work' (Phillips *et al.* 2002: 10) and a helpful contributor to crime prevention partnerships (DETR 2000; Tilley 1992). As well as supplementing police data for crime audits, the Service's direct experience in dealing with offenders, its community focus, its interest in disadvantaged groups and its recognition of the complexity of victim-offender relationship offers a uniquely 'broad orientation to community safety/crime prevention' (Tilley 1992: 26). With these perspectives, the Service is well placed to assist partnerships to assimilate and respond to the concerns for quality of life that tend to infuse local residents' reports of their crime and disorder problems (Audit Commission 2006a; Mair and Jamel 2002; Clear and Cadora 2003). Thus, in a number of areas, it has taken advantage of an opportunity to demonstrate a broader competence in crime-related policy and practice than might be implied by its traditional remit for individual offender supervision.

Elsewhere, however, more equivocal findings on the Service's contribution are reported (HM Inspector of Constabulary 2000; Mair and Jamel 2002; Newburn and Jones 2002), again suggesting that its response has been uneven. It is unclear how far the Probation Service is culpable here. For example, Newburn and Jones's (2002) case studies of five CDRPs, supplemented by a broad national survey, reveals that the Probation Service was not included in preliminary consultations in some areas, despite its explicit inclusion in statute as a relevant agency. Furthermore, only 52 per cent of community safety coordinators responding to the national survey reported that consultation with the Probation Service was successful. Nevertheless, this apparently disappointing figure places the Probation Service third in rank against, predictably, the police (96 per cent) and police authorities (54 per cent), despite its exclusion from consultation in a number of areas. Somewhat curiously, this study does not list the Probation Service among agencies approached during the interview phase of data collection, so that probation officers' perspectives on their involvement, or lack of it, are unavailable. Thus, whether its absence was due to neglect on the part of the primary partners of police and local authorities or to inaction on the part of the Service itself is not explained. Failure to include, at least explicitly, the Probation Service in evaluative studies is noticed elsewhere. For example, in Bradley's (2002) survey of community safety partnerships, the only available category of agencies into which the Service might conceivably fall is the inaccurate and unlikely one of 'other council departments'. This neglect has been repeated at the practice level: for example, the majority of multi-agency domestic homicide reviews in London failed to invite a contribution from the Probation Service (Richards and Baker 2003).

Mitigation has been offered for the Service's absence from CDRPs. For example, there are 373 CDRPs in England and Wales (where they are called Community Safety Partnerships) (Audit Commission 2006a). Inevitably, then, the Service's participation is frequently limited by the multiplicity of local partnerships within single probation areas, creating problems of servicing all groups and constraints on its financial contribution. Geographical complexity, staff shortages and financial strictures rather than lack of commitment have been advanced as factors reducing the Probation Service's capacity for participation (Phillips *et al.* 2002).

Targeted groups

Multi-agency collaboration has become an increasingly popular approach to interventions with offender groups of special interest. The previous Conservative government initiated this trend in 1995 with its mandate for an integrated, multi-agency approach to drug control centring on the establishment of local DATs comprising senior representatives from health, social services, probation, police, education and relevant voluntary organisations. Once again, we see the determination of Government to see the implementation of policy in the requirement that DATs develop action plans to tackle drug problems in their localities. Indeed, the authorship of the document setting out this integrated policy sets a laudable example of collaboration between government departments (Lord President of the Council *et al.* 1995), contrary to earlier Conservative policy, which emphasised law enforcement as the primary route to drug control (Home Office 1988b).

The Crime and Disorder Act 1998 imposed a duty on local authorities, in collaboration with police and probation services, to ensure the availability of youth justice services in their areas. Specifically, each area was required to establish multi-agency youth offending teams (YOTs) for service delivery, drawing on practitioners from the police, probation, health, education and social services (see Morgan and Newburn, this volume). Evaluations of partnerships between YOTs and other service providers have found mixed benefits and problems (e.g. Minkes *et al.* 2005). Somewhat disconcertingly, a recent inspection of YOTs, led by the probation inspectorate, contained no direct comments on the Probation Service's involvement (HM Inspectorate of Probation 2004). A criticism common to most agencies, however, was a growing tendency to second inappropriately qualified and inexperienced staff, who were also often recruited directly by the YOTs, leading to a lack of professional identity and connection with the 'parent' organisation that contradicts the original policy ambition for combining specialist expertise.

One area in which service delivery in youth justice is developing an interesting lead is in revitalising the use of volunteers, a field of activity that in previous years was a strong feature of probation activity, but more recently has been in 'almost terminal decline' (Morgan 2006: 62; HM Inspectorate of Probation 2003: para. 13), a trend reportedly attributable to the mistaken assumption that volunteering has itself declined or, to the extent that volunteers are available, their contribution is of less value to a more professionalised service. These assumptions the YOTs have challenged with considerable success (YJB 2006: 6).

The Criminal Justice and Courts Services Act 2000 required Police and Probation Services jointly, as the responsible authority, to make arrangements for assessment and management of risks posed locally by known sexual, violent and other potentially dangerous offenders. As part of their implementation of this mandate, they were required to involve health and social services and local authority housing departments (Home Office 2001). The Criminal Justice Act 2003 added the Prison Service to the responsible authority. These multi-agency groups have enjoyed a bewildering variety of names (Maguire *et al.* 2001), currently being labelled as Multi-Agency Public Protection Arrangements or MAPPA (see Kemshall *et al.*, this volume). At least one source attributes much of the early pioneering practice developments in public protection prior to legislation, including inter-agency information sharing and liaison, to the Probation Service (Maguire *et al.* 2001). Again, the Service appears to have capitalised upon an opportunity for raising its profile as a contributor to community safety through these activities.

A recent evaluation of practice found that senior management from all key agencies was well represented on the strategic management boards that were established to monitor local MAPPA effectiveness (Kemshall *et al.* 2005). This represents a considerable advance on the patchy response to other multi-agency collaborations, for example in the areas of crime reduction and the Supporting People programme, perhaps attributable to the potentially high level of public interest in the management of serious offenders. Positive links were also developing with other multi-agency collaborations concerned with public protection issues, such as child protection. However, the evaluation found evidence of 'risk inflation', serving to connect less dangerous offenders rapidly to resources while detracting attention from those presenting the highest risk. And while partnerships recognised the importance of measuring the effectiveness of interventions and frequently claimed an impact on risk reduction, clear criteria for substantiating these assertions were undeveloped.

Social planning and provision

The popularity of partnership is not confined to criminal justice, but is increasingly spreading throughout a range of social welfare issues. An example of this is the Supporting People programme, launched in 2003, which was intended to provide housing-related support to sustain vulnerable groups in independent living via collaborative planning and commissioning through local government, probation, health, voluntary sector organisations, housing associations and other relevant agencies. A recent evaluation of the Supporting People programme acknowledges the general strength of Probation Service involvement (Audit Commission 2005a).

More specific evaluations of the progress of Supporting People are now emerging through published inspections of individual local programmes. As with CDRPs, the Probation Service's contribution is frequently hampered by lack of staff capacity to cover all meetings, particularly given the multiplicity of local authorities within individual areas (e.g. Audit Commission 2005b), as well as high staff turnover (e.g. Audit Commission 2006b, 2006c). However, in strongly performing programmes, this can potentially be compensated by developmental work undertaken outside strategy group meetings (e.g. Audit Commission 2004b). Moreover, where attendance is adequately supported, the probation representative's presence facilitates learning from different boroughs, thus turning a handicap into a strength (e.g. Audit Commission

2005b, 2006c). In strongly performing programmes, democratic governance arrangements permit effective participation in decision-making, Supporting People strategies are integrated into other aspects of local planning and crime reduction priorities are featured in service development (e.g. Audit Commission 2004b, 2005b). Indeed, the Probation Service's involvement in a range of crime-related partnerships, including DATs, domestic violence fora and CDRPs, facilitates its importance as a key coordinator of information contributing to local needs assessment and strategic planning (e.g. Audit Commission 2004b, 2006b).

Given that access to Supporting People provision is necessitated by the lack of alternative funding in the Probation Service for housing-related support for offenders, since its entire accommodation budget was transferred to the scheme, it is surprising to find, in at least one area, a lack of clarity 'about the nature of (its) representation on Supporting People and the role and accountability of probation personnel' (e.g. Audit Commission 2006b: 17). Such role confusion has at times appeared to be pervasive among all organisations within the core strategy group (e.g. Audit Commission 2006c). Where the Probation Service itself is unclear about the accommodation needs of offenders, its influence on provision is inevitably further reduced, even in relatively good local programmes (e.g. Audit Commission 2006b, 2006c). The Probation Service's ability to influence planning and commissioning is also weakened where local authorities fail to provide strategic leadership and to develop effective and democratic consultative relationships with their partners (e.g. Audit Commission 2004a, 2005c). In these circumstances, even regular attendance and active participation on the Service's part may yield little positive progress (e.g. Audit Commission 2005c).

The importance of sustaining Probation Service representation on core strategy groups cannot be overstated. In poorly performing programmes, the most challenging groups, including offenders and others vulnerable to criminal involvement such as the homeless and drug misusers, are often inadequately serviced (e.g. Audit Commission 2004a, 2005c). Failure to establish clear priorities against which to evaluate services produces an environment in which providers deliver according to their own preferences (e.g. Audit Commission 2004a), which are likely to favour less demanding client target groups. Conversely, the challenge to maintaining and developing the quality of housing-related support for the most vulnerable groups is further illuminated in the finding that the other primary partners of health and social services have, in some areas, inappropriately offloaded their statutory responsibilities for care to Supporting People providers, thus deflecting the costs of delivery (e.g. Audit Commission 2004a, 2005b). Such practices inevitably weaken the effective management of high-risk groups by placing the burden of care on housing support workers who are untrained for such roles.

A second example of the Service's involvement in social planning and provision can be found in the area of employment and training. Since 1998, the Probation Service has been required to broker multi-agency agreements for services to improve offenders' access to employment and training opportunities (Fletcher 2001). This is an interesting field of activity in that policy responsibility for community-based learning and skills provision for offenders was transferred from the Home Office to the Department for Education and Skills (DfES) in April 2004, with delivery based on partnership between the DfES Offenders' Learning and Skills Unit, the Learning and Skills Council and the National Probation Service (Home Office 2004a). This move suggests a significant shift towards integrating offenders into the mainstream of educational provision. However, the challenge of increasing the employment prospects of a group with complex needs is formidable, particularly when funding arrangements encourage the relevant agencies to focus on short-term outcomes (Fletcher *et al.* 1998).

But what is partnership for?

This accelerating demand for partnership development reflects growing appreciation that complex social problems, including crime, cannot be adequately addressed by the uncoordinated efforts of well-intentioned organisations working in isolation. Salutary experience in diverse fields including social welfare, drug prevention and public health has testified repeatedly to this apparently obvious point (Annie E. Casey Foundation 1995; Johnson *et al.* 1990: Orians *et al.* 1995). In their determination to enforce partnership, however, policy-makers appear to have identified a disappointing gap between principle and practice, evidenced in the inertia of many organisations that continue to protect autonomy at the expense of mutual advantage. Nevertheless the current explosion of 'collaboration mania' (Mattessich *et al.* 2001) threatens to undermine the value of a good idea through indiscriminate application. Experienced enthusiasts for the prevailing collaborative mood tend also to counsel the greatest caution in practical application (Annie E. Casey Foundation 1995; Huxham 1996; Mattessich *et al.* 2001).

A major pitfall in transforming this good idea into effective practice lies in the ambiguity of its purpose. While there appears to be universal agreement that partnership is a good thing, there is not necessarily a similar consensus as to precisely what it is good *for*. Indeed, very often, apart from value-laden assertions as to its anticipated benefits, partnership development has been a largely atheoretical process of local pragmatic adaptation to central demands. Nevertheless, an analysis of collaborative activity to date suggests at least three quite different conceptualisations of its purpose (Rumgay 2003).

Firstly, partnership may narrowly be understood as a redistribution of responsibilities, in which the responsibilities of one organisation are transferred to another (Reid 2001). This perspective may represent a positive appreciation of the expertise of alternative agencies along with financial inducement to those that might find engagement with offenders an unappealing prospect. However, it potentially underestimates the demands on alternative 'in-house' expertise in liaison, project support and quality maintenance in the delegating agency (Rumgay 2000; Reid 2001). Organisational accountability may further be compromised when different services, such as tenancy support, drug counselling and skills training, are dispersed among disparate agencies.

An alternative conceptualisation of partnership views it not as a *cause* of system fragmentation but as a *solution*, through effective integration of systems of social provision (Locke 1990; O'Looney 1997). This ideal, however, is easier to agree in principle than to achieve in practice, due largely to the inertia of organisations that find maintenance of the *status quo* to require considerably less effort than internal change (Agranoff 1991; Armstrong 1997). Even among those willing to take the challenge, diversity of opinion is likely to arise as to the precise form and depth of inter-agency relationships that are necessary to attain the goal of system integration. Possibilities range from mechanisms of liaison that preserve individual organisational autonomy to collective power-sharing, planning and resource commitment (O'Looney 1997; Reilly 2001). Moreover, despite its objective inefficiency, agency isolation has particular immediate advantages in saving resources by moving problematic clients between alternative social welfare and criminal justice systems, disguising through this perpetual motion between agencies what is in effect an abdication of responsibility (Pumariega *et al.* 1997).

Finally, at its most ambitious, partnership may be perceived as an opportunity for 'grassroots' empowerment of weaker organisations and individuals, including small local voluntary agencies and service users. An aspiration to nurture the local voluntary sector featured in several early probation area partnership plans and, indeed, many small organisations owe their origins to pioneer probation officers seeking to extend the range of local support services relevant to offenders. Drug misuse agencies are an example of provision that has often been inspired by probation officers' efforts in their communities (Rumgay 2000).

Empowerment of this nature is nevertheless not without challenges. For example, Women's Aid, as an organisation dedicated to campaigning on behalf of and providing assistance to women fleeing domestic violence, appears to be an attractive candidate for the Service's support. Indeed, that organisation has been keen to demand financial support for capacity building to enable small voluntary agencies to participate effectively in consultation and tendering for contracts to deliver services under the new vision for NOMS (Women's Aid 2005). Women's Aid points out, not unreasonably, that it, and organisations like it, are not funded to engage in policy consultation, despite the obvious necessity and burden of commenting on Government proposals pertinent to its cause. Empowerment for such organisations, therefore, implies funding for engagement in the policy process, for building capacity to compete in the market for service provision and for resourcing service delivery to performance standards (Women's Aid 2005). Empowerment, it seems, is not a cheap pathway to expanding the voluntary sector.

Moreover, vital differences on policy issues are not to be silenced through the process of empowerment. For example, Women's Aid, while supporting rehabilitative interventions with domestic violence perpetrators to an extent, also favours imprisonment as a means of holding offenders accountable, protecting present and future victims and recognising the harm caused to children: indeed, it presses for a domestic context to violence to be treated as an intrinsically aggravating factor to the offence (Women's Aid 2003a, 2004). While the organisation expresses concern about Government expectations of information sharing between partners as a potential hazard to victim safety

(Women's Aid 2005), elsewhere it strongly advocates information sharing between the family and criminal courts to enhance victim protection and for information about an offender's post-release plans to be discussed with victims (Women's Aid 2004). The organisation strongly opposes the use of restorative justice interventions in domestic violence cases (Women's Aid 2003b).

It is not the purpose of this chapter to debate these arguments in themselves or to suggest that they are erroneous, but simply to point out that each and every one presents a complex and potentially combative issue for the Probation Service to resolve in its dealings with a prospective partner, given its necessarily holistic approach to securing the interests of both offenders and victims. For example, Women's Aid's preference for holding offenders accountable through prosecution and imprisonment contradicts general Probation Service interests in assisting projects that pursue diversion from criminal justice processes: indeed the latter approach might be acceptable to the many women who do not want their abusive partners pursued through the courts but simply for the violence to stop (Hoyle 1998). Similarly, the tension between public interest in victim protection and citizen's rights to confidentiality, which, as we have just seen, may be a source of internal confusion within an organisation, has received inadequate attention in government enthusiasm for the benefits of collaboration (Perri *et al.* 2006). Even in cases of multi-agency domestic homicide reviews, agencies have withheld information on grounds of confidentiality (Richards and Baker 2003), yet perhaps also to protect themselves against criticism.

While none of these issues are necessarily irresolvable, it should be borne in mind that this is only one of many potential partner organisations with which the Service may engage. A full-throated partnership approach, particularly one based on agency empowerment, accommodates differing viewpoints on the definition and resolution of social problems in ways that promote the collaborative enterprise, enabling all participants to contribute. Yet no commentator, however enthusiastic for the principle of partnership enterprise, has ever suggested that this is easy: not only are agreements between multiple partners difficult to forge, but they are also subject to constant renegotiation (Mackintosh 1993).

Partnership futures

Examination of Government strategy in the development of different varieties of partnership shows a common thread: early facilitation of voluntary participation, followed by mandate and the requirement for swift and visible evidence of compliance in the form of published plans. The success of this tactic in stimulating partnership activity has been considerable, despite continuing evidence of the difficulties of transforming action into effectiveness. The result has been an extraordinary and rapid proliferation of partnerships across a range of criminal justice and allied interests. Moreover, the partnership enterprise has been accompanied by an extraordinary expansion in directives and infrastructures (note the plural) ostensibly intended to support its healthy development. For example: probation areas are required to submit their plans, updated at six-monthly intervals, for expenditure on contractual relationships (Home Office 2006); local Multi-Agency Public Protection Panels are required to submit business plans in light of national steering guidance (Home Office 2005a); and the policy drive to raise the level of basic skills among offenders has resulted in a bewildering multiplicity of acronyms, sub-groups and partnerships, close examination of which reveals that many activities are concerned with consultation, dissemination, staff training, performance monitoring and evaluation rather than with front-line delivery (see, for example, Home Office 2004b). The Service is confronted with an extraordinary array of guidance documents, separately extolling the virtues of partnership with statutory organisations, voluntary sector agencies and businesses, which, to the perplexed observer, are barely distinguishable in their import (e.g. NOMS and YJB undated a, b, c). In the interests of criminal justice system efficiency, a further bureaucratic tier of partnership has been introduced, since 2003, in the form of 42 Local Criminal Justice Boards comprised of chief officers of police, probation, courts, Crown Prosecution Service, YOTs and prisons, under the coordination of a National Criminal Justice Board, mandated to improve cooperation between these agencies. Partnership has itself become an industry, spawning an expanding population of consultation groups, steering committees, working parties and inspectorates designed, perhaps unintentionally, to have the effect of perpetuating the *process* rather than producing the outcomes of multi-agency collaboration.

And what of the quality of this frenzy of activity? As we have seen, the Probation Service, in common with other organisations, has received mixed evaluations of its partnership activity, revealing tensions between enthusiasm and reluctance, commitment and capacity, professional integrity and situational opportunism. While the partnership enterprise still enjoys wide acceptance in principle, the impact of this proliferation on practice may be less positive. As policy and legislative demands on professional time and resources for sustaining partnership obligations increase, organisations inevitably begin to develop informal strategies for reducing the load (Lipsky 1980; Rumgay and Brewster 1996). While multi-agency collaboration should, ideally, provide a counterbalance to this tendency, collusion to alleviate the strain is an equal alternative. For example, while MAPPA are intended to enhance the quality of attention to high-risk offenders, an increasing caseload, bringing with it additional demands on the resources of partner organisations, may encourage concealed, informal reassignment of offenders to lower priority categories (Maguire *et al.* 2001). For the Probation Service, the problems of finding capacity to fulfil these expanding partnership commitments is particularly acute: for example, in honouring its commitment to Supporting People, 42 Probation Service areas must deal with 150 administering authorities (Audit Commission 2005a).

It has long been understood that policy intentions are susceptible to distortion by those mandated with implementation. Not least among the factors influencing such distortion is the opportunity that particular policies may, unwittingly, present to pursue self-serving organisational interests. Thus, for example, the requirement for broad consultation in the development of local CDRP audits and strategies offered a forum for police not merely to discover public opinion as intended but also to *educate* the public about their problems (Newburn and Jones 2002). Indeed, in many examples of public participation in tackling local social problems, it appears that officials perceive their role in terms of explaining why change is not possible. Thus while much Government rhetoric has lauded the benefits of community engagement, strategic decisions remain largely the province of the primary organisations, taken in isolation from the activity of public consultation. This outcome has been, at least in part, the result of conflicts between responding to locally defined needs and the necessity of delivering centrally prescribed performance indicators (Newman 2004).

The Probation Service's response to demands for multi-agency collaboration has shown similar interesting and self-serving variations. Its mixed reaction to the introduction of contractual relationships reflected alarm about job security, which was alleviated by strategies for neutralising the perceived threat. Conversely its helpfulness to CDRPs and MAPPA is suggestive of shrewd exploitation of public relations opportunities.

This latter point is not necessarily a criticism of the Service's approach. The best contractual partnerships, in preserving professional territories, have allowed both partners to play to their strengths (Rumgay 2000). Even in the relatively restricted field of contractual partnerships, the Probation Service equally has been at its best when sponsoring projects that contribute to the overall health of local communities. Successful early contractual partnerships did not conform to a predetermined model but rather responded to the form of local problems and the available opportunities for tackling them. Thus, for example, an urban environment spawned a structured programme for young drug-involved offenders, while a rural area gave rise to a confidential outreach service for substance misusers in the general population (Rumgay 2000). Multi-agency collaborations, therefore, might justifiably be understood as opportunities to demonstrate the Service's relevance to pressing local concerns and its importance as a presence at the negotiating table (Rumgay 2004).

While the early pressure to develop contractual relationships caused the most obvious consternation in the Probation Service, their significance in the partnership enterprise to date has in practice been relatively small in comparison with the scale of mandated multi-agency collaboration in relation to crime prevention and community safety, targeted groups and social planning and provision since the mid-1990s. Nevertheless, they currently occupy centre stage again as, post-Carter, NOMS prepares the ground for market testing the entire range of probation services. Thus the view of partnership as responsibility transfer has surfaced as a crucial driver behind contemporary policy for the Probation Service. There are, however, very real challenges to the pursuit of this programme in terms of sustaining quality and accountability in conditions of potential fragmentation of service delivery (Smith *et al.* 1993).

The prospect of managing offenders through a battery of supervision services, each contracted to different providers while at the same time preserving the integrity of the multi-agency collaborative strategies, is self-evidently a recipe for chaos unless stringently controlled. For the purpose of maintaining effective ground-level supervision of individual offenders, NOMS appears to have placed its faith upon the primary, if not perhaps the single, strategy of 'end-to-end case management'. It is suggested here, perhaps somewhat contentiously, that this term, if it is to signify *effective* practice, represents a return to the early Probation Service practice, then known as 'one-to-one supervision', of designating a single probation officer to work with each individual offender from the point of entry into the criminal justice system to the point of departure. NOMS visionaries appear unable to concede this point, despite its obviousness to anyone with some knowledge of the history of probation practice. Indeed, recent commentary from the centre on the implications of the offender management model does not even acknowledge the existence of probation officers, preferring to refer to 'offender managers' of previous decades as if they are actually to be found in the archives of probation history (Home Office 2005b).

It may be argued that 'offender management' is qualitatively different from earlier one-to-one supervision, requiring the direction for and enforcement of attendance at discrete programmes rather than an individualised relationship with the offender. However, it is suggested here, in common with other commentators (e.g. Burnett and McNeill 2005; Raynor and Maguire 2006) that this process cannot be accomplished effectively without such a relationship. This is particularly clear when considering the management of risk. The fragmentation of client contact between different agencies, leading to a diminution, rather than enhancement, of individual care has been a recurrent theme in the inquiries after homicides by mentally disordered people (Munro and Rumgay 2000).

We now see that theme recurring in recent reviews of practice following serious offences committed by offenders under supervision. Thus the supervision of Anthony Rice (HM Inspectorate of Probation 2006a) was fundamentally flawed by lack of clarity as to lead responsibility for the case, which facilitated an accumulation of misjudgements, miscommunications and mistaken assumptions between different agencies. In this case also, the review team concluded that, even while the *quantity* of contact was sustained at the required level, the *quality* of supervision was undermined through the probation officer's commitment to a high workload spread over a large geographical area – an arrangement that might well be envisaged under NOMS. It seems, then, that directing the offender to alternative agencies for substantive rehabilitative input will not reduce the necessity for substantive contact with case managers. The case also reveals the inability of the Probation Service to control effectively internal decisions by partner agencies that alter the quality and quantity of service delivery. Indeed the review team acknowledge that high-risk offenders are so hard to accommodate that supervising officers are poorly placed to challenge the effectiveness of an agency that is prepared to receive them. In the absence of an appropriate agency from which to commission service, offender managers may resort to attempting to provide it themselves (HM Inspectorate of Probation 2006b), a role for which they will, in future, be poorly equipped.

Similar findings are reported in the review of the cases of Damien Hanson and Elliot White (HM Inspectorate of Probation 2006c). Here, the involvement of specialist teams disrupted the continuity of supervision, diluting rather than enhancing the attention that was paid to high-risk individuals. Indeed, the *expectation* that contact would be transient shaped the practice of specialist agents. Staff were distracted from the task of risk management by bureaucratic demands to meet other performance targets. This case also illustrates how, while initial plans for the management of an offender may be defensible in principle, the complexity of implementation creates many points at which errors of judgement and communication may jeopardise its effectiveness in practice. Burke (2005: 23) remarks on the threat to 'rigour and coherence in the assessment and management of serious, dangerous and highly persistent offenders' inherent in the proposed separation of offender management and service delivery.

If contestability in practice results in full-throated fragmentation of service delivery by different specialist providers, end-to-end case management will need to prove sufficiently robust to sustain continuity of contact with and supervision integrity for offenders to achieve effective risk monitoring and reduction. Yet, there is no clear safeguard against the potential for offender management to be shaped primarily by the large bureaucracy of NOMS in general and of the Prison Service in particular rather than by responsiveness to individual needs (Burke 2005). The dilemma for the voluntary sector in contemplating its participation in this enterprise is also particularly acute here. On the one hand it is lauded for its 'grassroots' responsiveness to unmet need (Etherington 2006). On the other hand it is argued that the strength of NOMS lies in its capacity to determine services to be delivered under contract: 'separating out decisions about what needs to be provided from those who provide services allows for responsive and effective public service provision. This is what commissioning is *about*' (Lowit 2006: 24, emphasis added).

Moreover, if the problems already noted of servicing partnerships in conditions of staff shortages and high turnover are anything to go by, the contradictory outcome of end-to-end case management will be repeatedly disrupted relationships between offenders and their constantly changing supervising officers. The chances of any supervising officer remaining in post long enough to accompany an offender from end to end of a sentence appear, ironically, to be diminishing. Creating continual uncertainty about job security by threatening staff with withdrawal of their contracts to provide and oversee carefully managed, coherent, individually tailored supervision appears an unlikely strategy for promoting that aim (Liebling 2006).

The Home Office points to the success of prison privatisation in changing custodial institutions for the better. 'Performance testing and competition for new prison contracts has' allegedly 'already had a major effect on driving up standards across the custodial sector' (Reid 2006). Yet this claim, both in itself and in its transferability to the Probation Service, has been questioned by several commentators. The professional association, Napo (2005), challenges the evidence base for asserting a causal link between contestability and a reduction in reoffending rates, points to the failure to include the bureaucratic costs and complexity of implementing the new structures in the reckoning (similarly Burke 2005) and highlights the poor quality and expense resulting from recent privatisations of probation hostel facilities management in 2002 and of the management of probation premises in 2003. Liebling (2006: 73) concedes that, while the benefits of prison privatisation have to date been less clear than is claimed, the urgent challenge of rectifying 'escalating costs, overcrowding and the under-management of culturally resistant prison staff' called for a radical approach in the early 1990s. Liebling observes, however, that not only does the Probation Service present none of those disadvantages, but that, far from recalcitrance, it has in the past decade shown remarkable compliance in delivering punishment in the community, increasing its enforcement rigour and embracing public protection. What, then, are the problems that contestability is designed to resolve? And with what evidence of their likely success? Liebling suggests that this approach risks producing incapacitation rather than invigoration of the Service.

A more optimistic view is promoted by the Confederation of British Industry. Reasserting the claim of positive results of prison privatisation, and giving examples of good practice in private-voluntary-public partnerships, the organisation 'believes that the new market in offender management will be a key tool for NOMS in delivering value for money and targeted interventions' (CBI 2006: 4). In the light of repeated delays to the implementation of Carter's proposals, it goes on to complain that '(w)ithout action from government, a major opportunity will be lost' (ibid: 1). However, we do not need to deny that good practice may be achievable with the help of private contractors. At the time of writing, the most problematic issue is the continuing lack of clarity on the organisational future of the Probation Service and the nature of its relationships with partners. Poor implementation of post-Carter policy is likely to lie at the root of many future difficulties. It is a singular irony of Government partnership policy that the Probation Service was entirely ignored in its pre-emptive and public determination of the organisation's future (Burke 2005).

Meanwhile, as voluntary agencies have combined to express their poor appetite for competing with an organisation that has long been regarded as an ally (Clinks undated), the Probation Service is 'preparing for contestability', with the explicit 'intention that, where services are eventually contested, they are won by the public sector provider (i.e. the National Probation Service (NPS))' (NPS 2006: 1). The expense of this endeavour in financial and human resources, planned to include training in 'advanced bid techniques', a mock contestability exercise, consultation with commissioners, business efficiency initiatives, a 'value for money' project, a 'business alliances' project and a 'competitor intelligence' project, is unclear, but common sense suggests it will be substantial. Moreover, there appears to be a distinct conflict of interests emerging as this combative preparation for competition emerges from the centre of the National Probation Service at precisely the same time that the same centre is required to implement policy on contestability.

The question how the quality of community supervision is to be ensured within such a competitive climate looms large but is, to date, unanswered. The experience of contracting for community care services has revealed the difficulty of measuring the effectiveness of the separate elements of provision, of determining meaningful measurements of quality in the complex field of social care and of agreeing the criteria of assessment between different professional perspectives and priorities: in such a context, professional networks characterised by reciprocity, complementarity and trust are more suited to the task of delivering high standards of delivery (Flynn *et al.* 1995; Forder *et al.* 1996; Johnson *et al.* 1998). Yet, over and above delivering the complexities of ground level supervision, there still remains the plethora of local multi-agency collaborations to be tended if the Probation Service's generally positive contribution is to be maintained. The cost of establishing and sustaining good practice in a field of activity in which, as we have seen, standards vary widely is extensive. For example, the Supporting People programme alone has given rise to a massive exercise in appraisal of each local partnership. Nevertheless partnership activity in itself receives little if any funding to support it, despite its formalisation in statute, leading, it has been alleged, to unconstructive competition between voluntary sector partner agencies over the limited available sources of financial aid (Radford and Gill 2006).

An accumulation of evidence reviewed in this chapter suggests that in sufficiently supportive circumstances the Probation Service is capable of making a valuable contribution to the well-being of local communities. Yet, amid this climate of uncertainty and perpetual change, the health of its partnership enterprise is in jeopardy.

Further reading

For a full discussion of the background, policy debate and practice implications of current moves towards contracting for community supervision services see Burke (2005) *From Probation to the National Offender Management Service: Issues of Contestability, Culture and Community Involvement.*

For an illuminating set of exemplars in community-based justice, including innovations in voluntary involvement, probation practice and relationships between the statutory, voluntary and private sector, see Clear and Cadora (2003) *Community Justice.*

For an example of the evaluation of the Safer Cities Programme, focusing on the quality of multi-agency partnerships see the DETR (2000) *Partnerships in Community Safety: An Evaluation of Phase 2 of the Safer Cities Programme.*

For general introductions to issues in multi-agency collaboration see Huxham (1996) *Creating Collaborative Advantage* and Balloch and Taylor (2001) *Partnership Working: Policy and Practice.*

For a comprehensive critique of problems in evaluating multi-agency collaborative projects see Rosenbaum (2002) 'Evaluating multi-agency anti-crime partnerships: theory, design and measurement issues'.

For a critique of the 'What Works' initiative in effective probation practice contrasted with opportunities in partnership and collaborative work see Rumgay (2004) 'The barking dog? Partnership and effective practice'.

References

Agranoff, R. (1991) 'Human services integration: past and present challenges in public administration', *Public Administration Review*, 551: 533–42.

Annie E. Casey Foundation (1995) *The Path of Most Resistance: Reflections on Lessons Learned from New Futures*. Baltimore, MD: Annie E. Casey Foundation.

Armstrong, K.L. (1997) 'Launching a family-centered, neighbourhood-based human services system: lessons from working the hallways and street corners', *Administration in Social Work*, 21: 109–26.

Audit Commission (2004a) *Supporting People Programme. Liverpool City Council*. London: Audit Commission.

Audit Commission (2004b) *Supporting People Programme. London Borough of Brent*. London: Audit Commission.

Audit Commission (2005a) *Supporting People*. London: Audit Commission.

Audit Commission (2005b) *Supporting People. London Borough of Tower Hamlets Inspection 2005/2006*. London: Audit Commission.

Audit Commission (2005c) *Supporting People Programme. London Borough of Barking and Dagenham*. London: Audit Commission.

Audit Commission (2006a) *Neighbourhood Crime and Anti-social Behaviour: Making Places Safer Through Improved Local Working*. London: Audit Commission.

Audit Commission (2006b) *Supporting People Inspection. Bristol City Council*. London: Audit Commission.

Audit Commission (2006c) *Supporting People Inspection. Bedfordshire County Council*. London: Audit Commission.

Balloch, S. and Taylor, M. (eds) (2001) *Partnership Working: Policy and Practice*. Bristol: Policy Press.

Bradley, J. (2002) *Cracking Crime Consultation: Participation and Consultation in Crime and Disorder Partnerships*, Policy Support Series No. 2. Birmingham: Bostock Marketing Group Limited.

Burke, L. (2005) *From Probation to the National Offender Management Service: Issues of Contestability, Culture and Community Involvement*, Issues in Community and Criminal Justice Monograph 6. London: Napo.

Burnett, R. and McNeill, F. (2005) 'The place of the officer–offender relationship in assisting offenders to desist from crime', *Probation Journal*, 52 (3): 221–42.

Carter, P. (2003) *Managing Offenders, Reducing Crime: A New Approach*. London: Home Office, Strategy Unit.

Clarke, R.V. (1980) 'Situational crime prevention: theory and practice', *British Journal of Criminology*, 20: 136–47.

Clarke, R.V. and Cornish, D.B. (1985) 'Modeling offenders' decisions: a framework for research and policy', in M. Tonry and N. Morris (eds), *Crime and Justice: A Review of Research*, Vol. 6. Chicago: University of Chicago Press.

Clear, T.R. and Cadora, E. (2003) *Community Justice*. Belmont, CA: Wadsworth/Thompson Learning.

Clinks (undated) *Response by CLINKS to the Home Office Consultation 'Restructuring Probation to Reduce Re-offending'*. Clinks.

Confederation of British Industry (2006) *Protecting the Public: Partnership in Offender Management*. London: CBI.

Department for Environment, Transport and the Regions (2000) *Partnerships in Community Safety: An Evaluation of Phase 2 of the Safer Cities Programme*. London: Department of the Environment, Transport and the Regions.

Etherington. S. (2006) 'The transformation of public services – the voluntary and community sector and the criminal justice system', in N. Tarry (ed.), *Returning to Its Roots? A New Role for the Third Sector in Probation*. London: Social Market Foundation.

Fletcher, D.R. (2001) 'Ex-offenders, the labour market and the new public administration', *Public Administration*, 79 (4): 871–91.

Fletcher, D.R., Woodhill, D. and Herrington, A. (1998) *Building Bridges into Employment and Training for Ex-offenders*. York: York Publishing Services.

Flynn, R., Pickard, S. and Williams, G. (1995) 'Contracts and the quasi-market in community health services', *Journal of Social Policy*, 24 (4): 529–50.

Forder, J., Knapp, M. and Wistow, G. (1996) 'Competition in the mixed economy of care', *Journal of Social Policy*, 25 (2): 201–21.

Her Majesty's Inspector of Constabulary (2000) *Calling Time on Crime: A Thematic Inspection on Crime and Disorder*. London: Home Office.

Her Majesty's Inspectorate of Probation (2003) *2002/3 Annual Report*. London: HM Inspectorate of Probation.

Her Majesty's Inspectorate of Probation (2004) *Joint Inspection of Youth Offending Teams: The First Phase Annual Report*. London: HM Inspectorate of Probation.

Her Majesty's Inspectorate of Probation (2006a) *An Independent Review of a Serious Further Offence Case: Anthony Rice*. London: HM Inspectorate of Probation.

Her Majesty's Inspectorate of Probation (2006b) *Offender Management Inspection: A Report on Offender Management in Cheshire*. London: HM Inspectorate of Probation.

Her Majesty's Inspectorate of Probation (2006c) *An Independent Review of a Serious Further Offence Case: Damien Hanson and Elliot White*. London: HM Inspectorate of Probation.

Home Office (1988a) *Punishment, Custody and the Community*. London: Home Office.

Home Office (1988b) *Tackling Drug Misuse: A Summary of the Government's Strategy*. London: Home Office.

Home Office (1990a) *Supervision and Punishment in the Community: A Framework for Action*, Cm 966. London: HMSO.

Home Office (1990b) *Partnership in Dealing with Offenders in the Community*. London: Home Office.

Home Office (1990c) *Partnership in Crime Prevention*. London: Home Office.

Home Office (1992) *Partnership in Dealing with Offenders in the Community: A Decision Document*. London: Home Office.

Home Office (1993a) *Probation Statistics England and Wales 1991*. London: Home Office.

Home Office (1993b) *Probation Service Partnership Policy: Submission of Partnership Plans 1993–1994*, CPO 23/1993. London: Home Office.

Home Office (1993c) *Probation Supervision Grants Scheme: Arrangements for Grants to Local Projects 1994–1995*, PC 16/1993. London: Home Office.

Home Office (2001) *Criminal Justice and Court Services Act 2000: Sections 67 & 68, Guidance for Police and Probation Services*, PC 44/2001. London: Home Office.

Home Office (2004a) *Learning and Skills Provision for Offenders in the Community: Draft Policy Framework*, PC 21/2004. London: Home Office.

Home Office (2004b) *Basic Skills Update. December*. London: Home Office, National Probation Service.

Home Office (2005a) *MAPPA National Business Plan 2005/08*, PC 88/2005. London: Home Office.

Home Office (2005b) *The Implications of the Offender Management Model for Service Delivery Structures*, PC 83/2005. London: Home Office.

Home Office (2006) *Voluntary, Community and Private Sector Alliances*, PC 07/2006. London: Home Office.

Home Office Standing Conference on Crime Prevention (1991) *Safer Communities: The Local Delivery of Crime Prevention Through the Partnership Approach*. London: Home Office.

Homel, R. and Clark, J. (1994) 'The prediction and prevention of violence in pubs and clubs', in R.V. Clarke (ed.), *Crime Prevention Studies*, Vol. 3. Monsey, NY: Criminal Justice Press.

Hoyle, C. (1998) *Negotiating Domestic Violence: Police, Criminal Justice and Victims.* Oxford: Clarendon Press.

Huxham, C. (1996) 'Collaboration and collaborative advantage', in C. Huxham (ed.), *Creating Collaborative Advantage.* London: Sage.

Johnson, C.A., Pentz, M.A., Weber, M.D., Dwyer, J.H., Baer, N., MacKinnon, D.P., Hansen, W.B. and Flay, B.R. (1990) 'Relative effectiveness of comprehensive community programming for drug abuse prevention with high-risk and low-risk adolescents', *Journal of Consulting and Clinical Psychology*, 58 (4): 447–56.

Johnson, N., Jenkinson, S., Kendall, I., Bradshaw, Y. and Blackmore, M. (1998) 'Regulating for quality in the voluntary sector', *Journal of Social Policy*, 27 (3): 307–28.

Kemshall, H., Mackenzie, G., Wood, J., Bailey, R. and Yates, J. (2005) *Strengthening Multi-agency Public Protection Arrangements (MAPPAs)*, Home Office Development and Practice Report 45. London: Home Office.

Liebling, A. (2006) 'Lessons from prison privatisation for probation', in M. Hough, R. Allen and U. Padel (eds), *Reshaping Probation and Prisons: The New Offender Management Framework.* Bristol: Policy Press.

Lipsky, M. (1980) *Street-level Bureaucracy: Dilemmas of the Individual in Public Services.* New York: Russell Sage.

Locke, T. (1990) *New Approaches to Crime in the 1990s: Planning Responses to Crime.* Harlow: Longman.

Lord President of the Council and Lead of the House of Commons, Secretary of State for the Home Department, Secretary of State for Health, Secretary of State for Education and the Paymaster General (1995) *Tackling Drugs Together: A Strategy for England 1995–98*, Cm 2846. London: HMSO.

Lowit, N. (2006) 'The National Offender Management Service – the case for change', in N. Tarry (ed.), *Returning to Its Roots? A New Role for the Third Sector in Probation.* London: Social Market Foundation.

Mackintosh, M. (1993) 'Partnership: issues of policy and negotiation', *Local Economy*, 7 (3): 210–24.

Maguire, M., Kemshall, H., Noaks, L. and Wincup, E. (2001) *Risk Management of Sexual and Violent Offenders: The Work of Public Protection Panels*, Police Research Series Paper 139. London: Home Office.

Mair, G. (2004) 'The origins of What Works in England and Wales: a house built on sand?', in G. Mair (ed.), *What Matters in Probation.* Cullompton: Willan.

Mair, G. and Jamel, J. (2002) *Crime and Disorder Partnerships in Liverpool.* Paper presented at the European Society of Criminology Conference, Toledo, 5–7 September.

Mattessich, P.W., Murray-Close, M. and Monsey, B.R. (2001) *Collaboration: What Makes it Work*, 2nd edn. Saint Paul, MN: Amherst H. Wilder Foundation.

Mayhew, P., Clarke, R.V., Sturman, A. and Hough, J.M. (1976) *Crime as Opportunity*, Home Office Research Study No. 34. London: HMSO.

Minkes, J., Hammersley, R. and Raynor, P. (2005) 'Partnership in working with young offenders with substance misuse problems', *Howard Journal*, 44 (3): 254–68.

Morgan, R. (2006) 'Working with volunteers and the voluntary sector – some lessons for probation from youth justice', in N. Tarry (ed.), *Returning to Its Roots? A New Role for the Third Sector in Probation.* London: Social Market Foundation.

Munro, E. and Rumgay, J. (2000) 'Role of risk assessment in reducing homicides by people with mental illness', *British Journal of Psychiatry*, 176: 116–20.

Napo (2005) *Restructuring Probation – What Works? Napo's Response to the Home Office Consultation Paper 'Restructuring Probation to Reduce Re-offending'.* London: Napo.

National Offender Management Service and Youth Justice Board (undated a) *The Reducing Re-offending Civic Alliance.* London: National Offender Management Service and Youth Justice Board.

National Offender Management Service and Youth Justice Board (undated b) *The Reducing Re-offending VCS Community Alliance*. London: National Offender Management Service and Youth Justice Board.

National Offender Management Service and Youth Justice Board (undated c) *The Corporate Alliance for Reducing Re-offending*. London: National Offender Management Service and Youth Justice Board.

National Probation Service (2006) *NPD Business Development Unit*, National Probation Service Briefing Issue 33. London: National Probation Service.

Nellis, M. (1995) 'Probation partnerships, voluntary action and community justice', *Social Policy and Administration*, 29 (2): 91–109

Newburn, T. and Jones, T. (2002) *Consultation by Crime and Disorder Partnerships*, Police Research Series Paper 148. London: Home Office.

Newman, J., Barnes, M., Sullivan, H. and Knops, A. (2004) 'Public participation and collaborative governance', *Journal of Social Policy*, 33 (2): 203–23.

O'Looney, J. (1997) 'Marking progress toward service integration: learning to use evaluation to overcome barriers', *Administration in Social Work*, 21: 31–65.

Orians, C.E., Liebow, E.B. and Branch, K.M. (1995) 'Community-based organizations and HIV prevention among Seattle's inner-city teens', *Urban Anthropology*, 24 (1–2): 36–58.

Phillips, C., Considine, M. and Lewis, R. (2000) *A Review of Audits and Strategies Produced by Crime and Disorder Partnerships in 1999*, Policing and Reducing Crime Unit Briefing Note 8/00. London: Home Office.

Phillips, C., Jacobson, J., Prime, R., Carter, M. and Considine, M. (2002) *Crime and Disorder Reduction Partnerships: Round One Progress*, Police Research Series Paper 151. London: Home Office.

Pumariega, A.J., Nace, D., England, M.J., Diamond, J., Fallon, T., Hanson, G., Lourie, I., Marx, L., Solnit, A., Grimes, C., Thurber, D. and Graham, M. (1997) 'Community-based systems approach to children's managed mental health services', *Journal of Child and Family Studies*, 6: 149–64.

Radford, L. and Gill, A. (2006) 'Losing the plot? Researching community safety partnership work against domestic violence', *Howard Journal*, 45 (4): 369–87.

Raynor, P. and Maguire, M. (2006) 'End-to-end or end in tears? Prospects for the effectiveness of the National Offender Management Model', in M. Hough, R. Allen and U. Padel (eds), *Reshaping Probation and Prisons: The New Offender Management Framework*. Bristol: Policy Press.

Reid, B. (2001) 'Partnership and change in social housing', in S. Balloch and M. Taylor (eds), *Partnership Working: Policy and Practice*. Bristol: Policy Press.

Reid, J. (2006) 'Foreword', in National Offender Management Service, *Improving Prison and Probation Services: Public Value Partnerships*. London: Home Office.

Reilly, T. (2001) 'Collaboration in action: an uncertain process', *Administration in Social Work*, 25: 53–74.

Richards, L. and Baker, Commander A. (2003) *Findings from the Multi-agency Domestic Violence Murder Reviews in London*. London: Metropolitan Police.

Rosenbaum, D. P. (2002) 'Evaluating multi-agency anti-crime partnerships: theory, design and measurement issues', in N. Tilley (ed.), *Evaluation for Crime Prevention*, Crime Prevention Studies Vol. 14. Monsey, NY: Criminal Justice Press.

Rumgay, J. (2000) *The Addicted Offender: Developments in British Policy and Practice*. Basingstoke: Palgrave.

Rumgay, J. (2001) 'Accountability in the delivery of community penalties: to whom, for what and why?', in A. Bottoms, L. Gelsthorpe and S. Rex (eds), *Community Penalties: Change and Challenges*. Cullompton: Willan.

Rumgay, J. (2003) 'Partnerships in the Probation Service', in W.H. Chui and M. Nellis (eds), *Moving Probation Forward: Evidence, Arguments and Practice*. Harlow: Pearson Education.

Rumgay, J. (2004) 'The barking dog? Partnership and effective practice', in G. Mair (ed.), *What Matters in Probation*. Cullompton: Willan.

Rumgay, J. (2005) 'Counterblast: NOMS bombs?', *Howard Journal of Criminal Justice*, 44 (2): 206–8.

Rumgay, J. and Brewster, M. (1996) 'Restructuring probation in England and Wales: lessons from an American experience', *Prison Journal*, 76 (3): 331–47.

Smith, D., Paylor, I. and Mitchell, P. (1993) 'Partnerships between the independent sector and the Probation Service', *Howard Journal of Criminal Justice*, 32 (1): 25–39.

Tilley, N. (1992) *Safer Cities and Community Safety Strategies*, Crime Prevention Unit Series Paper 38. London: Home Office Police Department.

Whitelaw, W. (1982) *H.C. Deb.*, Sixth Series, vol. 21, col. 1122, March.

Women's Aid (2003a) *Women's Aid Full Response to 'Safety and Justice: The Government Consultation Paper on Domestic Violence'*. Bristol: Women's Aid.

Women's Aid (2003b) *Women's Aid Consultation Response to Restorative Justice – The Government's Strategy*. Bristol: Women's Aid.

Women's Aid (2004) *Women's Aid Response to the Sentencing Advisory Panel: Consultation Paper on Domestic Violence and Sentencing*. Bristol: Women's Aid.

Women's Aid (2005) *Response to 'Managing Offenders, Reducing Crime – The Role of the Voluntary and Community Sector in the National Offender Management Service'*. Bristol: Women's Aid.

Youth Justice Board (2006) *Annual Report and Accounts 2005/6*. London: YJB.

6, P., Bellamy, C., Raab, C. and Warren, A. (2006) 'Partnership and privacy – tension or settlement? The case of adult mental health services', *Social Policy and Society*, 5 (2): 237–48.

Chapter 20

Community penalties, sentencers, the media and public opinion

Rob Allen and Mike Hough

'I don't think probation means anything to many people' (Interviewee, MORI 1998)

Introduction

For most of the postwar period British penal policy in general, and policy on probation and community penalties in particular, evolved with very little regard to public opinion. Public opinion was something to be *managed*, but it was not regarded as something that should be a significant driver of policy. Since the early 1990s, however, there has been a radical shift towards a greater responsiveness to public opinion. Several factors are responsible.

In the first place, the authority of 'expert opinion' and the legitimacy of professional judgement has waned, not just in penal policy but across the political landscape. This is a trend associated by sociologists such as Giddens (1990, 1991) with global patterns of development in 'late modern' industrialised societies linked to declining levels of deference and greater democratisation in decision-making. Secondly – a linked phenomenon – the reform agendas of British public sector services by both Conservative and Labour governments over this period have emphasised the need for greater responsiveness to the public as both paymasters and consumers of public services. Thirdly, penal policy has become increasingly politicised. While this process of politicisation has been evolving over a much longer period,[1] it was in 1992 that, as Shadow Home Secretary, Tony Blair famously mounted a credible challenge to the Conservatives as the party of 'law and order' by promising a new Labour government that would be 'tough on crime, tough on the causes of crime'. Since then, both parties have taken care to ensure that their penal policies resonate with public opinion, at least as it is constructed in, and reflected by, the popular press. (As we shall discuss, claims that the public want much tougher punishment need to be critically and carefully assessed.)

Fourth, there has been a growing political recognition of the centrality of public confidence in the criminal justice system; there are important linkages between compliance with the law and confidence in the fairness and effectiveness of the system (see Tyler 2003). The authority of the police in particular, but also that of the other agencies of justice, require institutional legitimacy, and Government needs to be sure that public confidence in justice is not ebbing. Since 1998, the Government has monitored 'key performance indicators' relating to confidence in justice. More recently there have been government initiatives to promote community engagement in community penalties.

Finally, there have been several tragic high-profile cases of offenders who have committed grave crimes while under probation supervision. The Probation Service has been required to supervise increasingly more – and increasingly risky – offenders on release from custody, and this makes it virtually inevitable that not all risks will be managed effectively. This has been reflected in the growing number of inquiries by HM Inspectorate of Probation into grave crimes committed by those under probation supervision (see, for example, Morgan 2004; Bridges 2006) In particular, the series of murders committed from 2003 onwards[2] by offenders under probation supervision on licence have thrown the Probation Service under the political spotlight and sensitised politicians further to public opinion about the Service. Such is the concern at the time of writing that in March 2006 the Home Secretary had reportedly described the Service as 'the dagger at the heart of the criminal justice system, undermining public confidence in criminal justice as a whole' (*Daily Telegraph*, 21 March 2006). Eight months later, his successor made it clear that 'the Probation Service is letting people down, and needs fundamental reform' (Home Office press release, 7 November 2006).

All these factors mean that much more weight is being attached to public opinion about justice, and how people think about community penalties is an important component of their views on justice. This chapter provides an overview of the field. It does not aim to be comprehensive or international in its scope. Other publications deal with the subject in more detail (e.g. Roberts and Hough 2002; Roberts *et al.* 2003; Hough and Roberts 2004a; Roberts and Hough 2005). Here we describe the main contours of public attitudes as they relate to probation work and community penalties; we examine the 'drivers' of public opinion, and consider the relationships between public opinion and the views of sentencers and other criminal justice professionals. The chapter concludes with a discussion of the policy implications of this body of work.

However, it is worth stating at the outset that the substantial structural changes proposed at the time of writing for the Probation Service carry implications for what both sentencers and the public make of the Service. In particular the controversial proposals published in 2005 to restructure the Service could easily be seen as a vote of 'no confidence' by the Home Office in the ability of probation to protect the public and reduce reoffending. At the very least the uncertainty generated by the apparent confusion about the future of the Service is likely to do little to foster a sense of public confidence. On the other hand, there is little or no evidence that quite significant reforms to the Service in 2000 made much of a difference to public attitudes. In particular, it is not at all clear that changing the names of penalties has achieved the desired outcome of boosting public confidence.

Measuring attitudes to probation and community penalties

Before presenting substantive findings, something needs to be said about the measurement of public attitudes in this field.[3] Measuring opinion about probation work is inherently more problematic than opinion about more visible parts of the criminal justice system such as the police. Most of us have at least some direct contact with the police over a five-year period, and a third of us in any one year can be counted as police 'users'. Our ideas about the police are grounded in personal experience as well as what we read and hear in the media. The range of information in the media – whether in documentaries or dramas – is also wide, and we are exposed to differing, often conflicting, viewpoints. Most people will have thought about the police and policing at least to some extent.

By contrast only a very small proportion of the population have any contact with probation officers, either professionally or socially. Probation work, including most forms of community penalty, is largely invisible to the public. Knowledge about probation work is very limited, and what little information people have is gleaned from media reports that relate to high-profile tragedies, often prepared by journalists with little knowledge of probation work.[4] Certainly people will answer questions about probation put to them by survey interviewers: less than one in five of the population offer 'don't know' as the response to a regular British Crime Survey question about the competence of the Probation Service. If the findings presented in the next section are any sort of guide, less than one in five of the general public could honestly claim to be in a position to offer an informed answer.

Of course, misinformed or uninformed opinion is politically important to chart, if only because it is these opinions that most people take into the ballot box. But documenting opinion does not imply responding to public opinion, and certainly does not imply doing exactly what the majority state as their policy preferences. The risks of penal policy by plebiscite are obvious.

The findings presented in this chapter are drawn from social surveys and polls. The great strength of the survey method lies in the replicable generalisations that it can support. A properly conducted survey enables one to generalise, on the basis of the responses of a population sample, to the population from which the sample is drawn. But polls can also mislead. Pitfalls included:

- unrepresentative samples;
- questions which offer insufficient or inappropriate response options;
- questions which are framed in biased or leading terms;
- failure to permit respondents legitimate indecision;
- failure to give respondents enough thinking time;
- failure to give respondents enough information on which to base a response.

These issues have been discussed in more detail elsewhere (e.g. Roberts and Hough 2005). The key point to emphasise when considering attitudes to any form of punishment is that loose and broad questions will certainly yield answers *of some sort*, but these will often be loosely thought-through and broad answers based on very little knowledge of the issues.

In other words, the strength of surveys and polls – their standardised and replicable method – can also be their weakness. Large-scale surveys do not have the flexibility to deal with a respondent who asks for more information before committing themselves to an answer. 'It depends' is probably the most thoughtful response to a wide range of survey questions – even if it is deeply unhelpful to those asking the question. As a general rule, the solution to this set of problems is to be found in asking questions that are as specific and as unambiguous as possible, that anticipate the supplementary questions that respondents might reasonably want to ask about the sort of offence and offender that is under consideration.

The general public

When the Home Affairs Committee published their report *Alternatives to Prison* in 1998, they concluded that securing public support was central to the development of community penalties. They argued that 'Unless the public has confidence, far from reducing the prison population there will be calls for increasing it' (Home Affairs Committee 1998). More recently the former Lord Chief Justice Lord Woolf said that 'neither the public, nor sentencers have sufficient confidence in the community alternative' (Woolf 2002). The very sharp increase in the prison population in recent years suggests that these warnings were right. But how punitive is the general public and what do they really think about community sentences?

In common with the general public around the world, it is certainly true that people in England and Wales don't know a great deal about community penalties or the organisations which supervise them. A recent review of international findings noted that 'most people are unfamiliar with the alternatives available to judges in their particular jurisdictions' and that 'even probation, the most widely used and oldest community sentence in most countries, is little known to large numbers of people' (Roberts and Hough 2002). This does not of course stop people having views and attitudes about how to deal with offenders. Views and attitudes about sentencing are complex and sometimes contradictory but it is possible to discern some level of public support for the idea of community penalties, both for adult and young offenders. The public are not generally as punitive as is often supposed although there is considerable variation according to age, class and political affiliation. Attitudes are less punitive towards individual cases than groups of offenders. Evidence about levels of public confidence in the agencies responsible for the implementation of community penalties is more mixed, however.

What do the public know?

The British public know little about the criminal justice system in general and sentencing in particular. Research carried out for the Review of the Sentencing Framework in 2001 found, for example, that 52 per cent of the public thought that sentences in the Crown Court were imposed by the jury rather than the judge. Less than a third of people could recall three or more sentencing disposals unprompted. Somewhat implausibly perhaps, only 67 per cent remembered prison,[5] a half community service and 49 per cent fines (Home Office 2001).

People substantially underestimate the extent to which the courts sentence people to prison. In the mid-1990s, over half of BCS respondents made large underestimates of the proportion of adults convicted of rape, burglary and mugging who went to prison (Hough and Roberts 1998). For example, people typically said that the courts sent half of convicted adult rapists to prison when the correct percentage was 97 per cent. A survey conducted for the Sentencing Advisory Panel confirmed this overall picture, showing that people consistently underestimated the degree to which courts actually imposed prison sentences (Russell and Morgan 2001). This pattern of findings has continued, although the gap between perceptions and reality may be narrowing slightly (Allen et al. 2006).

It is only by implication that these findings shed light on perceptions of the use of community penalties: those who underestimate courts' usage of custodial sentences *presumably* overestimate their use of community penalties. However, it seems just as likely that many respondents will not have thought through precisely how rapists, for example, are dealt with other than through imprisonment.

Certainly, the general public know very little about the work of the Probation Service and less about youth offending teams (YOTs). A MORI survey carried out in 2002 found that 7 per cent claimed to know a lot about what the Probation Service does, two in five (43 per cent) said they knew a little, while half said they knew hardly anything (35 per cent) or nothing at all (15 per cent) (MORI 2002). More recent research found that only a quarter of people had heard of youth offending teams and one in eight knew what these teams do (Hough and Roberts 2004b). Only 11 per cent of people are aware of anything in their own local community or area which has benefited from unpaid labour by offenders serving their community sentence.

The low visibility of community sentences was confirmed by work undertaken by one of the authors for the Esmée Fairbairn Foundation Rethinking Crime and Punishment initiative (Hough et al. 2003). We found that some sentencers, let alone members of the public, were poorly informed about the full range of community penalties and about their benefits. Most sentencers recognised that the general public knew little about most community penalties. Research on the role of the media in shaping attitudes found that most viewers had very little understanding or knowledge of alternatives to prison (Gillespie and Mcloughlin 2003). Surveys carried out by the Henley Management College found that many people know little or nothing about prison alternatives (Macmillan et al. 2004). There is a particular lack of knowledge among the public about where community sentences have been successful.

What do the public want?

On the face of it, evidence from opinion polls suggests that people in Britain have harsh attitudes towards offenders. Three-quarters of BCS respondents say that sentences are 'too lenient', and between a quarter and a third will 'strongly agree' that this is the case (Russell and Morgan 2001; Allen *et al.* 2006). There are four other types of survey evidence which suggest the picture is a lot more complex and that unequivocal public punitiveness may be something of a myth.

First, as discussed in the previous section, surveys suggest that demands for tougher sentences arise in part from an underestimate of the severity of sentences which are currently imposed. Close analysis would suggest that there is something of a 'comedy of errors' in which policy and practice is not based on a proper understanding of public opinion, and that the same opinion is not based on a proper understanding of policy and practice. When people are made aware of the actual use of custody, not surprisingly far fewer say that the courts are 'much too lenient'.

The second *caveat* about punitiveness is that the public are severe when confronted with a question about sentencing in general, but more lenient on a case-by-case basis. Support for custody as a sanction falls when even a few details about the offender's life are presented to respondents. This is partly because when answering a general question about offences, the public tends to exaggerate the seriousness of the crime. In this way a 'typical' burglary is erroneously associated with damage, theft of high-value goods and persistent offending. This is what people have in mind if they are given only basic information about a case, and a more detailed description of the same offence produces a more measured response.

Especially in relation to young offenders, the public's tolerance for lenient sentences is really quite marked. For example, one of the authors mounted a survey of attitudes to youth crime, including questions about sentencing (Hough and Roberts 2004b). Just over half our sample (52 per cent) said that a community penalty with reparation was an acceptable sentence for a violent 16-year-old robber with three previous convictions. Guidance from the Lord Chief Justice and from the Sentencing Guidelines Council is very clear that such a case deserves imprisonment.[6]

The third reason to question public attitudes to punishment is that when asked to rate imprisonment as a policy response to crime, people show a good deal of scepticism. In a MORI survey conducted for the *Daily Mail* in 2000, only a third of respondents agreed with the statement 'Prison works – the more prisons the better', with well over half disagreeing (MORI 2000). Figure 20.1 shows that about half of the public think that offenders come out of prison worse than they go in and a third don't know (Esmée Fairburn Foundation 2004) and broadly similar proportions of the population agree and disagree with the proposition that numbers of people in prison should be reduced. When asked how to deal with prison overcrowding, building more prisons is a relatively unpopular option with the support of only a quarter of people. Figure 20.2 shows that more than half would prefer tougher community punishments to be developed or more residential centres built so that drug-addicted offenders can receive treatment (MORI 2003a).

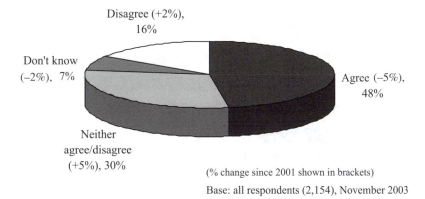

Disagree (+2%), 16%

Don't know (−2%), 7%

Neither agree/disagree (+5%), 30%

Agree (−5%), 48%

(% change since 2001 shown in brackets)

Base: all respondents (2,154), November 2003

Source: MORI (2003a).

Figure 20.1 To what extent did respondents agree or disagree with the statement 'Most people come out of prison worse than they go in'?

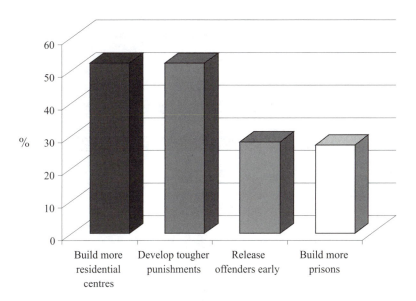

Source: MORI (2003a).

Figure 20.2 How would respondents deal with prison overcrowding?

It is clear that when presented with a range of policy options, public enthusiasm for prison evaporates. Asked what would do most to reduce crime in Britain six out of ten people say better parenting (MORI 2003a), 55 per cent more police, 45 per cent better school discipline and 41 per cent more constructive activities for young people. As Figure 20.3 shows, only one in ten people think more offenders in prison is the answer. When asked in 2001 how the public would spend a notional £10 million on dealing with crime, the most popular option was to set up teams in 30 cities to work with

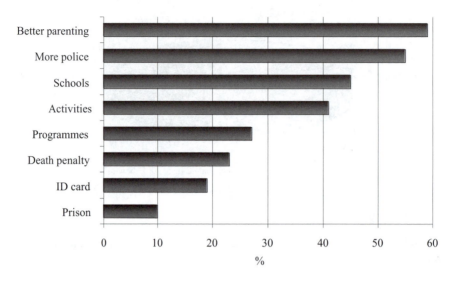

Source: RCP (2002a).

Figure 20.3 Which two or three of the following factors would do most to reduce crime?

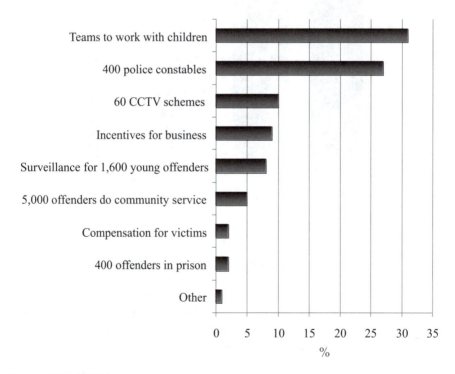

Source: RCP (2002a)

Figure 20.4 How respondents would spend £10 million on crime reduction.

children at risk (RCP 2002a) as illustrated in Figure 20.4. Only 2 per cent chose to spend the notional £10 million on prison places.

Finally, the superficiality of public attachment to prison is suggested by what people say they want sentencing to achieve. Research suggests that they think it should aim to stop reoffending, reduce crime or create a safer community. Very few people spontaneously refer to punishment or incapacitation. When asked in research for the Home Office Sentencing Review to rank specified purposes of sentencing, the largest proportion rated rehabilitation highest (49 per cent) with three-quarters of the public believing most offenders can be rehabilitated. A small absolute majority support the philosophy underpinning restorative justice (Home Office 2001).

These four factors – lack of knowledge about the current system, relative leniency on individual cases, poor ratings of prison as a response to crime and commitment to consequentialist purposes for sentencing – mean that, in the words of the Home Office Sentencing Review, 'tough talk does not necessarily mean a more punitive attitude to sentencing' (Home Office 2001: 118).

Specific attitudes to community penalties

Given that at least part of the purpose of community penalties is to provide rehabilitation (e.g. through programmes to address offending behaviour) and reparation (through unpaid work), they should in theory have some appeal to the public professing support for these objectives. There is indeed evidence of some support for community penalties – a recent review concluded that the public is 'probably ambivalent' (Maruna and King 2004). In the 1996 British Social Attitudes Survey three-quarters of the sample thought offenders who were not a big threat should spend time helping in the community. Nine out of ten agree that there should be more use of intensive community punishments to keep track of young offenders (RCP 2002a). But it is not clear how much such support extends to penalties being imposed as *alternatives to prison*. There is, however, a relatively high level of support for a combined prison and community penalty disposal with almost three-quarters in research for the Home Office Sentencing Review thinking three months prison plus three months in the community more constructive than six months in prison (Home Office 2001).

It is the reparation element within community sentences which seems to resonate most strongly with the public. There is more scepticism about the value of straight probation. In a 'deliberative poll' study of 2001, 69 per cent of respondents agreed that more offenders 'who are not a big threat to society' should be 'kept out of prison, but made to spend a certain number of days helping people in the community', whereas only 45 per cent agreed that such offenders should be 'made to report regularly to probation officers'. When asked about a specific case, that of a first-time burglar aged 16, 78 per cent of respondents agreed they should be 'made to do community service' and this was the most popular sentencing choice. Focus group research by Strathclyde University has confirmed that people want non-custodial sentences that get offenders to pay back and learn their lesson (RCP 2002b). Research on the reputation of alternatives to prison found a need to benefit victims and communities as well as offenders (Macmillan *et al.* 2004).

In most of the studies covering non-custodial sentences, the potential of these alternative sentences to cut crime goes relatively unrecognised. In the survey for the Home Office Sentencing Review on the impact of information, only 40 per cent of the general public respondents felt community sentences were effective in reducing crime (Home Office 2001).

As far as confidence in the actual delivery of community sentences is concerned, recent work undertaken for the Home Office has suggested that there is a clear correlation between how much people know about the different constituent agencies of the criminal justice system and their perceived effectiveness. The police are, by far, the most well known agency and are rated as having the greatest impact on crime in the local area. At the other end of the spectrum, relatively few know much about youth offending teams, which consequently are not typically rated as being particularly effective.

Nevertheless, in a MORI poll 59 per cent said they were very or fairly confident in the Probation Service – higher than the CPS, courts and prisons and second only to the police (MORI 2003a). This is perhaps surprising given the lack of knowledge about probation; it is also rather inconsistent with findings from the British Crime Survey, which shows the Probation Service now securing ratings similar to magistrates and judges, the Prison Service and the Crown Prosecution Service – but well below those of the police (Allen *et al.* 2006).

Variations in attitudes

Most studies have shown that older people are more punitive than younger and manual occupations more punitive than non-manual. The British Crime Survey (Mattinson and Mirrlees-Black 2000) found, for example, that older people are the most likely of any age group to think that sentencing is too lenient: 56 per cent of respondents aged 60 and over said sentences were 'much too lenient' and 28 per cent said they were 'a little too lenient' (among 16 to 29 year olds, the rates were 37 per cent and 34 per cent respectively).

There are interesting age differences between types of offence, however. According to the 1992 British Crime Survey, the old are more tough-minded about the punishment of property offences than the young. However, young people are less tolerant of violence than their elders, for example, and far fewer of them advocate community penalties for perpetrators of domestic violence or sexual offences such as date rape and marital rape (Hough 1998).

The Rethinking Crime and Punishment survey found that while slightly more people are likely to see reducing prison numbers as a 'bad' rather than a 'good idea' in overall terms, the reverse is true among those in social classes A and B and those who read broadsheet newspapers (MORI 2001). People who fear crime are more likely to think that courts are lenient and advocate heavier sentences. But surprisingly, victimisation does not seem to affect punitive attitudes. The BCS has also found that black and ethnic minority respondents were less punitive than white respondents. They were much less likely to think that sentencing was too lenient than were white respondents (67 per cent vs 80 per cent). In particular, half of white respondents (50 per cent) said sentencing was 'much too lenient', whereas only 36 per cent of ethnic respondents said likewise. This is likely to reflect the fact that ethnic minority respondents were more likely to give a correct answer (22 per cent) about the severity of current sentencing than were white respondents (15 per cent). Seventy-four per cent of white respondents considerably underestimated the proportion of burglars jailed (giving an answer of 30 per cent or lower), while only 64 per cent of ethnic minority respondents did so.

International surveys suggest there are important cross-cultural differences in attitudes. The International Crime Victimisation Survey suggests that in comparison with many other countries, the British tend to want to use prison more readily. Using a burglary case study the survey found UK countries consistently near the top of the table in terms of preference for prison (Van Kesteren *et al*. 2000). On average 34 per cent of respondents from 16 countries preferred prison, with a range of 56 per cent in the USA to 7 per cent in Catalonia. Just over half of the British sample opted for prison. Interestingly, most of the countries with above average support for prison have cultural origins in Britain, America, Canada and Australia. The exceptions are Japan and the Netherlands, both of which have seen sharp increases in popular support for prison in recent years. On the whole, the countries in the least punitive half of the table share a mainland European or Scandinavian heritage. In all these countries community service is more popular than prison.

Quite why this is so is not clear. Analysts have pointed to a range of possible explanations including deep-seated differences in traditions of tolerance or social solidarity and varying levels of experience of detention, for example in wartime. One possibility is that Britain's tradition of educating its elite in boarding schools has shaped attitudes to a range of residential institutions including prisons. It was Evelyn Waugh who observed that prison holds no terrors for those who have endured the rigours of a public school education (Allen 2002).

There are some more predictable links between ideological beliefs and attitudes to crime. Studies, mainly North American, have shown that highly religious people and those with a strong belief in a just world – the belief that good things will happen to good people and bad things will happen to bad people – held the most punitive attitudes to offenders. Other studies have found that Christian fundamentalism strongly predicted support for the use of punitive criminal justice policies (Wood and Viki 2001).

Not surprisingly conservative beliefs – measured by agreement with statements endorsing traditional social values – are linked with punitiveness and liberal political views with more lenient attitudes. This is confirmed by detailed analysis of survey data in Britain. The British Social Attitudes Survey in 1999 (National Centre for Social Research 1999) found that support for stiffer sentences ranged from 59 per cent among salaried Liberal Democrat voters to 90 per cent among working-class Conservatives (and, surprisingly, working-class Liberal Democrat supporters). Among Labour voters, 70 per cent of salaried, 77 per cent of self-employed and 85 per cent of working-class respondents supported a tougher approach.

A similar pattern was found in MORI's poll on attitudes to burglars conducted early in 2003, in the wake of a media rumpus about lenient sentencing. Conservative voters favoured imprisoning a first-time burglar by 50 per cent to 41 per cent, Liberal Democrat voters favoured community service by 54 per cent to 38 per cent while Labour supporters were equally divided. When, in work undertaken for RCP (Allen 2003), MORI asked if it was a good or a bad idea to reduce the prison population, they found that respondents intending to vote Conservative were more likely to think it a bad idea (53 per cent) than Labour voters (45 per cent) or those supporting other parties (37 per cent).

Research carried out for the Coulsfield Inquiry found sharply contrasting attitudes to punishment between the residents of two high crime areas. More punitive attitudes were prevalent in an area where residents felt a strong sense of rootedness but experienced increasing disorder in public space and a lack of optimism about the future. Less punitive attitudes were present in an area with more of a sense of social control and safety (even where crime rates were equally high). In both areas most residents were positive about the idea of offenders moving out of crime and going on to lead useful lives. The researchers found reasonable public support for the idea that offenders should be allowed to redeem themselves and this is the case in areas with high punitiveness as much as in other areas (Bottoms and Wilson 2004). It is this notion of redeemability which may lie at the heart of the difference between people with more or less punitive attitudes and propensity to support community penalties (Maruna and King 2004).

What drives public opinion?[7]

The previous section has charted the – fairly complex – terrain of public attitudes to community penalties. We have seen that on the surface, at least, there is a great deal of frustration with the lenience of the courts and a desire for tougher punishment. By implication this would mean a public desire for *less* use of community penalties and an even less prominent role in the system for probation. On the other hand, there is good evidence that beneath this layer of punitive attitudes a large proportion of the population is sceptical about imprisonment and optimistic about preventive, rehabilitative and reparative options. What are the factors that shape this multi-layered set of attitudes?

We have argued that in part, the image of a highly punitive public derives from surveys and polls whose methods presuppose accurate information about offenders and about sentencing. Asking someone if the courts are tough enough is a sensible question to ask of someone who has *some* idea of current practice. At one level, the answers of the demonstrably ignorant are of limited value. That is not to discount their views altogether, however. They represent an important political fact: a large proportion of the population distrust the courts and think they are doing a bad job. They think that the system is doing far too little to protect them against crime. People *do* actually believe that the courts are too soft, even if careful survey research suggests that if asked to pass sentence, a majority would behave much as magistrates do. Several factors shape both the 'surface' punitiveness that polls can readily describe and those that emerge when people are given information and time to think.

It is important not to dismiss surface views as *superficial* views. On the contrary, popular punitiveness may be shaped by more powerful factors that the more rational, knowledge-based opinions that can be elicited by careful survey questioning. Public attitudes are emotionally as well as intellectually grounded, and if one is to understand public attitudes one needs to look beyond the rational. Understanding the emotional or dispositional side of opinions is just as important as the informational side.

Unpicking these aspects of public opinion is a complex task. It draws one into diffuse issues as broad as the symbolic meaning of crime and punishment in the face of rapid social transformation. Indeed it is these broad symbolic and emotional dynamics that have dominated much sociological discussion of public attitudes to punishment (see especially Bottoms 1995; Garland 2001). Reducing down the voluminous literature that examines the place of crime and punishment in the public psyche three main factors have been identified as associated with popular punitiveness:

- the pervasive experience of insecurity in late modernity, and the ways in which crime and criminals can become identified – or misidentified – as a source of this insecurity;

- the transformation, through political rhetoric, of popular fear, sense of threat and insecurity into emotions of frustration, anger and entitlement;

- the use of crime as a symbolic issue in response to which politicians can present themselves as determined, decisive and effective.

If this sociological analysis is broadly correct, then there are two types of problem that have to be dealt with in making sense of public attitudes. First, at the cognitive level is the level and quality of information. Second, at the emotional level are the fears, frustrations and uncertainties that characterise life in late-modern industrialised society. To these two levels could be added a third – the political level, the 'hardening of attitudes', the retreat of liberalism and the amplification of popular fears by the media (see Roberts *et al.* 2003 for a fuller discussion). This third level really reflects the interplay of the former two. Politicians, doing what politicians do, will work with the available resources to maintain their electoral base. Few have qualms about exploiting public fears and uncertainties. Although we may be critical of politicians for using crime as a symbolic issue, it could be argued that this is a perennial aspect of political life and it is naive to expect otherwise.

A model of influences

Public opinion is clearly the product of a range of influences and most of those who have examined the formation of public opinion stress the highly interdependent nature of the various influences. This idea of a complex interweaving of influence and response is a common conclusion of those who have examined the relationship between media, crime and public policy.

In explaining the development of public opinion and its role in policy, the primary relationships must be between the public, political decision-makers and the news media. Of secondary importance are the efforts of lobby groups and various vested interests across the political spectrum that try to influence the shape and direction of public debates. Public opinion exists within a dynamic framework dominated by political initiative, the media and special interest groups. A useful model that captures the interplay of these forces was proposed by Kennamer (1992) – see Figure 20.5.

In this model the news media have been located at the heart of the process. It might be objected that both politicians and the public have access to other forms of information about crime and punishment, and that we are exaggerating media power. However, in complex industrialised democracies it is only through the media that each element can be represented to the others. At the start of the twenty-first century, the media are the main conduit for expression, for conveying positions and expressing postures. And in performing these functions, the media are shaped on the one hand by commercial imperatives – to maintain circulation and revenue – and on the other, by the political agendas of their owners and editors.[8]

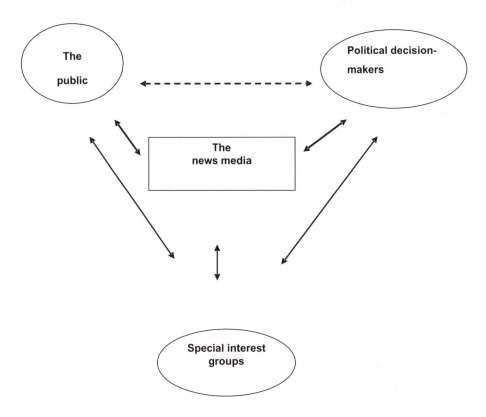

Source: Adapted from Kennamer (1992).

Figure 20.5 A model of the interaction of media, public opinion, special interest groups and political decision-makers.

A fuller account of the construction of opinion about crime and punishment would take account of further factors. Clearly, direct experience plays an important role, as does the experience of friends, relatives, colleagues and neighbours. Some communities, especially inward-looking ones in areas of intense deprivation, may be relatively insulated from the news media, especially the national press, and direct experience may be very salient. There is also the role of media dramas and 'soaps', which must shape conceptions about the criminal process among some groups as much as, or more than, any news media.

If our analysis is correct, the dynamic between politicians and the media places those in charge of probation work very much 'on the back foot'. Given the subtle association between the threat of crime and the more diffuse uncertainties of late modern societies, it takes a brave politician to challenge media representations of crime. Only a slight misjudgement of tone will convey the impression of complacency or weakness. Advocacy of community penalties – which both the main political parties have done – tends to be cautious and tentative. The risks of being portrayed as a wishy-washy liberal – 'soft on crime' – are significant to any politician with an eye to self-preservation. The result is that deep irony whereby:

- most categories of crime have been falling for a decade – but the falls have gone largely unnoticed by the public;
- court sentences have got progressively tougher over the last decade and a half – but the greater severity has gone largely unnoticed by the public;
- the media pressures for tougher sentencing continue.

Sentencers' views

Sentencers' views of community penalties and the Probation Service are obviously of critical importance. It is largely the decisions of sentencers that determine the volume of community penalties. Clearly, sentencing outcomes depend on many factors, including:

- guideline judgements and guidance from the Sentencing Guidelines Council;
- the guidance issued by the Magistrates' Association;
- the recommendations made by probation officers in their court reports;
- the availability to the court of particular sentencing options.

Nevertheless, sentencers who have confidence in their Probation Service and who believe in the value of community penalties will make greater use of the latter than those who are sceptical about probation work. Surprisingly, there is little recent survey work on sentencers' views about community penalties. One of the few pieces of relevant research was carried out for the Home Office Sentencing Review (Home Office 2001). In this, self-completion questionnaires were completed by ten groups of professionals, including magistrates and judges. Sample sizes for each group are small, as the total sample was not much larger than 1,000.

Some interesting patterns emerged. As Figure 20.6 shows, not far short of two-thirds of magistrates thought that current sentencing practice was too lenient. This is both important and puzzling – in view of the fact that magistrates pass the majority of court sentences. The probable explanation is that lay magistrates sit too infrequently to form an impression based on experience of actual sentencing practice and thus rely on the impressions they gain from the media.[9] To this extent, therefore, magistrates seem genuinely representative of the public from whom they are drawn.

It is striking that those with more experience of the courts – district judges, solicitors, barristers and probation officers – were much more likely to say that sentencing practice was about right. This could simply reflect a process of acculturation, whereby everyday practice ends up as seeming 'about right'. Equally, it could reflect fuller understanding of offenders, circumstances and motivation. At the same time, it is noteworthy that fully 95 per cent of police respondents – who presumably are equally well aware of offenders' circumstances – thought that the courts were too soft.

Both judges and magistrates generally appeared to reflect a view of sentencing in which the primary purpose was to punish, with rehabilitation as the most significant secondary purpose. In contrast, lawyers, probation and the CPS tended to rank rehabilitation higher than punishment as a sentencing aim. Deterrence came fairly low down the list for all groups. Unsurprisingly, a majority of magistrates (61 per cent) were keen to have a greater say over the content of sentences they passed – implying a greater degree of control over probation work – a view less popular among judges (46 per cent) and

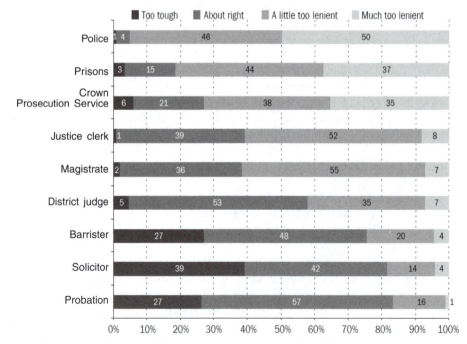

Source: Home Office 2001

Figure 20.6 Perceptions of current sentencing practice.

(of course) by probation staff (27 per cent). A majority of magistrates (57 per cent) supported restorative justice schemes, as did a minority of judges (34 per cent).

Greater insight into the complexities of the sentencing process and the factors taken into account by sentencing can probably be gained from qualitative work. One of the authors was involved in just such an exercise, designed to offer some explanation of the very rapid increase in the prison population in the 1990s (Hough *et al.* 2003). The study demonstrated clearly that there were two main reasons for this increase: sentencers were imposing *longer* prison sentences for serious crimes, and they were more likely to imprison offenders who ten years ago would have received a community penalty or even a fine.

We argued that tougher sentencing practice had come about through the interplay of several factors: an increasingly punitive climate of political and media debate about punishment – as discussed above; legislative changes and new guideline judgements; and sentencers' perceptions of changes in patterns of offending. However, the sentencing statistics did not lend support to sentencers' beliefs that offenders are becoming more persistent and committing more serious crimes.

In our interviews with sentencers we found clear evidence of a sentencing culture at both Crown Court level and magistrates' courts whereby imprisonment was a punishment of last resort. What made this 'last resort' appropriate was either that the offence was so serious that no other sentence was possible, or that the offender's past convictions or failure to respond to past sentences ruled out community options. Despite this, of course, the threshold at which the 'last resort' was activated had demonstrably changed over time.

An important feature of our analysis was that sentencers did not appear to be sending people to prison for lack of satisfactory or appropriate community options; they claimed that they impose community penalties whenever the facts of a case merit it. They generally expressed satisfaction with the quality and range of community sentences, and with the management and enforcement of these sentences, though there are widespread concerns that the Probation Service was underfunded.[10]

Perhaps of most importance for the present discussion, sentencers felt that they were able to resist pressures to 'get tough' from the media and the public, and that it was critically important to do so. At the same time, however, they felt a duty to ensure their sentencing decisions reflected and reinforced the norms of wider society. The study found overwhelming evidence that they had done exactly this.

Enhancing knowledge and confidence

Efforts to enhance knowledge and confidence have fallen into three main categories; first, through strategies to communicate accurate and accessible information about crime, the options available to the courts, and their effectiveness and costs; second, by work to increase the visibility of community penalties; and third, through attempts to involve ordinary people more in the work of the Probation Service.

Communication

The Home Office Sentencing Review (Home Office 2001) found that it was possible to raise levels of knowledge through printed information, a video and attendance at a seminar. Interestingly, the 'informed public' who had been given key facts were less punitive in their sentencing preferences than the general public. The review recommended that the Home Office should be required to disseminate information about the effectiveness of sentencing as part of its duties under section 95 of the Criminal Justice Act 1991, and should consider ways of increasing public knowledge about how sentencing is intended to work and how it is working in practice. One of the respondents to the consultation on the Sentencing Review suggested that schools should be required to promote understanding of crime and the justice system.

Research has shed light on other ways that public attitudes can be changed. One of the authors reanalysed the results of a deliberative poll carried out in 1994 in which a random sample of the public was exposed to a weekend of facts and argument about crime and punishment (Hough and Park 2002). We found that information and discussion could trigger significant shifts in attitudes about the best ways of controlling crime. For example, 35 per cent of participants initially thought that 'sending more offenders to prison' would be a very effective way of reducing crime. After the weekend, only one in five took this view. While 50 per cent initially thought that 'stiffer sentences generally' would be a very effective way of reducing crime, ten months later only 36 per cent thought the same. Support for community penalties was originally quite high and remained largely unchanged. By no means all people adopted more liberal views after the event; many adopted tougher views. In general, people adopted less extreme views after the event, with a net shift in a liberal direction.

The Local Crime Community Sentence project has found that case study presentations by probation officers and magistrates to community groups can increase the public's confidence in community penalties. Research shows that their programme of interactive presentations to local community groups including pensioner groups, students, business groups, Neighbourhood Watch, Victim Support and women's groups has been successful in raising confidence in community sentences. Talks based on case studies given to over 1,000 participants across England and Wales have shown that over 65 per cent of people who thought prison worked for low-level offenders at the start of the presentation had changed their minds by the end and nearly 90 per cent of the participants felt more confident in community sentences as an effective response (King and Grimshaw 2003).

As well as informing what people *know* about crime and offenders, there is a need to influence how people *feel* about the subject. As discussed above, there is an important emotional element to attitude formation, as well as a cognitive one: attitudes are formed on the basis not only of what people think but also what they feel. There is good reason to suppose that, however compelling the content and logic of information, attitudes to crime contain a strong emotional element. This may be based on personal experience, although on the whole victims of crime do not appear to be more punitive than non-victims. Attitudes may also be based on very local experience. In one study, those who believed that juvenile courts were doing a 'poor' or 'very poor' job were most likely to say that teenagers hanging around the streets locally presented a very big problem. Anxiety about crime – or indeed an anxious disposition[11] – could serve as an important mediating variable. Helping people to feel safer seems a prerequisite for developing more constructive attitudes. People high in anxiety (or in certainty) are low in persuadability. Influence is also needed to counteract the effects of the media.

Simple information may be sufficient to dispel common myths but a good deal more work needs to be undertaken to identify the impact which different messages have on the public. Focus groups conducted by Strathclyde University (RCP 2002b) suggested that key message strategies to engage public support for non-custodial sentences include:

- instilling a sense of responsibility and discipline;
- having to work hard, emotionally and physically;
- putting something back;
- paying back to victims;
- restriction of liberty and requirement to change behaviour;
- treatment of causes of offending.

Messages that focus on the costs of custodial sentences, the rising prison population or humanitarian arguments seem to be less persuasive. Reformers have often produced information about the costs of incarceration, assuming that people will be sufficiently shocked to find out that it costs £35,000 a year to keep someone in prison that they will change their views about the desirability of doing so. However, American evidence suggests that for the general public cost may be a marginal issue if they think that there needs to be a 'war on crime'. For some, the lesson may be that prisoners should be kept in more Spartan and inexpensive conditions, while for others '... jail is cheap at the price; just think of how much more it would cost repeatedly arresting and processing and trying and monitoring him on probation or on community service, which won't work anyway' (Marrin 2002).

Visibility

One difficulty for those concerned to raise public awareness of community penalties is their lack of visibility compared to prison. While what goes on inside prisons may be a mystery to most people, the external physical characteristics of prisons make clear their role in detaining or punishing citizens behind closed walls. Community penalties lack any equivalent assets (real or symbolic) which illustrate their purpose. The physical location of probation premises is in fact a source of considerable problems. Efforts to expand the stock of probation hostels have often met with considerable opposition from local residents. Much of the work of the Probation Service – basic day-to-day supervision of offenders, the delivery of offending behaviour programmes, the arrangement of housing, work or drug treatment does not lend itself to being made visible in the eyes of the public. One aspect of work which has attracted attention from politicians has been the unpaid work undertaken by offenders in the community – labelled as community service from 1974 to 2000, community punishment until 2005 and since then as unpaid work.

In the mid-1990s, Conservative Home Office Minister Michael Forsyth suggested offenders might wear some kind of uniform while doing their unpaid work in order that the public might see that they were being punished. Concerns about stigmatisation and the possibility of vigilante attacks led to the proposal being dropped but it has emerged as an idea from time to time since then – most recently by Hazel Blears in May 2005 (*Observer*, 15 May). While it has never been adopted as Home Office policy, some probation services – notably Durham – have required supervisors to wear jackets labelled 'Community Punishment'.

Recent efforts have concentrated more on drawing attention to the work that has been done rather than to the workers. Plaques for example have been placed on buildings, parks or other environmental features which have benefited from unpaid work hours. The Home Office has also promoted Clean-up Weeks in 2005 and 2006 designed to raise awareness of environmental projects.

The Home Office has further launched its own 'Visibility Agenda' designed to increase public awareness of unpaid work and its Five-Year Strategy (Home Office 2006) contains ambitious targets for increasing the number of unpaid work hours completed by offenders in the community. How this impacts on public attitudes remains to be seen. There may be a case for placing more stress on the continuity and underlying values of the Probation Service and less on the rebadging of probation functions in ways that run the risk of appearing gimmicky. Whatever the case, there can be little doubt that the recent cases in which offenders under probation supervision have committed grave crimes provide the Service with the worst sort of visibility that it could wish for.

Community involvement

A further way of promoting positive change in attitudes is to encourage greater public and community involvement in the criminal justice system. There are a number of reasons for supposing that the 'seeing is believing' inherent in involvement will not only help to inform and influence attitudes but might bring about a more fundamental reorientation towards offending. It has been estimated, for example, that only one in five of the population has been into a prison in one capacity or another. For the vast majority opinions on prisons are second-hand.

Two insights from social psychology suggest that increasing involvement can impact forcefully on attitudes and might therefore be a way of producing more positive opinions towards offenders. First, the so-called 'contact hypothesis' argues that prejudice can be reduced through contact between groups, but only under certain circumstances: when the contact is intensive and frequent; has support from the leadership of the groups involved; and where groups are of equal status. These are obviously problematic but not impossible criteria to meet when one of the groups consists of offenders. Second, there is evidence that people who express emotional attitudes to an abstract issue (crime) may develop different attitudes when given responsibility for solving a practical problem in the real world (an individual offender). It is a psychological commonplace that attitudes and behaviour are often not closely related. This suggests that the more people involved in direct work with offenders in one way or another the better. A MORI poll for Rethinking Crime and Punishment in 2004 found considerable appetite for such involvement. Twenty-eight per cent of people said they would be very interested and 36 per cent fairly interested in having a say in the type of unpaid community work that offenders are sentenced to. A three-year pilot project in the Thames Valley is currently underway, which aims to identify whether such involvement can be introduced and whether it impacts on confidence (Allen 2006).

The project 'Making Good' is an initiative led by the Thames Valley Partnership in collaboration with the Thames Valley Probation area and funded by the Esmée Fairbairn Foundation. The aim is to test whether the 267,000 hours of unpaid work undertaken by offenders in the area each year can be organised in a way which better responds to the needs and priorities of local communities and produces more visible results. It will focus its efforts in four pilot towns. Early work suggests that although the Probation Service enjoys constructive relations with some local authorities, most members of the public are unaware of the work that offenders do and have limited opportunities for influencing it. Work is underway with community organisations such as tenants and residents groups and Neighbourhood Action Groups to establish suitable local forums which can help identify unpaid work projects.

What is distinctive about the Thames Valley pilot is its effort to embed this aspect of probation work in the structures of local governance and to link it with broader initiatives to regenerate deprived areas. There are theoretical grounds to expect that this might provide a route to improving the perceptions not only of local people, but of the media and sentencers. An evaluation being conducted by the Centre for Crime and Justice Studies will provide empirical evidence in due course.

Conclusions

In the meantime, the uncertainties about the future structure of the Probation Service may well have a negative impact on perceptions of its work. In 2004 the Government unified the Prison and Probation Services into a single organisation, the National Offender Management Service (NOMS). At the time of writing, proposals for probation under NOMS included:

- dismantling of local (i.e. county-level) probation boards and replacing them with fewer probation trusts;

- the introduction of internal markets in probation work;

- exposing various aspects of probation work to 'contestability' – where private and voluntary section organisations are invited to tender for the work, in competition with the Probation Service;

- new structures for coordinating prison and probation work.

Any large-scale change programme, particularly as contentious as the Government's proposals for probation, brings with it upheaval, an inward-looking focus, risks to staff morale and political and media controversy. We have argued elsewhere that to pursue several strands of such a complex reform agenda in parallel is a risky enterprise (Hough *et al.* 2006). The question of relevance to this chapter is whether the new arrangements will improve the perceptions of the public, media and sentencers or weaken them.

There are three grounds for concern. First, the organisation of Probation Services is likely to be considerably more remote than currently. Whether the key role is exercised by the Regional Offender Manager at the level of the nine English regions and the whole of Wales, or the probation trusts – likely to be at the level of the 24 new police force areas, retaining a responsiveness to the needs and demands of local areas will be a crucial challenge. The dismantling of probation boards potentially removes an important link with local communities.

Second, whatever the merits of contestability as a way of driving up standards, it is difficult to see how a fragmented and changing cast of service providers will easily be able to form the strong relationships with statutory and civic society organisations which appear a prerequisite for confidence. For example, research has shown a higher rate of congruity between the proposals made by probation officers and the sentencing decisions made by courts when the report writer is known to the court (Gelsthorpe and Raynor 1995). Senior probation officers seem particularly respected by the courts if there is an opportunity to form a relationship over time. Such relationships may not flourish in the quasi-market conditions proposed for NOMS.

Finally, there appears more general disquiet on the part of sentencers about the proposals. The Home Office sees no conflict of interest in the idea of a private company preparing pre-sentence reports yet a sentencer made it clear in evidence to the Home Affairs Committee in November 2005 that she for one would struggle to take such a report seriously. Any diminution of sentencer confidence in community penalties that could result from the changes being proposed could have a potentially disastrous impact on the numbers going to prison.

Notes

1 Downes and Morgan (1997) regard the 1970s as a watershed decade. However, neither the 1970s nor the 1980s saw the relentlessness of competition between politicians in 'out-toughing' each other that emerged later.
2 Key cases were the murders of PC Gerald Walker in 2003, Marian Bates, Robert Symons and John Monckton in 2004 and Mary-Ann Leneghan in 2005.

3 For a fuller discussion, see Stalans (2002).

4 Nor is there any significant coverage of community penalties in television and radio dramas. Doubtless with worthy intent, scriptwriters for series such as *The Archers* sometimes sentence their characters to community penalties, but television 'soaps' that set out to dramatise probation work are few and far between.

5 Perhaps the remaining third of respondents took for granted that imprisonment was an option or in some other way misunderstood the question.

6 At the time of writing, a draft guideline recommended three years' detention for an offence of this sort when committed by a 17-year-old first-time offender. A 16-year-old could expect some discount for being a year younger and some discount for pleading guilty, but his previous convictions would make it hard for a judge to justify a community penalty. See http://www.sentencing-guidelines.gov.uk/docs/robbery-draftguidance.pdf

7 This section draws on Indermaur and Hough (2002) and Roberts *et al.* (2003), to which the reader is referred for a fuller discussion.

8 There are news values that are shared by much of the written and broadcast media that render crime stories particularly valuable commodities in maintaining circulation figures. But it is hard to argue that press barons are simply driven by commercial considerations.

9 Unfortunately, judges, who would have much greater sentencing experience, were not asked this question.

10 Had the study been carried out a couple of years later – or focused its work on London – a different picture might have emerged.

11 An obvious, but largely unnoticed, predictor of anxiety about crime is the tendency to worry about other sorts of hazard such as road accidents and accidents in the home (see Hough 1996). Worried people worry about all sorts of things, including crime risks.

Further reading

For an introductory text that summarises what is known about attitudes to the criminal justice system, we suggest Roberts and Hough (2005) *Understanding Public Attitudes to Criminal Justice*. Chapter 4 examines community penalties, among other issues.

For more detailed examination of the topic, we suggest Roberts and Hough (2002) *Changing Attitudes to Punishment: Public Opinion, Crime and Justice* and Roberts *et al.* (2003) *Penal Populism and Public Opinion. Findings from Five Countries*.

On youth justice, the best source is Hough and Roberts (2004) *Youth Crime and Youth Justice: Public Opinion in England and Wales*.

Rethinking Crime and Punishment – The Report from the Esmée Fairbairn Foundation (2004) describes a three-year grant-making initiative aimed at changing public attitudes to prison and alternatives. Practical initiatives to inform attitudes are also discussed in Allen (2005) 'What works in changing public attitudes: findings from rethinking crime and punishment', and in his (2002) article '"There must be some way of dealing with kids": young offenders, public attitudes and policy change'.

References

Allen, J., Edmonds, S., Patterson, A. and Smith, D. (2006) *Policing and the Criminal Justice System – Public Confidence and Perceptions: Findings from the 2004/05 British Crime Survey*, Home Office Online Report 07/06. London: Home Office. Available at: http://www.homeoffice.gov.uk/rds/pdfs06/rdsolr0706.pdf

Allen, R. (2002) '"There must be some way of dealing with kids": young offenders, public attitudes and policy change', *Youth Justice*, 2 (1): 3–13.

Allen, R. (2003) 'Attitudes to punishment: values, beliefs and political allegiance', *Criminal Justice Matters*, 52: 12–13.

Allen, R. (2005) 'What works in changing public attitudes: findings from rethinking crime and punishment', in P. Mason (ed.), *Captured by the Media: Prison Discourse in Popular Culture*. Cullompton: Willan.

Allen, R. (2006) 'Rethinking crime and punishment 2', *Criminal Justice Matters*, 62: 35.

Bottoms, A.E. (1995) 'The philosophy and politics of punishment and sentencing', in C. Clarkson and R. Morgan (eds), *The Politics of Sentencing Reform*. Oxford: Oxford University Press.

Bottoms, A.E. and Wilson, A. (2004) 'Attitudes to punishment in two high crime areas', in A.E. Bottoms, S. Rex and G. Robinson (eds), *Alternatives to Prison*. Cullompton: Willan.

Bridges, A. (2006) *An Independent Review of a Serious Further Offence Case: Damien Hanson & Elliot White*. London: HM Inspectorate of Probation. Available at: http:// inspectorates.homeoffice.gov.uk/hmiprobation/inspect_reports/serious-further-offences/HansonandWhiteReview.pdf?view=Binary

Downes, D. and Morgan, R. (1997) 'Dumping the hostages to fortune', in M. Maguire, R. Morgan and R. Reiner (eds), *The Oxford Handbook of Criminology*, 3rd edn. Oxford: Oxford University Press.

Esmée Fairbairn Foundation (2004) *Rethinking Crime and Punishment – The Report*. London: Esmée Fairburn Foundation. Available at: http://www.rethinking.org.uk

Garland, D. (2001) *The Culture of Control: Crime and Social Order in Contemporary Society*. Oxford: Oxford University Press.

Gelsthorpe, L. and Raynor, P. (1995) 'Quality and effectiveness in probation officers' reports to sentencers', *British Journal of Criminology*, 35: 188–200.

Giddens, T. (1990) *The Consequences of Modernity*. Cambridge: Polity Press.

Giddens, T. (1991) *Modernity and Self-identity*. Cambridge: Polity Press.

Gillespie, M. and McLoughlin, E. (2003) *Media and the Shaping of Public Attitudes*, Briefing Paper. London: Esmée Fairbairn Foundation.

Home Affairs Committee (1998) *Alternatives to Prison Sentences*, Third Report, Session 1997–98, HC 486. London: HMSO.

Home Office (2001) *Making Punishments Work* (Halliday Report). London: Home Office.

Home Office (2006) *A Five-Year Strategy for Protecting the Public and Reducing Re-Offending*, Cm 6717 London: HMSO.

Hough, M. (1996) *Anxiety about Crime: Findings from the 1994 British Crime Survey*, Home Office Research Study No. 147. London: Home Office

Hough, M. (1998) *Attitudes to Punishment: Findings from the 1992 British Crime Survey*, Social Science Research Paper No. 7. London: South Bank University.

Hough, M. and Park, A. (2002) 'How malleable are public attitudes to crime and punishment?', in J. Roberts and M. Hough (eds), *Changing Attitudes to Punishment: Public Opinion Around the Globe*. Cullompton: Willan.

Hough, M. and Roberts, J. (1998) *Attitudes to Punishment: Findings from the 1996 British Crime Survey*, Home Office Research Study No. 179. London: Home Office.

Hough, M. and Roberts, J. (1999) 'Sentencing trends in Britain: public knowledge and public opinion', *Punishment and Society*, 1 (1): 11–26.

Hough, M. and Roberts, J. (2004a) *Confidence in Justice: An International Review*. London: ICPR, King's College London. Available at: www.kcl.ac.uk/icpr

Hough, M. and Roberts, J. (2004b) *Youth Crime and Youth Justice: Public Opinion in England and Wales*, Criminal Policy Monograph. Bristol: Policy Press.

Hough, M., Allen, R. and Padel, U. (eds) (2006) *Reshaping Probation and Prisons: The New Offender Management Framework*, Researching Criminal Justice Series Paper No. 6. Bristol: Policy Press.

Hough, M., Jacobson, J. and Millie, A. (2003) *The Decision to Imprison: Sentencing and the Prison Population*. London: Prison Reform Trust.

Indermaur, D. and Hough, M. (2002) 'Strategies for changing public attitudes to punishment', in J. Roberts and M. Hough (eds), *Changing Attitudes to Punishment: Public Opinion Around the Globe*. Cullompton: Willan.

Kennamer, J. (1992) 'Public opinion, the press and public policy: an introduction', in J. Kennamer (ed.), *Public Opinion, the Press and Public Policy*. Westport, CT: Praeger.

King, J. and Grimshaw, R. (2003) *Evaluation of the Local Crime Community Sentence Project*. London: Magistrates Association and Probation Boards Association.

Macmillan, K., Money, K. and Hillenbrand, C. (2004) *The Reputation of Prison Alternatives*. London: RCP Esmée Fairbairn Foundation.

Marrin, M. (2002) 'The ugly truth is that Britain must build a lot more jails', *Sunday Times*, 10 March.

Maruna, S. and King, A. (2004) 'Public opinion and community penalties', in A.E. Bottoms, S. Rex and G. Robinson (eds), *Alternatives to Prison*. Cullompton: Willan.

Mattinson, J. and Mirrlees-Black, C. (2000) *Attitudes to Crime and Criminal Justice: Findings from the 1998 British Crime Survey*, Home Office Research Study 200. London: Home Office.

Morgan, R. (2004) *The Events Leading to the Death of PC Gerald Walker at the Hands of David Parfitt and the Manner in which the Case was Subsequently Dealt With*. London: HM Inspectorate of Probation. Available at: http://police.homeoffice.gov.uk/news-and-publications/publication/operational-policing/parfitt-walkerinquiry.pdf?view=Binary

MORI (1998) *Re-branding the Probation Service Research Conducted for the Association of Chief Officers of Probation*. London: MORI.

MORI (2000) *Crime and Justice Survey for Daily Mail*. London: MORI.

MORI (2001) *Public Attitudes Towards Prisons: Report to Esmée Fairbairn Foundation*. London: Esmée Fairbairn Foundation.

MORI (2003a) *Public Confidence in the Criminal Justice System – Survey Conducted in 2003*. London: MORI.

MORI (2003b) *Mori Poll 24th January*. Available at: http://www.mori.com/polls/2003/burglars.shtml

MORI (2004) *Attitudes to Crime and Prisons – Survey Conducted for Esmée Fairbairn Foundation*. London: Esmée Fairbairn Foundation.

National Centre for Social Research (1999) *1999 British Social Attitudes Survey*. London: National Centre for Social Research.

RCP (2002a) *What Does the Public Think About Prison?* London: Esmée Fairbairn Foundation.

RCP (2002b) *What Do the Public Really Feel about Non-Custodial Penalties?* London: Esmée Fairbairn Foundation.

Roberts, J. V. and Hough, M. (eds) (2002) *Changing Attitudes to Punishment: Public Opinion, Crime and Justice*. Cullompton: Willan.

Roberts, J. V. and Hough, M. (2005) *Understanding Public Attitudes to Criminal Justice*. Maidenhead: Open University Press.

Roberts, J. V., Stalans, L. S., Indermaur, D. and Hough, M. (2003) *Penal Populism and Public Opinion. Findings from Five Countries*. New York: Oxford University Press.

Russell, N. and Morgan, R. (2001) *Sentencing of Domestic Burglary*, Sentencing Advisory Panel Research Report 1. London: Home Office.

Stalans, L.J. (2002) 'Measuring attitudes to sentencing', in J. Roberts. and M. Hough (eds), *Changing Attitudes to Punishment: Public Opinion Around the Globe*. Cullompton: Willan.

Tyler, T.R. (2003) 'Procedural justice, legitimacy and the effective rule of law', in M. Tonry (ed.), *Crime and Justice: A Review of Research*, Vol. 30. Chicago: University of Chicago Press.

Van Kesteren, J., Mayhew, P. and Nieuwbeerta, P. (2000) *Criminal Victimisation in Seventeen Industrialised Countries*. Netherlands: Dutch Ministry of Justice.

Walker, N. and Hough, M. (eds) (1988) *Public Attitudes to Sentencing*. Farnborough: Gower.

Wood, J. and Viki, G.T. (2001) *Public Attitudes to Crime and Punishment*, Report for Esmée Fairbairn Foundation. London: Esmée Fairbairn Foundation.

Woolf, Lord Chief Justice (2002) *Making the Punishment Fit the Needs of Society*, Speech to Prison Service Annual Conference, 5 February.

Glossary

Accredited programmes
Generally, though not always, cognitive behavioural groupwork programmes designed to address offending behaviour and approved by the *Correctional Services Accreditation Panel* (formerly known as the Joint Accreditation Panel).

Approved premises
Hostel-type residential accommodation managed either by, or on behalf of, the Probation Service for persons either remanded on bail with a condition of residence or offenders released from custody on licence with a condition of residence.

ASBO
An Anti-Social Behaviour Order, as introduced by the Crime and Disorder Act 1998 s.1. Anti-social behaviour is defined as acting 'in a manner that caused or was likely to cause harassment, alarm or distress to one or more persons not of the same household as himself'. ASBOs are civil orders but breach of an ASBO is a criminal offence. Local use of ASBOs and other powers introduced to address ASB has, where appropriate, been encouraged and overseen by the Anti-Social Behaviour Unit (ASBU) within the Home Office.

Audit Commission
The independent public body established in 1982 to ensure that 'public money is spent economically, efficiently and effectively in the areas of local government, housing, health, criminal justice and fire and rescue services'.

Assessment
The process of evaluating the risk of reoffending and causing harm (to self or others) principally by identifying those criminogenic (predisposing) factors associated with the same. To this end various assessment tools are used of which the basic tool, for both the Probation and Prison Services, is OASys. Within the youth justice system a slightly dfferent risk assessment tool – ASSET – is used by youth offending teams (YOTs).

Association of Chief Officers of Probation

ACOP, as opposed to ACPO (the Association of Chief Police Officers), was the body which, until its dissolution in 2001 on the establishment of the National Probation Service, represented the chief probation officers heading the then 54 local probation services. From 2001 chief officers of probation areas were eligible to join the Probation Boards Association but there ceased to be an association for chief officers per se.

Breach

Not conforming to the requirements of a criminal court order with the prospect of being 'breached', taken back to court or referred to the Parole Board, for failing to comply with the terms of the order. In the case of a community penalty, or the terms of release on licence from a custodial penalty, breach proceedings will generally be the responsibility of the probation service. Breach proceedings may lead to resentencing or recall to prison.

British Crime Survey

An annual survey (since 2001, though first undertaken in 1982, and initially conducted less frequently) with a sample of some 40,000 households asking respondents about crimes committed against them in the previous 12 months, and their experience and attitudes on a variety of other crime and policing-related issues. BCS data are used alongside police-recorded crime data to develop a more complete picture of trends in the incidence of crime.

Case management

NOMS and the Probation Service use the term 'offender manager' for the role of 'case manager' or 'care co-ordinator'; 'offender management' for 'case management' or 'care co-ordination'; and the term 'sentence plan' or 'supervision plan' for the 'case' or 'care plan'. Essentially, there is a separation of 'case management' functions from 'interventions'. 'Case management' includes proper assessment and case planning, as well as oversight of the delivery of the case plan and action where the plan may break down. The aim is to offer 'end-to-end' case management with a single 'case manager' to ensure continuity of interventions. This all replaces casework which denoted individual work with offenders in previous eras of probation practice.

CDRPs

The local authority-based Crime and Disorder Reduction Partnerships (on which the Probation Service is represented in each area) which, since the Crime and Disorder Act 1998 s.5–6, have fulfilled the duty placed on all local authorities and police forces to formulate and implement crime reduction strategies based on periodic audits of crime and disorder locally.

Community Orders (sentences)

Generally any criminal court sentence served in the community involving some form of supervision, traditionally undertaken by the probation service, but not necessarily. Thus fines, compensation orders and discharges are excluded but electronically monitored curfew orders and unpaid work (formerly termed *community service*) are included. A variety of different community penalties, in addition to the probation order, were introduced from the early 1970s onwards but in 2003 all were replaced (Criminal Justice Act 2003) by the single portfolio community order to which twelve different requirements may be attached.

Community Service

A new sentence, the community service order, was introduced by the Criminal Justice Act 1972, during which an offender convicted of an imprisonable offence could be required to undertake between 40 and 240 hours unpaid work. The Criminal Justice and Court Services Act 2000 renamed the CSO a community punishment order and the Criminal Justice Act 2003 replaced all community penalties with a generic community order within which the requirement to undertake 'unpaid work', now of between 40 and 300 hours, became one of twelve possible requirements. Despite these changes 'unpaid work' remains widely referred to colloquially as 'community service'.

Compliance

The opposite of breaching (see *breach*) the requirements of any criminal court sentence, both *community orders* and the terms of any release from custody on licence.

Contracting out

Probation services and the management of prisons, or services within prisons, may be delivered in-house (by the Probation or Prison Services) or they can be contracted out to voluntary sector or commercial providers. Since the early 1990s successive administrations have sought to encourage the development of a 'market' in the provision of community-based and custodial provision and this is an explicit aim of the *National Offender Management Service* through competition or what they term 'contestability'. It follows that contracting out may amount to privatisation, but not necessarily.

Criminogenic

Any factor or circumstance, which may or may not be causal, positively correlated with the onset of criminal behaviour or reoffending. These factors and circumstances are the focus of risk assessment tools such as *OGRS* and OASys.

Desistance

The term now generally used for ceasing to commit crime. Certainty of desistance comes only with death. Thus patterns of desistance are identified in terms of significant reductions in the frequency and seriousness of offending. In this sense desistance is best considered not as an event but a process without a definitive end.

Discrimination

The practice of singling out one or another more or less discernible social group for more favourable or unfavourable treatment, particularly with regard to race, sex, sexual orientation or belief. The discrimination may be conscious or unconscious, overt or covert, implicit or explicit.

Diversion

Measures whereby a person, in the case of the probation service either an offender or a person accused of an offence, is diverted for whatever reason from being subject to a more serious intervention. Most commonly involving diversion from prosecution by way of a pre-court police caution. Or, for example, the provision of bail support schemes designed to divert to community services and controls persons charged with, or convicted of, an offence from being remanded in custody prior to trial or sentence.

Drug Action Teams

The local partnerships, established by the Home Office, combining representatives of the local authorities (social services, education, housing), the health, prison and probation services and the voluntary sector, to deliver the National Drug Strategy. Each DAT has a co-ordinator responsible for day-to-day management.

Drug Treatment and Testing Orders

A community sentence introduced by the Crime and Disorder Act 1998 s.61. Orders run for from 6–36 months where the court is satisfied that the offender is an illicit drug user and may be susceptible to treatment. Compliance with regular testing and treatment is required of the offender and – an innovation – there are regular reviews of the offender's response by the court. Following the Criminal Justice and Court Services Act 2003 these provisions become one of twelve requirements which may be attached to a *community order*.

Enforcement

Involves implementing probation service *national standards* for the supervision of offenders subject to either *community orders* or having been released from custody subject to supervision or on licence (*parole*). National standards include rules stating when *breach* proceedings should be brought for offenders' non-*compliance*. Successive government administrations have placed increasing stress on enforcement and later editions of national standards have tightened the circumstances in which *breach* proceedings must be brought. But there is growing recognition that if supervision does not enable compliance, enforcement can be counter productive: those offenders presenting the highest *risk* and most in need of support are liable to end up in custody and the benefits of offending behaviour interventions lost.

ETE

Education, training and employment. This has become a major theme within government policy in England and Wales in a number of different spheres, including criminal justice: it is seen as a pathway out of crime.

Governance

The legal (statutory) and managerial framework whereby a public service is authorised and made accountable for the service it delivers. Accountability involves both *for* and *who* elements, that is, accountability for delivering certain services to a given standard and being accountable to someone for that standard of delivery. Governance arrangements therefore include, among other things, ministerial and local powers, standards of service delivery and grievance and inspection mechanisms.

Managerialism

Managerialism (or 'new public management') refers to the movement which has reshaped public services over the past two decades. In the probation field managerialism has involved a shift from character-driven values (represented in individual casework) to system-driven values. Managerialism thus revolves around the economy (value for money), efficacy (the simplification and acceleration of procedures) and effectiveness (the achievement of specific outcomes) of the system. Staff behaviour is regulated and incentivised through organisational procedures such as key performance indicators in the service of a published goals or targets.

National Association of Probation Officers

NAPO was originally founded in 1912 as a trade union and a professional association for *probation officers*. In 2001 It changed its name to Napo – the Trade Union and Professional Association for Family Court and Probation Staff (the acronyms NAPO and Napo tend to be used interchangeably). The name change reflected the changes to the nature of Napo's membership and to the re-structuring of the Probation Service in 2001.

National Offender Management Service

The National Offender Management Service (NOMS) was established in 2004 following the comprehensive correctional services review conducted by Patrick Carter in 2003. Carter proposed that criminal justice system agencies (especially prisons and probation) should work more closely together to deliver a service fit for purpose in relation to *public protection* and reducing reoffending. This was envisaged as a way of maximizing scarce resources. Instead of relying solely on line management, the NOMS' aim is to establish a clear distinction between the purchaser of services and the providers. NOMS provides a national framework and ten regional offices for the commissioning of services. Also, colloquially, known as the 'Never Once Met Service' or 'Nightmare on Marsham Street' (the London address of the Home Office Headquarters), reflecting widespread ambivalence about the new framework. In late March 2007 the government announced that it intended splitting the Home Office, with NOMS, and responsibility for the Probation and Prison services, being transferred in May 2007 to a new Ministry of Justice.

National Probation Service

The National Probation Service for England and Wales (NPS) was created in 2001 following the Criminal Justice and Court Services Act 2000. Replacing 54 independent local probation services, it comprises 42 local probation board areas coterminous with police force areas and gives a national identity to the probation service. The NPS has to date been led by a National Probation Directorate (NPD) within the Home Office though most of its functions have already been taken over by the *NOMS*, to which most NPD staff have transferred. As of March 2007 there remains a Director of Probation who line manages all chief officers and, through this arrangement, promotes consistency in practice.

National standards

National standards specify how offenders are to be supervised and managed. They include the process and timeliness of the allocation of new cases, first appointment, assessment, frequency of contact, sentence planning and review. They also cover the standard of reports, including *pre-sentence reports*. National standards were first issued in 1989 in relation to *community service* (unpaid work). The most recent regulatory standards (2005) are based on the principles of offender management and the requirements of the Criminal Justice Act 2003.

National Vocational Qualifications

National Vocational Qualifications (NVQs) are work-related, competence-based qualifications. They serve to show that a candidate is competent in the area of work the NVQ represents. NVQs are based on national occupational standards. These standards are statements of performance that describe what competent people in a particular occupation are expected to be able to do. They cover all the main aspects of an occupation, including current best practice, the ability to adapt to future requirements and the knowledge and understanding that underpin competent performance.

OGRS

The Offender Group Reconviction Scale, a statistical reoffending risk score first launched for the probation service in 1996. The original purpose of the scale and score was to assist officers in their writing of *pre-sentence reports*. OGRS calculates, on the basis of a very limited amount of information, the likelihood of an offender being reconvicted for any offence within two years of their release from custody or from the start of their non-custodial penalty on this occasion. OGRS is based on a logistical regression analysis of a large sample of offenders convicted in the recent past and whose subsequent reconvictions have been traced through the Home Office Offenders Index. Unlike OASys, OGRS takes little time to apply but may be a poor guide to an offender's risk of harm or reoffending, particularly where the offender has little known offending history.

Parole

Parole means early release from prison on licence (and a promise of good behaviour). The licence agreement involves supervision in the community and may involve other conditions (for example, a stipulation as to where to live). The Parole Board, a non-departmental public body (NDPB) was established in 1967 to advise the Home Secretary on the early release of prisoners. Under the terms of the Criminal Justice Act 1991 and the Parole Board (Transfer of Functions) Order 1998, the Parole Board has delegated authority to decide applications for parole for those sentenced on or after 1 October 1992 to a determinate sentence of from four to less than fifteen years (other prisoners serving shorter sentences being released at the half way point automatically). The 1991 Act, as amended by the Crime (Sentences) Act 1997, and the Criminal Justice Act 2003, also gives authority to the Board to direct the release of life sentence prisoners (lifers) and those serving sentences for public protection. For other classes of prisoner, the Board makes recommendations to the Secretary of State.

Pilots

Pilots are essentially designed to tease out problems and test preliminary activities and interventions before such interventions are rolled out on a national basis. For example, within the Effective Practice Initiative for the Probation Service under the heading of *What Works* a number of 'pathfinders' were identified; these were programmes thought to be especially promising in terms of their potential effectiveness. 'Demonstration projects' are also relevant here insofar as they might be used as a prototype to show what might be possible in terms of implementation and effectiveness.

Pre-sentence reports

The preparation of pre-sentence reports (PSRs) is a key task of the Probation Service and probation officers. Reports take three principal forms: 'stand down reports' can be delivered after a short interview with the offender in the precincts of the court; 'fast delivery reports' are completed and delivered between one and five days of a court appearance; and 'standard delivery reports' – for which probation officers are allowed three weeks or more preparation time. The production of reports has been a central part of the Probation Service's work since its very earliest days. The purpose of 'social inquiry' or 'enquiry' reports, as they were known in the past, was to enquire into the background or home circumstances of the offender to assist the court in deciding on a suitable sentence. PSRs are today designed to present relevant information about an offender, an assessment of their risk of harm and reoffending, and a realistic proposal for sentence to the court.

Prisons and Probation Ombudsman

The Prisons and Probation Ombudsman is appointed by the Home Secretary and investigates complaints from prisoners and those subject to probation supervision, or those upon whom reports have been written. The Ombudsman is independent of both the Prison Service and the *National Probation Service* (NPS). The Ombudsman is also responsible for investigating all deaths of prisoners and residents of probation hostels and immigration detention accommodation.

Probation Boards

Probation Boards were created as part of the *National Probation Service* on 1 April 2001 by the Criminal Justice and Courts Act 2000. Boards operate within the provisions of the Act and relevant subordinate legislation, and comply with any directions given by the Secretary of State. They are corporate bodies, enjoying their own 'legal personality' but are also subject to numerous legal and financial restrictions. The Probation Board is the employing body of all staff in its local area (except the chief officer). The Board comprises a chairman, a chief officer and not less than five other members (typically, judges, magistrates, and community members). Appointments are made against a published schedule of competencies. The government has announced that it will introduce legislation to transform Probation Boards into *Probation Trusts*. Trusts are to become one of a number of possible providers of probation services under contract to the Secretary of State via *Regional Offender Managers*.

Probation Officer

'Main grade' probation officers (or offender managers) undertake a range of statutory duties related to the assessment and supervision of offenders. They work directly with offenders subject to community penalties (including supervision, unpaid work, drug and alcohol treatment) and those sentenced to custody, both during and after their release. Probation officers prepare *pre-sentence reports* and engage in the management, supervision and *enforcement* of *community orders* and prison licences. Probation officers generally have a qualification in probation studies (or equivalents). They are employed by a local *Probation Board* (which may be replaced by *Probation Trusts* in the future).

Probation Service Officer

Though not qualified as probation officers, probation service officers (PSOs) are similarly employed by local Probation Boards (soon to be *Probation Trusts*) to undertake the direct supervision of a wide range of offenders. They are given training in assessment and methods of working with offenders. They may have their own caseloads and work in much the same way as qualified colleagues. The basic distinction between PSOs and probation officers is that of expertise in (and responsibility for) risk assessment; unqualified officers do not prepare full pre-sentence reports (though they may produce short 'stand down' or 'fast delivery reports'), nor do they supervise offenders assessed as high risk in terms of harm.

Probation Trusts

A new type of probation body first identified in the 2005 Home Office consultation paper *Restructuring Probation to Reduce Reoffending*, a paper which sets out how the government intends to introduce commissioning and contestability in the provision of probation services and the organisational changes required to do so. At present, *Probation Boards* are the employing bodies for all staff (except the chief officer) in their area. The government has introduced a Bill to transform Boards into Probation Trusts which will operate with greater independence than Boards. Trusts are to have a role in providing probation services under contract to the Secretary of State via Regional

Offender Managers, to whom Trusts will be accountable for performance against contract. The Probation Boards' Association, amongst others, views these changes as a step further towards centralisation and has generated a good deal of opposition to their institution.

Prolific and persistent offenders

A sub-group of offenders who commit a high volume of crimes and/or who persist in committing crimes. There is no agreed definition as to what counts as prolific or persistent. The national implementation guide for the Criminal Justice Act 2003 states that persistent offenders are 'those who continue to offend over a period of time'. Prolific offenders are defined as 'those who offend with a high frequency, possibly committing a range of different offences, and rapidly building up a substantial history of convictions'. In September 2004, the Home Office launched a national Prolific and other Priority Offender (PPO) Strategy, requiring that a PPO scheme be established in every *Crime and Disorder Reduction Partnership* in England and Wales.

Procedural justice

Procedural justice relates to fairness and consistency in decision making in the administration of justice such that, for example, everyone has the right to a fair trial. The assumption is that everyone is 'equal before the law'. This contrasts with substantive or social justice which emphasises social inequalities between people in relation to the law, recognising differences in decision-making outcomes – for example, equal fines imposed on poor and wealthy alike – between those who are disadvantaged and those who are not. For example, in probation practice, procedural justice might mean ensuring that everyone has a right to be considered for 'unpaid work' as a requirement of a community order, but substantive justice might mean ensuring that working hours are arranged so as not to exclude those offenders who have childcare responsibilities.

Public protection

Public protection is the priority of offender managers (*probation officers*) and the work of the National Probation Service. Responsibility for public protection within the *National Offender Management Service* (NOMS) headquarters lies with the Public Protection Unit. The Unit develops strategy, identifies targets and priorities, and supports practice in the field. In local areas probation officers are involved in Multi-agency Public Protection Arrangements (MAPPA) and Mental Health arrangements. Risk assessment is a key part of identifying priority work with offenders. Those classed as Level 3 in terms of risk of harm automatically require a certain level of intervention and support. The MAPPA came into being in 2000 when the Criminal Justice and Court Services Act placed a statutory obligation on the Probation and Police services in each area to establish arrangements for the purpose of assessing and managing the risks posed by certain offenders.

Randomised Controlled Trials

Experiments in which interventions in relation to one group of people are compared and contrasted with another group who have not been subject to the same intervention. Having their origins in the field of medicine and pharmacology, with neither patient nor doctor knowing which is the placebo and which is the pill with curative potential, RCTs have entered criminological discourse and are now being promoted by government as a good test of the effectiveness of interventions. Their use is controversial because it is difficult, on ethical and operational grounds, to replicate the 'double blind trials' of medicine in criminal justice decision making and allocation procedures.

Regional Offender Managers
The ten (one for each of the nine English regions plus Wales) regionally-based commissioners of probation services who, alongside the *National Offender Management Service* Headquarters staff, it is intended will in future determine which among potential providers – the 42 *Probation Trusts*, and voluntary and commercial sector organisations – is to deliver probation (and prison) services currently delivered largely by probation areas and the probation service.

Rehabilitation
The proposition that it is possible to change offenders' attitudes and behaviour by working directly with them – individually or in groups – in order to bring about a reduction in offending. In the probation setting, early forms of rehabilitation revolved around individual casework and the notion that it was the probation officer's task to 'advise, assist and befriend' offenders. Rehabilitation has more recently come to be associated with *What Works* principles of intervention where demonstrable research findings in relation to effectiveness are used to guide and shape interventions with targeted groups of offenders.

Responsibilisation
Refers to the ways in which responsibility for the control of crime has been dispersed amongst a wide range of bodies and authorities, including individual members of the public, communities, and statutory bodies beyond the criminal justice system. The government's aim is to promote partnerships to tackle the problems of crime and social order.

Restorative Justice
Has its roots in indigenous forms of justice (in Australia, New Zealand and Canada, for example). It involves processes designed to repair personal harms and social ruptures to communities resulting from crime. One common process is the restorative conference – involving crime victims, offenders and their 'communities of care' (those who know them best, including families) – meeting to resolve the harm done through discussion, apology and reparation.

Rights culture
A movement which reflects the centrality of human rights to live life with dignity. The aim is to guarantee such rights in society by building a culture where rights and certain freedoms can be taken for granted.

Risk
The concept of risk has a foundation role in modern criminal justice systems. Late modern 'risk society' is manifested as a series of intersecting and overlapping trends, tendencies and techniques, centred on the assessment and management of risk and shaping the practice of agencies and practitioners. 'Risk assessment' instruments such as OASys and Asset have been developed for use with adult and youth offenders respectively (see *assessment*). Criminal justice practice is increasingly characterised as relying on actuarial ways of thinking about and managing offenders; that is, a calculative approach to risk and a risk assessment approach to offenders.

Senior Probation Officer
The first line managerial grade in the *National Probation Service*. SPOs are usually qualified and experienced *probation officers* employed by local *Probation Boards* (which may be reconstituted as *Probation Trusts* in the future) to manage and account for the work of a team of offender managers.

Sentencing Guidelines Council

The Council was set up under s.167 of the Criminal Justice Act 2003. It receives reports from the Sentencing Advisory Panel and sets sentencing guidelines for judges and magistrates. The establishment of the SGC represented a radical change from previous practice: sentencers are obliged to take into account the guidelines or give reasons for departing from them, although there remains scope for discretion.

Service Level Agreements

SLAs define the terms of engagement between agencies or tiers within agencies. That is, they comprise the rules (where legal contracts do not apply) governing the relationships between different parties, for example, between purchasers and providers of services. Such agreements typically include reference to service definition, problem management, fees and expenses, warranties and remedies, security, legal compliance, termination, and other relevant factors.

Social exclusion

This is sometimes seen as a particular condition relating to poverty or as the result of some other obvious social inequality. The condition which has come to be called social exclusion is to be found in any society where one social class or group has been able to expand its power and influence, to increase its prosperity, or to impose its culture, at the expense of another. It is argued that those in privileged positions should have some sense of responsibility towards those who are less fortunate. To this end there are government inspired community programmes, ranging from additional resources to specific intervention programmes for those most excluded, designed to facilitate social inclusion.

Victim Impact Statement

A statement taken from the victim of crime which records the harm done to them as a result of their victimisation. Such statements are used at different points in the criminal justice system depending upon the jurisdiction in which they are being used; they may inform prosecution and sentencing decisions.

Victim Support

A UK-based organisation that seeks to offer victims of crime assistance in the aftermath of a crime. The organisation comprises a federation of local Victim Support groups.

What Works

Both a question and a movement which emerged in the late 1980s signifying a renewed interest in the effectiveness of community penalties. The movement is grounded on systematic research reviews using meta-analysis to combine the results of large numbers of studies to reach overall conclusions about what kinds of projects and initiatives have produced promising results in terms of effectiveness at reducing reoffending. These analyses in turn generated a series of conferences, *pilot studies*, and pathfinders designed further to explore the effectiveness of offender interventions.

Youth Offending Teams

The multi-agency, local authority-based and managed teams (comprising seconded social services, probation, police, education and health workers) who deliver youth justice services (for 10–17-year-olds) and whose work is overseen on behalf of central government by the Youth Justice Board. YOTs undertake work (initial assessment, reports for courts, supervision, etc) equivalent to that of the probation service for child and young person offenders.

Other useful sources of information

For further details on some of the key concepts mentioned above, you may find it helpful to consult *The Dictionary of Probation and Offender Management* edited by Rob Canton and David Hancock (Cullompton, Willan Publishing, 2007), as well as *The Sage Dictionary of Criminology* edited by Eugene McLaughlin and John Muncie (London, Sage, 2005, 2nd edition). More detailed discussion of key concepts may be found in *The Oxford Handbook of Criminology* edited by Mike Maguire, Rod Morgan and Robert Reiner (Oxford, Oxford University Press, 2007, 4th edition).

The National Probation Service website (http://www.probation.homeoffice.gov.uk/) gives access to policy and practice documents, including many Probation Circulars, as does the site of the **National Offender Management Service** (http://www.noms.homeoffice.gov.uk/). http://www.probation2000.com/ is generally a useful resource and in particular can help to track down elusive circulars and documents.

Other useful resources include:
http://www.direct.gov.uk/CrimeJusticeAndTheLaw/fs/en
www.crimeinfo.org.uk and
http://www.homeoffice.gov.uk/rds/pubsintro1.html – where many of the publications of the Home Office Research Development and Statistics Directorate (RDS) can be found.

Index